THUS SPAKE
THE CORPSE

AN EXQUISITE
CORPSE READER
1988-1998

VOLUME 2–FICTIONS, TRAVELS & TRANSLATIONS

*Edited by ANDREI CODRESCU
& LAURA ROSENTHAL*

BLACK SPARROW PRESS
SANTA ROSA–2000

Black Sparrow Press books are printed on acid-free paper.

LIBRARY OF CONGRESS CATALOGING-IN-PUBLICATION DATA
VOLUME 1
Thus Spake the Corpse : An Exquisite Corpse Reader, 1988-1998 / edited
   by Andrei Codrescu & Laura Rosenthal.
       p.   cm.
     Contents: v. 1. Poetry & Essays
       ISBN 1-57423-100-6 (paperback)
       ISBN 1-57423-101-4 (cloth trade)
       ISBN 1-57423-102-2 (signed cloth)
     I. Codrescu, Andrei, 1946–   . II. Rosenthal, Laura, 1958–   .
   III. Exquisite Corpse.
   AC5.T45   1999
   808.8—dc21   99-32586

VOLUME 2
Thus Spake the Corpse : An Exquisite Corpse Reader, 1988-1998 / edited
   by Andrei Codrescu & Laura Rosenthal.
       p.   cm.
     Contents: v. 2. Fictions, Travels & Translations
       ISBN 1-57423-141-3 (paperback)
       ISBN 1-57423-142-1 (cloth trade)
       ISBN 1-57423-143-X (signed cloth)
     I. Codrescu, Andrei, 1946–   . II. Rosenthal, Laura, 1958–   .
   III. Exquisite Corpse.
   AC5.T45   1999
   808.8—dc21   99-32586

TABLE OF CONTENTS

3. TRAVEL & TRANSLATION

TO THE READER
OF THE SECOND VOLUME OF
THUS SPAKE THE CORPSE

You are now holding in your hands the second volume of ardent compilations from the fiery pages of *Exquisite Corpse*, the journal that for more than a decade delighted the indignant and the sophisticated and gave heart-burn to the fearful and the tenured.

The first volume, *Thus Spake the Corpse: An Exquisite Corpse Reader 1988–1998*, published by Black Sparrow Press in 1999, contained poetry and essays. We were delighted by the reception our readers gave this anthology. The fans of the *Corpse* were pleased to revisit their favorite poets and essayists, while new readers banged their disbelieving fists on unread stacks of *New Yorkers* and recent poetry compilations and cried out as one, "Where were you when we were dying for lack of real poetry and speculation?" These are our readers: histrionic, yet concerned. There is no need to elaborate here on the relative fame (very great in some cases) of our collaborators, some of whom catapulted from perfect obscurity to the highest ranks of our poetic culture, while others, who were already there, merely moved the breakables out of harm's way. Suffice it to say, the *Corpse* set some standards. Pissed some people off. Made itself at home. Will not be replaced.

This second volume contains "Lives of the Poets," a vivid, sometimes naughty, barely legal, collection of writings on contemporary poets. The critical method evolved herein rarely makes any distinction between verse, biography, memoir, or polemic. We should mention only the Ed Dorn controversy to see hackles rise. (We trade hackles on the NYSE.) The end result, we believe, has been highly beneficial to keeping Dorn's work alive. Even today, in the pages of the on-line version of *Exquisite Corpse* (www.corpse.org), there are lively discussions about this formidable poet, with many quotations and explications of his poetry.

Also in this book, you will find "fiction," an over-rated form of writing that is a great cash cow for MFA programs and publishers today. Fiction, as practiced in those quarters, is a sad common agreement to value the delusions of hagiographers, despite a century or so of decadence. Pretending that "fiction" is somehow a more

ANDREI CODRESCU & LAURA ROSENTHAL

11

sensitive record of our personal and national travails than journalism is a good tactic for selling ersatz writing and keeping innocents in the dark. The fact is that we only agreed to call our prose efforts "fiction," because it is easier than calling them "prose efforts," which might have even our stoutest admirers head for the hills. The "fiction" herein bears no resemblance, though, to what passes by the same name in approved circles. Just how that can be, you can find out by reading.

Our third and final section of Volume Two is complex and charming like *The Thousand and One Nights*. In "Travel & Translation," you will encounter highly idiosyncratic reports from many parts of the world, including hot spots like Lebanon and Bosnia. These are writers' reports, often written for reasons diametrically opposed to those of travel writers for the glossies. What many of these writers hope to find is amazement, in some pre-Frederick Jameson sense, or "the marvelous," as André Breton called it. You will also find, in the context of this geography, a hefty body of translation. The texts translated here originate in a great many languages and have in common a view of translation as vertical travel. The 12th-century poetry of Lu Li and Weng Li, for instance, recently found in manuscript, is proof, if any is needed, that contemporaneity is a matter of inclusive time-travel. There are also discussions of translation here, seen as an urgent critical field.

Ranging across the body of the vast *Corpse* in order to pick its most delicious parts has entailed many days and nights of labor. Some of us have been on tranquilizers since. In addition to the two editors, whom you see hanging limply from the lip of a precipice trying to decide whether to sleep or to jump, we want to thank the indefatigable assistants: Rex Rose, he of the eagle eye, Dan McNamara, the Hunter of Typos and Enemy of Tedium, and the in-coming House Power, Mark Spitzer who, despite providing incendiary text to the book itself, has proven himself a scrupulous and impeccable editor.

Owning both volumes of *Thus Spake the Corpse*, you can rest assured, dear reader, that you have missed very little of the decade that just fizzed out, even if you just woke up. (Wouldn't that be nice.)

Baton Rouge, August 29, 2000

12

THUS SPAKE
THE CORPSE

1
LIVES OF THE POETS

CRANBERRY JUICE IN A GLASS

*Based on a few events from Charles Olson's
life in Gloucester, Massachusetts*

Was it *"They that go down to the sea in ships. / That do business in
great waters,"* or was it blueberries in the center of the Cape, in Dog-
town Common where long ago dogs and old people were the only
survivors of a war, or was it rocks and sand dunes as varied as the
people who lay on them in the sun that made Mr. Maximus come
and cling to this fishtown on the coast of the Atlantic, it is not for me
to tell. It could be these and other reasons. There were reasons too
for wanting to sip cranberry juice with Mr. Maximus in a cafe by the
waterfront, or anywhere for that matter. And watch ice cubes in his
glass, stirred by an occasional glint of sun rays coming through the
window, change into a potion reddish-pink and crystalline. Mr. Maximus was the chief poet of the town, and beyond. He liked the town
and strolled around listening to gossipers, talking to fishermen and
local intellectuals. No thought passing through the streets escaped his
scrutiny, and conversation with him would have been most entertaining.
But as it happened it was not through conversation but through his com-
ings and goings, as he tried to carry this town on his humongous shoulders, that I was gradually drawn into the vortex of Mr. Maximus' deeply
personal event.

Winter is the time of year, more than any other, when I think of
the slow passing of Mr. Maximus. For it was on one of those cold days
that many stood at his gravesite: poets, friends, gravediggers, while scant
snowflakes were falling and they lowered his coffin into the ground.
With eyes big and flat, bigger than most peepholes and feeling heavy like
an old toad on its way to the mortician, this is the time to look through
the window and watch a fishing boat cut through the frigid waters of the
harbor. While the sun is setting the water is a deepening blue, the sky is
taking on emerald and the crystals of snow under my window become
pink, one of the shades of cranberry juice in a glass filled with ice cubes.
(Heck, why not just say "the colors of Fitz Hugh Lane"—he painted this
harbor, not I.) As the day darkens it is time to watch the boat move along
the distant horizon where it becomes no more than a brightly shining
light on its way to the fishing grounds, and like Our Lady of Good
Voyage bid it back, safely. Living on the Fort that juts into the

DANUTA BORCHARDT

17

harbor, Mr. Maximus would have watched it too. He must have watched many boats come and go and disappear into the fog. He must have known that their fate was guided by the sound of fog horns, bells and buoys and yet....

Not far from the Fort was a buoy by whose song this side of town rose and went to sleep. But Mr. Maximus tired of listening to it moaning and moaning into his bedroom ear. Sailors lost their bearings a few yards off shore, half the town slept well past the hour of noon, fish started jumping to see why it was so quiet one day when he prevailed on the city fathers and mothers to have the buoy shushed. I too missed the sound, but Mr. Maximus' ear was big, bigger than mine, and probably heard too much, much more than its simple rhythmic chanting. "Hey," I thought, "he must have had his reasons," but I started to watch more carefully what Mr. Maximus was up to. Especially when his battles with city hall moved closer to my home. Preservation of old houses was no matter to some, but Mr. Maximus led his life caring, as I soon realized. He fussed and worried about an old abandoned house that stood almost, but not quite, on a curve in my street. It had style. Gray, weathered clapboards (the more they weathered the more stylish they became), gingerbread on the pillars that propped up the overhang. Rats were popping their heads through the cracks but mostly wiggling their behinds and long tails after. City fathers wanted to straighten the street. "It's not quite on the curve," Mr. Maximus argued for the house and for the rats. But he lost. The house was razed and the rats moved on. The street was never straightened because there were other houses there, on the curve exactly. And so he went on gabbling and gibbering by the waterfront or, as I occasionally noticed, in the most dingy of diners while eating the best buy in town—scraps of roast beef and mashed potatoes, with gravy, sometimes a spoonful of green peas thrown in. The diner was not like one of those roadside establishments where truckers eat, where they serve hefty meals, homemade meat loaf, banana cream and coconut custard pies. No saucy comments from the waitress here either, only a smudge of brown stuff from the previous day stuck to Mr. Maximus' plate. Not that this was the fault of the high school kid washing the dishes. He insisted he was hired to shove them in the dishwasher, not to scrub them first. "What's the point?" the kid went on. The cook argued with him for everyone to hear what the point was, but Mr. Maximus told the cook not to squelch the teenager's independent thinking. There was once a movie house in town built originally as a live theater (a small stage, orchestra, balconies, velvet curtains), this known only to historians and to a few very old people, the same people who, as children, saw the elephants of the Ringling Bros. Circus stomp down the narrow Main Street winding to the contour of the waterfront. Mr. Maximus had a habit of sitting in the back of the cinema, watching whatever

18

films came into town. In the back, so that he would not obstruct anybody's view. He was so huge that were I to bump into him in the street my forehead would barely reach the middle of his torso and I would see nothing on either side of Mr. Maximus, no street, no sidewalk, only his torso spread wide. As I walked into the cinema that night I saw Mr. Maximus sitting in one of the back rows, his threadbare coat over his shoulders. I sat in one of the front seats. They were playing *Blowup*. I never cared for the shapes that leaves and branches take on when no one is looking, or shadows that they cast on the unwary, at night especially. I watched the final denouement of the film, when a man's face and below that the point of a gun come into focus on a photo of shrubs in a park, and I sensed my terror mounting. The gun was pointing at me, I was sure. Were I to turn around would Mr. Maximus pass me a slow, reassuring wink? I did not turn around, but that same night I unwittingly put my foot in his heart. Feeling almost certain that Mr. Maximus did not have a car, I went up to him after the movie and offered him a ride home. Maybe a glass of cranberry juice in my home first? Gracious acceptance magnifies those around as they walk beside him, pure and elated. "Thou leadeth me" they sing in their soul. But 'tis all for naught if the giant cannot fit into a VW Bug. We walked up to the car. The small curved form of my Bug looked at me with questioning headlights. Mr. Maximus stood tall, like a Martello tower over the Irish coast on watch for submarines, waiting for me to unlock the door. Too late now to decline the ride as graciously as he had accepted it. I pushed and shoved and squished him till he was in. Sweat on my brow, flushed with embarrassment, it felt hot in the car. But unsuspecting, without grief in my heart, I took him to my home where for several hours his words filled my living room. He did not tell me though, but others did later, that his beloved wife had died in an accident, in a VW Bug. Never again did I have a chance to sip with Mr. Maximus the juice from cranberries—skimmed off from flooded salt bogs—as they are bobbing up and down, little red balls on the water, and pressed into "Ocean Spray" or "Sweet Life," as sweet and sour as life. But as I look in the night at the copse of bushes where the old house once stood and out of the intertwining branches, I see his face take shape, I know why he does not bless me with a wink. Yet there is the comfort that the sun will light up the snow again, and with the hues and warmth of early morning offer me a thin film of potion, reddish-pink and crystalline. Were I to stick out my tongue and lick it.

PETE SEEGER ON CHARLES OLSON

I have been reading with interest the poetry newsletter, *Exquisite Corpse*, and came across the article on Charles Olson. I never got around to reading his poetry, but you might be interested to know that I did know him. It was a little bit over 50 years ago. I briefly had a job as a cook in Boston when I was a student, and the man I was cooking for invited Olson and another Harvard instructor around to supper; and I made so bold as to enter into the conversation and ended up getting fired a week later. But I stayed briefly in touch with Olson for a few months before I left college, and then lo and behold, a full four years later, I'm walking down Eighth Street in Greenwich Village, and I run into this huge tall guy who, of all things, remembers and recognizes me. "What are you doing these days?" he says.

"I'm living around the corner with some other guys, and we make a living singing songs, calling ourselves The Almanac Singers. Why don't you have supper with us?"

So Olson comes to supper and is completely charmed by Woody Guthrie and ends up asking Woody to write an article for a little magazine he is editing called *Common Ground*. The article was a beautiful description of folk music by one of the folks, "Ear Music, " and started off with Woody explaining that by this term, he does not mean you pluck a guitar with your ear.

Next thing, Angus Cameron, one of the editors at Little, Brown Publishers sees the article and writes a letter to Woody asking him if he'd like to try writing a book. And Woody says, "Sure I'd like to try." And during the next year he's pounding out page after page rapid-fire, and in 1943, a little more than a year later, the book, *Bound For Glory*, is selling medium-well. At any rate, you might be interested that that's how Charles Olson helped to get Woody into being a published author.

ROBERT DUNCAN:
THE LIMITS OF ALLEGIANCE

Poet Robert Duncan formed his social and political ideas far in advance of many of his own associates, including his ideas regarding sexual liberation and the status of homosexuals in America. In 1944, he sought to publish in the leftist journal *Politics,* "The Homosexual in Society," a criticism of the hypocrisy of the straight liberal critics who depreciated or ignored the contributions of gay artists—and also of the insular behavior of

20

what he termed a "homosexual cult of superiority" that maintained a private autonomous zone mirroring the hierarchy of the straight world in order to save itself. The article also called for homosexuals to come out by declaring their oppression a "battlefront toward human freedom." Before and after its publication, Duncan, anarchist, faced criticism from all quarters.

The editor of *Politics*, Dwight Macdonald, was concerned about the future of Duncan's career if he published the piece under his own name. "Outing" himself that way even in a literary world that included W.H. Auden and Stephen Spender would expose him to ridicule and blackballing, but not from heterosexuals only; the problems that the gay poet had to face in 1944 did not come just from straight society. Sure enough, in its wake, Parker Tyler, editor of the surrealist journal *View*, attacked Duncan's description of a homosexual elite "filled with an unwavering hostility and fear" for the heterosexual world. Tyler believed Duncan to be full of self-hatred and guilt. But Duncan had insisted upon affixing his name to the piece, writing to Macdonald that "The whole thing has no meaning if it is not signed" (Faas, 150).

There were more problems "at large." John Crowe Ransom, then editor of the conservative *Kenyon Review*, called Duncan's essay "courageous," but in the same breath rejected Duncan's poem, "An African Elegy," after having already accepted and typeset it. Ransom explained his last-second rejection by saying that since he had learned Duncan's sexual orientation, the poem could only be "obvious homosexual advertisement and, for that reason, not to be eligible for publication" (Ransom, 319). According to Duncan biographer Ekbert Fass, Duncan himself allowed that the sexual inferences in the poem were "inescapable" (a word suggested by Ransom in examining his own reading of the work). But later Duncan argued that the theme of the poem was "not homosexuality, but the unknown" (Faas, 153). "Negroes, Africa and the black of love are all symbols of subconscious forces," Duncan wrote in a letter, yet Ransom wasn't persuaded to print the piece. Why did Duncan choose Ransom's journal for his poem, an organ of the New Criticism and the Fugitive Poets, bards of the Solid South and stepchildren of T.S. Eliot? Fugitive magazines ought to have been the last that Duncan sought out. Poetry to them provided an escape from personal emotion; Duncan's romantic work, even without homoerotic content, didn't fit this script. But an unknown writer as Duncan was at the time would look high and low for reputable magazines that might bring out his work, sometimes with more hope than foresight.

Kenyon Review was reputable, maybe, but not very open-minded. Writing to Duncan on October 26, 1944, Ransom observed that while the "homosexuals" possess "this superior perception, sensibility, I do not doubt, in many cases," they should "sublimate their problem, let the delicacy and subtlety of their sensibility come out in the innocent regions of life and literature,"—whatever those may be— "in the same sense, that is, in which repressions cause great works of art which have no recognizable relation to the repressed desires." Behavior that would be viewed by mainstream society as aberrant would especially find no place in Ransom's magazine. In addition to asking what areas would be innocent enough for the gay writer to repress himself in, one wonders what would happen to the "homosexualist" who was discovered dallying there. Where Duncan saw homosexuality simply as one of many ways of loving and experiencing the world, Ransom evidently regarded it as an abnormality so unthinkable that he was ready to call the law: "I am not sure whether or not state and federal laws regard it so, but I think they do; I should not take the initiative in the matter, but if there are laws to this effect I concur in them entirely" (Ransom, 320). His "get out of town, boy," attitude shows the depth of resistance to candid discussion on the subject even in the most elite intellectual circles of the World War II years.

Still, the real controversy behind Duncan's article lay **not in** revealing his identity as a gay man, but in his criticism of alleged **self-seg-regating** homosexual cliques. "Although in private conversation, at every table, at every editorial board, one *knows* that a great body of modern art is created by what almost amounts to a homosexual cult; although hostile critics have opened fire in a constant attack as rabid as the attack of Southern senators upon 'niggers'; critics who might possibly view the homosexual with a more human eye seem agreed that it is better that nothing be said" (Duncan, *Politics*, 209). Denial and fear weren't the exclusive property of the gay elites or homophobes Duncan criticized but also of the "liberal body of critics" who feared to criticize either or to be associated with the topic. "Pressed to the point," Duncan continued, "they may either, as in the case of such an undeniable homosexual as Hart Crane, contend that they are great despite their 'perversion'— much as my mother used to say how much better a poet Poe would have been had he not taken dope," i.e., pointless moralism on one hand, and outright denial on the other that homosexual artists had contributed anything at all to modern art.

But what Duncan's article aimed at mainly was the alleged ingroup hostility of homosexual elites. These were the "most articulate members" of a shadow society who "have been willing to desert that primary struggle" (i.e., for total human liberation) in order to gain at the price if need be of any sort of prostitution, privilege for themselves, however ephemeral..." (*Politics*, 209). The creation of elites whose troubling difference is condoned as long as they mirror the elitism of the dominant social order is nothing new. For instance in Jim Crow New Orleans, an individual who could disguise his identity could "passer blanc,"

22

and benefit from the privileges accorded to whites there, just as a "straight-acting" homosexual could disguise himself or herself today, say, in the offices of a conservative political party. Yet light-skinned blacks (the term itself upsets conventional notions of race) such as James Weldon Johnson emerged from a life of passing to join the struggle. What Duncan wanted was for gays to emerge then, twenty-five years *before* Stonewall. But Duncan's criticism also reported a cult of superiority comparable to the exclusive Creole hierarchy. He proclaimed that these homosexual elites had cultivated "a secret language, the camp, a tone and a vocabulary that is loaded with contempt for the human," which survived far beyond the limits of rank and file "queers" (*Politics*, 210).

Those people he attacked must have felt themselves betrayed. If they were not honest about their orientation but responded, they were outed, and straight society would have another excuse to keep gays locked in the closet. Even the left couldn't openly face the homosexual question; Macdonald's suggestion to Duncan that he publish the article anonymously indicated this lingering disability. Mainline Marxism regarded homosexuality to result from capitalism's repression of women; even according to some contemporary traditional Marxists, homosexuality is an abnormality that will disappear with the triumph of the proletarian revolution and the liberation of women from their inferior (and unlovable?) social status. Duncan's anarchistic limits of allegiance to what might be called "interest groups" even today might be considered divisive and homopohobic by single-issue reformists whose dependence upon mainstream political parties eliminates the possibility of a more fundamental movement for total human liberation. But what some gays in the forties read as denunciation and betrayal by a still unknown writer was actually a call to "take in his own persecution a battlefront toward human freedom." What Duncan wished for was a gay movement that openly joined with labor and racial-equality activists. What he was risking was rejection not only by the Ransoms of the world, but also by the left and the gay world itself. In a time when the working class movement had enslaved itself to Stalinism, progressive forces were also divided over fighting against the Axis or non-cooperation with any state's war. Shadow societies like the gay community remained deep in the back of society's mind, their political potential unexplored.

It wasn't identity as a gay man alone that Duncan wanted to carry into battle. "What I think can be asserted as a starting point is that only one devotion can be held by a human being a creative life and expression and that is a devotion to human freedom, toward the liberation of human love, human conflicts, human aspirations. To do this one must disown *all* the special groups (nations, religions, sexes, races) that would claim allegiance" (*Politics*, 211).

What Duncan valued above all was the "struggle of all humanity for freedom," a conviction that he didn't profess lightly. He had only a few years before he objected to military service by writing to his draft board: "The illusion of possession is a manifestation of the ego; possession of a body, a name, a person, an object, a country, a law. In so far as we defend or seek to secure these, then we yield to this illusion, we dwell in the ego separation and we are at error" (Faas, 139). He could have ended up as did poets William Everson and Robert Lowell, among others, in detention as a conscientious objector; instead, after induction and training, he was detained as a psychological case by officers unaccustomed to that kind of philosophical speculation among draftees, and eventually discharged.

To his list of ego attachments Duncan could have added, "a clique, a claque, a cabal." Duncan's rigorous self-examination and spiritual-psycho-logical studies had led him into regions where personal identity dissolves and sympathy must be extended to the suffering of any soul regardless of its current existence as a straight, a gay, a German, a Jew. It wasn't through desire to betray his "own milieu," as Parker Tyler charged, or his own self-hatred. Nor was it a matter of convenience. Duncan's struggle with his homosexual nature took the same forms of crossdressing and rough-trade cruising as thousands of other men have also pursued. He was far from a model of easy self-acceptance. His internal struggles pushed him to study shamanistic practices of transvestism (Faas, 95) in which the male shaman dresses and behaves as a woman in the belief that only through experiencing the totality of human feeling can an individual pass into the spirit world and gain wisdom. As early as 1939 he declared himself a "shamanistic poet" and filled notebook pages with poems of ritual dismemberment. His detachment was hard-won and real. His anarchism was based in spiritual conviction that eschews allegiance to a part for loyalty to the whole, and rejects conventional partisan politics completely.

One can easily see the result of Duncan's policy of intense self-examination: "Faced by the inhumanities of society I did not seek a solution in humanity but turned to a second out-cast society as inhumane as the first" (Politics, 210). These private communities "offered a family, outrageous as it was, a community in which one was not condemned for one's homosexuality, but it was necessary there for one to desert one's humanity for which one would be suspect, 'out of key'" (Politics, 210–11). Therefore Parker Tyler's accusation of "a confession of a more or less personal guilt-feeling." It's possible to read this that way only if you ignore Duncan's strong sentiments regarding "those troubled emotions, the deep and integral longings that we as human beings feel, holding us from violate action by the powerful sense of humanity that is their source, longings that lead us to love" (Politics, 211). He

24

sensed as a source of love in self-doubt the need for forgiveness and the need to forgive. Duncan characterized gay alienation in the 1940s as the "gaiety" of a closeted population, "a wave surging forward, breaking into laughter and then receding, leaving a wake of disillusionment, a disbelief that extended to oneself, to life itself." Ironically, this sounds like the result of the kind of self-evasion that Ransom recommended as the correct "sublimation" for gays. Realizing that you can't openly love or return the scorn of a scornful society leaves the "different" person crowded out of his own life by emptiness and impotence. The solution Duncan argued was not to extend alienation into numbness and decadence but to realize the universality of alienation and to seek its reversal in love and political action.

WORKS CITED

Bertholf, Robert J., and Ian W. Reid, eds. Robert Duncan: *Scales of the Marvelous.* New York: New Directions Publishing Corp., 1979.

Duncan, Robert. "The Homosexual in Society." *Politics* I, August 1944.

Faas, Ekbert. *Young Robert Duncan: Portrait of the Poet as Homosexual in Society.* Santa Barbara: Black Sparrow Press, 1983.

Ransom, John Crowe. *Selected Letters of John Crowe Ransom.* Edited and with an introduction by Thomas Daniel Young and George Core. Baton Rouge: LSUP, 1985.

LIVES OF THE POETS: O'HARA, SCHUYLER, GINSBERG

TOM CLARK

City Poet: The Life and Times of Frank O'Hara by Brad Gooch. Knopf.

Brad Gooch's *City Poet*, a first biography of the poet Frank O'Hara (1926–1966), is also an extremely informative gossip-survey of the social and sexual mores of the New York avant-garde art scene of the Fifties and Sixties.

Indeed, at times this book resembles a slightly out-of-focus photo in which the background comes out sharper than the foreground figure. Somewhere around the middle O'Hara seems to get lost in the sheer abundance of juicy but sometimes redundant or even irrelevant information about the doings of his glamorous surrounding cast.

Gooch, a poet, novelist and slick-magazine journalist (*Vanity Fair, Harper's Bazaar*), knows the territory. He was a Columbia College student of Kenneth Koch, who, along with O'Hara, John Ashbery and James Schuyler, made up a group of poets known through their association with the Downtown Manhattan abstract expressionist painters as the New York School.

We see O'Hara most clearly in the early parts of the book. A New England Irish Catholic and parochial school upbringing is shown to be the oppressive breeding-ground for his rebellious attitude—one that grows more pronounced with his emergence from family into successive new worlds of the U.S. Navy, Harvard, and graduate school in Ann Arbor, each a fresh stage for the assertion of hard-won personal and artistic freedoms.

Freedom is in fact the key theme in Gooch's portrait of O'Hara. "Born in pain," the poet would one day melodramatically conclude a long autobiographical poem about growing up, "he will be the wings of an extraordinary liberty."

Gooch traces O'Hara's decisive rejection of the faith of his childhood to a traumatic experience of Catholic mourning rites at the death of his father, which occurred when the high-strung, creative young man was an 18-year-old Harvard freshman.

Turning away from the church's harsh view of death, sin and the hereafter would mean for O'Hara a compensatory embracing of life, and all the confusion and complication that came with it. One might say he summed up this critical turning by ironically subverting the catechism definition of sanctifying grace in another of his best-known lines, "Grace to be born and live as variously as possible."

But ghosts of the poet's past were not so easily dispelled, suggests the biographer. The traumatic imprinting of those paternal funeral rites may have continued to haunt O'Hara in later years, when, as his friend the painter Grace Hartigan told Gooch, the poet seemed "overly conscious of death": he often appeared to be at once spurred toward life by it, and unconsciously seeking it.

This can be seen, as Gooch observes, in O'Hara's 1955 elegies on the premature death of the actor James Dean. Obviously identifying deeply with Dean's persona—after seeing *East of Eden* he'd told a friend he noted in the Dean character much of himself, "a naughty boy wondering why he's different"—in these poems O'Hara made the actor a tragic figure of "pride / and speed."

In Dean's early and violent demise, O'Hara may have found the objective correlative of his own self-destructive urges. His poems to the dead actor read now as eerie presages of his own fate.

Taking after his mother, a volatile, anxiety-prone, alcoholic woman who as the years went by became the principal nemesis of his life—harder and harder for him to get along with even as he increasingly came to resemble her—O'Hara had a penchant for reckless plunges. This risk-taking tendency came out with a vengeance once he got to New York in 1951. From that point, his romantic commitment to art

26

and love, the two grand ideals in his life, became the only constant in an existence otherwise bewilderingly various.

A Christmas job at the Museum of Modern Art, selling postcards at the front desk so as to gain daily free entry to the museum's Matisse exhibit, eventually grew into a curatorship which O'Hara held until his death. Despite his obvious competence at the latter post, however, it was not easy for him to hold onto, his job security in time becoming compromised by an increasingly defiant public openness about his gay life style.

A frantic whirl of one-night stands and hopelessly one-sided loves, the sexual promiscuity practised by O'Hara in his heyday may provoke moralistic reaction in some readers today. But Gooch is careful to point out that the poet's sexuality was at a deep level an expression of the same libertarian impulse that also drove him as an artist. If the poet was, as Gooch says, desperately "dedicated to the sexual hunt," it was also true, as O'Hara once told a close friend, that for him "there were other reasons to be homosexual than the sexual one, that he loved the freedom."

The alcoholism, neurotic anxiety, insecurity, depression, insomnia, and death-obsession that troubled O'Hara's later years will come as news to those taken by his reputation for casually tossing off his funny, urbane, boldly straight-from-the-heart "I do this I do that" poems. The famous nonchalance now looks to have been deceptive.

Brad Gooch reports those disturbing problems and symptoms candidly, and even suggests that O'Hara's shocking death, following his being struck down by a beach buggy on Fire Island, contained suicidal elements. But the inner turmoil that from this account was clearly afflicting the poet toward the end of his life, leaving him in one friend's view a "wreck" in his final days, remains in large part mysterious.

In this otherwise highly entertaining and readable book, Brad Gooch suggests the depths of a "hunted and haunted" O'Hara lurking nervously beneath the generous, civilized, witty external demeanor, but never quite sounds them.

SCHUYLER'S TERRIFIC EAR

Collected Poems, James Schuyler. Farrar Straus Giroux.

James Schuyler (1923–1991) was one of the very finest poets this country has ever produced. Despite winning a Pulitzer Prize for poetry with *The Morning of the Poem* in 1980, during his lifetime Schuyler's work never had a wide following outside New York, and even among the poets of the New York School his achievement was largely overshadowed by that of his friends John Ashbery and Frank O'Hara.

The main reason for this lies in Schuyler's notorious

27

refusal, through most of his career, to do readings or public appearances, the principal source of poetic reputation in our increasingly post-literate culture. He was simply more interested in doing his work and living his life than in gratifying his ego by getting famous, something which made him a rarity in his field.

But Schuyler's genius has long been no secret to those who still care about the art (as opposed to the celebrity cult) of poetry. A while back, Ashbery, who ought to know, called him "simply the best we have." The fresh evidence of *Collected Poems* which expands on and now supersedes the 1988 Schuyler *Selected* with a substantial infusion of poems from his earlier, in some cases long-out-of-print collections, as well as thirty *Last Poems* the poet had been assembling for a new book at the time of his death—dramatically confirms that judgment.

Though his terrific ear for the idiomatic spoken language gives all his work a fresh contemporary ring, Schuyler's main greatness lies in his contribution to, and revivification of, the somewhat anachronistic mode of pastoral. Since he wrote about his life not only in the relatively withdrawn locales of Maine and the outer reaches of Long Island but New York City, with Schuyler it was often a slightly ironic *urban* pastoral, in which the flora (like roses, one of his favorite subjects) grew not in wild plots but in pots.

No other American poet has ever done so much with the momentary immediacies of our airs and atmospherics, the fleeting weathers of our days. The one who perhaps comes closest is Elizabeth Bishop: in many respects Bishop is indeed Schuyler's closest similar as a poet, sharing his dynamic lyricism, his founding of the poem in the felicitous *objet trouvé*, his brilliant intimist's touch and painterly way with luminous details, and most of all his subtle particularizing skills in the witnessing of adjacent nature.

In life they shared also a stance of public reticence, but while the reticence was maintained also in her poetry by Bishop, Schuyler's verse became over the years more and more emotionally expressive and open, allowing in all the sweetness and power of excited personal feeling.

In his mature work, heartbreaking intensities of love, loss and joy arise out of, yet are never detached from, the poet's endless inventory of daily miscellany and trivia. There are times when the verse seems almost to lift off the page in half-manic flights of euphoric, elated emotion; other times, often within a brief space of a few lines, a tragic understanding suddenly pervades, and the poem is brushed by dark wings of mortality.

Given Schuyler's quirky, mordant sense of humor, this often happens, as it does in life, in the most banal, commoditized moments—as when the poet, musing about death, speculates that it will take him "with a lifetime jar of Yuban Instant in my right hand,/in my left, Coleman's Mustard"; or when he writes of falling in love as "a calm secret exultation / of the spirit that tastes like Sealtest eggnog."

A splendid example of Schuyler's accumulative or incremental method is the long poem "A Few Days." The shape of this very characteristic Schuyler poem—which circles through some 1200 lines of expansive, seemingly random reflection and gossip before contracting abruptly into a quiet, elegiac conclusion at the news of his mother's death—is the shape of experienced temporality itself, all the dissonances and vicissitudes and daunting complexities faithfully captured, but the preciousness of the instant never forgotten. That sense of wonder, basis of Schuyler's *carpe diem* philosophy of living, shines through with a clarity of epiphany.

"Tomorrow is another day," he writes. "But no better than today if / you only realize it. / Let's love today, the what we have now, this day, not / today or tomorrow or / yesterday, but this passing moment, that will / not come again."

Schuyler's pastoral mode seems to me to recall, at times, that of the "mad" English shepherd-poet John Clare. Schuyler more than once spoke of Clare's *Shepherd's Calendar* as a favorite work, and scattered through these pages are many of his own poems on the seasons, composed over the years in hopes of gradually assembling a month-by-month seasonal calendar like Clare's.

And like Clare, Schuyler was institutionalized after several schizophrenic episodes, in the wake of which he wrote the series of long, thin-lined lyrics from the 1970s volumes *The Crystal Lithium* and *Hymn to Life* that ripple through the midsection of this book like pennants of alternately agitated and ecstatic feeling.

The special effervescence, buoyancy and depth of Schuyler's poems, which seem to happen as if they were bubbling up out of the unconscious, are so spontaneous as to defy theory and theorizing: as he announces in one poem, his intent in writing was "merely to say, to see and say, things / as they are."

In an age rigid with theory, that alone makes reading him all over again a unique pleasure.

THE LIVING PERSONA

Selected Poems 1947–1995. Allen Ginsberg. HarperCollins.

As would befit a national treasure, in assembling his *Selected Poems 1947–1995* Allen Ginsberg has entrusted his verse of the past six decades to an informal poll of poet-friends, who—as he relates in his "Apologia of Selection"—picked their "most vividly remembered" favorites to go with "pivotal scribings" of the author's own choosing. The product, gathering a range of work from Ginsberg's very earliest pieces through signature works like *Howl* and *Kaddish* to recent books like *White Shroud* and *Cosmopolitan Greetings*, is a volume that, as the poet puts it, "summarizes what I deem most honest, most penetrant of my writing."

Insistently, relentlessly "honest," even flagrant, in its attempt to expose the living vividness of the persona at its center, Ginsberg's poetry carries on and carries over into postmodern format the large-scale autobiographical expansiveness of Walt Whitman.

> I am the King of the Universe
> I am the Messiah with a new dispensation
> "Proclamation"

The public performer-poet figure, famous and knowing it, and the aging private man, with his hypochondriac catalogues of trivial symptoms, merge in Ginsberg's latest poems into a curious authorial entity that's so prominent in the foreground one can neither ignore nor see past it.

> It's true I got caught in the world...
> It's 2 a.m. and I got to
>   get up early
> and taxi 20 miles to satisfy
>   my ambition—
> How'd I get into this fix,
> this workaholic show-
>   biz meditation market?
> If I had a soul I sold it
>   for pretty words...
>
> "After Lalon"

If the narrative of elder-statesmanhood here is to be credited, living almost every minute of your waking life in public tends to obscure the dividing line between public and private. Much of the disarming humor—and humanity—of these poems, in fact, derives from Ginsberg's ceaseless confessions of the private weaknesses that render the public man a believable if semi-comic figure.

> sit solitary by the sink
> a moment before brushing hair, happy not yet
> to be a corpse
>
> "Autumn Leaves"

The most recent things here are a handful of uncollected pieces, including an unfortunately representative late-Ginsbergian declension into doggerel called "The Ballad of the Skeleton" ("Said the Presidential Skeleton/I won't sign this bill/Said the Speaker skeleton/Yes you will," and a few moving stanzas about homelessness, to the old hymn tune "Amazing Grace," that echo the poet's earliest Blakean lyric visions ("I dreamed I dwelled in a homeless place/Where I was lost alone /Folk looked right through me into space/And passed with eyes of stone..."

Managing history has become a tic with Ginsberg; tireless in his efforts to transform it, or anyway to annotate it to his liking, he's apparently driven to set the record straight. Here he provides introductory comments, in some detail, on the historical development of his poetry, as well as extensive endnotes that identify persons and places mentioned in it. The introduction veers dangerously toward the self-congratulatory, and the notes at times seem unnecessarily explanatory, descending to the very basic. Maybe it's ungrateful to view these gestures of reader-friendliness as the proverbial gift horse. But Ginsberg's bid to control reader response risks actually limiting it. These poems weren't all that difficult anyway.

EILEEN MYLES ON JAMES SCHUYLER

DANIEL KANE

On February 20th, 1996, I got together with poet, performance-artist, and all-around great writer Eileen Myles to talk about the time she spent taking care of and befriending the poet James Schuyler. Schuyler, member of the so-called "New York School" of poets, which included John Ashbery, Frank O'Hara, Barbara Guest, and Kenneth Koch, was perhaps the least known of the bunch until he published the book *The Morning of the Poem*. This book earned him a Pulitzer in 1981 and the wide audience he always deserved.

I was really looking forward to talking to Eileen about Schuyler's apartment at the Chelsea Hotel, the galleries he visited, his poet-friends, the flowers he surrounded himself with, the boys he kissed...

DK: I've just had a really weird day today, actually. I run this poetry group in a lockup schizophrenic ward uptown, and we used Schuyler's Payne Whitney poems, the ones he wrote while he was a client at that mental hospital...

EM: Yeah?

DK: ...and it was really rough! Some of the patients got upset by the fact that it was so specific to their experience as patients in a mental hospital, and others seemed to be happy that someone could put order into what they were going through...

EM: Right, right.

DK: ...but anyway. Schuyler's poem "A Few Days" was published in 1985, so I was wondering how long you'd been working for Schuyler prior to that time.

EM: Well, it was sort of uneven, because I started working for him I think in May of '79 and then it was pretty constant for 5 or 6 months. By constant I mean like 7 days a week. I think after he got out of the hospital, that's when he got installed in the Chelsea Hotel, and that was when a coalition of friends—mainly the Frank O'Hara Foundation—decided that they should take care of Jimmy and hire someone to take care of him there. And basically my main function *really* was to give Jimmy his pills, because he had burned his previous room down by taking them all at once. So that was the deal, that was why I was there 7 days a week initially. I kind of invented this position of a person who was with Jimmy which continued long after I left. So I was there for 5 or 6 months pretty constantly, and then after that I handed the job on to Tom Carey and Helena Hughes, and then I'd just kinda fill in for them and just slowly became a friend of Jimmy's. It was just kind of a quick, intense marriage.

DK: So you kept in touch with him after you officially stopped working for him?

EM: Oh yeah, of course. But the job was a treat—I got it because I was at St. Marks one night at a reading complaining about my life and how was I going to make money and what was I going to do, and I was talking to Charles North who said "Well, I know a job you could have, but I don't know if you'd want it." And Jimmy was already at that moment probably one of my favorite poets in the New York School and maybe in the world, and I had always been told he was unmeetable, so it was an incredible coincidence.

DK: I was looking at the poem "A Few Days," where Schuyler introduces you by reporting how someone asked him if you were his niece. Schuyler responded by saying—this is from the poem—"No, Eileen Myles is / my assistant: she comes and makes my breakfast and lunch, runs errands / to the grocery store, the P.O., the bank, mails letters and always arrives with / that morning's *Times*." You've started talking about this already, but as a poet yourself, someone who's expressed great respect for him in the past, did you see this job as a *job* or did you feel you were getting into an apprentice situation as a writer?

EM: There's no way one can separate it out that way. What I saw it as was access to Jimmy, you know, and my favorite sort of joke in my head was that the Frank O'Hara Foundation had two functions at that point in time; supporting Jimmy and supporting me. It was access to Jimmy, for sure, and like I said, I really did simply need to make some money so it was incredible—because what I was doing as well, I mean—that's what I was doing actively. What I was doing passively was sitting in Jimmy's room for *hours* reading.

DK: Reading to him?

EM: No, no! We'd just sit there *reading*. He would lie in his bed and read, and I would sit in my chair and read. I would mostly read books I'd pick up off the floor, because his room was strewn with books, and we'd intermittently say "something something something" to each other, you know, it was just really funny. It was like I got to be his roommate. And I got to show him my poems, and I got to see new poems of his, so that it was all those things. I don't really—the word mentor isn't a word that I generally use. You know, it's become so formalized in writing programs, but Jimmy really certainly was that to me, and I had massive respect for him. And it was reciprocated, he was very generous and admiring towards me and my poems and it was important to me...

DK: So, if you don't mind me asking, what was Schuyler reading at the time? I find it so curious that you saw what was going on in his mind.

EM: Oh, you know, endless Virginia Woolf and all sorts of British—he loved serial British novels. The Lucia books?

DK: I never heard of them.

EM: It was some odd British novelist that writes *hundreds* of novels. He always had piles and piles—what is that British magazine—*Country Living* or something?

DK: Oh, *Country Living*, there's a poem in the *Collected* that refers to that magazine. I think it might actually be called *Country Life*.

EM: Yeah. And you know, *The New Yorker*, he was just always reading *The New Yorker*. Of course, everybody on earth sent their books to him, so he would look at those.

DK: So who were the contemporary poets he was into at the time, besides all his friends?

EM: Hmmm...it's hard to say who he was into. There were people whose work was around, like Bill Corbett, whose book I remember him reading, and Gerritt Henry and, God, I can't remember any language poets; I don't think that was much up his alley.

DK: I was curious about that actually, because Ashbery seems to have a kind of a *fatherly* attitude towards the language poets, you know what I mean?

EM: Yeah, but he also tilts towards the kind of abstraction that Jimmy does too, though in a very different way.

DK: That's why I've always liked Schuyler *better*, to tell you the truth. At least for my reading, he seems to have Ashbery's

33

playfulness and appreciation for the abstract but he's also interested in talking about the *real*, in the sense of the "real" as promoting an environment which maintains the use of language for utilitarian communication. Like "pass me the salt," for example.

EM: Right. Well, the thing is, for all of Schuyler's and Ashbery's "togetherness" they're such utterly different writers.

DK: Absolutely. This is a corny question, but do you think your experience living with him gave you greater insight into his poetry?

EM: Yeah, but in the funniest way, which was that I could see Jimmy in some pretty amazing states psychologically and seeming very disturbed or...there was a real storm brewing in some way that was very visible, and yet the poem that he would write in that same moment would seem incredibly sedate and condensed and...I mean, I really felt that I was literally seeing the way in which poetry helped him keep balance, and the values that seemed so "Country Living," that his work can be read as exuding, were in some ways the conditions of his sanity. He was weighing himself down with his perspective on the world and naming each object. I think it's completely all over his poems, that kind of inventory that he does, and often the poem ends with a weird explosion and the viewer's eyes go up, and it seems like the poem is a countdown.

DK: Yeah! That's why I'm so interested in "A Few Days," especially when it's compared to "The Morning of the Poem." In a way, I've always read "The Morning of the Poem" as kind of the pictures you see before *dying*.

EM: Yeah, exactly. Totally.

DK: ...but I always got the picture of "A Few Days" as a more bitter version of "Morning of the Poem," in the sense that mortality seems a lot *uglier* than it did.

EM: Yeah, I'm sure so often you have that feeling. What could be worse than being stuck in life, and a sense of a glorious end, and all the probably attendant metabolic excitement of moving towards one's death, and getting beautiful flashes of the tastes of life and...You know, how many times have you heard that! Someone almost died and they were strangely rescued, only to be furious. "A Few Days" certainly isn't as great a poem as "The Morning of the Poem."

DK: No, it's not. The way I always thought of that was because he just seemed a lot more pissed off. I'm curious to see whether you thought that also.

EM: I don't know about "pissed off" but it certainly wasn't as transcendent. It didn't have the same arc to make. And plus it was...I think we've all done that too, it's like you write a poem and then you do it again. It's hard not to echo something you've done, and you do do it.

DK: Especially after winning a Pulitzer, I imagine.

EM: Yeah, yeah. I think too, that the freshness of invention is ... despite the fact that "The Morning of the Poem" is so much about death, what could be more lively than finding a new way to write a poem? And Jimmy said ... I think he was up at his mother's house and he was reading Whitman.

DK: I've got an interview where Schuyler discusses that time in his life. It's an incredible story. His reaction was ... he was trying to read so he could fall asleep, and actually ended up picking *Leaves of Grass* for his bedtime reading. He said—I think it was to Geoffrey Stokes from the *Voice*—he told him something like "Of course I stayed up all night and up through the next morning, and I said to myself, well, I'll never write as well as that but there's nothing to stop me from at least trying." That's what the long poem "The Crystal Lithium" and ultimately "The Morning of the Poem" came out of.

EM: And also the intention ... I don't know if he said it there or wherever ... but the idea of writing one of those long line poems ... that's the thing that I got out of him having read Whitman. Let's write something wide, which Jimmy didn't do. It was a whole different vision.

DK: Do you know if he used carriage returns as a way to break the line or did he just go to the end of the page and arbitrarily end the line there?

EM: Well, I think his lines were absolutely longer than what you have in the book.

DK: It's interesting to think of that in the context of the difference between prose and poetry. "The Morning of the Poem" is such a poem, but it could be read as almost a novella in a way.

EM: Yeah, totally, and of course if you've read his novels it's the same voice too.

DK: The stuff after the Ashbery collaboration, *A Nest of Ninnies*?

EM: Yes, the novel *What's for Dinner*. Also, if you haven't read it yet, track down *Alfred and Guinnevere* if you want a real treat. That's an *incredible* book. His novels are so far superior to what he did with Ashbery.

DK: That's good to know. You know, I never run into those books for some reason, I never see them anywhere.

EM: Well, *What's for Dinner* is a Black Sparrow book, and *Alfred and Guinnevere* is way out of print, so you'd have to find it. I've never found it, I read Jimmy's copy.

DK: I want to ask you a question about his *room*, which you wrote about in your book of short stories, *Chelsea Girls*, the actual room Schuyler lived in the Chelsea Hotel. Would you say that the way he decorated it and filled it recreated the atmosphere of his life, at least as we see it in the poems—for example the way he talks about light and flowers and autumn? Was that available to him in an urban setting?

EM: Well, he had a great room at the Chelsea. He had a room with big windows and a little porch—not a porch—I mean, somebody might use it, but he didn't—but it had these great French windows and there was plenty of light, and there was a chair right by the window. When I'd come in in the morning he would be sitting there reading. People always brought him flowers, myself included, so there were always these really terrific lush flowers there. And just so many books, so many books. And somebody had taken it upon themselves to build bookshelves. I mean people took care of Jimmy, and it was great—things developed according to who decided "dammit, he needs bookshelves." In that sense, it was just this very rich setting.

DK: Full of orchids?

EM: The flowers represented the people who had come to see him that week, so his friend the painter Darragh Park would bring these, and this person brought that. Everybody knew he loved flowers.

DK: You know the cover of Schuyler's *Collected Poems* that Darragh Park created—is that Schuyler's room?

EM: Let me just look at it…I think so. (begins search for book) Oh yeah, that's absolutely the room.

DK: That's good to know. You know, there's a section in *A Few Days* that I found so tantalizing, when Schuyler says—this is from the poem— "Eileen and I did the galleries and I/watched the women's feet." I'm curious, what was it like to "do the galleries" with Schuyler, keeping in mind that so many poets and critics have always talked about Schuyler in terms of his painterliness.

EM: Right, right. He was just very great. He was just a very careful looker and…doing the galleries was no different from taking a walk with him, which had that funny pace because by that time…no, by that time he hadn't lost…he lost a couple of toes, from diabetes a few years… when did that happen? Maybe five years before he died? So that in the course of walking with him, we'd be walking down the street and suddenly he'd stop cold, and you'd just be standing there and you'd think "Why are we stopped?" And then everything would become very visual and you'd stand there *looking* at everything because Jimmy would be looking at everything. He would be completely quiet. There was this very weird…I mean I just found Jimmy, in a passive way, was one of the most dominating human beings I've ever met in my life. That's what you were around all the time, and so looking at art with him was…you simply felt he was happy, he was very quiet, he would look at things, he would point out some little thing in a painting. He was just deeply appreciative and you felt like you were in a very palpable space. I'd say more fun than looking at paintings with him was going on 10th Avenue, there was an incredible florists', and he would like to go in there and look at flowers. That was like being in Heaven with God. That was really funny. That was an amazing experience. You just felt like you were *in the garden*, and he was just totally happy. If I would pretend that I knew anything at all, he would be very quick to say "No, those are the delphiniums." He knew his flowers inside out, or at least to me it looked that way.

DK: Well, he's definitely the late-20th-century flower poet of all time! I can't think of any other writer who refers to his knowledge so elegantly and yet so humbly when it comes to roses.

EM: Yeah, yeah, well, he read Gilbert White, for sure, too.

DK: Do you know of any painters that stuck out for you, in terms of what you'd see with him, someone who he's especially fond of?

EM: Alfred York I think might be what we looked at, a British painter who does flowers. I mean, it was somebody like that. We would go see Ann Dunn's work. People he knew, pretty much.

DK: You once said something which got printed in the *Village Voice* a couple of years ago, an article about poets' influences. You talked about Schuyler. You said "I'm convinced that Schuyler died exhausted, having held so much together for us." I was confused by that, and I was wondering who that "us" is—is it second generation New York School or is it everyone?

EM: I think *everyone*. I always experienced Jimmy's vision very intensely, and it seemed to me…just the way…the thing I was talking about earlier…you could see him just really cooking. And yet he'd just be looking out the window and be writing a very sedate poem. And there was just this way in which seeing him be that way and then looking at what he wrote made me understand what a completely intense act poetry is. There's a way in which every poet cooking at that level is really making the world. There's a way in which…is the world inventing the language or is the language inventing the world? It really is a bit of a godly feeling, because his counting means it's all really really really there. His counting and his naming is exactly the profound act of language. There's an incredible generosity in that too. I mean, yes he's saving himself, but I do feel that he's saving all of us.

DK: Like Whitman.

EM: Yeah, sure! But a much more private Whitman. So I just think he was done, and you know there's a really beautiful poem that is in...I guess it's in the *Collected*, or is it in the *Selected*, they have some new poems?

DK: Well, I have it right in front of me...

EM: "Six Something?"

DK: Let me just check this out. (looks at Table of Contents) Almost there. All right, here we go. O.K., I have *Last Poems*.

EM: Yeah, it's in there. "Six Something." That poem was one of his very last poems, and it says I think exactly what I'm saying.

DK: You want me to read it?

EM: Yeah, yeah, go ahead.

DK: O.K.

SIX SOMETHING

on June 5th, 90:
closed shops and well-washed
bluelessness, and
across the street
a man finishes
his polishing. I
count seedlings:
always counting,
cars, trees, not
infinitudes of
leaves. The Veterans
Building hides all
the Empire State Building
excepting its antennae
rising in stages
first woven then
slim out of thick
to an ultimate
needle taper pricking
the day: its
point a test
of clarity. And
where is God
in all this?
Asleep? Resting?
and if so, from
what? Eternity
is tireless

surely, like:
rest now forever
blessed tired heart,
wakening otherwhere
in bell-like blue.

EM: I mean isn't that glory, at the end of your life you know what you did and you're doing it one more time?

DK: Yes, yes, absolutely.

EM: I mean, that's kind of "The Morning of the Poem" all over again— you know, "how I made it." I don't know, it just makes me cry. Such a classic, so perfect. You know, I also think … you can look at "The Morning of the Poem" and you can look at "A Few Days" and see one being a greater poem and stuff, and yet of course as long as he was going to be alive he's going to have to keep writing. But the thing that seems to me that he was doing since "The Morning of the Poem" that was really important was he had … he finally had a reading career! I mean, what was that, 65 and he did the first reading of his life.

DK: Well, there's that almost legendary DIA reading in November of 1988 where it seems that every poet from the country attended.

EM: Right. And after it he said to somebody "Why didn't anybody tell me it was this much fun?" And then he had, what, 5 more, 10 more readings? It was just like that was the last blossoming it seemed, where he got not only to be a great poet but got to be a great poet in public who people got to hear and see.

DK: So he didn't read in public simply because he thought it was never going to be terrific?

EM: I think he was terrified of it! I think he was totally terrified. I don't know that he believed, besides publication, that poetry had an outside.

DK: Even though all his friends were out there?

EM: Yeah, but I mean that act of being out there representing the poem with your own body and voice. To me, I think it was terrifying to him. I mean he only did it because DIA paid $3,000 a reading.

DK: Sure … good reason to do practically anything!

EM: Reason enough! By the way, have you talked to Nathan Kernan?

DK: No, I haven't.

EM: He's writing a biography … well, he's editing the diaries, Schuyler's diary, and accompanying them at the front is a biography, like a short biography, and I think he's probably waiting to be Schuyler's biographer, so *he knows everything*. He was a friend of Jimmy's late in his life but he's read all the letters and has talked to all the people and

it might have been him who told me this thing which is amazingly interesting which was about some kind of interview that Jimmy gave in the
70s, and what Nathan told me about the interview was that Jimmy ... he
didn't hesitate or slur or falter at all! He talked in perfect sentences all the
time.

DK: Now was that unusual?

EM: People don't talk that way. With Jimmy, it was just kind of like the
concise quality of his mind was almost monstrous in its beauty, you
know what I mean? There was this way in which he was so self-contained that his language could frequently come out that way too, so that
there was just an awesomeness to his quietness and then his remarks, and
his capacity to represent himself as a poet in such a lucid way despite the
chaos of his life. There was a *completeness to his mind*. Jimmy sort of
falls into the category that maybe ... well, I don't know if this is true. I'm
just thinking of memorial services, there are two kinds. One is the kind
where you hear people get up and talk about a person, and the person
endlessly becomes more complicated and grand, you know, an *endlessly*
different human being. And then there's the other kind of person who ...
you just keep hearing about the same person. And I think Jimmy was
definitely a case of the latter. Almost the more you can gather, the fuller
picture you get, but in some ways it's sort of always the same picture, I
think. He had the art of the devastating remark—the way of putting
something perfectly and quickly. There was just a verbalness he had *in
the world*, in life, in his timing, in the room that you sat in with him. And
that's who wrote the poem.

DK: You say he perfected the art of "the devastating remark." That
reminds me of that final line from Schuyler's poem "This Dark Apartment": "You said so."

EM: Yes, yes. That *three beat ending*, preceded by the lines "But they
weren't lovers. You were."

DK: Now he was doing stuff like that from the *beginning*, from *Freely
Espousing* on, that kind of almost savage treatment of people.

EM: "Get away from me you little fool!" right? Isn't that one of the most
violent lines? Now where is that coming from?

DK: "Country Life" is also sort of a little bit in there, that almost aristocratic *disdain* for silly people, for the people that want his attention *for
no good reason*, you know? I've always been attracted to that in the
same way that I'm terrified of my own father, who's *British*. There's that
same kind of aristocratic British scariness going on, which is also
absolutely charming at the same time.

EM: Mmm. Jimmy was a surprising man. Like suddenly he had a
lover in the last few years of his life! He had this boyfriend

who just kind of came out of the blue. Suddenly there was Artie, and it was like Jimmy's Eros, which everybody had thought was long gone and sort of came out in sonnets to Tom Carey and stuff like that was just, you know ...

DK: So sexuality was still there for him in the end?

EM: Yes, I think absolutely.

DK: Because in the "The Morning of the Poem" he's a little bit upset that he's losing his erections and all that kind of stuff, which also of course ties into the whole elegiac sense of that poem.

EM: Right, so "A Few Days" might have been a lesser poem but he had other things going on in life!

JUST A MOMENT: PAUL BLACKBURN AND THE FRAGMENTATION OF THE NEW AMERICAN POETRY

BOB HOLMAN

"It's a Martian thing. You wouldn't understand." Paul Beatty

You can sit in the I can't call it a park, let's just call it a triangle, the one created by Stuyvesant and 9th and the fence round St. Mark's-in-the Bouwerie, tipping into Second Ave and find yourself *In. On. Or About the Premises.* The premises are of course Paul Blackburn's the map the poem "The Slogan." The Church, did it break Paul's heart, is the question, and NO, is the answer.

Paul Blackburn is the subtle father of the Poetry Project at St. Mark's Church, the pre-spirit. Three trees were planted outside the Parish Hall near 11th Street, the one dedicated to Blackburn growing next to Frank O'Hara's who died in 1966, the year the Poetry Project was founded, with the third dedication to Wystan Hugh Auden, who was a parishioner at St. Mark's, often heard coughing in a back pew. Ted Berrigan's tree grows there now, as does Michael Scholnick's. The subtle father led a vision that grows as trees do.

In the early 60s, at Mickey Ruskin's Deux Magots and later at a coffee shop on Second between 9th and 10th called the Metro, Blackburn ran a poetry reading series that included as regulars Beats, New York School poets, Deep Imagists, Black Mountaineers, Umbra poets, Patarealists, and 2nd Ave poets, among others. He wielded a big bucket, and had a way of standing so that to get in, you'd either be squeezed or drop something in. "Something for the poets?"

41

he'd ask. The different groups coexisted because Paul knew how to do it.

This was the flowering of the coffeehouse poetry scene. Paul would go from reading to reading, hauling his jumbo public-high-school issue Wollensak reel-to-reel, recording open and featured readings all over town. At night, he'd record jazz or rock off the radio, or read (rewrite?) his own poems on tape. He was a walking exponent of the oral tradition. His tapes, collected at the University of California at San Diego Library, are a document of an era, with the word at the center and poets breathing them in and out.

Blackburn held court long afternoons at McSorley's, this before the word "writing workshop" was invented. There he embodied what was to become the definition of what the Church, especially through the "workshops" of Alice Notley and Bernadette Mayer, would be: a place to inspire, not define.

First the Poem.

Then, the Theory.

But back at the Metro, the center wasn't holding. A minimum was instituted: 25 cents, the price of a cuppa. A Goldwater poster appeared on the wall. Blackburn's sensibility, the owner of the cafe's lack of sensitivity, the changing of an era. In 1965, LeRoi Jones led a walkout and the New American Poetry fragmented.

The rest is the end of history.

AN ABSOLUTELY GIFTED WRITER: MEMORIES OF JAN KEROUAC

GERALD NICOSIA

I knew Jan Kerouac as a writer before I ever met her as a person. Early on in my research for *Memory Babe*, I read a chapter from an "autobiographical work" by her tentatively called *Everthreads*; it was published in the *City Lights Journal*, No. 4, in 1978. Her writing was unbelievably lively, sensitive, humorous, and thoughtful for a young woman of twenty-six. The little excerpt recounted her adventures with several different men in Central America, and it evoked the place and the characters with tremendous vividness. But what was really special about the piece was Jan Kerouac herself—the sense of this mind that loved to rove and play with itself. I remember she wrote something about how wherever she traveled, she'd always ask herself *how she wound up there*, and the game of finding an answer kept her from ever getting bored.

When I met Jan a few months later, I was—like most other men on the planet—captivated by her stunning good looks and scintillating intelligence. She seemed to have something interesting to say about almost everything, and—what was immediately apparent—she loved language. Putting words together for her was making something permanent, something of beauty that would last, unlike the fragile earthly beauties of home and family that kept fading beyond her grasp. I remember her telling me, many times, how she hated the fact that words kept changing their meaning and pronunciation through time. She hated the corruption of language and had a special outrage at the mispronunciations of news telecasters and advertising spokespeople.

I was on the road constantly in those days doing interviews for my biography of her father. Jan was on the road because it was her way of life—and remained so almost to the very end. We met in San Francisco, at Carolyn Cassady's house in Los Gatos, at her mother Joan's house in Kittitas, Washington, and at the house of artist Stanley Twardowicz in Huntington, Long Island. Later, Jan would come to stay at my home in Lyons, Illinois, and then in my new home in San Francisco. Whenever we met, she always carried the manila folder with "Everthreads" scrawled in large letters across it. I was only two years older than Jan, but I had a couple of degrees in literature, and Jan looked to me to tell her whether what she was writing was any good. I was able to help with a little grammatical editing; but as far as I was concerned, Jan's work was basically untouchable. It already bore the mark of a unique vision and a unique voice. She was not writing because she was a famous man's daughter. She was writing because she had already lived far more broadly and intensely than most people, and because it was important to her to preserve as much of her life as possible in language. And for someone with almost no formal schooling, she picked up new words, and even the basics of several foreign languages, with an amazingly sure grasp. She was a living argument for the fact that language ability is indeed in the genes.

I began sending out chapters to various magazines and publishers as she wrote them. A lot of the replies were nasty, like one from a woman editor at *Playboy*, who said, "We don't need an 'On the Road with Kerouac's Daughter.'" Jan would spend her life, and her literary career, always trying to be seen beneath her father's huge shadow. But she considered herself a very different kind of writer than Jack Kerouac. "I'm more subjective," she told me once, speaking about how her own emotions interested her more than action-packed adventure. Ironically, though, when *Everthreads* was edited, packaged, and marketed as *Baby Driver* (a title which was forced on Jan by the publisher and which she always hated), it was the picaresque aspect of the book that was touted—the wild woman in her fast Caddy—and not the mind and soul explorer that truly made her and her work so special.

Of course it was miracle enough that the book did get out. Jan had gotten halfway finished and then put the manuscript on the shelf. She was living with her mother and working in a corn cannery, and she thought of going to college because in Washington she could get an educational subsidy. Larry Lee and Barry Gifford brought her down to San Francisco for the ten-year anniversary of her father's death, a gala celebration which also marked the publication of their oral biography *Jack's Book*, at the Old Spaghetti Factory in North Beach in October 1979. One night while she was in town, we sat at the bar in Vesuvio's, and she told me she had given up writing because she could never earn a living that way, and that college might at least land her a decent job. I told her my two degrees had scarcely earned me anything, and I promised her that if she kept writing, I would do everything possible to see her published.

Before she left the Bay Area, I introduced her to Joyce Cole, who was just starting her own literary agency. With the encouragement of both myself and Cole, Jan kept writing for another year, till the book was finished, though she still labored at lousy jobs like short-order cook and dishwasher. Then Cole managed to sell the book to St. Martin's, where a sharp editor, Barbara Anderson, did a good job of focusing on the most interesting parts and giving some order to what had been a fairly rambling narrative. Jan's instinct was always to include everything. I think, had she had the time and a crisis-free life, she would like Proust have finally put together one huge, all-inclusive autobiography. She had invented the title *Everthreads* because her mother was a seamstress, but it also reflected her view of her life as one long, entangled continuum, from which past, present, and future were never completely separable.

In the last two years, when she could no longer see enough to work on a typewriter, she was trying to put as much of her life as she could remember on tape. Sadly, the kidney failure was also beginning to take away significant areas of her memory too, and the loss of whole chunks of her experience grieved her even more than the freedom she'd lost having to do dialysis four times a day.

It was Barbara Anderson who structured *Baby Driver* with chapters alternating between Jan as child and Jan as hell-raising young woman. It made the book a neater product, but Jan was never completely happy with it. She wished that she'd been able to find a structure to convey that the two Jan Kerouacs were really one and the same: a more complex truth, even if literarily less clever.

After the publication of *Baby Driver* in 1981, several years went by before I saw Jan again. She was making the most of celebrity, traveling everywhere, lecturing and reading her work, going through men, drink, drugs, and every sort of experience at a frighteningly fast pace. In 1985, just back from Baja California, she stopped in San Francisco to see me, to have lunch, show off the new paperback edition of

Baby Driver with a picture of her leaning against a big car, and to tell me about her next novel. She was calling it *Loverbs*, a title which meant to convey that action was somehow her way of searching for love. The more I got to know Jan, in fact, the more I came to realize that where everyone saw this fantastically gorgeous, sexy, daring young woman (for whom taking off her clothes at parties was no big deal), there was really inside Jan a lonely, rejected little girl dying to be truly loved. That she never found that one big, true love was perhaps the greatest tragedy of her life.

Loverbs was finally published as *Trainsong*, a title which came from the area of Eugene, Oregon, near the railroad tracks where her mother lived. By and large, the book got better reviews than *Baby Driver*, and with good reason. Carolyn See in the *Los Angeles Times* picked out the tremendous sadness that underlay much of Jan's adventure writing, and it was that exquisite chord of sadness—like a Beethoven sonata—that touched me most when I read the book. My favorite passage in it will always be the scene at Allen Ginsberg's house in Boulder on October 21, when she looks into the blue flame of the furnace grate and says "Daddy," wondering how she can ever find her father again after so much lost time.

When Jan died, she was struggling to finish her third novel, *Parrot Fever*, which would have completed the trilogy of what it meant to be the daughter of the Beat Generation's greatest icon. That book marks a great deal of growth in her as a writer. She was writing in the third person, to obtain greater objectivity, and she had split herself into two half-sisters, both of them scarred by a missing father. One had gone into the depths of life, into drugs, stripping, and petty crime; the other had become a rootless wanderer and a writer. Somehow she wanted to make sense of her schizophrenic life by bringing both those characters together at the death of their mother—which was to be the death of Jan's own mother, Joan, on Mother's Day 1990. The theme of the book was to have been loss and rebirth, something Jan knew in her soul since she was old enough to notice that "Daddy" wasn't there.

Because she was working on tape at the end of her life, it is unclear how much of *Parrot Fever* was completed. Ideally it will be published with the other two novels someday as part of the trilogy she intended—a movement from joy and exuberance through pain, sorrow, and loss, to final understanding and redemption. No other child of a Beat hero has attempted such an ambitious chronicle. Even in its incompletion, Jan Kerouac's work is a literary milestone that will surely gain in recognition and admiration as time passes, and her accomplishment can stand free of the adversity and controversy that were, besides his name, a famous father's only legacy to her.

DEAR FRIENDS OF MY FATHER, JACK KEROUAC

Last June, I was removed by police from a conference about my father, Jack Kerouac, at New York University. My only "crime" was that I wanted to announce that two major libraries—including the Bancroft at UC Berkeley—were prepared to offer one million dollars for the deposit of Jack Kerouac's entire literary archive. But the family who now control that archive, the heirs of Jack's third wife Stella Sampas, led by her brother John Sampas, clearly do not want to make the archive available for study, because it is of more value if sold off piecemeal.

My father did not want the Sampas family to control his archive. The last letter he ever wrote, on October 20, 1969, to his nephew Paul Blake, Jr. (my cousin), stated: "I just wanted to leave my 'estate' to someone directly connected with the last remaining drop of my direct blood line ... and not to leave a dingblasted f—ing goddamn thing to my wife's one hundred Greek relatives." This letter has been certified as authentic and is currently on deposit in the Berg Collection of the New York Public Library.

The Sampas family will do anything to keep me from speaking out about their excessive commercial exploitation of my father's papers, artworks, and belongings. They have even threatened me with a libel suit if I continue to speak. And they have made certain that I can never be part of any events that celebrate my father, which they also are a part of. In eight years of Kerouac celebrations in Lowell, Massachusetts, staged by a committee of which John Sampas is a prominent member, I have never once received a single invitation.

Once again, my father's work is being commercially exploited by both the Whitney Museum and the Sampas family, at the Beat Culture and the New America exhibit, funded largely by AT&T, and once again Jack Kerouac's only child has been excluded. I wrote to Lisa Phillips, the curator, almost a year ago, and, predictably, received no answer. It is clear that I am not wanted there, because my presence would antagonize the Sampas family, whose Kerouac properties are worth so much money.

This kind of commercial glorification of my father's work, at the expense of the human values he stood for, is a travesty and a disgrace, and should be stopped immediately if his spirit is truly to be honored.

AMPLITUDE

TOM CLARK

Jack Kerouac: Selected Letters 1940–1956, Edited by Ann Charters, Viking.

The publication of the first volume of Jack Kerouac's letters puts in the hands of the general reading public a central element in the Kerouac canon, opening up key areas of the writer's work and thought previously accessible only to his biographers and a few other "inside" witnesses. As amply evidenced here, Kerouac was a great letter writer who wrote letters with a passion many other great writers' epistolary productions sadly lack. Certainly there's no mistaking in Kerouac's eloquent letters the pain and bitterness he felt while living in poverty as a rejected novelist through the very years when he was composing his finest works, *On the Road*, *Visions of Cody*, *Dr. Sax*, and *The Subterraneans* among them.

In a 1959 letter to Carolyn Cassady, a particular friend to whom he dared show his most vulnerable side, Kerouac confided his personal straits just after completing *The Subterraneans*. Living in his mother's modest home on Long Island, he saw no career success in the cards for himself: "I have $30 to my name & hope to earn some cash in Xmas rush baggageroom work if possible in this overcrowded frosty fag town; the least of which I can say for it. I always end up knocking off a couple more prose masterpieces ere the publishers repeat & make known to me thru masks of 'luncheon' & 'contracts' their dark contempt for the dedicated prophetic & pure scribbler beholden to no contract but that which the stars drew up, in the end to no revision but Time's own sea of it, to no commercial slant but the sun's on the commerce of the brow, to no hope of earning but the harvest after sleep." Like so many other passages in his letters to Carolyn, this one discloses much about Kerouac: his devotion to writing as a spiritual vocation, his purity of motive, and total, disarming honesty; but also his self-isolating hypersensitivity, manifesting itself in the misplaced homophobic vocabulary used to express his profound distrust of the East Coast intellectual world in general and the New York publishing industry in specific.

A more virulent strain of the latter appears in letters to his friend Allen Ginsberg, who for a brief period in the early '50s acted as Kerouac's soi-disant literary agent in New York City, and to Ginsberg's friend Carl Solomon, editor at a paperback house where Ginsberg was trying in 1952 to peddle the as yet unpublished *On the Road* (the book had by then undergone a sea-change into the sprawling manuscript later published as *Visions of Cody*). Increasingly impatient with what he regarded as weak-kneed prevarication and delay on the part of his New York contacts, Kerouac finally blew up. In a subjective tantrum-letter sent off from his impoverished exile in Mexico, Ginsberg, Solomon, and John Clellon Holmes—another writer Kerouac suspected of cashing in vicariously on his own breakthroughs—were accused of manipulative and envious interference in his fate, and dismissed as "parasites." "If instead you were men I could at least get the satisfaction of belting you on the kisser—[but] too many glasses to take off," Kerouac angrily told Ginsberg. "You are all a bunch of insignificant literary egos ... My whole record in NY is one long almost humorous chronicle of a real dumb li'l abner getting taken in by fat pigjaws ... the time has come for all you frivolous fools to realize what the subject of poetry is ... death ... so die ... and die like men ... and shut up ... and above all ... leave me alone ... & don't ever darken me again."

Such occasional irrational outbursts, it must be said, once again reveal only one aspect of the many-dimensional Kerouac personality encountered here. The heroic amplitude of his artistic project, as well as the care he invested in it, always remain looming somewhere in the background behind the temporary frustrations, confusions and embitterments.

The popular, partly self-created misconception that Kerouac never altered or revised his spontaneous prose outpourings, already long-belied by biographers, is disproven decisively by the extended rehearsals of literary works to come contained in the correspondence. One series of 1950s letters in particular, provoked by receiving a long, rambling, Proustian "confessional" letter from his road buddy Neal Cassady, shows Kerouac working his way through the "inside" story of his own life. This deliberate, self-conscious trial-run material, sorted and carefully re-shaped, would supply foundations for the novels that turned Kerouac's personal story into his fictive autobiographical "legend"—the myth of the truth of his soul. "Someday I'm going to write a huge Dostoevskyan novel about all of us," Kerouac exclaimed excitedly to John Clellon Holmes from Mexico City while at work on *Dr. Sax* in the summer of 1952. "What I am beginning to discover now is something beyond the novel and beyond the arbitrary confines of the story ... into realms of revealed Picture ... wild form, man, wild form. Wild form's the only form holds what I have to say—my mind is exploding to say something about every image and every memory ... I have now an irrational lust to set down everything I know."

As we just now begin to map fully the fallout of that creative explosion, these letters offer an invaluable blueprint to the intricate, high-yield ballistics that went into creating it.

SPARROW AND THE BEATS

I went to the Beats Exhibit at the Whitney to protest it. My friends, The Unbearables, had called a protest on the second day of the exhibition—the first free night. (The Unbearables are a group of writers who give long, democratic readings and protest Wrongs. So far we have protested the poetry in *The New Yorker*, The Kerouac Conference at NYU, and this.)

I wasn't sure what to protest about "Beat Culture and the New America: 1950–1965" until I ran into Mike Tyler at the Nuyorican Cafe.

"Did you see the ad in *Paper*?" he asked. "AT&T is sponsoring the exhibit."

I went to my local Gujerati newsstand, and there was the ad in *Paper*, showing a collage of Beats, the famous bell logo, and announcing: "Communication. Whether it's poetry, jazz, or your grandmother calling you for Christmas, we're involved. AT&T." Or something like that.

So I wrote this flyer, and mimeographed it at St. Mark's Church.: "We would like to thank AT&T for generously supporting the Beat exhibit. This demonstration, against the exhibit, is brought to you by Pepsi, the drink that *demonstrates* its taste again and again. Give the gift of life. Give Pepsi."

Then I wrote a second flyer, explaining my first flier: "I envision a Future where not only cultural rebels are underwritten by corporations, but the rebels *against* the rebels are similarly sponsored. Thus, rivalries between Schools of Art are actually advertising wars."

We gathered outside the Whitney at 6:00 on a Thursday, and began handing out pamphlets, shouting inflammatory slogans ("The Revolution will begin on E. 75th St.!" I prophesied), and confounding the populace, who could not decide if we were part of the exhibit.

At 8:00 the flow of visitors slowed, so we went inside. Immediately I was depressed. "Beat Culture and the New America: 1950–1965" was so *quiet*. It reminded me of the Asian Peoples exhibit at the Museum of Natural History, where you see, within glass, wooden Siberian tribesmen ladling out stew and curing venison—except this exhibit had wooden bohemians and artists; Poets Under Glass. It was so funereal.

And the artifacts! This was an art museum, so the curators had to produce *art* to illustrate Beatdom (although "Beat" was never, to my knowledge, an art movement) and they poured on paintings—canvases by Kerouac, Burroughs, Julian Beck (of the Living Theatre) and even *worse* paintings—particularly on the *left* side of the exhibit, entitled "San Francisco." (Michael McClure's art was both bad and giant.) On the *right* side, "New York," they had Great Art (Jackson Pollock, Franz Kline, Larry Rivers) by non-Beats.

It became painfully obvious that the curators, who

49

had collected the Beat material, shouted: "Oh no! We're doomed! This stuff is awful!" and threw in 3 walls of great abstractionists (which no one as far as I could tell, looked at).

So what *were* the Beats? Clearly, a bunch of hopped-up guys (and 3 gals) who painted bad paintings, wrote immense novels on speed (we see the Sacred Scroll of *On the Road*—with no paragraphing—written in three days on Seconal) and gave intense poetry readings in tenements on E. 3rd St. For it is in their photos that Beats truly live. The fatalistic French charm with which they smoked, leaning against walls, in photographs by Allen Ginsberg, excites a painful nostalgia. Life was a Mystery then, which Beats knew they could intuit, with enough drugs, coffee, and sleeplessness. Their artifacts were largely inane, but their passion for them was holy and pure. (My God, I'm *writing* like a Beat!)

Then I put on headphones to hear the Music That Inspired Them (Miles Davis' "Round Midnight") and thought, "*This* is the *real* art"— cool, perfect music, like water descending a mountain.

RONNIE BURK

AN OPEN LETTER TO ED SANDERS: I DON'T CARE IF JACK KEROUAC WIPED HIS ASS WITH THE AMERICAN FLAG, DON'T FORGET THE INDIANS

"Constitution written by a bunch of gangsters to exploit a continent" is what Charles Olson told me.

—Diane DiPrima
Revolutionary Letter #61

Imperialism: The policy of extending a nation's authority by territorial acquisition or by the establishment of economic and political hegemony over other nations.

—The American Heritage Dictionary

July 4, 1994
Dear Mr. Sanders,

I was not satisfied with our brief exchange at the NYU Beat Conference during the "On The Road" panel discussion (Saturday afternoon, 5/21/94 Loeb Auditorium).

To refresh your memory: I walked into the auditorium and found a couple of people on the panel and in the audience

50

commenting on how free we all are in the United States. To my utter amazement one guy went as far as to tell the story of how he was descended from the Mayflower set. I had to blink my eyes to make sure I wasn't at a meeting of The Daughters of the American Revolution. I turned to the woman sitting next to me and asked her. "What does this have to do with the intellectual avant garde?" Finally unable to tolerate such nonsense I walked up to the microphone and got in line to challenge all the jingoism I was hearing.

Reminding the panel and the audience that in fact this country was founded on slavery and genocide I asked "is beatism a patriotic trip?"

After a few stand-up routines from Hunter S. Thompson you thoughtfully answered that Jack Kerouac folded the flag and that "yes" you believed it was possible to be a "patriotic rebel." You further stated that unlike Russia who had just recently freed their slaves this country had freed its slaves a hundred years ago and no longer practiced genocide. There was little time to discuss these points but I was able to thank you for answering my question and reminded everyone "don't forget the Indians." I would like to take the time now to expand on my initial question and respond to your answers.

Your use of the "better than Russia" argument only serves to confirm my own belief that McCarthyism never ended in this country but was institutionalized as the presidencies of Nixon and Reagan, both rabid McCarthyites, indicate. As for the notion that the United States freed "its slaves" let a recent political prisoner Assata Shakur set the record straight:

"I don't work for nothing. I ain't gonna be no slave for nobody. Don't you know that slavery was outlawed?"

"No," the guard said, "you're wrong. Slavery was outlawed with the exception of prisons. Slavery is legal in prisons."

I looked it up and sure enough she was right. The Thirteenth Amendment to the constitution says: "Neither slavery nor involuntary servitude, except as a punishment for crime whereof the party shall have been duly convicted, shall exist within the United States, or any place subject to their jurisdiction."

Well that explained a lot of things. That explained why jails and prisons all over the country are filled to the brim with Black and Third World people, why so many Black people can't find a job on the streets and are forced to survive the best way they know how. Once you're in prison, there are plenty of jobs, and if you don't want to work, they beat you up and throw you in the hole. If every state had to pay workers to do the jobs prisoners are forced to do the salaries would amount to billions. License plates alone would amount to millions. When Jimmy Carter was Governor of

51

Georgia, he brought a Black woman from prison to clean the state house and baby sit for Amy. Prisons are a profitable business. They are a way of legally perpetuating slavery. In every state more and more prisons are being built and even more are on the drawing board. Who are they for? They certainly aren't planning to put white people in them. Prisons are part of this government's genocidal war against Black and Third World people.

—*ASSATA an autobiography by Assata Shakur*

Which leads me to your statement that this country no longer practices genocide.

On January 1, 1994, in Chiapas, Mexico an uprising by the Mayan peoples of the Lacandon rainforest occurred in direct response to the United States' implementation of the North America Free Trade Agreement (NAFTA) and the obvious genocidal implications of that treaty. NAFTA threatens to deepen levels of poverty and starvation upon millions of Indian peoples throughout Mexico.

In the United States, the Hawaiian people have initiated their own Sovereign Rights movement precisely because the Hawaiian people are dying out like an endangered species of bird. Their numbers since the annexation of Hawaii by the United States have dropped by such a degree that it is predicted that by the early part of the 21st Century there will be no more Hawaiians in Hawaii.

Aside from the continued maltreatment of Native Peoples by the United States government, we have the consequence of AIDS. Perhaps or perhaps not a biological weapon, the United States government's response, or lack thereof, can be described as genocidal given the effects this disease has had on African, Latino, White, Gay, and Addicted people here in the United States.

Then there is the foreign policy of this country, most recently Haiti and Iraq, and let's not forget, the horrible war against Viet Nam. No, to flatly say the United States no longer practices genocide as policy is more than arguable: it's simply not true.

With the collapse of the Soviet State, United States hegemony around the globe remains unchecked. In Eastern Europe there are reports that old style National Socialism is being revived and mutated within the old Stalinistic bureaucracy. Here at home increasing repressive measures, a move towards the construction of more and more prisons and cuts in social services for the poor and working people, spells trouble for millions.

For all these reasons and more, it is my belief that it is the intellectual responsibility of writers, poets. and artists to be ever-vigilant against the jingoistic trap of national chauvinism. Fundamentally, the very notion of a United States founded on genocide, slavery, and colonial wars is inherently a racist and imperialistic notion. There is nothing rehabilitative about our thoroughly corrupt bourgeois society. Thus the fallacy that one can be a "patriotic rebel."

Certainly Jack Kerouac, great and prolific writer; subject of legend: chronicler of the post-war "American" scene; heroic figure of our time, is worthy of our highest esteem. To base, however, a politic on his own distorted, albeit romantic, view of the United States, is as moronic as it is naive.

There is a story that Ken Kesey tells of a drunk Kerouac walking into a room of dope-smoking hippies sitting on an over-stuffed sofa draped with the "American" flag. "You can't do that," admonished Jack Kerouac, "you can't sit on the flag like that." I believe that was the moment that Jack Kerouac consigned himself to the history books. Time had passed him by. The Viet Nam War had charged a new generation with a new revolutionary impulse in direct opposition to the imperialist nature of the United States.

Thirty years later I found myself in an auditorium in New York City hearing people telling another generation all that crap about Old Glory and all in the name of Jack Kerouac. Knowing that Walt Whitman supported the United States' invasion of Mexican sovereignty in the Mexican-American War and that Gertrude Stein wrote speeches for Petain and after the war wrote paeans to the Dough Boys, my argument is simply this: there is a fine line between national chauvinism and social fascism. Fascism is as intolerable in an intellectual as much as it is in a goon.

I write you, Ed Sanders, because of my concerns over the rise of fascism across Europe and the reactionary isolation I sense deepening here in the United States. The century is closing, and as I told Dr. Hunter S. Thompson, "this is no laughing matter."

FROM THE DADA ARCHIVES

Dear John Cage,

Now that I know that you are editing *The Corpse* I can write you after the fact. Having never met you altho I did see you at a concert you gave in Boulder on the very night Nixon resigned. It was a fiasco. Now Nixon is back like his artistic double Andy Warhol. What I find most fascinating about all of you is your tremendous flair to bore me to death. I remember that afternoon before your concert Nixon was on TV giving his resignation speech. I turned the color dial and his face went green. It was my best collage effort and nobody noticed. Funny now that I think about it. Kerouac dead his prose selling sports cars on the telly. Warhol dead sells khakis for

RONNIE BURK

53

Gap along with that other scam artist Avida Dollars. Frida writes from the grave, the last of the Stalinist heroes, her diary will make some publishing honcho millions. Nixon's flawed postage stamps are worth $8,000 apiece. There seems to be no end for the dead to arrive more famous more exploitable than ever. A whole new definition for deadbeats is in order. I must warn you. Any more articles about Andy Warhol and I will have to stop sending you poems. It's not like I can threaten to cancel my subscription.

PAT NOLAN

IN MEMORY OF TED BERRIGAN

Life wriggles across
        the microscope's slide
from left to right
        so I'm given to assume
though I only know
        one thing for certain
a scratched ass is a contented ass

the anchor of dogma drags bottom

whine and growl on
        the distant highway
machines hiss as
        they plow through
the orange air
        here it's only
the dominant silence
        of a beating clock

guitar riff winds down
        the scale of my nerves
            and for my ears alone

where I am stretched out
        in memory of Ted Berrigan
in the recumbent position
ashtray and book at bedside
that faraway look pen in hand

"I don't want to confuse things with ideas now"

feeble buzz

Kerouac's winter fly
in the corner of the window
           after the sun's gone down
as I
           great reclining buddha of evening
contemplate these illusions
           our past and future lives

A LITTLE KNOWN FACT

KEITH ABBOTT

On the first Monday of April, 1985, I happened by the Café Mediterranean on Telegraph Avenue in Berkeley and stopped for a cup of cappuccino. I took the table nearest the front door, as it was the only one available. I was watching the street scene when I thought to look around the back, to see if anyone I knew was there.

Seated at the third table from the back was Ted Berrigan. His beard was neatly trimmed and he sported grey, rather than black, heavy rimmed glasses. He was still portly, but not heavily so. His pearl-buttoned, short sleeve shirt revealed arms that were much thinner than the Ted I knew. With a mild-mannered air, he stared out in his Irish fashion, head tilted back as if expecting news of a vaguely thought-provoking nature. In short, he looked like an off-duty scholar, having a cup of coffee.

I took my cappuccino and asked if I could sit with him.

"Sure."

I introduced myself and asked him if he was the poet Ted Berrigan.

He admitted he was.

I went on to say that I wasn't sure if he could remember, but I had been introduced to him sometime in 1975 when he flew into San Francisco for a reading.

"Oh, that wasn't me. That was Ted."

"You almost say that..."

"Well, he was my stand-in."

"Really? When did you switch?"

"Around 1965. When I came out here for the Poetry Conference, I was tired of taking speed and staying up all night and talking. I was getting confused. I needed a way out. Plus I wanted to start my thesis on F. T. Prince. So, I found this guy who looked kinda like me, and we traded places. I'd sent the joker some poems from time to time, but after a while they started coming back covered with coffee stains and this weird grade school handwriting. So I figured he took over."

"What about your friends?"

55

"To tell the truth, most of the people I ran with were high. None of them knew the real me. I told this guy to grow a beard real long, look at people crazy, and nobody would bother him. I guess he passed."

"That's amazing. Are you still writing?"

"Oh yeah. Sonnets—but they're not ready yet." Then, more darkly, "Not ready by a long shot."

TROUBADOUR OF CONCRETE ALLEYS

TOM CLARK

Cranial Guitar: Selected Poems by Bob Kaufman. Introduction by David Henderson. Edited by Gerald Nicosia. Coffee House.

Bob Kaufman's career in poetry, as David Henderson correctly suggests in his generously informative introduction to Kaufman's *Cranial Guitar: Selected Poems*, resembles nothing else in the annals of American literature.

This is one poet who never taught creative writing, held a residency, did a conference, sat on a committee, published an essay or gave a lecture. He produced only three slim volumes of poems and a few songs and broadsides, achievements for which he was elected to no academies.

An enigmatic, wiry, mostly silent Black man, Kaufman appeared a frail, waiflike, otherworldly figure. Wandering the streets of North Beach for some three decades until his death in 1986, he may have looked to some people like a head case, druggie panhandler, or saintly mendicant Buddhist bum. "He was actually the man that Herb Caen coined the term 'Beatnik' to describe," one witness testifies here, "because he was in the news all the time for being busted." Yet latterly, as Henderson reports, Kaufman has become legendary not so much for his eccentric lifestyle and manifest personal trials as for his literary art, and "various schools of American poetry have sung his praises."

This strange troubadour of concrete alleys and canyons was indeed the real article—a poet whose surprisingly delicate, transformative lyric touch gave birth to an art of sudden, unexpected graces, stunning emotive moments of soulful lament and desperate elation: "All those ships that never sailed /...Today I bring them back /... And let them sail/Forever."

Ravaged by the random sufferings of the American street and warmed by the casual glance of Eros, cool in its quiet truth to consciousness and wild in its classic command of poetic phrase and tuning, this is work that echoes an unlikely range of American songsmiths from Billie Holiday and Charlie Parker to T. S. Eliot and Hart Crane. It's probable that no other poet—not even Kaufman's Beat colleagues Kerouac, Corso and Ginsberg—quite so vividly exposed the apocalyptic condition beneath the surface normalcy of our midcentury culture.

> Alien winds sweeping the highway
> fling the dust of medicine men
> > long dead
> > > in the California afternoon
> Into the floating eyes
> > of spitting gadget salesmen,
> > > eating murdered hot dogs,
> in the California afternoon.

Kaufman's poetry reflects a state of trancelike acquiescence in language's psychic origins, a reliance on chance verbalizations and prelogical images that express an instinctive undertow of feeling: "The mind for all its complicated reasoning / Is dependent on the whim of an eyelid, / The most nonchalant of human parts ... "

Certainly the metamorphic quality in these poems, their evident trust in a semi-systematic derangement of the senses, suggests the strategies of surrealism. But with Kaufman it may be truer to say that such strategies are less inherited than held in common.

The only thing doctrinaire about this poet is his subscription to the poetic, a loyalty that for him appears to have precluded considerations of the business end of fame, publicity and career which today's poetry industry takes for granted.

> Eaten with remains of torn flowers,
> Overwhelming afterthoughts of binding loves,
> > classic pains,
> Casting elongated shadows of early pieces of
> > blue,
> Stringing hours together, in some thin melodic
> > line,
> Wrapped around the pearl neck of morning,
> Beneath the laughter of sad blue seabirds.
> > *"Picasso Balcony"*

JOHN KEHOE

CHARLES BUKOWSKI DEAD AT 73:
POET WHOSE SUBJECT WAS EXCESS

Well, no, I did not know Charles Bukowski that well, certainly not as well as I wanted to, even as hard as I tried to, but he stiff-armed me like he did nearly everybody else. Did you ever see his entry in *Who's Who*? In the space where it gives an office or home address Bukowski put this: Don't try.

It was no act. He often wrote about how he did not like people, how they disgusted and demoralized him. When he was just starting to get famous, when he was still living on DeLongpre Avenue in Hollywood, the parade of strangers knocking on his door was amusing for a while. When it didn't stop it became, he said, annoying and finally a torment. He stopped answering the door. Finally he had to move.

Around that time I wrote him a letter or two. I was working for a little local magazine, my first job, and I got fired from it. I wrote him a letter about that and he called me. In an unguarded moment he invited me over to his house. We'd never met.

Although I was broke I wanted to make a good impression, being raised that way where you bring the host something nice, so I did something I don't often mention even though it seems, on the surface, a Bukowski-ish kind of thing to do. I smooth-talked the liquor store clerk and had him put a couple of bottles of good California red, two six packs of Pauli Girl, cigars, cigarettes, pretzels and various counter items into a box. While the clerk was bent over totaling up the bill I picked up the box and ran out of the store.

Bukowski was great that night. My photographer buddy Tim Petros came with me, and we drank what we'd brought and then started on Bukowski's stuff and it was fucking great. Linda Lee was there, who was then his girlfriend and later his wife, and she was funny and pretty—we just had a great time. Bukowski challenged me to a fistfight out in the garden, he laughed at something I said, and finally he gave me a tour of the house. He showed me the room he worked in, he showed me his typewriter, the view from his window, his ashtray. I was reeling, just reeling. Understand I was just a kid, a baby. Nobody special, fired by a lousy magazine, a wife and a six-month old, and Bukowski was showing me around.

Then Bukowski did something that, I'm not sure how to say this, changed my admiration into love. Made me want to honor his memory, as I'm trying to do now. He said to Petros in that half-growl, half-whisper, he said, "Hey, man, make your living—take some pictures of us."

I got flustered. "Oh, no, I don't want to do that," I said.

"Come on, man," Bukowski said. and he put his arm around me and turned us to the camera.

"Look, he's *blushing*," Linda Lee said about me. Petros took a picture and I expected Bukowski to let go, but what he did was tighten the grip and say to Petros, "Come on, man, take another one, what's with you, man?"

We stayed for a little while after. Petros was so drunk by the time we left I had to fireman-carry him to the car, which was his, and dump him in the backseat. I drove home, over the Palos Verdes peninsula, the eucalyptus trees in full stinking bloom, the eager-beaver cops idling at the stop signs watching us pass by. I was pretty drunk too. This was years ago; I can't drink that way any more.

This past Friday I was sitting on the couch; it was late at night, 1:30 or so, and I was reading the paper and I saw his obit. I cried. Swear to God I burst into tears. We were not close; I'd managed to get him good and pissed off at me through a few stupid letters in the years since, and when he did reply to me he was terse. Usually he didn't answer at all. But that didn't matter. Knowing that he was dead was like a kick in the balls.

The other thing is Bukowski as a symbol. Anybody who does it, who sits behind the typer and tries to make sense out of their lives via the characters and keys, and sends it out and then has it come back, fluttering into the mailbox like a dying bird—they get to thinking there are other ways to live. But there really isn't and Bukowski, Bukowski, he never quit. He kept on doing it and he was close to or past 50 years old when he started to happen. He was writing when he was 20.

And when he hit, it came pretty fast and good. That house was nice, and there was a BMW parked in the driveway. The important thing is he never sucked ass, never did anything but stay true to what compelled him. For 30 years—30 years!—he got nowhere but he was indestructible, he was tireless, he was magnificent.

So that's it. He's dead; he was not my friend, we were not close, I understand he could be cruel to people, I know he swaggered and postured, but he was not that way one night. I'm here to testify, I'm here to signify, I'm here to say he was a great man, pure and complete, I'm here to say in a place where it can be heard one less giant walks the earth, one less.

JOEL BROUWER

ELEGY FOR BUKOWSKI

Every American morning
someone wakes still drunk
lumbers to the can
and groans out their beershit.

This endless fountain
your perpetual flame.

The ponies are forever
heaving down the backstretch.
Someone
has his last fin on
Fool's Errand, who will
lose.

She is dragging
your empty chariot
behind her.

MARK SPITZER

DINNER WITH SLINGER

Back in Poetry School, I didn't give a rat's ass about Ed Dorn, and he didn't give a shit about me—cuz in his Literature of the High Plains class, I was the guy who sat in the farthest corner, stoned outta my gourd, writing poetry and not paying any attention to him—why should I? I mean, the class was the Ed Dorn Show: each week he'd get up there and rant about different atrocities, and to pay attention to this was to embellish an ego the size of Charles Olson.

So it went on like this for a few months: Col. Wingnut and Gruff Dave coming on over to my subterranean earwig-hole which Kowalski and I rented up on 4th Street—and then we'd all do bongs and eat a herd of "free rangers" (which is what Gruff Dave called pota-toes—and margarine was "sauce")—and then we'd make a stop at Liquor Mart and get some beer and go to the Ed Dorn Show—

—of which the highlight happened mid-way through the semester, when the class found itself sitting there—and Dorn raging back and forth, ranting that if somebody thinks he doesn't have a teaching method, and if that somebody wants an instructor with a teaching method, then that somebody should get the hell out of his class and go take a class from some nun—

—and then Dorn (obviously drunk) goes on, howling

about how he doesn't drink, and he doesn't do drugs, and blah blah blah (the wind-bag)—until finally Gruff Dave (after forty-five minutes) jumps in and says: "Excuse me, Ed, what are you talking about?"

And Ed turns to him and says: "What am I talking about!?! I'll tell you what I'm talking about! I'm talking about an individual here who has a complaint against me! I'm talking about the individual who went whining to the Chair that I come to class drunk and high, and that I don't have a teaching method! As if the Chair cares! I mean, the Chair's a friend of mine! I see him in the hallway! He comes up to me and says, 'I know you didn't do it, Ed,' and I say, 'Yeah, I know!' "

—and then Ed rants for the remaining fifteen minutes before the break—but before he even gets that far, he manages to drive the accuser forth: the guy is in his early 40s, balding, and wearing a gay white suit—and he gets up, walks out, leaves the classroom, the class—and he never comes back.

But wait! There are more anecdotes—which I'm gonna use to illustrate this guy before blasting on into the story—

And the first has to do with squawfish—a subject I did a project on—cuz (thanks to "horsepower") they're an endangered species—and their upstream runs are dammed, and the Navajos don't give a damn, cuz concrete means jobs, and Camaros with V8s, and "home entertainment centers"— which leads to a drunken discussion in Dorn's kitchen (at the end-of-the-year class party)—in which I find myself outright lying to him (a notorious promoter of "the outrageous statement," anyway) telling him that squawfish swim a hundred miles to lay their eggs, that the males guard the young—and that with the full moon, squawfish rise at night, to croon their noodling fish tunes—

and Dorn is nodding impatiently back—cuz he's an expert on "the West"—and this is common information—which is something I'd know if I read more Brautigan or Edward Abbey!

And another thing: back in 1990 when I first came to Poetry School—I didn't know anybody and I was at a party for new grad students—and that's when I met Dorn, all craggy-faced and slugging on a bottle of Jim—and he starts in lecturing me about how the Brazilians are coming up to the Dakotas, abducting children, then taking them down to South America to stick 'em in "the deep freeze" for body parts—

(and I notice—while he's raving on—he's not really speaking to me, he's speaking to the booze, the wall, no person; he's just shooting off his mouth—with all the indifference of some crabby old granddad shouting at the six o'clock news—and not expecting any response)

(and it's also apparent that both of us would rather be talking to somebody a bit more nubile)

And then the last anecdote has to do with something I'm not supposed to talk about cuz I promised Mona Groan I'd never

61

reveal what she confided in me—having to do with the infamous Christmas party when Ed got all drunk and cornered Mona (my girlfriend at the time, in an on/off, on/off relationship based on sex and petty judgments)—

—and Ed, forcing her up against the bar wall, he told her: "Ya know what I'd really like to do? I'd like to stick my tongue in your pussy!"

—to which Mona, incensed, objected, yelling at him "Don't you know who my father is!?!" (another prof in the English Department) but Dorn didn't care—he grabbed her instead, shoved her up against the bricks, stuck his tongue way down her throat, and squeezed her boobs with all the grace of a rapist.

So yesterday, me and Extreme are cruising down to Denver (cuz he's graduating from Poetry School), and Dorn is throwing a dinner for those who defended their theses—

—and I don't know what the hell I'm thinking, but I wanna talk to Dorn—cuz he's Dorn—and if he was me and I was him, he should talk to me—so I should talk to him—

—and when we get there the place is full of studii and profs and food and booze—and Ed recognizes me but can't tell me from the 3000 generic-others he's had the pleasure of hating over the last how-ever-many years—and I see an Ezra Pound C.D. sitting there—so thinking back to Hemingway's *Feast*, I figure here's a good place to start a conversation up with him—so totally blunder, asking him: "Isn't Pound supposedly the ugliest poet ever?"—then quick, I remember—it was Wyndham Lewis, so amend the question—

—and Dorn (à la baseball hat, erosion-face and Don Johnson-looking with his t-shirt under blazer), says: "Number One, Wyndham Lewis wasn't a poet! And Number Two, Ezra Pound was known for being quite dashing!"

—And Dorn just keeps on going, attacking and attacking, smashing the bones of my stupid statement into a mush while I stand there thinking, I should (theoretically) be enjoying this—and I should (hypothetically) be valuing this—cuz I'm talking to such a historical guy—who is (in effect) shrinking me, just for the sake of shrinking me—so he becomes a giant—

—end then I realize something I forgot: if you're not a "nudie gal" beneath your clothes—then when it comes to this arrogant blow-hard, Communication=Antagonism.

So I turn him off—wander outside to get some air—thinking: whenever I consider going back to school, it's dynamics like these which make me see the lameness—and thus the conclusion: "Fuck em all...just write..."

So I'm standing there in Dorn's backyard talking to Peter

Michelson—who's the professor I modeled the Grizzly Professor on (a character in a big fish story). And Peter's a guy I used to feel all threatened by (like the time, all liquored up at Matt Cooperman's house when he told me, "Spitzer you asshole, you can't get to Iowa City on a river!")—but mostly it was his towering presence, and the fact that he's so calculated and intellectual, and I'm just the opposite: spur-of-the-moment and absurd—

—But now, cuz we don't have to deal with each other—my tension's gone away—so the subject of our conversation is Lorna's house—cuz Lorna, who's a big time Chicana poet and ten years older than me and already part of the modern canon (meaning she's in the *Norton*)—she got an NEA and went to Mexico, leaving her place with the Griz—and then Daddy-O (who just sold two big books to two big publishers)—he came on up from San Diego to rent the joint—and when he got there the place was soaked in cat piss and dog piss (and maybe even human piss) and the electricity was cut off, and no heat and no phone—so Daddy-O was ticked and telling everyone this drama—and then he asked me if I wanted to live in "the shit-hole," cuz already he paid two months rent on it—

—so I said "Yeah" and spent a week scrubbing the place—and I even yanked the carpet also—which is what Peter and I are yucking about—cuz when I first took a class from Lorna, we (the students) were sitting around in that very house—and each of us had to address the question, "Have you ever had to scrub somebody else's toilet before?"—

—cuz this was one of those confessional-type workshops, in which troubled students become empowered by digging up dirt—so by the end of the semester, as it turns out—everybody in the class, except me, admits to being raped.

Then Peter and I look over at the back steps—where it's the Ed Dorn Show again—and he's got an audience gathered all around—and he's wavering, and trying to pull himself up the stairs—but the hand rail is elusive—and Ed is stumbling, falling up, shouting (who knows why?) "Pollocks! Pollocks!'

And a few drinks later, inside—he's sitting at the table—a group of brown-nose groupies all around him (laughing at his jokes, agreeing with his blurtings, applauding) and he (Dorn) is eating chicken *mole*, and ranting at them—about how he's an expatriate in his own country—and how he should've been born in Europe—so therefore he's gonna sue!

—to which someone responds: "Who ya gonna sue Ed? Your parents? The government?"—and "HELL NO!" Dorn exclaims, "I'll sue the Indians! It's their country isn't it!? I'll sue the Arapahoes! That's what I'll do!"

So I decide to sit and listen to his wisdom (and "Hey! Is that whiskey!?" he demands, "Screw this wine shit!")—and then

63

we're sitting there with a bottle of Johnny between us, and he's telling me about how his new house is all a buncha bullshit: 200 feet this direction, 500 feet that direction—owned by some shifty East Coast bank investing in the hypodermics sucking dry the Ecuadorian rainforest—which has more species in its one jungle than the rest of the planet even knows exist—and how us Americans are bleeding that country for the equivalent of 13 days use of fuel—thanks to George Bush and his mutant son who ripped off Denver then fled ...

—and "There should be no cars!" Dorn lectures me, "No cars, no planes, no trains, just horses! Hell, every day I walk five miles to visit a friend!"

—And I laugh—right in his face—and Extreme, behind me, yells out: "That's a load a crap Ed!"—and Ed—he stares his disappointment into me (as if I, like everybody, am supposed to believe his myth of the moment, and take it, and repeat it, for the sake of his own secret legend)—

—and "What!? What!?" Dorn demands, "You're saying I don't have any friends!?"

—and "No," I shoot back, "I just don't believe you're that honorable Ed!"

—to which he replies: "Bomb the Chinese! That's what we gotta do! Bomb the Chinese! There's a war coming up! A big war!"

—Which, of course, leads to the Apocalypse (a discussion of)—Dorn claiming that Eliot's whimper is just an exaggeration.

—and "What whimper?" I ask—as Dorn slaps his forehead, gripping his head in disbelief—cuz I don't know nothing—cuz I'm just some stupid guy—another anonymous member of the decade ...

"Where the hell do you go to school!?" Dorn demands.

"University of Colorado," I tell him, "... went ..."

(and Extreme, still behind me—he says, "You taught him Ed!")

—But still, Ed won't tell me what the whimper is. Instead he's voicing his disgust:

"Jesus Christ! The whimper! It's the most famous line in all of Literature since 'to be or not to be!'"

—and "hmmmmm ..." Extreme ponders, reaching for some bourbon, Isn't it something like: 'the world won't end with a bang, but rather in a whimper?'"

But Dorn doesn't answer cuz two giggly blonde grad gals walk on in with shapely calves—so Ed pays attention to them (his eyes lit with orgy-scenes)—and eventually, Extreme and I say later-date, and take off to buy some pot.

And as we're driving, I hear myself say:

"Ya know, Dorn's wrong. There will be a whimper, even if it's a monotonous, three-century whimper. I mean, what the hell is he talking about? If he's a guy who supposedly speaks for some sorta disenfranchised generation, then his voice is a whimper. I mean, that's what he does. He whimpers for those who don't."

I dunno," Extreme says. "Why even try?"

—and I say: "But what he's talking about—it's like the whimper of a collective, historical consciousness—that's what he's talking about. It's like he's saying there will be less than a whimper cuz the world's so fractioned—cuz individuals are so involved in their own dumb things—cuz the media's been dulling us—cuz stupid fuzzy dice which double as air fresheners dangling from our rear-view mirrors and all the bullshit that we feed on, and capitalize on—instead of what we used to do, which is read more—and appreciate Art more, which is intelligence—supposedly..."

—and Extreme (interrupting): "I wonder who the 'Poet of our Generation' will be?"

—and me: "That's what I'm talking about. There won't be a 'Poet of our Generation,' cuz people stopped caring about that thirty years back, thanks to t.v...and gasoline—which is the focus of our collective consciousness now, if any—which is why the 'Poet of any Generation' doesn't exist ANYMORE, and isn't a concern ANYMORE—which is why Frank O'Haras don't count—which is why the game is over."

—and "Damn." Extreme says. "We were raised on Corporate Shit. Suckled on Nothing."

—and "Yeah," I agree. "But there will be a whimper, cuz even a little population, like say 300 people—when they get wiped out, there's a whimper cuz ya can't measure how big a minimum whimper is."

—and "Awwwww, quit yer whining," Extreme tells me—and we get off at Colfax, stop at a cash machine, punch some buttons—and receive $120 for an ounce of shwagg—

"Damn," Extreme says, "we suck."

"Yeah," I say, "let's go get fucked up."

SHALLOW SPITZER

"Heaven has no rage like love to hatred turned,
Nor hell a fury like a woman scorned."

—WILLIAM CONGREVE,
THE MOURNING BRIDE

Substitute "failed grad student" for "woman," and you have a fair description of Mark Spitzer's piece, Dinner With Slinger (EC No. 50, p. 45, under the heading "Visiting Hours"—quite appropriate: it is one sick piece).

ANSELM HOLLO &
JANE DALRYMPLE

65

The comic bathos of Spitzer's feeling so *refusé* by a mentor that he resorts to clumsy character assassination is enhanced by his obvious regret that he is, indeed, not a woman. He clearly believes that the mentor would have been more forgiving of his smugness and obtuseness if he, Mark, had been a Marcia.

Be that as it may, from a purely literary point of view Spitzer's piece could have benefited from more consistency in the naming of the dramatis personae. His fellow "students" (sub species "jackoff") are given cutesy monikers like "Col. Wingnut," "Extreme," and "Kowalski" (and, who knows, maybe "Mark Spitzer" is a pseudonym as well?). Their erstwhile (yes, the gods be thanked erstwhile!) mentors are not permitted such disguises, although Lorna Dee Cervantes is referred to only by her first name, with surely unwarranted familiarity.

Aside from conveying hearsay information that Spitzer himself states was confidential, the attack is set in large part in the home of Edward and Jennifer Dorn, a home that for all their years of teaching has been generously shared with students and friends for discussion and debate, sometimes over a bottle, often over dinner, and always with gracious hospitality. That Spitzer would abuse such hospitality with very little grace or genuine humor shows not only that he is a lightweight, but also that his feeling of being paid insufficient attention is entirely self-inflicted.

As for the over-all style of the piece, it is a prime example of how the use of the dash (—) does not a Kerouac make, nor does the use of the hash and the booze, for that matter. The piece comes off as scurrilous and mean-spirited. a self portrait of the author as shallow, narcissistic, and vindictive.

Spitzer's confusion and resentment is quite in tune with an era of popular culture dominated by types like "Rush" Limbaugh and "Newt" Gingrich, both of whom are working hard to ensure the extermination of the species Academic Liberal (not to even mention Radical—they're assumed to have died out already). If Spitzer (probably rightly) feels he has to give up ambitions to become the "Poet of Our Generation," or to get any other kind of recognizably human life, he may find gainful employment in the swelling ranks of political media Philistines—provided that he gives up those "ounces of shwagg" and Joins the Church of Rushing Newts.

GAMBOLING EXHIBITIONISM

TED GROSSMAN

This letter is written to call attention to irresponsibility and a contagious imbecility that has infected your pages. It is chilling to think that a journal devoted to publishing progressive work would debase itself and its readership by airing such a spiteful and partial piece. I refer to Mark Spitzer's "Dinner with Slinger." To publish unfounded and hateful gossip about a poet/teacher firmly committed to the art of writing and clarity is beyond comprehension. Spitzer is deserving of scorn, not publication.

My point is not to discuss Ed Dorn's merit as a writer. Others more capable have done that, and more will do so in the future. But some note must be made to his role as a teacher. Sure, Ed does not effect the sobriety of a government official, but neither is he the figure seen through the inflamed eyes of Spitzer. The spirit of the piece displays pettiness, loathing and personal frustration: the light breezy, self-deprecating pseudo-beat style cannot conceal Spitzer's puritanical inflammations, nor his obvious animosity toward someone he rightly feels inferior to. We are forced to endure a series of partial, one-sided anecdotes, mingled with falsehoods; misrepresentations of private occasions; misconstrued personal encounters; all couched in a sickening spread of professed humility, absurdity and spontaneity, which only thinly disguise a calculated and pernicious attempt to denigrate Ed Dorn.

At times Spitzer sounds like a puny gossip, as well as an offended boarding house matron. But he really is a gamboling exhibitionist, a devoted pupil of his own failings.

As I said, there is no doubt that Ed Dorn is a difficult hombre. This is in part because Ed is first of all a poet and last of all a poet. He is almost always speaking to the one most intelligent person he knows. It's just that a lot of other people have to serve as stand-ins: many with little ability, often missing his meaning, failing to respect his stance and approach. Ed is constantly challenging. His reputation and commitment, as a poet, to honesty and polemics and confrontation are well known. This commitment is seen in his teaching as well. Dorn works with his students and he works them, makes demands, outrageous connections and claims, constantly pushing them to get to the point, to participate in their own education. He often offends the coddled psyches of students by refusing to affirm the prevailing doctrines and dogma they blindly and religiously accept, as if the ideas come directly from the secret source of truth and justice. And he has a lot of contempt. If he offends one's sensibility over issues of race, religion, ecology, whatever, it is all part of an educating process. I know of no other teacher more committed to the education of his students, as he was educated by his masters at Black Mountain and beyond. (Actually, what seems to have offended Spitzer the most is some assumed preference Ed has for good-looking women as opposed to him, note the puritanical parenthetical observations. Whether the facts, presented as truth, are in fact so, is surely impossible for us to tell).

When I was a student the Dorn house was a warm, friendly, human place, full of activity and dialogue late into the night. It was the farthest thing from perverse. It felt alive with ideas and caring in the most unpretentious, unsickly manner. Ed may not have spent his time sending out Christmas cards, but he would sit down with you in his kitchen, brew up a cup of tea, read over your work and give his opinions, which were usually so sharp and concise as to alter the pivot on which you claimed to stand. Then he'd launch into an outrageous and fully informative discussion on anything from the latest in *The New Yorker*, to the trading habits of the Dutch, to the water system in Boulder. If there was something else to drink, we would drink it. He wasn't holding your hand, but he would shake it warmly when you left. I don't think this kind of experience was singular, I know it was not.

As a more public figure, Ed took the Chair of the Creative Writing Program when no one else would, and worked to save it from insensitive and cost-cutting administrators. When several students could not find a professor willing to work with them on their theses, Ed stepped forward and volunteered to take them on. This was in addition to his already large number of students.

In fact, both Ed and Jenny Dorn were always committed to the well being of their students, running two magazines which students could work on, throwing parties, attending student readings, socializing afterward, and always giving a lively spirited time. On my first day of class Ed looked at my small frame and, with a sly grin said, "This is a graduate course." I told him I was a graduate student. And he asked, "Are you sure?" I understood immediately the roles being taken and was only too willing to submit my student's arrogance to my teacher. By trying to understand what he expected of me I also knew what I expected of him, and could receive from him. And my expectations were always surpassed.

As for Mark Spitzer, you could always see how much he needed attention, and the closer you got to him those needs grew exponentially. In his own masochistic way, he's probably greatly anticipating the responses that will come, in print, because that's all he cares about, seeing his name in journals. He does not deserve that kind of satisfaction. I mean he feels owed, that's for sure, that's why we get this pro pot smoking, anti sex, drink, talk, ego (other than his own); this self-protective irony, this cloud of private hate. What's the point in publishing it? It's obvious he is anxious for justification, trying to hoist himself up in a public forum by an attack. After the body of his story is spent trying to trash Ed, we get this small-minded footnote, bemoaning Spitzer's own non-status, blaming the lack of a generation poet on TV and gasoline. Instead of the what, he's only interested in the how. All we seem to have from Spitzer is an embarrassing lack of passion for anything but his own ego, a mind entrenched in stupidity and sloth, as if that's what pot smoking does to you. The stupidity of the attack and the grotesqueness of its publisher disgraces your readership.

SPITZER'S SHWAGG

Like, c'mon guys! Is that overreacting or what? I never had the fortune to attend Mr. Dorn's lectures and I don't wish to incur Mr. Hollo's wrath—I've read and enjoyed his work in Codrescu's *Up Late* and in *The Corpse*—but isn't all that en masse pro-Dorn flag waving a bit of self righteous pig shit? In and of itself, Spitzer's piece is not bad; I went scouting for my #50, having prepared myself to jump into the demon's fiery breath, and *mon dieu*, it was rather sweet! Since I never met Mark Spitzer, I can't vouch for his character, but his piece seemed to me an honest and healthy expression of his personal experience, and not at all a bad piece of writing. It does not deserve all the hullabaloo, does not deserve the comparison with the Newt & Rush gang, and mostly, does not deserve all the hatred: Spitzer's write was not, by any stretch of the imagination, hateful. Perhaps a circle jerk with all parties involved, peace-piping an ounce of Spitzer's shwagg might restore some humor.

JULIAN SEMILIAN

WHAT'S A MOTHER FOR?

My son, Mark Spitzer, knows *mole* from brown gravy.

NANCY MACKENZIE

69

MAGGOT INSPECTS
MOUNTAIN PALACE

A few days ago I made the westward trek through the bovine death-camp corridor that is Interstate 80 across Nebraska. Sick, hungry, sportin' a hollow highway gaze, I stopped in Sterling, Colorado, where judging from the smell there is an industry built on the daily incineration of "non-edible" carcass parts. From a pay phone I got final directions to the house of the fabled "mountain gals" which, it turns out, is merely a haven for writers in the overly colonized foothills north of Boulder.

So then I get there expecting vibrant poetic happenings only to discover that the hottest thing going is this clique vs. clique-oh-yeah-says-you bantering born of a high-schooler-infested Beverly Hills McDonald's, splayed out in a literary glossymag. I'm more accustomed to reading about subjects like political prisoners on death row in America or nuclear waste dumped in the Mississippi River—dry stuff, I know, but I thought you might be interested in adding to the dialogue someone who doesn't even have an address, let alone a degree in writing.

Consider the possibility that Spitshit (I like that) actually LIKES Dorn—as someone who can keep up with his own ravings and crassness. I don't know these people, but I wouldn't take one of Mark's mad dissing sessions literally. I've seen what this dude eats. He cares much less for taste and aesthetics than he does for raw fuel value. Mark is usually concerned with deeper truths—like the drama of the human psyche. Some folks wrestle with it, try to ride it. Others repress it like their own body odor, which the television has so taught them to fear. Seems there is a little circle in your readership so eager to preserve the image of their friend and mentor that they cannot see what else the story might be about. Loyalty is cool, but I think y'all need to chill out. If Dorn is such a big guy, he can probably take it.

As for those who claim Spitzer's writing is beneath the dignity of a journal, or beneath their dignity to read, I know you. You are the lowest of the pretentious bourgeois. You work at those I-80 slaughter farms, doing the feeding, prodding, chaining, electroshocking, hormone injecting, executing, and eviscerating while turning cold, deaf ears to the horrified screams of helpless animals. But it would elevate your dignity to enjoy a steak with your publisher at an upscale joint for the stiffly dressed. Appalled at the notion of wielding a chain saw and felling thousand-year-old trees, you'll gleefully line your humble rose beds with redwood chips.

Is this a personal counter-attack on those critics?

Wake up! Sometimes one must put down the Proust and pick up the speculum. I don't see Spitzer putting himself morally or professionally above any of his characters. He's down in his own shit as well as theirs. This is integrity.

POPE HAD MORE VIGOR

The Ed Dorn brouhaha was fun, I thought. Pope's *Dunciad* having come up in #51 (in a letter on an unrelated matter), it occurred to me that Spitzer's piece on Dorn, and the ensuing retorts, compares favorably in cattiness with some of Pope's attacks on his literary contemporaries; and Pope would have found the idea of a poetical plastic-worker irresistible, surely. But Pope's satire drew its vigor and urgency from a conviction that literary taste could be a significant cultural and moral force—while the Dorn storm seemed for the most part just cattiness for the sake of cattiness. I mean, *sub species aeternitatis*, how important is Spitzer's being in deep doo-doo? And how much difference does it make if the "Am Po scene" is ridden by politeness or rich in vitriol?

> What dire offence from amorous causes springs,
> What mighty contests rise from trivial things.
> —*Pope*

The Dorn storm was interesting in somewhat the same way the supererogatory complications of soap operas, or the intra-mural toothpick-duels of university faculty politics are. Life being at bottom conflict, we love a rumble. In collective circumstances like ours, in which the most important conflicts tend to be beyond our understanding, not to mention our influence, and leave us feeling inevitably that we are *not getting into it* sufficiently, assassinating characters is better than just sitting there. Of the Dorn controversy one might say something like what George Lukacs once said of detective stories and romances in the nineteenth century: They did not depict characters in conflict with institutions, the forces of history, class barriers, or Nature—so they were really just plots without content. But they could hold people's interest because they invoked the archetypes of dramatic form to which our fascination with conflict responds. Much ado about nothing beats nothing, hands down.

JAMES GALLANT

SECOND CHALLENGE, CORPSE HIRING SECONDS

PETE SNIEGOWSKI

I have never seen such a craven display of obsequiousness in my life. For those of you who lionized Dorn in your letters, get this straight: *there is no correlation between brilliance and the possession of morals.* Picasso was an asshole. John Ruskin showed a mean penchant for little boys in his later years.

As for Anselm Hollo's far-fetched accusation of hard-right beliefs and behaviors on our part ... *sigh* ... quit using the "slippery slope" argument. Just because one member of the age group accuses one of his teachers of lechery doesn't mean we are all strapping on jack boots. It's a very annoying and lame tactic.

The Corpse may have leapt at the chance to stage this fight, but the truth is that present combatants have been fingering their swords for years. Unfortunately, I have no interest in attacking Dorn, suffice it to say I like the guy. I'd rather go after the PC brute squad.

And who is this Schroth guy? If "Spitshit" is the best you can do pal, take up plumbing, it fits your scatalogical scant. Jesus ... and Jason, nobody gives a damn what award you won or who bought you a beer. If the writing fails, there is always the trust fund, right?

And finally, my dear Mr. Hollo, next time you want to refer to me as a member of the "sub-species Jackoff," it may help to know me (Kowalski asked me to echo his sentiments here). So here is your big chance. *You* and *me* (bring any seconds you want—I got my boys). Strap a trash can lid to your forearm with duct tape, grab a length of 2x4 and meet me by the dumpsters behind King Sooper's anytime you like.

EDITOR'S NOTE

The literary jeu just got rough. Ooops. When we first read Spitzer's bit of lit spite we were amused, seeing in it a certain vitriolic mode all-too-absent from the politesse-ridden Am Po scene. Also, a generational burst of overdue rancor. We were not surprised by the volume of letters from The Slinger's friends and ex-students but we were taken aback by their chief argument, namely the upstart's lack of "manners." As if that were the most burning issue on the haunted landscape. As if Dorn & company & the noble savages of Beat did not sear the late American canon with their invective fury so as to better rise into amusement & righteousness. Not since the days of Dorn's own ROLL-INGSTOCK's AIDS Award did we hear such moan—from the other side. OK, Spitzer was a rude guest. Nonetheless, we have to say that he only vented in public a tiny bit of that swirling mass of orality that is the "lives of the poets." Would you that we rather waited for Ted Morgan's pompous biography wherein the late Dorn "lapsed into nostalgic Beatnik stupor after the fire-engine *mole*"? Spitzer doesn't know *mole* from brown gravy: it's not his fault. But his point is clear: nobody gossips about his generation. Not until now anyway.

STAGGERS, CRINGES

I stagger, cringe. You published Mark Spitzer's ad hominem attack on Dorn. Ashamed to think I laughed at your anecdotes, veered my attention to your words, sung your praises to well-connected, disinterested friends. I've been duped. You've proven yourself foolish— negligent by betraying a part of kitsch above religion and geography.

Mark Spitzer's not worth my time. A peer in graduate school at Colorado, I felt bad for him, horny spastic scribbler. He often looked cold in gold boots.

At UC Berkeley I thought I'd been inspired, great teachers whose business consists of lifting and slapping idiotic "A" students into something else. Thought at my younger age that would continue at Colorado, then probably someplace further for a further degree. Right off, I walk into Ed Dorn's office, and the first thing he asks is whether I know *Moses and Monotheism*. A short meeting. Days later, I rapidly tap my foot while declaring Freud was a self-hating Jew. I've never had a teacher like Ed, as generous, as protean in his assiduous precision. He asks students to bridge gaps in their essential education so they may learn what he knows and will share. An ingrate could see an opinionated maverick as a windbag (watch Spitzer call Olson one, too, and Pound). When there was nothing for Ed to add, he hushed. After a talk I gave on Auden's "September 1, 1939," Dorn re-recited the final ten lines by heart, nodded and said, "Yes. Yes." To some, Dorn was summoned to fill in the blanks, to etch characters into blank glowers.

One doesn't feel blessed to have an intellectual such as his influence and then ignore malevolence vomited his way. Dorn has one-upped his teacher Charles Olson. Asked of the parameters of their relationship, Dorn will call Olson his teacher, period. To myself and to others who deserved it, Dorn has offered his hospitality, his wisdom, his attention, and his oft-shocking but ever-brilliant images of action and reaction. How could you publish such an irresponsible piece here in the US, now in 1995? Come clean. Were you signing books when you met Dorn? Were you distracted by family? Are you blind? By intent, you've

JASON HORWITCH

73

aided in a poet's undoing. Free thinkers such as Ed (you've relinquished that title?) could aid this republic; instead, they're cast into academia and required to briefly tutor the physically stalwart sons of American men, a minimum amount of kindness in these adults.

Ed Dorn bought me a beer after I'd defended my thesis. My thesis won the Harcourt Brace Imaginative Writing Award. I've made my living as a professional writer. I am grateful for Dorn's guidance and sorry you took a cheap shot. Must've taken little effort to plant this loaded, resilient weed.

SOUR GRAPES FOR DINNER

JANET RODNEY & NATHANIEL TARN

The piece "Dinner with Slinger" in the last issue of *The Corpse* was a character slur of utmost stupidity on one of our surviving poets of substance who should rather be commended for not selling out to the bureaucracies of the poetry programs in our universities. Dorn represents what is independent, idiosyncratic and brave in the poetic world and if the result is a thorny and difficult taskmaster for the meek, they would do better to choose a different path. It would be good to remind the "student" in question that by so writing he aids and abets the reactionary forces in our society. These are only too happy to seize upon this kind of occasion to destroy the freedoms of expression and individuality in the arts and in the culture at large.

FUCK PROFESSORS

RONNIE BURK

After reading all the hoopla in the last *Corpse* I went back and read Spitzer's piece. Ohmiiigawd! It's *Wayne's World* goes to Naropa! I can't wait for his next installment. Will he trash Ginsberg? Tell stories about William Burroughs' smelly socks? Spitzer's actually very funny. I'd like to meet the guy, we could swap stories. I am certain he could get a job writing for *Saturday Night Live*. Lord knows they could use a shot in the arm. Maybe the *Rolling Stone*, after all didn't they launch that blathering idiot P.J. O'Rourke? The Hollos take themselves and Dorn far too seriously. Fuck professors! Long live the proletariat revolution! I read *The Corpse* for laughs and to see my name in the funny papers!

ED DORN: STRANGE JOURNEY

RICHARD CARR

Way West—Stories, Essays, and Verse Accounts: 1963–1993;
Edward Dorn; Black Sparrow Press.

The subtitle of Edward Dorn's *Way West—Stories, Essays. and Verse Accounts: 1963–1993* is descriptive of the book's contents except for one omission: editorials. It may not seem like much, but *Way West*, as a "selected works," could be called as easily, and maybe more appropriately, the author's selected opinions. That we have Dorn's opinions, however, is not a Socratic caveat intended to weaken Dorn's assertions, but a Socratic reminder that in the epistemological flux bequeathed to us by the post-moderns (or by Socrates himself), we must still ask how opinions are derived.

How does Dorn work? If we looked solely at his *Rolling Stock* editorials, we would judge the magazine an outlandish rag and Dorn an even more outlandish muckraker. I don't know about the magazine, but Dorn, muckraker though he may be, is more than just a loud voice on the literary scene. To be sure, Dorn wades in the muck, laughing and making us laugh, but his two hands, openness and insight, remain clean. He shows us loner railroad workers and hard-luck families forced into a life of migration, yet he is also quite capable of floating us through the drug haze of a quirky intelligentsia. In one essay Dorn enters the current debate on whether Columbus is a hero or an oppressor, arguing that he is neither, and asserts the national and international priority of English, but then in the next essay he finds it somehow relevant to show us Montana cowfolk snarfing fried calf testicles. While much of *Way West* has the flavor of freelance reporting, particularly as the book progresses, it becomes clear that Dorn's reports are shaped by his own experience of the land and its people. Dorn derives and presents his opinions, then, through a kind of anthropological journalism in which observation and interpretation are one.

"In Memoriam: Richard Brautigan" is very much a work of journalism, and the piece in fact appeared in the *Denver Post*. But instead of gathering his information from the wires, Dorn relies on his personal experiences with Brautigan as friend and one-time neighbor. The essay seems to give the "facts" of Brautigan's life, but it really offers the "facts" of Dorn's life. Nonetheless, Dorn picks his facts well, and we feel that, through Dorn's observation and interpretation, we've gained some further understanding of Brautigan's life and work.

One fiction piece, "Of Western Newfoundland, Its Inns & Outs," is written from an anthropological perspective. A carload of tourists visits rural Newfoundland but finds it impossible to interact with the tightlipped locals. The visitors, thus forced to observe only, fall into interpreting the native culture and finally determine that the local taste for pork and beans—"Pork, and Beans. In that order"—places the natives at the transition between hunting and agriculture. In a spooky scene at the end of the story, the travelers have bedded down at an inn but panic when the lights go out and they seem to hear the pattering of dolls' feet. Without further explanation, the story ends. Here we recall that the story is written from a limited third person point of view, and we realize that it is Dorn, at an additional anthropological remove, that is observing and interpreting the behavior of travelers abroad.

A number of the pieces in *Way West* combine the journalistic style and the anthropological perspective. Covering various events—from the 1981 MLA convention in Houston to the Testicle Festival in Ryegate, Montana—sometimes actually on assignment and sometimes just out of curiosity, Dorn observes people and places without, apparently, participating in their activities. That his observations are interpretive is most clearly seen in the fact that "Chaps/Houston" MLA is written in verse. At the same time, we get the impression that Dorn does participate in these events, for in Ryegate, at least, we know he does eventually sample the local cuisine.

In some ways Dorn's anthropological journalism is reminiscent of Hunter S. Thompson's "gonzo" journalism. Both writers like to go to where the action is, ostensibly to observe but actually participating and interpreting at the same time. Even Dorn's occasional companion, Dobro Dick Dillof with his curious musical instruments, parallels Thompson's Samoan attorney and sidekick. And in expressing their opinions, both writers take full advantage of the dynamic of irreverence that is the life-blood of American English. Lacking intimations of dangerous insanity, however, Dorn's work is not so excessively deranged as Thompson's. Nonetheless, relying more on the good humor made possible by openness and insight, Dorn's *Way West* is a pleasingly strange journey.

DON BAPST

PAUL HOOVER'S POETRY WORKSHOP

He liked playing teacher.
He knew a lot about poetry.
He knew a lot of literary gossip too,
like "The Time I took Robert Bly to Lake
Michigan and He Ran Around in Circles" and
"The Fringed, Spanish Hat that Melville Wore
when He Courted Hawthorne from a Horse."

My favorite classes were (in no particular order):

The one where we drew pictures of ourselves—I
did something abstract and geometric. It became
the cover of my chapbook. Paul drew himself like
Apollo, with big muscles, torpedo dick, and little
gleam marks emanating from the smiling face.

Then the time we listened to Thelonius Monk,
Billie Holiday, Divine, Falco, James Brown,
and Annette Funicello. Two women stopped in
to listen to the music. "What class is this?"
"Advanced Poetry." They left immediately and we
started writing. My poem was called "dancing."

Best of all was the time Paul totally lost it.
He looked up from one of his poetry books
with wonderfully crazy, human eyes and asked,
"Did you ever just feel like a corpse?
Sometimes you feel okay, but then you just
don't sometimes. You know?"

Another time, or was it the same time? he looked
around the room and started complimenting people
on their looks. I remember at one point,
"Don's hair has been looking great lately, hasn't it?"

I guess I forgave Paul's armchair liberalism for
moments like that. I was motivated in ways
he hadn't even thought of.

VISION/REVISION:
BORGES, HOLLO, CREELEY

PART ONE

Every writer creates his own precursors

—JORGE LUIS BORGES

I published some poems, did a few public readings, won a contest,
and then suddenly was introducing myself as a writer. Of

CASEY BUSH

course, there is a point where formal instruction must end, in order for a truly informal education to begin. In my case, it was sometime in the mid-1970s; I had taken too many English classes to apply towards graduation, and needed to learn another language. The Dean of Arts & Letters was not sympathetic: "You must read the Masters in the original..."; but a department counselor knew how to get around the foreign language requirements. "Why not try movie classes in the Romance Language Department? It's all subtitles." Classes of Buñuel, Fellini and Truffaut followed, and soon I discovered a course entitled "The Novel in Translation," with a largely French speaking bunch studying mostly Sartre and Camus in English. The instructor, Professor Josephs, looked like a miniature Peter Lawford and wore a beret on overcast days. He approached his subject with a reverential awe; early on I called him out on the existential yin-yang: "Isn't it all covered by Murphy's Law?" Josephs responded in kind. The standoff lasted half a semester and came to a boiling point when I was assigned to conduct two class periods in a discussion of Jean Genet's *Querelle of Brest*.

At the first session, in order to emphasize Genet's romanicization of murder, I displayed a number of deadly weapons including an ice pick, a poker, switchblade, a few unusual gardening tools, framed by a hangman's noose and a shotgun. Despite that preparation, Josephs pulled out his notes and began class without me: "Well, what do you think Freud would have said about Querelle? Does this inversion of conventional morality deserve such an eloquent spokesman?" As usual, all the French students were too meek to respond, so I answered that question with another question. "Why not just use a Darwinian perspective on all those tarantula-style relationships? I mean, what part does the deviant play in Evolution?" "And just who do you think you are?" Josephs picked up a weeding claw and used it to point at the shotgun. "I could lose my position for allowing firearms on campus." He then proceeded to read me the Riot Act but after class insisted on providing me a ride home. "Just so you aren't detained by Security," he explained.

The next evening, at the library preparing for the second class period, I stumbled across a friend, Jan W., who immediately divulged, "Anselm will be in town on Thursday." Anselm Hollo, the Finnish-born but thoroughly American poet, translator from a dozen languages, was responsible for the English version of *Querelle*. "He's being flown in from Baltimore for some kind of public television project." The previous spring Anselm had been poet-in-residence at Michigan State. Jan and I had met in one of his creative writing classes. At that time Anselm was a bachelor, yet *Deutschland & Other Places* by his former wife, Josephine Clare, was required reading for his students. Over the course of that season, Anselm had taken up with Jan, who was from Michigan's Upper Peninsula near Marquette on Lake Superior, an environment not unlike Finland. Her voice had a trace of accent that leaned towards the Winnipeg "eh." When Anselm's short stay at MSU was over, the two of them moved to Ann Arbor for the summer, where he paid the rent by translating a pharmaceutical text for Parke-Davis. When Anselm took a faculty position at the University of Maryland, Ms. W. returned to East Lansing.

My library search had produced significant returns. Although I arrived early to the next class, I found Anselm and Josephs already introduced and thoroughly engaged. "Borges," Jan winked, explaining the cryptic content of the conversation. In his seventies and totally blind for thirty years, Jorge Luis Borges was visiting Michigan to collaborate with an MSU professor. Although still a card-carrying member of the avant-garde while being conspicuously overlooked for a Nobel, the Argentine master of letters had caused a minor sensation with a series of public lectures. "I've been told," Josephs remarked, "that among his intimate friends he prefers to speak Old English."

Josephs provided a brief introduction as Anselm lit up a cigarillo and stated, "The first word took me an hour to translate." He puffed on the stick, eyeing his audience. "The opening sentence required an entire day's labor," he paused. "The initial paragraph demanded a whole week of time," the translator stated emphatically. "Remember, this wasn't just translation from French to English but a rendering of Genet's mongrel lingo into Hollo's mongrel American. Let me provide some examples." An inspirational class period followed, with Anselm's eloquence and insights charming the Professor. Afterwards Jan had to rush Anselm to the airport while Josephs quietly took me aside. "Now don't think I'm still not pissed off about Tuesday." He tried to sound tough. "But I would like to make an appointment for you to meet Borges during his office hours." I was flabbergasted. Although Borges sat in on those classes that interested him, my most intimate exposure had been at a public reception where students were allowed to ask embarrassing questions. Josephs read my incredulous expression correctly. "Actually, it's only a half hour. This next week is my turn to provide an appropriate..." "But what could we possibly talk about? I've only read a few stories from *Labyrinths* and *The Book of Imaginary Beings*," I objected, cutting him off. "Don't be absurd," the Professor scolded me. "Borges doesn't want to talk about his own work. He wants to meet young writers. You must bring your own manuscripts and be prepared to read them." I left Joseph's office in a daze.

That evening I checked a Borges collection out of the library and soon became entranced. "The cross was not invented, it was discovered. The Romans were using it as a symbol long before Christians began using it." It all seemed so mathematical. "For us the word 'thousand' is almost synonymous with 'infinite.'" To say 'a thousand nights' is to say infinite nights, countless nights, endless nights. To say 'a thousand and one nights' is to add to infinity. Let us recall a curious English expression: instead of 'forever,' they sometimes say 'forever and a day.' A day has been added to forever."

That contemplation was broken by a phone call from Jan. "Want to hitchhike to Baltimore this weekend?" Anselm was barely out of town, but she was already in hot pursuit. "There will be plenty of poetry. Robert Creeley is doing a reading at the University of Maryland." Easily persuaded, I arranged a ride out to the highway at 4 A.M. and twelve hours later, after a series of adventures, we were deposited onto the streets of Baltimore. At a derelict intersection, three corners vacant and a gas station, Jan approached two men in a convertible stuck at the pump. "How about a ride downtown?" The motorists were enthusiastic until I bounded across the road. "And suckass too?" they moaned. As we drove through the urban grit of Baltimore I noticed a warm breeze that seemed momentarily to reverse the seasonal progression; fallen leaves had returned to their branches, and everything was green.

PART TWO

distracting particulars
are to be avoided

—ANSELM HOLLO

We were soon delivered to a four-story brownstone located immediately adjacent to downtown. "Thanks, fellas," Jan said, absently dazed from the day's travel. "Hey, fuck you," our chauffeurs squealed out, hurling an empty beer bottle against the curb. Anselm was immediately out on the street. "What was all that about?" pointing towards the shattered glass. "Where've you been, I was worried." "Oh, I can explain it all," Jan assured him. "So how'd the drive go? Did you have problems finding a parking place?" Anselm asked, quickly drawing out the truth. "We hitchhiked, Anselm," Jan immediately confessed. His eyes lit up as she continued. "Five rides, right to your door."

"Oh yeah, I heard right to my door." Anselm laughed and then proclaimed our safe passage a miracle. We had just caught Anselm headed out the door to a Halloween reading at which he was the featured poet. We piled into his Pinto and the Finn cautiously guided it through the street. Young trick-or-treaters darted out from behind parked cars, mostly ghosts, skeletons, witches, and pirates. Inside the lecture hall, people had arrived early to drink wine and toast the poets. Anselm introduced me to one of the other readers, Joe Cardarelli and his spouse, Marta Backstrom, and then announced that he had arranged for me to stay with them. "Shower even works," Joe offered. A few minutes later Mr. Cardarelli took the stage as the first reader, launching into a half-hour of poetic intimacy, blending the cosmic with the compassionate. In his turn, another Baltimore poet, Kraft Rompf, hypnotized the audience with the kaleidoscope of his vision. Next, Anselm was introduced, and he quickly launched into an extended poetic exploration of gender relations entitled "The Anima Abstract." I was immediately lost in a tailspin of associations in which it seemed easy to recognize both the presence of Jan W. and Josephine Clare. In the psychic fallout of that performance, the hall emptied slowly as we made plans for the following day. "Joe can put you on the right bus in the morning," Anselm determined. "We'll need your backbone." I had been drafted onto a moving crew that was going to unload a printing press.

The drive to Joe and Marta's proceeded in silence. Marta quickly disappeared while Joe led me upstairs and produced an end-of-day beer which he poured into paper cups. I fell easily into dreamland and woke the next morning curled up on the couch. Downstairs, in the kitchen, I looked in the refrigerator and found the last of a carton of orange juice, which I instinctively drank. As the mucous membranes in my throat bathed in vitamin C., Marta joined me in the kitchen. To my dismay she immediately looked for a glass of juice.

"Sorry," I sheepishly held up the empty. "Oh man," Marta hissed and then corrected herself, "I mean oh men!" "But, but," I stammered. "I mean oh shit," she clarified. "It's just this whole damn thing with Anselm and Jan." I didn't even know where to begin. We both sat quietly for a moment, long enough for me to gather that I was an unwanted guest. "And besides," Marta continued, "Grandmother is in the hospital again this weekend and yesterday was my birthday ..." Our conversation fell off as Joe entered the kitchen and began to make breakfast. After properly feeding me, Joe provided directions and an assurance that we would meet again the following evening just before Creeley's reading.

Arriving at the Maryland Writer's Collective I found Anselm and Jan browsing through a collection of poetry chapbook and magazines that spilled off the shelves and largely lay scattered in piles across the floor. "Check it out," Anselm greeted me, "straight from the Winter-Water-Wonderland." Sure enough, there was a Xerox magazine with MSU professor Albert Drake on the cover ready to tap a keg of beer. I was impressed that a publication held together by a single staple had traveled from East Lansing to the East Coast. At the back of the building, Anselm introduced a lively gray-haired man who stood on the tailgate of a truck. "This is Charlie Plymell and his Cherry Valley Press."

"Ho, ho, ho," Charlie laughed right in my face. "Another scrawny poet! Only needed three healthy farmboys to load the damn thing, but you can see it's gonna take a dozen of these literature types, maybe a whole funeral procession of citified artists to unload, ho,

81

ho ho!" Although the name was familiar, I scanned my skull unsuccessfully for a clue to his identity, until he offered it himself. "Thank Buddha Allen didn't tag along," Plymell stated, "or he'd have us all chanting, trying to levitate this load, complicating physical matters with spiritualistic techniques." I mentally paged through an edition of *Planet News* and "Wichita Vortex Sutra," realizing that Charlie was a midwestern Carl Solomon, a fellow traveler who brought Ginsberg so much extra mileage. "The plate-maker first," Plymell announced to a gathering crowd. Over the course of an hour, three refrigerator-sized appliances descended from the truck and floated across space on a row of hands into the basement without touching the ground, handled with reverential awe, disappearing into the storage room.

Charlie thanked all the help as Anselm and Jan headed out to the airport to pick up Creeley. We arranged to meet later that day, and I set off across downtown Baltimore on foot. Over the next few hours I conducted a self-guided tour of the city, traversing the warehouse district, some humongous housing project, and a highway under construction. I caught up with the poets on South Broadway at a shabby bar set among a group of recently renovated storefronts that stretch down towards the waterfront area known as Fell's Point.

PART THREE

we are
as we find out we are

—ROBERT CREELEY

Anselm and Jan were at the back of the long narrow drinking hole with Robert Creeley and a small entourage. As I shook Creeley's hand he leaned forward and momentarily forced me to look directly into the empty socket of his left eye, the scar of a childhood accident. Although I had known about Creeley's enucleation, no picture on the back of a book could have prepared me for that gnarled misshapen contraction of flesh that sat proudly on his face. He wore no patch and did not use a prosthesis. I swallowed something in my throat, smiled weakly, and ordered a beer. For a moment I had interrupted a discussion, but the current of ideas continued without missing a beat., Creeley lecturing extemporaneously, intellectual cyclops at the hurricane-center of ideas.

"History is just a collective lack of imagination," Creeley pronounced dramatically and immediately reinforced this with an appropriate quote. Pitchers of beer, hamburgers, and deep-fried oysters passed around the room as Creeley continued to hold court. Between bites someone who, like myself, must have been startled when introduced to the poet, naively asked: "Mr. Creeley, when was it that you lost the use of your eye?" Creeley placed an oyster back on his plate and put his napkin onto the bar, raising himself up on the stool. He slowly and purposefully turned his head so that his empty socket was trained upon the unfortunate individual who had asked the question. "I never lost the use of my eye," he said. "I just found new uses for it." While exhibiting a huge mental wink, the poet's face was totally impassive. It was from that point that I began to notice how Creeley communicated his negative vision, using his disability so that it seemed to constitute a great advantage. Shortly thereafter Creeley took off, toting a knapsack of books over his shoulder like a body bag. We all stuck around through a few more pitchers of beer, trying to sort out impressions.

That evening I was taken in by Kraft Rompf, who lived in a large house that he was in the middle of remodeling. "A fix-it-up from the City," Kraft explained as he turned on the living room light, revealing a collection of couches and chairs all covered by sheets to protect them from the dust. Kraft introduced me to his refrigerator which was stocked solely with beer, and we faded off into the evening. The next afternoon we headed back to Fell's Point. At an art gallery, we met up with Anselm, Jan, and Creeley, surrounded by a small contingent that included Joe and Marta. There Creeley lectured much as he had the day before, pulling books out of his pack and reading text in order to qualify his points. "All this popular psychology." he lamented. "How is the serious student of the human condition able to see past the hype?" He picked up another book from the pack and turned to a selection that brought emphasis to his pronouncement. After finishing off the beer and some whiskey, we set out for UMBC. At the university library, Creeley shook all the appropriate hands before stationing himself behind a desk rather than approaching the podium. He spilled his duffel bag of books onto the floor in front of him, like a plumber looking for a wrench. Half the audience had come up from Fell's Point, while the rest consisted of overdressed professors and under-dressed students. Creeley began the reading with an apology.

"I brought all these with me," he gestured to the books that almost covered his feet, "and then forgot to pack anything of my own." A groan of disappointment rose from the crowd. "But fortunately, Anselm was kind enough to let me borrow my own work from his library, a few titles from the Scribner's series." Creeley opened *For Love* and began to read aloud. In the middle of the second stanza he interrupted himself and explained, "That's an example of the overwhelming dynamics of human relationships. What metaphor can handle all those emotions we accept as natural? I dedicated this book to my second wife." He then reached down to the floor, picked up a book and began to read a pertinent passage. The method of the address was not new, only the setting. He turned to another poem, seemingly paging through the book at random, announced the title, read the first line and then caught himself as though in the process of telling a lie. "You can imagine

83

how old this poem is," he sighed. "How many lives I have lived since then." Although I had acquired a taste for his discourse, those around me began to whisper disparaging remarks.

"So Scribner's was held to its contract and published *Pieces*," Creeley waved a book in the air. "But they didn't like it. Not enough titles, too loosely organized." He then read snippets from that volume, providing appropriate interruptions, that were equally tantalizing and mystifying to some, aggravating and obnoxious to others. When Creeley finished a poem without a footnote, the performance was over, and he accepted the light round of applause with a nod. His impish grin seemed to indicate that he enjoyed the thankless task of defying taste in order to define it. As the reading broke up, a contingent headed out for dinner at a family-run Italian restaurant. All the central tables were connected to accommodate our party. I sat next to Joe and Marta.

"How's your mother?" I turned to Marta. "Grandmother," she corrected me. "Mother's a problem too, for that matter." I had brought up the wrong subject, but it was quickly forgotten as the head of the English department at UMBC, Anselm's boss, decided to confront Creeley about his performance. "Now Bob, why couldn't you just read some of your poems, forget all that other stuff. That's what we came out for." A murmur went around the table. "The point is," Creeley stated, "to read my poems alone would be like presenting a scientific paper without quoting the source material." The argument soon crested and conversation returned to small talk. I awkwardly tried to apologize for intruding on Joe and Marta but they both assuaged my guilt.

It was then, during the main course, that we noticed the guest of honor at a table directly behind us, intervening in the affairs of total strangers, father, mother and daughter, like a therapist with a search warrant. "Pardon me," Creeley began, "but I couldn't help but overhear your squabble." "It wasn't really like that," the father squirmed, flanked by the silence of both his wife and daughter. "We can keep it down." "Oh no," Creeley laughed, "I'm at the loud table over there. He pulled up a chair and continued, "What I can say is that you have a love triangle going on here." All three members of the family put down their silverware. "And it's your daughter here," Creeley gestured towards the teenager, "standing between you and your wife. The child is bearing the brunt of your struggle." Joe, Marta, and I all exchanged expressions of total disbelief. If the charge of self-indulgence had been raised over Creeley's reading, it paled in comparison to this encore. Because the restaurant was packed to the brim, the general commotion ensured that only the three of us sitting closest were privy to Creeley's unusual encounter group.

"Now, sir," the father objected, "I don't think this talk is proper..." "And it seems," Creeley continued, "that you have grown

84

to hate your wife and have replaced that former affection with an interest in your daughter." None of us could believe our ears. "I said," the poet-turned-psychoanalyst emphasized his point, "that you have transferred your marital love onto the product of that union." The wife, who up to that point had kept her head bowed as if in prayer, sat straight up and offered the first admission of Creeley's diagnosis. "If what you say is true, what would you suggest we do?" The husband cast an intense stare of hate across the table, while the daughter tried to appear oblivious. "If you want my opinion," Creeley began slowly. "No, my good sir," the wife intoned, "we need your opinion. I'm so mixed up with all of this. They plot against me." "No," the husband objected. "They do," she insisted.

"Mother, stop it," the daughter projected her presence. "You are embarrassing us all." The mother continued to stare at the poet. "Now, now," Creeley backed off in order to charge forward. "I don't need to know the details, but, for me, the hardest thing in life is to come to grips with one's basic desires and motivations. And in order to realize your desires, you must act out your innermost fantasy." He then turned toward the father and said in dead seriousness, "Which in your case means making love to your daughter." "And for you," he turned to the mother, "you need to have an affair and break the bonds of this emotional prison that is surrounding you. Of course, it all may lead to divorce." And without breaking stride he turned upon the daughter. "And for you, you need to run away from home, take the Greyhound to San Francisco, and give your parents some time to themselves." Just as quickly as he had descended upon them, Creeley withdrew, shaking hands all around the table, and then returned to his seat next to Jan and Anselm. Flabbergasted, Joe whispered over his beer: "He just told the old man to fuck his daughter!" The room was alive with whirling voices but I could only concentrate on the one speaking inside my own head.

After dinner, our entourage continued into the night, finding refuge at the abode of Roxie Powell, beatnik turned bureaucrat. He had spent over a decade in Vietnam pushing paper for the State Department. "Saigon was an incredible city," he reminisced. "You could get anything you wanted, and be able to afford it!" Powell had obviously spent it all in Southeast Asia as his apartment was completely bare of furniture, with only a stove and refrigerator. Everybody sat on the hardwood floor, soon filling the studio with beer, wine, smoke and talk. As the night grew late, Creeley and Powell entered into a series of reminiscences that quieted every other voice. "Well, the last time I saw Carolyn Cassady…" Jan and Anselm gave me a nudge, and we headed out the door into the early morning.

"I've decided to fly back later this week," Jan admitted. "Anselm doesn't want me hitching." I wasn't surprised. "And we were thinking, what with getting Bob to the airport and Anselm having classes today, maybe we could take you to the interstate right now." I had no objections, and Anselm drove out of town on a quiet section of I-70 where he could easily turn around. The last I saw of Anselm was his smile illuminated beneath a cigarillo. Twenty hours later, after an extended day spent aboard a succession of strange vehicles going nowhere fast, the fates delivered me to East Lansing in an icy rain, well after midnight, a veritable zombie. The next morning around noon, stumbling toward the shower, I found a note taped to the telephone which read: "Borges, 3 P.M., November 4, Room 53f2—Josephs."

Alternately elated and anxious but not quite recovered, I stuffed a few of my poems into a folder before walking across the subarctic campus. After checking in with the department secretary who motioned me down the hall, I knocked on the door of Borges' office. When there was no answer, I gently pushed it open and found Jorge Luis Borges facing me behind his desk in an unlit room. He was dressed in the usual dark blue suit; his head was propped up on one hand, eyes open though not quite aligned, staring in different directions. The dreamy left orb was pointed toward the ceiling while its steady companion on the right gazed straight ahead. His shallow nasal breathing at first seemed adequate for a meditatively conscious state, but his true condition became evident when one of those light inhalations got caught in his throat and his mouth partially opened as though to yawn, but instead produced a moderate snore; he was totally asleep. It then happened that I witnessed a short run of rapid eye movements, his steel-blue orbs flitting around the room as though beholding some scene which I could not appreciate. The blind poet was dreaming with his eyes open wide. I left the self-described "anarchist, anti-nationalist, atheist" as I had found him. Retreating down the back stairway, I constructed an account of that interview to satisfy the curiosity of Professor Josephs.

POSTSCRIPT

A decade later, at the Portland Poetry Festival, I briefly talked to Robert Creeley about that time in Baltimore. He read his poetry in the amphitheater at Washington Park and made it through every poem without interruption except when Mark Sargent's one year old son bumrushed the stage; Creeley pulled his glasses down his nose and remarked, "Ah, there's the hope of the future." As Melita led a loudly protesting Alekos back to his seat she noted, "The hope of the future needs to take a nap."

The last I read about Borges was an AP story entitled "Author erases suicide from life story" which reports that he outlived the prediction of his own demise as portrayed in a story entitled "August 25, 1983." Borges explained, "I have thought about suicide many times. When I wrote the story I elected a date I believed would most certainly be posterior to my death. It was like choosing the year 2000." Borges admitted the date had snuck up on him and said he would have committed suicide "But laziness and cowardice prevent me." By way of explanation he admitted to being busy working on new fiction, a essay on Dante, and a translation of the 17th-century German mystic Angelus Silesius. Since then, Borges has been called to an afterlife that he still doesn't believe in.

Last I heard from Anselm Hollo he was happily married—not to Jan—living in Boulder, hanging out with the Naropa crowd. A poem contained in Anselm's book *Sojourner Microcosms* (Blue Wind Press, Berkeley, 1977) crystallizes my memory of that Halloween weekend.

OCTOBER 31ST

for marta backstrom

all saints, all persuasions
& to be sure quite a few holy
fools among them
filed past your crib, double-time

when you were born
all hallows' eve

the night human beings
change the way they look

to allow their dead
to come back & visit
in disguise

a hospitable time

FICTION WORKSHOP: NOTES ON
BLOOD AND GUTS IN HIGH SCHOOL

To: Kathy Acker
From: John Gardner

Kathy,

A basic characteristic of all good art—all man-made works that are aesthetically interesting and lasting—is a concord of ends and means, or form and function. The sine qua non of narrative, so far as form is concerned, is that it takes time. We cannot read a whole novel in an instant, so to be coherent, to work as a *unified experience* necessarily and not just accidentally temporal, narrative must show some profluence of development...any narrative more than a few pages long is doomed to failure if it does not set up and satisfy plot expectations...The most important single notion in the theory of fiction I have outlined—essentially the traditionalist theory of our civilization's literature—is that of the vivid and continuous fictional dream. I'd like you to think about this as you revise the novel. What's at stake for Janey? You might take a look at the novel Cormac is writing—I'm sure he'd be happy to give you a few tips.

Dear John,

If you're using Tampax tampons for the first time, please read these directions carefully.

Every day a sharp tool, a powerful destroyer, is necessary to cut away dullness, lobotomy, buzzing, belief in human beings, vivid and continuous stagnancy dreams images accumulation.

HELLO, I'M CORMAC MCCARTHY WHO LOOKED FAULKNER IN THE EYE WITHOUT BLINKING.

Don't bleed don't bloody genres Janey's underwear John Gardner's underwear white virgin red bleeding hole through poetry literary pulp romance mystery fiction trash cyber feminist punk genres no bleeding with two companions John Grady sets off on an idyllic sometimes comic fuck you to a place where when a tampon is inserted properly you shouldn't feel a thing. Dreams are paid for THIS MESSAGE HAS BEEN PAID FOR in blood.

Use a tampon with the minimum absorbency needed to control BODY SLAVERY MIND SLAVERY locked up in a slave trader's room is easy your menstrual flow in order to reduce the risk of getting TSS.

JOHN GRADY: I AM AN APPARITION OUT OF THE VANISHED PAST

88

FATHER: Why don't you just dwell on memories of

how good things were? If you feel uncomfortable, the tampon is probably not far enough inside you.

JOHN GRADY: In this headlong deficit the blood JUST REMOVE THIS TAMPON AND TRY AGAIN WITH A NEW TAMPON of multitudes might ultimately be exacted for the vivid and continuous fuck you of a single flower. THIS HAS BEEN A more comfortable and discreet kind of feminine protection PUBLIC SERVICE paid for by Tampax Flushable Applicator New York Times Book Flushable. Flushable. GardnerMcCarthyAckerFaulknerFlush.

ALFRED CHESTER: GOODBYE TO CHRISTENDOM

EDWARD FIELD

Except for some juvenilia from his early Paris years, most of Alfred Chester's reviews and literary essays were written between 1962 and 1964, a period when he was one of the most sought after and talked about writers on the New York literary scene. This was in sharp contrast to the neglect a few years later, after he had rejected writing criticism as a betrayal of his talents, and then had progressively withdrawn when his book of short stories, *Behold Goliath* (1964), and his novel, *The Exquisite Corpse* (1967), failed to get more than cursory critical attention.

In the early fifties in Paris, he had served briefly as Book Review Editor for a little magazine called *Merlin*, edited by Alexander Trocchi. But a projected essay on James Baldwin and Ralph Ellison for *Merlin* never materialized. In 1953, an essay on Djuna Barnes, "Watchman, What of the Night?" appeared in the Dutch magazine, *Litterair Paspoort* #VIII, along with an interview. Both have only survived in the Dutch translation, and therefore the versions, retranslated into English and included in the volume of his essays, *Looking for Genet, Literary Essays & Reviews* (Black Sparrow Press, 1992), are twice removed from the language of the original and, necessarily, mere approximations. Even allowing for this double distortion, the Djuna Barnes piece is clearly juvenilia, and even might be a clever term paper, one that perhaps had received praise from the teacher, and that Chester had brought to Paris with him when he dropped out of Columbia Graduate School in 1951.

But the interview with Hans de Vaal, a young Dutch writer he met in Paris, is a more interesting document. It has clearly been worked over, for Chester's answers are too long and elaborate to be spontaneous. But as an expression of the young Alfred Chester's ideas and enthusiasms it has special significance in light of later developments: For instance, he speaks of Countess Elizabeth de Breza, the disciple of Chopin and piano teacher whom he is to write about so vividly in his story, "Head of a Sad Angel." Furthermore, it is startling to see the beginning of his fascination with Paul Bowles, who led him to Morocco, and madness, 10 years later. And *The Exquisite Corpse*, the novel that he is to write there, will be a vivid demonstration of the very ideas he discusses with de Vaal in this interview, where he speaks about the novel as "a continually changing entity." He even defines for de Vaal the Pirandellian ideas about madness and identity that obsessed him throughout his life and were so crucial to his thinking.

The Dutch, an extraordinarily open-hearted people, if somewhat overidealistic and naive, even innocent, to our eyes, are always the first to accept everything new from America, and here we see the interviewer taking the young author as seriously as he took himself. But the interviewer's pomposity is clearly a game, for going out for coffee at the end of the interview seems as important to him as the discussion of literature. Ah, the Dutch, how charming and civilized they are. When Alfred Chester died in 1971, I first learned of it when someone sent me a clipping from a Dutch newspaper. He was remembered there, even after years of silence, whereas in his own country the death of an important writer was ignored in the press.

Locating a copy of this early publication in Amsterdam was for me a small adventure of literary sleuthing—though nothing special, I am assured by academic friends, in the life of a research scholar. For over a decade, I've made it a project to collect and type out Alfred Chester's marvelous letters for future publication. In transcribing the correspondence with Theodora Blum (McKee), I came across several mentions of an essay and interview to come out in Holland in a literary magazine. Alfred was terribly broke at the time and reported to her on March 3, 1953, that he was being "paid 2500 frs. for an article on Nightwood." (In old francs, this sum translated into about seven dollars.) Again, on April 17, 1953 he wrote, "*Litterair Paspoort* came out with my photo and five large pages all about me." Reference was also made in a letter of November 22, 1953, of a recent story in *Elsevier's Weekblad*, a more popular Dutch magazine, about the literary expatriates in Paris: "There on page 25 you will see a picture of me among many thousand other American writers." And here the fledgling author lists the literary people he knew in Paris that year. "I am the queer-looking bit standing between a North Korean Don Juan and Austyn Wainhouse. Sitting below me is Jean Garrigue and to her right is Miss Alice Jane Longee of Limerick, Maine (the backer of *Merlin*). At the extreme right is C. Logue, the human diphthong. Above him is Miss Mobile, Alabama (Eugene Walters), and above her is George Plimpton. To GP's left is William Pene DuBois, partly obscured by James Broughton (whose film opens soon in London) and to Miss Broughton's right is William Gardner Smith who they tell me publishes in Pocket Books. As you can see, I have arrived." This was only a year after Alfred Chester's first publication, an essay "Silence in Heaven," in *Botteghe Oscure*, but he was already making enough of a name for himself among the expatriate literati in Paris to merit inclusion in the photo.

The mention of the publication in Holland was a slim enough clue, but a year or two later, when I was visiting my sister who lives in The Hague, I made a trip into Amsterdam, less than an hour by train, to inquire at one of the libraries about *Litterair Paspoort* in which the interview and essay had reportedly appeared. But I was not overly hopeful of locating an obscure little magazine that had probably only existed for a few issues nearly forty years before.

I was not encouraged by my first attempts: The libraries I visited either did not have the magazine in their collections, or were closed for remodeling. Finally, I was directed to the main library of the University of Amsterdam, a bland, modern building which lay in the heart of the tourist belt with its merchant houses on picturesque canals, and which I had passed many times before on the No. 2 tram from Central Station to Leidseplein and never noticed. I doubted that they would allow someone with no academic credentials to simply go in and use the facilities. New York University only allows me, even as an alumnus, to use its library if I pay a fee.

But the Dutch were extraordinarily civilized about this too, and treated me as seriously as they would a visiting scholar, instead of a crazy American with a wild idea. And predictably helpless, I was unable to read the instructions in Dutch on the computerized file catalogs, but a librarian patiently punched in the request for me—research librarians are a remarkable breed. When the file of *Litterair Paspoort* glowed on the screen, and under Issue #VIII of 1953, the name of Alfred Chester in the Table of Contents, I will confess my hair stood on end and my heart beat, as if I had gotten a communication from The Beyond.

In a few minutes, the issue itself was delivered across the counter into my hands. I looked at it for a long time, this magazine the size of *Harper's* or *Encounter,* with a photo I had never seen of a young Alfred Chester, before spreading it face down on the glass table of the photocopying machine, feeding my *quartje* into the slot and pressing the "Print" button.

Until the early sixties in New York, the only critical prose Alfred Chester had written, after the Barnes piece, were reader's reports for The Book of the Month Club (on whose legal-size forms he also wrote long letters to friends). But this latter job was simply one of his desperate freelance devices to earn some money, just as he had once written a dirty novel for a few hundred dollars for Olympia Press in Paris. He had never seriously considered turning pro, for in spite of his delight in appearing in the literary group photograph, like many in his generation he was an extremist about Literature, and a believer in Art as Redemption. It may sound strange to today's generation that one should write for posterity, rather than immediate recognition, but, in that not-so-long-ago-time before it became perfectly acceptable to aim at celebrity, we all shared a general contempt for writers who "sold out," and expected a true artist to reject fame even if it pursued—as, later, in Morocco, Alfred Chester rebuffed a *Time Magazine* reporter and photographer who persisted in trying to interview and photograph him (yet afterward, how bitterly he resented his book not getting attention). Occasionally, though, his scorn of writers of his generation who wrote for television and the movies seemed less idealism than jealousy. As he wrote from Paris in February 8, 1954 to Theodora Blum: "... it is kind of unpleasant to be getting nowhere what with Eugene [Walters, who had had a short story done on television] and Manny [Rubin, an old classmate who was writing movie and TV scripts] and James Baldwin (to Hollywood yet for 25 Gs) rolling it in hand over fist."

Generally, after thirty, one can't help beginning to feel like this, especially if you're still living in poverty, struggling to pay the rent, while around you your peers are advancing their careers, or at least settling down to the serious adult business of raising a family. In 1959, 30-year-old Alfred Chester returned to New York after nearly a decade in Paris—to "face reality"?, deal with unfinished business?, to grab for the gold ring of success? His novel, *I, Etc.*, after years of work, was still an enormous, shapeless manuscript, from which he rescued various chapters to reshape as short stories. He was still in 1959 committed only to fiction, and continued to write startling stories, among them "From the Phoenix," about the recent breakup with his long-time boyfriend who had left him and gotten married. Though he had had no problem producing his first novel, *Jamie Is My Heart's Desire* (published in 1956, but written several years earlier), he had struggled for years since then, agonizing over his inability to complete another. But, as if fiction wasn't enough or he was trying to expand his horizons, he also dabbled at playwriting, and wrote four one-acters of a projected series. (One of these has survived, and has been issued as a pamphlet by Kent State University.)

The irony was that the minute he turned to criticism, editors started telephoning him, and he was faced with the shocking but undeniable fact that as a critic he was a rising star on the scene. Though flattering, this was very hard for him to swallow. But understandable—Alfred's critical prose was high powered, racy, and iconoclastic. He was called a "sport" in the critical field for his original, off-center, ruthless, and devastating analyses. To a certain extent one could call this approach to reviewing Literary Criticism as Entertainment, just as Tom Wolfe a few years later invented the essay of Social Criticism as Entertainment.

Editors soon expected from him more than book reviews, they wanted controversial re-assessments of major literary figures that they could feature. He was willing to oblige them, and produced, one after another in the next two years, essays on Updike (a famous roasting), Nabokov, Burroughs, Rechy, Albee, Salinger, Genet and others. He worked with great intensity, laboring for long hours through draft after draft, often resorting to dexamils, a then-easily obtainable version of speed that gave him *sitz-fleisch* at the typewriter.

Whether it was Norman Podhoretz, editor of *Commentary*, or William Phillips of *Partisan Review*, who first enlisted him in the criticism racket is hard to establish. It was probably *Partisan*, though the essay on Updike appeared first in *Commentary*, which came out monthly, and only later that year was the Henry Miller piece published in the quarterly *Partisan Review*. I ought to emphasize that *Commentary* at that time was not the stodgy parochial journal it is today, but like *Partisan Review*, was one of the hippest possible organs on the New York intellectual scene.

But *Partisan* was not so hip as to allow some of Alfred's more *outré* remarks on Miller. Deleted by the editors after Miller's brag, "... having taken on his (Miller's) six-incher, she will now be able to take on stallions, bulls, drakes, St. Bernards," was Alfred's reaction that ran: "Six whole inches? Eeek! Ooh-ooh! Help!" Or something close to that—I was laughing so hard when he read it to me in manuscript, I may not have got the exact words. That summer *Partisan* further demonstrated its prissy puritanism by rejecting his Genet-like story, "In Praise of Vespasian." "Our objection is not to the subject [homosexuality] or its detail but rather to the rhapsodic treatment. The piece is very well written but the writing is more celebratory than analytical or just plain fictional-prosaic," they wrote. This is so obvious an evasion it doesn't need any analysis. Perhaps it was just typical of the hypocrisy of the time, even in the highest intellectual circles. Thank God for Gay Liberation, is all I can say.

His attacks on and ridicule of some of these major authors was not expediency. He continued to express doubts about them in his correspondence. A year after the essay on Salinger had appeared, he wrote that "his spiritual quest leads nowhere." And his put-down of Burroughs (whom he had gotten to know in Tangier) was confirmed in a letter to Norman Glass on May 3, 1964:

> My review of *Naked Lunch* is true. I looked through the book at Paul's [Bowles] the other day. I also listened to some taped cutups (boring)... I don't like his easy assimilation of the vocabulary of Industry and Wall Street. Remember, remember, he is the Burroughs Adding Machine. With them, of them, against them.

He is the world of science and mechanics... He obviously believes in assimilating the machine and using it to personal advantage.

Of course, with criticism taking over Alfred's life, his fiction had to suffer, and it was with a feeling of loathing for the literary marketplace that he turned his back on his New York success and left for Morocco in the summer of 1963. But even there he had to eat, and was forced to continue to write reviews, though less frequently. Besides the study of Jean Genet for *Commentary*, he reviewed *Candy* by Terry Southern and Mason Hoffenberg, and a last, but enthusiastic piece on Truman Capote's *In Cold Blood* for *Book Week*, at that time a supplement of the *NY Herald Tribune*. Richard Kluger, the editor, also offered him $100 a throw for a monthly column, a significant sum in Morocco at that time, enough to live on for a month.

A vivid picture of Alfred Chester at work on the Genet essay (during the holy month of Ramadan) is given in letters he wrote from Morocco:

> January 20,1964: My Genet essay tears everything down, the whole of western civilization. It must be there by the 1st, and my column is due today for the *Trib* and I haven't even begun it. I want to write about Mailer as a postscript to the Genet. The Genet says that when Christ died in the 19th Century, Europe woke from a sweet dream with a bloody knife in its hand. It couldn't face its guilt, 2000 years of godless murder so it had to go on believing in dead institutions. *Freud comes briefly to Europe's rescue with his brilliant diversion. He makes guilt personal; though he too denies God, he fouls from the target by making it possible for a man to ignore history in favor of his childhood. We pay attention to our mouths and anuses (tr. assholes). What a relief to be guilty of nothing worse than coveting mama. (And what a perfect totalitarian weapon psychoanalysis potentially, if not actually, is. It reduces all opposition to expressions of personal and misdirected hostility. It makes all protest infantile.)* ... On and on goes my inexorable logic, until the coup: Hitler had the genius to turn Christianity inside out, to make that of which the Christians were most guilty into the ideals of a new order. Conquest, murder, betrayal, all the crimes of man that had been for twenty centuries blessed by God, again received the blessing, and along with it the blessing of bread.

(The fascinating thing about this and the following quotes from the piece he is writing, and my justification for reproducing them in full, is that all this material was deleted by the editors of *Commentary* from the essay as published. Unfortunately, the original manuscript, which Alfred said was three times as long, thirty pages, has disappeared. Knowing him, I'm sure he would have rewritten all these pieces for his collected essays, and put back much of the deleted material, as well as adding to it, if he were alive.)

Later in the same letter, in his eternal identity crisis, he writes:

I just have never faced myself, really. That probably sounds so boring to you, but it is causing me gigantic anguish. Even my criticism. All I ever do in it is try to show the writers up. I am campier than Rechy, beater than Burroughs, more brainy than Nabokov, more zen than Salinger, etc., etc. All you have to do is turn the dial and I'm it. Even all this is just because of Genet probably. I'm Genet now. Is there any hope of ever being Alfred?

It is nevertheless true that if his stories sometimes seem to be written by different authors, as critics have noted, in his essays we hear a single, unmistakable, authoritative voice. But after the lapse into self pity, he returns sure-footedly to the Genet essay:

When one looks back at the slaughtered of Christendom—the American Indians, the Negroes, the Moslems, the Christians themselves, the Asiatics and Africans—six million Jews are a drop in the bloody bucket. Hitler was no uncouth accident in the ladylike history of Europe. He was the history of Europe, he was Europe merciless up to its very last gasp. And if we don't know of the crimes of the humanists, it is probably only because the humanists won the war…To a melody by Mozart, enter Jean Genet, whom François Mauriac has accused of being in league with the devil.

And later:

I finally ran out of dexamils and to my surprise I went right on working, just as many hours and just as clear-minded. Lots of coffee though. I don't need liquor either, though I might if I started on a novel. I can't write at all with kif except analytical horrors.

Tuesday. Strange you mention the golden chalice. I use it in the Genet. I say: *He holds the golden chalice in his hands but he knows the Holy Water has dried out of it leaving a crust of blood around the edges.* I thought I was making up the expression as an image of the cup, the holy grail. But I guess I wasn't. Yes, I think it is the cup of the tarot, since I've always assumed, or was told, that the tarot cup is the grail.

…But no one can be thrown out of civilization because each man contains the whole and tells the truth about the whole. A state executes in order to disavow everyone's guilt. The execution of Eichmann, for example, makes all the rest of us seem innocent, when in fact the only honorable and honest thing would be to have the whole human race hanged in Jerusalem. Do you think *Commentary* will be amused by that?

And on January 29, 1964—

It is eight p.m. and I've been at the Genet since eight in the morning and yesterday and forever and it is supposed to be there this week and I'm exhausted. It gets more and more brilliant, but I hate it more and more. And the letter comes from Irving Rosenthal in Marrakech saying money is absolutely the only justification for writing essays and book reviews in which case you don't tell your friends about it. So I've written him a letter (Hitler being his favorite hate) beginning Mein lieber Adolf and telling him I didn't know the law. And that if he was cold there was a surplus of fuel at Auschwitz. But it's made me depressed because it's true and I'm working like a dog... What I say in the Genet is just telling the truth. He (Genet) is making the real Christian ideals—murder, pillage, treachery and robbery—into his own ideals. As he's in jail he has nothing to lose. It takes me thirty pages to say it, but that's a good sign. I'm beginning to get my wind back. I don't come out in farts now, but in streams of shit. Note how long my letters are... From last part of essay: *America is Europe's knight in shining armor. But the love-starved maiden needs something a lot warmer in her arms than a coffer of jewels. Beauties have been known to fall in love with beasts before; or, as Confucius said, a hot dragon is more fun in bed than a cold dollar bill*... I really need a rest after this.

... Dris woke me at five this morning and I finished the Genet in time to get it to the post office before noon when it closed for the weekend ... The Genet is called, "Goodbye to Christendom." [It was published as "Looking for Genet."] I do hope they print it. It will bring me $300 and cause a little stir.

It is easy to see why he called it "Goodbye to Christendom," and why *Commentary* had to rename it when they threw out that whole aspect of the essay. Besides the unlikelihood of a Jewish magazine publishing an attack on Christianity, they probably did not appreciate that he was writing from outside the Christian world, from the liberating vantage point, for a Jew, of a Moslem country.

I read it over this morning and could hardly believe how good it was though it reads like I'm in the middle of a nervous breakdown. It must be the dexadrines I use to keep going. I alternated between dex and librium as you can't get dexamils here. At night I had gin and kif to unwind with ... The Genet is really an apologia per mia vita. It tries to explain my dybbuk ... The essay is really such a vicious attack on everything except Genet, you, God and myself, that I don't even know whether they'll have the nerve to print it. ... By the way, my Genet ends up talking about Kennedy. I quote Mailer's passage about the subterranean river of American life, *It was out of this river that the assassin's bullet came, regardless of who pulled the trigger or why. We accept, with the authorities, the guilt of the lonely psychopath because it tells a truth if not a fact. It dramatizes the refusal of Unreason to be silenced any longer by man's, Europe's, idea that he, Reason, rules the world. Humanism, however pretty, isn't for us because nature isn't human, and man willy nilly is of nature. Nature is unreason and God. It is the madness that runs through our lives and connects us to the stars in a way no rocket ship can ever duplicate. It connects us to all living things and to ourselves. To name this madness Holy doesn't promise peace or prosperity; it promises only a reason for being, a reinvestment of life into the dead matter of which the universe is now composed.* Nice, yes?

But in a later letter, he adds: "I feel as if mama's going to slap me hard for writing such mean things."

Writing a column for the *New York Herald Tribune* aimed at a mass readership was at variance with Alfred's image of himself as a writer for the literary few, but he could not ignore the fact that he was being widely read for the first time. It disturbed him, and he wrote me in February 19, 1964: "Edward, am I going mad or is it possible that people do actually write nasty things about me in newspapers? ... Someone called Jimmy Breslin ... writes: "Behan at least tries to write for the entertainment of the reader. He is not some outlandish homosexual trying to sound off on human destiny between paragraphs about his boyfriends." I just read that and I thought that man is talking about me ... I keep thinking I am mad. I mean, suddenly I think How can I write about being poor, and Dris, in the *Herald Tribune*?" But the columns brought him some diverting correspondence: A theatre group in Washington D.C. asked for permission to stage one of them, paying him $5 per performance, and a psychiatrist wrote, "Dear Scabrous Fungus Collector ... I'd order you to douse the glim of your horrible light of darkness if I had the power and if I didn't like the twisted macabre stuff ... "

But with the upheavals of his life in Tangier, encompassing stormy relations with his boyfriend, feuds with the Bowleses and others of the literary colony, bouts of near starvation, breakdowns and strange ailments, the "monthly" *Book Week* column came out only sporadically. And as he started to concentrate on writing a new novel, which eventually became *The Exquisite Corpse*, he devoted less and less time to criticism and the column, dropping this kind of work entirely after he suffered a final psychotic attack.

When he returned from Morocco to New York in the winter of '65–'66, he began his novel *The Foot*, much of which has been lost. And as his mental state deteriorated and he embarked on desperate voyages, his literary production became sporadic. There is firm evidence that he wrote a story called "Trois Corsages," about his three friends, Harriet (Sohmers) Zwerling, Susan Sontag, and Irene Fornes, but this too has been lost, along with most of his unfinished and unpublished works. In his madness, I believe he destroyed much correspondence and many manuscripts himself, but some things were in the hands of his agent, Ted Chichak of the Scott Meredith Agency, who now denies any knowledge of their whereabouts.

After much erratic wandering, Alfred Chester settled in Israel sometime in 1970, where he wrote a final essay, "Letter from the Wandering Jew," that was never published. (It exists thanks to Theodore Solotaroff who photocopied it when it was submitted to him at Harper & Row by the same Ted Chichak who refuses to search his files for surviving manuscripts.) If Alfred Chester's charm has disappeared, along with his sense of humor (either due to a state of mental deterioration or on his way to death), this final essay reveals a new identity, no longer worried about who he was, whether he had an "I" or not. To paraphrase his early mock-formulation, *il m'encule, donc je suis*, he now suffered, therefore he was. Unexpectedly for such a previously elegant, often humorous writer, he let out, at the end of his life, a hurt, angry bellow of rage and despair at a world he couldn't stand, almost Céline-like, not caring what anyone thought, and mixing large complaints with petty gripes—it was all the same to him by now. With a sour, don't-give-a-shit tone, he did not try to pretty up his feelings, and snarled and snapped unreasonably at his imagined persecutors. And the fact that he sent this piece to his agent meant he wanted the world to listen. As a record of his last lonely years, when he rejected his friends, as well as the literary world he was part of, it is unique testimony.

In a commentary in *The New York Review of Books*, that could apply just as well to all of Alfred Chester's critical work, Gore Vidal wrote that he "... was a glorious writer, tough as nails, with an exquisite ear for the false note; his review of Rechy's *City of Night* is murderously funny, absolutely unfair, and totally true, a trick that only a high *critic knows how to pull off.*"

ABBIE HOFFMAN: REQUIEM FOR A HEAVYWEIGHT

MIKE GOLDEN

It seems only appropriate he went out with Sugar Ray Robinson, who was called *pound for pound, the greatest fighter that ever lived*, a description a lot of us felt fit Abbie just as well. As big a thorn in the ruling power's side as he was, even the system he fought all these years will miss him, because he was not only Tom Paine incarnate calling *them* out on the carpet for their bad shit, he was *The Colgate Comedy Hour*, *Laugh-in* and *Saturday Night Live* all rolled into one humongous ball of energy and humanity. Not that he wasn't co-opted just like everything and everyone else—he was one of the first to learn that the system eats everything, including revolutions in this country, and the best you can do is digest it and try to make waves in the languid sea of mass unconsciousness. Not an easy thing to do when you're hanging ten, of course, but our Dear Abbie understood McLuhan better than McLuhan, and knew how to feed the beast whether the beast was hungry or not.

Not to say he didn't get tired. Accumulation does it to everyone, and if your own system goes as haywire as society itself, there's not much you can do except fight it until you go under. What the exact circumstances of his passing were it doesn't matter. It doesn't matter whether he did himself in, spontaneously OD'd or he was offed by the CIA, because the body is just one thing, the first thing to go, and in Abbie's case even that's immaterial.

When I first saw the headlines I thought of something Maurice Girodias said to me about Mason Hoffenberg: "Mason is dead," Maurice grudgingly acknowledged, "but he is not that dead." Abbie is dead, but he is not that dead. His influence, his spirit lives on in all of us who were inspired by him. Not meaning to get metaphysical here, but perhaps now that he's free of the restraints of the body, perhaps now that he's crossed over to the next level, whatever that is, he'll be able to infiltrate that same spirit into a different plane. If there's a bureaucracy on the next level, which I suspect there is, they obviously have more need of Abbie's talents now than the virus which society has become does on this level.

Technology at this point seems to have trashed any sort of working ideology, and while Abbie was in the middle of the transition, there was a definite void, a philosophical hole that couldn't be filled by the old rhetoric. Feds and Heads, Cowboys and Indians, cyberpunks vs. corporate chippies, the name of the game is always changing, and Abbie, who had been riding point on the great tidal wave of change practically his whole life, was certainly more adaptable than most of us. And probably still is, even out on the bardo plain. He was a warrior, and his sword was his tongue. His strength was his sense of humor. His blessing was his great heart. His gift was the total contribution of his essence to making sure the American Dream lived up to its promise. That it didn't, that it couldn't, in no way diminishes his contribution. Ultimately we're all fighting a losing battle, unless we, like Abbie, understand that the fight itself is the victory. More than anyone else who came out of that shattered propinquity known as the counterculture, he was the spirit of the 60's. And he'll live on as long as individuals stand up to the inevitable oppression any society—be that a government, a church, a school or a corporation—passes on to its citizens. And for that we thank him.

THE FEMALE NUDE AS SCULPTOR

MICHAEL ANDRE

1. Everybody's on a first name basis with Madonna and Colette, but Marisol's been famous longer. New York Telephone insists on a last name and therefore Colette, to enter the phone book, is Colette Colette. Marisol uses her last name, Escobar. I don't know about Madonna. The bride is stripped bare of her last name. Patty Hearst when she married the SLA became Tanya; with the bad girl fame of Tonya Harding, some newscaster first named her, and I thought briefly we were back in the '60s. Literary critics seem always to call Emily Dickinson just Emily.

Marisol's a multilingual Venezuelan New Yorker. I asked her if she was any relation to the more famous Pablo Escobar, the cocaine cartel overlord, and she said, no. But she did once tell me she grew up mostly in Europe particularly France. High school on Long Island taught her English and trend and rendered her persona American, fashionable and exotic.

2. I was assigned to review a retrospective of her prints by *ARTNews* in 1973, and wrote: Images of a shoe, purse, spoon, her face, her feet and especially her hands form these prints Marisol began in 1961. There is an ambiguous play between the outline and hatching and blank paper. At times a complicated image suggests a symbolism similar to Redon. Generally she seems more interested in duplicating through etching some inexplicable mental afterimage. Hands and other images were often traced from her own body, and her process is enmeshed in all life's processes.

3. Painting participates in the history of ideas. But, as Ad Reinhardt is reported to have said, sculpture is what you bump into when you're looking at painting. On the other hand, if music is for elevators, then a wise Philistine will stay out of rooms where painting is hung. Sculpture cannot be avoided, unless you stay out of parks. Only architecture is a less avoidable, more public art.

4. Sculpture could be anything. It could be a tree or a trash can. You can inspect it. But a painting is artifice. The subtler the painting, the better. My ex-wife, a guerrilla girl who no longer speaks to me, may perhaps have done an advertisement for her point of view: the only way a woman artist can get into the Metropolitan is naked. But isn't that the dispensation of sculpture, or art—clothes?

5. Marisol's *Memorial for Merchant Marine* in the water at Battery Park is dwarfed, of course, by Bartholdi's *Liberty*

Enlightening the World, but nicely endures fog and storm anyway. The theme is analogous to *Burghers of Calais*. Three sailors are on the bow of a sinking ship: one stands and calls, another kneels and a third lies on the deck, hand reaching into the waters, trying with his outstretched hand to lend life, as God to Adam, to a fellow sailor already overboard.

Sculpture is dependent on architecture, as Serra (with *Tilted Arc*) found to his chagrin. But to my mind Serra and Richard Nonas and Carl (no relation) Andre are boyishly playing with construction materials; contrast their work with the organic yet powerful pseudo-phallocentrism of Louise Bourgeois. With Bourgeois, the object of the sculptor objectifies; that is, in effect, the nude takes Pygmalion's chisel and sculpts a penis.

With Nonas, sculpture becomes architecture. Sculpture is primal like speech—or building.

Michelangelo signed the Sistine Chapel, "Michelangelo, sculptor." Today, would he have signed it, "Michelangelo, multimedia artist"? I asked Colette if she was a sculptor and she said, no, a multimedia artist.

Donatello's *David* is a favorite Renaissance sculpture—masculine yet sensual, amused yet martial, it embodies both Strength and Youth. But Leonardo gave the painter the edge; Leonardo was the man who advanced painting beyond the conquest of pictorial space—something the Greeks or Romans, according to the standard art histories, did not achieve. Sculpture could not hope to surpass the Age of Pericles; ye olde S-pose was the breakthrough into realism so long ago achieved that it no longer seems to be part of a developing science.

6. Marisol's *Last Supper* appears and disappears in the American wing of the Met at curator's whim. I miss it, but not as much as an Aphrodite, sexy now and sexier originally painted trompe l'oeil like a nude Hanson or D'Andrea. I became an art critic when I realized at age 14 I could not spend the rest of my life studying *Playboy* nor possibly make a living with such study. But is a painted nude stripped of its paint nuder or just naked? Aestheticians of the airwaves might call it the Problem of Cher.

7. Robert Creeley's *Presences*, about Marisol, appeared in 1976. I quoted him in a 1975 review in *ARTNews*: According to Robert Creeley, Marisol first used her own person as model because she worked late at night, and models weren't available at those hours. Her new series of drawings, at Janis, is also night work. For one thing, many of the drawings are on black paper. As white paper negates space, black paper suggests infinity, the reaches of the sky at night. She has chosen, secondly, to color her works with a species of rainbow hatching which flames in a manner suggesting, with vulgarity, psychedelic or X-ray phenomena. But the black is here, most importantly, the setting for sexual encounters, probably with the self. A nude profile is perhaps Egyptian,

perhaps Vogueish, and certainly narcissistic. Her traced hands clutch at traced buttocks and breasts. Vaginas flower.

Creeley made his remark about Marisol in a prose poem, "Presences." Marisol for dark reasons has touched off considerable poetry. Language has been integrated into these new works: "Marisol, I love you," Marisol has scrawled on one. In another the instruction reads, "lick the tire of my bicycle." Marisol's language is admirably fresh; it highlights the gulf between poetry and painting and, as well, the novel importance of these works.

Art generally has been static, a single moment in time; but literature, like music, has generally been temporal, a succession of moments. Duchamp, in *Nude Descending a Staircase,* attempted to portray succession. That, too, is Marisol's goal. Just as she maintained the flatness of the picture plane by portraying herself in profile, she destroys logical "illusionistic" time by using the same model—probably herself—in numerous positions in the same work. She is simultaneously the sadistic rider and the masochistic horse in *Paul Revere.* Like certain seraphim, Marisol appears in several places at once. It's a smart development of Duchamp, and it also develops women's erotic art. As John Cage says: "The trick is, without any apparent means of transportation, to suddenly appear in a different place."

8. Not all sculpture is of bronze or marble. Philip Corner gave me a broken drummer's baton rubber-stamped "piece of reality."

John Chamberlain took the Duchampian ready-made forward as a material, car as wood or marble or bronze. Is this John Cage's noise? Picasso, though he used ready-mades, seems to subordinate them to the "science" of cubism.

Hannah Wilke made photographs of herself as a nude and beautiful caryatid; she also made ceramic vaginal flowers, and I was clumsy enough to break one. I've never seen Greek or Roman sculpture that wasn't, to some degree, broken. Wilke's posthumous show at the Ronald Feldman Gallery features photos of herself sick and dying. Hair, fallen out from chemotherapy, is framed; Joel Fisher, who is balding, also used his hair, in the making of paper finding ideographic lines. In the days of body art, literal body parts, human hair as at the Holocaust Memorial, become objects of veneration as well as *objets d'art.*

Before Charlotte Streifer Rubinstein wrote *American Women Sculptors,* even before Jack Burnham wrote *Beyond Modern Sculpture,* Herbert Read's *Concise History of Modern Sculpture* lamented the loss of mass in sculpture after Brancusi, Moore and Arp. Abetted by technology, a sculptor like Fisher can "scribble in air" with his hair. It's elegiac homage to one's own decay. Who wasn't once the beautiful helmet-maker's wife?

9. Plato and Bertrand Russell might think ideas are forever, and some sculptors like the late Don Judd surely believe their sculpture lives in the world of ideas, forever secure within the human spirit; but the truth, most people think, is less grand and more comical. Phidias chiseled some stone, perhaps he had a speech impediment and therefore would not know how to say yes to Socrates (everyone is Plato teacher's foil); Pericles looked the other way when Phidias put his hand in the till, the original NEA scandal; perhaps Phidias couldn't sit still at assembly, perhaps he was an idiot savant who could represent anything in marble but was otherwise incompetent and chiseled merely to earn drachmae. Rodin and Michelangelo share the prestige of the broken fragments of Roman copies of Greek originals. Greek and Roman science is considered wrong but curiously Greek and Roman poetry, such a Homer and Vergil, are considered—despite the great barrier of their "dead language"—the equals of Shakespeare and Milton; and no one would compare Ashbery and Creeley, for instance, to Milton or Shakespeare. Roman painting, which does not have our perspective, enjoys little prestige. It is one area where the "ancients," to use the time-honored term of the Renaissance, remained "primitive," to use the newly "in-correct" term, which is yet indispensable if art is to be viewed as an ongoing historical process. Art is viewed as a kind of Darwinian evolution, a history of ideas; is it? Is all great art on the flaming tip of the arrow of art history?

10. My knowledge of the literature on Marisol is thin. As the editor of a little magazine *Unmuzzled Ox*, I became friends with Suzanne Zavrian and got to know her magazine *Extensions* in the early '70s: *Extensions* published sapphic homages to Marisol by the pseudonymous, M. Trap. Life for Lesbians in the late '60s was yet without honor. That's where I first heard Marisol's name; Marisol is not gay, in fact she had an affair with a principal contributor to early *Unmuzzled OX*, the woolly beatnik Gregory Corso.

11. Sculptors used to embody drama; their peers were the playwrights. They'd represent and summarize human situations. Rodin's *She who was once the beautiful helmet-maker's wife* or Michelangelo's homoerotic, grandiose *David* have all the dramaturgic resonance of literary representation. At some point in this century sculptors eschewed mimesis for invention.

    Even Rodin clearly followed rather than led the Impressionists. But Calder and Tinguely, Moore and Caro are less like Joyce and Proust and more like Schoenberg and Stravinsky. Cubism, of course, was the turning point: painting became like sculpture in that it represented reality on several planes at various angles; but sculpture became like music not literature. Think of Brancusi and Serra. Performance art took on the dramatic function of the sculpture of the past. Much performance art exists after the performance as photography and has the erotic charge of, say, Crito's Roman copy of the Greek Aphrodite at the Met. The late Hannah Wilke, along with preeminent performance artists of our generation whose work merges with sculpture. They make body art. Why do I describe Marisol as a performance artist? Because she incorporates her face and other body parts in otherwise impersonal work. Rembrandt painted the best self-portraits, but always in costume; Marisol, like Colette, Wilke and Schneemann, uses at times her own nude figure. Is such self portraiture narcissism? Not unless Joyce's *Portrait of the Artist*, the most accessible masterpiece of literary modernism, is also so dismissed.

12. I reviewed her sculpture at Marlborough for the November *Art in America*.

Marisol's partial self portrait as a *Tablita Dancer* seems to metamorphize out of a tree. Bark and wood grain conspire to make the artist her own totem. All this new work concerns the different sculptural possibilities of wood. *Tablita Dancer* is merely the most resonant mimesis, leaning most on nature. Like Oldenburg, unlike Serra, in other words, there's more to Marisol than formalism.

The allusions to totem poles proliferate with native American subjects, such as *Wolf Robe, War Bonnet and Coup Stick, Horace Poolaw* and *Blackfoot Delegation to Washington, 1916*. But often the bark of this natural material has been stopped, and the wood has been sawed, painted, hammered, and only then touched by the artist; it is carved and assembled into witty and offhand representations. Here she makes "assemblages" from used or "found" materials. It just happens that the material she has found is probably the same material used millennia ago by the first sculptor.

Sometimes she halts with a drawing on wood, at other times she carves the image in the drawing; always there is visible awareness of the spontaneous creative process. The colors of the sanded wood harmonize with the colors she paints. As a dare, she carves feathers from wood, the subject diaphanous, the material heavy and industrial.

Humans in Ovid are forever turning into trees. Ovid's *Metamorphoses* consists of one creation or origin myth after another. Augustus disliked Ovid's wanton ways and exiled him to the provinces. Marisol is similarly deracinated, notorious in Caracas, a trilingual French Venezuelan New Yorker.

Two of her pieces are local to TriBeCa: *George Summer* and *George Winter* both portray George Grimm who habitually sits on the stoop of Marisol's building smoking cigarettes in summer and cigars in winter. Some of the ensemble pieces such as *Cuban Children with*

Goat and *Children Sitting on a Bench*, clearly based on photos, suggest to me the poignance of Marisol's vantage as a childless woman of a certain age.

The basis of her preeminence is Pop Art, which is to the School of New York as Impressionism was to the School of Paris. It is universally likable. The pedestals of these sculptures are ad hoc and witty found objects, sometimes sawed police barricades, at other times pushcarts ready to be wheeled into the Museum of significant twentieth-century art.

These sure-handed vigorous pieces enhance Marisol's status as the finest American sculptor.

13. Idols are religious sculpture which as genre date to the era of cave painting; they predate not only written poetry, but writing. Are Diana and Aphrodite idols? Dennis Oppenheim represents the sculptor as shaman. His burning antlers could light Lascaux.

Marisol transforms herself in her art into our idol. In the '60s she embodied chic fame and art glory.

14. Moving up 57th Street from Janis to Marlborough, she has switched from the gentleman dealers of the '50s, where she began, to the great mega-dealer of the '90s. Janis seemed to be keeping her art secret. I once gave Carol Janis, who took over the gallery from his father many years ago, a copy of a signed limited edition of *Earth Egg*, a book I had published by Gregory Corso, Marisol's old friend, with the understanding he would try to sell it. It stayed on his shelves. After a year, I asked if he had had any luck, but it was still there in the same place. After another year, I asked for it back. Offended, he handed it over. It was very dusty.

The gallery itself, with its tiny windowless sixth floor exhibition space, reminds me of the basement of the Met.

Connected to this is the fate of the other book on Marisol to which I am in some sense personally connected: Robert Creeley's *Presences*. Creeley is an excellent poet and essayist, but when Abrams asked for a text, Janis did not advise Marisol or Creeley that what was needed was an essay. Instead, Creeley turned in a creative manuscript, like the ones he's also done for Robert Indiana, R.B. Kitaj, Jim Dine and Francesco Clemente. It's art writing not art criticism, a one-eyed poet on a one-named sculptor. Abrams rejected it, and consequently no major art historical book has appeared on Marisol. Creeley's own publisher at the time, Charles Scribner, Jr, was a gentleman of the Carol Janis school. He published the book. It sold few copies. It was really meant to be hung on the wall, page by page. Scribner's eventually got swallowed up by a larger, more efficient publisher.

15. Arman's *infinite typewriters* + *infinite monkeys* + *infinite time* = *Hamlet*, in his retrospective at the Brooklyn Museum, sums up the problem of photography and sculpture alike: if you play second fiddle, even if you compose like Corelli or finger like Paderewski, it avails. Not. What's Arman's first name? What's Hamlet's last? "What's in a name?" Arman accumulates. Christo covers and does not strip nude.

16. Frailty, thy name is woman, Hamlet said. The minimalists were men, and the abstract expressionists, such as David Smith, were men. But by 1976 in a piece in the *Village Voice* on the alternate space Buecker & Harpsichords, I remarked that Buecker exhibited sculptors who were generally nice little old ladies, specifically, Lily Ente, Sari Dienes and Louise Nevelson. Sari Dienes challenged me, admitting that she was indeed old, but was not otherwise a nice little lady; Sari then wanted me to edit a cookbook of her unwritten improvisational recipes. Nevelson's dramatic yet frail appearance in black, often completed with a cape, dramatized and signed, so to speak, her stark, cerebral black sculpture. Nevelson's bohemian manner irritated the art establishment until one day she was recognized as a genius—a very old genius, as it happened. Michelangelo may conceivably have been gay, but chiseling the marble *Pietà* with a mallet does not seem like work for the frail. Colette's *In Memory of Ophelia* and *All Those Who Died of Love and Madness* (Berlin, 1976) with Tabea Blumenschein upset my one-time roommate Laurie Anderson: both Tabea and Colette were nude and supine in public for weeks.

17. Marisol's *Portrait of Nevelson* (1981) uses blocks of wood, appropriate for an artist who stacked and painted wooden boxes. It's not quite the pathetic fallacy, as is Sari Dienes' portrait of John Cage made of mushrooms. Sari's portrait won't last. But, then, not marble nor other gilded monuments to the rich will outlive a powerful rhyme, wrote Shakespeare. Ente, Dienes, Nevelson and Wilke are dead. Marisol is the eminent American sculptor. The status of women and the status of statues is less shifty than meets the eye. Hierarchies of painting, poetry and sculpture, or of men and women, are, in other words, equally suspect. Wasteful war, in any case, shall as Shakespeare put it statues overturn: unswept stone, besmeared with sluttish time.

2
FICTION

THIS STORY

DANA WILDE

PREFACE

This story is handicap accessible. It can be read by anyone without regard to race, gender, nationality, ethnic origin, age, religious preference, sexual orientation, physical or mental ability, or political sympathy. Although it is made entirely of words and nothing else, and realizes this, it is intended to be realistic. Its characters are pretended to have realistic pasts, with realistic ancestors and realistic homes which are nonetheless fabrications of the author.

The author and the narrator are not the same person, and therefore the attitudes of the narrator should not be construed to be the attitudes of the author. It should be understood that the attitudes of the author must also necessarily have influenced the attitudes of the narrator. But every effort has been made to carefully eliminate from the voice of the narrator as many personal biases as the author is aware of; the narrator is explicitly and implicitly of no particular gender, race, ethnicity or national origin; the narrator claims no special knowledge of any characters other than him or her self, either fictional or reality-based, and therefore understands that no particular truth resides in this story, except by accident.

No reader, of no matter what race, gender, nationality, ethnic origin, age, religious preference, sexual orientation, physical, mental or emotional ability, or political sympathy, should be offended by any statement, event or philosophic or political assumption that might inadvertently be made in this story. No part, and no combination of parts, of this story should be construed to imply that the author or narrator has in any way sought to prefer or promote any values or beliefs that are held in either the culture or society occupied by the author or narrator, or the fictional culture or society occupied by the characters; since the fictional culture or society is realistic, it should be understood that no narrative remark about, or description of, that culture or society is intended to imply a preference for, or a promotion of, the values of the culture or society upon which the fictional culture or society might inadvertently have been modeled.

This story explicitly assumes that all its female characters are equal to all its male characters, all its homosexual characters are equal to all its heterosexual characters, all its Aboriginal, African-American, Asian, Hispanic, Native American, Polynesian and other characters are equal to each other and to all Caucasian characters. In certain instances some characters are more equal than others, but in no case is the overbalance of equality intended to give any particular privilege or personal advantage to the character who is in that instance more equal than other characters. If, for example, it is stated by the narrator or a character that another character is "beautiful" or "good looking," this is not to be construed to mean that any other character is not beautiful or not good looking. Accordingly, no remark, event or description in this story should be construed to mean that any human being who is not a character in this story is in any way different from any other human being.

No event in this story is intended to imply, either directly or indirectly, the superiority or inferiority of any person of any race, gender, nationality, ethnic origin, age, religious preference, sexual orientation, physical, mental or emotional ability, political sympathy, or moral disposition to any other person, whether real or fictional, of any race, gender, nationality, ethnic origin, age, religious preference, sexual orientation, physical, mental or emotional ability, political sympathy, or moral disposition.

In addition, no appellation applied to the race, gender, nationality, ethnic origin, age, religious preference, sexual orientation, physical, mental or emotional ability, political sympathy, moral disposition, or physical appearance of any character should now or at any time in the future be construed as a slur against any human, whether living, dead or fictional. This story seeks to employ descriptive terms that are most widely acceptable to each specific group (and in some cases individuals) being described or referred to. Should a descriptive term or phrase, through forces beyond the control of either the author, narrator or political advocates working in either the fictional or reality-based society, become at some unforeseen point in the future offensive to the group or individual the term applies to, then the reader should feel free to strike that term from the text of the story and substitute a more acceptable term. For example, were the currently-accepted appellation for children between the ages of 12 and 20, "teenager," to become offensive to any reader of any age, but particularly to a reader 12–20 years of age, then the reader is required to substitute an acceptable term of the reader's own choice each time the word "teenager" appears in the text of the story. (For example, the term "intermediately spatiotemporally challenged individual" might be utilized in place of the term "teenager.") In order to minimize the possibility of offending any group or individual, appellations normally used to describe generalized races, genders, nationalities, ages, ethnicities, religions, sexual orientations, physical, mental or emotional abilities, political sympathies, moral dispositions, or physical appearances, have been deleted from the story as often as possible.

No event in this story should be construed to grant or intend to grant any special privilege or advantage to any character, no matter what the event. All characters in this story are accorded equal rights and opportunities for employment, government benefits, race, gender, nationality, ethnic origin, age, religious preference, sexual orientation, physical, mental or emotional ability, political sympathy, moral disposition, physical appearance, and spiritual redemption. In the interest of fairness, some allowance is occasionally made in this story for previously-existing underprivileged statuses of certain characters. Any appearance of underprivileged status in this story is due solely to the story's intended realism. No prior judgment is made by the author or narrator as to the fairness or unfairness of any character's social or cultural standing.

No race-, gender-, nationality-, ethnic origin-, age-, religious preference-, sexual orientation-, physical, mental and emotional ability-, political sympathy-, moral dispositions, physical appearance-, or spiritual integrity-based quotas are imposed on the characters, events or settings in this story. This story intends the distribution of its characters according to race, gender, nationality, ethnic origin, age, religious preference, sexual orientation, physical, mental and emotional ability, political sympathy, moral disposition, physical appearance, and spiritual quality to match percentage distributions of humans in each category with the distributions assumed to exist in the fictional society in which the story takes place. No such relation between fictional and reality-based societies is assumed or proposed; in fact, no relation between this story and reality is assumed to exist at all. Subsequently, the omission of any characters representing any particular race, gender, nationality, ethnic origin, age, religious preference, sexual orientation, physical, mental and emotional ability, political sympathy, moral disposition, physical appearance, or spiritual magnitude that has a higher percentage distribution in the fictional society than in the story is strictly accidental, and should not he construed to imply any prejudice against the omitted character, or any special privilege to any included character.

In fact, anything may be added to or deleted from this story at the discretion of the reader, provided the addition or deletion does not give offense or privilege to any other reader or any fictional character of any race, gender, nationality, ethnic origin, age, religious preference, sexual orientation, physical, mental and emotional ability, political sympathy, moral disposition, physical appearance, spiritual or any other conceivable human quality.

No petting is allowed to occur in this story without the prior written consent of the characters.

In addition, this story provides a totally smoke-free environment for its readers.

≈

THE STORY

A human female and a human male copulated a number of times.
The female gave birth to an infant.
Later, the [human] male and [human] female died.
The infant grew to adulthood. Later, it too died.

POMBO

CLIFF HUDDER

Let me finish. I savor nightmares but when I am making dog or
giraffe, or making monkey, and the nightmare walks in the middle of
day, white-faced like wearing dead human's skin, then I do not like
it, and I tell you also he frightened the child and everyone else at the
corner of Decatur and St. Ann. Pombo you are bad.

He comes walking a dog that *is not there*. I twist the balloon
ears onto a *real* balloon dog I am making—for a child—but Pombo
frightens the child with his hard white face, black eye-rims, his tuxedo, gloves, umbrella. He holds a long stiff leash at the end of which
is nothing. I do this for the children and here he comes, he frightens
them.

"We went in there and the bar was closed," says a man to a
woman, a couple who happen to come just then. Two of them coming
from the iron rows across the street, stopping to look at Pombo just as
the child and the child's parents stop watching me, the balloon in my fingertips, watch to see this nightmare on the corner coming. Pombo follows the invisible dog right into my face.

He lets the invisible dog piddle my leg. NO! I say.

Pombo has been away but now, for some reason, thinks he can be
back.

There's more.

Because Pombo had not been seen for weeks and weeks nobody
knew: Did Pombo live? Did Pombo die? (I hoped.) Now he was here
after weeks, but who could tell: with the white face and the painted
frown and the deep wrinkles of sad white—was this a living creature or a
corpse erect? I could not tell because for weeks I had not seen him, and is
anything ever the way we remember?

The child went up to him, particularly close to his whiteness and
his smell.

I shook my red sleeve—long and red and hot, but the coat is
something I do...for the children. I flap the sleeve and rattle the
animals tied at my waist and they stretch and complain and I

nearly stomp the foot of a giraffe...which would make for collapse. Sweat runs down my legs—as if the dog that is not there actually did piddle. (I wear shorts for the heat; I do enough for the children and always have; what do they ever do for me but look with brown animal eyes, arms soft, totter on over-wide hips?) My sensibilities are affected. I say:

NO. I say, YOU HAVE BEEN GONE!

Pombo's handkerchief flies. He looks up Decatur in a direction; he looks up Decatur again in another. He bends a soundless rasp or cough into this handkerchief; one cough up the barrel of the iron cannon on its big-wheeled cart; one toward the Café du Monde (his mouth makes no noise but his lungs do, which spoils the effect), then he folds the handkerchief away.

I stomp. My red cap with the white fuzz-white ball (brown from river air, street breeze, coffee air) flips. NO! YOU HAVE BEEN GONE IT IS MINE! I DO NOT CARE IF YOU'VE HAD A BAD COUGH YOU LOOK DEAD GO AWAY. GO REST... because I am thinking now of the terrible corner. *This* is the good corner, here in front of the Café du Monde, the pedestrian walk, but before I was at the terrible corner. Beyond Royal, beyond Bourbon, beyond Rampart Street. If I go there it will rain. Nobody will come to the terrible corner where nobody ever comes only perverts. Beyond jugglers and the parks, fire breathers, musicians, rope trickers, beyond the man who bends his legs behind his ears, the Tarot reader, the Crystal Oracle—the terrible place I was before where the children never come with their round brownness and if I go back there and stand in the rain—it is sure to rain—I will get a bad cough.

YOU CANNOT HAVE IT BACK!

Pombo hides away the handkerchief, pounds his chest with sounding slaps. His chest is broom-handle hard. Pombo breathes in: one suck up Decatur, one suck up Decatur the other way, shoots his arms out hard toward the cracks in the sidewalk where I stomp, and the child and his parents have backed away. "Why is the clown mad at Santa?" asks the child, walking away from the dog I haven't finished making, haven't yet squeaked the last ear in place.

"That's not a clown, sweetie," says the mother.

Bad Pombo flicks his hands at me like flicking at an insect in the afternoon. Here: he turns his back, backs into me the dark back of his jacket and he tugs his sleeve and his other sleeve and begins to lean upon a post (or possibly a window sill) that does not exist.

Pombo is bad.

This is not all. NO, I say, YOU HAVE BEEN GONE AND THIS IS MINE, a place nothing like the other with its rain where the parents and the children never come except to come past and I do not touch the children...NEVER...but I see myself going back there now and can't stand it. I do stomp the giraffe's foot then and it collapses: KABOOM!

The mother pulls the child by hand, the father puts his arm around them both, his camera snicks the buckle of his belt and NO! I scream. COME BACK! I am screaming. The giraffe bursts into collapse.

Pombo holds up his glove white fingers. Pombo listens up St. Ann. Listens with the other hand toward the Café with its caffeine air which affects my sensibilities. The tilting top hat is on top of his ears which are as full of hairs as the ears of a pervert, but he shakes his head, pretends to not hear, leans against a wall that *cannot be seen.*

"That's not a clown," says the father (who is pulling his family away), "that's a mime," and the other couple who found that the bar was closed: the man is laughing and pulling at the shirt of the woman. The woman says: "Let's get a drink."

"This is great," says the man.

"Let's go find someplace to go somewhere and find a place to get a drink."

"This is great! Two mimes in a shouting match."

I AM NOT A MIME! I scream so loud it might open my head. I cry and stomp. KABOOM! A dachshund goes and KABOOM! A monkey. They collapse. I AM AN ARTIST OF BALLOON, I say, AND NOT FINISHED WITH THIS DOG, which I hold out to the cringing child though its one ear (the dog's) is not right and is collapsing. I didn't twist enough.

"Why is Santa yelling?" The child bawls. There could be tears in his round eyes, his face is red and wrinkled like a cloth, his parents are scuttling him toward the Café—they are not happy. LOOK AT WHAT YOU'VE DONE, I say to Pombo. LOOK AT WHAT YOU'VE DONE TO THE *CHILD!* I stomp the animals. LOOK, POMBO, WHAT YOU'VE DONE TO THE SPIRIT OF CHRISTMAS. *KABOOM!*

"Get it?" says the man. "Mimes?"

"A drink," says the woman and Pombo leans on nothing, pats his mouth, popping on the death whiteness of mouth. He yawns.

KABOOM! KABOOM! It is the caffeine air, it is that I'm hungry, it is my sensibilities, my boots stomp all of them down, my animals. TAKE IT, I say, YOU ARE BAD! YOU ARE A NIGHTMARE MOTH-ERFUCKER. SHIT-MIME. SHIT POMBO. People force across to the other side, across Decatur Street, the mothers hold the ears of children in the spirit of Christmas. YOU ARE BAD. LOOK AT WHAT YOU HAVE DONE!

I squish away with damp legs, sweat down them like the red coat is a squeezed sponge. I wipe my eyes with the red hat's white puff. I stand beyond the Tarot reader on the pedestrian street. I stand beyond the Crystal Oracle with his bulging eyes. But I still see Pombo. On *my corner*. I keep going.

HE IS BAD! I scream down Pirate's Alley and ... and ... and there's a pervert in a sleeveless shirt who steps off of Royal to say: "Sweetness." "Sweetness," he calls, "ain't it so?"

This is all.

At the place no one comes, no one came. Not the firebreather or the rope-swallower or the shit-eater, none of them come here, this is the end. I come here, there is no other place for me, and on the first day there was rain, and on the second day it rained and some perverts came but no one else; and on the third day it rained and I shivered. It rained the red-wet suit down my legs, me alone, north of Rampart, where people pass with children quick on their way someplace else but it's not so awful, it's not so bad, it's not like God is dead or something ... but the whole time I wonder:

Is Pombo real? Was anything about him solid to the touch? His sills and posts and dogs? His wheezing lungs? His walls and cubes and tables and the "rocking chair" he sits on (with his stick legs crossed)? His filthy coat? Is any of it in this world at all?

If so: has it done anything for us lately?

Could such a toweringly dead-like thing return and make a threat to me? So, grim in twilight, on the third day, I go back to Decatur and St. Ann; I go to make sure. I "tip tip tip" in the rain and hold down my bad cough with my hand. His umbrella is out, his back is turned, the back of him like a mystery the other side of which must exist. I tap his shoulder and he, off balance, turns to me and—in a surprise move—I poke his eye like THIS!

"Ouch!" says Pombo.

I laugh down Pirate's Alley HO, HO, HO. Pombo you are bad (HO HO), I'm sorry (HO) I hurt you but you hurt me first.

THE HI-SPOT

Looking back on the Hi-Spot, I regard it as one of the lowest points in my life.

I signed on there as a dishwasher in the early months of 1983 in order to make extra money for a trip I was planning to Europe with my girlfriend. The pay was five dollars an hour, a

KIRBY OLSON

rather extravagant sum, especially if you consider that it included dinner and tips and that, many nights, there were no customers—or so few that I was able to spend the majority of my time studying German.

So, what is there to complain about?

This.

The place was staffed by abused children who had turned 22 and graduated from college. They had abuse envy. The hierarchy of the establishment turned the outside world, to a certain extent, upside down. There were no racial minorities on the staff, so people made much of the fact that they were misunderstood Jews, or badly underestimated lesbians, or slightly retarded Presbyterians (the church had stunted their mental growth). Nearly everyone had been abused by their parents as infants, or claimed to be, and blamed every mental ailment on this, just as a century earlier every physical ailment was put down as consumption.

The suffering was enormous among these well-educated white youths, and in retrospect I weep great wells full of tears for them.

We were a tiny, poorly-managed link in the food chain. A yuppie outpost in one of Seattle's poorer neighborhoods, our clientele consisted of misfits. Not the ones you see standing on a corner raving about Joseph Mengele and the Vatican's legacy of nerve gas plots against the West, but rather those who don't get along too well with their families, and so have to pretend that the other people at the café *are* their family, while they each sit at separate two-person tables, reading the funnies. By their clothes, you know these people had once aspired to be hippies, or would now, if the time was right. They were generally bathed, but not necessarily well; they were generally polite, but not necessarily people you would hire to teach the finer points of etiquette. Still, forks with crud glued to them were often returned with no apparent hostility.

The staff, as I saw it, was made up of artists with talent, artists with no talent, ecology freaks, more than a handful of extremely bossy bulldykes, and a ragtag bunch of intelligent, articulate drifters with lots of opinions and limited, but definite, senses of humor.

I liked the artists with talent and could put up with the ecology freaks. The rest I would have gladly shoved into the garbage disposal, but their hard faces would have broken the grinder. Anyway, I did not have such luxuries of opportunity.

The hegemony, both in terms of numbers and in terms of ferocious vociferousness, lay in the hands of the bulldykes and their pets. These were also the cooks. To get a decent breakfast or dinner you had to be nice to them. I was.

My girlfriend was one of the first to be ostracized. The last heterosexual to work in the kitchen, she was conveniently scapegoated for everything that went wrong, and she left in tears.

Soon, the entire staff began to change over—and every time a pleasant and potentially-fuckable waitress left, she was replaced by a tobacco-chewing she-wolf. All the heterosexual men were long gone except me and a newly-arrived German immigrant. He was the other dishwasher, so I rarely saw him, but we left each other funny notes in German, informing each other of things like towel shortages. Why didn't I quit? I stayed out of curiosity—I love to watch, as they say—and I had a window that looked both into the kitchen and out on to the floor … plus I already had a set date for departure on the big silver bird to Europe. There was no reason for anybody to kill me off, as I was already due to expire, and it seemed foolish for me to find another job, since this one only taxed my powers of observation and my ability to amuse myself rather than any powers of physical endurance or, God forbid, speed.

What amused me most intensely was to sit with the cooks. I found their savage, S/M, drug-taking lifestyle to be extremely glamorous in a *film noir* sort of way, and often asked for blow-by-blow accounts of fist fucking, needle sharing, what it was like to sit on the breakfast cook's face, etc. The cooks, to their credit, were cooperative towards my research and seemed to treat me as if I were no threat—much the way lions and tigers, not being natural enemies, regard each other with curiosity, rather than with the animosity reserved for those considered to be an actual ongoing hazard to their habitat. I was a fly on the wall; circumspect, but amicable. As a poet, I was considered to be preternaturally good, above suspicion. The cooks, too, wrote poetry—which usually complained about the purposelessness of cooking, or the occasional waitress-hating poem.

Y was my favorite, as she was the clearest case. Abused as an infant by her truck-driver pa, she was Jewish and lesbian, used heroin and had an IQ of about 106. Her plan for world peace was striking. Throw all heterosexuals in the oven and flick the switch. Like Bakunin's slash and burn economics, there was no tomorrow. First, erase; then, grace!

X was my least favorite. Infinitely more sophisticated than Y, she was a full-blown hysteric who practiced scat-singing as if it was more than an expression of her neurosis. She was slumming after her expensive education in this land of demented fry-cooks with easy-overs sliding around in pans like the uneasy eyes of Laura Mars. She was a gifted accordion player and accomplished vocalist who could as easily be hired for a traditional wedding as for a Japanese jazz tour. She had a brain the size of a silver dollar, with an unusually sharp finish. She hated working and didn't feel it was her lot in life. She was not as well-organized as the cooks with humbler origins—and often burned her pots, or sent me a pot that was red hot without telling me, so she could amuse herself over my ouch. She bore watching. I often burnt my hands during shifts

117

she worked, and the pots she didn't burn me with were already so deeply scalded that they required extra elbow grease on my part. What she really got burned up about was if I tried to suggest new working methods for her, which I invariably did at every staff meeting.

Together, X Y Z and the other lesbians who worked at this joint developed a similar logic, which went like this. We are women. We have been abused. We have cunts. Anyone with a cock is evil. Anyone with a cunt who allows it to be touched by a cock is evil. In order to distinguish between us, and them, sophisticated determinants are seldom employed. After I left for Paris and the German was accused of being a Nazi and hounded out the door, the dykes were left to themselves. Who did they now have to blame? Well, so-and-so once had a boyfriend. Bang, gone. She doesn't like to share in group sex, therefore she is a throwback to the heterosexual couple. Gone.

The world shrank, and the owner, an eminently fair woman who had left her husband to participate in the shenanigans, suddenly had a light come on in her head. The situation was unhealthy, because suddenly she, as capitalist owner and therefore exploiter, was now being scapegoated. The staff rationalized theft of her cakes and pies and money with the saying, "Property is theft." If property is already theft, why not steal it back, the logic went.

The parasites were decimating the host, and the host started plucking them and booting them out the door. They came back to kick at and slap her, calling her politically incorrect—a real smack to a woman who had spent her life on peace marches, thinking she was rebelling against her martial father.

Daughters all over the country are accusing their fathers of abusing them as infants. They have no proof, just a dark hunch. They may be right. But in this country we have always said that a person is innocent *until proven* guilty. How does one prove a rape in infancy? Is it not often a vicious circle, exploited by therapists and by young liberal women, driven crazy by their privileged upbringing, who need to make an indictment against someone in order to show that they, too, are fighting against an oppressor? When it comes to the point that every father stands accused of a crime no one can really remember (and much less prove) and thus men in general are seen as co-criminals, or even as subhuman; then only women will any longer be seen as responsible human beings. When only women really *exist*, they will no longer be women. Women only exist today as a category of *human being*, and when women are the ONLY human beings, they will no longer think of themselves as women, but simply as the only human beings.

At that point, they will begin to tear each other to shreds, just as the women at the Hi-Spot did. Human beings, whatever else they are, are animals. We live in a food chain. We exist in a predatory state. We try to form cooperative bonds, but often they can exist only in relation to an enemy. When men have disappeared in the ovens, new scapegoats will be made and made to feel nonhuman. This low road to the ever illusive utopia is the legacy which the left has left us, and we see the same logic operating in every movement touched by its insanely cheerful spirit. The world has seen it in Pol Pot and I have seen it at the Hi-Spot. What is saddest is that it is always those on the bottom of the pile who suffer from such logic, as they take it too seriously, and they take it too far: actually pulling guns on the upper class, as poor Y did later in our story. She then was wanted in several states for armed robbery and finally ended up in San Francisco as a prostitute with AIDS. X, more sophisticated and with many more ideas in her head, was able to balance the theories of lesbian superiority with intelligent capitalist survival skills, and, with a nice family background and good skills, conveniently slipped off to New York City, got a boyfriend and became a famous singer.

WHAT'S NEW, PUSSYCAT?

MAGGIE DUBRIS

"If you don't get rid of that fucking cat I'm going back to Ohio."

My roommate Lindy tossed a shoe at Baby Beano, who ran hissing behind the stove, and picked up her fork.

"Shivonne, I'm not kidding, I'm sick of this shit." She shoveled frozen pie into her mouth. "No work, nothing to eat, and I have to fight with some psychotic feline over every pathetic bite I take."

"You know, if I ate that fast I wouldn't even be able to taste it."

"I don't have to taste it, I ate this kind before, I know it's good. All of which has nothing to do with that horrible little Beano."

"He's hungry," I said.

"He's hungry, fuck him. He's lucky we don't eat him. I don't even think he's a cat, I think he's just … a friendly rat."

Beano crept slowly along the wall, eyeing her plate.

"And another thing." She began to gesture wildly, her mouth full of pink meringue-like matter. "I'm not going for one more waitress job. They don't want waitresses in this city. They want naked waitresses. Why don't they just say that in the ad, huh? Naked Waitress Wanted. How hard is that to spell?" Pink bubbles sprayed from her mouth. Beano shot out a claw, hooked a clump of pie and capered back to his spot behind the stove. She threw the tin onto the floor. I took another bite from my own pie.

"You know, this is just part of being a poet," I said. "I

119

don't imagine Rimbaud complained about the cat. I don't picture Baudelaire entertaining thoughts of moving to Ohio."

"This isn't Paris. We have to get jobs."

"We will, there's jobs everywhere. We're poets, we're not subject to the constraints of the dominant culture."

"Yeah well I'm hungry. I'm getting tired of eating frozen pies and I don't like stealing toilet paper from public bathrooms and the landlord hasn't forgotten about us no matter what you might want to believe." She began to wheeze loudly. "And that creature is giving me asthma. Either he goes, or I go."

I picked up Beano and put him on my head, where he lay purring like a coonskin cap with a motor in it.

"That's not cute, it's perverted," Lindy said. Beano hissed and dug his claws into my scalp.

"Okay, I'll find him a better home. And we'll get jobs." Skin drums pounded on the street outside my window, summer New York night coming down, a thousand poets walking the streets on fire and wonderful, headed my way.

"Tomorrow. Definitely." I tossed Beano toward the pie tin and ran out the door.

Morning. Drinking sour black coffee as we had run out of powdered milk and I forgot to pocket any more packets of sugar. I sat poring over the *Voice*.

Subjects wanted to test pharmaceutical products. Must be 18–24, in reasonable physical condition, not squeamish, not pregnant. Good veins a plus. Top pay for qualified individuals.

Student needed to distribute flyers, 3 hours/day, late nights only, prefer reliable sort. No prudes. Room for advancement.

Business opportunity for self starters. Foolproof product, low overhead, high return. Get in on the ground floor. Commission only.
Hard workers wanted to open oysters looking for pearls. Low pay, long hours. Call Wed. only, 6am-8am.

Blind sculptor requires model, $6/hour, Brooklyn location, can accommodate unemployment/welfare/SSI .

Janitor needed, must be reliable, part time, flexible hours, top pay, must have experience. Great opportunity for artist or free thinker.

Janitor. I could handle that. A bit of mopping up, hose out some toilets, dust a radiator or two. There was no phone number, just an address. 222 E. 14th Street. I decided I should wear a bra for the occasion, pulled on my cleanest T-shirt and jeans, and headed on over.

Pink signs lined every window. TOPLESS BODY RUB $10. I checked the address again and climbed the stairs: stained linoleum, dust balls lining the floorboards. A bloodbank on the right, winos lined up with their sleeves rolled above their elbows. On the left another pink sign. WHAT'S NEW PUSSYCAT. I knocked on the dented steel door. A man opened it. Black pants, black shirt, white tie, needlenose boots, but still not hip. A blobby white nose and skin that would probably dent if you pressed a finger into it.

He looked me up and down. "You here for the job?"

"Uh-huh."

"Okay, come on." I followed him into a small room with what looked like a doctor's examination bed with a towel laid across it. Beside was a small table with a box of tissues, a bottle of rubbing alcohol, a can of baby powder, and a squeeze jar of baby oil. He stared at me as though he was waiting for something.

"Go on, take off your clothes," he said.

"Take off my clothes? Are you insane, Lindy was right. Why didn't you just put it in the ad, naked janitor wanted? You pig." I began to stalk around the room, knocking bottles from the table, grabbing the towel and twirling it over my head. "What kind of an asshole are you, I must have some asshole magnet embedded in my forehead. No matter where I go, bang, I smash right into the biggest asshole in the vicinity. I can't believe you want me to take off my clothes for a janitor job."

I looked up to aim the towel at him. He was plastered against the door laughing.

"You think this is funny?" I said, "I had to walk all the way up here, I could be interviewing for that pharmaceutical job."

Finally he stopped. "I take it you're not Angelique?"

"No I'm not Angelique. If I had a name like that, I'd change it."

"And you're here for the janitor job."

"That's right."

"Well it's still open, lucky you. You know how to clean?"

"Of course I know how to clean, how could someone not know how to clean?"

"None of the last fifteen janitors did, we had one last week trying to mop up with the broom. Claimed that was how they did it back home. Which was Jersey, by the way. Maybe it's good you're a woman, I'll show you where the mop is."

"Wait a minute, how much do I get paid?"

"Don't worry, you'll be richly compensated. Same as all the other damn janitors in the city."

A bucket. A mop. A bottle of TopJob. It seemed easy enough. The bouncer at the blood bank winked at me as I passed. I decided to start at the bottom and work my way up. Sprinkle, swab, step. Sprinkle, swab, step. The dust balls turned to black threads and stretched from stair to stair, the winos plastered themselves against the wall but refused to move their swollen feet.

"Hey baby, you're supposed to sweep first," one of them said.

I continued along my appointed path.

"You're supposed to sweep, then wet mop, then dry mop, didn't your mother teach you 'bout mopping?"

I glared at him.

"You don't take advice from a man, you never going to learn. You never going to be no crackerjack mopper. Nobody wants a janitor can't mop."

I walked to the top of the stairs and poured the water out, winos leaping as it cascaded a brown waterfall to the landing where it slowly soaked away.

"I'm done," I said to the asshole. "When do I get paid?"

"You got to do in here too. Let me introduce you to the girls."

Four girls sat on the couch watching TV. A black girl, a Spanish girl, a white girl, and a Chinese girl. All wearing leotards. I waved hello. They continued to stare at the box until he flipped it off.

"Jezebel. Rosita. Taffy. Jasmine. This is ...?"

"Do I get paid in cash or check?"

"Cash."

"On the books or off?"

"Off."

"Good. My name's Evangeline."

All four girls burst out laughing.

"Hey Evangeline, you got your period yet?" the black girl said. "Your mama know you're hanging around here?"

She didn't look that much older than me. Maybe twenty, at most. "I'm a poet," I said, "and since I haven't lived with my mom in three years I don't imagine she cares."

"Glenn what are you doing bringing this baby in here?"

"Evangeline is the new janitor. Get used to it Jez, especially if you want her to perform the usual janitorial duties."

"What's that supposed to mean?" I said.

"Don't worry about it babyface, just start mopping that back room."

"I need a broom."

"You need a broom. Unfortunately, the broom is ruined on account of your predecessor; you'll have to go out and buy one.

122

And get a gross of rubbers while you're at it."

"A gross of rubbers? Where am I supposed to get that?"

"At the One World Bargain Discount Store. Right up the block, you can't miss it."

When I got back there was a rabbi standing in front of the desk. He nodded at me. "Awfully young."

"She's the janitor," Glenn said. "So that's ten dollars, plus another ten for the extra half hour." The rabbi handed over a fistful of crumpled bills. He waved to Rosita.

"Bye sweetie," she said, "see you next week."

"I don't know how you go with a nasty old man like that," Jasmine said after he'd left.

"He's all right, he just wants me to think up games. Last week he was a fireman, this week he was a cowboy. I don't care, he tips good." She handed Glenn fifteen dollars.

"I tell you honey, they can't tip enough for me to act like I like it. That one this morning, twenty-five dollars, a straight fuck, he's taking forever to finish, and then he has the nerve to say, 'Can't you move around a little or something?' I laughed in his face. I said, 'Listen baby I already got to change the towel, you want me to change the sheet too you better give me another twenty bucks.'"

I swept out the back rooms, wiped off and straightened the tables, sprayed Lysol around and mopped. I didn't have to touch the linens. That was the girls' responsibility.

"You should get some incense or something," I said to Glen as he handed me a twenty. "It smells like a hospital back there. Is this all I'm getting?"

"Is that all you're getting? You were only here two hours, and you trashed the best room during your interview. What time you coming in tomorrow?"

"I don't get up early."

"Just show up before three, we don't want you around during the rush."

"So you're working in a fucking whorehouse," Lindy said.

"It's not exactly a whorehouse. I mean, it couldn't be, it's right there on Fourteenth Street. If it was a real whorehouse the cops would shut it down."

"Great. Not only does the whole neighborhood think we're dykes, now they're going to think we're whores as well."

"They don't think we're dykes, we've slept with half of them."

"They think we're the kind of dykes that sleep with men. They don't connect that one thing has to do with the other, you better not get high and start bragging about this job or our gooses'll really be cooked."

"I got paid cash. Let's go to Tad's and get steaks. One of these girls is going to take Beano, I can feel it in my bones."

I showed up at noon. It turned out that was the time they opened. "Perfect," Glenn said, "you can join us. We're doing a process."

Everyone was sitting with their eyes closed. "Do I get paid for this?"

"Yeah, we'll start you at noon. Sit on the couch and close your eyes."

I sat beside the other girls.

"Evangeline, assume a position of neutral repose. Your legs are not crossed and your hands are not touching. Good. Now close your eyes and find a space. I want you to locate a space in your left elbow. Good, fine. Now locate a space in your right shoulder. Okay. Now locate a space behind your left eye. Be entirely within that space. Fine. Create before you a chalkboard, and intend for yourself by writing on that chalkboard. Intend for yourself how many customers you will satisfy today. Be sure you make that number a large number. Good, fine. Intend for yourself a profitable day."

I wrote the name of the girl who would take Beano. Rosita. She looked like the kind of person who could be pushed around by a cat.

"You create your own universe," Glenn droned on, "you deserve what you get, and you get what you deserve. Good. Fine. Great. When you're ready to smile, open your eyes."

In a couple days I got to know the routine. Never show up before two or I might get sucked into a process. Never show up after five or it was too busy to clean. The girls sat on the couch all the time, watching TV and talking about tricks and their lives. They all had fake names so if a trick met them on the street they could pretend they didn't know him. Jezebel lived uptown some place and went to church on Sundays, had a husband and two sons who thought she worked in an office. Jasmine never talked except to bitch about the men, the other girls said she lived with her parents. Taffy took pills all day and didn't consider herself a whore. "This place is different than the other houses, the people here are so nice, don't you think so?" I nodded as I mopped and dusted. Rosita was the only one I really liked, but she had a baby son with asthma so I knew she would never take Beano. Taffy was my next hot prospect. She was always telling me how lonely she was.

"Hey Taffy, do you like animals?" I said one day. There were no customers and they were waiting for a delivery from the coffee shop down the block.

"What do you mean by animals?" She always spoke very slowly, as if she were a very thoughtful person, but really it was just the pills.

"Like, a nice little cat."

"Oh no, cats are carnivorous. I could never live with a carnivore."

"Cats are dirty," Jezebel said.

Jasmine nodded. "But they make good soup." I couldn't tell it she was joking or not.

I was at a dead end. I had figured a whore would be the perfect new mom for Beano, but they were all so uncooperative. One day Rosita beckoned me over.

"Evangeline, listen, did you ever smoke pot or anything like that?"

"I'm a poet, I'm into derangement of the senses."

"Right. Well, one of the things the janitor generally does is go cop for us. We'll cut you in or however you want to work it."

I copped at the lot on Sixth Street, three ounces a day, and they went through it all. For my days off I bought double so they didn't run dry. Lindy was doing nothing but lying around the house in her underwear, spraying the roaches with fluorescent paint, wheezing and bitching about Beano. I was beginning to doubt that she was a real poet after all. She didn't even want to drop acid anymore.

"I wish I had my TV back," she said one night. We had been robbed six times since we landed in town. The last time all they got was a bowl of pennies and a five-dollar alarm clock.

"A TV? What for, just look out the window if you want to see people get shot."

My new fan was trained on her face, giving her voice a strange vibrato. "It looks more real on TV. Anyway, I thought we were supposed to meet Allen Ginsberg by now."

"Come on, we can't be bound by the parameters of time. If we want to be poets, we have to break free of the whole time/matter continuum. We don't try to control things, we embrace chaos. Anyway, he's not all he's cracked up to be. If you're a girl, you have to buy him drinks."

"Let's kill Beano then, maybe I'll feel better," she said.

"I love Beano, I'm finding him a home with the whores."

"No. You can't give him away, he couldn't live without you, but he was a bad mistake. You should kill him. It would be best for everyone. You have one week. If he's not gone in a week, I'm taking the bus back to Ohio."

Glenn was waiting for me when I walked in the door. "I want you to have a look at this," he said, holding up a copy of *Screw*.

125

"I think I'll pass."

"No, you're in it, listen to this." He flipped through the pages, cleared his throat. "What's New Pussycat, a spotless establishment on East 14th Street, offers an alluring array of girls ready willing and able to cater to your every whim. A real find, and the price is right."

"That's really heart warming," I said.

"It's more than heart warming, it's your doing. 'A spotless establishment,' Al Goldstein himself wrote that, he made a visit. A couple weeks ago."

"Do I get a raise then?"

"Evangeline, this isn't about money. It's about agreements. You create your own money situation, that's not up to me. Here, I made you a copy."

He handed it to me as if it were the dead sea scrolls.

"Great," I said, "I'll send it to my Mom. She'll be so proud."

As I was mopping out the back I set my plan into action. I ran shrieking to Glenn. "A mouse, there's a mouse. He's shitting in the middle room." I had dropped some pepper corns around, figuring he couldn't know any more about mice than I did. All the girls screamed. "It was big, it had a long tail and I had to beat it away or it would have bit me."

"Sounds like a rat."

"No it was a mouse, a horrible little mouse."

"Okay, go down to One World and get some poison."

"We can't have poison in here, we'll all get sick."

"I'm environmentally sensitive," Taffy said, "I can't be around toxins."

"Anyway, the mice go into the wall and die and stink up the place. You never get rid of that smell."

"Shit," Glenn said, "are you sure it was a mouse?"

I nodded. "I could loan you my cat."

The whores began to snicker. "Cats are dirty," Jezebel said. "Anyway we already got enough pussy in here. You let a cat in, board of health will be here like that." She snapped her fingers and I shot her a look.

"You would have to pay me, of course," I continued. "He's a wonderful cat."

"Did I tell you this girl was trouble Glen? Now she's trying to sell her little pussy to you. I bet there's not a mouse back there at all. "

"There's a mouse. I have to go clean up mouse shit now. And you're the one who's going to be in trouble if that mouse pops up at a sensitive moment."

She laughed. "You got that backwards honey. I am not

going to be the one who's in trouble. I don't stick no part of me in some stranger's mouth."

I stomped off to clean the rest of the rooms, making sure I left the pepper corns lying obviously in a couple piles by the door.

Something struck me as odd as I dragged the mop along the hall floor trying to make it looked like I had shined it all up on my way to get paid. The television was off and I could hear what sounded like walkie-talkies. I tiptoed to the doorway and stuck my head around. Jasmine, Jezebel, Taffy and Glenn were up against the wall, arms and legs spread. A bunch of burly white men with guns hanging from their belts frisking them. I stared for a few seconds. These had to be cops, they all looked like they should be mowing lawns someplace. I snuck back the way I'd come. There was no window I could crawl out of, no real place to hide. The only ones they hadn't got yet were Rosita and me, and Rosita was in deep shit if they decided to make a search now.

I turned the knob as quietly as I could and tiptoed into the back room. The rabbi, clad only in white socks and a black hat, was getting a blow job.

"Shut up," I hissed, "don't make any noise, there's cops out there."

Rosita stood up. The rabbi looked like he was about to faint. "Oh, my children, my wife, my heart." He began beating his palm against his chest.

"No no no don't do that, just get dressed, I know how you can get out of it. Rosita you got the pot?"

"I'll put it under the mattress."

"It won't work, that way we all go down. We have to eat it."

"Eat it? There's two ounces, what if we die?"

"We won't die. My old boyfriend had to eat half a key once, he was okay."

We began stuffing pot into our mouths. It tasted horrible. I had never eaten it not in brownies.

"I wish we had some lemonade or something," Rosita said.

There was nothing to drink in there, only baby oil and rubbing alcohol. The rabbi fumbled with his buttons, mumbling in some language I couldn't understand.

"This is what you do," I said. "Wait till we finish this pot, then run out and act disgruntled. Like you don't hardly speak English. Say, I come here for topless massage, I take off top, girl sprinkles baby powder on me, that's it, I have bad back, I want real massage or I want money back you thief. Just keep saying that. Act happy to see the police, like it's a wonderful coincidence that they've arrived in the nick of time. Just keep demanding your money back, that's the only English phrase you're really familiar with. They'll be pushing you out the door in no time."

We finally choked down the pot and the rabbi ran off to perform his charade.

"Do I have stems in my teeth or anything?" I grinned and she peered at my mouth.

"No. Do I?"

"No."

"What should we do?"

"It's better to give ourselves up I think. There's no way out anyway. I'll explain that I'm the janitor and you're my associate."

"They're not going to believe I'm your associate dressed like this."

"I guess not." She was wearing only the leotard and spike heels. "I know. We can make you a gown thing out of a sheet, and ditch the shoes. You could be kind of, a nun-like person. Just pretend you don't speak much English."

"That's your big trick isn't it? Pretend you don't speak much English."

"Do you have a better one? I bet you never even thought about it. I think about these scenarios all the time, that's how come I know what to do. That rabbi's probably halfway to Brooklyn by now. Too bad I'm such an apple-face, those cops'll take one look at me and know I speak English. With my luck, they'll probably know I'm from Ohio too."

We sauntered into the main room. I was holding the mop and she was draped so only her eyes were showing.

"Okay," I shouted like she might be deaf, "so in here we gotta mop, we gotta dust, they want the walls wiped down, the whole she-bang. I'll have to show you since you don't speak much English." I nodded to the cops. "How you doing, fellas. Now the steps are our responsibility, too. We might as well start out there, come on." We headed for the door. A hand grabbed my collar.

"What the hell are you two supposed to be?"

"I'm the janitor. This is my associate. She doesn't speak much English."

"Hey, no problema. My Español is excellente."

"She doesn't speak that. She speaks ... Wolof."

"She speaks Wolof, huh?"

"Yeah, that's right."

"So how about you translate?"

"No. I don't speak Wolof, you'll have to find an indigenous person of some sort. Anyway, we have to get going, we have twelve other buildings that have to be cleaned by six. It was nice to meet you."

He seemed to consider this, but never let go of my collar. "I'm glad you enjoyed meeting me. That's really important, because you're going to have a lot of time to get to know me. And your little Wolof buddy too. What's your name anyway?"

"Bonnie."

"Well Bonnie, do you have any ID on you?"

I gave him my iciest stare. "I didn't know I was required to carry ID. Or has a fascist police state been declared while I was mopping the bathroom?"

He sighed and looked disappointed. He had kind of long hair, for a cop. "I really am trying to help you," he said.

"Then pay my rent when I lose all my contracts because of you. And she has to be home before sundown or her husband will beat her. "

"Bonnie, if your name is Bonnie, one last time, do you have ID?"

I dug around in my pocket and pulled out a laminated card. He let go of my collar and studied it. "Bonnie Aqua-Fresh. Very nice address in Gramercy Park, kind of ritzy for a janitor, Miss Aqua-Fresh. And date of birth, well this would make you how old?"

"Twenty-four. "

"Twenty-four. So refresh my memory, what grade were you in when Kennedy was shot?"

"I went to a free school, we didn't have grades."

He shook his head and tossed my ID on the table. "You don't honestly think I'm going to believe from a piece of Playland ID that you have some ridiculous name like Bonnie Aqua-Fresh and are twenty-four years old? You look about sixteen."

I burst into tears.

"It's okay honey, we'll get you back to your Mom and Dad."

"My name is Bonnie Aqua-Fresh," I wailed, "and all my life it's caused me nothing but trouble and now here I am about to be thrown in jail and I'll lose my job and wind up out on the streets and my poor friend will probably have her hand cut off or something if she ever gets out of jail because that's the sort of thing they do in her country."

I was starting to feel kind of nauseated. I hoped I wasn't going to throw up the ounce of pot right there in front of him.

"Can I have a glass of water at least," I said. He went over to the cooler and filled one for me. "Here. Now sit on the couch, your friend too."

I made a series of elaborate gestures at Rosita. "She needs a glass of water too."

"All right, all right, just sit on the couch, you can both have glasses of water, but no one's going to the bathroom till we get to the precinct. Got it?" I nodded.

The rabbi was nowhere to be seen. All the girls had been

searched and were chained together, a pair of cops ogling them as two others rifled the desk, Glenn beside them his hands cuffed behind his back.

"I'm starting to roast in here," Rosita whispered from beneath her layers of sheets.

"Shh. It's the pot, don't worry about it. He almost believes us, I think he's going to let us go.

The door rattled and in walked a man who looked as though someone had recently ironed him. Blue pants, white shirt, blue hat, a badge so shiny it nearly blinded me, topped with a tower of medals that listed to the right from sheer weight.

"Holy shit, they sent a fucking brigadier general." I laughed so hard I choked. When I regained my senses the general was looming over me. The pile of sheets that was Rosita shook so hard the couch bounced.

"Who are these jolly little idiots?"

The cop in charge of us rushed over. "We're trying to figure that out, Sir. This one claims to be the janitor and the other one speaks something called Wolof—"

The general pulled the sheet away from Rosita's face. "She's Spanish, she doesn't speak Wolof, who told you she spoke Wolof?"

"The other one."

"Nice try honey, what do you take us for, a bunch of philistines?"

He plucked at Rosita. "These are bed sheets. You don't speak Wolof. And I bet my next paycheck you are wearing a leotard underneath all this."

"How come I have to have this handcuff on me and they all got their handcuffs off, I don't think this is right." I rattled my chains. The whores were all in a big chicken-wire cage with a bunch of other whores I didn't know, smoking and chatting, and I was sitting next to the long haired cop, chained to a blue pipe. "Why don't you just put me in there?"

"Because, Miss Aqua-Fresh, we have certain procedures, and you happen to fall into a different procedural category than they do." I had already been fingerprinted, now he was looking through a loose leaf binder of runaways from all over the country, stopping every so often to compare me with some loser's high school yearbook photo. I started crying again. I had to cry every fifteen minutes or so, otherwise I was afraid he would start to wonder why my eyes were so red.

"What are you crying about now?"

"I want to talk to my friend."

"Oh Jesus Christ." He uncuffed me and dragged me over to the cage and cuffed me to it. "Don't start crying again that you got no place to sit down, this is the last time I'm moving you."

"Hey 'vangel, I mean Bonnie." Jezebel sidled up to me.

"You want a cigarette?" I nodded. She lit one and handed it through. "Look, I been thinking, I'll take your cat. In my church they got a lot of mice, a lot of children just love little cats and things. He'll be spoiled rotten, you want me to take him?"

I sniffled. "Yes."

"Then stop crying; the minute we get out of here I'll take your cat. We'll be out twelve, fourteen hours at the most. Just plead down to dis con, it's nothing. You got a record?"

I shook my head.

"So it's nothing. No real shit." She handed a few more cigarettes through and went back to her buddies, a bunch of girls in tube tops and silver hot pants I had never seen before in my life. They laughed and slapped each other's palms like it was some kind of twenty-year reunion. Rosita was huddled in the corner of the cage. She looked really paranoid.

"Psst, Rosita."

She didn't move. "Rosita, come on." Finally she slid herself over, her butt always in contact with the bench, as if she were afraid she might fly into space if she lost touch for even an instant.

"Are you okay?"

"I feel really weird."

"Me too. They can't tell."

"What about my baby?"

"Isn't someone watching him?"

"The girl next door."

"She won't leave, she'll know something happened."

"I'm supposed to be home, she got her own life. Anyway, he knows if I'm not there. He'll think I ran off or some shit."

My stomach growled.

Rosita jumped. "What was that?"

"I'm starving."

"Me too. What time is it?"

"I'm a poet, I don't wear a watch."

"Well they have to feed us some time."

"Hey," I yelled, "what about our rights? We need some food."

The cop came over, folded his arms. "You have a right to one phone call, you don't have a right to food. I don't think the founding fathers had your particular interests in mind when they wrote that damn bill. You ever had jail food?"

"I'm starving, look." I sucked in my stomach and pulled up my shirt.

"Stop that. We'll get you some sandwiches."

A few minutes later a matron came in carrying a stack of napkins wrapped in plastic. The cop threw one to each of us.

"What are these?"

131

"Sandwiches. Baloney sandwiches." I looked at mine closely. Sealed in plastic, twin slices of white bread, a thin brown line between them.

"I can't eat baloney, I'll have a fatal reaction."

"Then take the baloney out and give it to one of your starving sisters, maybe you can get some mayonnaise in return." He went back to his binder. I handed Rosita my baloney and ate the soggy bread.

A big fat matron walked in. "All right ladies, you all know the program, let's go." She unlocked the cage and all the whores filed out.

I tried to follow but I was cuffed to the chicken wire. "Wait a minute, what about me?"

She bustled around, like I didn't exist, chaining all the whores together in a long line. From the back, she looked like she had poodles in her pants. I couldn't take my eyes off her butt. I blinked and looked away and looked back. Started laughing, then buried my face in my hand and pretended to cry instead.

"Don't worry," Jezebel whispered, "they can't prove anything, just keep your mouth shut. If it gets too bad, say you feel sick. They have to take you to the hospital, it's a law."

The door opened and out they all went. It was just me and my nemesis, the cop who had the nerve to pretend to be hip. I hung from the wire, trying to sit on the floor. He ignored me. "What about my rights?" I said.

"You have the right to remain silent, how about you take advantage of that one."

I tapped my foot and smoked a cigarette. I'd given them up due to lack of funds but it tasted pretty good right then and it kicked the pot into high gear. If I didn't get something to eat soon I'd probably go into some kind of coma.

"Can I have some potato chips?"

"No."

"Well how about rice and a soda?"

"How about you tell me your name first?"

"I told you already, what good did it do, you got me chained here, I can't even sit down. I didn't do anything."

I began to cry again. He ignored me. "Can I sit back on the bench next to you?"

He sighed and muttered under his breath, cuffed me to the pipe again, where I stared over his shoulder.

"I feel sick," I said, giving him my most pathetic look.

"You're young, you'll live."

"No, I can't breathe. There must have been traces of baloney rubbed off on the mayonnaise. "

"You know this is only going to delay your progress through the system."

"I don't care, I'm sick. I want an ambulance, I don't want to die." I began to weep against his arm.

"Stop crying. We'll get you an ambulance, just shut up and keep still."

Two pimply perverts showed up, one clad entirely in green, the other in white pants and a dentist shirt.

"I can't breathe," I said.

The dentist seemed to be in charge.

"You look all right to me."

"I'm not all right, I can't breathe. Are you a doctor?"

"I know what I'm doing. You're talking just fine, you can breathe."

"I can't breathe through my nose."

"You don't need to breathe through your nose, breathe through your mouth."

"I don't need to breathe through my nose? You think my nose is just there for decoration? Oh, well maybe God made a mistake in giving us all noses, perhaps I should just crack mine off and throw it on the floor. Is that what you think I should do? Crack it off and tromple on it."

"What the hell is she in for?"

"It's a long story," the cop said, "and she won't shut up until she sees a doctor. Let's just get this over with."

The whole way in I harangued the dentist.

"I know what you want, you want me to be like you. If I can't breathe through my nose, oh no big deal, I'll just breathe through my mouth. That's what you would do isn't it? Who cares, I'll just breathe through my mouth. What kind of world would this be if everyone just accepted things like that? I'll never be like you; you'll never break me." The cop slumped against the bench pretending to sleep.

"I'm starving," I said to the cop. We had been waiting four hours and they hadn't even taken my name yet. I had the feeling the perverts from the ambulance had told the nurse some lie about me. "Go make them give me dinner, tell them I might die otherwise."

"No."

"Then let's get some pizza, no one would miss us."

"No."

"If I was in jail, I would have got dinner by now."

"If you were in jail you would have got beat up by now is what you would have got, the last thing they want in jail is some little wise-ass from Minnesota."

"I'm not from Minnesota; I wouldn't be caught dead there. I don't even have a Minnesota accent, for a cop you're not very clever."

133

"So where are you from then?"

"I'm from Hell. How does it feel to be an expendable pawn of the ruling class?"

"It would feel a lot better if I wasn't stuck on overtime babysitting the world's most irritating janitor."

"So why don't you let me go? What am I being charged with anyway, no one ever read me my rights."

"You're being charged with being a public nuisance. It's a Class B Misdemeanor. You could do up to six months, how does that sound."

It sounded like he was just blowing smoke. "I think you're scared to go out for pizza," I said. "You're just as hungry as me but you don't have the balls to do it."

"Look, Aqua-Fresh, if I wanted to go out for pizza, we'd be sitting at Ray's right now."

"I wouldn't tell anyone."

"I don't care if you tell someone, I'm a fucking cop, I can go out for pizza anytime I want. Why the hell are your eyes so red, you look like a damn rabbit."

A man rolled by on a stretcher, blood spurting in a geyser from his chest. I started to cry again.

"All right, all right, why are you crying now?"

"That man's going to die, he's going to die, didn't you see him?" The high seemed to be lasting forever. I was running out of reasons to weep. "I'm hungry and you hate me and that man's going to die, how can I live in a world like this, I wish I was dead."

"Look, we'll go out for pizza, will you stop crying if we go for pizza?"

I sobbed. "I don't know."

"Come on, let's try it."

He uncuffed me on the way out. We stood at the tables in Ray's eating slices with extra cheese. I was done with mine before he finished salting his.

"Can I have some of your mushrooms?"

"Just go get another slice."

"I don't have any more money."

"What did I do to deserve this?" He handed me two dollars.

"I need a soda too."

He tossed a handful of change in my direction.

"You could be kind of hip if you weren't a cop," I said, chomping on the crust. "I'm still hungry. Can you buy me a pack of cigarettes?"

"I have the feeling that you will be hungry for the rest of the night," he said. "In fact, I have the feeling that you ate your parents out of house and home while lecturing them on the evils of the ruling class and that is why no one has put out a bulletin for you. As far as I'm concerned, Miss Aqua-Fresh, if you were to walk out that door right

134

now it would not disturb me in the least. A warrant would be issued for Bonnie Aqua-Fresh, who lives in some apartment that doesn't exist, and you could hustle your little ass back down to Playland and get yourself another piece of ID, this time in a more believable name. Maybe, Elinor Oldsmobile or Mary-Jo Texaco."

"You won't shoot me if I try to escape?"

"No, I won't shoot you. In fact, I'll fall down on my knees and thank God that I'm finally rid of you."

"I think I should get some money for false imprisonment. I could have been working all this time."

His face turned as red as the sauce that smeared his lips. "If you don't get out of here in the next twenty seconds I swear I'll cuff you so tight you'll lose both your hands."

I bolted out the door.

There seemed to be a great commotion going on on my block. Fire trucks everywhere, black hoses strewn all over the sidewalk. It smelled like a barbecue, and flames were shooting from every window in our building. Lindy sat on the curb across the street, elbows on her knees. Next to her was my fan, a pile of notebooks, and a backpack. Between her legs an undulating pillowcase.

"Here's your stupid cat," she said, tossing the pillowcase at me. I untied the end and Beano leapt out and attached himself to my head.

"You saved him."

"What else could I do, I couldn't let him roast in there." Her face was covered with red scratches.

"What happened?"

"The landlord burned it down."

I nodded. "Good thing we didn't pay the rent."

"Well, I got everything we had left. The fan, our poems, the money, and Beano."

"That's all we need. This is all for the best anyway, the place was getting dirty, it was time to move. I don't think it was Beano you were allergic to anyway, I think it was mold from the walls. We'll find a much cooler apartment. The whorehouse got raided, I just escaped from jail."

"Are they looking for you?"

"They're looking for Bonnie Aqua-Fresh." I pulled the ID from my pocket and gave it one last look, then sailed it into a pile of flames that had just tumbled from the roof.

"I can think up a better name anyway. Artrina Rimbaud. That has a nice ring to it, don't you think? Come on, lets get out of here."

I picked up the notebooks and she took the fan and the backpack and we headed east.

"Let the towns light up in the evening," I recited, "My day is done, I'm quitting Europe."

"Sea air will burn my lungs," she joined in, "strange climates will tan my skin. To swim, to trample the grass, to hunt, and above all to smoke; to drink liquors strong as boiling metal—like my dear ancestors around their fires."

We walked a ways in silence. "Let's buy some real food," I said.

"No let's just get a couple pies. I'm starting to get used to them. We'll get Beano one of his own."

The stars revolved above us blotted out by the lights of the city and we went to the river with its oily salt air and smoked and ate the pies with our fingers and drank beer, waiting for the sun to come up. Beano chased rats as our new lives shimmered just below the horizon, unimaginably glorious, about to burst forth.

THE APACHE KID

HOWARD MCCORD

I have twice been on mysterious Jungle treks that were finally as empty as dreams; if what we sought was found, I did not know it. The way was hard and long, and the goal obscure. or worse. never shared with me. There were good reasons, doubtless, I should be ignorant. Tactical reasons, security reasons. I did not complain, for who, engrossed in such a mystery, can complain? I would not have had the pleasure of the mystery, had I complained. But the small way, however steep, that Charlie and I had to go to search out the grave of the Apache Kid, was as clear as the air over the San Mateos.

The place was known, at least to a few, perhaps. It was generally known, let us say. It was on Cyclone Saddle, a little to the NW from the trail coming up from Cold Spring Canyon, between Apache Kid Peak to SE and West Blue Mountain to NW. Some years past the grave was marked, but no longer. Somewhere I saw an old photo of the grave, a neat rectangle marking it out, and a headboard. The Forest Service says of old—that there is a tree blazed with two old crosses near it. Charlie Mangus, David Burwell, and I had decided to re-discover the spot, and celebrate that old Apache spirit we would pay homage to, described by Ed Dorn with these words:

> The most absolute of the predatory tribes
> Apache policy was to extirpate
> Every trace of civilization
> From their province
> —*Recollections of Gran Apacheria*

Massai, later known as the Apache Kid, was the son of White Cloud and Little Star, Chiricahua Apaches, and born at

136

Mescal Mountain near Globe, Arizona. A member of Geronimo's band, he and his friend, Gray Lizard, escaped from the prison train carrying the Apaches to Florida after their surrender to General Crook in 1886 General Miles, in his Personal Recollections, remarks on their escape. He made the long journey home with Gray Lizard, who went on to Mescal Mountain. Massai paused long enough in the Mescalero area, at a spot called the Rinconada to steal a woman, and then headed into the San Mateo range, just west of the Rio Grande at the northern end of the Jornada del Muerto. Exactly how he escaped from the prison train, and made the walk back without being seen, so far as we know, is an Apache secret, or as unknown a thing as how many breaths he took on any given day. It was not worth remarking on.

His wife told afterwards that at first he kept her chained, but not long. They raised five children in the San Mateo, and she said Massai was "not blood thirsty. He never killed anyone unless he was running short of ammunition or grub or needed a fresh horse, or something like that." At least, that's what Eugene Manlove Rhodes reports (*New Mexico Highway Journal*).

Massai escaped from the train in 1886. He got back in the San Mateos in 1887. He lived there close to twenty years He was outside all law but for his own as long as Eyvinder of Iceland was, and neither was the worse for it.

St. Augustine, quartered by Christianity, said, "Love, and do as you will," depending on love to give control. I don't know what Massai thought. He wanted to be free, and to live as he liked. He felt no need to love anyone who did not love him. One version of the story has Massai picked up by Anglos as an infant, after a slaughter of Apaches in Skeleton Canyon, near Duncan, Arizona. This was Nana's band. The infant was fed burro milk, and raised by someone until he was sent east to an Indian School, where he perfected his English. In this story, he left school, bummed his way back, stole a wife, and went on as in story. Annette Smith is telling this, and it can be found in Chaparral Guide. The Apache Kid would go to gambling halls to win money for his family, and sometimes people would be found dead in their cabins. Horses would be stolen. A man must do what a man must do, *nicht wahr*?

We drove the Jeep up White Mule Ridge to trail 87, not marked. But it was there. You can't miss a canyon that big. David was ill. He tried to walk in with his pack, but fell after two hundred yards, his legs giving out. We left him at the Jeep with a quart of Scotch, much water and food, and instructions to fight off the devils, no matter which direction they came from. Stay naked during the day, drink the Scotch, and we would be back on the morrow. Devils are everywhere. Charlie and I made a stumbling passage down the first quarter-mile of trail, which dropped from the ridge to the arroyo. Then we began a pleasant walk up the bottom of the canyon. The trail was plain, but without sign of any passage. In three miles, as it narrowed and steepened, we walked quietly, and stopped when we heard a rock click on the hillside south. We looked up, and two mountain lions were bounding up the hillside to the crest. First time either of us had seen lion in the wild. They were yearlings and still hunting together. In a hundred yards, we kicked out a squad of mule deer from the brush, and they went clattering over the slope in their haste to escape. We had interrupted two lions' stalk for breakfast. Two more miles and we had come to such a narrowing of the canyon as to send us up the hillside in a series of switchbacks. We were at about 9000 feet, and I was breathing hard. Too many years at 600 feet. We decided to lay our big packs aside and continue with water and light gear only. This made the switchbacks easier, but they were still pitched at the angle of agony, and my method was will-over-sense: some few steps up, then rest, then some few more steps. I am old and wicked, and doubtless about 10,000 feet is my maximum without acclimatization. The col, Cyclone Saddle, was about that. Finally, we reached it. Beautiful ponderosa still, some aspen, and miles to see to the NE. I looked across the Jornada to the Oscuras, out of which such heavy storms had marched towards us two years before, as David and I walked the Jornada. A bit south were the San Andres, grey-brown and distant. I rested to find my breath and, after five minutes, began to amble through the trees in the saddle. This was an area of two or three acres, a rough park high up, with an Apache buried somewhere under the rocky skin. I could not imagine digging any grave here. If he were buried on this col, it would be only a foot or two down, and then be heaped with stones. He kept his wife and children nearby. They lived high to avoid those searching for missing horses, or out to avenge a death. Winters must have been very hard, even when they moved down in the canyons. It was more than two miles to the nearest spring, called on the map, "Twenty-Five Yard Spring."

Henry Walter Hearn was in on the killing of the Apache Kid, and wrote up an account of it. In the December 1, 1988 edition of the *Magdalena Mountain Mall*, the tale was reprinted. Hearn says on September 4, 1906, Charles Anderson came by his place and asked him to help tail someone who had broken into Charles' cabin, broke the dishes, slashed open the pillows, and left the place in a terrible mess. He had also stolen some horses. Hearn couldn't go that day, but four days later he met another of Charles' friends riding to get fresh horses for Charles. Harry James and Jim Hiler. Hearn came along then, and got Bill Keene and Charlie Yaples from the R bar R Ranch. They went by the Winston store to get some cheese, crackers, and sardines to take along. and he picked up his .30-30 Winchester and two .30-40s (probably 1895 Winchesters, but perhaps Krags). Six of them rode out toward McClure's place at Poverty Springs. The six split up, three going to Adobe Ranch, and Hearn and two others went to Sorrel's Ranch. There they found that Charles and his two friends had gone into the San Mateos. Cebe Sorrel went over to Adobe to fetch the other three, with word to meet at old Fort Ojo Caliente. About sundown, they finally spotted some sign on a faint old Indian trail. They followed it until they could no longer see. They unsaddled and lay with their heads and shoulders on the saddles, but did not sleep. All night long they watched a campfire in the distance. As soon as there was light enough to see by, they headed toward the fire. In about a half an hour they came upon Charlie's stolen horses.

Bill Keene, Mike Sullivan, and Cebe Sorrel went ahead, leaving the others behind, watching the horses and keeping guard. The three came upon two Indians. The first one was unarmed, carrying a rope: the second had a .30-40 rifle and a rawhide scabbard. They shot the first Indian, and when he went down they shot the second one. But then the second one jumped up, gave a war-whoop that could be heard a long distance, a blood-curdling yell, and ran down the hillside on the San Marcial side. He left a blood trail, but they did not follow it. The dead Indian had three bullets in his heart.

There was a considerable reward for the Apache Kid, but the men did not claim it. Charles Anderson said, "We weren't just dead sure right then that it was the Kid we killed. Maybe we had killed some wandering Navaho. Uncle Sam had a way of making a whole barrel of trouble for anybody that killed one of his Indians. John James made the gruesome suggestion that they cut off the Kid's trigger finger, but they just buried him there on the saddle.

The article goes on to say that a year later Tom Wilson and H.A. Faust opened the grave and took the skull to the Smithsonian Institute. It was identified as the Apache Kid's. How this was done is not reported. Some years after that George Messer of the Forest Service blazed the trees near the gravesite so it could be found again. The Apache Kid's wife stole a horse and rode to the Mescalero Reservation, and later her children were brought there. That is where Eve Ball interviewed Alberta Begay, the Kid's daughter, in the early fifties and included it in her *Indeh: An Apache Odyssey*.

Another twist in the story is given by Ball who quotes a letter from Mrs. Evelyn Dahl, "who carried out years of research on the Apache Kid," and relates that she had heard that the body was not buried at all, and Ed James, who caught up with the posse after the shooting, found Bill Keene boiling the Apache Kid's head in a vat. The Kid's family was hiding in the brush, says Alberta, and watched the men build a big fire. After they left, the Kid's wife went to examine the ashes and found the Kid's belt buckle.

So perhaps what we look for is less than a grave, but a

death site. An ash deposit and bits of bone, long blown away and ground into dust. After a half hour of wandering on the saddle, I found what might have been a broken headboard, and some worked sticks that might have been posts for a small fence, and a long heap of stones about the size on would expect to cover a body. Charlie and I decided this was the place, and so we had a drink to Massai's memory, took a photograph, and turned back down the trail.

Jason Betinez, in his memoir, *I Fought With Geronimo*, says the wounded Indian was Massai's son, who survived and fled with family across the Jornada and on to the Mescalero Reservation.

As with most histories, it is probably safe to say that if things didn't quite happen this way, they happened in some similar way, maybe. After the Indian's death, the problem with horse-stealing, cabin burglaries, and murders seemed to have stopped, so most people think it was the Apache Kid who was killed that day. Whatever, Charlie and I can now point out where he just might be buried.

The downhill walk was fast, and we decided to push on and get back to David and the Jeep to make sure he was OK. We had no need to camp for the night just yet, and so we pushed hard and covered ground We were back before the sun went below the mountain ridge behind us, and found David working on the Scotch bottle, just about naked, and doubtless many dead devils out there in the bush. We rested a while, then drove out the ranch road to the highway and headed for a steak supper in San Antonio, there on the Rio Grande in the Bosque del Apache. The Bosque is a National Wildlife Refuge on the Rio Grande fly-way, and thousands of birds stop by on their migrations, the thick woods entwined with old river channels, cat-tails, tamarisk, cottonwood, and the ghosts of many old Apache warriors who gather by the river to listen to the cries of the birds in the old language they remember.

ERIC KRAFT

HAVE YOU EVER WONDERED WHY MICROPHONES DON'T RESEMBLE EARS?

from *Leaving Small's Hotel*

Because I am a shameless eavesdropper, I have often wondered why microphones are not made to resemble ears. After all, the point of a microphone is not that someone is speaking, but that someone else is listening, or will be listening. That is also the danger of microphones.

What we say never gets us into trouble unless it's heard. Shout it at home in your cork-lined room, and you're safe. Tell someone, and you are asking for trouble. Speak it into an open mike, and you're courting disaster. Yet who among us, upon discovering that an idea has popped into our minds, can resist whispering it into an attractive ear or a microphone?

Consider the case of Bob Balducci, who rose to fame as a ventriloquist and ended up as assistant to a dummy.

For quite a few years when I was a boy, "Bob Balducci's Breakfast Bunch" was a program everyone knew. The Breakfast Bunch was broadcast from a restaurant where an audience of little old ladies sat at tables eating breakfast. The clatter of cutlery was always in the background. Bob ended his final program with his usual routine: "Well," he said, "that brings another gathering of the Breakfast Bunch to a close, but it has been so wonderful being here with all of you lovely ladies this morning that I think we ought to do it again tomorrow ... don't you?"

The audience chorused, "Yes, Bob," and the lively Breakfast Bunch theme came up over their applause.

Then, thinking that he was off the air, Bob turned to his second banana and alter ego, Baldy the Talking Dummy, and asked, "What were the last words of our dear departed Uncle Don?"

"Gee, Bob," said Baldy. "I haven't thought of Uncle Don in years. I used to listen to him all the time when I was a little splinter. Poor guy."

"I asked you what he said."

"He said, 'That ought to hold the little bastards for another week.' Too bad the mike was on. That was his best show."

"And his last."

"Yeah."

"But in our case," said Bob with an audible sigh, "there's gonna be a whole new batch of desiccated old bats tomorrow."

The microphone was on.

Like Uncle Don before him, Bob went down. The program went on, though. It was still called "Bob Balducci's Breakfast Bunch," but every show began with the claim that Bob was on vacation. Someone was always filling in for him.

I knew that Bob wasn't on vacation. All I had to do to find him was tune in late at night, and there he was still on the air—in a way. His new program was called "Baldy's Nightcap." Its star was Baldy the Talking Dummy.

Bob had only one line on Baldy's show: "Yeah." Sometimes it was, "Yeah?"

At least once in every program, Baldy would ask, "Bob?"

"Yeah?"

"Aren't you the guy who insulted those desiccated old bats?"

141

"Yeah."

"Baldy's Nightcap" had a simple format. Baldy talked. That's all he did. He didn't play music or interview guests. He just talked. He seemed to be just letting his thoughts run on, talking to a friend—me. Often he would begin by asking, "Have you ever wondered..." and go on to explore some question that he had been wondering about.

Sometimes he would employ a prop. I remember his saying one night, "You're probably wondering why I've got this log beside me. Well, you know what? I think it might be one of my relatives," and he went on to reminisce—complain, actually—about growing up as a dummy in Falling Rock Zone, Minnesota.

He never offered much detail about his private, off-the-air life. He was wary, I suppose, of suffering Bob's fate. He claimed to live in a cave, but he never said a word about how he spent his days. It was as if he were someone else during the day, or asleep, or in a box.

I would lie there, listening, and sometimes I would fall asleep, and wake, and sleep and wake again. It wasn't that Baldy was boring, but he spoke with an infectious weariness that seemed to have begun long before the show came on and would continue long after it was over.

He always ended the show in the same way, with a look at the news, followed by the words "Good night, boys and girls. Remember what Baldy says: stay in the cave. It's a nasty world out there." Sometimes, he would add, as if to himself, almost inaudibly, "That ought to hold the little—" and then the microphone would be switched off abruptly leaving a wooden silence: dead air.

THE DAUGHTER OF MR. YUMMY

One night, late in the spring, forty years ago, when all of the summer and most of my life lay ahead of me, fertile as a field growing wild, five of us were spending the night in my back yard: Rodney Lodkochnikov, Marvin Jones, Rose O'Grady, Matthew Barber, and me. Rodney was known as Raskol, and Rose called herself Spike. The rest of us used our real names. We were sitting around a fire toasting marshmallows.

We had been talking about the difference between the ideal and the actual—along the lines of "Why don't the insides of the frog they give you in biology match the drawing in the book?" In the aftermath of that discussion, a silence had fallen. Within it, we toasted the marshmallows and waited for a new topic to suggest itself.

Matthew's marshmallow burst into flame. He pulled it from the fire and, as he rotated it to char it on all sides, asked, "Can you imagine being someone else?"

"Who?" I asked.

"Nobody in particular. Just not being yourself. Being someone else."

142

"Yeah, but who?" asked Spike.

"Anyone," said Matthew. "Someone who doesn't exist, but might have existed. Somebody new." He blew the flame out and began waving the marshmallow in the air.

"Come on," said Raskol, stirring the fire.

"Okay, okay," said Matthew. "I mean, what if some other sperm had reached your mother's egg before the one that did?"

"What are you getting at?" demanded Spike. She clenched her jaw and squinted at Matthew.

"Well," said Matthew, "what I mean is—"

Spike interrupted him. "What I mean is, are you suggesting something about my mother?" She leaned toward Matthew. The fire separated them, but even so Matthew pulled away.

"No," he said. "No, of course not. I mean, I am suggesting that she gave birth to you—" He paused, smiling, hoping for a laugh, but Spike didn't even return the smile. "—and to do that she had to have some sperm—"

"Do you want a fat lip?" asked Spike.

"No, I do not want a fat lip, thank you."

"Then stop saying things about my mother."

"I'm not saying anything about your mother. I mean, except for—"

Spike leaned closer. The flickering flames lit her from below. "I'll defend my mother's good name against all comers," she said.

"I'm sure you would," said Matthew.

Spike squinted at him again. "Are you suggesting that it needs defending?" she asked.

"Oh, come on, cut it out," said Marvin.

Spike grinned and shrugged and said, "Okay, okay. I was only kidding." She tossed some twigs into the fire so that it flared dramatically, shrugged again, and added, "For all I know, I'm the milkman's daughter."

The rest of us thought about this in silence for a moment. Mr. Donati, the milkman in Spike's part of town, was a short, bald man, heavy, always sweating, with black hair everywhere. Spike looked nothing like him.

"Nah," I said.

"Not a chance," said Raskol.

"Highly unlikely," said Marvin.

Matthew squirmed in place and scratched his ear. When he had something to say he could not allow himself to say nothing, however prudent that might be. Finally, he said, "Mr. Yummy."

None of the rest of us said a thing. We studied Spike, sidelong, and, trying not to let it show, compared her with Mr. Yummy.

He had been delivering the Yummy Good brand of baked

goods in Babbington, where we lived, for as long as any of us could remember. His route took him around Babbington and round and round again, and because he worked at his own pace, no one could predict when he would arrive with his tray of Yummy Good goods. His appearance at the back door, raptap tapping in a jazzy way he had, was always a pleasant surprise. Whenever my mother heard his rapid tapping, she would call out, "Just a minute!" and run into the bathroom to fix her hair and lipstick. His customers called him Mr. Johnson, but their children called him Mr. Yummy. He was ageless, and he was handsome. He had a big smile and freckles, like Spike.

"Now you're talking!" she said. "Look at these freckles. Look at this smile."

She smiled her smile, and in the firelight the truth gleamed. Spike was the daughter of Mr. Yummy. There could be no doubt about it.

"I never noticed before," I said, shyly.

"Maybe you never saw me in the right light," she said. That must have been the case, because after that night she became, in my mind, the daughter of Mr. Yummy, and Mr. Yummy became the father of all those things in life that I misunderstood, a role that he still plays.

THE ROCK AT THE MOUTH OF THE CAVE

One spring night, forty years ago, I was camping in my back yard with four friends: Rodney "Raskol" Lodkochnikov, Marvin Jones, Rose "Spike" O'Grady, and Matthew Barber. Spike brought our meandering conversation to a sudden end when she suggested that she might be the daughter, not of Mr. O'Grady, her apparent father, but of the man who delivered the Yummy Good brand of baked goods door to door in Babbington, a man we called Mr. Yummy.

In the embarrassed silence that followed, Spike stirred the fire while the rest of us tried to think of a way to change the subject. This wasn't easy. The thought that Spike might be the daughter of Mr. Yummy stood in the way like a fat man in a narrow tunnel, as plump and sticky as "Little Yummy," the cartoon fatty who promoted Yummy Goods' products on television. We sat there, working hard to squeeze past the thought and on to something else, working our jaws over our gum, ruminating vigorously.

When the ideas came, they seemed to come all at once, as if we had squeezed past Mr. Yummy and tumbled into a vestibule from which many passageways radiated. Each of us scrambled into one and asked whatever question he found there.

"Any more potato chips?" asked Raskol.

"Will good eventually triumph over evil?" asked Matthew.

"Are flying saucers real?" I asked.

"Do all hermits live in caves?" asked Marvin.

"Do they fake those nudist camp pictures?" asked Spike.

Another silence fell. I spent some time wondering about whether the potato chips were all gone, about the likelihood that sweetness and light might eventually prevail over the forces of darkness, whether life was present elsewhere in the universe, and whether all hermits were troglodytes, and I suppose that the others thought about those things, too, but when we finally spoke, we all asked the same question: "What pictures?"

Grinning, Spike produced a folded magazine from her back pocket.

After we had looked at the pictures very thoroughly and tried to explain how the photographer had made the black rectangles stay in place on the people's faces, fatigue settled over us, and we ran out of conversation.

"We can still catch a little of Baldy," I said to Marvin. His question about hermits living in caves had been inspired, I knew, by listening to "Baldy's Nightcap." This was a radio program hosted by a dummy, Baldy. His ventriloquist, Bob Balducci, was relegated to the background as file clerk, gofer, and yes-man, or in Bob's case, yeah-man. Part of Baldy's routine was the pretense that he lived in a cave.

"Oh, sure," said Marvin.

He turned his radio on. I coveted Marvin's radio. It resembled a small piece of luggage, with a real leather case. The radio took a while to warm up, as radios did in those days, so the sound of Baldy's voice came upon us gradually, as if he had been waiting outside the bubble of firelight and now, when we summoned him, joined us there, within the shrinking sphere.

Baldy was bringing his show to a close, ending, as he always did, with the news:

"The hour is growing late," he said, "It's time to see what's going on in the hideous world outside the cave. Bob?"

"Yeah?"

"Did you roll the rock in front of the cave?"

"Yeah."

"Good boy, Bob. Let's see..." There was the sound of rustling newspaper. "We've got the war in Korea ... some bombings ... refugees ... corruption here and there ... here's something: 'Ferry Capsizes, Ninety Dead.' What is it with these ferries? They go down like rocks! Bob?"

"Yeah?"

"Bring that ferry file to me, will you?" A pause. "Thanks. Nice work, Bob. What have we got here? A hundred orphans on their way to a free lunch ... ninety lepers going to a clinic ... two hundred virgins off to dance around a maypole. They always take the ferry! And down they go! Let me tell you something, boys and girls: if you see a ferry pulling away from the dock with a hundred nuns on a pilgrimage, stay off it!

145

That boat is headed for the bottom! Bob?"

"Yeah?"

"Make sure that rock is in front of the cave."

"Yeah."

"Well, it's time to say good night, boys and girls. Remember what Baldy says: stay in the cave. It's a nasty world out there."

Baldy's closing theme came on, and Marvin clicked the radio off. Silence fell into the dying light. I squirmed lower in my bedroll and pulled the blanket over my head—to make a little cave.

MASTERS OF THE ARTS

One of the two is almost always a prevailing tendency of every author: it is either not to say some things which certainly should be said, or to say many things which did not need to be said.

—FRIEDRICH SCHLEGEL
Aphorisms from the Lyceum

Among my tutors when I was a boy were three who almost certainly never thought of me as their pupil: a nondescript man who lived across the street, his wife, and a ventriloquist's dummy.

The dummy was the host of a late-night radio program called "Baldy's Nightcap." His show was nonstop talk, a monologue, a seamless stream of Baldy's reminiscences, thoughts, and feelings. He was a master of the art of frankness, of revelation, and I wanted to learn the trick of it.

The man who lived across the street, Roger Jerrold, was, I believed, a spy, but he kept it hidden behind a seamless front of conventional behavior. He was a master of the art of concealment, and I wanted to learn the trick of it.

Because the spy business required a lot of travel, Mr. Jerrold was rarely around. His wife, Marilyn, was left alone for days and even weeks at a time. She was a pretty brunette with a trim figure. I thought about her quite a lot, especially on rainy days.

On rainy days when Mr. Jerrold's car was not in the driveway, I would cross the street to visit the Jerrolds' two boys, who were younger than I. Often I would play marbles with them indoors, within a ring of string that we laid out on the living room rug. If Mrs. Jerrold was passing when I bent over to take a shot, I could see some distance up her skirt. The effort required to obtain this view affected my shooting, giving me a handicap that made my games with the boys closer than they would otherwise have been.

In shooting position, I could also see under the living

146

room sofa, and one rainy day I discovered a tape recorder under there. This was a surprise, because almost no one had a tape recorder in those days. They were specialized gear, little used by the general public but widely used, of course, by spies.

Mrs. Jerrold paused as she was passing and said "That's quite a position you've twisted yourself into."

"I was—ah—looking under the sofa," I said.

"Oh, really? See anything interesting?"

"A tape recorder," I said.

"A tape recorder? " She dropped to the floor and looked under the sofa. "What is that doing there?" she wondered aloud.

"Do you think I could try using it?" I asked.

"You can have it, for all I care," she said.

"Really?"

"Well, no, I guess not. It's Roger's. But I never see him using it, and it can't be getting much use under there, so I don't see why you shouldn't use it. Be my guest."

I slid it out from under the sofa. I opened one of the boxes beside it and found inside it a reel of brown recording tape.

The reel fit onto a hub on the top of the recorder. On a metal plate riveted to the lid was a diagram showing how to thread the tape along a pathway from the full reel to an empty one on the other hub. Eventually, I got the tape threaded in a way that seemed almost right.

I found a pair of earphones clipped into the top of the case, put them on, and plugged them in. I shifted the machine to "play," the reels turned, the tape began running, and somewhere along the tape's path the recorder worked the magic of playing sound, but that aspect of the machine—its essence, after all—was to me what technologists call a "black box," a device that we can appreciate for its product without understanding its process, its mystery. Ask a black box, "How do you do that?" and it answers with a silence that seems to say, "I do what I do, and you do not need to know the trick of it."

Through the earphones, as if inside my head, I heard Mrs. Jerrold's voice.

"Oh, yes," she said, huskily. "Again. Again."

I listened to enough of the tape to conclude that Mrs. Jerrold had mastered the art of frankness to a degree that even Baldy the Dummy would have envied. More remarkable still was the fact that she had kept this talent of hers so completely hidden from me. She must have learned the art of concealment from her husband.

I said, suddenly, "Hey—I've got to go."

I put my jacket on and zipped it up, rewound the tape and put it back into its box, closed the tape recorder and pushed it under the sofa, twisted myself into shooting position, and—working under the sofa—shoved the tape box under my jacket. I took it home with me, even though I didn't have a machine to play it on, because I knew that it could teach me things that I wanted to learn.

A CASE OF THE FAMILY ILLNESS

I suffer from a couple of forms of inherited mental illness that have been passed along on both sides of my family for generations. We get the idea that we can do things that a moment's reflection ought to tell us we cannot, and we are easily sidetracked.

To give you just one example: once, when I was about twelve, I got the idea that I could build a tape recorder. I had come into possession of a recorded tape, but I had no means of playing it and didn't have enough money to buy a tape recorder, so I decided to build one. If this seems preposterous to you, you probably have a good grip on reality and are not related to me.

Not only did I suppose that I could build a tape recorder, but I expected to be able to build it out of common household junk. If that seems unlikely to you, then you have never come across a copy of *Impractical Craftsman Magazine* (not its real name). I think it is safe to say that this magazine has been responsible for more wasted hours of labor in the basement workshops of America than any other single cause.

I walked to the drug store to get the latest issue. It had just arrived, but the stockboy hadn't put it on the rack yet. Men with nothing better to do were lined up at the coffee counter, waiting, staring into their cups with the desperate empty eyes of the addicted. I took a stool at the end of the line and ordered a Dr. Pepper. When the stockboy emerged from the stockroom with a bundle of magazines in his hands, the men rose and followed him. So did I.

"All right, all right, stand back," the boy said. He removed the last few dog-eared copies of last month's issue and began, slowly, putting this month's in its place.

The cover offered to show one how to "Build a Photo Enlarger from War Surplus Bomb Sight!" I wasn't going to be sidetracked by that. I had already tried to go into the photography business, and once was enough.

From a company that advertised in *Impractical Craftsman*, I had ordered a Deluxe Developing Kit and E-Z Darkroom Instructions. To give myself something to do while I was enduring the pain of waiting for the kit to arrive, and to recover its cost, I advertised myself as an expert in photographic services. I had a little printing set—actually a Little Giant printing set—from another enthusiasm, another ad. I printed some flyers and distributed them throughout the neighborhood.

I set up a basement darkroom and picked up a roll of film from my first customer, Mrs. Jerrold, who lived across the street.

I'm sure you have already guessed the outcome. I worked on her pictures for an afternoon, and then I gave up. I put the results in an envelope, walked across the street, and knocked on her back door.

"I have your pictures," I said when she opened it.

"Oh, good," she said. "I can't wait to see them. There should be some nice shots from our vacation."

"Yeah, there probably were," I said.

"Were?"

"Not all of them came out."

"Oh."

"A couple of them came out."

"A couple?"

"And some of them came out partway."

"Oh."

"There was a really good one of you in a bathing suit," I said, with genuine enthusiasm.

"Was?"

"Yeah. I was trying to get it just perfect, you know, really perfect, but at first it was sort of too light, and then it was still too light, and then it was a little too dark, and then it was black."

"How much do I owe you?"

"Oh—no charge."

"I must owe you something."

"No, no. We only charge if the whole roll comes out. That's our policy."

I closed up shop.

The equipment remained in the basement, but it began a shove toward the farthest corner. All the equipment abandoned in the cellar—the gear for my mother's failed projects, my father's failed projects, and my failed projects—shoved miserably, humiliated, under pressure from the equipment required by our new projects, into the corners, where it accreted in heaps.

There were no plans for a tape recorder in *Impractical Craftsman* or the other do-it-yourself magazines. For a moment I was tempted by the idea of building the enlarger, since there was a surplus bomb sight in the cellar left over from my father's attempt to build a theodolite and make big money in surveying, but *Cellar Scientist* (not its real name) had plans for a flying saucer detector, and I decided to build that instead.

FLYING SAUCERS: THE UNTOLD STORY

Dudley Beaker was a fussy, educated man who lived next door to my maternal grandparents. Encouraged by my mother and tolerated by my father, he took an interest in my development. He never missed an opportunity to correct my course, and I came to loathe him for

149

that. I kept my loathing to myself, lest he discover it and correct the tendency, but it was bound to come out some day, and, under the influence of flying saucers, it did.

Flying saucers were a craze when I was a boy, but I couldn't make myself believe in them. I tried. I wanted to believe in them. I understood that it would be fun to believe in them. I followed the reports of spottings in newspapers and tried to swallow them, but it wasn't easy. The photographs were especially hard to accept. I kept seeing flying hub caps, pie pans, and Jell-O molds instead of saucers.

One of the magazines devoted an entire issue to "Flying Saucers: The Untold Story." It began with a summary of saucer sightings from earliest times to the present and ended with plans for a saucer detector. I built a detector, but only for the sake of scientific inquiry. I didn't expect it to detect anything.

When I finished the detector, I was proud of my work, of course, and, full of enthusiasm, I brought it up from the cellar to show it to my parents. I brought the magazine, too, so that they could see how well I had reproduced the detector pictured there, which was built by professionals.

Dudley Beaker was visiting. He and my parents looked the detector over, and I explained what it was supposed to do. My parents admired it, as parents will. They praised my effort and execution, just as they would have if I had made a painting, written a novel, or cleaned my room.

Mr. Beaker, however, took it upon himself to go further. He had to consider the worthiness of the underlying goal. "I'm beginning to think that the human race will never grow up," he said.

"Huh?" I said.

"People still have a need to believe in things."

"Yeah, I guess so," I said.

He went on: "They won't accept ideas based on logic and evidence—"

"Like what, Dudley?" asked my mother.

He said, "Oh, quantum physics or evolution, for example, or the dignity of labor—"

"I worked pretty hard on this," I said.

Ignoring me, he continued: "—but quite a lot of them do believe in God, and astrology, and flying saucers."

"One of the articles traced saucer sightings back to prehistoric times," I said.

"Stop and think a minute," said Dudley. "If there were sightings in prehistoric times, how could we know about them?"

"Well—"

"Do you know what *prehistoric* means?"

"Yeah," I said, "before recorded history—"

"Yes, and—"

"—but you know that's not accurate."

"—and—but—what?" he spluttered.

Having made a start, I plunged on, and to my surprise, I discovered as I spoke that I knew more than I realized, that in reading about flying saucers I had actually picked up something that might be true. "It would be accurate to say preliterate," I said, "but it isn't accurate to say prehistoric, because they recorded history."

"Oh? And how did they do that?" he asked.

"Cave paintings," I said.

"Really?" said my mother. "That's fascinating. They kept their history in cave paintings? Why did they paint in caves?"

"Well, they *lived* in caves," I said, guessing. "And caves are a safe place to work, where the painters wouldn't be interrupted by saber toothed tigers, and other people wouldn't be criticizing them all the time."

"Are there flying saucers in these paintings?" asked my father.

"You can judge for yourself," I said. I flipped the magazine open to the cave paintings.

Mr. Beaker took one look, shook his head, chuckled, and said, "You know, flying saucers are presumed to be ships from other worlds, and in a sense of course, this is true, since most of them come from the world of the—" He paused and took his pipe from his pocket, and then finished with a sneer in his voice: "—imagination. "

He would have called himself a realist. He was one of those people who prefer the examined life to the imagined one, who disparage that alternative world where I live so much of the time, the world in which survivors of prisons and concentration camps dwell while they endure their trials. There they can keep self-respect alive, and thought, and will, and hope. Mr. Beaker had driven me there. When I had looked at the cave paintings earlier I hadn't been able to see anything that looked like a flying saucer. Now I could. Now I *believed*.

TWO WORKS

CATHERINE SCHERER

I have seen in the aisle of the supermarket a car trying to make a U-turn. It splattered cans everywhere. "Woman driver," several of the women customers hissed at the driver, a youngish man with electric hair that, when he plugged it into the socket of the cigarette lighter, blazed with a neon glow. Near the meat department a food-demo lady was frying hair. In the pan the locks curled into crisp ringlets that she assured shoppers tasted as good as fried pork rind. Several women and one man volunteered locks of their hair to be fried and the demo lady, all the time thinking of her husband, sheared them off with scissors that had tiny, tinkling bells tied to the blades. The electric frypan sizzled in perfect pitch with the scissors' bells.

The demo lady thought nothing good of her husband, whose mouth was abusive. The only thing he had liked about her when they married, he told her, was her long chestnut hair. The very next day she had had it shorn off and the wisps spit-curled like a lamb's wool. It pleased her to think she had found a way to deprive him, even if only of so little. Standing in the checkout lines the customers grew garrulous; it was a day marked by complaints. Even the police, on the TV news the night before, had committed a public indecency. The Noon Report was replaying the tape. In line the customers were watching on the TV monitor provided by the management to distract them during the long wait. They saw again the police carrying a woman out of her house after a domestic dispute. In the rough handling the police had bunched up her skirt. "You can see way up underneath," a woman was saying, "you can see her hair inside." "You'd think the police would realize children watch the news too," someone else said. It was a scandal that people talked about in silky whispers, as scarcely audible as wind blowing through a woman's long hair.

RULES FOR WRITING RIGHT

1.

A grave marstake in grammar mars the grace of written prose; a gaping lapse in marvelled sentence slows the grailseeking eye to a snail-snacking pace. And no mistake, mars may lead to marstook meaning. Mar- and under- stooking stand exposed as meandering all balk to grabble and marking commarication fleet as grass, for grave grass is serious and luxuriating for a grademarred day, but then it is grabbed and grated into the grackling fire—all for want of a market in unmarted grand mars.

So guard grammar dear as did our dear granmas and granpas when grammar schools were gratified to teach with grace a graded grammar correct and unmarred. Graze in the great fields of grammar and grapple if granted with its intricacies—that thou may be judged worthy of the grace of good and godly grammar. For prose sings, Mark me, do not mar me.

2.

Be punctilious about punctuation, period.

3.

Speling shuld, of cours, be coreect.

But spieling is les dealmanding, alowing more leaweight for comefusing and bewildmeant. But wen in doughs, insult a dictionnary.

STORIES

PHILIP HERTERPHILIP HERTER

THE PRICE IS RIGHT

My wifey and I were sitting around our house, watching TV in the family room, eating microwave popcorn. The airconditioner pumped in that invigorating, ionized air.

"Hey," I hollered, "get in here and take some blood!"

Among other things, the wife and I want to know the cholesterol level in our blood down to the tenth of a milligram.

She came out of the bathroom holding her home pregnancy test, "It's pink, it's pink, what a delightful shade of pink, what do you think? It's pink."

"I never thought you were pregnant," I told her with my mouth full of those golden-flavored kernels, "just like last month. Pee-Ess, I hate rhymes."

"Pee-Em-Ess, better that we know for sure." She was right of course, but a little snippy that I was not as excited as she.

"So let's get this underway," I told her, rolling up my sleeve.

"Not the sleeve, silly, we only need a pinprick from the middle finger."

She checks my cholesterol level once a week now, and my blood pressure, just to be sure. We investigate each other's urine for trace substances that might threaten us. We always pass. We are legally married and stay true to one another like we stay true to our diets. We keep the most intimate records of our internal lives in a blue ledger book on the coffee table.

We are pornographers, the wife and I. We love knowing our levels. As we approach our one thousandth day of marriage, we want to chart where we stand in our lives. We love knowing procedures. We want to know exactly where to grab our wrists, where to place them under the diaphragm of the blue diner (first ask in a clear voice, *Are You Choking?*), how hard to pull up and in, between a squeeze and a jerk, to send the tracheal blockage flying. It is usually a chicken bone or hunk of poorly masticated steak. Vegetables and baked goods are rare, percentage-wise. Pastries and desserts less common still. We want to know exactly how many shots of icy vodka it would

153

take, during the first trimester, to generate a citizen with the brooding, flat forehead and long jawline of fetal alcohol syndrome, like the guy at the Mobil Mart.

Anything can kill, anything at all you can put in yourself, any ignorance,

While she performed the procedure, I looked at the radon meter on top of the piano and did not feel a thing. My wife is really good.

Wife drank her filtered water with the pH paper still floating at the bottom of the glass. Pinkish-purple, almost alkaline, almost acid. Neutral, just the way she likes it.

"What's the Ultraviolet Index today, have you heard?"

I had not. Going out just complicates everything.

"Well," she said, reading the LED, "you're pumping a one seventy-one today. A little sludgy."

"It must have been the omelette yesterday. That's what." She forgave me my elevated lipoproteins with a little kiss to my forehead.

We brushed. We flossed. We brushed again with hydrogen peroxide. We chewed lime red tablets to reveal the plaque on our teeth and we watched "The Price Is Right."

"That woman is nuts, thirty-five hundred for a refrigerator freezer?" My wife has little patience with fools.

"It has an icewater dispenser in the door, and an ice cream maker. Built in."

"She's listening to her husband that's why," my wife goes on, "they should make that against the rules."

"Keeps the excitement that's all, all that screaming."

I know she is right. "The Price Is Right" is no way to learn the value of things. The value of some things can only be learned by learning the value of everything. How much does a sheetmetal worker in Ohio earn? How much does it cost to have a Malaysian wrap copper wire around an electric motor? What's the ecology tax on 35 cubic feet of deep cooling Freon? How many dollars does it take to bring the word *Whirlpool* to our ears?

"Of course she lost it, the bitch." My wife hates when contestants fail to win the sports car. "I know the price of that convertible, where Carol Merril is now standing, down to the dime. The bitch."

My wife was looking at me like she knew. I knew that she knew. For fun, we could plug into the actuarial tables on the Internet. We could rehearse our familiar satisfactions, knowing with statistical precision how many years we have left, what our chances are. Instead, she switched to the shopping network. Nothing sexier than value. Bargains are hot. The jewelry, the clothing. Our erotic life is so lush sometimes I embarrass myself just thinking about it.

In my lap, my wife became a blur of hair and sofa cushions.

"You can swallow it," I urged her, firm in my faith, "you've only had about, what, 36 percent of your RDA of protein. She looked up at me from under heavy-lidded eyes.

"It's only amino acids, just the building blocks, I could take 500 megs of lysine, eat a handful of peanuts... do the same thing."

I wavered for a minute, trying not to interpret the insult, but I knew she was right. Wild thing that she was, her lip on me was sex itself. She moved me.

"The microscope is set up," she gasped, panting. "I should prep some slides, we could see your motility."

Together in our living room, with the TV down low, we watched my little fishes swim heartily from one side of the circle of light to another. They migrate with a singular fury. They know one thing, they don't need to know more. That makes them beautiful.

This is how we live now that information has become local.

My wife and I rested comfortably in the afternoon sunlight of our bed. We know exactly what we are. We have all the maps. We know where the sex offenders live and we know where the toxins are buried. We know what the sun is doing and where the comets are headed today, 41 days before the equinox. We are content in the knowledge that we can get an extra kidney, a next extra cornea, even a heart, lungs and liver, god forbid, knowing almost everything it is possible to know, almost, for now.

FROM *BABY FARM CIRCUS*

He was a whistler, bred in the bone. He was sure, they were sure. But something else sung when he whistled, premeditated anger hit the air. Thoughts of the revolution vibrated in the atmosphere.

What revolution?

The fifty-two months before, The Only One, The One Not to Be Involved In, The Mistaken Premise, The Violence, The Troubles, The Erroneous Situation, The Late Riser and Never Leaver.

It's a labor of love mother! her sweaty face screamed, transformed with new lines, creases that would never leave her. In the hospital green and absolute her own shocked mother, mouth slightly open and breathing hard, stood beside and held her hand. The daughter, bathed in light with her legs spread like a chicken wing about to be pulled apart, dropped, squeaked, eeked and gave slippery forth to this life two blue baby boys. Battered, beaten and small, their minute hands, the nails marvelously long, gripped tightly around empty throats.

The sun shone down on a shiny red truck pointed directly at three unframed doors with glass knobs lying in the grass. A monarch butterfly perched on the middle door, contemplated spreading its wings just once more. She remembered and did not care to look at the life she had given her sons. Her loins and heart at that instant felt as fierce as an idling truck. As fierce as her mother's face at the moment the pair drew their first vicious breath. A tag team surrounded the moment history will regret.

Babies conceived in ditches will have a mark on them like two different colored eyes or harelip or maybe even two different colored twins. Those are the stains of illicit lust. Sometimes you can have two different babies in one body and that's schizophrenia, or one baby in two bodies and that can be a half wit, and that's the worst. Those boys will never drive that truck, they are for horses, that's their speed, and there will be no women for them, no more women, only cities and blood.

Fierce, their teachers called them. They were split, divided, and each time came back stronger and more coherent. Always they were reunited and the women were satisfied. It seemed one breast, one brat, did not age as quickly. At the beach the boys' sandcastles turned into cement. And those two insisted on building every thing life sized. Their eyes stared hard into each other's faces. This was not unique. They eyed each other, even as the tide raised its hand, they stared blue eye into identical blue eye. Their hands and faces merely machinery for el ojo claro, their marvelous fingers grew violet, the lips deep lapis foamy and palms wet, their hands beautiful as marble, alive with grace, gripped around each other's throat.

She who wasn't his mother and he who didn't get speared, who were they? They lived in a time when there were no more warriors. She was timid of music and the games, and she bore the reflection in bronze. He marched for her. She held the substance of a warrior for her own reflection and she wouldn't share those pearls with anyone.

He had to live for two. To "carry on" for the shy girl and her representational warrior, for the Spartans and the Athenians, for the rich and the poor, for the slaves and the freemen, for all men and women. Two conversations, the sadly true and the pitifully false, made it worse. He looked into the face of absolute authority and thought of something far removed like the face of a boy he knew in summer camp. He lived in a dream, he read dreams and considered the future while we ate refrigerator food and one more thing: he worshipped the woman for her instincts and they shot him.

"A Chinese princess with white hair parted on the side. Her eyes shone black under the bleachers, as black as the big top during the pony show. She was perfect and her hair was white and her mouth was red and her round brown shoulder split her hair in half. It hung over me like a forked tongue when she kissed me. My brother saw and he saw her mouth and he saw what she was doing and now we are different and we always will be. She was perfect, she was smoking me and I was a cigarette. The moments I lived in her mouth I couldn't have imagined inside quintuplets."

"I called him the lonely planet boy, because when I met him, he and I went to the Neptune Club, near the sea green palms. He called me Venus, and his dog's name was Pluto, though later I found out it was Bluto. But it was so outer space, you know, I had to call him the lonely planet boy, it just made sense. It seemed like a fine name for him, don't you think? Of course, I had to call him something. Lonely planet boy. He was like that when we first met, lonely. When he finally settled down I didn't know him at all."

She stands in the field like justice herself. The soft hands almost translucent around the brown gun stock. Graceful aging arms like teak handrails. Hair glowing white in the moonlight. The fine hair around your temple feels it and you think of the triangle formed by the spread legs for symmetry, balance and strength. Center of gravity hovering low, down around her knees. Her white hair split over the round shoulder peeking through disintegrated lace in the mottled moonlight. See the hair on the top folded over the free eye squeezed shut. The ends thick as rope ends split like a forked tongue frozen in the infrared light of a beanfield at midnight.

As he plowed the dirt, looking for his woman, or any mate, he flecked through these thoughts: he could sculpt a fountain of bronze with his mother as the central feature; this was possible. His brother and himself could be represented below her, resting in the shade of her triangular paps. A painting of the statue, more correctly a fresco, would be installed in the patio of a villa in Sardinia, belonging to an Italian-American pop singer. He thought of going to church to pray to the heavens for the preceding thoughts to bear truth. He considered the likelihood of getting a stomachache from God. He saw faith was a lie and fate was a fib and destiny a bad map. His religion turned into a cul de sac.

He remembered a poster. Mad! Anarchic! Delirious! After all that, he wandered home with a better idea how to get to the place of the circus, the spot of trampled earth where his family home would stand.

"Jesus was an even man, he was fair and square. He had an even keel and two holy hands. I'm gonna climb that hill, pal. I'll find that man with the spikes and behold him, I will spread my hands for him, yea, though he be friends with the hammer. "

The old truck is still there, the front fender is all shiny like somebody's been leaning against it. And even though the fields are just grass now and don't seem near as big, there's still something there under all that forage. A suggestion where nothing grows. There are spots where the grass dies early each year, and comes up later each spring, and they mark attacks of passion.

Esplendor en la Hierba.

RAT TANGO

"Take here dis lady in Detroit bludgeon her husban', chop up da body, den cook it. Talkin' 'bout payback! Whoa!"

"Baby, you oughtn't be readin' dem kinda lies is put inna newspaper. Ya know dat shit jus' invented, mannipilate y'all's min'. Make peoples crazy, so's dey buy stuff dey don't have no need fo'. Stimmilate da'conomy."

"Wait up, Jimbo, dis gal got firs' prize, She skin him, boil da head, an' fry his hands in oil."

"What kinda oil? Corn oil? Olive oil?"

"Don't say, Lady be from Egyp', 'riginally. Twenny-fo' years ol'. Name Nazli Fike. Husban' name Ralph Fike, Police found his body parts inna garbage bag, waitin' be pick up. Whoa! Ol' Nazli was stylin'! Put onna red hat, red shoes an' red lipstick befo' spendin' hours choppin' on an' cookin' da body. Played Ornette Coleman records real loud while she's doin' it. Tol' police her ol' man put her onna street, shot dope in her arms, an' was rapin' her when she kill him in self defense."

"Bitch was a hoojy, begin wit'."

"Jimbo, how you know? Plenty guys lookin' turn out dey ol' ladies."

"Was a hoojy."

"Aw, shit!"

"What?"

"She ate parts da body."

"Cannibal hoojy."

"Dis disgustin'."

"What else it say?"

"Can't read no more."

BARRY GIFFORD

Jimbo Deal got up from the fake leopard-skin-covered sofa and snatched the newspaper out of Baby Cat-Face's hands. He and Baby had been living together for six weeks now, since the day after the night they had met in Inez's Fais-Dodo, and he wasn't certain the arrangement was going to work out. She had a tendency to talk too much, engage him in conversation when he was not in a conversational mood. At thirty-four years old, Deal was used to maintaining his own speed. Since Baby Cat-Face, who was twenty-three, had come into his life, he had been forced to *adjust.*

"Woman ain' be clean fo' way back, Baby, you read da res'. Run numbers on guys since she come from Egyp', seven years ago. Car thef', drug bus', solicitin' minors fo' immoral purpose. A hoojy, like I claim. Foreign hoojy."

"Husban' put her up to it," said Baby. She lit a cigaret and stood looking out the window down on Martinique Alley. "She been abuse' as a chil', too."

"Dat's what dey all usin', now. Abuse dis, abuse dat. Shit. Says she be foun' sane an' sentence to life imprison. Shit. She probably be queen da hive, have hoojies servin' on her in da joint. Big rep hoojy like her."

"Quit, Jimbo! Cut out dat' hoojy' shit, all ri'? Tired hearin' it."

"Troof, is all. Since when you don't like to listen da troof?"

Baby sucked on her unfiltered Camel, then blew away a big ball of smoke.

"Swear, Mister Deal, you da mos' truth tellines' man in New Orleans."

Jimbo tossed the newspaper on the coffee table.

"I got to get ready fo' work," he said, and left the room

BabyCat-Face smoked and stared out the window. The sky was overcast. It was almost six o'clock in the evening and Baby was not sure what she was going to do while Jimbo pulled his night shift at the refinery in Chalmette, She saw two boys, both about twelve years old, one white, one black, run into the alley from off Rampart Street. They were moving fast, and as they ran, one of them dropped a lady's handbag.

"Baby!" Jimbo Deal shouted from the bathroom. "You gon' make my lunch?"

Baby took a deep drag of the Camel, then flicked the butt out the window into the alley. It landed, still burning, next to the purse.

"We got some dat lamb neck lef', darlin', ain' we?

"What you want, baby I got it. What you want, baby I got it."

"Say, what?" Baby Cat-Face said to the red-haired, café-au-lait woman who was singing and dancing the skate next to the jukebox, her back to Baby.

159

"Huh?" the woman said, doing an about-face, keeping her skates on. "How come there ain't mo' Aretha on this box? Re-s-p-e-c-t, find out what it mean to me," she sang-shouted, beginning to swim and shimmy. "Sock-it-to-me sock-it-to-me sock-it-to-me!"

The woman wiggled and shook, causing Baby and another patron of the Evening in Seville Bar on Lesseps Street to grin and clap.

"Down to it, Radish!" shouted a fat man standing next to the pay phone. He banged his huge right fist on the top of the black metal box, "Be on time! Ooh-ooh-ooh!"

The dancing woman looked at Baby, and asked, "You say somethin'?"

"Thought you was talkin' to me, was all," said Baby, "You say 'baby.'"

"Yeah, so?"

"That's my name, Baby."

The woman smiled, displaying several gold teeth, one with a red skull painted on it. "Oh, yeah? Well, hello, Baby. I'm Radish Jones. Over here playin' the telephone's my partner, ETA Cato."

The fat man nodded. He was wearing a porkpie hat with a single bell on the top that had DALLAS printed on a band around the front of it, and a black silk shirt unbuttoned to the beltline, exposing his bloated, hairy belly.

"Happenin', lady?" he said.

"ETA?" said Baby.

Radish laughed. "Estimated time of arrival. Cato's firs' wife name him, 'count of his careless way 'bout punctchality. Come we ain't seen you in here before, Baby?"

"Firs' time I been, Radish. My ol' man, Jimbo Deal, tol' me check it out."

"Shit, you hang wit' Jimbo? Shit, we know da man, know him well. Don't we, Cato?"

"Who dat?"

"Jimbo, da oil man,"

Cato nodded. "Um hum. Drink Crown Royal an' milk when he up, gin when he down."

"Dat him," said Baby.

"Where he at tonight?" Radish asked.

"Workin'."

"Well, glad you come by, Baby, We front you a welcome by."

"Rum an' orange juice be nice."

"Say, Eddie Floyd Garcia," Radish called to the bartender, "lady need a rum an' OJ."

The bartender mixed Mount Gay with Tang and water and set it up for Baby.

"Thanks, Eddie Floyd," Said Radish. "This here's Baby."

"Hi, Baby," the bartender said, "Round here we call dis drink a Rat Tango, as in 'I don't need no rat do no tango at my funeral.' "

Eddie Floyd Garcia, a short, wide, dark-blue man of about fifty, winked his mist-covered right eye at Baby. Up close, she could see the thick cataract that covered it.

ETA Cato traded off dancing with Radish and Baby to the juke over the next couple or three hours, during which time they consumed liquor at a steady clip, Eddie Floyd making sure to keep their drinks fresh. It was a slow night in the Evening in Seville. Other than a few quick-time shot and beer customers, the trio and Eddie Floyd had the place to themselves. Baby learned that Cato worked as a longshoreman on the Celeste Street Wharf, and Radish did a thriving nail and polish business out of her house on the corner of Touro and Duels called The Flashy Fingers Salon de Beauté.

Sometime past two A.M., Radish decided that ETA Cato had danced one too many times in a row with Baby Cat-Face. Johnny Adams, the 'Tan Canary,' was seriously wailing "I Solemnly Promise" when Radish flashed a razor under Cato's right ear, cutting him badly.

"Damn, woman!" Cato yelled. "What you do that for?!"

Radish Jones shook a Kool from a pack on the bar, stuck it in her mouth, but couldn't quite hold her lighter hand steady enough to fire up the cigarette.

Eddie Floyd Garcia grabbed a rag, vaulted over the counter, and knelt next to ETA Cato, who had slid to the floor, holding his right hand over the cut. Blood was jumping out of his neck.

"King Jesus! King Jesus!" screamed Baby, backing away.

Eddie Floyd applied pressure to Cato's wound with the rag, but the bleeding did not abate.

"Call a ambulance!" Eddie Floyd cried. "Look like a nerve be sever'."

Radish did not pay any attention to Cato's predicament, absorbed as she was in her attempt to torch the Kool. Baby grabbed the phone and dialed 911. When a voice answered, she started to talk, then stopped when she realized it was a recorded message requesting that the caller please be patient and hold the line until an operator became available.

Baby forced herself to look at Cato. He coughed, lurched forward and fell back against Eddie Floyd. Cato turned toward Baby and opened his eyes wide. She thought he was going to say something but he died with his mouth half open, staring at her. A human being came on the line and asked Baby, "Is this an emergency?"

HARIETTE ON THE MEN'S PLANET

ME, JANE AND THE MEN'S PLANET

Jane listened to all my complaints while I was going out with Martin, a former rock drummer turned video store employee. His wife had left him, ironically, for a successful rock drummer, so he lived in Brooklyn with his half St. Bernard/half Gordon Setter dog and his pottery collection. The pottery was insured for theft but not for breakage. The dog had an enormous fringed tail, like the trim on a Davy Crockett jacket, and the vases and bowls were displayed on the coffee table, but the dog never knocked any of it down, bless her little canine heart. "Pottery," Martin told me, "is a very high aesthetic." In her "good-bye and drop dead" letter, his wife wrote, "It was practically kinky the way you would sit for hours, gazing at your goddamned dishware." I asked him about their sex life. "She didn't want to do it in front of the dog," Martin told me. For the first three months, we really got it on and the dog didn't seem to have an opinion either way. Periodically, his mother, a tiny but domineering modern dance teacher with a high, squeaky voice, would telephone and ask, "How come you never call us?" "I don't know what it is you want from me!" Martin would scream back. Eventually, I became suspicious of Martin's sexuality. We couldn't just fuck, we couldn't make love, sex couldn't be an expression of, say, tenderness, he had to always be looking at me from behind with my legs spread really wide and my tits hanging down. He often verbally compared the vista to scenes in the porn videos he took home daily from the store he worked in. As he lost the few inhibitions he had, he grew progressively more fixated with sticking his tongue up my ass. Finally, I told him, "You've been living alone with a dog for too long."

Meanwhile, Jane had auditioned for a commercial and on the set met an amnesiac named Gerard who had been in a bicycle accident in France. He had also been kidnapped as a child. He sent her a greeting card addressed to "my little snowflower of tragedy." She had to tell him what restaurant he had made reservations at five times. Next there was Jeremy, the self-hating Jew who insisted his last name was pronounced "Sha-pie-ro." A former San Franciscan and doubtless member of a "men's group," he boasted to Jane that he had a chance to go to L.A. for a week to make a couple of thousand dollars as an art consultant or something, but had decided to stay in New York and care for his friend's cat instead. Jane is a black belt in karate, and talk of cuddling up with little kittycats is not the way to her heart. Along came a dreadlocked jazz musician with an enormous tongue that he maneuvered halfway down her throat, but he never called back. "Be wary of the black jazz musician syndrome," l advised. Then I gave her a nugget of wisdom gleaned over two decades of fucking. "Don't sleep with them on the first date. Men like to go out with a woman, and then go home and jerk off, fantasizing about doing it with her. If you deprive them of this opportunity they get resentful."

Jane was becoming seriously depressed when her aunt invited her to attend a ritzy wedding in Scotland, held by business associates of her late husband. Tom, the brother of the bride, a handsome and witty accountant, told her "the angels stopped in the heavens when they made you" and Jane was charmed. The next day, he sent orchids over to her hotel. They spent the night together, using fresh figs and papayas from a giant gift basket of fruit as accessories. Jane returned to New York with pheromones spritzing all over the air and announced, "I'm getting married and moving to Glasgow." Bonnie said, "Can I start an artist's colony there?" Maryann asked, "Is he politically correct?" I decided to reserve judgment and watch how things developed when Tom came over to stay with her for a couple of weeks. Jane, Bonnie, Maryann and I all worried about how an accountant from Glasgow would adapt to Avenue C, but he acclimated just fine. Jane reported that he was self-reliant while she was rehearsing her performance art and entertaining when she wasn't. Suddenly, she called me in distress. During a dinner party with four of her friends, Tom had lapsed into a catatonic state, complete with closed eyes and junkie-like nods. Could he be a borderline schizophrenic? "Honey," I told her, "Remember that he is from the Men's Planet so you have to expect a little weirdness sometimes. At least he isn't sticking his tongue up your ass. Let that be our litmus test." This mollified her, and she and her Scottish beau explored all of Manhattan's finest sex shops, since Tom was possessed of a fervent desire to buy her a super premium, state-of-the-art vibrator. Partly he wanted to watch her get off with it, and partly he hoped it would enhance whatever erotic phonecalls they had when he went back to Glasgow. She could just plug it in and buzz away. Inspired, she started sending him erotic faxes, suggesting many creative uses for kilts. Fortunately he was the boss and could send his employees out of the office. He sent her poems by Byron which he had copied in longhand and I said, "Byron! Jane Darling! This is major-league. This is Mr. Right! No jaded New York guy would ever dare to send poetry... much less Byron!" A week later, Jane turned thirty-five—her sexual prime—and quite naturally developed an urge to get tied up and spanked. I recalled with fondness my first inclinations in that direction as well as memorable scenarios. But when she faxed Tom images of punishment rooms in Victorian boarding schools, he was appalled. He whined that he "didn't understand" the impulse. Good-bye, Tom. Jane started seeing a neighborhood playwright, an ex-alkie and ex-junkie with a face that was rusted as an old beer can, who worked, as so many

163

ex-alkies do, as a bartender. He lived in a furnished room and had a large tattoo of a bulldog with blood oozing from its fangs on his left forearm. They were fucking and spanking zestily until she invited Tattooman over for pasta and he told her he couldn't make that kind of commitment. "Tell her that there are a lot of guys out there who would tie her up and eat pasta too," said our Mature Friend, a literary agent who followed each action-packed moment closely. "At my age, it isn't often that I get a chance to listen to pretty girls talking about their sexual problems," he admitted. But by this time Jane was truly distraught. She asked, "Har, is something wrong with me?" "Absolutely not! " I adamantly replied... I regaled her with tales of just a couple of past amours. There was Saga, the Yugoslavian journalist whose lineage could be traced to Tito, who spoke constantly about how his retired father would go out fishing in a boat, and his retired mother would come outside and ring a giant bell for him to row back when she wanted to ask him a question. He had been married and had two sons, but he told them that he was going around the world fighting for peace and justice and split. Meanwhile he was going around the world fighting for drugs and pussy. Then there was Charlie, the communications professor who had the audacity to criticize my writing. He was half Italian and tried to uphold his macho image by hanging out in pool halls. He usually got involved with neurotic tight-assed Wasps who had hysterical fits and rejected him, but me he liked to tie up and eat out, and he liked to preface the act by doing a little blow. Then, after I fractured my spine and was lying on a heating pad taking anti-inflammatory medications at 10 A.M., he came running into the room with a vial of coke and a pair of handcuffs. "No, Jane," I told her, "We are legendary-type babes whose every conversation is worthy of a Henry Jaglom filmscript and they, darling, they are from the Men's Planet."

THE APARTMENT

Deanna, one of the tenants in my building, could complete the daily crossword in the *N.Y. Times* but had no common sense whatsoever. A Scorpio, she probably had Pisces rising. Her cleaning lady, Sara, a Brazilian lesbian with no top teeth, was an animal fanatic and a know-it-all. She lived in East Harlem with twenty-seven cats and two dogs. She couldn't bathe in her own apartment because the bathtub was entirely filled with kitty litter, so she showered in clients' homes. Sara's favorite item of apparel was a man's sleeveless undershirt, which highlighted her muscular arms.

Deanna was close to 50 and was warm, loving, and generous. In fact, she had been President of the Baptist Students Union at college until she smoked her first joint. The only time she was rude or nasty was when you asked her for some pot. She liked to maintain a hefty stash.

She was also a slurry, sloppy but amiable drunk. The more

looped she got, the more sentimental she became. Once I was hanging out there and she got a call from an uncle in his 80's.

"Oh, my dearest darling, I love you, I'm going to move down to Tennessee and take care of you," she slushed.

"Yo, Deanna, shut-up!" I kept saying.

Her cat Tubby had been neutered long ago and ever since had maintained a permanent vigil on the kitchen floor, hoping to guilt-trip someone into throwing him some extra kitty nuggets. He must have weighed twenty pounds. Deanna explained that neutering a male cat would cause him to overeat. Every time she drank, she would pick him up and sob, "I should never have cut off his balls! " She was the kind of person who liked to say the same thing all the time. I wondered if she realized she was doing this.

Three times a year, Deanna's sister Denise from California would visit and spout annoying new age truisms about self-esteem and co-dependency that would impel Deanna to drink and smoke even more.

Her best pal Bettyann was the grimmest person I had ever met. Anxiety, and not maternal instinct, oozed from every pore. Nonetheless, at age 37, she decided she wanted a baby but she didn't have any prospective "fathering" candidates. So she picked up a guy in a bar and told him that if she got pregnant, she was having the baby. He, naturally, thought she was kidding. Pretty fucking funny. Then, when Hillary the Horrible was born, she was enraged when the poor schlub wouldn't play daddy.

When Hillary the Horrible wasn't hurling paint on to a wall or sticking a crayon up her snatch she "liberated" toys from her one terrorized playmate. Her desire to eviscerate a small dog recalled Jeffrey Dahmer. Dear Deanna benevolently looked on. "She's a sociable girl," she would say fondly.

Deanna was but one of a whole building full of eccentrics, myself included. We had a tenants meeting and it was like a scene out of Fellini's "Satyricon." Jean-Claude, replete with toupee and wooden leg was there, as was Catherine, a tall, elegant blonde filmmaker who had recently married a short, beer-swilling, tobacco-chewing illiterate black guy with a giant tumor in his cheek who used to stand out on the street asking me to "give him some pussy." Iona the opera singing cat lady was resplendent in sequined headdress. She had written a letter to the tenants and posted it on the bulletin board in the lobby describing how her apartment was "hot as a Brazilian jungle." Once she approached me, looking like a corpse in her long maroon velvet gown, with her pasty white skin and overly dyed black hair, and said, "You think you're better than me. All you have is an ego and nothing to base it on." I was tempted to reply, "You're right, I do think I'm better than you and I have a lot to base it on," but I didn't, because I know she's crazy and I feel sorry for

165

her. The next day she said, "Hariette, I'm sorry. I'm on Prozac and it makes me very aggressive." Elmer D., my psychotic downstairs neighbor, never one to miss out on an opportunity to give the landlord a hard time, was there as well. He was crazy but I didn't feel sorry for him. I didn't even feel bad that he had purportedly spent his adolescence in a juvenile detention home, forcibly fellating older male inmates.

Janine chaired the meeting. The subject was the rock club that Ron Wood had opened up in our basement. The noise was preventing people from sleeping and functioning. A representative from the club patiently listened to everyone's complaints.

"I have something to add," Iona trilled. "I am a cat, meow, meow, meow!"

Janine, a bi-sexual poet/junkie/stripper from Smith College, had been my entree into the building. I had been teaching writing in San Francisco during the heyday of gay liberation. I even saw two guys fucking on their front porch. On every corner was a bar outfitted with "glory holes." Walking down Castro Street, I felt like a Black in South Africa. Starved for testosterone, smarting from rejection, I moved back to Manhattan.

Janine had offered to sublet me her apartment. She lived on and off with her boyfriend on 14th Street. In fact, many prior subletters' possessions were still under her bed, along with a broken stereo receiver, a broken manual typewriter, and a steamer trunk filled with waterbugs. On the wall were seven broken mirrors. Janine later explained that this was some kind of voodoo ritual.

My mother and my nuttiest brother, Karl, helped me to move in. Karl had just gotten a doctorate in Soviet history but had been unable to secure any teaching jobs. Apparently, he had been going to job interviews wearing overalls, since he considered business suits to be "bourgeois." My second nuttiest brother, Leon, moved to Canada to escape fascism when Nixon was elected president. My third nuttiest brother, Frederick, published a newsletter detailing trade agreements between socialist and capitalist countries. By 1992, he was unemployed. I would have been named Rosa, but then my grandfather, Harry, died.

Have you ever heard the expression "red-diaper baby"? I was told the phone was tapped as soon as I learned how to speak. Till the age of 6, I feared that the family dog was really an FBI agent dressed in a dog costume. There was a Marxist literature class at my summer camp. The terms "bourgeois decadence" and "capitalist alienation" were thrown around my childhood home as casually as curses in a naval barracks. My family hoped I would one day write a "socialist novel." The fear and paranoia my parents instilled in me about the FBI, CIA, etc. persisted until I became a crime writer and attended the Secret Service Christmas party in Washington, D.C. on December 23, 1987. All the feds present thought I was a DEA agent and tried to hit on me. A lifetime of fear evaporated. Just like that.

Standing in Janine's bedroom, I noticed a whip on the wall over the dresser. I hoped my mother would not see it, or, if she did, would repress the perception entirely, as parents, both left-wing and right, tend to do when dealing with uncomfortable truths. Naturally, on cue, Karl said, "What the fuck is a whip doing on the wall?" I later asked Janine.

"When I was at Smith, I supported myself by working as a stripper," she said. "So when I was onstage I would call men up and then whip them. I considered this a feminist act."

For the first few months, Janine kept telling me to be extra secretive.

"If the landlord finds out I'm subletting, he'll kick you, me and all our stuff out of the apartment."

I pictured a paunchy, cigar-chomping, greasy-haired thug surrounded by leg-breakers kicking down the door. Then, one day the bell rang and a really handsome blond guy in Ralph Lauren threads said, "Hi, I'm the landlord. You must be the person who's been subletting since January. I just came by to check the radiator."

I convinced him to rent me the first apartment that became available in this rent-stabilized building. In N.Y.C. today, this could take a decade. But there was a family on the top floor with a foster daughter. The Chinese husband died of a heart attack. The Irish wife, Gladys, became an alcoholic and attacked the Indian daughter with a knife. The city removed the child from the home and rescinded Gladys' support payments. Without that income, Gladys couldn't afford her rent and was evicted. Gladys moved into the Women's Shelter and grew a moustache and I was poised to replace her when the landlord, who is Ukranian, told me he was morally obligated to rent it to recently emigrated fellow Ukranians.

"Don't talk to me about moral obligations," I exclaimed. "Your Cossack ancestors conducted pogroms against my Jewish ancestors in Russia, and drove them from their villages, so, karmically, you owe me a home."

I moved in the next day.

FRENCHIE

It never occurred to me that Frenchie might be a homicidal sociopath until I asked him if he had ever killed anyone. This occurred on New Year's Eve. We had been seeing each other since September, always just hanging out at my apartment because, as I learned, free-lance fashion photographers are paid even less frequently than free-lance investigative reporters. He couldn't even afford a bottle of wine, so he brought carbonated apple cider, 2% alcohol. I was naturally eager to spend time chez lui, but he emphatically refused to invite me over. Towards the end of our relationship, I began to wonder what artifacts his apartment contained—a wife, stacks of "Blueboy" and "Huge," ninja throwing stars, decomposing corpses?

I was drawn to Frenchie's classy, refined features, avant-garde sensibilities and European manners. He was an intriguing jumble of contradictions. He always wore black leather jeans and motorcycle jacket, travelled by Harley and was into biker culture. Yet his diet consisted of miso soup, brewer's yeast, tahini and antihistamines for chronic allergies. He claimed the drugs fatigued him, so I always initiated sex. I liked to moan "baisez-moi" and "lechez-moi," conjuring up memories of erotic escapades sur le Rive Gauche in 1984. But I quickly realized that the idea of fucking a French fashion photographer was more of a turn-on than the act itself. In fact, I was so perplexed by Frenchie's lack of libido that I brought one of his letters to a graphologist. The expert promptly pronounced him a closet case. This resonated. Frenchie performed when challenged, ate pussy passably, but I often wondered whether his mind was on a pair of hairy buttocks while his tongue was on my clit.

I could understand him secretly hating women. His mother died when he was a baby, leaving him unprotected in the care of a brutal, dictatorial French patriarch. Dad was also an avowed Marxist. Frenchie rebelled by becoming a rightwing paratrooper and fought in Algeria, but by the time I met him, alas, he was listening to left-wing radio incessantly. His all-purpose explanation for every geo-political crisis around the globe was "American imperialism"; he perceived more CIA conspiracies than Oliver Stone. Irritated, I reminded him of French anti-semitism and general obnoxiousness. I added that I had heard enough "dialectical materialism" from my wacko leftist family to last a lifetime, and pleaded, "Can we, like, talk about Truffaut?"

New Year's Eve began oddly. That afternoon, Frenchie had bought me a beer and falafel and then uncharacteristically emoted, "You're too nice for me. I can't handle it. I like bitches who treat me like shit, like my last girlfriend."

My friend Jane had invited us to a party. I revelled in the buzz I copped off the 12% alcoholic content of my glass of red wine. Frenchie slunk around in black leather.

Just before midnight, he discovered the host's collection of hunting knives. Removing them from their case, he ran his fingers over the blades, his eyes glowing. Someone asked me, "Who the fuck is this psycho?"

Curious myself, I asked him the fateful question.

"I'm not sure how many people the actual total is," he replied thoughtfully. "Aside from all the kills in combat in Algeria, I ran someone over on a dark country road in California. Then there was this fight with a biker. And I was in a motorcycle accident. Another time I was in a bar and this guy kept bothering a chick. I punched him out and his head made a strange thud when it hit the floor. I didn't stick around, but I'm pretty sure he was dead..."

"Do I pick them or what?" I asked Jane.

She walked me to the door as I bade Frenchie, "Bonne Année et au revoir!"

TIM

"What kind of music do you like?" the handsome but shabbily-dressed new sublet tenant asked me in the lobby.

"Reggae. Rock and roll. Classical. Why?"

"Do you like jazz played on a string bass?"

"No. Why? Are you giving away your old tapes or something?"

"I'm playing a gig tonight at a club in Soho. I'm a jazz musician. Do you want to come?"

"Well, uh, sure. I haven't really done anything all weekend." He *was* cute. "How much does it cost to get in?"

"I'll put your name on the list."

All day long I wondered... is this, like, a date?

The only thing I knew about the new sublet tenant was that he was subletting from Ron, a club-footed, red-faced, chain-smoking, misanthropic pseudo-writer who was mean to my neighbor Patti and played choral music at midnight in bouts of manic elation. This did not reflect well on Tim. But I hadn't gotten laid since last June, during an ill-fated reunion with the Mature Friend (see "Me, Jane, and the Men's Planet"). It had been three years since our last lovemaking session, and, on my part, it was mainly a sympathy fuck. The Mature Friend had confided his distress over the fact that, now that his hair was white, women on the street no longer made eye contact with him.

"I feel invisible," he said piteously.

"Don't worry, I'll re-invigorate you," I promised.

The ingrate unbuttoned my blouse, unhooked my bra, and laughed.

"Your tits are the same size, but lower," he announced.

That evening, buoyed by images of sturdy young manhood, I sped-walked to the Soho club. It was a filthy little dive.

"Five dollars," said the woman at the door.

"I'm on the list," I countered.

"There is no list," she replied.

Tim greeted me.

"I got here late so it will be a while. Why don't you sit with my friends?"

I was led over to two women. Margo was Scandinavian.

169

She had erect posture and a clenched face, was obviously a tyrannical personality. Sort of like Helga, She-Wolf of the SS.

"I smell something sweet. Are they burning incense?" she said bitchily.

"It must be my perfume."

I met her gaze until she turned away.

Aduki was a goody-goody Japanese, who sat immobile and silent, with her hands folded on her lap.

"It's chilly in here," I said.

Margo got up, located the window, and slammed it shut.

Tim played jazz viola. The same old standards I'd heard 100 times. But he was talented. He had incredible rhythm. And I loved the way he worked that bow. I imagined his hands all over my body.

He was up there for two hours, cracking jokes, relating mildly witty anecdotes. When it was finally over, he came to our table.

"Why did you ask me if I like string bass when you play viola?" I asked him.

"Did I say that?"

"I felt honored to be here," said Aduki.

Afterwards, Aduki, Tim and I went to eat at an East Village luncheonette. Tim had brought along special tablets he takes to avert intestinal spasms.

"I haven't been hungry in three years," he confided. "It all started with this raw chicken I ate in Japan."

"Where are you from?" I asked him.

"Texas."

"Waco?"

"No. Why did you say that? Everybody keeps talking about Waco. Is something going on there?"

"Don't you read the papers?"

"Not in five years."

I was ready to invite him up to my apartment, but Aduki was fiercely possessive.

"Are you taking a cab home?" I asked her, hopefully.

"Yes, but I'm not leaving yet." She accompanied us to our building.

"Tim, I need to use your bathroom," Aduki said.

"You can use mine," I cheerfully volunteered.

"No!" Her eyes flashed.

I said goodnight.

The next day I consulted my gay buddy Freddy, who has an answer for everything.

"If it was like a date, but he's fucking this Japanese chick, why did he invite her?" I inquired.

"He's probably not fucking her, but she was probably so out of it, she didn't realize what was going on. You know how Japanese people are. They're in their own world."

"So what's my next move?"

"Just wait, honey," Freddy counseled. "Just wait."

A week later, I encountered Tim in my lobby. There were a dozen holes in his baggy cotton pants. He looked like a little lost puppy.

"Tim, no offense, but may I make an observation?" I asked.

"Sure."

"You look like you need for your mommy to come to New York from Waco and buy you some clothes and make you dinner."

"Would you make me some dinner?" he pleaded, instantly infantile. "Would you? It could be like a potluck-type thing. We could share expenses."

I don't like little boys—to fuck, but then, I cannot resist a culinary challenge. So, mindful of his intestinal spasm problem, I prepared a soothing repast of coq au vin with wild mushrooms, mashed potatoes, and a spinach salad with a honey-grapefruit dressing. I put on sexy black lingerie, lit candles, slipped Mary Chapin-Carpenter on the tapedeck.

Tim arrived with a bottle of $2.99 Spanish wine that was half-empty.

"I brought this to the studio last night," he said, "but there's probably enough to get us pretty blitzed."

I resisted the urge to call him a cheap scumbag, reassured that getting blitzed was usually the preliminary to getting laid.

"I love this kind of food," Tim exclaimed. "My old girlfriend, Tracy, used to cook turkeys all the time."

"Turkeys? For two people? How long did they last?"

"A couple of days."

Liar! I thought. A fucking turkey would last two people three weeks. He's just upping the ante, the manipulative little shit. Now, if I want to get laid, I'll have to start cooking him turkeys.

"Tracy was a WASP who was really into responsible journalism," Tim continued. "She had all these rich friends who gave fancy dinner parties."

Somehow, I couldn't envision Tim attending with his torn pants. What kind of a guilt thing was this Tracy babe working out?

I turned the conversation back to myself.

"Why did you invite me to your gig?" I asked, blatantly fishing for a compliment, such as, "Because you're so pretty, sexy, interesting..."

"Because you walked through the door," Tim replied. He yawned, announced that he had to be in the recording studio in the morning, and left.

171

It was another lonely night with my mechanical friend, Mr. Good-vibes.

Two days later, there was a message taped to my door.

"I lost your phone number. Call me, Tim."

I decided I would call him and ask to borrow $10, for an "emergency" and then keep it. I had spent $20 on food for this "potluck," and he had brought a recycled bottle of wine. If I recouped half my losses, I could just chalk up the whole experience to yet another example of ignoring my instincts. And the truth that the friends of assholes are invariably assholes, too.

Amazingly, he brought the ten bucks over immediately.

Then I got the message on my answering machine. 11:00 on a Wednesday night.

"Hello Hariette, Tim here, you know, in 5G. Listen, I bought this piece of really cheap fish and I put in the freezer. I just took it out to cook it and it smells really disgusting, really spoiled and putrid and rotten, and I was wondering if I could bring it up to you and you could smell it and tell me if I should cook it."

I called him back.

"Tim, let me get this straight. You want me to smell something vile and disgusting? Is this supposed to be an enjoyable experience for me?"

"Is that bad?"

"Tim, do me a favor. Lose my phone number again."

Maybe I should move uptown. I heard that on the Upper East Side men bring flowers and perfume...

JANE'S WEDDING

My friendship with Jane ended abruptly a year ago. Billy the Fireman was the catalyst.

"I'm dying to fuck this gorgeous fireman," Jane had gushed. "I know it's meant to be because the last time I walked by the firehouse a firefly flew onto my shoulder and stayed there for like five minutes."

"Jane, I'm sure he's married."

"No, he told me he's single."

"What is he—late 20's, Irish-Catholic, lives on Staten Island?"

"How did you know?"

"Jane, when I wrote all those crime articles for *Penthouse* and interviewed about 50 cops, they were all married, they all fucked around, and they all lied like dogs about it. One guy swore up and down he was single, then a woman cop told me he had a week-old baby. Firemen are probably worse because they can sleep at the firehouse."

"Billy's different. I sent him an invitation to one of my performance pieces."

"Did he show up?"

"No."

"Did he mention receiving the invitation?"

"No. Maybe it got lost."

Jane ignored Aunt Hariette's excellent advice and procured a dinner invitation from Fireman Bill.

"Make me two promises," I urged. "Try to find out if he's married, and don't fuck him on the first date. He's not one of your musicians or playwrights. Trust me, he's got retrograde sexist values."

"How can I find out if he's married?"

"Ask him for his home phone number. Ask how many kids he has. You're an actress. Act!"

I waited up for Jane's report. She delivered it in her princess Di voice.

"We had a lovely evening. He picked me up in his car and took me to an Italian restaurant, where we had a delightful meal and a bottle of red wine. Afterwards we went for a pleasant stroll and stopped off for a nightcap."

"Okay, and then ..."

"We talked about our brothers, how his are always borrowing his car."

"Did you talk about his wife?"

"I did not feel it was appropriate, under the circumstances, to ask him such a personal question."

"I see. Did you think it was appropriate, under the circumstances, to sit on his face or suck his cock?"

"Certainly not! He insisted on coming up to my apartment. We made out, and when he wanted to go further, I told him it was simply not my custom to engage in sexual relations on the first date."

"Good. Because if you had there would be no more cozy dinners, no cocktails, no holding hands. Next time, he'd call you at midnight, come over, get his rocks off, and leave. I've been there, Jane. It's not great for your self-esteem."

Jane waited for Fireman Bill to call again, but he never did. She blamed yours truly and dropped me as a friend. I was relieved because I had grown sick of her selfishness. During 10 months of friendship, she had left at least 20 identical messages on my answering machine. In her Melanie Griffith voice: "I need a favor ..." But whenever I asked her to do something for me, she would blatantly refuse, or promise to and then forget about it. Then she'd rationalize by saying, "I'm a flake." In the Melanie Griffith voice again.

I had given Jane many items of fab footwear, including a pair of barely-worn $215 Stefan Kelian ankle boots. She gave me a bright orange rayon skirt. I donated it to homeless people.

Then, a month ago, I received Jane's wedding invitation. An enclosed note explained that her fiance, Sy, age 45, was a fellow aspiring actor. I hoped that getting engaged had mellowed Jane out. Even though she lived on Avenue C and practiced karate, I knew that she was a middle-class girl from Long Island whose goal in life was to snag a hubby.

We made a movie date.

When I called to finalize arrangements, Jane said, "I don't really have the money for the movies. How about a drink and dinner?"

"Um, okay. Where should we meet?"

"I can't afford to eat at a restaurant. I thought I'd make something here."

"Well, okay, but I have a touch of the stomach flu and can really only eat bland things."

"What if I make some some fresh corn and tomatoes?"

"Jane, did you ever take Home Economics in high school? Corn is the hardest food to digest, and tomatoes are really acidic."

"How about a tabouli salad?"

"Scallions, lemon juice, tomatoes … are you listening to me?"

"Well … well …" She was sputtering now, practically hyperventilating. "I'll make a green salad with some tunafish."

"Let's order Chinese food. I'll get egg drop soup."

"Fine!" She slammed down the phone.

I took a cab to Avenue C. My bad back was spasming up. Jane's building was located next to a vacant lot, where a group of homeless people built a nightly bonfire. On her front stoop, two crackheads were beaming up.

Sy answered the door. He was about 5' tall, with a chinless, flabby face. Jane is gorgeous—that's how she gets away with all her shit. Sy probably thought he was really lucky. Poor schmuck.

I sat on a beanbag chair and popped some codeine.

The phone rang in the bedroom and I heard Jane inviting someone over. The evening had metamorphosed from a movie date into a party. I hoped Jane wasn't talking to Sara. She seemed normal, even intelligent, when I met her at Jane's. Then I went to her play, "Housework." Two women held up banners embroidered with "herstorical" facts about female domestic workers in America. Jane pounded on a table, repeating "Po-ta-to!" over and over. Then she wandered into the audience, singing a Native American song and making odd hand gestures. Other cast members fell down, as if drunk.

"Wasn't it brilliant?" Jane asked me afterwards.

Jane entered the room, perky as Liza Minelli. She gave me an anemic embrace and began complaining about how her mother would only buy her thrift shop clothing.

"She just has a problem with giving," said Jane.

Calling Dr. Freud, I thought. Dr. Freud to the white courtesy telephone, please.

I showed Jane a silver, garnet and marcasite ring I'd scored from a street vendor.

"He sold me this for $22, but I think he undercharged me. What do you think it's worth?" I asked Jane.

"$1,500?" she suggested, without a trace of irony in her voice.

Possibly, she's totally nuts, I thought.

I was astonished when a cute, hip-looking guy in his mid-thirties arrived. He had hazel eyes and curly hair. His name was Peter and he worked as a cameraman.

Sy said, "Hariette, I hear your parents were Leftists. Mine were, too."

"Where did you go to summer camp?" asked Peter.

"The commiest camp in America," I replied. "Paul Robeson's grandchildren were counselors there."

"My stepfather believed Stalin didn't kill enough people," said Peter.

I was awestruck.

"You've actually out-Commied me."

After Peter left, I asked Jane, "Is he single?"

"Yes. He just broke up with someone."

"Where does he live?"

"Three blocks away from you. He has a very tidy two bedroom apartment with no roommates."

"Call him tomorrow and ask him what he thought about me, okay?" I said excitedly.

"No!" Jane snapped. "I'm leaving town tomorrow and I won't have time to make any phone calls."

Yet, the next morning, inevitable as air pollution, was Jane's four word message on my machine. In a whiny, demanding Joan Rivers voice.

"I need a favor."

The day before the wedding, I called Jane and asked for a description of the eligible single guys who would attend.

"You've already met Chayo," Jane said, referring to an obese Puerto Rican community activist. One night, he and Jane had watched a nature documentary about a goat giving birth. The farmer had to insert a chain into its uterus. Chayo got a hard-on and started kissing Jane.

"Call me picky, but eligible men doesn't include anyone who weighs 350 lbs. and gets off on goats."

"Maybe Chayo's changed," Jane countered.

"Jane..."

Her voice took on a hysterical, Sean Young edge.

175

"There's Peter, my brother Salaam, and Sy's boss, Al Rivera. He owns three restaurants."

Jane's brother, Salaam Schwartz, had converted to Islam in the 70's. That left Peter and Al.

I wore a low-cut black lace mini-dress and French black textured stockings, the kind that induce Pavlovian responses on the Men's Planet. Salaam immediately cornered me. He fasted on Ramadan, prayed on a rug facing Mecca, abstained from alcohol. But, apparently, he still indulged in sexual fantasies. Blatantly undressing me with his eyes, he complimented my legs and added, "Among other alluring accoutrements, your perfume is divine."

I tried to escape, but he followed me around the room. I was tempted to yell at him, "You are a traitor to the Jewish people!" Finally, I spotted Peter, and gestured for him to rescue me.

"Mmm, you're wearing lots of lace," Peter said.

Salaam was outta there.

Peter and I talked about movies and music. We seemed to have similar tastes. Then we sat down—at different tables—for dinner.

I had been seated next to Wentworth, a pudgy Black poet with a chronically sweaty face. At one of Jane's parties, he had observed, "You seem like the type of person who would make someone else suffer rather than suffer yourself."

"You say the sweetest things," I'd replied.

Looking at Wentworth's damp cheeks, I lost my appetite.

I found Jane and asked if she would introduce me to Al Rivera.

"No!" she snapped. "I can't see anything. I don't have my contacts on."

Why had I ever let her back into my life?

Salaam initiated the post-dinner speeches with an Arabic prayer from the Koran. Jane's other brother, totally shit-faced, followed with a rambling obscene joke about a rabbi's wife stuck on a toilet bowl.

"That was appropriate," I said to Peter.

Peter suggested that we share a cab home. He got out with me and asked if he could read some of my *Penthouse* articles.

"Come on up, I'll give you a couple right now," I said. "I just xeroxed some clips."

Peter took the articles, pled fatigue, and split.

The next morning, he left a message on my machine expressing admiration for my work and a desire to see me ASAP. An incipient boyfriend loomed. I blasted The Pixies' "Here Comes Your Man."

Peter and I played phone tag for four days. Finally, we spoke, and he invited me to the movies that night.

Peter paid for the tickets. I handed him my bottle of Pellegrino water in its brown paper bag to smuggle in his briefcase. Inside, he handed it back to me, saying, without a trace of irony in his voice, "Here's your beer."

A Pall Malls smoker, Peter coughed up phlegm throughout the flick. I thought the story was contrived and derivative; he found it fresh and original.

Announcing that it was his custom to end an evening with two martinis, his "Father's drink," he took me to a local bar.

"Those women over there are lovers," he observed. "The women I fall in love with always turn out to be dykes."

"Oh, bullshit," I said.

"Did you read the book *Damage?*" he asked. "I cried at the end."

Maybe we didn't have the same tastes after all.

Peter had alluded many times to his original screenplay, at the wedding and on the phone. Clearly, he believed himself to be the next Quentin Tarantino.

Finally, I asked him about it.

"It's about this guy who tortures and murders his pregnant wife," he said.

"I see."

"How often do you wash your hair?" Peter asked.

"Every day. Why?"

"I only wash mine once every four months. The rest of the time, I just put water and gel on it. You only need to use shampoo three times a year."

I had a vision of cooties crawling all over my pillow. Nonetheless, I was trying to be tolerant. When Peter asked if he could come get some more of my clips, I acquiesced. We sat together in my big white armchair. After ten minutes, I said, "Peter, are you going to kiss me or what?"

He replied, "Hariette, I'm not attracted to you."

I said, "Then get the fuck out of my apartment."

He pouted. "Can I still read your writing?"

"No."

"That's not fair!"

He slammed the door, leaving behind a tacky umbrella.

I donated it to homeless people.

MARIANNE STEELE

It was not long before I met up with the wildest white girl on the circuit, Courtney. She had milky white skin, short blonde hair and neon green eyes. She was 19. Courtney made her entrance by colliding with the dressing room door at Da Tong. The first thing she said at the top of the three metal steps was "Jesus fuck!" She was wearing a tee shirt and a skirt the color of oil rags and sandals with lots of heavy black straps on them. Her hair stuck straight out all over. She looked like a white slave. Fingers stood right in front of her, eyeing her up and down. She was incredibly well built, as tall as Fingers. She pushed passed him and he shoved her in my direction saying.

"That one America also. You talk her flash."

She and her pile of bags landed next to me. She turned around to Fingers and said, "Asshole. Don't push me around, I'm warning you." Then she said to me, "No shit, America where?"

"San Francisco."

"No shit? Me too. Who sent you here? Aiko? That bitch."

"Must be the same one."

Courtney dumped the contents of her bag on the counter and sifted through till she found what she wanted. A small plastic case. She popped it open and rolled out three silver pills.

"Silver bullets, shit only three left. Do you know where I could get some more?"

"You can probably buy them in any drugstore, I've bought valium several times without any hassle."

She took one and washed it down with a can of Mr. Brown, a cold sweet coffee drink. "Yeah? I'll get me some later but now I need these to get me going." She talked constantly while she got ready for her show. All about herself and her family. She was not in this racket for the money, she said. Her family had plenty of it. She was here for the fun of it. She claimed that her grandfather was the eyeglass king of San Francisco. Having the largest chain of eyeglass stores in the city. "It's old money," she said," he's been there for fucking ages." Her father was an author who had co-written a book called, *Holy Blood Holy Grail*. She promised to get me a copy. And her mother was an ex-hippy psychologist. But no one could control her, she said with pride. Even her mother the ex-hippy psychologist wanted to slap her with an incorrigible youth charge and turn her over to a foster home. She turned 18 before they could pull it off. "Like, I got sick of the bullshit so I left. I got this job modeling in Tokyo. But my god it was so false like getting up every morning early and everbody putting on their light pink blushes and rose red lips, going out to the shoot and then having dinner with the clients afterwards. Look pretty, be nice, oh god it made me

178

sick! So I split from the agency and found plenty of work in the underground theaters. I got busted by foreign affairs police doing a porno show. Then it turns out my fucking visa is expired. Deportation, you know what I'm sayin? Blacklisted, I can't go back."

She put on black lipstick and brown blush and a heavy black line under her eyes. She yanked off her clothes and threw them on the floor, standing there naked she said, "The real reason I came here is because I'm interested in religions." She ran through a quick comparison of Buddhism, Taoism, Christianity, Greek myths and Satanism. I hardly heard a word she said because I was looking at her body. Beautiful skin, beautiful breasts, really a work of art. Her costume was an old black Salvation Army dress. It was visibly torn and filthy. Dressed in it she looked like some beautiful ghost from a train wreck.

Fingers came to herd her on to the stage. He used his good hand to point. "You America, afta dis." He looked at her and frowned. "Get ready, get ready!" He yelled.

"I am ready asshole."

"Shoes," he said pointing at her feet.

"Why don't you go and fuck yourself."

"Ayia! America!" He groaned.

Courtney made a point of creating trouble. I'd heard about her for weeks. She fought with theater managers and always was late and used drugs openly and to excess. She was speeding on silver bullets when I gave her the run down on how to flash at Da Tong.

"Today, I heard there are police so you can't get naked on the stage, you got to come down here get the cape and remember to flash only to the left and right from the catwalk. The police always sit in the back row center. If you face him with all you got all hell is going to break loose."

She came over to me and shot me with those wild bulging eyes. "You gotta be fucking kidding me!"

"No, he can't get upset about what he does not see."

"Come on come on !" Fingers shouted.

She hit the stage to the sounds of "White Wedding." A short while later we heard Fingers shouting.

"No, no! side side, no center!" The music cut and everybody ran. Courtney flew back into the room, jumping down from the top step. Fingers was right behind her yelling.

"You flash, no good!" Then he turned to me. "I tell you talk her flash!"

"I did! Take it easy Fingers, it's her first time. Next time better, o.k.?" After he was gone I said to her. "Don't piss him off! No matter what you do make it look like a mistake, but don't blow the flash again, the way he feels about you now you better be careful."

"So what's there going to be, a raid? Jesus I got to get out of here. Come on show me where I can get some drugs." I took her to Spikes in Kaosuing. He supplied just about anything from his drugstore. He never asked for prescriptions and was a favorite with the white girls. Silver bullets were no problem, but seconal he could not supply. "Only in hospital," he said.

Courtney attached herself to me that week. She talked non-stop about herself and her philosophy and her punk scene in San Francisco. She had memorized long, really long monologues from Shakespeare and she would recite them to me along with her favorite satanic poems. She had a way of making me think she was a mad genius. She was definitely mad, and clever and beautiful. She got her seconal by staging a completely convincing psychotic fit in the dressing room. They took her to the hospital where she asked right away for seconal from the doctor who examined her. He said she was just nervous, he was reluctant still.

"I fucked him for it," she said shaking the little bottle. "Jesus he was easy, have one open wide." She sang.

Courtney would do anything for money or drugs, she was a punk who wore a noose around her neck as she slam danced her way through life. Courtney's dance was the wildest I've ever seen, but she was so damn beautiful to look at. Till you met her and saw her eyes then her beauty became almost frightening. It was as much her eyes, her hair, her skin, the powerful electric charge coming off her that made everyone a little afraid of her. She towered over most Chinese, they never pushed her around after getting a look from those demonic green eyes. While I was never into the punk scene in San Francisco, it was my home and I had a good time relating with her in our own language, in northern California jargon. It takes care of a certain homesickness when you can tramp over every detail of home with someone. 49er's, North Beach, Mission. That's where she mainly hung out, in the Mission District, the same one my mother grew up in when it was an Irish working family neighborhood. Now it's called Little El Salvador due to the large population of Latin Americans. It's also a hang-out for punks and drunks and because it's usually warmer down there than other parts of the city, the homeless. We stayed together constantly that week. Went shopping, she actually found an English copy of her father's book in a small bookstore in Kaosuing. She hit me in the chest with it. "Read this." We lay for hours during the hottest part of the day on my bed under the fan. Courtney would tank up on drugs and then beg me to stay with her while she flew. It was only her mouth that flew. She talked away telling me every intimate detail of her life and her relationship with her family and all their problems. She began pressing me for solutions, answers. I told her, "Hey I'm not your psychiatrist." But I listened to her and stayed with her when she took drugs. I usually had a couple of valium to counteract her force.

By some coincidence we were booked in the same theaters for three con-secutive weeks. It was my last three weeks with the Polo agency and I'd managed to save up some money. I'd never gotten a new contract from them but when I paid off all the advances, fines and even air tickets, I fought over that one. That I should have to pay back Lynn and Bill's air tickets was outrageous. But Mr. Yeh had it deducted from my salary, did-n't even tell me how much it was. I eventually got my full salary and still had every bit of cash I took from Mr. Chia and those others. As hardened as I'd become I could only think of that money as filthy. I held on to it, greed I guess, or simply survival. It added up to around five thousand dollars. By now I knew lots of people in Taipei most connected with the theaters and some not connected at all with the sleazy side of town. I was introduced to Liv by my friend Jim. We were old friends after having lived together in California till he went off to the Peking Language Insti-tute. He now lived in Hong Kong. He flew right over when I wrote and said I was in Taipei in this crazy job. He spoke Mandarin fluently and had a talk with Mr. Yeh and Dandy. It didn't go so well. They were sus-picious of this outsider friend of mine who could speak Chinese so well. He showed his concern to me though. "Are you sure you want to be doing this? I could get you out of it I think. Do you think you are in any danger? I'll give you Liv's number, she's a great gal, a really good friend. If you need help or just want to talk to someone call her. I'm going to see her tomorrow, she's having a party for a client at her apartment. You should come over there later and I can introduce you." Liv offered right away to hold any money I got in a safety deposit box in her office. So every time I was in Taipei I called her and we had coffee together and dropped off my cash with her. She was slightly amazed at my line of work but wasn't judgmental about it. From Liv I collected all my cash and checked into a first class hotel with a swimming pool. I invited Courtney to share the room with me as she was booked nearby at Ching Ing. She brought along her drugs and a guy named Taco. "As in burrito," she said, introducing him. "Don't worry, he's not staying but he got this great way for us to make some easy money. Fuck this dancing scene. We can sit on our asses in a nice hotel like this one, all we have to do is a couple of guys a night and we can make double what we make working for those jerks. And now you are not working, what are you gonna do when your money runs out? And believe me they're sucking it right out of you in a place like this."

"A couple of guys a night?"

"More if you want," Taco said, "if you want to make money, as many as you like!"

"Yes well Taco how much?"

"Well Miss Courtney, because her skin is so white, she can make maybe ten thousand NT's a day. But for you I think the price will be lower because your skin is covered with black points."

"They're freckles!"

"Yes," said Taco.

Get lost you scum, I thought but I was polite. "Well this is something to think about, how about I let you know later."

He sat up. "But I have work for you tonight! It's very good, never mind, these are," he searched for the word, "dentists! They want to have the company of some foreign girls tonight. Courtney said you would come."

"She did?! Courtney where did you find this guy and why did you say I would go out with a bunch of dentists!?"

"O.k., fine. Don't be a friend, just dump me on a load of dentists by myself. Besides, look at what I got." She got rid of Taco saying, "Goodbye taco burrito, you can pick us up at nine." She dragged me into the bathroom and pulled out a vial of something white and fluffy, dipped the end of her cigarette in it and twirled it around till the end was caked with the powder. "We'll do it this way for now, but we can chase the dragon later if we need to.

"What is it, cocaine?"

"It's horse, sweetheart, come on ride with me baby." She inhaled deeply and passed the cigarette to me. "Now," she pinched my lips together and kissed me on the mouth, "go and get on your pinks and lipstick and it'll all be over before you know it."

I got very high my first time on the heroin. I'll try it just once, I thought. One time doesn't make someone an addict. First it made me feel ill and I thought, there see I don't even like the high. Then I began to feel so heavenly I wanted to go floating through space with her. The stuff certainly made her less aggressive and she was well behaved through dinner. For some reason Taco came along with us, to keep an eye on things, on us, on the money. By the time dessert came we both were coming down from the first hit and felt a need of more. I wanted to touch paradise again. That's how it made me feel, what could be so bad about that? We drove to a Japanese tea house in Bei Tou. All were given kimonos to wear and seated on tatamis around a low table. The waitress crawled in on her knees to serve warm sake to everyone. "Jesus look at that." Courtney said out loud. "Don't crawl for these bastards! How can you do that?" Luckily the girl did not understand. Courtney was getting fidgety. I could see her aggressiveness coming back. I had a thought to warn at least Taco, but it was too late. She stood up and stripped down to her underwear and started to dance. Her nearly six-foot milky white frame covered one end of the shoji screened room. I doubted the dentists had this kind of entertainment in mind, they all looked a little uneasy at first but they were so polite as to go along and even clapped for her. One of the younger dentists, fired up with sake, got up to dance with her. I'm sure he never slam danced with anyone before, especially not this

American punkster drunk on sake. He was eventually knocked down and crawled back to his place at the table. When no one wanted to dance with her after that she grabbed me and said, "Come on let's go check the bathroom for dragons."

Taco said, "Where are you going?" The evening was not going well particularly from the Chinese point of view. Even I could see that. Taco could see that and the dentists were trying not to show it. What is to them an evening spent with charming women with possibilities of building into an erotic experience for one or all of them, is certainly not what Courtney or I came up with. Especially not after we drifted from the bathroom and sat down stupefied. I stared across the table at her and lost myself completely looking at her half-naked body and imagining making love to her. She would be like a huge wild cat, I thought. And the dreamy fantasy went on and on till I didn't know any difference between my fantasy and the seven dentists seated on tatamis.

Taco took us out for some air. I remember getting out of the car after a long drive, at the beach. It was late at night, cool, and the big moon was shining on the water. I wanted to follow the moonlight across the water and drifted off.

"Sit down!" Taco yelled. He came across the beach and we three sat in the sand. Taco cried. Probably because we had embarrassed him, or more likely because he lost money.

Courtney never stopped talking all night. She talked about the sweep of Christianity across Europe and how Buddhism went the other way from India to China and how she herself was spinning in circles as a result. All night as the moon passed over our heads she gave us the history of the religious world. Till the first light showed far out in the mist that lay on the China Sea.

"I want room service, and I want it quick, I'm starving. Two of everything, eggs, toast, coffee and, do you want pancakes? Yeah send up some pancakes."

I lay in bed with my eyes closed. The depths of my sake heroin hangover were bottomless. I hurt in every point imaginable. I groaned and tried to move, my bed was full of sand.

"You just fell of the horse honey, you have to get right back on." She handed me a silver bullet and began to pack the end of a cigarette. I pushed it aside.

"Jesus the sun's not even up yet."

"It's been up, it's going down."

If I could have turned myself inside out and rinsed every part of me in clean water I would have. My soul felt dirty. With my eyes closed I saw demons and hell. "I don't want that stuff, sure it would take away this horrible feeling but ..."

"You scared to get hooked?"

"My body wants it but my brain doesn't."

"You want to relax a little? You want to feel better? You want to stop being so uptight? Ah shit, here." She thrust the cigarette at me. I took it.

Our room had an assortment of room service dishes scattered here and there, under the bed, on the chairs. My red boa draped over the wall light and the contents of Courtney's numerous bags emptied across everything. She had a strange assortment of junk. Even several tubes of oil paint that had been stepped on and smeared into the carpet. Across the mirror, in red lipstick was written, "freckles are a curse." The only thing she kept track of was a small plastic cow from a child's farm set. Her sacred cow she called it. If she prayed she prayed to it. We had made a little shrine on the bed table between the two beds and there sat the sacred cow and my contribution, a seated Buddha figure. I was praying for some relief now and it came after a few minutes, like angels returning. I was high again. Room service arrived. Courtney kicked a path clear so the boy could wheel in the cart. Behind him were two maids, they looked over the mess shaking their heads, they were afraid to come in. The boy then opened the refrigerator and made a list of the contents for the bill. "We haven't touched anything in there, look! why don't you just take it all out now."

She shoved him aside and began tossing bottles and cans on the bed. The maids rushed in to gather them up. They saw the paint on the carpet, the lipstick on the mirror and all the spilled and leftover dishes and they erupted into a Taiwanese chatter as they tried to recover some of the dishes. The room service boy translated for them. "They can not clean this room, they must notify the manager," he announced.

"Fine, good, notify God while you're at it, now get out of here!"

All of them glanced around worriedly, saw our little shrine, complete with incense. The boa, the Buddha, and the cow. That really startled them and they left quickly.

"It's pretty bad in here," I said noticing that they missed the dishes under the bed. The oil paint was tracked all over the place and my dress with Courtney's menstrual blood on it lay crumpled up on the floor. She hadn't bothered to wash it out after she borrowed it. It looked like a planned effort to create chaos and disorder. "You are like a pig pen," I said, "everywhere you go a pile of garbage gathers around you."

"You calling me a pig!? Miss neatness and purity? Then why don't we divide the room and you can keep your side all neat and clean and pink and pure. And, you better not insult me again you fucking prude!"

"How can you call me a prude? You don't know me well enough, obviously. Didn't I take one of those dentists into that small room and fuck him, the oldest guy there, he must have been seventy! You

184

just sat there with your tits hanging out and punched that young one in the face when he tried to touch you."

"So you did make money. You bitch! How much did the old fart pay you!"

"Not much, three thousand, I left it on the front seat of Taco's car."

"You what!?"

"Just forget it. I didn't want that old man's money, it stank like the whole experience. I want to forget it ever happened."

"That's very touching. You know I think you are one of the stupidest women I've ever met. I could have used that money, why didn't you give it to me?!"

"Shit, why? You wrecked that shoji screened room, freaked everybody out. It wasn't the kind of evening anyone would pay for. Besides I just wanted to get rid of it, so I left it on the seat of his car."

"Why don't you just get the fuck out of my life!"

"I think now that's a good idea, but this room is in my name. I've got to pay whatever damages, don't I? Look, I'm checking out, whatever you do in this room after I'm gone, is on you." I got out of bed, high but at least I could move without pain.

"So, you think I'm a pig, a wasted pig. Get out of here. I don't need you, or this. She threw the vial of powder at me as I tried to pack my things. I put it in my bag. "I'm going to get rid of this, where is my other shoe?"

"Right here!" She threw it at me, it missed me but hit the wall hard. Next came the ashtray which was heavy glass. It broke in two and took a chunk out of the wall. After that followed the breakfast dishes which scattered into powdery bits. Then she grabbed the serving tray and flung it like a frisbee into the mirror.

"Courtney, stop!" I screamed dodging all the flying glass.

"Fuck you! How dare you walk out on me! You think you are so good, so wonderful. You were just as willing to sell off your ass, you even did! And now you want to play Miss pure, always doing the right thing, god you make me sick!" Her rage built. It lit up her eyes and curled back her upper lip. Like a demon she flew at me. Tackled me to the floor and sat on top of me with her hands pressed around my neck. I looked as hard as I could into her wild green eyes. Tried to look past the fierce beast she had become. Tried to see whatever was left of this girl inside. All I could think of to say came out very calmly. "Courtney, stop."

"Bitch, go ahead and leave me, get your stuff and get out of here."

I waded through the debris to the door and down to the lobby. I checked out and took my cash out of their security box.

Apparently the front desk hadn't been notified of the damaged room upstairs. Lucky for me, I could not have faced another scene. I was just about out the main door when Courtney ran out of the elevator and yelled across the lobby. "Give me back my heroin!" I did not look around to see if anyone heard it. I just walked over and handed her the vial then turned and walked out the doors and onto the street. I was afraid to look back in case she was following me. I didn't want to go back in for another hit even though I was needing one badly. I was hoping I would never see her again. The next several days were hellish for me. I hid myself away in a mountain guest house near some hot springs and went through the sickening process of getting the heroin out of my body. I sweated then froze, threw up nothing and shook all over. When I didn't leave my room for four days the guest house manager came to my room. He took one look at me and asked if I had malaria. If so he would have to notify the health authorities. I told him I had eaten something bad in Taipei and it made me sick. Once he felt convinced it wasn't malaria he brought me hot water and a bowl of rice.

BASEBALL

DON MONACO

Tim turned the corner and an orange was rolling toward him across the squares of concrete sidewalk. He would have to step aside to let it roll, but he bent and snapped it up as though it were a ground ball and looked to his left where first base should be, and there a young girl with a baseball cap and a big leather mitt stretched toward him, awaiting his throw.

Without interrupting his scooping motion he pitched a medium speed strike into her glove.

The coach had moved him to second to support the new kid at first. His natural hard throw from third had to be controlled, modified from second, especially if they were using oranges now in practice, having run out of hardballs.

Well, that's the way pre-season goes. You had to roll with the fruit of the season. Luckily oranges were often in season, and he didn't mind grapefruit. But there was a time when the front office, overriding the manager, had purchased a crate of hard pears with the idea that the uneven roll, the tricky shape would train the infielders to keep their eye on the ball. He hadn't liked that.

The new kid at first waved to him. She had made him a little uneasy the first day she came into the locker room. But he had also felt uneasy the first day a black had been put on the team. He was old enough to remember those days. Then, because the coach had

186

seen him talk to the black—they were called Negroes then—he made Tim his road roomie. He took a lot of ribbing from the guys the day that was announced.

He walked over to the first baseperson.

"Nice game," he said.

"You threw a couple of those into the dirt a purpose," she said. "A purpose," he thought. He hadn't heard that phrase since his growing up in Kentucky.

"Yea," he said. "You looked a little cocky." Tim wondered if that was the right word. "Henny" certainly sounded wrong. "I wanted to see how you'd handle a couple in the dirt. You did OK."

"When're you guys going to get done testing me?" she said. She took off her cap and a flood of short curly black hair popped out from under her cap. "They were swearing in the locker room this morning like it was going out of style. That was for my benefit too. It was like that for years in the minors. Now it's going to go on here?"

They turned toward the dugout and she banged her glove on her knee as they walked. The dust of the long afternoon was deep in the cloth of their uniforms. She was long limbed, muscled and very loose jointed. At bat, she came around on the ball in about three stages. He often laughed, but like Ty Cobb she "hit it where they ain't." Cobb never hit a long ball either.

"Riding you won't last," he said. "They know if you ride somebody too much it'll hurt the team." He had the urge to pat her on the behind. The loose uniform didn't hide her figure.

Billy, the fat round-faced manager, met them at the dugout steps.

"I've been trying to figure out your roommate, April," he said, looking first at the woman, then at his second baseman. "Think I've figured out someone. I chose this man because he's mature, he's helped us in the past, rooming with new players, and you're standing next to him."

Damn, Tim thought, just because I helped the first black player on the team get oriented and accepted, he's picking me because she's the first woman.

April burst into laughter bending backwards, then forwards. While her laughter continued, Billy covered a small smile.

But maybe he picked me, Tim thought, because she's black.

Suddenly he felt a healthy slap on his behind. April had quite a wallop.

"Don't you worry a bit, Tim," she said, laughing again. "I'll bring you along slowly." She flipped the orange to him, and he caught it with his bare hand.

Tim thought this was going to be a very interesting season.

Timothy Collins continued to stare at the orange as his fingers held it across the seams. A very fat white-aproned Oriental stepped up to him from the crates of fruits and grabbed the orange out of his hand, and put it back into the display crate outside the grocery door.

As Tim continued his walk to work he knew this incident was recorded by the mirror-windowed van that cruised just behind him. But it would appear so innocent. Billy, code name Chang, in a clever Oriental disguise, would later take the cocaine-filled orange out of the street display and distribute its contents. Tim would be eating the real orange, the orange he had palmed, at his desk, remembering the easy pick up of twenty thousand, and the pleasures it would bring.

April, his newly-hired black secretary, dumped his bulky mail onto his desk. The new shipment would be marked "Rush." He permitted himself a small smile.

CRUISIN' AT THE A&P

KEN MCLAUGHLIN

In the afternoons on these long summer days when it's too hot to do anything else, and there's nothing to do anyway because this is a little pissant, southern, industrial town, and I'm flat broke because I quit my fucking job two months ago, and even my car has been repossessed, I like to walk over to the A&P and look at the guys. You can always find a good-looking man or two, anytime of the day or night—it's open 24 hours. I guess they have to shop like anybody else. Maybe there's not a higher percentage of them in the store; it's just that you can see them better. For the purpose of inspecting merchandise, I've found, fluorescent panel lighting is far superior to the dim, smoky effect in bars, or worse—the strobe thing in discos.

Sometimes Yvonne goes with me, but sometimes I go alone. If I go alone I always wish Yvonne were there, so at least I could carry on the pretense of a conversation while wandering the frozen food aisle, managing to discreetly cross paths with some dark-eyed beauty or other, possibly even managing to furtively brush up against one as I avoid knocking over the Velveeta display (precarious stacks of things in the middles of aisles are an easy excuse for momentary, though often quite intimate, physical contact). But if I go with Yvonne I always wish she'd stayed home. She has an annoying habit of stopping dead in her tracks in the direct line of vision of some guy she's staring blatantly at, and saying quite audibly something like, "Fuck me! Would you look at that butt." Or worse, "He's your type. He looks Chinese."

It works very well for Yvonne. She's caught the attention of many a three-night stand this way (she goes through boyfriends the way other people go through video rentals). From her, obscene behavior in a grocery store seems just charming. But I prefer to keep a low profile, since this is a redneck town and, being male myself, the physical encounters that could arise for me are probably of the less pleasant kind. I could get beat up.

Of course, this has never happened. If there's one thing I am, it's discreet. And if there's another thing I am, it's manly—in a sensitive and shy sort of way. Nobody ever suspects I'm queer. Which is probably why I don't have sex often. Even though at the moment I'm completely available, because the man I love is out of town with his wife and child, probably flirting his brains out with any person he meets on the street, male or female, that he's not even going to ever actually do anything with. Not that I'm unavailable when he's here—we're just friends. I'm free. Free as a bird. Free as the fucking wind.

So, after a while of me witnessing Yvonne's prowess in this bizarre version of that supermarket grab gameshow, where the prizes seem to be even those guys who are supposed to be my type, we can usually manage to scrape together enough money to buy a cheap six-pack, and with the help of a new friend maybe even a pack of cigarettes, because we certainly don't have enough money to buy beers at The Morgue, which is the only bar in town we ever think about going to. We just go back to her place and sit on the porch, and drink beer and smoke cigarettes, and watch people sweat by on the street, and comment on the beauty of heat lightning flashing in a polluted evening sky.

Actually, all the A&P's in town have changed their names. I don't know if this is a universal phenomenon or only local. It doesn't really matter. Yvonne and I will always call it the A&P, because we're southern and fixed in our ways.

UP FOR B & E

First time I saw him he was standin out by the truckstop sign with his thumb up for a ride into Booneville, and I knew right then he was bad business, nobody you'd take to meet your mama. I knew he was a drifter.

I was right. Trouble is, before he drifted out, he drifted in, and oh lord, I mean in. He comes here, see, and he swings himself down onto the counter stool like he's a-mountin a real good lay—an I'm over there, behind him, servin some truckers a mess of biscuits and sausage gravy, and I can't help it, I says to myself, Wooo-ie! Lookit that!—and I swear to god he spun that stool-top and looked me clean in the eye. He knew exactly what I was thinkin. Hi, he says, real slow, but what he meant was somethin too obscene to put on paper.

PAT SCHNEIDER

189

Hi, I says, and I was meanin the exact same thing. He stood up kinda slow motion and started toward the door, and then he turned and looked back at me. You comin or not, he said, and I swear to god I put down the two coffees and the side of homefries I was still balancin, put em right down on the counter in front of Joey Barstow. He's one of our best regulars. Hey! I didn't order me no homefries, Joey says, and then my brother-in-law, he turns around from the grill and yells, Where you think you're goin, Maxine?—shit, he acts like he owns the whole god-dammed truck stop, not just a fuckin franchise on the restaurant part.

I didn't say a word, I just sorta floated outa here and straight into the second trailer of an empty rig. This guy says hey, what if the fella drives this comes out and takes off? I says, sorta teasin, Yeah, what if? But I knew who the driver was, and I knew he was just gettin started on a big mess of biscuits and gravy, and he was good for at least three cups of coffee after.

Well, this guy was somethin else, let me tell you. You know them thick quilt things they have in some trucks?—he spread one of them things out and then he picked me up and laid me down and spread me out and oh my god there was stars a moving around inside that rig I ain't never, never been touched like that—so gentle I wanted to cry, and so sure of himself.

But you know what's really weird? After he finished, after he rolled offa me, you know?.—he didn't groan or cuss or jump right back up like they usually do. This guy was weird. He cried. He did—he put his hands up over his face and he cried. Real hard, I mean. And for a long time. I didn't know what to do. I wanted—you know, I sorta wanted to smooth his hair down, like if he was a little boy—but I didn't know what the hell to do, and just about as I was startin to get scared, like maybe this guy's crazy or something, you know?—he wiped his face on his sleeve, and sorta shook himself, and jumped down outa the trailer, and turned around and helped me down as nice as you please.

Man, that is one complicated dude. He followed me back into the restaurant, and when my brother-in-law came over and said real nasty, Get the hell back to work, Maxine—I told him, Shut up, Leroy, I'm hav-ing me a coffee break if you don't mind. I sat down on a stool between Jimmie Barnes and Andy Konachek on purpose so's this guy won't think I'm encouragin him none. He stands there behind me for a little bit, like he don't know what he's supposed to do next, and then he goes to anoth-er stool way down at the end of the counter. Well, I couldn't sit there all morning, not with LeRoy throwing them eggs and homefries around on the grill like he was premeditatin murder. Sure enough, though, soon as I stood up, this guy comes around fast and gets up real close to me and asks me won't I go on with him. Just like that! I mean, give me a break! What's really weird is that I might a done it. No joke, until he started crying out there in the rig, I tell you I woulda done it in a second. No, honest, I woulda! But I just said, No, I gotta get back to work. That's when he split.

This here picture?—that's him. Right there, page one, mornin edition. It's not a very good picture; you can't see how cute he is; I mean, the way he looked when he was first turnin around on that counter stool. It don't surprise me none that he's up for breakin an enterin. Like I said, he was weird. Still, if you don't mind my sayin so, them as he broke an entered, they might even be thankin him for it, you know what I mean?

—More coffee?

URBAN JEWISH WHITE TRASH STORY

MAXINE CHERNOFF

Not only in towns named Shirley and Lead Bottom do bad things happen to good people. Not just to Billie Jean or Roy, Jr. It can be Detroit or Queens or Los Angeles. It can be Chicago, a middle-class neighborhood of optometrists, steel workers, leather salesmen, and minor insurance agents, where disaster may strike. Its cousin, Fate, already led you here when your father, anonymous victim of world economic crisis, quit school. He had hoped to become a doctor and control the destinies of those he loved. Failing at that, he became a man with numbers stuck in his head. Like the wizened men you see on Crete in cafes, doing math problems for pleasure, your father loved the cold logic of sums. His numbers arrived without life, and it was up to you to resuscitate them. "I have so little to work with!" you complained to no end, for this is what you were given, this is what you made of it, and what it made of you.

On your block itself, there were countless dangers beyond the vague threats of polio and nuclear emergencies. The boy next door, Stevie, whose mother was Glamorina of the recent divorce, was left in the yard in his underwear in bone-chilling weather. There Stevie is, trembling near the gate, where he must stay until she has finished entertaining the man she's brought home from a date. Through the fence you feed Stevie crackers. Like a dog, he crunches on them gratefully. You offer him an old sweater. Instead of thanking you, he aims his penis at you. A wet stream shoots through the mesh that separates you as you jump back and stare. "Aren't penises long as hoses?" you ask your sister later. "You're thinking of elephant trunks, crazy person," she says before she tells your mother on you.

You stop asking questions, which is dangerous, because

191

sometimes you could use more information. Mr. Morales next door is a foreman at the steel mill. What does it mean that he is also a money-lender and that the labor his plant needs is shipped straight to his basement on Constance Avenue? One of the men has steady eyes and shows no fear. He walks down the street in daylight. "Sweet sweet little Mama," he whispers to you as you pass him. Having not yet discovered shame, you have no modesty. It doesn't occur to you to close your Venetian blinds or ask your mother why that man watches you undress every night. It seems as much a part of your weekly routine as Saturday night baths and Sunday school. When you move away many years later, Mr. Morales plants an open-mouthed kiss on your surprised lips. "I'll never see you again," he blinks sadly. "I should have closed my blinds," you lament, eight years after the fact.

The Morales family is your substitute for asking questions. You learn so much from them. Freddie, the eldest son, drinks heavily. He shoots a gun in the alley on New Year's Eve. "Don't take rides from him ever!" your mother has warned. After a fight about the rent, Freddie threatens to send the severed head of his family dog home in a box. You watch the mail for weeks. What shape will the box be? What color? Will the mailman shake the box wondering what it holds? It never arrives, but the dog returns. Freddie too. Bearing a knife, he chases his mother, who is trying to collect his rent. She shows up breathless at your door. You have been watching "American Bandstand" and practicing the vaguely obscene gestures of the dance called The Jerk. "He's trying to kill me," she says quietly. You show her to a chair. "I shouldn't sit. I've peed my pants." "Don't worry," you reassure her. "We have plastic covers."

It isn't a neighbor but a stranger who touches you first. You are on a trip with the Girl Scouts to the Wisconsin Dells. A fat theme park Indian, authentic but in bad faith about his work, grabs your nub of a breast. You don't register it until your sister sees the photo and makes a remark. So much that happens is only given a name later, you note after your Wisconsin experience. You are learning. When Bobbie L., a demented boy with tight curls and a three-year stint in eighth grade, knocks you off your bike and grabs you in the same place, you know something is wrong, but you don't say anything. Your sister would laugh. Your father would calculate the probability of such an event occurring, which is high in a city. "I'm not surprised," he would say with the glint of sad circumspection that makes you anxious for his health.

One Halloween at Missy's house down the street, her mother is preparing dinner. But you see that her hands are trembling as she slices the London broil. When she finally sits down with you, she bursts into tears. She's been frightened by a boy who reached into her car and grabbed her purse off the passenger seat. "I've learned my lesson!" she announces, wiping her eyes and sniffling bravely. The doorbell rings. It's Ronnie Roberts, the cutest boy in eighth grade, who is dressed as a bum. He is reaching his hand out to grab you there again, but you're ready. Your knee shoots up into the extra-long crotch of his hobo pants. There are so many stars in the October sky, you think as he writhes on the porch. You are learning to protect yourself. You aren't like Missy's mother's purse, sitting there for the taking.

Once when your mother got off the Jeffrey Express at your corner, a tall black kid snatched her shopping bag. Against the advice of experts, including your father who lectures the family on miscellaneous dangers, she held on and wrestled it back. "You son of a bitch!" she called him, your mother who never swore. In telling the story, she made a point of her race neutrality. "You son of a bitch!" could be aimed at anyone. Her open-mindedness was a point of pride.

This event has some vague correlation with the invention of refrigerator art in your household. The collage shows the Montgomery bus boycott and newspaper photos of Cheney, Schwerner, and Goodman. You'd think someone had an ideology looking at it, but your mother never speaks about the cause of civil rights. A few months later, she tapes up pictures of astronauts. The white wall of your refrigerator commemorates seasons, minor holidays, and family victories. When your father bowls a 700 series and his photo makes the local paper, your mother creates a three-dimensional bowling display. The street thief has brought out your mother's artistic side. You want to thank him. But your father is driven to another conclusion. He buys a handgun and does target practice in the basement. Your family closes its ears and turns up the TV as bullets ricochet off the washer and utility sink.

Down the street, Sharon Silverberg dies of cystic fibrosis on the night that Teddy Kennedy's plane crashes in a storm. You were supposed to babysit for her that night, but first she was hospitalized and then she was gone. She couldn't eat ice cream. You would serve her marshmallow whip with colored sprinkles if she managed to swallow at least half of her bird-sized meal. Her skin was as white as paper. She slept in an oxygen tent and was the bossiest kid you knew. Two doors down, tiny, stooped Mr. Bernstein has a massive stroke. His son who sells furniture fashions a crank bed for him that is placed in the center of the picture window. As often as not, his father is asleep in that bed. But sometimes, when you ride by on your red Schwinn singing songs from *West Side Story*, you see his passive face in the window. His eyes appear to cry without his volition. Ancient Mr. Bernstein reminds you of saints that your friend Kathy Kaszmarek has in her big saint encyclopedia. You'd like to own that book, but you know your parents would say no.

Across the alley from you, Martin Morley's father gets killed in a car crash. The policeman comes to your house first, thinking it is the Morley's. You know before Martin or his mother that his father is dead. When Darlene holds her breath to scare her mother, she isn't dead. She is just making a point about power to her mother Irene, who had replaced Glamorina as your next door neighbor. Three doors down, Ellen, who is a devout Catholic, tries to smother the fourth child she and Frank have had in six years. She is sent to a rest home and given a prescription for contraceptives. The doctor is Jewish, she tells your mother upon her return to the block. You notice that the baby she tried to kill is prettier and more alert than the three she has tolerated. You question her intelligence. Across from you, Mrs. Neilson's husband falls off the roof he is shingling and breaks his neck. "He drank too much" is part of the story your family hears upon their return from Niagara Falls.

You wish sometimes that your parents drank. It would be sophisticated for them to hold a martini or a highball like the classy adults you watch in movies. You've since read that Jewish men suffer from a higher rate of depression than their Christian brothers, who rely more on liquor to fix their moods. Maybe a Tom Collins or two could have helped your father through his dark middle years.

When your grandmother tries to commit suicide on a bench facing the lake, the police come again. "We're off to the hospital," your parents whisper. "Don't go anywhere." Where are you supposed to go at one in the morning? You turn on the television and watch *The Best Years of Our Lives*. One nice man in it has a hook for a hand. Maybe your grandmother has chopped off her hand, you think. Two weeks later she comes home with a big bandaged fist, where the IV incision has gotten infected. By now you know she had taken pills. You stare at her vials of medications when you visit her apartment. There are blue satellites and long yellow rockets. You glue some to a barrette and hide it in your drawer, the way your father hides things in his. Between the handkerchiefs and old wallets, you've seen rubbers, World War II shrapnel, and photos of the South Pacific. When your sister can't find a clip for her long hair, you offer her the barrette. "You're sick!" she shouts. The year you start college, you pry a few pills off the barrette and try them. The blue ones make you sleepy. Your grandmother never misses them.

"I don't believe in God," you tell the rabbi after your grandmother tries to kill herself. He doesn't seem surprised, which distresses you greatly. "Then I'll give you a different part," he shrugs in response to the context, the recitation of a Sabbath prayer in a play your class is performing. "You can be a prophet. They were all crazy."

When your family moves away, when they take their lives to the socially engineered suburbs, when your father's attitude improves and the refrigerator door is once again bare, you think the story will end. But that is another story. It will wait in the wings like a patient, hopeful understudy until someone gives it a name.

THE MELANCHOLY HOUSE OF GATES

PETER WEVERKA

MEMORANDUM
Date: July 13, 2051
To: Detective John Wimkey
From: Detective Ronald Kite
Re: Bill Gates' whereabouts/demise

Sorry I can't be there to deliver this in person and answer your questions, but after you have read this memo you will understand why it is utterly impossible for me to leave the Gates Mansion. The news isn't good, John. It's not good on several fronts. In fact, the Gates heirs have not been completely honest with us. We were charged with finding out whether Bill Gates is still alive inside his vast mansion. The answer: he is and he isn't.

Just like we planned, I was able to enter through the east wing, the former servants' quarters. As you know, Gates built the place at the turn of the century as "the first electronic smart house." The inhabitants wore computer-badges so that the house would know exactly where they were at all times. The house would open doors for its inhabitants as they came to doorways, would play their favorite songs as they walked from room to room, would regulate the temperature so that only rooms with people in them were heated, etc., etc., etc.

It still does all that. The house still works. Tell Sarah in Research she did a great job. As soon as I got in the house, my sensor told me that the silent alarm had gone off, but by listening for music, by seeking out a part of the house that was still heated, I was able to find a corpse with a computer-badge still stuck to his rotting clothes. I pinned his computer-badge on my shirt seconds before the robots arrived.

"Sorry to bust in, dude," one said, "but Bill was like, wondering if you've seen a stranger in the house?"

The robots, believe it or not, carried skateboards and looked to be dressed for the beach. The Gates touch. His goons were dressed for a beach party.

"Haven't seen a thing," I told them.

They quickly left. The corpse had been there, I'd say, for at least a decade. A virtual-reality helmet was strapped to his skull. Strapped to his pelvis was a virtual-reality codpiece. Probably one of Bill's old programmer cronies dead in the throes of ecstasy.

I began exploring the mansion. Please appreciate the doublebind I was in, John. I had been sent to ferret out the mansion's deepest, darkest secret, yet the mansion knew exactly where I was at all times and wouldn't permit me go in certain rooms or down certain passageways. I'd go room to room thinking I would find Gates at any minute, then a door wouldn't open or one of Gates' robots would appear and kindly tell me that lunch was served or offer some other distraction. If I demurred, the robot would say, "Now now, we have to eat, don't we?" and I would be whisked to a dining room for a meal of Doritos and Twinkies. Or else I would be taken to Gates' private movie theater to watch Stephen Spielberg movies.

Wherever I went, I heard music (that rock and roll pabulum). The volume and intensity never changed, no matter how fast I ran through the halls, because the house knew where I was and would activate the speakers in hallways as I came to them. When I opened a window to get some fresh air, the breeze wouldn't come in, because the house regulated the temperature at a steady 23°C, no matter the time of day or the weather outside. The house, sensing when I stood up, flushed the toilet beneath me when I rose from the seat.

It's still there, John. All Gates' riches are still there. I spent a fascinating afternoon with the DaVinci Notebooks (until a robot showed up and insisted that I play a computer game, Interactive Leonardo!, instead). The Renoirs, Van Goghs, and Christopher Lanes are still there, gathering dust. I even found one or two collections that the public doesn't know about. Gates' medieval torture devices, for example. Computer hardware had been attached to some of the machines, as if Gates or someone else had tried to modify, or modernize, them.

I spent two weeks exploring the maze-like mansion before I got the lay of the land. It took me two weeks to understand how the parts of the vast mansion fit together and which part of the mansion I was being excluded from. I was being kept out of the west wing. Whenever I made my way to the west wing, Gates' robots stopped me. Now I knew where Gates was.

Weak from a diet of junk food, delirious from not being able to sleep on account of the loud rock and roll music that the house blared at me, I nevertheless continue to pursue Gates. Doors in the west wing were closed to me, so I tried climbing down laundry chutes and heater vents, only to be rebuffed on the other side by a smiling robot who asked how I got to be "such a lost little puppy," or some such thing. But I was determined to find Gates, and I kept trying, and finally I had the good luck to stumble across another corpse in a crawl space. What was that corpse doing there? John, *we are not the first whom the Gates heirs hired.* We're not the first by a long shot. They hired others to find out if Gates is dead, four others to be exact. I found all four corpses.

I took the first corpse's computer-badge. Now I had the power of two. His badge combined with my badge gave me access to a few more rooms, and in one of those rooms I found another corpse. I put his badge on, too. Now I had the power of three. You get the idea. I found the corpse of each detective they hired before us. I got the badge of each detective who died of junk food malnutrition and lack of sleep. Each had tried and failed to find Gates, but had not tried in vain. Each bequeathed me his computer-badge. And with the power of four, I found Gates.

I found him in the west wing, in a room decked out to look like a spaceship in an early science fiction film: high ceilings, swivel chairs, huge computer screens with flickering, ever-changing images. An entourage of robot nurses and servants eagerly attended to Gates's every wish.

In silken robes much too big for his shrunken body, he looked like a weak, feeble Chinese king. I might not have recognized Gates if not for his trademark horn-rim glasses.

"Mr. Gates," I asked, "how are you today, sir?"

They turned him about in his wheelchair so he could face me. A robot gently grasped his skull-like head in her hands and lifted it in my direction.

"Fine and dandy is what Billy is today," the robot said.

"Do you need any help Mr. Gates?" I asked him. "Would you like me to help you?"

"Mr. Gates is as happy as a clam and he doesn't need any help, thank you," said the robot with a smile.

Trapped, I decided. Gates was trapped by his robots, was trapped by the software he had so lovingly created. They invited me to dinner. Gates never said a word. While one robot spoon-fed him, others kept up a lively conversation and spoke and answered in Gates's name. Whatever they said, it always began with "Bill thinks" or "Bill says" and ended with "Isn't that right, Bill?" or "Bill's nodding because he agrees." He couldn't swallow, much less talk. I looked closely at the green pallor of his skin. I looked closely at his shrunken head and the black patches on his scalp. I was, I realized, eating dinner with a dead man.

When the robot who had been feeding Gates turned aside to get more popcorn, I grabbed the handles of Gates's wheelchair and pushed him down the hall as fast as I could. The music started. Gates keeled over and nearly fell out of his wheelchair, but I managed to prop him back up and still elude the robots who chased us. Doors opened for us instantly. This was, after all, Bill Gates who I was pushing, king of the house, and he could go anywhere and do anything. I heard the robots right at my heels. It was as if I had robbed the queen from the center of the hive and now the swarm chased me because of it.

At last I came to an octagonal room and slammed a door behind me. Robots beat at all eight doors. Then I had an idea: I unpinned Gates's computer-badge and pinned it to myself. Five or six of the doors crashed open.

"Leave us," I commanded. "Leave us this instant."

Gates had spoken. All the robots went away peacefully.

Is Bill Gates dead? The answer is yes and no. He programmed his own soul into the software on the computer-badge that I now wear. Gates, more than any other software robber baron, perfected the idea of "service software." He thought software should serve in every way, even if it meant robbing people of their free will. At the end of his life, the robots he programmed carried his corpse through all the motions of a normal life. Not only did they feed him, they made conversation for him. They made decisions for him. They lived in his place.

Bill Gates, his corpse stinking and rotting in the octagonal room, is dead and yet still alive. He is alive as long as the software on the computer-badge I wear functions. And that's the problem, John. Gates programmed the software to slowly take over his duties and responsibilities as he grew older. Even as I write this, Gates's robots are wiping my brow with warm wash clothes and massaging my back. I need to reprogram the software to make it think that Gates has grown younger and stronger, to make it think that Gates can once again make decisions on his own. But I don't have the knowledge to do that. I don't know enough about programming. Besides, computers aren't used to relinquishing power. Once they have it, they never give it back.

STORIES

HYPERACTIVE BEFORE MY TIME

I guess what really got me to hating Commies was that article in *Life* about the two-headed dog. Hideous black-and-white photos billed as a miracle of Soviet surgery. The dogs looked stupid; tongues out, eyes glazed. Russians didn't even have a sense of humor about it. Didn't graft the head, say, of a Chihuahua onto a St. Bernard. Oh no; although they dress like the Three Stooges and jabber worse than Donald Duck, Commies don't know how to be funny. They simply stitched the head of a corgi onto a lab mix. Both heads similar in size.

The fear was next they'd do this to people. Soldiers show up with two heads. Soon whole divisions of the Red Army boast twice the eyes, twice the ears, twice the thinking power.

In future negotiations we might find ourselves dealing with Krushchev and Castro *on the same body*; presumably that of Krushchev. The Russians had already launched Muttnik—the space pooch. (Who had died out there spinning around.) No telling what data obtainable when they orbited a two-header. Maybe enough to jump years ahead on The Bomb. Relegate our own to the level of firecrackers and sling-shots; leave America defenseless.

The dogs had died. The lab head first. But not before both survived several hours; thereby advancing the frontiers of science. Russian science. They weren't about to share. Only eager to gloat over the proof of their triumph.

A tear splatted the slick photo. I wasn't scared, I wasn't sorry. It was a tear of envy, a tear of rage.

I slapped the *Life* onto the dinette table. Swore then and there, from that moment on, to play catch-up. Why, I'd surpass the damn Russians—make a *six-headed* dog!

I stepped outside for a walk around the neighborhood.

Our family dog was a German shepherd. She had a long neck. I figured, if I limited myself to dachshunds, cockapoos, schnauzers and such, I could easily splice on six heads collarwise. For a seventh—bonus—the skull of that obnoxious Pekinese up the block right between Trudy's ears. I'd show those godless Commies.

My penny loafer kicked a piece of gravel. It skipped across the sidewalk and into the driveway where it belonged.

Hell, I could never transplant a dog head. I was only in the fifth grade. A straight-A student, sure; but it took at least college for brain operations.

Russia was a nation of idiots. They couldn't understand our way of life. But that didn't mean they hadn't done their homework. Especially in areas with potential military application.

I rounded the corner—saw Mrs. Bernstein's dachshund with her butt up against the butt of Buddy, the Sinclair's sheltie. They faced opposite points of the compass. They were panting hard, but at the moment not moving. They had apparently just undergone a struggle. Had some vandal epoxied together their rears?

I approached the dogs standing anxiously on Mr. Johnson's lawn. Examined where the long-haired miniature collie's rump met smooth dachshund butt.

Nope. No evidence of glue or cement. No strings attached. No rubberbands.

Holy cow—a double dog! Had the whole world gone crazy?

Then it hit:

I could transplant *tails*. No harder than pinning one on a donkey. I could use Band-Aids and mercurochrome. Give the dog beer so she wouldn't hurt; wouldn't feel the stings of tails stuck around her neck. She could wear the Pekinese number like a pompon.

Since these two bowsers were totally immobilized, the de-tailing should go easy as candy from a baby. Trot home for safety pins and scissors. Tell Mom it's an art project for school. Perform the transplant down in the basement underneath Dad's workbench. Trudy likes to hang out there on hot afternoons anyway.

Neither the snipping nor the pinning would be a picnic. But in the advancement of science, what mattered the discomfort of a few canines? Besides, this would be less hazardous than a head job. And I could apply what I learned from the tailing toward making the cranial procedure safe and painless.

Meanwhile, soon as I'd pinned on the seventh tail, I'd phone *Life*. Have them send out a photographer. Prove to the world America was still in the competition.

At school, once the mag hit the stands, they'd promote me up to the ninth grade, maybe the tenth. No sense holding back a young scientist contributing to the defense of the Free World.

I hurried back home.

Mom knelt out in the backyard doing her Sunday weeding. Dad snored in his armchair—bowling on the TV.

I sneaked into the Singer. Appropriated scissors, couple dozen safety pins, needle and thread (realized sewing would make the job more permanent).

Removed a can of National Bohemian from the fridge. Dad wouldn't notice. He stayed so neutralized all weekend, I doubted he could tell the difference between six and five.

Slipped down into the basement.

Sure enough, there lay Trudy—stretched out in the shadows on the cool cement floor. I lifted the church key off Dad's tool rack. Cracked the National Bo. Poured cold beer into the dog's dish.

After a minimum of coaxing, she got to her feet. Padded over. Lapped curiously at the brew, wrinkling her nose as it fizzed. She'd never before sampled beer. Me neither. But it was cold, wet, foodlike. She caught on fast. Got into it. Slurped the bowl dry.

The dog was a good eater. She wasn't afraid to gulp a novelty.

She belched lightly. Walked over to her spot in the corner. Circled once. Flopped back down onto the cement.

Good. While I was out gathering tails, the beer would be taking effect.

I contemplated a moment her own long, curved, bushy endpiece. What was a tail, anyway, but an extension of the spine—a sort of antenna for the radio inside the brain?

A shiver coursed my spine: what if all those tails pinned and sewed to her neck increased Trudy's intelligence? With a thousand such dogs, the Free World might be safe forever!

I bolted upstairs. Tiptoed hastily through the living room. Carmen Salvino bowled a strike. The crowd cheered. Eyes closed, Dad grunted between the snores. I darted out the front door.

During Korea, Mr. Johnson had been a prisoner of war. He owned the most immaculate lawn on the block. His wife had just left him. There were no children. Rumor hinted his captors had done something unmentionable to that part of his body it isn't polite to discuss.

By his own admission, the Koreans had forced him to eat dogs. Maybe that's why his only pet was a black and chrome Ford Fairlane, which he kept brightly waxed.

Anyway, I found the double dog where I'd left it—square in the middle of Mr. Johnson's crewcut lawn. They had moved around a bit. The dachshund now faced the house, the sheltie the street. They weren't panting so hard. But they were still stuck tight.

"Nice doggie," I said.

Easing the scissors from my pocket, I patted Buddy's butt, then the dachshund's. They rolled their eyes. Lolled tongues. Looked unsure; although patient.

Something stank. I sniffed lightly. Like when you ate a lot of onions the night before, and your hand is on the lever, but you just don't quite wanna flush? Whatever, I didn't let it interfere with the job.

I lifted Buddy's feathery little tail out from the junction. Gently wedged the scissors at the base of his spine. If I cut quick, I doubted he'd notice. Hurt no more than trimming a giant tubular toenail.

I took a deep breath. My lungs filled with the stench, my mind with concentration. Precision was the order of the moment. This was for Ike, for America, for The World. Dirty godless Commies...

"Screw in my front yard, will ya?"

I looked up to behold Mr. Johnson emerge from the side of the house with a running hose in his fist. He had evidently been washing down the Fairlane. Flushed scarlet from his short thick neck to the peak of his bald dome, he screamed, "I'll kill ya—eat yr fuckin asses for *lunch!*"

I jumped back just as the water hit the junction full blast. Both dogs yelped, writhed, whimpered. Till a miracle occurred: they came apart. Poof! No more double dog.

In a flash I saw they had been pegged together by an appendage which on the playground kids call a *wiener*. Doubly odd, because wiener is another name for dachshund. But this was no time for reflection. I turned my back on the explosion of water, flesh, profanity. For dear life I sprinted home.

I rushed into the house.

Broke stride. Choked back my breath. Both precautions unnecessary—Dad still slept, the TV blared an ad for a cigarette if only you bought a carton everything would be gay, smooth, cool. I disappeared into the basement.

Boosted myself up onto the edge of the dryer. Sat catching

my breath, smelling bleach, Tide. Turned the gaze on Trudy.

She lay utterly passed out. Anaesthetized. Her jaw yawed open; her tongue kissed the cement like a pool of bubblegum. The beer had worked like a charm.

Suddenly the last idea of that hectic afternoon materialized:

Why not graft onto a human an *entire* dog? Use the peg between my legs—known to science as the *penis*, rhymes with tennis, sits above two balls, tied at love. Such a gambit would never occur to the Russians—mired in their Communist rules.

I smiled to myself, slipped down off the Maytag. Stepped over to the dog.

It took an American to arrive at the logical conclusion. We are a free people. Not a pack of zombies worshipping a red flag. We can vote. We can choose. We can *think*.

Would be strange at first, learning to walk on six legs. But at my disposal I'd have the dog's nose, her keen ears, her speed. She could bite the hell out of anybody who got too close. With practice, we might learn to sprint up to forty miles per hour. Come in handy if the Russians landed. Say there was an engagement with an isolated pocket of defenders—only the dog and me could get through.

Carefully I lifted her limp tail. Bent down on my haunches.

I needed to inspect what kind of socketry she had down there. I'd never before examined the dog this close.

Damn!

I let the tail clump back onto the cement.

The scissors. Back on Mr. Johnson's lawn I'd left Mom's *tool!*

I hurried upstairs, out of the house, into the sunshine. Noted briefly Dad had rolled over on his side, was no longer snoring; breathing heavily, mouth dropped open. A thought squirted I could peg that mouth. Dad was a ghost—floating through life, working in a Government office. Give him a taste of reality. But it was just the ghost of a thought. There were ghosts on the TV screen. But I had no time to monkey with rabbit ears.

I was down to the curb before the screendoor banged. On the way, nearly tripping over the scissors. What?

I stopped dead. Scurried back to the stainless steel stuck in a clump of crabgrass. We suffered from a crabgrass infestation. Nobody knew why. It was a mystery. Mom kept after it. Today, this was the only patch in sight. I knew, by late afternoon, Mom's trowel would get it.

I drew the tool from the tangled roots. Attached was a note:

"Keep your kid off my front yard. It ain't no whorehouse for beastialty."

I didn't understand all the words. But the gist was: nobody needed to see this. I crumpled the scrap of paper. Jammed it into my pocket. Likewise the scissors. Crept back into the house.

The TV concerned itself with a repeat of a John Wayne movie. Conestoga wagons wobbled fuzzily through sand. The screen was snowy, the movie old—pre–WW II. Oxen bellowed. Horses neighed. Dust swirled. A Hollywood orchestra aped cowboy schmalz. I hated John Wayne. His movies were endless. Even *Iwo Jima* was mostly talk, cigarettes, less than 20% firepower. I sympathized with Dad sleeping through this one.

Infiltrated the sewing room. Inserted the scissors back into the middle drawer of the Singer. Silently closed the drawer. There. I was blame free. Everything back in place.

I pulled out the wadded note. Put it in my mouth. Thoughtfully chewed. Ink, paper, touch of scissors oil, suggestion of crabgrass. I wandered into the dinette.

Eyed the *Life* on top of the laminated drop-leaf table:

Filthy propaganda. Sure, Muttnik rang the bell. Thanks to a dog, the Russians were still a few years ahead in space. This however—I sneered at the photo of the two-headed freak—merely constituted an attempt to bulldog the American public with a farce our science wouldn't touch with a ten-foot tongue depressor. This wasn't science—this was the *circus.*

Less than an hour ago, I'd been a believer. I suddenly saw how easily a brain could get washed.

Dad sometimes muttered the Koreans musta washed Mr. Johnson's brain. He and Dad never saw eye to eye. Anymore, they didn't even speak.

OK—I'd scrap all designs on canines. Avoid altogether Mr. Johnson's yard. Devote more time to the new math—*that* way beat the Russians.

I heard Dad, out in the livingroom, stir. The TV was selling women's underwear. The ad where the bra comes to life. I liked that one. It held my attention. Aerodynamics, drama, girlie jokes—all rolled into one.

But right now I didn't have time for such trash. I'd go wash the hands. Have another go at the math homework. It was the least I could do to help America catch up.

Soon Mom would finish with the crabgrass. Come in, heat up supper. I swallowed the chewed-up note. (Gah, yuk.) Confident, as I stood at the sink, mixing hot and cold to the precise temperature, that even if tomorrow bits bobbed up in the toilet, nobody but nobody would ever know. It would be scientifically impossible to reconstruct the evidence from whatever traces survived digestion.

I was glad I didn't need to hurt the dog. Or put her life at risk by grafting onto her neck extra heads.

I worked the Lifebuoy between my palms. Spread lather over the backs of my hands. Trudy was my friend. We played fetch and took walks together. Hell, someday we still might try that six-legged maneuver. Seemed harmless. I'd keep a hose handy in case we got stuck. Worth a little discomfort and embarrassment. After all, there were possible military applications.

This Cold War was a bitch. We had to make so many *sacrifices*.

Russia was a cold, cold country. In Russia, people lived like dogs. To them, the life of a dog meant nothing.

I replaced the Lifebuoy in the dish. Washed and washed and washed. Rinsed thoroughly. Dried. Marched down the hall to my room and the homework.

FINGERPAINTING IN THE VOMIT

In elementary school, I dug fingerpainting hydrogen bomb blasts. I made heavy use of oranges, yellows, reds. All afternoon I spent perfecting my mushroom cloud, till I caught the teacher's eye, and she asked what it was, and I'd carefully explain it was a thermonuclear detonation. A fusion bomb. *Not* a mere A-bomb. A hydrogen bomb is *triggered* by a fission bomb—that's how weak an A-bomb is compared to the mighty fusion-powered H-bomb. I wasn't a genius. My IQ was, and probably still kind of is, 127. I was a precocious little smartass who had absorbed Walt Disney's cartoon movie *Our Friend the Atom*. And here I kneel, 127 years later, fingerpainting in the vomit.

Probably the Quaalude on top of the Rainier ale, after the MDA. Quaalude is related to barbiturates, and when mixed with booze, Green Death in particular, will surely make you puke. Green Death is the brew that slew the Northwest. By alcohol content, it is only twice as strong as your run of the mill malt. But there is something special about Rainier ale that puts you on your butt faster than a mule kick to the breadbasket. Perhaps the effect of light bent through the green bottle?

Nuclear explosions fuse sand into green glass. This was noticed at the first burst, on the New Mexico desert, when thousands of hunks of green glass were found littering ground zero. I once saw a TV sci-fi show in the 50s, where the hero trapped the aliens by spotting a trail of green glass left by their nuke-powered spaceship.

Few folks on the street or in the lab agree what MDA stands for. Some say methylene-dioxy-amphetamine. Some something else that ends in *-amine*. I used to deal the stuff, and jokingly tell my customers: Most Die Afterwards. An apt label, since forebodings of doom are often experienced under the drug's influence.

MDA appears to fall near the middle of the psychomimetic spectrum determined at one end by methedrine, at the other by mescaline. Yielding an effect that is wiry, but also visionary. Resulting in a heady sex trip. People claim there is nothing like sex on MDA. I wouldn't know. The stuff immobilizes me; shrinks my unit to a lump of ABC chewing gum; makes me too paranoid to communicate, much less to initiate the Big Tickle.

Hence the Rainier ale—to oil my joints. Get me to feeling whole; so I can walk around and utter stupidities, or at least monologue at the wall intelligently.

After the six-pack, I went to a party and took some Quaalude. Once lewded-out, I sampled the bourbon, then somebody suggested I take five more hits. I must have, because childhood memories besieged me, as I lay on the bathroom floor, supposing people actually were peeing in the toilet, and not my ear. Quaalude, besides knocking you flat, and being an aphrodisiac, induces memories from childhood you'd thought long lost; or maybe you never had lost, but you're too high to remember.

In second grade, I became obsessed with computing people's energy. Again, I had learned the formula from Walt Disney: 34596 followed by six zeroes, times the weight, equals the energy. I would amaze my contemporaries by converting their mass into energy, all according to E equals mc-squared—the motto of the Twentieth-Century Genius.

The fat girl got a little embarrassed. Although her blush was more fueled with pride at the string of numbers announcing the energy she could become. Was there not also a tinge of lust to that florid, pudgy visage? There was. The next day she tried to dryhump me in the coat closet. I was too slow to figure out what was going on. I was only seven. Besides, my IQ was thirteen points under the minimum for genius. Today, I would've slammed it to her. Puking, flaccid, stupid— what the hell? The only reason to refuse a fat girl is because you are a sadist.

One afternoon I stuck a wad of ABC gum at the bottom of my mushroom. Teacher came by, and she already knew this was little Willie's rendition of a thermonuclear explosion. But she had to ask about the gum.

"That's the hospital we dropped it on," I said, realizing—as I spoke—I had made a mistake. The Hiroshima device was *not* thermonuclear; just a firecracker of a fission bomb. But, although teacher was twelve at the Attack of Hiroshima, when I was negative five, she didn't catch my lapse. She smiled. Moved onto the next child, who was touching up a landscape of lollipop trees, smeared flowers, happy puppies.

At least—I coughed bile—I hadn't told the *truth*, that it was Already-Been-Chewed doublemint. *Not* the nature of the bolus at the bottom of tonight's H-bomb.

Trying to visualize myself as negative five, into my head popped remembrance of the genie in the bottle.

A fisherman netted the bottle. When he went ashore and uncorked it, into the sky mushroomed smoke, atop which glowered the hateful genie. The fisherman tricks the genie back into the bottle. And the captive grants him three boons. Humankind has not yet done this with atomic power, despite the efforts of Disney's animation.

I sniffled, swirling curlicues into the cloudcap. Tonight, I brought up the same problem, staggering out of the bathroom. My interlocutor, perhaps not quite as stewed as me, claimed, since it was July 4, it was time to go out on the lawn and hurl crackers. He had a dozen M-80s and a few cherry bombs.

I used a thumb to make upthrusts in the stem of the mushroom. My canvas was troweled cement—probably on my hands and knees down in the finished basement, sunrise, nobody around, everybody passed out. My thrusts and turbulences held true in the soupy medium. Dinner I had eschewed; not wanting to mingle food with MDA. Thus, no chunks. Save the masticated cherry bomb, which I moved to the center of the base of the explosion.

I feared at first it was a tampon, because of the dream, while on the floor, and somebody pissed, while probably changing one.

I was porking Patsy, the fat girl, back in second grade. She met my every thrust with a hump. Together totaling but fourteen years and 190 pounds, we mated faster than helium fused by a righteous mass of Plutonium. So frenetic grew our rut, my cock popped off. Snapped at the base. Horrified, but still horny as a nine-peckered Sal Mineo, I groped inside her yoni. Eventually finding the thing, but it slipped my grip; till I located nature's equivalent to a Tampax string. I removed the devil by this bizarre appendage. Held it up to the light, as Patsy humped away.

A sort of hydra sprouted at the bottom of the penis. The hydra waved in the light, indicating it was out of its element. I crammed the organ back into the hole above my testicles. With a *whoosh!* it took, sucked back on solid as ever.

Having flushed, the anonymous waddled out of the bathroom. And I was left with the castrated half-thought: nukes will destroy even menses. As human life, vertebrate life, possibly *all* life goes up in a cloud of idiocy and confusion. Tell Disney that.

"I'll swallow that bomb!" I screamed into the night, snatching out of his hand an about-to-be-lit. Tasted worse than maggots in shit. He shoved me away, grumbling I was too loaded to appreciate our nation's birthday.

I reeled inside, down to the basement, to be left alone, to vomit.

Why no green glass on the beach around the fisherman's bottle? Can the genie in Rainier ale be tamed? Is drunkenness a boon likelier than nuclear benevolence? I am high as a kite, diddling with my puke— are you somebody pushing a button?

Then came the whirl into unconsciousness. To awaken here, fingering the hospital at ground zero.

TAKING CARE OF THE POOR

Slaps a thin record in a fairly new green folder on my desk. Green means the middle two digits of the case number are between 40 and 49. The State stocks folders in nine other colors. Brown is 50 to 59, blue is 60 to 69, so on. I look up. It's Rob Hardesty.

"Here's a plum for you." He smiles under his thick black mustache. Except for his New York accent, Rob could be a stand-in for Burt Reynolds. A shade younger than the swaggerer from *Deliverance*.

"I couldn't figure it out." He purses his lips, shakes his head. "You got time for it?"

"Maybe." I peer back down at the paperwork he has interrupted. Rob is a new worker. Hired permanently three months ago. I'm a temporary. An emergency hire. I come and go. For fifteen years I have been coming and going. On the average, I work about ninety days a year. No benefits, no vacation, no retirement—just enough to squeak by at my accustomed poverty level. One of my chores, one of my many chores, is to assist new workers with their thornier cases.

"The hospital is calling," he says above my head. "They seem pretty desperate for their money. The bills exceed $100,000. I did my best. But I can't make it fit the format. The whole debt accrued in less than one twenty-four hour period. I'm sorry to hit you with this if it's a bad time…"

I smile up into his frown. That's all I needed. The magic word. A brief sorry.

I tell him this is a sorry place, and it's always a bad time. But a hundred thou is a lotta dough. No wonder they're complaining. It's part of our job, after all, to see the hospitals get paid… get paid *something*. Sure, I'll do it.

"Thanks, man." He shakes his head one last time—not so sadly, more businesslike. Hitches his belt. Struts back down the aisle to his own desk.

Leaf through the folder. Papers seem to be here, but not in order. "Consent to Release Information" shouldn't be on top. Should appear below prior history.

Undo brad. Note "Consent" form signed by guardian. How old is this person? Thumb down a dozen pages till I reach "Hospital Admit Sheet." Place "Consent" on top of "Admit." Reorganize a few pages in prior history. Reinsert and fold back down brad. Gaze at "Initial Food Stamp Interview," now correctly positioned as first page of file:

DOB: 5/2/76. Just turned seventeen at time of interview.

No permanent address. Living on the streets. Currently unemployed. Not in school, schooling incomplete. Single. No dependents.

What was this person in for? How did she ring up in less than one day a hundred thousand dollars?

Flip back to "Admit Sheet." Her name: Plumb, Tracy NMN. DOB: 5/2/76. Admitted: 6/15/93, 14:52. Parent: Unknown. Guardian: Joellen Thompson. Method of Arrival: Puget Sound Airlift from Renton to Soundview helipad, Samaritan ambulance from helipad to emergency room.

Then a code I don't immediately apprehend: SIGSW. Rest of the page crammed with letters, figures, shorthand. Discharge must be on back. Turn sheet over ...

Discharged to: Mortuary.

Tracy (No Middle Name) Plumb didn't make it.

Oh yes, GSW—gunshot wound. And SI, well, that must be ... self inflicted.

I scan the next sheet, the "Operative Report." Heart rate 30, BP extremely low, difficult to ascertain; trauma-induced coma. Skip past the prepping, the putting of the patient on a ventilator, the palping of the entry wound in the left parietal, the excision of the skull.

The proof of the pudding: a small caliber bullet lodged deep in the left temporal lobe ...

In a failed attempt to revive a seventeen-year-old suicide, they spent 10 percent of a million dollars. Why not spend that much working to keep the bullet out of her head in the first place?

Using the eraser end of a pencil, I page back to the food stamp interview. My eyes light on the blank below the question *How do you get food if you have no income?* (The Federal Government requires this question be answered in writing, so the worker can determine if perhaps the client is capable of existing on air, dirt, rainwater or other sources of free food, and thus can be declared ineligible for food stamps, thereby saving the government up to $100 a month.)

Six weeks before her suicide, Tracy Plumb had penciled: I just don't eat. The irregular scrawl of a street kid telling the truth: I just don't eat.

"Can you take a phone call?"

I squint up from the record. Betsy Feldman, my leadworker, is leaning over me.

"It's from Soundview. Rob says you have the record."

"Tracy Plumb?"

"Yes. I know you're swamped with those cases I loaded you up with this morning. But," she rolls her computer-weary eyes, "they say they don't wanna talk to Rob anymore on this particular problem. I thought maybe ..."

I say sure. I was just familiarizing myself with the case. Put it through.

Betsy's menopausal face yields a taut smile. She rushes back to her desk to transfer the call.

When it rings, Pavlov flipflops—my mouth dries. I pick up the phone.

It's Harry Smart, from the Medicaid unit up at Soundview. I've never met Harry. Few in my hundred-person office ever have. But we all at one time or another—some of us more than once a day, day after day—deal with Harry over the phone. Good old disembodied Harry. He's the chief liaison between our State-run County Medicaid Office and the largest hospital in the state, which is owned and operated by the University—yet another organ of the State.

He wants to know why "that idiot" Rob Hardesty mailed a Medicaid coupon dated *backwards?*

I say into the mouthpiece that Rob is new, and assuredly has an IQ of at least 101—what more do you want from a State worker?

Harry's high voice keens into my ear he doesn't care if Rob was born yesterday—there's no excuse for generating a coupon dated: valid June 15 through June 14. It'll bounce. The computer will never take it. Soundview Hospital is gonna wind up eating the entire hundred thousand bucks!

I gaze down at the "Education" section of Tracy Plumb's food stamp application. She dropped out in the tenth grade, due to a drug problem. Needed to find work to support her habit. "Doesn't make sense to me either, Harry," I say. "First I've heard of it. I haven't even looked at the bills yet. Can I call you back in half an hour?" She worked part time at McDonald's for a year. Fired for not showing up twice in one week. Unemployed since. Ineligible for Unemployment Compensation. On the waiting list to get into Treatment. "Probably a simple mistake. You know how complicated our calculations get. I'll shoot you a corrected coupon in this afternoon's mail."

A frantic female voice in Harry's office butts in. I hear the rustle of a hand covering his mouthpiece. Over the line a less-than-polite conversation ensues unintelligibly.

I thumb sixteen pages forward to the eight-page computer print-out "Itemized Billing Statement" received over six weeks ago from Soundview billing department and filed by Rob in the correct (for once!) spot.

I scrutinize the "Date Incurred" column. Nothing on the 14th, nothing earlier. Nothing on the 16th or after, because the 15th was her last day on earth. No, this child's first and only contact with the medical establishment occurred entirely on the 15th of June. Had she managed to get into Treatment, had any other kind of routine medical or psychological care been available to her income bracket, she already would have received Medicaid and this conundrum been avoided.

But America firmly believes in waiting till the wolf snarls in the kitchen before arriving on the scene to offer assistance ... our fixation with stepping in at the eleventh hour, only then rolling up our sleeves to pitch in wholeheartedly with our most sophisticated weaponry ... did I say *heart*?

"Look, I gotta go," Harry's voice comes back over the phone. "Some other goddamn pressing issue has come up. I can't submit this absurdity. I may as well throw the account into collection."

"Harry, wait!"

"It's not my job to decipher the nightmares you clowns create. Nice chatting. Bye."

Slowly responding to the click on the other end, I cradle my own receiver. My eyes drift back down the columns of dot-matrix figures:

6/15/93	ventilator	$8,000.00
6/15/93	IV hookup	$2,587.00
6/15/93	syringe	$5.98
6/15/93	shunt	$125.00 ...

Why didn't she aim better—irredeemably blow out her lights before the meddling medics arrived? Is it that hard to shoot out some vital center in your own brain? Even so, the best they could've made of this teen was a cabbage.

Shame she couldn't afford a shotgun. Open her mouth, jam the barrel against her palate. Disintegrate the entire brain pan with one blast—four pounds of slop to decorate the ceiling. Try to make *that* show a pulse. Lucky to be able to steal a tiny caliber target pistol ... lucky Tracy "I Just Don't Eat" Plumb.

The phone rings. It's Joellen Thompson, the guardian. Per regulation, she also received a copy of the medical coupon in today's mail. Understandably, she doesn't understand it. She called Rob. Rob turned her over to Betsy. Betsy gave her my number.

While talking to the guardian, explaining neither do I know what's going on, I wheel my chair over to my monitor. Get into the coupon generation screen. I re-input the data: name of client, dates of service, name of provider, client DOB, SSA# ...

"The man at the hospital," she says in my ear, "says I'm stuck with the whole bill if you people won't cover the charges. Threatened me with a collection agency. I'm the eighth or ninth foster parent Tracy had. She ran away from me two years ago. Am I really gonna owe a hundred thousand dollars just cause I signed that form at the hospital that afternoon they helicoptered her in and I ... I mean, she ..."

"Look," I speak into the mouthpiece to cover the catch in her voice, as I type into the computer under the field "Client's

Address": *General Delivery, Seattle, WA 98111.* "I'm going to get to the bottom of this, Ms. Thompson. I'm redoing Rob's calculation this instant."

She sniffles, sighs; but does not sob. "I only got a part-time job at Fred Meyer. This is a one-bedroom. I let Trace have the couch when she was with me. Hardly blame her for moving on. I don't know where she got the gun. Said she had a boyfriend down in Renton. I seen him once, waiting out in his car at the curb. I'm not the one to judge, but frankly he looked more like a pimp..."

The Welfare Manual demands I type in all eight pages of bills. But I hit the *pagedown* and *area total* keys simultaneously, then type $100,000, thus lying to the computer in a relatively truthful manner. Into the mouthpiece I mutter, "You've been dealing with Harry Smart at Soundview?"

She says yes, *Harry*—latching onto a familiar chair thrown overboard shortly after they kicked her off the boat into these cold roiling seas of bureaucracy. "He's a nice man. Been very patient with me through all this."

"He's an asshole!" I almost find myself blurting. Instead type in the six-digit case number.

I reflect, well, Harry is overworked at his toil of striving to squeeze enough money out of the Medicaid system to keep the hospital solvent. Even if we get this coupon to work, Soundview grosses only $12,000—Medicaid pays about 12 percent on most procedures, and its acceptance renders pursuit of any other source of payment illegal. On the other hand, he'd never get more than a thousand or two out of a little old lady struggling to make ends meet as a part-time department store clerk. Of course, he's a State worker like me—gets paid the same whatever happens. Although we are both audited, supervised, under pressure to produce.

The computer doesn't accept the case number. I typed the last digit wrong. I type back in all six digits.

"Sir...are you still there?"

"Harry is a hard worker; one heckuva good guy. Look, Ms. Thompson, can I call you back in half an hour?"

"Can a collection agency repossess my car? All I got's a 1978 Valiant, worth about $500. Puddle-jumper takes me to and from work. Ain't even insured. Also I got no other insurance..."

I confess to know nothing of collection agencies. Except they phone a lot. Sometimes call all hours of the night. But I doubt *legally*...

The sob finally escapes: her faced with financial ruin, Tracy dead, she doesn't understand why...

"I don't either understand why the coupon came out backwards!" I type the address of Soundview Hospital. The cursor jumps to the field labeled "Guardian's Address." "You're still at 526 Melrose, 98102?"

"I...yeah. Lived here since '74. This is low-income housing. Can't afford to move."

"OK. I'm completing the rework. In the unlikely event it still comes out backwards, I'll call the State Office to determine the difficulty. Can I call you back in forty-five minutes?"

"Sure. This is my day off. Will they garnish my wages? I hardly get nothing as ..."

"I'm hanging up now, Ms. Thompson."

"Please don't not call back like Harry sometimes. I'll be here all day, right by the phone. I, uh ... OK."

"I told you two hours ago—I threw that case into collection. Old what's-her-name the guardian is now 100 percent liable. I don't have time for this! Do I hafta lodge a complaint with your ...?"

"Harry, I have since spoken with the State Office." Six experts. Six different humans puzzling over my question; grumbling at me for calling; putting me on hold; transferring my quirky query ... till the *seventh* was able to finger the crux of the screwup. "Harry, there's nothing wrong with that coupon. It's *supposed* to read backwards."

"You redid Rob's work?"

"Yes. Mine came out backwards, too. Down at State Office I finally reached a programmer who understood enough about how Medicaid meshes with hospital billing systems. It seems the computer is rigged to reject any eligibility period shorter than two days; most periods of course last thirty days to six months. This prevents the accidental typing of the same date in both the 'Period Begins' and 'Period Ends' boxes. The computer is trying to help us. Just like the surgeons tried to help Tracy Plumb."

"We have lots of stays of only one day ..."

"Yes. But then they follow up as outpatients or next month see a doctor for cast removal, prosthesis fitting, chemotherapy, whatever. It's unusual for you guys to kill a new patient utterly within the confines of one calendar day."

"I thought she killed herself ..."

I tell Harry to please be quiet. Just resubmit the coupon.

"I tore it up."

"I'll mail you my regenerated coupon. The thing'll read 6/15 through 6/14—just like the one Rob sent. That's how the computer alerts itself the client is eligible for coverage of one day and one day only."

"That's stupid."

"Yeah. You're Smart. I'm Medicaid—we're Stupid. Did you notify the collection agency, can you still call them off?"

He says if he hangs right up he can retrieve the letter just in time. Thing is, he called the guardian over an hour ago. Told her Medicaid refused to pick up the tab, she was liable, should make immediate payment arrangements with Ace Collections.

"You *didn't!*"

"I was tired of this crap. First Rob's three weeks late with his work. Then the coupon doesn't make sense. Then *you* claim you're gonna start the whole process over. We lose these accounts altogether if we don't initiate collection within a ninety-day timeframe. It's been eighty-nine days ... I gotta run down to the mailroom, intercept that letter to Ace before it goes out."

I ask how she took it—was Ms. Thompson reasonably OK with the disaster?

"She wept. I couldn't even get her to take down Ace's number, through all her blubbering." His voice breaks into a shriek: "I'm an ogre! an asshole! I made a *mistake!* Tried too hard to coax in a dollar to help keep this charity ward afloat. Now you call her back, tell her the good news, take all the credit. I'm running my ragged ass down to the mailroom!"

Click. Dial tone.

My cold sweaty index punches Joellen Thompson's number. I am two hours behind in my work. Behind the phone, to the left of the monitor, lurk ten other cases—stacked, waiting to be certified or denied by 5 P.M. I have worked through lunch. On the other end, the phone begins to ring. My stomach growls. I swallow dry spit.

Her phone rings and rings. Continues to ring. Clutching the receiver to my ear, I stand up. Glance over the top of my cubicle; beyond the hive of other cubicles; through the sealed-shut windows on the south wall of our 5,000 square feet of climatically controlled working environment.

Outside it rains. An all-day storm. Rain streaking the windows. Low, heavy black clouds causing traffic on the boulevard to drive with their lights on. Not at all an afternoon to leave the apartment.

A chilly ruthless afternoon in September. A time for hanging around the television. A soap, a magazine, a glass of economy port, maybe a nap.

Hanging around, hanging around ... a handful of pills, your head in the oven, a can of Drano, a bottle of bleach, a razor to the wrist. I'm not counting, but it feels like over fifty rings. Nobody could nap through that.

I hang up. Sit back down.

Leave it alone. Give her time. Let the situation ripen. Let it fall from the branch. If she's DOA or, better yet, dead on the *scene*, the taxpayer can heave a sigh of relief. No hospital in America will

213

spend a dime on attempting to revive a certified *corpse*. Besides, this is all fantasy. She probably took her puddlejumper out for a scenic drive on the Cascade Highway in the freezing downpour.

Let Harry call her in the morning.

It isn't my job to phone wild suicide suspicions to 911. My appointed task is either to deny, or to send out correctly-dated medical coupons. Which Rob already did. And I did again.

Grab off the stack the next record. A wrinkled yellow folder fat as a dictionary.

THE WILLIE SMITH FILE

Dear *Corpse*—

We heard fourteen gunshots just a moment ago. After all, it IS Saturday night on Seattle's lovely Beacon Hill. Perhaps someone did not get what they wanted. And when they fired upon the person who was thwarting his/her immediate desire, perhaps that person fired back. One never knows when one hears shots ring out down the block of a Saturday night. Perhaps it is merely the Mexicans playing William Tell with their myriad wives.

But we are so frightfully gunshy that we did snap off the lights and crawl to the phone. Dialed 911. Told the pimp answering on the other end that we had just heard fourteen gunshots possibly just down the block, although things echo weirdly around here, this is a largely Asian neighborhood, and Asians do love their fireworks. However, a gunshot does have a bit of nastiness no firecracker possesses, and we truly feel it was gunfire.

Sure, they'll send a cop out to have a look in, oh, maybe before Sunday sunrise. It can't be important—no corpses, right?

"Right," my wife breathed into the phone in our darkened bedroom, cradled the receiver. Come to Seattle, *Corpse*. You will no doubt recognize yourself here.

Past few months I have been working as a temp in a mental health clinic. I'm a medical records clerk. $7 an hour minus any benefits imaginable, including sick pay, paid holidays and the right to have more than two seconds notice before being told to vamoose, pack up and split; no more job. I have come to think of life as nothing more than a temp assignment in hell.

The job ends next week. I've saved enough to live for a good 4 to 6 weeks with nothing to do but drink beer, smoke, pray, dream, ejaculate & write. Is this Heaven or do we gotta get off already?

THE MORNING AFTER: On my morning constitutional through my trashed neighborhood I found nary a casing. Although I did, down the block, discover a stripped car, sat up on bricks, wheel-less, windows open, glove compartment yawned wide. A late-Seventies white Monte Carlo, license #949 EXD. I used to come home with lines of poetry in my head, upon returning from a morning constitutional. Now it's license numbers, bullet casings and the addresses of abandoned houses where I saw doors kicked in and evidence of crack squatters.

From the Sunday morning paper my wife reads me snatches of Ann Landers, whose entire column this week is devoted to gun control. I think back with envy to just-conquered Berlin and the marvelous gun control the Soviets effected back then in May of 1945. The Red Army proclaimed it a capital offense for a German citizen to possess a firearm. The squads of soldiers duly went from house to house searching for guns.

At one not-too-badly bombed-out house, they went inside and discovered a child's BB gun. The soldiers took the adult male of the house outside into the street and promptly shot him dead, despite his frantic protestations that it was only his child's BB gun. This is the kind of gun control needed in my neighborhood. How about yours?

God Bless America,
Willie

RIGOROUS APPROACH

Late May. The weather beautiful. Just got layed off. Can afford to coast a couple of weeks before again going out to look for an office temp slot.

But the writing won't come. Not a story, not a line, not a picture. I'm stumped. To kill time, to deaden the frustration—decide to translate a little French.

Say the Baudelaire poem about the infamous corpse. I pick up my tattered, stained *livre de poche*. I have most of the original by heart. Good thing, in light of this fly-specked, come-unglued copy. But I've drunk my coffee, sun floods the room, and the first two quatrains ring through clear as a bell:

> Do you recall the thing we saw, my soul,
> That lovely sweet summer morning,
> At the crook of a path: a horrid corpse
> On a bed seeded with pebbles.
>
> Legs in the air like a slut,
> Smoldering and sweating poisons,
> It lay opening—nonchalant and cynical—
> Its belly full of fumes.

I'm not troubling with the rhymes. Just arranging the scene, sticking to the point, getting the details sharp. I consider changing soul to *lass* and corpse to car*cass*. But realize I'd be sacrificing clarity on a tin altar. Poetry is nothing if not clear.

The meter in the first quatrain quasi scans. Becomes anarchic in the second. I let it be. I'm not painting by numbers. I'm sketching another human's dream. A guy who happened to be the Edgar Allen Poe of France.

> The sun beamed down onto this rot,
> As if to cook it to perfection ...

I'm on the brink of typing: "And give back to Great Nature a hundredfold/All which together She once joined," when my fingers fall off the keys.

This isn't writing. This is rote. The coffee is wearing off. I'm nervous, fingers cold. Don't want another cup. I never have more than one a day.

I stand. Cross the room. I want another cup.

Coffee rots the gut, chafes the nerves. Taken to excess, clouds the brain. I need all the guts, brains and nerves I can muster to keep writing. That is, if I'm ever going to again. Maybe another cup would help?

But instead of going downstairs, to the pot on the stove, I stride through the hall into the bedroom. Gaze out the window, as I seem to remember I often do when cast adrift.

"All which together She once joined," voices mechanically inside my head, as I fully open the curtain, disgusted with the cheapness of my line.

God—why does coffee crash? And why not "cooked *thoroughly*"? And how come I'm not at work today laying out newspaper clippings for microfilming? Because the job ended, thank God, although my bank account doesn't know what to think. I'll get another position soon. Some other goddamn office where they need a gentleman types 55wpm, filing and sorting skills.

"Give back *centuple* to Great Nature"?

My backyard is a steep little tenth of an acre. Narrow lot; not too deep, but quite tall. The two lots to the south are one monstrous blackberry patch; they belong to an agent who bought them after their houses burned down—just before the Korean War. He's been waiting since for the value of real estate to rise. This is a poor neighborhood—freeway a furlong to the east. An unmaintained, forgotten City Park uphill to the west. North lie the rest of the houses on the skinny block. All housing on the other side of the street demolished ten years ago to allow for the freeway.

An eight-foot cedar fence rims our yard along the back

216

and the north. The 480,000 cubic foot blackberry patch adequately shields the south. My wife bought the fence during the Reagan Error. Her small business was then doing well. I've personally never been flush enough to afford a fence, especially one of cedar, eight feet high.

For the past two Administrations, her business has been failing. I could worry about that, too, as well as the possibility I won't find work for a couple of months; so maybe we can pay the rent with Xerox copies of my translation fragments. Good as gold. Cooked to perfection. Legs in the air like a hot trollop.

And then it dawns, as I notice the white slashes between the slats. The *position* is wrong. The lines shouldn't be white, because the sun still shines from the east, hasn't yet swung around from behind the fence. The slits look gray. The corpse should not be putrid. The fumes are false. Or else the "legs in the air" is a lie.

Baudelaire meant the equestrian position. A *car* sits out there, parked against the fence. An oval, showing white through the eighth-inch slits. Swing my head back and forth—strobing, to make sure. The white strobes are in the shape of a long American sedan, maybe a Buick, Mercury, Olds. Hard to tell when all you've got is twenty slits to strobe.

I hurry downstairs. Unlock the backdoor. Climb the two-by-four steps to the top of the backyard. Place my eye at a slit.

The equestrian is a position of rigor. As if the corpse were riding a vertical horse into the sky; but never, of course, getting off the ground. "Legs in the air slut-like" handily describes the assumption of this pose. As if the lubricious carcass were in the throes of receiving a much-needed missionary.

A Chevy Impala. '67, '68, '69. Four door. Toothpaste bodywork. Pitted, peeling roof. I shuffle two slits north. Squat down further—hoping to see in the... yeah!

Only one head visible. Young guy in the frontseat. Moustache; long, sweaty hair; t-shirt. Hodcarrier, shipscaler, carpenter—just off graveyard? or early lunch?

I center him in the slit.

He grips the wheel with both hands. Stares expressionless through his windshield into the weedy alley between the other side of my fence and the overhanging trees of the overgrown park. His lips are pursed.

For a split second I focus on the roar of the freeway—a quarter mile to my back. Like holding a seashell big as God to your ear. The God man made.

Rigor only lasts a dozen hours. After which the corpse conforms to the ministrations of gravity. The equestrian position is the musculature's last hurrah.

Paragons appear in photos snapped a few days after the Battle of the Bulge, deep in the heart of Luxemburg, during late December

217

of 1944. These display men slaughtered (what was the sex of Baudelaire's carcass?) in the snow. Cold as it was, it took a few hours before their bodies froze solid. Allowing time for rigor to set in among numerous specimens. Many of whom assumed the equestrian.

Up from under the steering wheel pops the second head. Flowing amber ringlets of a recent perm. She sits up in the seat beside him, licking her coral lips. Her face is chubby. She is large-bosomed, inside the pink jumpsuit. Must be under twenty-five. Any older, with her figure and lifestyle, she'd be gone utterly to fat.

Her door swings open. Bangs into the fence. I jerk back. Musn't let her spot my eye at the slit.

Doors open, doors close. What are they doing—getting out their guns, climbing over the fence to kill me, rob my house? Nonsense. This is the usual alley fare: routine prostitution.

I squint into the blue as the 747 flaps-down for a landing at Sea-Tac—twenty miles to the south.

I'll wait till the jet din fades, before risking another peek. Give them time to settle into their next position.

Mathew Brady's Civil War daguerreotypes, on the other hand, never show a carcass in the equestrian. Because all of his pictures were taken at least two to three days after the battle. Brady's corpses are obviously putrid and full of fumes—lying swollen and slack in the fields and forests of summer. Unlike those frozen in rigor at the Bulge. How could Baudelaire make such a mistake?

The jet is gone from sight, its behemoth vacuumcleaner almost out of earshot. I frogwalk south a couple slats—figuring they probably climbed into the backseat.

I hunch at the right slit—lined up with the backseat. And see by shadowy motions that they are indeed both in the back. But this is a lousy peephole; slats nailed too close; less than a sixteenth-inch wide. Even pressing my eye against the splintery cedar, I discern nothing but a jumble of shadows.

I'll hafta stand. Leap up. Grab the top of the fence. Hoist myself off the ground so I can look over the fence down into the backseat. Unless...

I remember the cinderblock. Been a while since I had to peer over the top. And I felt so bad then I hid it over by the ... ah, here it is.

I upend the cinderblock against the fence. Climb onto it. Both feet shakily balanced, straighten myself. Lift my chin over the edge.

They are in full career. Him on top—one knee on the seat, one foot on the floorboard. Her head is jammed against the inside of the door. His eyes squinted shut. Still wears his grimy t-shirt. His jeans drape the frontseat. The lass has removed her pink jumpsuit and wadded it for a pillow against the vinyl handle of the door. Neither seems to

218

have had on underwear. It *is* a hot morning.

Her carmine toenails brush the ceiling of the Chevy. Her legs in the air like a ...

He is slamming to beat the band. She meets the occasional thrust. Actually showing clear interest, considering her trade. Perhaps this is a *good* trick. Most often out here, I see the trulls helping out oldsters, or fatsos, or other flaccid types. At least this guy has muscles plus dedication.

On brittle springs the Impala chassis jounces.

Her breasts are indeed sizable, and he seems to notice them too, opening his eyes, grabbing her creamy teats.

Carefully lower my chin. He mustn't see. Eye contact forbidden.

My heart races. What if he looks up? What if the poem concerns an *animal* carcass—did I really know what the bastard *meant*? When he opened his eyes, went for her bosom—did he *spot* me?

Lower my head all the way below the edge of the fence. Stoop a moment to collect my thoughts.

In the fourth quatrain, the evanescent rhyme *epanouir/evanouir*: to bloom/to faint.

> And the sky surveyed the superb carcass
> Like a flower in bloom.
> The stink was so strong, that on the grass
> You thought you'd swoon.

Obviously the thing smelled. But now I think of it, the title *Une Charogne does* mean carrion or decayed carcass. Was the poem about a shot duck, I mean *buck*, left to rot at the bend of the path? or is it a possum an 1863 bicycle roadkilled? No possums in France. Must it be *France*?

I detect the reek of their sex filtering through the fence. Am I imagining things? Don't dare sniff. Make too much noise. Even above the freeway they might hear. A lot of johns scare easy. Especially when in naked delicto. Rather, delicto with no pants. Delicto bareassum. What the hell do I have to fear?

Lift my chin back up over the fence.

Still, if the legs are up—why is the carrion sweating poisons, crawling with vermin, rotten enough to make my soulmate nearly swoon on the grass? Don't the rules of rigor hold trans-species?

He's still pounding away, his long wet hair slapping his shoulders. He has torn off the t-shirt. At every stroke his abdominals ripple. The whore has anchored her feet on the ceiling. Slamming him back parry for thrust. It's hard to believe this is prostitution, so viciously it resembles love.

I begin to harden. Teetering atop the cinderblock, groin

shoved against the cedar. Her boobs bobble—chocolate nipples pouted tall. Her belly awash with shivers. Can't glimpse her face; her head wedged against the inside door handle.

Heartbeat shudders my body. I struggle to keep my eyes from throbbing in their sockets.

Her pubic hairs glisten jet black. His—russet. They collide insistently, like slamdancing rats; his busy penis all but invisible from my angle.

Perhaps it is love. Neither whores nor lovers sport badges. Is my alley the only sanctuary from his wife or her husband where they can consummate their affair?

And even if this be a drab and her mark, have I the right to spy out in the open—where a glance from either participant could stop the act cold? I've seen it happen before. Caused it, by seeing: the scramble for clothing, the dive into the driver's seat. Ignition turned. Vehicle backed out of alley while engine still cool.

So what is my position, as blocked writer, uncertain translator, office temp temporarily between assignments—am I an ecstasy wrecker, a saboteur of whoopee?

I am ashamed of what might happen, of what I am probably doing, of what has happened in the past. I'm ashamed of being so human as to be ashamed.

I slip down off the cinderblock. Turn. Slink back inside.

> The sun beamed down onto this rot,
> As if to cook it to a *turn*(?)

I hurry past the coffee pot. Decide to stick with *perfection*. Settle on the humanness of Baudelaire's dreamy corpse. Leave by the front door on a hike to the library. Hoping to calm my heart, to soothe the clammy fingers of my mind.

Maybe I'll find a good action-packed mystery that is straightforward on the rigor.

There are a lot of days like this—when I don't write.

Dear *Corpse*—

I have once again been talking to cops in the middle of the night. This time due to my wife's car having been hit-and-run and destroyed where it was parked out front. SCREECH...BAM! Delightful way to be awakened at 1:20 A.M. of a Thursday. It's been a good two years since we last conversed with cops in the middle of the night—the time our door was kicked down and my wife's purse stolen, before we could bolt out of bed and race downstairs to respond to the explosive racket of a dead-bolted door being kicked down. Then pursuing the spoor woke us up; plus the rude awakening at 3 A.M. last year or so when a cop was banging on the door wanting to know about some whores in our backyard. I'm surprised the city doesn't raise our property taxes—just because of all the free entertainment.

I have also been talking to people about dead animals. Being a city boy, I had to be told about why Baudelaire's carrion has its legs up in the air, and how this lubricious position has nothing to do with rigor or the equestrian position. All I ever see around here is dead dogs, poisoned rats and smashed pigeons. None of them ever seem to have their legs in the air. But my country friends have finally gotten through to me that cow carrion and such, once bloated, frequently roll over on their backs and project hoofs skyward. Still, I can't help but wonder if perhaps Mr. Baudelaire were not daydreaming of the *decidedly* lubricious pose of the equestrian position.

The afternoon of the night my wife's parked car was anonymously totalled, the Rat Man payed me a visit. In response to our call to the Seattle Health Department's rodent hotline. I trusted this guy implicitly and was very pleased to make his acquaintance. He was in his late forties and had a heavy New York accent; he looked and he sounded like a man who would know how to kill a rat.

He wants me to lace the entire house with poison. A dozen baited paraffin bars in the crawlspace; bars under the sink; bars in the bathroom; bags of pellets in the attic. Then I am to search out their burrows in the backyard and cram paraffin bars down the entrances. The active ingredient in the bars and pellets is a highly sophisticated anticoagulant. Eventually causes the rats to choke to death, when their lungs fill with their own blood. Lovely way for a rat to perish, but I did feel compelled to ask about the hazards to my cats.

The Rat Man sneered: "*My* cat is still alive. Besides, if they start hemorrhaging, just feed 'em a shot of vitamin K. You should worry about a little blood about the nose and anus?"

I know my wife would never consent to put the cats' lives at risk. But I played along. Nodded—sure, I'd turn my house into a maze of poison.

Then he told me not to worry about the stench. "Ray-uts," as he New York-ed the word, "Ray-uts are gonna start dying in your walls. But I don't want you to worry about no stench." Indeed, the answer was simple: when I smell a poisoned-to-death rat in the wall, I at once drill a small hole where the stink is worst. Then eye-dropper in oil of wintergreen. He assures me oil of wintergreen—squirted in once or twice a day—perfectly masks the odor of putrescence. In any event, the remains will skeletalize within twelve to fifteen days. "Den, of couwrse, dere can always be a problem wit flies. But for da most part, dey'll be dyin inside the wall, too."

Remember I told you about my piece of tail? The 3 caudal centimeters I hacked off with an axe? I'm not a gun owner. But I do have this nice $25 axe. It's safer than a gun: ever try to commit suicide with an axe?

Haven't since last letter come any closer to gittin me my rat. I may not have to. Thanks to sixty of Susan's well-spent dollars we now own an ultra-sonic new age rat deterrent. Thru the grace of ultra-sonics, this device (about the size of a modest dildo) sets up a keening that drives Rodney mad. We all have our frequencies. This humanly inaudible siren sends rodents packing. So they go nextdoor and devour my neighbors alive. Soon she'll have one, too. Soon the whole world will possess these ultra-sonic marvels. Then Rodney will at last be conquered—banished from human society, driven out into the wild, there to take his chances with leopards, boa constrictors and Hondas.

What will happen, of course, is rats will become inured to ultra-sonic devices. Soon they'll be *attracted* to the shriek. You gotta hand it to rats—they are certainly more human than we are.

Meantime, the house appears to be rat free. Ganz Rattenrein. No scurrying in the woodwork, gnawing of the floor boards. No visits in broad daylight to spook my wife. No half-eaten raw potatoes left in the middle of the kitchen floor for discovery on the morrow. I kinda miss the little gray fucks. Wish one would show up right now, so I could allow it to bless me with the opportunity to whang it to death. Rats, whores, carrion misconceptions,

Yrs on his ass,
Willie

Dear *Corpse*—

As you can see from the enclosed police report, I was recently shot at in my own home. A disgustingly thrilling experience. My wife and I had committed the sin of going to the window and looking out to see why her car alarm was screeching at 11:45 P.M. It was screeching because these gentle Asian types had smashed in the window with a rock and were now attempting to snatch the radio/cassette player. But it's a theft-proof radio, and they couldn't get it, and so, as they strolled away from the scene and spotted my charming wife looking down at them from the second story window up here, they carefully aimed a revolver and squeezed off a round.

Susan felt the bullet travel under her chin, across her neck. I had my back to the window and was groggily wandering off to call the cops or maybe just take a crap, I forget. I screamed and threw myself at the floor. On the way down, I heard the report of the gun out on the

222

street. I had initially reacted to the feel of the slug passing a fraction of an inch over the back of my head. I almost joined you, dear *Corpse*. Closest I've come to violent death since I was in a logging accident back in 1970.

I bent my glasses, jumping down onto the floor. We had to replace the pane of glass, the sill now has a bullet-hole in it and there is a beauty of a hole in my plaster ceiling. Most experts agree it is nothing more than a .38 or maybe just a lousy little ole .32 magnum. Nothing really to get excited about—nothing like a .357 or a round from a rhino gun.

This getting shot at did not make me very happy. Nor did the thought of watching my wife die in front of me from a gsw to the forehead. Or just hafta live with her with half her jaw shot off and a $98,000 medical bill with nobody to help. Remember, surviving getting shot in the face is just the tip of the iceberg of agony.

We stayed away from the house for a month and went $2,000 in debt getting bars on all the windows and putting up other security measures. Tonight is our second night back in the house. Why don't I get a gun?

Because I am a chickenshit motherfucker. I'm not one of these brave writers like Hunter Thompson or that old wife-shooter Burroughs. Besides, I never learned how to use a gun. There is also the consideration that it might be thoroughly rotten karma to kill someone—even in defense of your own miserable squalid life. Plus the everpresent threat of suicide when you keep a gun around the house.

Still, Susan and I occasionally talk shotgun. Just a little lady's .410. Not one of these wall-busting 8 gauges or nothin. But I doubt it's gonna happen. We're pretty well caged in now with iron bars, filmguard, alarm system, deadbolts, steel doors and also rose boughs and blackberry brambles that I have strung with great personal discomfort over the balcony. I also sleep with my axe beside the bed. In case some cokehead uses a hollowcharge to blow through the steel door, bursts into the bedroom and begins blazing away with his lousy little .32 magnum. I can leap out of bed (yes, I sleep nude), grab the axe, take six slugs in the gut and still keep coming thanks to mere poetry power and cleave this varlet's skull in twain like Roland did to Arafat back at the Pass. It would be a pleasure to die on such a trophy.

On the way down to the floor, as the report exploded inside my ears, I felt filth, grime, guck, guilt, shame. These would have been my dying emotions and perceptions. I'm sure my body thought I was dying. For a few thousand microseconds, I thought I had been shot in the back of the skull. A quite frequently lethal sort of blow. Imagine that: death a one-way journey into filth and shame. Sounds like what I've been preparing for all my life. That pretty much sums up my writing. And now the dear sweet cherub god Ganesha, remover of obstacles, custodian of writing, propitiator of beginnings, has awarded me yet more time to become acquainted with shit and grief, before his petulant dad Shiva finally rings down the curtain once and for all.

Welcome to Seattle, *Corpse*.

Thanks for *Corpse* 43. Chris Waddington's "A Cold War Memory" was music to my ears. Very thoughtful bit of Americana. Waddington writes like Norman Rockwell withdrawing from prozac. Prose oozing with razor curveballs. Excellent control on his screwball. And when he comes inside with knucklers like "charms that didn't keep Dad from viewing the state as a textbook target for the Soviet bomber fleet"—whew, pitches like that ain't nobody gonna hit!

Been enjoying my *Corpse*'s so much, I am letting them stack up by the phone, so I'll have something to read, while repeatedly dialing 911, begging cops to hurry up and get to the scene of the latest shooting on dear old Sturgus Ave. Took John Law thirty minutes to answer our frantic calls during the recent attempted murder of my wife. If I'd been killed, it wouldn't be murder: they were shooting at my wife's face in the window. I just happened to be in the room. And if my brains had been splattered on the wall, it would've just been accidental homicide or manslaughter—probably reduced to reckless endangerment.

When the cop came, he said, hey—don't worry: this happens all the time.

"What!" my wife screamed in his face. "People get shot at all the time while they are inside their houses?"

The cop shrugged. He told a few stories about other shootings in recent weeks. He stifled a yawn. Smiled weakly. Said he was sorry this had to happen to us. By way of reassurance, he promised he would sit in his car and fill out the report right there, parked under the streetlight in front of our house. This would provide us a good extra 15 minutes of police protection.

I got mad at the cop. What an asshole I am. "Can we talk to somebody higher? I don't think you've done enough here, Officer!" This isn't a direct quote. I believe I used the word FUCK once or thrice, while addressing the public servant. These things happen to even the politest of *hommes de lettres*, immediately following their near shooting to death in their own home for some flimsy gang-related horseshit. My psychiatrist says I should go ahead and use dirty words, if it makes me feel better.

The cop shrugged. Sure, I could talk to the Sergeant—he comes on duty in about six hours. But he wouldn't actually be in the station till 7:30; and he NEVER accepts unsolicited calls until about 8:30, more like quarter after nine.

So, next day, my wife the community activist got on the phone to the Precinct Captain, the community interface cop, the cop in charge of district public relations, etc. We got invited down to talk to some cops. Important cops. A lieutenant, a sarge, the bullbeat cop of our

224

neighborhood, etc. They apologized for the blasé attitude of the investigating officer at the scene of our little fracas. We were assured: no, this kind of thing does NOT HAPPEN all the time in the fair city of Seattle. This is rather unusual that residents would be shot at inside their home during the course of a routine car prowl. Although there had been several recent incidents—even up in Mukilteo—of residents being shot, while Asian gangs were having their way with the individual resident's vehicle. He wouldn't go so far as to say this is the Asian gangs' M.O. Legally, of course, he can't say stuff like that. Besides, these guys are only committing a misdemeanor while they are smashing your car and methodically stealing the radio, the seats, the glove compartment contents, whatever else they feel they might need. No point in even arresting anybody committing a misdemeanor. Too bad about those guns they carry. We used to have a good law on the books—it expired or got repealed or something back in '71 ... but this law made it a felony simply to possess a handgun while committing a misdemeanor. With that law, we could send some of these murderers to jail for like a year, or at least six months. Now we are powerless to get them any time at all. They got a right to carry a gun when they are out late at night driving around practicing their tax-free profession. Car prowlers have rights in this country. You folks, neither of you folks was hurt—right?

"Fuck no, Officer," I muttered to the graymetal desk. "I feel fine as a fresh-fucked sodomite in hell. And my wife didn't even get her jaw shot off. I wanna apologize for making such a cocksucking nuisance of myself. Would you put us in for a few tickets to the policemen's ball?"

We have a great police department up here. Their motto is (forgive me, I have forgotten the Latin): "Officer—don't get yourself hurt!" The investigating officer actually divulged this. He didn't say it was SPD's motto, but he did say that's what they always told him in training, and at least once a week on a memo from the Chief. He also mumbled over his shoulder, as he was walking off to fill out the report in his car under the streetlight: "If they come back—maybe they'll shoot *me*." I always admire cynicism in a coward. It is perhaps the accomplished poltroon's crowning glory. Unless you allow the knack for suicide.

Because my wife raised hell, we got the P.R. cop to write the enclosed note to all residents on our block. Let me hasten to underscore: We have no "Block Watch map." The cop who wrote the note only thinks we do. We are a scared, incommunicative, depressed block.

Dear Neighbor:

At 11:45 P.M. on the night of August 4, 1993 two occupants of a home on Sturgus Avenue were shot at by car prowlers. The residents were awakened by the car alarm and arose to look out their bedroom window when one of the suspects fired a gun at them. The bullet went through the bedroom window, traveled under the chin of one occupant and over the head of another, and embedded itself in their ceiling. Fortunately, neither resident was injured, though they are understandably upset. The suspects are described as Asian, with medium to short hair, late teens to late twenties. They were driving a late-seventies model, white four-door American car, possibly Chevrolet. Four men total were seen that evening.

There has been much criminal activity recently on Sturgus Avenue, with the gang graffiti and continued car prowls. Please be aware of your surroundings at all times. If you see anything suspicious, please call 9-1-1 immediately. I ask that you do not put yourself at any risk, consider your own personal safety at all times. If you see anyone that fits the suspects' description in the recent shooting, please notify the police as soon as possible (and remember they might be armed). Don't forget to use your Block Watch map to communicate with your neighbors about the activity on the street. You need each other now more than ever. The Seattle Police Department's South Precinct commander, Capt. Ferguson, the Community Police Team and the patrol staff are aware of this recent unfortunate event. As your block watch coordinator, I am here to serve the block in any way I possibly can. So please keep your watchful eyes out for each other and your own property. If you have any questions please call me at 684-7555.

> *Very truly yours,*
> *Terrie Johnston*
>
> *Crime Prevention Coordinator*

Dear *Corpse*—
    Since the shooting, many of my friends urge me to get a gun. Even up the odds. Pack me around an equalizer. As I say, I did momentarily entertain the thought of purchasing a shotgun. I still daydream about my pumpgun. Conduct a daily inner debate as to whether she's a 16 or a 12 gauge. Imagine blasting crooks in two with double-ought buckshot. Somedays even envision sawing her off. The sawed-off—every home owner's dream. A shotgun is a beautiful weapon for cutting people in half or blowing holes in the wall the size of windows. But it's so unwieldy. Enter the flyweight, pistolgripped sawedoff. Unfortunately, a sawedoff is an illegal weapon, and I am a law abiding citizen. That's why I wanna get the gun in the first place, right? Because I'm a law abiding citizen. I mean, in this country, how can you obey the Law if you don't own a gun?
    There is ample literary precedent of gun ownership. This

century alone affords us such enthusiastic gunners as The Hem, Mailer, Burroughs, Thompson, ad cojones. How can you expect to learn to type if you haven't blown away at least a few birds or skunks or Japs in your life? All American writers typewrite. We're too pressed for time to settle for anything less.

Well, I taught myself to type. I never went to gun school. Dad never owned a gun. He grew up too poor to own a gun. Later never had the inclination. Maybe it was just repressed sissyism. Dad had also wanted to be a writer—another indication of sissyism. Only sissies want to be writers. Instead poor dear Dad wound up being a technical writer for the United States Army. All life is suffering. Nuff said.

So I had a rotten childhood that was totally deprived of guns. And here I am at 44, with distinct suicidal tendencies, about to go out and purchase my first sidearm? Or blunderbuss, I should say. You see, it's just gotta be a shotgun. The scattergun is made for the novice. You don't aim, you *point* a shotgun. If you only hit the bad guy with 5% of your pellets, and then only in the elbow, you still crash him to the floor unconscious where he perishes from arterial bleeding in five minutes unless urgent medical attention responds.

And I tell all my friends about the suicide-phobia. Plus the stat that gun owners are five times likelier to off themselves than nongunowners. They poo-poo me with stories of sleeping with the ole .357 under the pillow. Makes 'em feel better. Me, I'd just blow my head off during a bad dream.

My dead buddy Dana used to own a .357. Also a 9mm. He would come over and we would drink beer and smoke and take out his guns and play with them. I'd spin the cylinder of the .357. Dana would snap in and out clips into the black handled 9mm. We taperecorded these noises. Lovely clean sharp clicks. Click, click, click, SNAP. Nothing tighter than a gun being loaded up. Precise machines. Typewriters are by comparison inaccurate clunky beasts. Dana was always bugging me to go out into the woods with him and shoot some tincans. We could drink beer, smoke and bang off a couple dozen rounds. He really wanted me to do this. Dana and I were pretty tight that year. It would've meant a lot to him for me to go out and shoot with him. I loved Dana. He's been dead for almost ten years and I can still work up a tear.

But I told him: "Man, I'm a poet. I don't drive cars and I don't shoot guns." He winced. I could tell he wanted to bring up the usual objections: Burroughs, Thompson, The Hem. But he honestly loved me too much to press the point. We went on to have many a good time just *looking* at the rods, taking them apart and putting them back together.

I see guns wherever I go. Pawn shops, video stores, newsracks, tobacco shops. I pick up casings and the occasional live round, as I walk around town. I walk a lot. Since I don't drive, hate the bus,

227

walking is good for the spine, good for the psyche, the mood, the pneuma. Walking, I think about guns. Especially when I am not thinking about naked women, the grand obsession of my lifelong interior monologue. Will they get me in a drive by? Is some pimp pissed about me spoiling his open air whorehouse?

Yeah, I really fucked those whores. Haven't seen one over my back fence since we browbeat the City into dumping jersey barriers at the mouth of the alley. Couldn't blame the pimp if he smoked some crack one afternoon, saw me walking down the street and decided a dozen or so potshots might be in order.

Then there's the Vietnamese gangsters who shot at me back in August. Shot at my wife, to be precise. It was her face in the window they saw. What did they care if I was standing there three feet behind her, they couldn't see my skull from down the street. Once a slug is released, after the initial target is passed, or before, God and Her dice come into play.

A couple days after the shooting, I went to a community meeting with my wife. I never attend community meetings. I get too angry when I go. Tend to say bad shit. Maybe I'm afraid someday they'll cart me off for verbal assault. Anyway, this one I didn't miss, because the Precinct Captain and some of his closest associates had promised to attend.

The meeting was unusually dull, despite the presence of the Boys in Blue. And my anger failed me. I merely spluttered and dribbled like a limp dick. But as the meeting dragged on, some old African-American lady stood up and started talking about all the dogs that crap on her parking strip. Every morning she has to go out and scoop poop. Don't we have a leash law, a bag law, a *crap* law? She'd like to know what the mayor intends to do about this wild pack of dogs that is constantly befouling her lawn.

As she sat down and several folks around the table stifled yawns, my buddy X, the Japanese-American, leaned over and whispered into my ear: "Shoot the dogs with your gun!"

I turned purple, choking back laughter. Christ, funniest damn thing said all night. I envision this gray-haired old bat out there with a pumpgun blowing away a poodle in mid-defecation.

The whole meeting had heretofore centered on guns and their overwhelming presence and usage in our community. Now this whispered haiku of canine mayhem.

Frankly, what *is* funnier than a gun? A deadbaby joke? A flashflood in a fizzy factory? After all, it is *the* most surreal act. Firing at random on a crowd. Oh, Josephine—how positively su-*real!* Look—that old man with arachnoid membrane protruded from his skull! The baby spinning around with a sucking wound, the shlub and his frau with splinters in the breadbasket, the torso with everything loose shotgunned off—a scream! Yowl—funniest damn thing since a fart in a spacesuit!

Why this erotic fascination with instant death? instant maim? instant winging? or at the very least, instant terror?

Because it's cool. Guns are cool, *Corpse*. Cool for other folks to own. But not for me. I'm a writer, a beer drinker, a suicidal maniac and a hunter of words. You can take your gun and shove it up your fucking ass, fuckface. I WILL NOT OWN A GUN.

I am the bravest man in Seattle. I walk five to ten miles a day—totally unarmed. Except with mumbled lines of poetry in the making. Of course I write while I walk—when else would I have time, dodging bullets, earning a living, maintaining drug abuse, listening to Bach on my cassette recorder and writing about American writing while not really doing it.

Yrs in avoidance,
Willie

WILLIE, GET YOUR GUN

HOWARD MCCORD

Corpse 47 came in the door the other day, and I had a fine visit. "The Willie Smith File" got me going a bit—the quasi-moral questioning, indulgence and reticence combined, and more than anything, his "Man, I'm a poet. I don't drive cars and I don't shoot guns." I guess I have never felt that being a poet involved any particular inadequacies. Historically, I know where the image came from—Oscar Wilde in Denver, on his American tour, doing a campy version of Keats, Ginsberg with his Sunflower and dopey smile, and then TV—Ernie Kovacs in the late 50s, "Percy Dovetonsils," and the "Laugh-In" bumpkin, and the mewling poet is pop ikon. It's all part of the great American put-down of the artist, which is part of the game. But that poets themselves begin to buy such trash…this I don't understand. And "Burroughs, Thompson, The Hem," don't really counter the image. Willy Smith really wants to be a wuzz, and thinks he is a superior sort—"the bravest man in Seattle." Hell, maybe he is. Or maybe he's a damn fool. I'm not one privy to such secrets.

JIM GUSTAFSON

THE GREATEST MARDI GRAS EVER

I wake up at 2:15 AM on February 15th from a dream where my old friend Ace is stalking my sweet teenage wife. Her and I live somewhere like a treehouse or a Volkswagen van, and since Ace is a famous international assassin, we feel kind of unprotected. My teenage bride prostitutes herself to get enough money to check us into the relative safety of a suite at the Fairmont. But when we open the room instead of a mint on the pillow, there's Ace. "Don't drink those little bottles in the refrigerator, they charge you a fortune for them," he warns. Nice to see you too, Ace. A shiny high rifle is sitting on top of the television, slowly melting. My teenage bride, who for some reason is now wearing a thong bikini says "Oh no! He's come to kill us!" But she says it in such a B movie voice that I know it isn't true. In fact, I'm thinking, Ace is probably the guy she serviced to get the $1,200 this place costs. I make a note to ask her about it later. I also take note that in the beginning of this dream she was kind of pretty in a young dumpling way, but now she's absolutely scrumptious. And if she has this kind of earning potential, why the heck are we living in a treehouse??? Then we figure out she has the ability to travel back on her back, to drift through time and have sex with famous people in history. Crusaders, conquerors, and of course, writers. The good part is is they pay her in gold. Plus tips. She lies down on the big bed and closes her eyes while Ace and I plunder the courtesy bar, which has become affordable. A few whiskeys later she comes back into the room with a bag full of ducats, a long strand of black pearls, and a jewel encrusted chalice she probably got from some French pope! "Not a bad afternoon's work for a little gal from Point-aux-Chenes!" she announces, obviously pleased with herself. Meanwhile, out the window, Mardi Gras has begun. Just as suddenly we're riding on the dead poets float with Ted and Jeffrey and Yeats and Breton and lots of Bardic bead-throwers from all ages. My teenage bride is still butt-nekkid and is causing riots every time she harvests another 24-carat doubloon from her pussy and throws it into the crowd along St. Charles Street. Ace has a bag of magic sticks that turn into snakes in mid-air. And I'm throwing hand grenades that explode into bouquets of flowers upon contact. "This is the greatest parade in the history of Mardi Gras!" Ace exclaims as he throws a cobra into the throngs. I'll say! agrees my teenage bride as she pulls what looks like the Heisman trophy from her loins and after teasing the crowd, hands it to an old couple who turn young again when they touch it. My flower grenades are bouncing off wires and balconies and white roses are everywhere. Now all of this is a lot of fun but I'll be happy to get back to the hotel, providing, of course Ace hasn't glommed my gal. Which he has in the past...more than once. But this time I get to keep her as Ace has hooked up with someone who is either Kiki or Catherine of Aragon. "Meet you back at the refrigerator!" he shouts as they hop off the float and vanish into the mob. The greatest Mardi Gras ever.

ENLIGHTENED MULTIPLICITY

It's my enlightened multiplicity that most often sinks me into the ever-lurking Deep Shit. One minute I'm just your average wayward moose, freshfucked and big-racked stomping around on the outskirts of Medi-cine Hat or Waldoboro, and the next thing I'm speaking at an animation seminar in Denver about the history of deer, elk, and moose in cinema. Then there's one of those cwazy clicks, and I'm an utterly befuddled Okie who has just found Botticelli's Venus rising out of the pile of spare parts in the back of his compound. But before I can even scratch my head and begin to wonder if I can fuck her, I'm back at my desk, looking at a post card of Wrigley Field, wondering if I was there the day the picture was taken, and if I was, was I alone, was I drunk, was I living in Chicago or just visiting? I don't know if this tendency to fade into whatever I'm looking at a picture of is a good thing or not. It makes for a cheap vaca-tion. But at times I start to feel spread pretty thin. Everything I put on my wall has a purpose. Usually as evidence. Or to remind me that I was someplace or thought about some thing some time in the past, but in most cases, didn't deal with it adequately, or file this data away to play with at a time when my Imagination is stuck in money jail or I've admit-ted I'll probably be too broke to travel any time before the end of the century. I guess that I'm lucky that a bottle of Rebel Yell will take me to Chickamunga or a six pack of Pabst reminds me of a long dead favorite Uncle who fictitiously claimed to have been a bowling hustler. To take this further, I'm probably real lucky to have done enough stuff in my life that almost everything reminds me of something else. Usually a whole lot of things. This is also a form of steadily unfolding Hell that makes it impossible to formulate a new thought, especially at a critical moment, when I need one. I've only been a moose a couple of times before, and certainly never have I been a moose confronting a phalanx of cinematic eggheads. How do I know! I bellow. Yes, of course I know Bambi...it's a small town and a tightly-protective corner of the industry. It's these mul-tiple orgasms that turn into light, circumventing heat entirely, that tend to paint me into the corner of my delicious laboratory.

COMMUNAL MEMORY HA-HA

We're talking communal memory ha-ha here. Some kind of scam-o-rama for drug-resistant necronauts. Do you actually want to sit in some retro cafeteria and start listing every hallucination we ever shared? On a legal pad? Where'd you get a legal pad? Shit, I'm hallucinating even now while we speak over the ice telephone and you want to remind me of some pterodactyls we left bleeding in the road in 1968? How do you know it was 1969 and not 1107? It's time we stop reminiscing and get as real as what's left of our brains will allow. I'm out of toilet paper and your mortgage is overdue big time. I'm craving some macaroni and cheese and the headlight you need for your BMW costs more than you made in the last three months. Besides, what makes you think you remember anything the same way that I do? How about the color orange? You think sherbet and I think egg yolk, and no matter what color the Broncos' uniforms were on television, they were really a completely different color. Considering the television we were watching on and what we were on, that Super Stupor Sunday. And that day was completely different than this one, believe it or not, even if it doesn't seem like it. You want to go for double or nothing and try another color? Pink? You want to try what Lizzie Beck's pink tasted like? You'd say veal and I'd say swordfish and we'd both be romantic liars, because Lizzie was the most virtuous commune queen in the whole Midwest and neither of us got close enough to know what kind of toothpaste she used, much less anything more intimate! Crest gel?!? They didn't even make Crest gel until the 80s! And I'll tell you, we're all a couple of a bunch of deluded frauds and are wasting our time/space thingamabob if we're still trying after all these years to compare memories just to find out whose is worst. Besides, I can tell you right now, yours is.

BARTFLY

It was another crossed wire morning. Today I'm imagining that I'm Mickey Rourke and I've just signed with MGM to play Homer in the 2020 revival of *The Simpsons*. This is a pretty disgusting thought, but anything that relieves me from the tedium of the actual is as welcome as opiated lemonade at this point. In my quirky, pop-noir version of America's proto family, Homer is a traveling small arms salesman. He has been living on the road for oh these many years, and now wants to visit the family he abandoned to capitalize on the California Secession Conflict. Bart, naturally, is a corrupt attorney now, working out of a desk in the prosecutor's office, but freelancing as a baksheesh conduit between the nuke dealers and the suits. I'm not sure if they're happy to see each other. It's still early in the scrambled semotext some of us call Monday. By my second cup of coffee-flavored non-dairy creamer, I'm absolutely raging, as usual, about how destiny is a really sick practical joke. When you stop to think of it, doesn't a lot of the landscape remind you of rubber vomit and exploding cigars? And I'll tell you Marge, there are days when even I get tired of being a man of vision. Often when Mr. Coffee is hissing and the toast is crisping I think my life would've been better spent doing something else. I could've been a great hubcap finder. Or one of those rural village idiots working as an unpaid cage-cleaner in rural Alabama in the early 60s. I may have well seen those marches go by, but I didn't exactly understand what all the hubbub was about and besides I was busy tending to the hamsters. And so another morning opens like a security gate of a merchant who reckons this is the day he's going to get shot for twenty-four dollars. I'm both shopkeeper and robber in this pessimistic vision. But what remains most vivid is the screech of the gate rolling up. It reminds me of the time my exwife (who doesn't drink) went out and rented *Barfly* and bought a quart of whisky and invited her fnends, hi-falootin' dilettantes all, over to watch me guzzle and provide inside commentary. This is the old poet as a talking fright wig with a bottomless booze hole routine. "Drinks for all my friends!" they say at exactly the right time, like they're at *The Rocky Horror Show*. I'm not sure just how involved I want to get with any of this.

It's pretty much a full-time job remembering who's the cartoon and who's the drunk and whether the motorcycle in the bathtub is mine or Lisa's. I struggle to keep track, but when the mutt chews the radio cord and the roof starts leaking in the typhoon and the plasma from the jellyroll starts tasting like cheap rye, I have a tendency to let go of the ropes and to just let balloons take care of themselves.

I SHOULD HAVE KNOWN I WAS IN TROUBLE

I should have known I was in trouble when someone who I didn't know very well, a so-called "bar friend," referred to me as "the suicide expert." There's no denying that I'd had first-hand experience. That a number of my brander, ballsier, and most affluent friends had done the Dutch over the last decade or so. I'd become, for a while, a big time semi-official elegist … a chore I've since abandoned. Death was a constant source of aggravation in the 80s and early 90s. I noted at one point, actually fairly early in this cycle, that I was about ten elegies behind for friends and a hundred or more for famous folks. The deaths didn't bother me as much as the suicides. Regular death is there. But these self-killers, these people who I had genuinely loved, I couldn't fathom. It has taken me a long time to stop trying. It has also taken me a long time to be able to compare myself and my late comrades in their last days. "You know, everyone who I know who killed themselves stopped being funny in the last year or so before they croaked," I told Jesse. And it was true. This crew of zanies, this posse of wags, had grown pretty morose toward the end. I used to be the compulsive telephoner. And I called all of them up at least twice a week and tried for major yucks or even cheap giggles, but after a certain point it was useless. I even tried to make them funny in my dreams. At least until I dreamt that Gumption had put on his clown suit and stood in front of the barrel of the Human Cannonball cannon, then heard two days later that I was almost right. He'd bought a Brooks Brothers suit and a Michigan Twenty Gauge. Yowlp! I don't like it when my dreams make me nervous. Especially that nervous over that long of a period. "Promise you won't tell us if you dream about us," my friends pleaded. And for the most part, I've kept that promise. Once, in a fit of pique, I told someone I saw him choking at a baseball game. That his head was turned and he was scarfing a hot-dog and a foul ball clipped him square in the noggin, and the plump-when-you-cook-em frank inflated like a plastic Boy Scout after it got caught in his throat. He's still alive but speaks with a rasp and never to me. Which is one good thing about being a suicide expert. But I don't like the idea of using vision as a weapon any more than I like the idea of "fuck it" being the last thing anyone thinks before leaving this world. It's not so bad, I meant to say. It's pretty good, I tell myself, going out to rake the yard on the morning of some anniversary or the other. Next year will be the anniversary of my planting a new lawn, I think. I may well still be in trouble, but I'll be laying on the grass, not under it.

OLD AND FULL OF DAYS

For Kathy, who gave me life back,
and then filled it with love.

I am a forty-two year old single man with a double life and a part-time job.

This is the simplest way I can explain myself. To break my life down into an equation that is possible to understand, and take it from there.

I'm trying to be brave and big-spirited about the whole thing. I understand, or at least suspect, that the whole world as we know it has been defined mathematically, and that formula is stored on a hard disc that's stored in a vault in Fort Meade, Maryland.

Even if it isn't, it might be, which to me is close enough.

In terms of my own life, however, I have a tough enough time remembering how to work the money machine and whether I have ten or twenty dollars in my account this week. Yesterday I couldn't remember my four digit code. Which would've been bad enough under any circumstances, but since it's my birthday (the code) it's maybe X times as bad.

I would like to have ten times as much income and about one eighth of the aggravation. I would like a lot of things. But this isn't about what I want. It's about what I have. And how I got it.

I'm a forty-two year old single man with a double life and a part-time job. I also come complete with a complicated personal life and a history that is truly almost an embarrassment of riches. I have struggled mightily to put my memories to rest, but they just won't go away.

I used to say that I wanted a life as short and comfortable as a rich midget's favorite pajamas. This is typical of some exotic thought disorder I picked up somewhere along the way. I think it might've come from wearing too many lampshades. There might've been some leftover light clinging to some of them, and that light might've gone directly into my brain.

Have you ever met one of those old self-righteous geezers who say "I know what I know" and then go on to tell you? They are usually talking about fertilizer, hammers, one particular woman, or their useless sons. I don't know what I know. I fear that I don't know much of anything, or worst, that I used to know something but it's faded like a pair of old Levis. I shudder to think that my precious thought process has a rip in its crotch and is splattered with day-glow paint.

Still, I'm curious, make that obsessive, about finding out what I know. I used to tell my students that the human brain has a capacity for eighteen trillion information bits, and I was determined to use each and every one of them, a goal that I am no longer interested in attaining. But this is more than a fun fact to know and tell. Part of my problem, or one of my problems, is that my brain contains an abundance of the wrong kind of information.

None of the knowledge that I have will help me become a forty-three year old married man with two normal children and a position of responsibility with a prestigious conservative think tank.

Which is what I want.

But somehow I don't think the Great American Republic will ever embrace me as the jolly barbarian who perfected the theory of fascism with a human touch. Then again I know I'm a drunken chronic fornicator with a serious fondness for anarchy that is on record in at least fifteen states in seven countries.

I never said I was consistent.

I believe in wild vacillations and sudden dips in levels of specific gravity. I believe in both long term cycles and the magic of fractals, and that they are sometimes but not always the same thing. I also believe in Woody Guthrie, Nelson Algren, St. Dymphna, and Elmore Leonard. I believe in belief in a way similar to how some people love the whole idea of love.

I believe in multiple starts and that you have to start somewhere. Then you are compelled to go somewhere. Motion, I believe, is a constant that has to be reckoned with, pandered to, and thoroughly enjoyed. Even if it makes you sick.

Are you with me so far?

Thanks. And good luck.

I am a forty-two year old single man with a double life and a part-time job who could probably use a quadruple bi-pass and would love to get out from behind the eight ball.

I'm an idea man who would like to be an action guy. I live on a lunatic reservation that most people think of as a Major American City. At least part of the time. During the week. During the weekend I live with a beautiful, responsible woman in a posh suburb and drive a convertible.

During the week, I walk.

On weekends I make Jamaican Blue Mountain coffee and heat up croissants, then bring them to Katie on her veranda. We watch the ducks in the pond across the street, talk flipply about social issues, and make love almost incessantly. Too much, as we keep saying, but that doesn't change.

During the week I live in a slum downtown, in a building that features a couple of terrorists, a minor drug lord, a French feminist chemist who I think might be turning tricks, and a seventeen year old feral child who often forgets to put on her clothes before she runs down the hall snarling.

I also have a rich internal life and a good, though not as lively as it used to be, imagination. During the week I use my imagination constantly, sometimes as a condiment with my memory. Since my job isn't terribly demanding, at least in the hours category, I have time to think. I have too much time to think and too much to think about. I also have insomnia.

At least during the week. On the weekends I sleep like a baby curled up next to Katie and don't think at all if I can avoid it. On the weekend the hardest thing I have to contend with is withdrawal from the newspaper. My agenda was pretty crowded with vices, and after I tried and failed to give up booze, coffee, sugar, desire, and conspiracy theories, I decided to give up newspapers on the weekends. I read it when I come home on Monday morning.

I never said I was perfect. I am the least perfect person I know. I have flaws and fear sometimes that I am a walking embodiment of the Seven Deadly Sins. Maybe I should rotate them. Or concentrate on one per day. If this is Tuesday, it must be gluttony. Maybe I could have them sticked onto my boxer shorts. Why does it say "sloth" on your leg, Honey?

I tend to celebrate my imperfections while concurrently wallowing in guilt. Sometimes I feel like a defrocked missionary stewing in a pot of toxic sludge. I recognize that I am a sinner and want to repent. Or wanted to until I heard one of those egghead film critics on television say that repentance has been done to death.

And isn't it about time for a new wave of romantic musical comedies? So part of me wants to be a passion play while the other half wants to romp with Doris Day. Or better, with Sean Young in a remake of *Pillow Talk*.

Katie doesn't like it when I think of actresses, but I explain that actresses were a critical part of my daily life for a number of years, and I can't just stop thinking about them. They are a part of my life. One of many, many parts.

I'm not sure what it is I want to tell you, so I'm going to try to tell you everything. What I want to do is find out just what "everything" consists of. At least the best parts of everything, and the best of the worst parts.

I have to start somewhere, so let me say it again.

I'm a forty-two year old single man with a double life and a part-time job.

JEW STORY

To seek the origins of theater in History, and the origin of History in the past, is fucked. Waste of time. What would be lost if we lost the theater?

—GENET, "L'ÉTRANGE MOT D'..."

Filippo charged ahead with his scimitar, decimating several armies of marauding estate-dwellers then en route to a mirthful afternoon among heathens.

Cut: to the mirthful afternoon, never in fact occurring, but nevertheless quite real. The heathens are disporting themselves on the lawn, undoing knots as is their wont at top gallop atop fine creatures not quite equine but savage nevertheless, shouting at the same time stanzas of excellent poets to the assembled tribes of their vanquished, who can only look at the mounted victorious heathens with downturned head (eyes as far up as possible) and murmur little ditties from their own tongues, all about survival.

Out from the blue of the western horizon, on this never-to-be afternoon, arrive thousands of wealthy industrialists, men whose distribution systems call for evenings of talk over pricey liqueurs. There is clangor, a vast system of knocks recalling a metaphor about schools or some other industrial method, that arises from the protection the estate-dwellers are sheathed in from head to estate-dwelling toe.

"Hark," yells a victorious heathen, "I see something ugly." "Ugly," they all agree, and race charging away from their moment of glamour towards the confusing army, over the watchful eye of the downtrodden. There, bits of heathen, and then songs we know quite well, discussing the joy in discovering a new species of flower upon an oft-tread heath, the perfection of young Maribelle in treading upon same flower, the correctness of murdering young Maribelle for her

237

JACQUES SERVIN

insult to science, joy in discovery of other delights than young Maribelle—Oh wanton flower! for example, and How sultry the visage, for another—and all in all, there on the ax-heathen-lawn, a vast euphony of competing ideologies certain for one historical moment of concord, in thorough, replete *Weltanschauung*, that no one will out-envisage-completeness them.

Then, march home with second-rate heathens in tow, those still unminced, not required to keep their heads bowed any longer but still and all murmuring ditties. March home across barren wasteland and Jews, back to hearth and countryside and dementia and Jews, and evenings of solemn assurance that nothing will out-envisage-completeness our knights, who corner young Maribelle and discuss things like throwing the thong and maligning imbroglios.

"Huh?" young Maribelle says, for she is still young and innocent, her cheeks like apples, her lips little worms; when more crafty but still as virginal as is practical, she will say, instead, "I deplore the hating of throwing the thong, but I resent the damage it does my young suitors," upon which the suitors will race out to the countryside to throw thongs, getting damaged, which they know will touch young Maribelle, for whom the charade is a matter of not being rent into five. (This is why, even now, throwing the thong is attended by thousands and gets our best hunks, and wives will cook easy goods in its honor.)

But of course none of this happened, this once—not the heathens disporting, the wealthy attacking, the brave heathens rendered into fragments of heathen, the second-rate chained, the songs afloating through wasteland and hearth and horizon and Jews. Instead Filippo charged ahead full of terrific ideas and a consummate grasp on delivery of one thing from the next, and knocked the hopeful but overburdened and anyhow clumsy estate-dwellers from recalcitrant mounts, and hacked.

"Say, Filippo," they cried. "We are going out to do the thing that will benefit all, give the world its grasp, do the dirty devils, garnish euphoria for models of curtseying...."*

Filippo did not answer, but continued his hacking and knocking with furrowed brow and his tongue out the corner of his close-hewn lips,

---

* "The main current of eighteenth-century historical thought posited as the main impetus for the Crusades the salvaging of customs seen to be foundering under the weight of necessity, competing philosophies, alien mores (Jewish, Gypsy).... Even as late as 1830 the eminent German historian Ludwig Schwerster declared, authoritatively and seemingly without thought for substantiability, that the French Revolution resulted from a 'lack of conviction on the part of the Court as to the importance of its imaginary domain, i.e. form, elegance, and its rarefied mores.' He places the seeds of this doubt in the time of the first Crusades, and repeats the previously common (but by 1830 nearly unheard of) assertion that the Crusades were the first, and most misguided, attempt to shore up internal decay." (W.E. Kornfeld, *Medieval History After the Renaissance*, 1960.)

focused on doing this job right for once, so many others had tried, this was too much.

"Silly Filippo," they cried again. "Here, let us have a conference, let us discuss these merits or not in full, argent terms."

Filippo still did not answer, barely heard before he dismissed, knowing the error inhering in terms that yank error to mind, "merit," "full."

Filippo had been a well-balanced child whose efforts in the fourth grade had not held a candle to his efforts in the fifth, and so on.

"Filippo!" the estate-yellers yelled. "For heaven's sake get a grip, adorn yourself with some accolade, get brave, don't be a dipsticked coward and give in to primal, unthinking patterns, let us knights get a move on towards the fields we feel, after all, we have a certain right to, so that afterwards we may come charging back in a certain, after all, splendor, through marshlands and terror and momentum and Jews—come on, guy."

"Nope," Filippo murmured under his breath, which was harsh and rasping what with the marauder decimation he was engaged in.

Afterwards he took a warm bath among the beautiful men he had had imported from Malaga for this and other occasions, who perpetuated his youth in the Roman empress tradition and sang between gasps little ditties of Malaga, about seasides and villas, and beautiful boys troubled by want, and Jews.

CHAPTER 9: IN WHICH THE HOOK MAN AND HIS FAITHFUL FOLKLORIST COMPANION INVESTIGATE THE SPECTRAL GLOBETROTTER, GRAVITY

MATT CLARK

"A student told me about this," Brautigan says.

We're driving away from town, south, past the abandoned Rock Shop, past creaking University Stadium. Alpine falls behind us like a toy on a sand-box hill, Fisher-Price village, Lilliputian college-villa. Midget post office, five-and-dime, movie theatre, barbecue joint, halls of learning, all of them shrinking behind me until they are gone. (Or maybe I'm getting larger, like a fifties monster-movie radiation victim grown to dwarf loved ones and enemies, finally falling dead amongst a

239

mob of olive-green tanks and collossal-boot flattened bazooka shooters.)
The city evaporates. Ahead of us, sunburnt mesas glow red in the waning
daylight, monsters bigger even than myself.

"How come you've never invited me to your class?" I ask.

"What? Class? Why would you want to do that?"

"You could introduce me. As an artifact or witness or text.
Something."

Brautigan shakes his head. "We'll see," he says, then changes the
subject. "This particular phenomenon is not uncommon. I've read a
number of reports placing it in almost every midwestern state. Big in
Missouri for some reason. But I had no idea it was here until this student
told me about it." Brautigan steers with his left hand on the wheel, right
resting on the stick shift, comfortable, at ease, relaxed, like it feels good
to drive that way.

"I like it," I mumble.

"What? The Volkswagen? Thanks. Had it forever."

"My father, he really would have liked it."

"Ah, yes, wind in his hair," Brautigan acknowledges. "The open
road."

We roll over a snake warming itself on the asphalt.

"Ooops," Brautigan grunts.

I turn around quickly to see if the snake has survived or if it lies
segmented and writhing, hopeless. But the road behind us is empty: the
snake has either high-tailed it onto the shoulder to take inventory of its
squashed parts and curse us, or it's hanging onto the bumper even now,
slithering up over the downed rag-top, tongue-flicking, spine-sore, hungry for revenge.

"They don't completely die until sunset," Brautigan says.
"Snakes."

"It is sunset," I remind him. "And that's not really true. That's a
myth."

"Really?"

"Really."

The car slows to a stop. "I guess," Brautigan conjectures, "this is
it."

We're parked in front of a railroad crossing. There is no flashing
light or jerkily lowering arm. Just identifying X signs on either side of the
road. The landscape is so unencumbered by anything you'd have to be
blind and deaf to miss a train bulleting through the desert here. On top
of that, this road is spectacularly lonesome. I suspect it peters out no
more than a mile or two ahead, the black tar and weather-cracked
cement dissipating into sand, hardscrabble and the occasional Apache
arrowhead. "Iron Horse," I say.

"What? Oh, yes. Well. Here we are."

"So now what?"

Brautigan gives the car a punch of gas, rolling us up onto the slight rise where road and rails mesh. "We pull up here like so, turn the motor off"—he does—"and wait for the dead kids to push us off the tracks to safety." He reaches behind my seat and begins to rummage around. I can hear a slight splash of water, ice against glass, glass against glass, glass and ice and water against styrofoam, skin against glass, water against water. "I have been told some level of intoxication is advantageous in conjuring them." He pulls his arm back into the front seat holding two beers. "Drink 'em if you got 'em."

The cooling engine clicks and creaks, groans, settles, hisses. It's dark out. The cloudy sky shields us from the stars and whatever moon is up at bat. When my eyes finally adjust to the headlights' absence, the road ahead becomes almost visible. A jackrabbit, its fur vaguely luminous, plops onto the center stripe, stops, sits up on its hind legs to sniff the air.

"Ah, peace at last," Brautigan sighs, taking a long pull on his beer. "Kids're having a sleepover at the house tonight. It'll be crank calls, water balloons and Ouija board hysteria till two at least."

"What dead children?" I ask

"What?"

"What dead children? Will push us to safety?"

Brautigan nods and belches. "Oh, the ones from the school bus that got stuck on the track when the train was coming and couldn't stop in time. They push us to safety. The ghosts, that is."

"Wow," I say.

"Well, in reality it's just the tilt of the road. It looks like we're sitting on perfectly level ground here, but that's an illusion. We're imperceptibly rolling right now. Eventually we'll gain momentum and roll over to the other side, Saved."

"How do you know we're not on level ground?"

"Good point," Brautigan admits. "I brought a carpenter's thingy. We'll get out afterwards and do some measuring. When we look for the fingerprints."

"What fingerprints?"

"The kids' fingerprints. That's the best plan, and a fairly recent development in this particular activity. After we're safely across we get out and—according to legend—find dozens of little fingerprints all over the trunk and bumper."

I think about the snake we ran over and wonder if he's anticipated our mission and is coiled patiently, nuzzled up against the license plate, waiting for us to investigate our mysterious source of motion. "Creepy," I say.

"You betcha. Another beer?"

I gulp the last of my first before accepting another. We take turns gulping and wiping at our mouths with the back of our hands, careful not to move in unison, fighting the rhythm our car-bound union nudges us toward.

"I feel like we're waiting for me to show up," I say.

"What? Huh?"

"Like we're waiting for the Hook Man to come get us," I clarify.

"Oh. Yeah. Scary. Yikes! You're in the car with me!" Brautigan laughs. "Ever take on a convertible before?" he asks.

I think back through the sundry vehicles in my history, the quarterbacks' nifty Firebirds (black with gold trim), the borrowed family wagons (baby seat strapped in the back), ailing Plymouths, Suburbans, Impalas, souped-up, customized farm trucks, Fieros (ripe to crash and burn), Mustangs (always red), ridiculous Gremlins, Corvairs, Pintos, stout Broncos, Jeep Cherokees, Chevy Blazers, fathers' AWOL Oldsmobiles, Lincolns, Cadillacs, Volvos, Audis, drug-money Jaguars, hand-me-down Skylarks, thoughtless Corvettes, Thunderbirds, Chevettes, sick-making Good Times Vans. "No convertibles come to mind," I tell the doctor.

"Really? Yes. Well, they're probably difficult to approach correctly. You'd risk observation before the ultimate moment."

Silence again.

"How many children are there?"

"I've got two boys and a girl," Brautigan answers.

"No. The ghosts. How many are there supposed to be?"

"Good question," Brautigan says. "I don't know for sure. Some research might be done on that. 'How many children would your average Joe expect to die in a school bus/railroad crossing tragedy? How many baby ghosts does it take to make a good story?'"

"What are their names?"

"The ghosts?"

"Your kids."

"Oh. Oldest is Kyle. Next is Amelia. Then Thad. It's Kyle's sleep-over, so—"

I hold my hand up to stop Brautigan from saying anything more. We're rolling. I can feel it. After Brautigan's voice stops, I can hear the tires humming, crunching gravel against the road. The speed we attain is unmeasurable in terms of miles per hour: faster than a snail, slower than a fire ant. A couple of yards beyond the tracks, we settle to a stop.

"I'll be damned," Brautigan says. He reaches beneath his seat and pulls forth a carpenter's level, then a flashlight. "Let's check it out," he suggests, sounding more Hardy Boyesque than professorial.

We get out and walk back to the tracks. Brautigan crouches with the level, sets it down, then he's on his stomach next to it, eyeing the bubble of air trapped and searching for an escape. "Oh, it's there all right. Just barely there, but there." He gathers himself and stands, turns the flashlight up under his chin, throwing shadows onto his face. "Gravity's a bunch of ghosts," he says Karloffishly.

I'm considering the back of the car from a foot or two away, examining for snakes and fingerprints. Brautigan's flashlight beam clarifies. "Nothing," I say.

"You sound disappointed," Brautigan snorts.

"I feel like the Easter Bunny at a court martial."

"I didn't get that."

"You don't believe in me," I moan.

Brautigan is flabbergasted. "Come again?"

"I watched you get off debunking a pretty nifty story that sounded perfectly plausible to me. Am I next? What kind of hardware will it take to exorcise me from your office into the vault of silly legerdemain? Will you tape-measure my conscience, then hacksaw my ego and sand down my id?"

We stand a long time then. Not talking. Me breathing hard. Brautigan's mouth agape. We're a weird tableau hinted at, then revealed by, then bathed in and dazzled with the headlights of an approaching car. Out a sunroof a boy's voice snipes, "Hey! Quit hogging the dead kids. Give somebody else a chance."

THE MITZVAH MOBILE: THE NEWEST RECESSION BUSTER?

BRAHM EILEY

Montréal (JP). Fresh information surrounding the abduction of high school students Timothy Pearson and John Wright, confirms the rumor that they are living within Montréal's Lubavitch community—an orthodox Jewish sect. The story is strikingly similar to the number of U.S. Servicemen missing in action who have purportedly integrated into Vietnamese society. The information comes from a letter recently received by Pearson's mother.

Due to the intimate and controversial nature of this situation, neither the Pearsons, nor the Wrights have been forthcoming with the press. However, the Pearson family has allowed this journalist access to the letter. With some omissions the contents are, for the first time, revealed below.

Dear Mom,

My name is Yitzhak and I am a Jew. I was once Timothy when I lived with you on the hill in Westmount. I didn't do this to hurt you. But today I can daven freely, dress like Jesse James, and be part of a community—a real community! I know my life before was traif and I owe my realization to the boytcheklachs from the Mitzvah Mobile. The truth is Mom, what did I have to look forward to? As the son of upper crusty Westmount WASPS I had few choices. Either I'd end up like Dad, slogging away at the law firm, drinking too much and chasing after girls with names like Megan. Or, going Third World, working for some alternative organization, drinking too much and being chased by girls named Megan.

The day John and I boarded the Mitzvah Mobile I was as skeptical as you are now. I still wonder why they let us aboard? But spreading the Jewish faith is a fringe job even within the Jewish faith. The Lubavitchers do good work. They save kids who are in trouble across the world. Not that John (Jacob) and I fall into that category.

We just thought that the Mobile was really cool. We liked the crazy hooplah we saw around the Mobile when it stopped in Côte Saint Luc. I know you told me I should never go there—that those people were below me, but you only made it more attractive.

I have to say that when we went home with the boytcheklachs, we thought—well at least they all wear black. And, I have to admit, now, a year later that I look pretty cool with my long blond hair, beard, (Jacob's dyed his) and used 40's suit. Kinda like the group ZZ Top—who you probably don't know.

I get a lot of attention here. We eat, kibbitz and put on tfillin together every day. It's not like home at all. I don't have to constantly mind my manners. As for the Mitzvah Mobile, I'm in charge of pumping out the Hebrew and Yiddish songs through the loud-speakers. I've recommended a new and better system which I'm convinced will get more kids off the sidewalk and on board to pray. The request has gone to the central office of the Big Rebbe— it's a big bureaucracy here—and I don't know what will happen. Although some of the boytcheklachs do share my disappointment when we cruise through neighborhoods and can't get a minion. We'll see what happens.

That's really it. I'm well-fed, feeling fine and am thinking a lot about making alliyah or some career through Yeshiva University—I always wanted to check out New York.

Kain Ehorah,
Yitzhak

P.S. Jacob, (John), is fine too. Although I think he's more into a job with the Lubavitchers.

I recently spoke with conversion expert Professor Michael Weinstein, who teaches in both the Sociology and Economics Departments at McGill University, about the Pearson letter. Weinstein speculates, that due to the continuous numerical decline in the Jewish faith—especially Orthodox—and the current long-term recession, both the Lubavitchers and the boy's interests mesh perfectly.

"If you notice, Pearson consistently mentions his economic potential in the letter. He is aware that there is a paucity of jobs out there and that the Orthodox wing of the Jewish faith is still a growth area. The Lubavitchers, on the other hand, are a quick people. John [Jacob] and Timothy [Yitzhak] must have impressed them with their discipline and intelligence. They were both straight A students at Lower Canada College—[a prestigious Montréal high school] and the Pearson boy for one shows a distinct sign of skepticism when it comes to his own faith."

Weinstein went on to say that this episode is atypical but could be a coming trend within all orthodox religious wings especially because of the cultural emptiness of mainstream religion and the current recession which sees no signs of abating.

Rumors are now circulating that teenagers south of the border have caught wind of the story and are seeking out their cities' Mitzvah Mobile. Good SAT scores are recommended.

STORIES

METAPHYSICS FOR THE TV GENERATION

If Superman arm-wrestled the Incredible Hulk, who would win, George Reeves or Lou Ferrigno?

If Jeannie on "I Dream Of Jeannie" had to do whatever her master Tony commanded her to do, what would happen if he commanded her to give him a blow-job? She'd have to do it, right? So how come he never did?

Same thing on "Bewitched." Why didn't Sam just make them rich, so that Darren didn't have to work for Larry Tate? Larry was a jerk. Why didn't Sam just like kill him or something so that Darren could take over the ad agency? Darren was always coming up with the good ideas anyway. Sam could do that, couldn't she?

Which was lamer, Dean Martin on "The Hollywood Palace" or Dean Martin on "Dean Martin Presents the Golddiggers"? Was there ever anybody lamer than Dean Martin? Doesn't he remind you of your father, maybe just a little bit? Why is that so?

Was there anything going on between Batman and Batgirl? What was the story with her anyway? Batman was really wealthy Bruce Wayne but Batgirl was Commissioner Gordon's daughter, so where did she get all her stuff from? They weren't rich.

Remember "The Real McCoys"? They were a bunch of hillbillies with no money or anything, right? So what was that all about? Why did they make a show out of that?

How come when they adopted Ernie from next door, they didn't change the name of the show to "My Four Sons"? Did one of them die or something? Is that why they didn't change it?

If Marcus Welby was such a great doctor and everything, why did he try to kill himself by getting drunk and running his car in a closed garage?

What happened to the guy who was on "Hogan's Heroes" and then was on "Family Feud"? The English guy. "Family Feud" is still on but not with the English guy. What happened to the English guy?

Remember how they used a laugh track on "M.A.S.H."? How weird was that? What were they thinking? How come television is so junky like that, with all those stupid shows and the fake laughing all the time? If it's funny, you laugh; if it's not funny, you don't. Do they think that by putting a laugh track in, they make it funny? Is it funny because there's laughter, or does laughter make it funny?

BIBLE COMICS

The battle was joined. It was Jesus Christ, Son of God and Holy Redeemer against Spiderman, the old webslinger, Peter Parker, a graduate student bitten by a radioactive spider and who had assumed supernatural strength and agility as a result.

Oof! Bam! Heavenly Father! Jesus turned the loaves into fishes and Spiderman found himself at the bottom of a huge pile of mackerel.

Spiderman squirmed out from under the mass of stinking fish and shot a sticky strand of web-fluid at Jesus. It coiled around his Holy Feet and Spiderman pulled hard. Ouch! Jesus went down like a felled tree.

All day they fought.

It was a draw. Jesus was thinking about Satan and how he'd have to get thee behind him pretty soon, like the day after tomorrow, so he offered the olive branch of peace to Spiderman. Spiderman was thinking if this didn't end soon he'd miss his date with Mary Jane, his girlfriend who didn't know his secret of being Spiderman, so the webslinger accepted.

They shook hands. "Judge not, lest ye be judged, Spiderman," Jesus said.

"Yeah, well, whatever," Spiderman said.

KEHOE RAPPED ON TV

PAUL GRAJNERT

It is obvious from his piece, "Metaphysics for the TV Generation" (page 14, No. 44, 1993) that Mr. John Kehoe does not watch enough television. The answers to his questions are: 1) Lou Ferrigno would win if the Incredible Hulk and Superman arm wrestled. George Reeves has been dead a long time. 2) Tony get a blow-job from Jeannie?! Come on! Tony was only interested in getting rockets off with Major Heally! (Hm?) 3) "Bewitched?" Let me put it this way—the only women allowed to use power (any power) on this program were witches (just replace the "w" in "witches" with a "b" and you'll get the message). 4) Dean Martin, unlike my father, is a genius. "My life is like one long bowel movement." Pure genius! Pure Dino! 5) Her dad's the commissioner! Batgirl comes from a long line of corrupt public servants. She was obviously trying to shed some of that family guilt. Batman and Batgirl?! Robin and Batgirl lost their virginity together. Duh! 6) "The Real McCoys"—Who cares! 7) Ernie was treated as an outsider—never really let in on all the family secrets. Later in life he killed Fred McMurray, but nobody knows this except me and *my* TV. 8) After being stuck in a 15" x 15" x 15" box for God knows how long, wouldn't you, like Marcus Welby, want to kill yourself. 9) Richard Dawson is no longer on TV. Isn't that the only thing that matters? 10) I never laugh when I think I'm alone? Do you? Is that normal? 11) And the answer to the question behind all of Mr. Kehoe's questions: The Seven Deadly Sins! (Gilligan = Ignorance, The Skipper = Gluttony, Mr. Howell = Greed, Mrs. Howell = Sloth, Ginger = Lust, The Professor = Pride, and Marianne = Avarice). Sherwood Schwartz (the creator of "Gilligan's Island" and "The Brady Bunch") = Dean Martin.

THE AMISH STORIES

DAVE BREITHAUPT

BLIND LEMON YODER: AMISH BLUESMAN

Blind Lemon Yoder relaxes on his front porch, blowing a mouth harp into his mike stand. The sound follows a wire to three speakers sitting in his milk house. He fingers a few chords on his Epson Soundmaster and sings:

> My baby left me,
> All dressed in black she was ...
> Oh yeah my baby left me,
> An drove away ...

247

His only audience however, is a herd of unresponsive cows across the road. Perhaps the cows had their own blues, the *Goin' to the Slaughterhouse Next Week Blues.*

Like his brother, Fidel Yoder, who preferred bright colors over the color black, he was exiled from the Greater Amish Community. In fact, if Blind Lemon could see, he would be able to gaze upon his rebel brother's farm down the road. He would be able to savor the Aqua-Shock coloring that made his entire farm vibrate like a swarm of day-glo bees in the valley where it nestled.

Blind Lemon's story was different from his brother's though. His episode of exile began at the Loudonville Amish Jazz Festival. This was a yearly event in the spring when the tribes would gather for a day of traditional Amish tunes.

Oh there was Marvin and Fred Yoder singing the classic *Today We Will Make Cheese,* and the Yoder Sisters performing the ever popular *Do You Need Another Quilt?* Then finally, it was Blind Lemon's turn.

The crowd was in shock almost before he began. Two hired boys, roadies from Danville, wheeled a couple of giant amps onto the stage which were wired to a small generator behind the curtain. They then led Blind Lemon to the stage and plugged his Epson into the amps.

The crowd was unable to stir until Blind Lemon tore into the opening of his *Barn Raisin' Blues* with a couple of Hendrix-like riffs.

> I'm sick ah barn buildin' baby,
> Don't wanna build no mo barns.. .
> Oh I'm sick ah barns baby,
> Don't need another one around.
> If I build another barn baby,
> Ah may jes curl up an' die.. .

Suddenly, as if released from a trance, the Amish crowd went wild. They did not like Blind Lemon Yoder going electric. A testimony to this fact was that despite his handicap, the crowd threw cheese wheels and fresh baked loaves of bread at him. The roadies quickly escorted him from the stage and that was the last time Blind Lemon Yoder ever played the Loudonville Amish Jazz Festival.

Nowadays, you can hear his tunes ambling over the fields as Blind Lemon sings to the cows across the road. You can here him sing all morning, except when Fidel decides to take his Harley for a spin on the track behind his Aqua-Farm, singing those blues as the brothers live out their days in exile.

FIDEL YODER: AMISH REBEL

This year he painted his house "Aqua Shock," including the trim, which was only a few shades darker. Not only was the house this color scheme, so was the out-house, barn, fence, weather vane, lightning rod, and mail-box. He painted his spread fire engine red with apple-green trim the year before. And before that, lavender and Van Gogh yellow. For you see, Fidel, formerly Marvin, was an outcast, a cast-away, banished from the larger Amish community thirty miles north.

His troubles began when a neighbor noticed a toaster in his kitchen and later, a BMW 350 motorcycle stashed under some hay in his barn. The Cuisinart was his final downfall. He was free to do as he pleased now.

Then he bought bargain paint from the local Odd Lots, colors nobody wanted or needed except for Fidel Yoder, Amish Rebel. He was sick of black. Tired of sitting in the dark. He stirred his paint with an electric mixer attached to thirty feet of bright orange extension cords. The righteous claimed you could probably see his spread from the moon. It did have a tendency to glow within the valley that cradled it. Don't need electricity with colors like that, said related Yoders as they stroked their white beards.

"Electricity," Fidel muttered to himself. "Gotta have it." As for his former Amish comrades? "Fuck 'em."

Just wait till next year. You'll see his farm from Mars. Maybe Pluto.

CIRCUMCISION SNIPPETS

Apparently there were two forms of circumcision among ancient Semites. The one practiced in more primal Palestine was performed by women with sharpened stones and the blood was allowed to drip onto and be absorbed by mother earth. The other more abstract practice in Babylon was performed by male priests, the blood caught in a silver bowl filled with water. We can presume it was drunk. But by whom? A sacred-being or the community?

The Americans lost in Vietnam because of historical continu-ity in the circumcision policy during the Second World War. It was then that secular foreskin snipping was generally introduced. So by the Sixties all the troops were circumcised, but all the Generals and the Politicians were not and wanted to save their skins.

Gone but not forgotten. During the Great War the Nobel Prize author Isaac Bashevis Singer, then a child, remembers being evacuated from Warsaw across Austrian lines to a village named Bilgory where there was more food and less plague. "I was able to witness," he writes, "holiday celebrations which had not changed for centuries ... Hay cov-ered the synagogue floor. It was an old synagogue, the Ark carved by an Italian master. On one of the walls hung the matzoh eaten at the end of Passover seder, the Aphikoman. *A metal vase filled with sand contained the prepuces of circumcised infants."*

It is now a few days before the New Year, a holiday celebrating the Bris of Jesus, his circumcision. To this day men get drunk and women weep when their Jewish sons get circumcised. This practice has found its way into Christian New Year's parties.

In the Uffizi Gallery in Florence my mother dragged me around looking for paintings of Christ's Circumcision and exclaiming loudly whenever she found one. Especially when sighting Andrea Mantegna's altarpiece done for the chapel of Castello di Corti at Mantua. And each time re-telling the story about how she cried at mine.

When my friend was pregnant with our child I secretly wished for, and got, a girl. Rationalizing to myself that I enjoy hanging out with women and that they have real role choice in modern western society, the deeper reason circled around circumcision. Should I or shouldn't I? By circumcising him, I fantasized, it would make us the same. Yet then he would be different from his European contemporaries, who remain uncircumcised. Or if allowed to be foreskinned it would make us genital strangers. But my most profound paranoia was this. If I hesitated my father would fly someone over the Atlantic to perform the bris, who would parachute from an airplane knife in mouth. And as it is written: I would have a Mohel on the roof.

THE SPANKING OF THE LAMB

And the Lord gathered the twelve around him and the Lord said:

"Which of you took five bucks from my wallet?"

And Peter, their leader of the twelve brought forward a small frightened lamb and Peter said:

"This errant lamb took your five bucks, Lord."

And Jesus held the lamb fast in his arm and did not ask for the five bucks back, but merely spanked the errant lamb once across his backside, and not too hard, and let him go.

When the twelve, who were gathered at a distance saw this they exclaimed among themselves:

"Surely our Lord is a merciful Lord."

And the Lord heard them and He said "that's right" upon which Jesus laid himself down beside the fire for it had grown late.

The following morning Jesus rose before dawn and went to the market to purchase the Sabbath bread. And it was at the checkout counter that he discovered 60 bucks had been taken from his wallet. And the Lord made haste back to where the twelve were still asleep, and with a length of cedar He walked among them.

And the Lord was not so merciful.

3
TRAVEL & TRANSLATION

FRANCE, 1945

That's it, I was in Compiègne
    I was nineteen, and so happy.

The farm in its snowy woods
    was so far behind, less than a fantasy
where the letters from home came from,
    distress and love—my uncle's
fatal heart attack after downing a pound
    of salami, which he was warned not to do.

I stood in the Forest, near the actual site
    where the railroad car stood where
the Germans signed ignominiously after WW I
    and where Hitler forced the French
in 1945 to return the favor, then carted off
    the car, chairs, inkwells, and table
whizzing it off for kerf, fertilizer
    for cabbages.

It was spring—I descended the Paris train
    amidst lilacs, rampant jonquils, and daffodils,
trilling birds, daisy-studded grass—
    all of France was a superb lawn!

I sang the only French song I knew:
    "Frère Jacques," beneath a cherry tree,
stood on one leg, and felt absurd.
    A widow in black, with a potato for a nose,
chained in sorrow, clanked, stared past me,
    and threw crumbs to some ducks.
I didn't ask then where I'd be years up the road,
    a rancid vest-pocket with heirloom
watch and tobacco grains, my uncle's.
    In qhoaw eooma qouls I play? For I knew then
in Compiègne that I loved men.

There's a full moon in California.
    Why won't it sail backwards? If I could
ride the Metro back to Compiègne, I would.
    If I could sniff spring haze,
the honey-colored palace, if I could smell
    the earthworms weltering through the lawn,
the beaked red palates of the ravenous, French, spring
      robins ...

BORIS VIAN

AN ALTERNATIVE TAIL

translated from French by Julia Older

In certain fair booths
filled with Peruvian alguazils
and large swordfish with death rattles in their ears,
next to the shaggy barbazons
of bouncing cournafluches
and windy-wrigglers from Malta,
you encounter gross people with canine eyes
who simulate a larval mania
and cover themselves with tawdry rags
hand-decorated by a lay brother
(who from childhood has specialized
in the question of color).

Naturally, for ten francs
you're almost permitted gravelly dust,
garlic fumes, the scraping of feet
on the hand-waxed wooden ramp,
and a dog-eared placard announcing.
"MY PARENTS WERE RAPED."

ALAIN BOSQUET

AN ATHEIST'S CREED

translated from French by Edouard Roditi

"I'm going down to the village,"
says God, "to feel closer
to those who still want to believe in me.
I promise whiter wool to the shepherd
and juicier pears to the pear-tree.
I'm wearing my wooden clogs,
my sweater and my cap.
I drink water from the fountain
but refuse to take the children
to school:
being a zealot is a sin.
I greet nobody
and pretend I'm passing by mistake.
A few old men
   want to drag me to the church,
      but I cannot kneel in front of myself!

256

I'm respected, which makes me happy.
Tonight I'll sleep
with my beloved comet."

God scolds his poet:
"I'm still awaiting your hymn to my greatness
and your ode to my glory;
don't I inspire you?"
The poet remains aloof,
worried by a syllable,
a verb that has wandered off,
the meaning of a word that keeps him awake.
God says: "You still have thirty days
to convince the crowds
of my eternity."
"It's useless," replies the poet,
"I am the god who replaces you;
I've even written a satire
to explain why
you can no longer be divine."

God says: "I felt like a fresh wind in my soul;
I was quite sure of myself,
and even chaos seemed friendly.
Between being and no-being
all conflict had ceased, that evening.
I somehow guessed
that time would be born from space,
and the latter from the former, with ease.
I thought that the unknown
should more wisely become knowledgeable,
and the indefinite
should at last define itself.
Suddenly, without shame, I had the courage
to create the universe."

"When I want to take shape,"
says God, "I have a spate of choices:
I can be oak or tiger,
I can become brook or sky.
Sometimes, I'm more subtle and become
an idea, a thrill, a bliss,
or else, in a malicious mood, a unicorn eating roses."
"When I want to take shape,"

says God, "I have no choice:
in the middle of a page, whatever the book,
I become the dullest word."

"You think," says God, "that God doesn't suffer?
He seems serene and sure of himself:
he has the power, I grant you,
but nobody dares criticize him.
You think he can bear his eternity?
He cannot conceive
his own death nor his suicide,
for God is not perfect."

Man sang:
"The tiger is born, the tiger leaps,
the tiger vanishes,
but you, oh God, you keep on living and living. "
Man sang:
"The rose blossoms and withers,
but you, oh God, you keep on living and living.
Man sang:
"The river flows, the river runs dry,
but you, oh God, you keep on living and living.
Man sang:
"The word is fit;
the word grows old but then gets lost,
but you, oh God, you keep on living and living."
God decided that man was right
and should therefore die.

THE FRENCH: THEIR CAUSE AND CURE

BOB BLACK

Like many others, I honor the extraordinary French contribution to
civilization. We need a way to keep the contribution and dispense
with the French. Perhaps they could be kept under house arrest and
only let out under supervision—doubtless the Germans could attend
to this—to write books, cook meals and oversee the hogs as they
root out the truffles.

Why the French are such puds is hard to figure. Once they cut
a great figure in the world when it was small. They've been washed
up lots longer than the English but are even slower to admit it, much
less enjoy it. Their impudence/impotence ratio is unacceptably
high.

They're not so good looking either. Speaking French is such an exercise in facial contortion that by puberty they've all got vertical lines in their faces. When the vicissitudes of age and dissipation etch the usual lines of latitude also, the French face resembles a tic-tac-toe board. Were Dorian Gray a Frenchman only Mondrian could do justice to his Picture.

"Hell is other people," a Frenchman once wrote. Other people— foreigners, Jews, Protestants, Alsatians, even Belgians—account for much of the best in French civilization. In olden times, Scots and Irish gave their armies some backbone; more recently the Foreign Legion's done their dirty work. Their kings, knowing the character of their subjects, preferred the protection of Swiss Guards. No tinge of chauvinism— a French word, of course enters into these observations. The French love each other no more than they love anybody else. Who is any outsider to question the French on a judgment of taste?

The best thing they ever did was invent "69."

DERRIDA AND LSD

KIRBY OLSON

Derrida's *Dissemination* was published in 1972, the heyday of the LSD era. Was Derrida aware of how many drug references he was making? Did Derrida take LSD? The experience of reading his texts is similar to what is often described by those who have taken LSD— one is knocked off one's center and participates in a kaleidoscopic series of interrelated puns and chance encounters which mushroom gaily, in a way that can be either playful or bewildering or both. Chance connections read like eternal insights into the nature of things, etymologies run wild; memory systems and sense organs blend; and a monstrous sense of humor gets off its leash. Derrida is a monstrous humorist in French (his American translators tend to make him seem dull and earnest in comparison); his level of punning is simply terrifying, the links he makes between chapters and books are not just sly, but uncanny; his sudden stabs of irreverence are more than clowning, they take out entire systems of thought by simply finding a loose thread, and giving a pull. The title of his book, aside from being about the spread of the seeds of thought through language; and the seeds of life through sperm; is also still a widely used term among drug-dealers, and the agents who attempt to prosecute them. Derrida constantly alludes to persistent fantasies of the period, such as turning on a whole city via the water supply:

Le sperme, l'eau, l'encre, la peinture, la teinte parfumée: *le pharmokon* pénètre toujours comme le liquide, il se boit, s'absorbe, s'introduit à l'interieur, qu'il marque d'abord avec la dureté du type, l'envahissant bientôt et l'inondant de son remède, de son breuvage, de sa boisson, de sa potion, de son poison.

Dans le liquide, les opposés passent plus facilement l'un dans l'autre. Le liquide est l'élément du *pharmakon*. Et l'eau, pureté du liquide, se laisse le plus facilement, le plus dangereusement pénétrer puis corrompre par le *pharmakon* avec lequel elle se mélange et compose aussitôt. D'où, parmi les lois qui doivent gouverner la societé agricole, celle qui protège sévèrement l'eau.

from "La Phammacie de Platon,"
in *La dissémination*, p. 175

Sperm, water, ink, paint, perfumed dye: the *pharmakon* always penetrates like a liquid; it is absorbed, drunk, introduced into the inside, which it first marks with the hardness of the type, soon to invade it and inundate it with its medicine, its brew, its potion, its poison.

In liquid, opposites are more easily mixed. Liquid is the element of the pharmakon. And water, pure liquidity, is most easily and dangerously penetrated then corrupted by the pharmakon, with which it mixes and easily unites. Whence, among all the laws governing an agricultural society, comes the one severely protecting water.

Dissemination, trans. Barbara Johnson, p. 152

The very last paragraphs of *Plato's Pharmacy* are knockings on the door, at once recalling the traditional drug paranoia—who is it?—could it be the police?—and recalling Coleridge's session in which his opium-laced vision of Kublai Khan was interrupted by a similar knocking. Derrida's book was conceived when the spirit of the Eleusinian mysteries was seen as a necessary antidote to the decades of rigid logic that had preceded them. Every notion was being reexamined. One of the central themes in the book is the bewildering question over what is alive and what is dead, a question not bewildering, apparently, to those actually on LSD, as the sense of self so completely disappears, the sense of being a subject is so completely abandoned, that the whole sense of personal immediacy that one usually has in life fades, and is replaced by an impersonal floating sensation of startling detachment. So severe is this change that one's very foundations for the belief that one is alive are deconstructed, leading those who partake straight to the medicine closet of Tibetan Buddhism and its main remedy for this state of non-corporeal reality, *The Book of the Dead* (currently in paperback with a preface by Timothy Leary). Derrida's book is obviously an extended allegory of the hallucinogenic experience, while *at the same time* being a serious investigation of Platonic themes, each providing insights into the other. Derrida is a survivor, who to my knowledge has left no trace of his own pharmaceutical history (for all the obvious reasons, the most obvious of which is that it's illegal, and further, frowned upon professionally. He was arrested in Prague in the early 1980s as an "intemational drug dealer," but the evidence looked trumped, and was likely political harassment because of his association through his Czech wife with the Charter 77 movement—which was preparing a more subversive remedy for the city's ills—laughter, jazz, and poetry). My understanding, based on an admittedly small sample of sixty people, who enjoy and do not enjoy reading Derrida, is that those who have taken LSD read in it a way of understanding the essential incommunicability of the hallucinogenic experience; while those who do not read Derrida with pleasure, or who read him with pain and puzzlement, are by and large those whom the drug experiences to be had in the late 1960s passed them by. There is another variety of Derrida readers who read Derrida in English, for professional reasons, which is another experience altogether, and which may produce either hot and contentious rhetoric, or merely a sense of pride at having completed an arduous task, or even a renewed sense of philosophy's possibilities, but not the sensation of walking on air which I believe it was originally calculated to produce. As time goes on, and more and more students have not taken the proper *pharmakon*, Derrida and other poststructuralists may come to seem even more of an aberration, a lyric explosion which resembles an extreme manic high, which they will merely shake their heads over. Socrates, who partook of alcohol, is likely to have a more enduring following. *Plato's Pharmacy* is a referendum on the LSD use of the period: is it a poison or a medicine? My own experience is that it left me unable to speak for close to a year. As a result, I turned to writing to regain control of language which, via the Egyptian God Thoth, deity of writing and magic, is another potable theme of Derrida's *Dissemination*. LSD is both a poison and a medicine. It leads to Mallarméan silence. It killed half of my friends. It gave the other half their first taste of Life.

JACQUES DERRIDA IN BATON ROUGE: THE PHILOSOPHER IN THE CITY OF FLAYED SKINS

I am asked by the *Exquisite Corpse* to interview the philosopher about his lecture, "Gift of Death—the Secrets of European Responsibility." There is something strangely funerary about all this. Was it to be a talk about the body of Dionysus strewn to the winds, with attendant bacchants and bacchantes? I consider the philosopher a friend, I have listened to him intently for years, my ear and eye riveted,

MARIA GOODWIN

261

not knowing whether what I saw or heard was his truth, or the fiction I needed to create as his truth. Reading his words makes me hear his voice.

My friend the philosopher has been too close to death this year, and that closeness comes only when the death is of another, and that other is beloved. I find myself too aware of this, wanting to protect. The interview is to be brief, but it is supposed to include one question—a question meant to elucidate a statement by Kirby Olson who pretends that Derrida's 1972 essay "*La pharmacie de Platon*" is a referendum on the LSD use of the period: is it a poison or a medicine?" I completely missed the Sixties myself, went straight from the Twenties to the Twenty-First Century. Someone capable of an oversight of this magnitude can be forgiven for overlooking most of Derrida's lecture, the topic of her absent summary. Moreover, we must concede that the lecture did take place during the missing period between the Twenties and the Twenty-First Century. (It seemed, in fact, to take up a large chunk of that epoch.) Furthermore, MG continues, her conversations with Derrida are not about things like LSD. When she "speaks with the philosopher" they "speak of Artaud, or of the Thirties, but mostly we speak of what I've seen in her work." Perhaps as she discourses on his works, he fills her in on the Thirties, which, like the Sixties, she missed. Finally, MG gets to her lamentable conclusion: "There is no way in which I can ask Derrida if he ever took LSD."

Cannot intrude. It would be out of line, and for me out of character. When I speak with the philosopher, we speak of Artaud, or of the Thirties, but mostly we speak of what I've seen in his work. We don't speak often enough. I have been waiting since 1983 for his visit, but this time he is not coming to see me.

Derrida arrives late. He greets me warmly, with our usual double *bises*. We use *vous*. I have never dared to go beyond that barrier. He looks more tired than I have ever seen him, almost weary. I have spent the morning listening to the Canadian novelist Nicole Brossard. She has spoken of her bilingualism, her double culture. She speaks as a feminine subject, that is as subject who can only speak when it writes. She speaks about how to write—the rites of writing: "ritual with trembling…ritual with shock…ritual with slippage…ritual with breath". It all sounds better in French—*tremblement, choc, glissement, souffle*. I am convinced. Her voice is lovely. Its accent antique. It echoes from elsewhere. (That is also the title of the Conference: "Renvois d'ailleurs.") Derrida enters. He sees a friend's face—mine. The greeting described above takes place. We are listening to V.Y. Mudimbe's fables and parables "From Nowhere and from Everywhere." Mudimbe speaks of Humanity, Nationality and the Politics of Identity. Identity is as transparent as the Identity cards which—I paraphrase—like economical tables condense us so we can be conceived as socio-historical events. Am I a socio-historical event? Is this Conference?

I have not told Derrida that I have secret orders and a mission, but I am prepared to listen to him. How can you prepare to listen to Derrida? By reading what he plans to speak about. Kant and Heidegger, Edmund Jabès and Lucette Finas fill my shelves since I've been listening to Derrida. Sarah Kofman and Jean-Luc Nancy too. And then there is Derrida himself. He writes books faster than I can read them, because there is always homework to do. You cannot read Derrida without reading what he is writing about, although it is common practice to dispense with the homework. I spent the evening before preparing, reading Kierkegaard—*Fear and Trembling*. I retain a quote from Johannes de Silentio's "Preface": "The present writer is nothing of a philosopher; he is *poetice et eleganter*, an amateur writer who neither writes the System nor *promises* of the System, who neither subscribes to the System nor ascribes anything to it. He writes because for him it is a luxury which becomes the more agreeable and evident, the fewer there are who buy and read what he writes." Johannes is ironic, Kierkegaard too.

We brave the "Tiger Lair" for coffee. I make my request. I couch it with the proper *formule de politesse*: "Je voudrais vous demander un service." Perhaps, it's the request for the favor. I have asked what I should not have dared. He is tired, and he doesn't like to give interviews. They always turn out wrong. Perhaps, Saturday, at the end of the Conference several questions. I thought we were better friends. But his refusal has nothing to do with friendship. He is tired. He fears interviews. I suggest instead producing a summary of the lecture. "Je ne voudrais rien faire pour incommoder un ami de longue date." Maybe I don't know what that word means—friend, or maybe I do. It has to do with obligation and concern.

The room for the lecture, an antiquated amphitheater in the Geology building, is packed. We are late because we have all been at a reception, the speaker, the colloquium organizers. I see a friendly face— Patrick Mensah's. He is surrounded by empty seats two rows from the back of the hall. He is one of the organizers of the Colloquium. The other is David Wills, an Antipodean. Derrida has come to visit David. David is translator and presenter. For a moment he peers over Derrida's shoulder. I have a postcard image of Socrates and Plato. And then they change places. Derrida begins. That voice—very fluid in English tonight. The translation is a good one. We learn first about the secrets of European responsibility, or how it is seen by the philosopher Jan Patocka in his essay "La civilisation technique est-elle une civilisation de déclin, et pourquoi?". I do not know this philosopher. I expected Kierkegaard, but he too speaks of fear and trembling—*mysterium tremendum*.

263

That mind which I know for its rigor moves point by point through its logic. The repetition turns to chant. I notice for the first time a woman signing for the deaf. She is smiling, her hands dancing. I *see*, actually *see*, Derrida's words for the first time. I cannot understand my eyes. I rely on my ears. They take me to familiar places, places where Derrida has been before—*don, crypte, secret*. Silences, omissions, names being obliterated, hidden under the palimpsest. Questions of name and signature and of the secret name one calls one's self.

The sacrifice of Isaac. Abraham has led us to Kierkegaard, to the trembling of fear and trembling. Abraham defies the ethical. Keeps silent when his son asks him about the sacrifice. I am transcribing my notes—"such a silence takes over his own discourse"—he speaks, speaking in order to keep the secret—"God will provide the sacrificial lamb." Derrida speaks of the responsibility of always being alone as soon as one speaks. There is a grave theological problem. I listen rather than care to argue. "Frightful mystery" which makes us tremble. Levels of obligation and of duty, risks of absolute sacrifice of the father ready to put to death his beloved son. Is there no darker thought? I am painfully aware of sacrifices. We have been sitting for more than two hours. I am on my third pen—blue, black, red. The woman with the dancing hands is still smiling, her fingers, still as nimble as hummingbird wings. Is God completely other? Where is Kierkegaard—"Tout autre est tout autre." I am riveted, but I have lost Kierkegaard. I am following Derrida. The last words in my notes—"he sees in secret"—*obscundito*.

It takes many minutes to empty the overheated room. Four hundred people turn into eight. We are having dinner. I have been included. The air-conditioning drones and now I am trembling from the cold. I hardly remember what we say while we are eating. There is talk of live Christmas trees planted in Derrida's garden after they are stripped of their ornaments at the end of the holiday season. Is Derrida a Druid? We have gone from the religions of the book to the religion of the tree. But of course they are one in the same.

I drive two of the speakers and Patrick back to the campus. There is talk of tobacco—fragrant Dutch blend. I hear my words turned back on me, echoing: "J'ai un service à vous demander." Now it is Derrida who is asking for the favor. He has spent three hours talking about a father sacrificing his son, and he cannot keep from thinking of his own. It's a postal problem. One only a father can solve. He needs to have a letter Fed-Exed to his younger son, with a photocopy of the genitor's National Identity Card, for an official purpose which needs not be disclosed. I accept to fulfill the request. I discover his secret name. I discover that it costs half as much to send a letter by Federal Express from Baton Rouge to Paris as it does in the other direction.

Is this autobiographical disclosure really necessary?

Derrida was to make others the following day. He spoke in "Le mono-linguisme de l'autre" about a child—himself—whose language, his only language, is not his own, about a child who loses the only nationality that he has—about what it is to be French, and not to be French, and grow up in North Africa during World War II. The Jews lost their nation-ality, and Derrida discovered that the culture which he thought was his was not. I am touched by his sincerity and simplicity. This is not the first time. I am moved by the disclosures. He understood what it was to be a "franco-maghrébin"—North-African French. But, then again, as he said, doesn't any one who writes learn that this duplicity of having a culture which is simultaneously one's own and not one's own—is the very nature of literary culture? Derrida's monolinguism seemed quite bilingual to me. Yes, we know writing and speaking are not the same.

I should speak of the response to Derrida—David's. I remember the title—"Faking It." It shifted between French and English and believ-ing and trusting—*croire* and *croire*, from parody to barely veiled aggres-sion. Does that have something to do with faking it? We move from solemn secret to performance. There was talk of false fathers and *pollu-tions nocturnes* which became *émissions nocturnes*—media productions, I suppose, to be broadcast on the networks of bad dreams. I woke up when I heard Gayatri Spivak speaking of "Identity as Wound, Decision as the Tearing of Time, Philosophy-Translation." Her voice is not Derrida's, but her own. Its inflections as soothing and startling as differ-ent and as seductive as his. I am again captured by a voice, by nimble fin-gers which punctuate with mudras. I like the way she presents herself—as a woman who always followed the Spirit and always did what she wanted. She spoke of Echo as analyst and Narcissus and—more family histories quoted her mother more than she quoted Derrida: "Speak the truth, work hard, help the poor." I think I would like Gaya-tri's mother. I wonder about translation. Did Derrida become famous because Gayatri Spivak translated him? Echo as Analyst. David asks a question about her garment—a Bengali sari. It fits her perfectly—the gar-ment not the question. I too ask her a question about love and sacrifice, about women's sacrifice of love when they follow the Spirit. She does not really answer me directly. I don't mind. I never asked the LSD question. I still don't understand sacrifice. I only condone those which are symbolic and leave no red stains—and never, but never let them be of love. I do like knowing the secrets—Derrida's, David's, Gayatri's?—and having a secret name and a signature, my own.

MAX CAFARD

DERRIDA'S SECRET NAME, OR, WHAT TRANSPIRED IN THE AUDITORIUM OF GAEA AND LOGOS

I recently discovered that Columbia University had decided to remodel the Audubon Ballroom, where Malcolm X was assassinated. The University decided to make it into a Biotechnology Center. There were protests against gutting the interior and effacing the traces of history. Columbia went on with its plans, but agreed to preserve the bullet-hole from the bullet that killed Malcolm. I imagine some future guide pointing out into space. "Over there is the famous bullethole: when the wall was demolished the hole was left intact, as you can see, for posterity." Inspired by Columbia, I have decided to create a Museum of Absences, which will contain famous holes, voids, vacuities, spaces, and other notable specimens of Non-Being. Columbia has been asked to donate its renowned bullet-hole. Richard Nixon has been requested to send the celebrated gap in his presidential tapes. Various dictatorships ("friendly" and "unfriendly," without discrimination) have been asked to be so kind as to send the Disappeared.

The immediate purpose of this communication is to request permission from *Exquisite Corpse* to include in the Museum's "Literature of Absence" collection Maria Goodwin's recent article "Jacques Derrida in Baton Rouge: The Philosopher in the City of Flayed Skins" (*Exquisite Corpse*, No. 37). The article is notable for the multitude of Absences contained within it. First, MG informs us that her purpose was originally to interview Derrida and to ask him about the obvious influence of LSD on his work. We find instead the Absence of that interview. Next, we discover that she proposes, in the Absence of the interview, a "summary of the lecture" that was given by Derrida. Fortunately, we are treated to no such summary, which is replaced by a few sketchy remarks about the content of the lecture. But finally, and most importantly, we discover the most significant Absence—let's call it the Dominant Absence—in the article. This is the Absence of Derrida's Secret Name. Ironically, the Dominant Absence depends on an abundant Presence. The Presence of "the philosopher,"Jacques Derrida. Let's examine the way in which MG presents this Presence.

MARIA ANNOUNCES HIS ARRIVAL

MG prefaces her announcement with an apology for her failure to submit "the philosopher" to the acid test. She associates LSD with the Sixties, which are curiously Absent for her. And that which is associated with the Absent, must, according to the rules of strict logic, also be Absent. She reports: "I completely missed the Sixties myself, went straight from the Twenties to the Twenty-first Century." Someone capable of an oversight of this magnitude can be forgiven for overlooking most of Derrida's lecture, the topic of her absent summary. Moreover, we must concede that the lecture did take place during the missing period between the Twenties and the Twenty-First Century. (It seemed, in fact, to take up a large chunk of that epoch.) Furthermore, MG continues, her conversations with Derrida are not about things like LSD. When she "speaks with the philosopher" they "speak of Artaud, or of the Thirties, but mostly we speak of what I've seen in his work." Perhaps as she discourses on his works, he fills her in on the Thirties, which, like the Sixties, she missed. Finally, MG gets to her lamentable conclusion: "There is no way in which I can ask Derrida if he ever took LSD."

We must consider further MG's inability to ask things of Derrida. At this point, I want only to note how close she came to the forbidden topic of hallucinogenic writing. Of their three acceptable topics of conversation, one is, of all things, "Artaud." Why did it not occur to her to delicately remark, "Jacques, something seems to have slipped my mind— what was it that Artaud used to do with the Tarahumaras down in Mexico?" They spoke of Artaud, the philosopher-poet who says he "did not renounce as a group those dangerous disassociations which Peyote seems to provoke and which I had pursued by other means." And who adds immediately, he who wished to "bring back" that which "lay hidden," and "that it serve, that it serve precisely by *my crucifixion*" [*Antonin Artaud: Selected Writings*, ed. Susan Sontag (Berkeley: Univ. of California Press, 1976), p. 391]. Can she speak of this to "the philosopher"? "No way."

"Derrida arrives late," she reports. (It is still well before the Twenty-first Century, however). "He greets me warmly, with our usual double *bises*." MG is slightly deceptive here. To an Anglo-Saxon audience this might appear to be a shocking profusion of *bises*. Actually, it is the minimum number of *bises* ever given by *any* French person in any century. "We use *vous*," she continues. This formality is, however, no reflection on the intensity of their friendship. No doubt for Derrida it merely indicates the multiplicity inherent in all subjects. But for MG, there is another rationale: "I have never dared go beyond that barrier."

MG does not dare. Derrida is a Presence to be reckoned with. There are questions not to be asked, requests not to be made, words not to be spoken. We are getting to her point. This is a story of "Fear and Trembling." Which is also, coincidentally, the topic of Derrida's lecture, which MG recounts briefly.

THE SCENE OF THE READING:
SUBTROPISM IN THE SUBTROPICS

"The room for the lecture, an antiquated amphitheater in the geology building, is packed." Note that MG employs the tense of Presence. But she is interested only in a certain Presence. She fails to note the *nature* (the *physis*, the physicality) of Presence, the nature of the Being-Present, for the audience. The physicality of four hundred people packed into a room without ventilation. The physicality of the dismal surroundings. The physicality of the intense, penetrating heat (an intensity that does not intend like language, a penetration that does not penetrate like Logos). A physicality that amplifies itself before a word has been spoken, during the long delay as the assembled multitude awaits what they have come for: the Presence of "the philosopher." From a certain point of view, this is merely a delayed gratification, and therefore no cause for complaint. From another point of view, it is not a delay at all. "We are late because we have all been at a reception, the speaker, the colloquium organizers." Some have already received the Presence, while others wait for their reception.

"The philosopher" enters. His Presence is applauded. MG informs us that she always prepares for Derrida's lectures by reading what Derrida plans to speak (or read) about. She is the auditor made in Heaven! Knowing that it is to be his topic, she has read Kierkegaard's *Fear and Trembling* (on the story of Abraham's willingness to sacrifice his son Isaac). She has discovered that Kierkegaard's pseudonymous author Johannes de Silentio "is ironic." She has discovered that Kierkegaard himself is ironic. She does not mention that Kierkegaard once called himself, perhaps not entirely ironically, "the master of irony" (he wrote a masters' thesis on the concept of irony).

"The philosopher" does not begin at once. The auditors are required to sit through a very long, adulatory introduction, by a certain David Wills, whom MG calls the "presenter." The presenter makes a feeble attempt to sound like an intellectual on LSD, but no one is convinced. The presenter concludes his remarks by presenting Derrida, who is then fully Present. "The philosopher" begins to speak, or rather, to read. This is "*lecture*" in the *sens littéral*. He spends several hours reading the long text, one that is obviously written for publication—not for oral delivery, in English translation, to this particular group of auditors in this particular Geology Auditorium, in, as MG would have it, this "City of Flayed Skins." As MG notes of Derrida at one point, "I have listened to him intently for years." The audience knew the feeling very well that night. Even MG shows some awareness of the conditions of Derrida's Presence. At one point she herself rises to the level of irony: "I am painfully aware of sacrifices. We have been sitting for two hours." But, in general, MG is overwhelmed by what merely bathes others in sweat. She takes copious notes. As she exclaims at one point: "I am on my third pen—blue, black, red."

The title of this text is "Gift of Death—the Secrets of European Responsibility." "The Gift of Death." No doubt after several hours many in the audience began to pray for that gift. As the temperature soared and the oxygen-supply plummeted, some may have indeed come close to the ultimate sacrifice. We the auditors became, collectively, Isaac, the child. We followed obediently, like little lambs. Our Father, Derrida-da finally spared us. He finally stepped back from the altar of sacrifice (a table conveniently placed before him).

What do we make of the reference to "European Responsibility"? It would not be difficult to conclude that Derrida, in subjecting the audience to such torture, was one irresponsible European. But this would be a merely ethical judgement. We had entered the realm of the Father, the realm of the Teleological Suspension of the Ethical. So the audience had no right to complain. What may not be entirely clear is the nature of the Telos for which Derrida so harshly suspended the ethical. There is only one possible justification: the entire event, the Presence of the philosopher, was a brilliant joke. Derrida's experiment: to see how long an audience could remain passive, could suffer, could offer itself sacrificially, hoping to be magically impregnated by the *logoi spermatikoi*, the seeds of his Logos, the phallic wisdom of the philosopher. Derrida would, through his ironic persistence in such a travesty, reveal the absurdity of his own power.

Unfortunately, this is only wishful thinking. The Spirit of Gravity prevailed. As Kierkegaard pointed out, the ethical is not suspended for the sake of the aesthetic. MG got her categories right. She reports that the reading was about the "*mysterium tremendum*." But it is clear that for her the true *mysterium tremendum* is Derrida himself. She exhibits a truly religious awe. It is for that reason that there are questions that "cannot" be asked of him. She calls him "the philosopher," unquestionably comparing Derrida to the Aristotle of scholasticism, the ultimate authority-figure among thinkers. But this reference, though not without validity, is deceptive. Is not the definition of a "philosopher" one to whom one poses questions—any and all questions? It is obvious that Derrida is seen as more than a mere "philosopher." As we shall discover, he is the One with the Secret Name, the Name that she cannot utter.

After several hours of reading, "the philosopher" stops, and the event is over. No questions are allowed, from the audience any more than from MG. The tired, damp throng files out. They may go forth into the world and report that they experienced the Presence of Derrida.

Whose Presence was this? It was not that of Jacques Derider, everybody's favorite pen-pal, the Jacques who cracked us up, and himself, in *La Carte postale*. Not that of the deconstructor of onto-logo-theo-phallo-centrism. It was the Presence of "Jacques Derrida," "the philosopher," and more than philosopher, the One with the Secret Name. It was a logocentric Presence. It was a theological Presence. It was a phallic Presence. MG writes of "*monolinguisme*" but she does not write of monotheism or monolingamism.

Who is this "Maria" and whose Name does she announce by its absence? She remarks that his words—his Logos—"take me to similiar places where Derrida has been before—*don, crypte, secret.*" What gift does he give? Into what secret places does he go? Does he leave stains? Or does he give immaculately? Will he come again?

Strangely, MG finds it worth noting that colloquium participant Gayatri Spivak's "voice is not Derrida's but her own," and that "her garment...fits her perfectly." (She does not note that Spivak had dyed her hair purple.) Of Derrida's garment we hear nothing, except perhaps a faint echo of "if I may but touch his garment...."

LIEBESDIENSTE

It should be clear now that the Presence of the One with the Secret Name was a service. The audience's reception of "the philosopher" was also a service. But we hear much more about services.

MG politely proposes to Derrida: "*Je voudrais vous demander un service.*" The favor is the interview, and perhaps a chance to pose *The Corpse*'s killer question. But no! Derrida declines, because "he's tired" and "he fears interviews"! Un-huh, let's not scare Derrida. Apparently, "the philosopher" has not entirely lost his sense of humor. Taking his latter comment seriously, MG suggests foregoing the interview and "instead producing a summary of the lecture." Why MG thinks that readers of *Exquisite Corpse* would be interested in her notes on a text certain to be published in full is not clear. In any case, she gives up on the interview. "*Je ne voudrais rien faire pour incommoder un ami de longue date,*" she remarks generously. But despite an *amitié de longue conservation*, Derrida doesn't mind imposing considerable inconvenience on poor MG. In lieu of an interview he demands of her three pens (blue, black, and red) worth of *incommodité!* MG says, later, "I only condone those [sacrifices] that are symbolic and leave no red stains." But here it is, a copious sacrifice of stains: black and blue, red. Jacques! Jacques! A paltry pair of *bises* and then this!

Later Derrida turns the tables on MG: "J'ai un service à vous demander," he declares. It concerns his son. As MG puts it, "He has spent three hours talking about a father sacrificing his son, and he cannot help thinking of his own." Perhaps the three-hour lecture was Derrida's mnemonic device for reminding himself that he had to send a letter to his son. "He needs to have a letter Fed-Exed to his younger son, with a photocopy of the genitor's National Identity Card, for an official purpose which needs [sic] not be disclosed." MG is a good friend, and is happy to accommodate "the genitor." A more calculating would-be interviewer might take advantage of the situation and tell "the genitor": I'll mail your letter under two conditions: 1) You disclose what the hell the official purpose is; and 2) You tell me whether you ever took LSD. But MG blows it, settling for the chance to see "the genitor's" I.D.

In fact, this turns out to be even more revealing [put that under erasure: "more revelatory"] than even the LSD question. As she informs the reader, she discovers something which finally gets us to the Dominant Absence of her article, and qualifies it for inclusion in the Museum of Absences. "I discover his secret name." She is gettng to the climax of her story. The *dénouement* of the Not. Derrida, we now know, is "the genitor," the Father. And we are now in the realm of the famous Name of the Father. Le Nom du P. (Pere, Phallus, Philosopher). She does not reveal to us that Name, needless to say.

Little did MG know that Derrida had played his old postal trick. He's been doing it ever since he wrote *La Carte postale*, the most brilliant philosophical joke of the century. At every appearance he earnestly asks someone to send a fake I.D. to his non-existent son ("Isaac," I believe). They talk about it for months afterward in the literature departments. MG fell for it. Derrida is a master at "Faking It." "Faking Id." "Faking I.D."

GAEA BEFORE LOGOS EXCEPT AFTER ARCHE

But an important question remains for us. Why was Derrida called to the Geology Auditorium—the Auditorium of Gaea and Logos? The Place of Gaea before Logos? Perhaps another mnemonic device was at work. That is, a device that undoes the vice of forgetfulness (a professional vice of philosophers). An urgent message from Gaea, by way of Mnemosyne, daughter and granddaughter of Gaea. Why was he called to the Auditorium of Gaea and Logos? For "the philosopher" to bring his Logos to his Auditors, but, perhaps more importantly, to give "the philosopher" the opportunity to listen to the voice of Gaea, who comes before Logos. Perhaps because "the philosopher" in his quest for Logos—even a Logos that purports to subvert the dominant Logos—tends to overlook the Earth. It escapes his notice. Perhaps if the Earth "had taken on the figure of a very rare and tremendously large green BIRD, with a red beak, sitting in a tree on the mound, and perhaps even whistling in an unheard of manner," Derrida would have noticed it! Or perhaps that of a tremendously large green Word!

The fate that brought Derrida to the Auditorium, the place of hearing, destined us to hear his Logos and for him to hear Gaea. As "the philosopher" droned on, Gaea took her revenge. The heat of her anger pervaded the atmosphere. Could he hear the groaning of Gaea, the flowing of her salty waters? The Word is indeed Flesh. The Soul is indeed something about the Body. About the Terrestrial Body also.

DRUNK IN MOONLIGHT
TALKING POETRY

STEFAN HYNER

A few days ago my neighbor came by for a visit. Since a hail storm had just destroyed his tobacco harvest, he'd brought along a couple bottles of local wine and we ended up talking poetry as the moon rose above the bamboo in the garden. I always share my copy of *Exquisite Corpse* w/ Hewel, who is 65 years old and never spent much time in school; the war wouldn't allow for it. After WW II he worked several years for the U.S. civil services where he discovered Olson, Creeley and Co. for himself. His knowledge of verse is by far deeper than mine, for he so easily draws together Walther von der Vogelweide, Villon, Whitman and Su Tung-p'o into one line of thought. We automatically came to speak of the statement by Mr. Scofield from Olympia. Here's an account of our talk as far as I can recall it.

H: Did you read the "Dark Concerns"? I'd call that an ignorant manipulation of the tradition of poetry, as if it doesn't always articulate its political and philosophical agenda. As the expression of sentiments, i.e. responding to external objects in song, poetry used to eulogize good and set right evil behavior. A practice of long standing. That today poetry is characterized by satirical allegory and laments is a sign of the time, like the hail ripping thru my tobacco leaves; it happens over and over again.

S: That's what the tradition is; outside the pale, it was there w/the first songs, the epic stories. What is the *Edda* other than a long song w/a political agenda, *Ulysses* and the *Tao Te Ching*?

H: That's memorable, and talking about it, the most memorable lately to me was Ed Dorn's "Abhorrences," very much articulating a political agenda too, right? And what's meant by real artists? Wanna know what real artists are? Those Polish guys who come here to help me harvest the tobacco; they get by like hermits.

S: Exactly, besides there's no room for personal preferences in poetry. It's tradition is a flower held up to expound the law.

H: And Mao's "Let a thousand flowers bloom" is where the

cynical comes in, when it's used to get rid of the poets after they expressed their sentiments clearly.

S: That's why others still kneel in the dark, thinking they have to be missionaries of some kind.

H: The sentiments we need to hear about all of this world, that is a burning house; still we have nothing lost.

S: A burning house. Ha-ha-ha.

H: Ha-ha-ha.

We'd gone thru both bottles of wine, the moon was disappearing behind the eaves, the dark came to sit w/ us, but we had nothing left to offer.

HOW TO SPEAK DUTCH

It's helpful to work up a mouthful of spit
in dealing with the three gutturals:
"g" and "r" and "ch" (like in "Bach")
are all gargled, but each is different.
It's like a heavy workout
of clearing your throat of phlegm.

When a word has "s-c-h" in it, "*schoen*," (yes, shoes),
you first say the "s," then "ch" (like in Bach)—
it takes a lot of practice.
Then try "s," "ch," followed by an "r," as in "*schrijver*,"
and I'm not even mentioning those weird vowels
and diphthongs all their own.
No one born Dutch will ever get right
the word for seagull, "meeuw."

A woman speaking Dutch must probably settle
for looking wholesome, even earthy, rather than elegant.
She is forced to work so hard
with her whole mouth and all her teeth
just to get around the words,
it resembles the juicy mastication
of the national treasure, the cow.
In fact, the women are cowlike creatures

EDWARD FIELD

273

popping forth the prettiest boys and girls in the world,
whose rosy innocence makes you long
to ravish the sex of your choice.

The vocabulary is mostly German,
but it's a more informal variety,
a low German closer to Yiddish.
so no wonder they understand the Jews.
Remember, these are the people the Germans
pushed into the practically uninhabitable
marshes along the sea.
The Dutch are not forgetting that.
But when the Germans need a host for a tv show,
someone to loosen up the audience,
they always get a Dutchman,
because the Dutch radiate good nature,
reveling in the jovial atmosphere they call "*gesellig*"
with its two impossible guttural "g"s.

But above all, the Dutch love the vowel "a",
pronounced "a-a-ah," and if you frequently say
Oh, yah! with a relaxed sigh,
before launching into the story of your day,
that is a good way
to begin to speak Dutch.

LINDENHOFFER

TEODOR FLESERU

You don't remember the red velvet robe you dragged everywhere and
you don't remember how upset you got when we tried to take it
away from you but I remember your whimpers as you swaddled
yourself in it and held dead silent inside till this worried us so much
that one night when you were soundly asleep I rolled you gently gently out of the robe, quickly cut it, sewed it up, stuffed it with feathers, took it back in our room, slid it under your head and watched
how without waking up you hugged the pillow, buried your nose
deep in it and drew a hard long sigh that went to my heart and I
cried thinking you must have been so fond of the robe because of my
telling you the stork brought you wrapped up in it—the robe I
bought for the wedding night from the old gypsy witch who got it
from a fancy city-woman who fled with the Germans when the Russians were coming; and when Father got a job here in town working long hours and earning good money we sold the cow and

roasted the chickens while the neighbors mocked us for quitting our house and the little village beyond the forest to move up here in this room, oh yes! it makes me smile now that I think back and see all our fortune piled in the middle of the room: the ripped mattress, two chairs, that little table, two forks, one knife and the clay cooking pot but as your first birthday present we bought the radio and what a black evening that was because Father caught pneumonia, fell to bed with sickness and though I told him his days weren't over and begged him to stay and fight on he left us, oh my, how angry I was with him! but had to grow strong and make up for I couldn't have left you small and alone, just with Nanya, that's how you called it, your pillow ...

When she did leave him alone, he was seven years old. It was dark, his nose bled and he took to the pillow; covered with stains, feathers shedding about the edges, its velvet case had turned rusty and exhaled a fur-like smell. He was to be moved across the street into the orphanage that used once upon a time to be a nunnery but the two men in charge failed to persuade him right away that leaving home was for his own good. He flung himself into a corner and cried. One of the movers, the one with the wiry mustache and ugly scar on his cheek, tried to untie the boy from the pillow but the little man, his face dirty with the night blood, held on to it.

He got to keep his pillow, though it was never easy. In the orphanage it would be stolen many times but friends always wrestled it back for him. It got worse during his military service: they kicked it around, polished their boots with it and threw it in the trash. He started to wonder whether he should get rid of it. One night, his arms wrapped around it, his hand slid through a fresh side split into a tight glove—it was a pocket, the robe had a pocket. It made him think of home and the red brick wedge-shaped building that capped a two-street dead end: on the right hand Yalta, on the left hand Athens; silent sunscreen windows shielded the National Office of Tourism on the ground floor, wherein at night one could see a large globe fuming lazily round and round; a sickle-shaped balcony bridged the nose of the building between the two first-story windows and every morning a red-haired child climbed out of one window, placed the cage with a colorful parrot on a little round table, then climbed back in through the other window; shaped on the corner, the second-story window cast an indifferent glance, its wooden shades rolled down most of the time and when they were up a bony face was seen peering through; and there was the attic with its oval window squinting incessantly over the roof tops. In the park between the building and the orphanage reigned an old chestnut tree known to everyone as the crows' headquarters. At dawn, the cawing would reach such intensity the windows rattled and the floors vibrated. They fluttered and cackled, soared and dived, chased after one another all day long, and only at dusk they stood still and glossy. And then a beggar's chant rose menacingly loud, soon to be swept up and away by a chance flurry of wind. In the park with green lawns and white benches, a row of aged statues withstood the tyranny of seasons; whether snowcapped, rain lashed, blossom decorated or painted with wet rusty leaves, they always looked onward, unabashed.

Yes, the little pocket had made him think of the park and the building, and in his dreams its facade resembling a giant's multi-eyed face twitched and frowned till the red bricks shifted about and light oozed thickly through the cracks; reeling hypnotically, the world-globe prowled through empty dusty rooms.

Back from the Army, he was irresistibly attracted in his daily walks to the building; he would examine it from a distance, but paid close attention to its real or imaginary changes; he entered it through Yalta, walked up and down the stairs and exited on Athens, or vice versa. One day, while he leaned against the lamppost, a first-story window opened and a man waved urging him to come upstairs, where he was treated in a friendly manner by the Leopolds who told him that the apartment he sought, the one above theirs, was occupied by a retired officer with no known relatives; he had been rushed into hospital the previous night and the doctor, a friend of theirs, thought he wouldn't make it back home standing.

He ran to his boss, explained the situation, mentioned that he had repeatedly turned down finer prospects, and claimed the apartment. He got it and moved in immediately. Over the weekend he whitewashed the walls, painted the doors, waxed the hardwood floor, greased the hinges, scrubbed the bathroom tiles, polished the fixtures, mopped down the spider webs, mailed the telephone application, and when everything was in its proper place, Vlad Dragan took the pillow out of the trunk, put it under his head and slept like a baby in his home at 33 Athens Street in Hermannstadt, a little town in the Carpathian Mountains of Transylvania, the heart of Romania, an Eastern European country, its map shaped like a fish, tail wriggling in the Black Sea. It was Sunday night and it rained monotonously.

POEMS

RICHARD COLLINS

276

THE NEW BUCHAREST

It's not chaos
Au contraire
So much ugliness can only have been planned.

Chaos is a lot of things
but ugly it's not.
Chaos is dangerous, meaty, random, rundown, violent, upbeat,
   beat-up, silly, weird, American, damned, joyous, turned
   upside-down, inside-out and sprawling, crawling, purple,
   howling, hungry, satiable, insatiable, curious …
Chaos is furious, never canned, inimical to man
Chaos is never planned.

Wandering these darkened streets
   empty of bistros on every corner
seeing the night-life with all its dangers
   bad taste, discos, risks, whackos
that isn't there, but could be,
   should be, should have been,
could have been, is, in absentia
   (all it has is a city dementia), then
I want a big stick of chaos in my hand
   to murder the little man
who turned the Paris of Eastern Europe
   into a plan.

AN AMERICAN SOCIOLOGIST IN ROMANIA

"If I see one more Gypsy kid without feet
I'll scream. You notice their mothers
never whack off their hands, oh no!
Hands we let them keep.
Those dirty little fingers are tools of the trade
valuable as ivory, pretty as jade,
and necessary.
For pushing the little Porgie-board
For pulling at your skirt, plucking at your heels
For wiping the eternal rosary of snot
For exploring pockets, for imploring
(I luff you, madame. Giff me a dolor!)
For adding up at the end of the day
all the little weightless communion wafers,
cinci lei, cinci lei, cinci lei …
coins in exchange for the phantom pain
(there goes one now, down the stairs on his stumps
into the underground. Shall we take the escalator?
Never mind that, we'll give him something later)
the day's gain."

277

EDOUARD RODITI

On Clowns: The Dictator and the Artist. Norman Manea, New York, Grove Weidenfeld, 1992.

Norman Manea has good reason to distrust dictatorial political power, if only as a survivor, in his early childhood, of the Romanian Iron Guard's anti-Semitic atrocities of 1941, then of the Nazi death-camps in the occupied Ukraine after his family's deportation from their native Romanian Bukovina, and lastly of the lunatic postwar totalitarianism of Romania's Communist dictator, Nicolae Ceausescu. Preceded by a brief "Author's Note," five of Manea's essays of recent years describe his experiences and considerations as a dissident writer under an authoritarian regime: "Romania: Three lines with a Commentary," "On Clowns: The Dictator and the Artist. Notes to a Text by Fellini," "Censor's Report, with explanatory Notes, by the censored Author," "Felix Culpa" and "The History of an Interview."

Manea's experiences as an artist who was tolerated, at best, as a kind of clown or buffoon under Ceausescu's own clowning regime as one of the world's most rigorously incompetent dictatorships leads one to suspect that there might well be more than meets the eye in Lord Acton's famous remark that power corrupts, but absolute power corrupts absolutely. There might indeed exist some kind of basic corruption in the character of any individual who, from the very start, seeks to acquire any kind of power. In our United States, we might therefore be wise to distrust on principle all candidates for the presidency. Wouldn't a truly wise and good man prefer Thoreau's idyllic life at Walden to all the worries and the flimflamflummery of the White House? Might not Reagan, for instance, have been corrupted by sheer vanity long before he even thought of embarking on a political career?

Manea appears to be tactfully aware of some such flaws in our own "American way of life" when he writes, for instance, that "even after the Communist mask had fallen from the tired, disfigured faces of the millions of captives of Eastern Europe ... on the other shore, a self-congratulatory society took the collapse of the *other* side as a vindication, all the while avoiding a sharp look at itself." Yes, President Bush went so far in avoiding again and again this kind of sharp look that he even declared that he had put an abrupt stop to the Gulf War in order "to save precious American lives," though he actually meant "precious American votes." Had he really been interested in saving American lives, he would long ago have displayed more interest in reducing the shockingly high rate of infant mortality in New York's South Bronx, for instance, where it is as high as in Bangladesh. But infants don't vote.

In the eyes of many an American reader, Manea's most revealing essay may prove to be "Felix Culpa." Here he discusses in detail the whole philosophical, literary, political and university career of the late Mircea Eliade. At the time of his death in 1986 at the age of seventy-nine, Eliade was Sewell L. Avery Distinguished Service Professor in the Divinity School of the University of Chicago and Professor on the University's Committee on Social Thought, a veritable think-tank of reactionary ideologies, closely allied with many of the leaders of American Cold War policies. Quoting extensively from Eliade's numerous Romanian-language publications that remain on the whole unknown in America, Manea proves that Eliade had never ceased to express, ever since 1933, overtly Fascist and anti-Semitic beliefs as an admirer of Mussolini, Hitler and Salazar and a supporter of the ideology of Romania's Iron Guard.

There appears to have long existed in some American intellectual circles a veritable conspiracy to rehabilitate former Fascists and to dismiss their Fascist declarations of earlier years as mere expressions of youthful inexperience, momentary aberrations or statements made under extreme pressure. One would be a fool, I admit, to take Gertrude Stein at all seriously as a political thinker of the same kind of aberrant importance as Ezra Pound; but she is known to have declared, in spite of being Jewish, that Hitler was, in her opinion, a great man, and her admiration for Marshall Pétain was so great and so overtly expressed that neither she nor Alice Toklas were ever molested, whether as Jews or as enemy aliens, during the German occupation, after Pearl Harbor, of what had briefly been the "Free Zone" of Pétain's France. Paul de Man, a notorious Belgian Fascist, found refuge, like Eliade, for many years on the faculty of an American University. In America's intellectual world, other notoriously Fascist thinkers and artists have continued to enjoy unquestioned respect, above all Heidegger and Borges.

Should we condone the Fascism of Heidegger, Borges, Pound, Céline, Gertrude Stein and Eliade, among others, as the mere clowning of court buffoons? But shouldn't we then extend this generous pardon also to those whom we might now declare to have been likewise the buffoons of Communist regimes? And shouldn't we also begin to wonder how we should handle the innumerable clowns and buffoons of our own increasingly corrupt and undemocratic regime, under which a quarter of the American population now lives below the official standard of poverty?

Norman Manea, as a refugee in our "best of all possible worlds," tactfully refrains from posing his American readers such disturbing questions. We can criticize him, at best, for perhaps overestimating the importance of Ceausescu as an impostor or a clown. Every political regime, all the way from that of Mobutu in Africa to our own, has its official buffoons at its head and tends to treat its serious writers and artists as mere clowns.

ELIADE FASCIST?

I read with interest the Roditi article on the first page of your latest. Eliade a fascist? The friend of Cioran? Gertrude Stein dug Hitler? I suppose now I have to check out Mr. Mania. I mean, it's possible, but I just read all of Eliade's expensive journals. Now what? On pp. 6–7 of Vol. 11 (July, 1957), Eliade talks about his American experience, and an anthropology prof at Chicago asks Eliade about his most impressive experience in the States, and Mircea says it is feeding squirrels in the parks. He's bowled over by the trust they exhibit!

In the last volume, #IV, Eliade changes his tune somewhat on this lion with the lamb routine. 21 July 1979, again he's in a park, this time in a dream, and "A well-dressed man is there, with many small animals around him. I don't know why, but I fold the manuscript and press it together, reducing it to the size of a sandwich, and try, for fun, to threaten a little rat with it." (No wonder Eliade was surprised at the trust of the squirrels!) "But," he continues, "the animal takes hold of the packet with his mouth and won't let go. Although he isn't biting it or chewing it, I observe that the manuscript is getting smaller. Impossible to pull it out of the rat's mouth. I have nothing handy with which to hit it. Alarmed, I beg the elegant gentleman, who is standing directly in front of me, to stab the rat. He replies that here he doesn't have the right to fire a revolver. ..." Hmmm. Are rats the truth of squirrels? Was it a real rat, or just *squirrelly?*

THE PASSION OF BENJAMIN FONDANE

With the renewed interest in Martin Heidegger's unrepented Nazi past, we learn that in 1934 he would refuse to greet his erstwhile teacher and protector, Husserl, in the streets of Freiburg. The author of Being and Time and Nazi-appointed Rector Magnificus and Führer of the University would cross to the opposite sidewalk so as not to have to say good-day to Husserl, *der Jud*, by then seventy-five, to whom he had dedicated his main work. Consistency required that Heidegger remove the dedication from his book, as well as Husserl's portrait from the University's hall. Well, after all, Peter too denied his Master thrice, yet on him was built, as on a rock, the most powerful church in history. But Peter, right after his triple denial had the decency, if we are to believe Matthew, of crying bitterly. Nothing suggests that Heidegger ever cried bitterly over his denial. Nor did he, as far as we know, ever utter a word, even after the war, about his treatment of Husserl (who died in 1938), or about

Germany's treatment of the Jews. All the same, a powerful church has been built upon Heidegger's rock, a church whose latter-day sects have come to dominate the discourse in the Humanities at our universities. That discourse, as it turned out, has no more reference to the human person, to live human beings, than the technical language of, let us say, Physical Chemistry.

The drama I want to tell is in many ways the opposite of Heidegger's betrayal. It also involves two men, two philosophers, a Master and a Disciple, a Father and a Son. If we look up Léon Shestov's name in *The Encyclopedia of Philosophy* edited by Paul Edwards, we find: "(1866–1938), Russian philosopher and religious thinker, was born in Kiev...Perhaps most strongly influenced by Pascal, Dostoïevsky and Nietzsche..." There follows a summary of his thought in two columns of small print, and an incomplete bibliography. He was the master. As for the disciple, Benjamin Fondane, a Romanian Jew born in 1899 who moved to Paris in 1923, he is not mentioned at all in that encyclopedia. Why tell the drama of two relatively obscure philosophers... In the hope that more of us will read them? Those of us who would defend a belief in the dignity of the person against the current critical attacks need all the help we can find. For the denial of the human being behind the word, the text, the artifact, requires only a modicum of ingenuity and dialectical skill plus a certain tone-deafness; but the opening of an I-Thou of author and reader, of poet and listener, the welcoming of a presence...that is something altogether different, and Shestov and Fondane, in their works and their lives, show us what that may be: they point to a way. Let me hasten to clarify the *Encyclopaedia*'s term, "religious thinker." Both Jewish, neither Shestov nor Fondane belonged to any synagogue; they were not men who had found a faith, a truth, a niche; like Pascal, they searched in pain. It is the search they tell us, not the results. They belong to that kind of philosopher for whom thinking is participation, witnessing. They seek to awaken us, to infect us with their insomnia, and they have nothing to say to those who have already found or to those who prefer to sit as mere spectators of reality. Nor do they have any special wisdom to impart. Often referred to as "the Russian existentialist," Shestov wrote with a style thoroughly purged of technical jargon: simple, unemphatic, striving for clarity above all, brightened by gentle, pungent irony. As the French poet Yves Bonnefoy has put it, "[Shestov's] *literary* quality is as unessential as it is evidently superb."

Benjamin Fondane arrived in Paris in 1923, about three years after Shestov. E.M. Cioran, a fellow Romanian who arrived in Paris in 1936 and who went on to become, in the words of Susan Sontag, "the most distinguished figure in the tradition of Kierkegaard, Nietzsche and Wittgenstein writing today," met Fondane in 1942 and remembers him as a man of extraordinary charm, with a captivating voice, a

281

fascinating talker wearing the attire of a *clochard fantastique*, a fantastic bum. Steeped in French literature like most educated Romanians of that time, Fondane, even before leaving his native country, had published poems and literary criticism in the local avant-garde reviews. Once in Paris, he met his compatriots Tristan Tzara, the father of Dada, and the sculptor Brancusi (later a witness at his marriage—the other was Shestov), as well as many others. But most importantly, in 1924 he met Shestov. While still in Romania the young poet had read the Russian philosopher's studies on Dostoïevsky and Tolstoy, and reviewed them for Romanian journals (Cioran told me that during the 20's and 30's Shestov was the most widely read philosopher in Romania). Fondane himself has recounted (*Rencontres avec Leon Chestov*, Ed. Plasma, Paris, 1982, p. 42.) how the meeting of master and disciple came to pass. "But it wasn't until 1926 that a serious contact was established between the two of us. He sent me a copy of the French translation, recently published by La Pléiade, of his *La Philosophie de la tragédie (Dostoïevsky et Nietzsche)*. I wrote a letter of thanks, in which I told him, more or less, how hard it was to follow him, for to reach and penetrate his thought it was necessary, according to his own advice, to have experienced some intimate disaster ... And I added: where is the man who, for love of Truth, would wish upon himself such a disaster? Who would willingly accept to be his disciple? A few days later I received an invitation from his daughter Tatiana. There were guests, for a soirée, at her place in rue de l'Abbé-Grégoire. Shestov received me saying, 'I am used to people writing to me that I'm so talented, how deeply I have grasped Dostoïevsky, that my style ...,etc., and now, perhaps for the first time, someone understands what the real issue is.' He showed my letter to everybody, making a great deal of it."

And so Fondane became Shestov's disciple; in fact, his only disciple, his son. Many had admired him, but nobody else had ever believed with Shestov that at the crucial moment, when our reason testifies unhesitatingly that there is not and cannot be any hope, given a grain of faith we can awaken from reason, from the impersonal It, as we do from a bad dream. Nobody but Fondane ever followed Shestov all along the arduous way leading, through the promise of a faith shining always ahead, into the realm of freedom where everything is possible, even canceling a tear, changing the past, restoring his children (his original children!) back to Job. For such is Shestov's doctrine. The dialectical skill and deep knowledge of the Western philosophical tradition that others deploy trying to dissolve the human personality into the It, he uses to insist that man can wrest from the It even what is most its: the irrevocable past. Under the Russian expatriate's tutorship, the Romanian expatriate read the philosophers. Husserl, Plotinus, Thomas Aquinas, the German idealists ... Husserl, because he was the thinker at the opposite extreme, the boldest and most articulate advocate of scientific thought, the champion of reason and the eternal truths, and therefore the one master Shestov chose to attack in order to free himself of those eternal truths. Incidentally, Husserl became the Russian philosopher's appreciative contender. "No one has ever attacked me so sharply as he," said Husserl, introducing Shestov to a group of American professors of philosophy, "and that's why we are such close friends." (See L. Shestov, "In Memory of a Great Philosopher" in *Speculation and Revelation*, Ohio U. Press, 1982. On Shestov's attack on Husserl, see the former's "Memento Mori" and "What is Truth" in *Potestas Clavium*, Ohio U. Press, 1968.) A characteristically noble gesture on the part of a man whose most famous disciple was later to deny him before the world. And always the one guiding idea, Shestov's stupendous *idée fixe*: to examine the credentials of philosophical reason; to expose the unreasonableness of reason's claim to sovereignty in all regions of experience; to return to us the absolute freedom that may have been ours before the Fall, before the eating of the fruit of Knowledge. Fondane, of course, had his own style, different from Shestov's—more aggressive, richer in imagery and rhetorical fireworks—and his own preoccupations, stemming in great part from his own continuing poetic practice in French. The nature of poetic inspiration, the denunciation of Surrealism in particular, and, in general, of poetry which pretends to the status of knowledge; the poetic and the existential experience of Rimbaud, of Baudelaire. These, and a vast array of other subjects, he brought to the crucible of Shestovian thought; all during the thirties he published sharply critical articles on major figures, the most formidable names: Husserl, Heidegger, Gide, Valéry, Bergson, Breton, Nietzsche, Lévy-Brühl, Freud ... (Fondane's *Faux traité d'esthétique, Rimbaud le voyou, Baudelaire et l'expérience du gouffre*, as well as a collection of his essays, *La Conscience malheureuse*, have been reissued by Editions Plasma, Paris.) And to all he applied the critical method described by Cioran: "Truly, [Fondane] wasn't so much interested in what an author says as in what he could have said, in what he *hides*, making thus his Shestov's method, i.e. *the pilgrimage through the souls*, rather through the doctrines."

In 1932, at the time Fondane published his article on Heidegger (included in the book *La Conscience malheureuse*), the latter's reputation was unblemished and his writings were being unanimously praised by the professional philosophers of France. Shestov's disciple was undaunted. Most critiques of Heidegger written in English charge him with logical inconsistency, empirical groundlessness, or false etymologies. Fondane goes instead to the intention behind, the *vis a tergo*. He sees in Heidegger's philosophy a compromise, a monstrous coupling of Kierkegaard's psychological contents and thought with Husserl's phenomenological method, and behind that compromise, a brazen

283

attempt at subjecting the actual, live experience to the dictates of Knowledge. Nothing could be more hateful to Shestov or Fondane, for in the uncompromising nature of the either/or, in the aggravation rather than the relaxing of the tension between Husserl's and Kierkegaard's opposite extremes, between Knowledge and Life, they saw the only chance of hope for civilization. To talk of Nothingness as if it were something is a logical contradiction, it has been often noted. Heidegger cut the Gordian knot by simply declaring Angst, or Dread, the feeling of dread before nothingness, to be prior to Logic. In doing so, the Freiburg Professor has a secret purpose, Fondane charges: to defang dread, to domesticate it, as it were (Fondane points out that he is concentrating on Heidegger's "*Was ist Metaphysik?*," his 1929 Inaugural Lecture, to which the quotations here belong). By affirming that "Dread is in secret union with the purity and sweetness of the creative yearning," Heidegger would have Dread perform for us a useful service: to reveal Nothingness, and therefore to make Metaphysics—the questioning about Being and Nothingness—possible and respectable and professorial again. To get Philosophy rolling ... Dread then, Pascal's abyss and Baudelaire's, the late Latin poet's anguished cry, "*Timor mortis conturbat me*," all these things, these awful, tragic things, looking at death in the eye, are neither ugly nor frightful; they become nothing but necessary, scientific steps toward Heidegger's metaphysical heights, from which we can, in the Freiburg's philosopher's words, "repossess for our understanding all of Being, as such and in its totality."

Dostoïevsky had foreseen the monstrously totalitarian vocation of "our understanding," and had replied, in his *Notes from the Underground*, "If you say that all this, too, can be calculated and tabulated—chaos and darkness and curses, so that the mere possibility of calculating it all beforehand would stop it all, and reason would reassert itself, then man would purposely go mad in order to be rid of reason and gain his point!" And Fondane himself responds to the future Rector Magnificus and Führer of Freiburg: "Tragedy—even the gods'—is not grand nor beautiful; human 'finitude,' its 'forsaken and humiliated' character; all that has, even on Heidegger's lips, a cracked sound that turns your stomach. Tragedy, even though accompanied by 'solitary grandeur,' makes whoever watches it sick and turns whoever experiences its deep meaning insane."

It is interesting to note that twenty-four years and a World War later, when Heidegger's doctrine of Dread had already become, in the guise of French existentialism, the world's most influential philosophy, another expatriate from an Eastern European country, the Polish novelist Witold Gombrowicz, criticized it in his Diary in very much the same terms as Fondane. "Historically speaking, the plunge of the human spirit into this existential scandal, into its specific helpless rapacity and wise stupidity, was probably inevitable. The history of culture indicates that stupidity is the twin sister of reason, it grows most luxuriously not on the soil of virgin ignorance, but on soil cultivated by the sweat of doctors and professors ... The imperialism of reason is horrible. Whenever reason notices that some part of reality eludes it, it immediately lunges at it to devour it ... life ridicules reason. This, reason could not bear and from then on its torments, which reach tragicomic heights in existentialism, begin. "This, which applies, *mutatis mutandis*, to much of today's critical discourse no less well than to the writings of Heidegger and Sartre, Gombrowicz wrote in Buenos Aires in 1956, when much of the century's horror had been played out, and probably without ever having read Fondane. But only a prophetic spirit, open to the passion behind the word and not merely to the grammar, could have seen it so clearly back in 1932.

In October 1944, Fondane died at the gas chambers of Birkenau, near Auschwitz. His master Shestov had died six years earlier, shortly after Husserl: both philosophical friends, old Jewish men, had been spared the worst. Fondane, who had been naturalized French, served briefly in the French Army, was taken prisoner, escaped, was captured then freed, spent some time recovering at the *Val de Grâce* hospital, and then remained in Paris during the Nazi occupation, hiding, with his sister and wife, in his own apartment at 6 rue Rollin, a few yards from the house which had been Descartes'. All along, Fondane knew his destiny was tragic. Victoria Ocampo, the Argentine *femme-de-lettres*, has recounted that on July 18, 1939, Fondane gave her a packet of letters from Shestov, as well as transcripts from conversations between master and disciple. "It is my most precious possession," Fondane told her, and asked her to open the packet and have the texts published, in case of his death. She tried to make light of the whole affair, but he insisted: the war was coming and he had the foreboding that this was the last time they would see each other. But why did he stay in Paris? His Argentine friends tried to persuade him to go back to South America, where he had sojourned in 1929 and 1936. He wouldn't leave his sister Line and his wife Geneviève; but even if they couldn't follow him across the ocean, why didn't they all hide somewhere in provincial France, as so many others did? Or simply change lodgings in Paris, a most elementary precaution? By 1943, it seems Fondane actually walked the streets openly, wearing his distinctive "fantastic bum" attire, until he was anonymously denounced to the Gestapo early in 1944. He was perfectly aware throughout of all the risks, yet, as Cioran remarked, seemingly fascinated by his own tragic destiny. In March 1944 Fondane and his sister Line were arrested and taken first to the Prefecture de Police, then to a camp at Drancy, near Paris. His wife Geneviève (née Tissier), not being Jewish, wasn't arrested. She retired to a convent in 1949, where she died in 1954. While Fondane was detained at the Préfecture de Police, Cioran went there with the Romanian Cultural Attaché, to try to get his friend sent to his native land. Fondane, the Attaché claimed, was translating an important Romanian poet into French, and was therefore of great value to the Romanian State. Although Romania was Germany's ally, he would have been safe there, Cioran tells me. But this ploy didn't succeed. Once at the Drancy camp, Fondane didn't even want his friends to do too much on his behalf for, he said, a Jewish doctor there told him, "While I'm here you have nothing to fear." One day, however, a prisoner failed to return from leave, and all the others were deported as punishment. In May, Fondane was sent to Auschwitz, where he was registered under his old family name, Benjamin Wechsler.

Thus ended Fondane's life. A dream of pristine, absolute freedom turned into a nightmare of brutal, absolute necessity. Is that grotesque paradox the meaning of our philosopher's death? I shall propose another possibility. With open eyes Fondane had become Shestov's disciple. Their letters, their writings give us a vivid glimpse of the high love between the two philosophers. Then, on November 20, 1938, Shestov died. Gone, as Plato was convinced Socrates was, to other gods who are so wise and good? Or simply dead, like a dog? The English poet David Gascoyne told Cioran that he was haunted for months by the image of Fondane whom he encountered by chance, on the Boulevard Saint Michel, the day of Shestov's death. Was this, then, Fondane's intimate, necessary disaster? How hard to come by, that beginning, that grain of faith. Perhaps farther on, deeper down, till every single trace of hope has been extinguished? His later poems suggest (but in these matters "suggest" is, I feel, too positive a word) that at some point after Shestov's death, and perhaps because of it, Fondane had a momentous insight. I do not know whether he saw it vaguely or distinctly, suddenly or by degrees: Shestov was wrong. Even if that most difficult thing were obtained—that seed of faith—even if one could erase Job's ordeal and Socrates' execution, even if one could cancel all the tears in the world...it would still not be absolute freedom. For it is not in eliminating suffering from the world, but in assuming it, taking all on oneself: there—tremendous there—resides the only real possibility of freedom. And how could he refuse such a gift?

> C'est toute la douleur du monde
> qui est venue *s'asseoir* à ma table
> —et pouvais-je lui dire: Non?

> All the pain of the world came to sit at my table—and could I say: "No"?

(Untitled, 1944. Fondane's poems are collected in one volume: *Le Mal des fantômes*, Ed. Plasma, Paris, 1980.)

But what is most significant for us lies on this side of their possible divergence on the meaning of freedom. The meaning of faith was the same for both Shestov and Fondane: to believe, despite the overwhelming evidence to the contrary, that each human being can be—and therefore is—unique, irreplaceable, infinitely important. If our animal nature makes that faith ever hard to sustain, humanistic culture at least used to come to the rescue. But what are we to do today, if literary texts are meant to refer to nothing but themselves and other texts, if paintings are supposed to be only about painting and music speaks to us only about the qualities of sound; when we open, for example, The *Times Literary Supplement* (May 13–19, 1988, p. 537) to find A.C. Danto writing with admiring approval that Diebenkorn's art, like his life, "is a systematic effort to expunge from itself whatever is other than itself." For what is true of much of present-day art is originally and primarily true of reason. In the finished mathematical theorem we are not expected to feel the mathematician's breath. It is of the essence of reason systematically to expunge from itself whatever is other than itself. And that means, above all, the live human person. With what passion would Fondane have written, had he lived to see them, against these exacerbations of reason! Yes, a belief in the person is difficult to sustain today. The lives, the words and the love of these two men, Shestov and Fondane, provide us with a precious help, an invaluable testimony.

HOWLING FROM THE MARGINS (ON READING CIORAN)

RICARDO L. NIRENBERG

"Parents are either provocateurs or simply mad. The vilest freak has the power to give life, to 'bring someone into the world': could anything be more demoralizing? How can one reflect without dread or revulsion on this wonder which makes of the first comer a half-baked demiurge? What ought to be a gift no less exceptional than genius has been allowed equally to all: such sham liberality disqualifies nature ... Flesh spreads upon the globe like a gangrene ... "

What can we make of these pronouncements? More precisely, what can we make of them in the context of 1992 and the U.S.A.? Here, with aphoristic insolence, the two pragmatic axioms of America, production and philanthropy—and the latterly-deduced corollary, equal opportunity for all—are being outraged. Perhaps we should fling back at the father those lines he attributes to parents, tell him that he is an agent provocateur or simply mad. And perhaps he would not disagree, if madness is the name for paroxysms of lucidity, and if "provocateur" be taken as one who calls forth a challenger. Let us, then, ask a double question: where is Cioran, the author, calling from, and to what is he challenging us?

My title already offers a partial answer: Cioran is calling, or rather howling, from the margins. The metaphor, almost dead from much use and abuse, stands or falls with the printed page and the book: margins make no sense among the illiterate. Among the literate, conversely, margins have too many meanings. Cioran's margins, as I will try to explain below, are the margins of primordial shame. For the time being, let us imagine the place Cioran is howling from as some remote outskirts of the vast metropolis of the written word. You may throw in, if you wish, mounds of burning refuse, slums, a slaughterhouse or two. "A physical craving for infamy. I would have liked to be the son of the executioner," he writes in *De l'Inconvénient d'être né* (1973). Joseph de Maistre, the reactionary writer Cioran has admirably dissected, maintained in a Hobbesian vein that public executioners were the base and mainstay of society; yet they lived without the city boundaries, feared and shunned, disreputable.

E. M. Cioran was born in 1911 in a small Romanian village of the Carpathians, a place as marginal to Western culture as one can possibly wish for. After moving to Paris in 1937, he single-handedly proceeded to revive the old genre of the French *moraliste* essay. Beginning with Montaigne, cultivated by Pascal, La Rochefoucauld, La Fontaine, La Bruyère, and culminating at the end of the 18th century in Chamfort, the form had fallen into desuetude and was therefore, at least *historically*, marginal. The fragment, maxim or pithy anecdote, characteristic of the genre, by its brevity and, above all, by its cavalier attitude toward the prolixities of proof and the web of the main text, is marginal in a second, logical sense. Aphorisms are noted for their lax posture regarding logical quantifiers—who is the referent? Humankind, some men, or only one?—and for their blatant inconsistencies: often a maxim is as persuasive as its contrary. La Rochefoucauld's "One is never as fortunate or as unfortunate as one imagines" may without much damage be changed to, "One is always more fortunate and more unfortunate than one imagines," and Cioran's "What I *know* destroys what I *want*" can as easily be inverted.

Cioran is marginal in still another and more fundamental, ontological sense: like his friend Samuel Beckett and unlike the vast majority of us, he miraculously and monstrously remembers the moment of his birth—and feels shame and undying resentment. Had he been able to speak, before they cut his navel he would have cried: NO! He would have turned his back on the light, refused to join the party. In 1949, as bigger thermonuclear devices were being developed and the poet Eluard thanked Stalin for relieving us of doubt and giving us happiness instead, Gallimard published Cioran's *Précis de décomposition*, his first book in French (translated by Richard Howard as *A Short History of Decay*). "Injustice governs the universe," he wrote there. "All that is built, all that is destroyed carries the imprint of filthy fragility, as if matter were the result of a scandal at the bosom of nothingness ... In this slaughterhouse, to fold one's arms or draw the sword are equally meaningless gestures." And a bit further on, "Chaos?—It is to reject everything we've learned, it is to be ourselves ... "

Filthy fragility, scandal at the bosom ... the *Chaos* that figures so prominently in Cioran's texts is not the "chaos" of physics, of dynamical systems too sensitive to small changes in the initial conditions. Nor is it the Anaximandrian *áperion*, at the beginning of Western Science, out of which the cosmos inexplicably precipitates, leaving behind a debt to be paid, an all-pervading guilt like the background black-body radiation. In one of his more recent books, *Avuex et anathèmes*, Cioran writes: "Another Yankee, this one a professor, was complaining of not being able to find a topic for his coming course. 'Why not Chaos and its charms?'—'I have no idea about that; I have never experienced that sort of fascination,' he replied. It is easier to communicate with a monster than with the opposite of a monster."

Cioran's Chaos carries, we see, a capital C and charms to which non-monstrous, normal people are immune, whereby it resembles Baudelaire's *gouffre*, a frightful place where nonetheless *tout n'est qu'ordre et beauté*, rather than Anaximander's *ápeiron* or a blur on the screen of an oscilloscope. Out of such Chaos Being does not precipitate but rather oozes; Being is sticky and so can never be completely detached: one does not feel the guilt of separation, but the shame of not being separate enough. "I long to be free—desperately free. Free as the still born are free," he wrote in *De l'Inconvénient d'être né* (translated by Howard as *The Trouble with Being Born*). Cioran would stretch the moment of his birth to fill all time.

Heedless of Cioran's "A curse on the mind with clear abysses!" let us look into the abysses a bit further. In *Précis de décomposition* whores and female saints occur frequently, but the word *mother* never does (except for figures of speech such as "Action, the mother of all vices"), nor does the word *child*. The image of the mother and child seems to have been struck out by a fierce and unforgiving iconoclasm; Thaïs and Santa Teresa are let in, welcomed with open arms; any hint of a nativity is kept out, the author's birth the object of a final curse. The biographical note that is attached to Cioran's books tells us that his father was an Orthodox priest, but there is no mention of who his mother might have been, and it is not (as far as I know) until *The Trouble with Being Born*, twenty-four years later, that she is mentioned at all.

So when we read in *Syllogismes de l'amertume*, "In the

edifice of thought I have not found a category on which to rest my brow. Chaos, instead, what a pillow!" we cannot avoid linking this ever-present Chaos to the maternal body, the great, the formidably absent one. Mother: origin and dissolution, dream palace and slaughterhouse, paradise and swamp. What is melancholy if not an impossible nostalgia for that union of opposites?

Mother—I mean the one we bear inside—is more than just a locus of nostalgia: she is also the memorial of that time when we were but little bundles of dependency, a reminder that we are not gods. Nero *had* to kill his mother, and Caligula surely would have killed his too, except she died before he reached the throne. This brings us back to what I called "primordial shame," by which I mean the consciousness of a predicament: we want to grab on to our extremely fragile autonomy, be sovereign individuals, while being aware of how utterly dependent we are on the world, on language, on the social. For the godless man there are only two clean, non-murderous, non-suicidal ways out of the contradiction: to renounce our proud autarky, dance with Necessity and chacha with Ananke (something far harder than it may sound), or to retire to some remote Thebaid, cease craving for sex and recognition, keep absolute silence. And then we stumble on a third way, not a way out but a way around, a shameful compromise, one of whose possible variants is this: to line our need for recognition with a need for infamy; to hire a whore if we are men and want a woman (thus remaining unattached, discharging our debt and paying the fine for our rebellious glands); and finally, if we happen to be writers, to speak out yet keep under the lee of silence by sticking to short and perfect paragraphs. This double consciousness (of our predicament and our cowardice) can be properly called shame.

With what strenuous efforts Cioran renounced his native marginal language, Romanian, in which he had already written four books, for central (and proud-of-it) French we can hardly overestimate: France is a country obsessed with the perfection of her tongue. "A man who repudiates his language for another," he wrote later, "changes his identity, even his disappointments. Heroic apostate, he breaks with his memories and, to a certain point, with himself." Yet, after his heroic divestiture and achievement, after his rebirth, his self-recreation, Cioran characteristically looks over the Pyrenees towards the country where he feels he should have moved *instead*: Spaniards have a tragic feeling, *el sentimiento trágico de la vida*, while the French, with the important exception of Pascal, never did. "They [the Spaniards], live in a kind of melodious asperity, atragic non-seriousness, which saves them from vulgarity, from happiness, and from success."

Voilà Cioran's aspiration: to be saved from vulgarity, from happiness, and from success. Can one justify writing successfully against success? (Cioran's books are well admired and they sell; recently, in an overall review of the state of French letters in *The Times Literary Supplement*, Marc Fumaroli, Professor at the Collège de France, called Cioran "a master of French prose," "a legend" and "a modern Socrates.") To that quibble he might arrogantly respond like Unamuno, "Contradiction? Of course! Contrary to what Hegel taught, what's real, truly real, is irrational," and leave it there. Let us, however, dwell a bit longer on the paradox. Mystics used to point out that impossibility of putting their experience of the Supreme Being into words, but our century has been the first to witness attempts to denounce Being, to put it to shame or to poke fun at it, notably by Beckett and Cioran. Language, social to the core, whose successful use entails, at the very least, a fine regard for rhetoric, a love of the well-turned sentenced which contradicts the professed devaluation of the universe, may not be the instrument best suited for such task. And so we end up in an impasse not much different from the classical "a Cretan says that all Cretans are liars." The howl seems better suited for the purpose, which is why Cioran writes (*Syllogismes de l'amertume*), "If I had to abandon my dillettantism, I would specialize in howling." And Wittgenstein too (*Philosophical Investigations*, I, 261.): "So in the end when one is doing philosophy one gets to the point where one would like just to emit an inarticulate sound."

Yes, indeed, but howling doesn't take long to become boring, and so, paradox or no, it's back to language. Not necessarily to one's mother tongue, though: rigorous French has attracted both Beckett and Cioran precisely because it was not their mother tongue and precisely because of its rigor—you need gloves and a scalpel to operate on Chaos and maternal flesh, you can't do it barehanded. Someone widely read ought to make a detailed study of the diverse strategies writers have used to curse or to murder their parents.

Curses. Or anathemas, as in the title of one of Cioran's recent books, *Aveux et anathèmes*. Contrary to the Homeric epic, which tends to reconcile us to the contingent, contrary to the confident Renaissance, our marginal Romanian, a Gnostic figure from the first, exhausted centuries of the Christian Era, uses language to set us apart, aside, on the margins, as lucid hence unhappy critics. "I'd rather sacrifice my life than be necessary to any one," for example. Or, "At a certain point, one begins imitating only oneself." "Anathema," however, besides the usual senses of "curse, execration," "a thing accursed or consigned to damnation," has another, earlier meaning: in the first book of the Odyssey, dance and song are called the *anathemata*—the graces, the ornaments of a feast. Cioran's curses are no coprolalia but rhetorical jewels, and like Chamfort's *Anecdotes*, they make us wonder that so many rich veins of meaning are condensed into a line or two.

291

The Temptation to Exist (translation by R. Howard, 1968), the first book by Cioran published in the U.S., was enthusiastically prefaced by Susan Sontag; the blurb speaks of a "Cioran mystique," "an underground classic." Favorable notices in *Time* and in *The New Republic* (the latter by Richard Gillman), were followed by laudatory articles in highbrow magazines: *Hudson Review, Triquarterly*. It is especially rewarding, however, to pause a bit on John Updike's critical judgment (*The New Yorker*, 1974). The title of his review, "A Monk Manqué"—euphonious but inept, since the monk in Cioran is not manqué, *plutôt réussi*—is only the first salvo of disapproval. What the American writer disapproves of most in Cioran is what he calls a lack of gentleness and seriousness. "Serious philosophers" (Updike mentions Wittgenstein, Nietzsche, Kierkegaard) "wish to relieve, through clarification, our limitations" or "to inflame them to the point of crisis and cure." Cioran, frivolously, "wishes only ... to give us *frissons* ..." To make us shudder, to shock us. Which brings to mind Victor Hugo's famous accolade to Baudelaire, "You have invented *un nouveau frisson*." Hugo thought it no mean achievement; Updike would rather have congratulated ... perhaps Auguste Comte, for trying to "cure" humankind of metaphysics? But clearly what the American writer holds against Cioran is his radical rejection of the great American values, productivity and philanthropy. Cioran is no Whitman. The pragmatic Protestant's revulsion against the son of the Orthodox priest inserted in the French, mainly Catholic tradition. And there is no reducing such difference: criticism is the Wars of Religion pursued by other means.

May '68 in France and the student unrest in the U.S. may have had something to do with the interest in Cioran among us twenty years ago. As things quieted down, it fizzled out. That is unfortunate, for we, perhaps more than any other nation in the world, are in need of Cioran. I don't mean it facetiously; I am aware that we need many other things, but, as Lobatchewski and Bolyai, those other marginals from the European Orient, allowed the unthinkable into geometry, it may be worth our while to let a bit of the same toxin seep into our Euclidean schemes. Tocqueville thought that we Americans need nothing so much as "a more enlarged idea of ourselves and our kind." In any case, it is a challenge.

And perhaps, too, there is nothing we need as keenly as a voice in praise of marginality as such; the U.S., who once took pride on being a melting pot, has now set out to eliminate its margins. Blacks, Jews, Native- and Latin Americans, Women ... "marginal" groups have been turned into academic studies: the *lógos*, as always, overflowing.

Margins, like Derrida's "margins of philosophy," are meant to be conquered, *aufbehoben* and surpassed—from the lectern most often. Meanwhile, although to be sure among us Reading and Literacy are academic studies too, reading is clearly disappearing and our college graduates are illiterate. A metaphysical question haunts our class-rooms: why should young souls be made to read any particular literary work instead of none at all? The envisioned human paradigm seems to be the Hermetic sphere whose center is everywhere and whose boundary is nowhere, which Pascal compared to the vast void of the universe; a sort of cosmic L.A. But such ideal, noble and worthy as it may be, is too improbable; the easy way out is to forget the book, instrument, justifica-tion and witness of past murders. The image and electronics will rule, and with the final disappearance of the book, there will be no more mar-gins and no more marginals in society. Cioran, however, old fashioned that he is, insists on being marginal. God (he says), in case such thing exists, cannot be other than the Great Marginal.

If you, like me, find commericial ads and PC blather relatively innocuous (after all, we've come to expect that garbage and hype), but retch when the univesity president praises you for "consummate profes-sionalism" and invites you to a meeting "to share your thoughts and expertise on how to empower young men and women for the coming information age," you will enjoy Cioran. You will find that your gall has been transmuted into gems.

My opening quote is from *Le Mauvais démiurge*, 1969 (translated as *The New Gods* by R. Howard), the book Updike reviewed. Cioran was writing such stuff while the students of Paris were rioting; in that same Quartier Latin where 19th-century Romanian intellectuals learned liber-alism and forged national aspirations, now, back from listening to the rebellious optimists at the *Théâtre de l'Odéon* exhorting to lift the paving stones and find the beach beneath (presumably the same beach equated to life in our bumper stickers, that other popular, pithy genre), up in his room Cioran struck his maxims. "Whoever hasn't died young deserves death." "To suffer is to produce knowledge." "First duty, on getting up in the morning: to blush for yourself." A madman who cares for objectivity, such is Cioran's self-contradictory self-assessment. One can find precious little in his writings that would place them in time, and almost no reference to the happenings, characters and inventions of our epoch. The aphoristic art, like that of epitaph, aims at timelessness, the same timelessness, ironically, which Cioran hated in the life of the peas-ants of his native land. A few years ago, my wife and I visited him in his garret, Place de l'Odéon. After five flights of stairs we were winded and marvelling at this man, almost eighty years old, who went through such ordeal several times a day. The wickerwork table, his bed, and out from the window, the roofs of Paris, the chimneys. Books everywhere: Chamfort at his bedside; and a few records: J. S. Bach, and Schubert's *Winterreise*.

The room harmonized with the man: spare and spotless,

unencumbered and luminous. We talked about the Russian Jewish philosopher Shestov—"Back in Romania, in those days, he was extremely influential; it was Shestov who introduced me to questioning and to perplexity. The one regret in my life is never to have met him." About Benjamin Fondane, poet and thinker, Shestov's disciple and Cioran's compatriot and friend, who moved to Paris in 1928 and was killed by the Nazis in Auschwitz—"A master in the art of giving life to ideas." Together we deplored Anglo-American analytic philosophy. He railed against solemnity, praised *Exquisite Corpse* for being free of it, and so went on talking tor a while, and even though he was kind and unassuming, gentle and serious (*pace* Updike), and not at all the misanthropic monster I had feared to find, I felt ill at ease and fretful. I had been pepping up my courage remembering his professed sympathy for failures, triflers and dilettantes, but now certain words he had written kept echoing accusingly in my mind. "Interview with a sub-man. Three hours of sheer torture if I hadn't constantly repeated to myself that I wasn't quite wasting my time, that it was my good chance to contemplate a specimen of what humanity will be in a few generations..."

As we were leaving, Cioran noticed—*trop tard*—the tray with glasses and the bottle of whiskey he had prepared for us but forgotten to offer. Out in the street, with great difficulty I tried to explain it to my wife. I felt like a fake and a snob: I had never suffered, never kept arduous vigils, never *lived* intensely enough to give me any right to babble about Unamuno and Kierkegaard, Shestov and Fondane. Me, disparaging analytic philosophy! And what did I know about it? Next to nothing; only this: algebra, analysis, language, are the public playing grounds of *essence*, an immense and liberal games arcade with free admission. Our existence, however, what we sometimes call "the concrete," can only be picked up and questioned at the price of sacrifice—or as the prize of godlike laughter and dance. Only by the Monk or the Corybant, the ascetic or the ecstatic. Unable of one as of the other, *homme sensuel—et intellectual—moyen*, I had no right to the margins I had been just now badmouthing the analysis of language the way someone well-to-do and progressive curses the American Establishment from a plush sofa in an Upper-West-Side apartment.

That didn't explain much: I was just regurgitating the Existentialist line. Only much later did I realize that my blushing was the natural reaction on meeting the Master of Primordial Shame. Cioran will not let you or himself out of the bind, out of the toils of lordship and bondage, freedom and necessity, raging in our hearts. Headsman, he slays in the grand style not just the pieties and prejudices of the times, but his own arduously acquired conclusions. "As long as there is a single god still *standing*, man's work is not finished." "Ascent to the sovereign zero whence proceeds the minor zero which we are." The great

294

ancient Skeptics, a Pyrrho, a Sextus Empiricus, practiced such discipline to achieve quietude and detachment; both Skeptic and Martyr, both victim and torturer, at the margins of both Paganism and Christianity, Cioran lies stretched upon the rack, quartered at noon. Now and then, in beautiful French, he calls upon the impossible balm: Chaos, or the Queen of the Night. And now and then, with each new book, we have his distilled howling.

BITTER BYTES FROM CIORAN FROM HIS *SYLLOGISMES DE L'AMERTUME* (1952)

ERIC BASSO

Reality gives me asthma.

For three centuries, Spain jealously guarded its secret of inefficacy. Today, all the western world possesses this secret. It didn't steal it; it discovered it on its own, *through introspection.*

Without God, all is nothingness. And God? Supreme Nothingness.

The unbeliever, bewitched by the Abyss, and furious at his inability to tear himself away from it, displays mystical zeal in constructing a world as bereft of depth as a ballet by Rameau.

One objection to science: this world is not worth knowing.

The man who has never been forced to act against his own nature, who has never imposed a long period of sexual denial on himself or known the deprivations of abstinence, will be as closed to the language of crime as to that of ecstasy. He will never understand the obsessions of the Marquis de Sade or St. John of the Cross.

Modern pride: I lost the friendship of a man I admired by repeatedly insisting I was more degenerate than he.

"Talent" is the surest means of falsifying everything, and of deceiving yourself. *True* existence belongs only to those whom nature hasn't overburdened with abilities. Likewise, it would be hard to imagine a universe more false than the literary universe, or a man more stripped of reality than the man of letters.

The duty of lucidity: to achieve an *impeccable* despair, an Olympian ferocity.

TUDOR ARGHEZI

THE CHIMING MAN

Translated from Romanian by Julian Semilian

He'd been born with an odd infirmity, an unheard of gift. His body, or perhaps his soul, chimed. Maybe his plasma had properties analogous to the storage battery which absorbs and stores electricity, generating in its turn energy and light; or maybe I should say he stored sounds, unwittingly, in his flesh; or, even, possibly, his blood stream accompanied itself with the music of the ocean waves. In any case, the man chimed like a little bell, like a violin, like a zither and all other tools of song.

Maybe his vibratory plight was purely a condition of his soul, like a reminiscence whose origins are lost, resembling the rosy undomesticated porcelain of the conch shell, which, without the tongue and the iron cherry inside, sings endlessly in the showcases of the natural science museums, ailing with nostalgia for the ocean roar.

Like a clock, each being of flesh vibrates, and lizards can hear a hum even within the most intrinsic recesses of a plant, which we, humans, could never make out: the heart pounds and races, the vein throbs. The chiming man enjoyed and suffered from uniquely different attributes, from fiddle strings and metal, which could not dwell along the all-too-well-known, though inconceivable biological throbbing, of the heart's amphora, living flask, strung up in the dark, and key to the associated enigmas.

As though assembled of nickel and pressed sheet metal organs, equipped with rivets, washers, forelock pins and nuts, locked in conical, cylindrical and circular gearing, his step at times rattled like an iron boot, his shadow collided with the moon like a chain-mail head shroud, with a clang like key chains or chain links, clattering in his kinetic construction of mechanical entrails, like a power plant at the instant of power up, at the hour of foggy mist of the industrial dawn.

When he lifted his mustache with the brush, before the looking glass, his mustache whistled like brushed crystal stalactites, strung around a lampshade. If he dabbed himself, upon awakening, with the sportsman's cold towel, his flesh would dimple like glass drizzled by winter's icy grits. He roamed like an unseen, endless chain, fastened to the planet's cannonball, which shuffled along.

Since childhood, his ear was bewitched by the silvery bell which escorted him everywhere, and which, even off-duty, marked the time of its rhythmical clinking. The little bell spilled down an infinite staircase, set off impelled by its own impulse, and, step by step, leap by leap, bolted through oblivion, pierced the earth, escorted the waters, shot out through the back of the world and, back again, backwards now, like a pearl, airborne creature forever soaring inside the entity of his soul, unfurling like the zigzag bellows of the concertina, folded tight as a book and unfolding in a gallery of chaos.

He pursued the little bell in the folds of his clothing and in his laundry, his pockets and sleeves; he sensed it on his chest and the little bell spilled down to his belt; he fumbled for it on his thigh and it slipped down his socks; he removed the sock and the sound plunged in his shoe; he flipped over his shoe and the little bell went hiding in his handkerchief. He then aimed to capture it about the pillows, amid the lacy cloth and the seams of the silk bedspread, on his bed. The bell cut loose like a sour cherry, lurking out of sight like a quicksilver seed, forgotten among the fretwork stitching. And all of a sudden, again, there it was, in the fluff of the pillow, pouncing on the sleeping man's ear, fleshy and crimson like the roseberry, among the rusty copper curls. The chiming man had been a pure hearted child and his eyes like mother of pearl had lain in wait ten years before he spied the semblance of the sleepless little bell.

Later, only later, and only then time and again, the sound swelled and proliferated. In his sleeping room it roamed, all night long, a resonant phantom, its chest a constellation of carillons, whispering halos. The careful clatter of tallied jewelry, gleaned, placed in a bag, then emptied again and again tallied, frolicked till the overflow of day. The man became accustomed to his dwelling mate and from time to time he chided his phantom in jest.

"Let me sleep. Haven't you finished yet, grandma?"

He liked to imagine that his grandmother was still living, and, in the dead of night, roused from sleep by rue or remorse, was caressing her ornaments of platinum and gold, with which she glittered in her youth. The clatter thinned out to a flaxen strand, and shattered to powder; from the former only a softer comrade lurked, shadow of a shadow, scrap of a crumb, fuzz of a fluff.

On the childhood's staircase the spherical little bell tumbled down to adulthood a gold coin, balancing on its brink, animated by an alien impulse but roaming of its own want. On the rim of a tread, the gold might pause an instant, prior to pushing down to the next. It spun like round a spindle, swelled like a circle, appeared to ponder when, wham! whooshed down the abyss, smashed into millions of rings, in frantic pursuit, like a hatching hen abruptly aroused, from under whose feathers the startled yellow chicks scoot and scramble. And, sinking into the chasm of the staircase, twirling like a drill at the bottom of a well, the gold rolled into the water tank's piggy bank, like a pealing echo of treasures and catacombs.

The man aged, unable to temper his orchestra, which now sang with hundreds of bagpipes and bull fiddles, thousands of uprights, flutes and Jew's harps, ebony nightingales and brass finches, organs, and string titmice. And all around him, too, matter which never resonated before, the clay and the log, began to sing, springing to life to delight and cuddle him. The rocks, tough and ruffled and unsensing, rolled to the side, swung open like eggs or boxes with lids and hinges, and out of every one shot out either a bird, or a white snake, or maybe an elf or damsel who sang then returned to stone, chaperoned by primrose mosquitoes and frosty butterflies.

I LOVE YOU

Translated from Romanian
by Sasha Vlad and Zack Rogow

The suave heteroclite objects, the button, the veins, a mustache, a guitar, lightning, the piano tossed out the window, a hat which a very beautiful woman eats macaroni out of, a few fingers, a tie pin, a couch on top of which a bed is rotting, a curtain under the moon, an apricot that's been bitten into, a bar of laundry soap next to a jewel, a spider next to a fork and the mythology of the orgy acquires a modern voluptuous meaning, the meeting between objects borrowing the nebula's velvet and the catastrophe of planets meeting, there are flames meeting water, there are voices meeting their echo, love rendezvous where paralysis is a character trait and cramps a way of living ferociously, quietly, minerally, I attend to this monstrous coupling of objects with the feeling that I participate as spectator-actor in the lovemaking between desire and pleasure in a world of dreams and vice, I breathe the eroticism of these metallic embraces, I listen to the passionate howls that atoms communicate to me, I thrust my teeth into wood to the point where they bleed, into stone, into paper, into rags, myself a rag among these objects of flesh in which I bury my crying more allusive than real, impersonal, ideal, here is this indisputable knife where my uncertain blood trickles, here is my living velvet suit and palpitating underneath it a specter, an appearance, I walk among these fully erect objects, fully certain, I hear their breathing accelerated by lust, their blood reddened by a spasm as by murder, here is this plush chair biting an artificial carnation, drinking its lips and tongue, writhing on this rug of hair which steam rises from, the comb biting the mirror, the mirror kissing on the teeth the smile of this celluloid doll transmitted by a woman's compact, major orgy at the edge of lovemaking, at the edge of dreaming, at the limit of fainting, hallucinatory coupling of possibilities and phenomena, of desires in a permanent state of readiness, where tensions don't disappear with their fulfillment, tensions grow higher with a flame after each satisfaction of pleasure, a state of strain, contraction, and howling, the silent howling of objects making love, their wooden or glass veins swollen to the bursting, with their teeth of frost and grass ready to burst, the bed where love is consummated now as big as the universe or my room, the bishop is no longer a madhouse chessman, he loves his queen with his hand on his heart, with a rose between his lover's teeth, his lover's teeth now a rain of stars in his uncombed black hair, his hair blown by the wind like walls turning into ruins, like acacia trees blossoming, lovemaking that escaped from the human jail now singing freely in a scale invented by delirious desires, glassy and cold desires like lightning, on the surface of the world or of my room lovemaking emerging from man, this compromise enters through the hottest door into ripe objects, these brides, these objects with disheveled hair, carnivorous, bloodthirsty, magic objects that surround me divulge their secrets one by one, these women with an unlimited number of sex organs where mystery wears a mask of stony cruelty, a virtual avalanche where snow is made of the void, an automatic mask, an automatic chair, an automatic flower spreading an automatic smell in an automatic room, Hero of Alexandria, Bacon, Van Helmont. and all those genius builders of automatons, whom I remember whenever I look at an object from outside as if it were inside, whenever I look at a door, an armoire with a mirror, a tie pin, a wax doll, I automatically automatize them, they acquire their own life (which the fabulistic cretinism of Aesop or La Fontaine tried to compromise in a didactic manner) a certain individuality, with a hallucinatory and mechanical walk that fills out my trips and fear, that fills out my dream and waking with a world of noises, colors, veils and hairdos undone, gloomy and sublime golems revealed inside the most common and most indifferent objects, I touch a fork and I trigger a whole network of possibilities, a very complicated machine is set in motion as if the fork were a factory of questions, impulses, and specters, inside it a door opens onto a corridor, at its end a mirror reflects me upside down in medieval dress, another door leads to the phosphorous room of my childhood where the sleeping beauty has been waiting a hundred years now for me and will never awaken, another door leads to a window or the bottom of a well, this fork put to sleep by my magnetic glance, my glassy eye, the fork crosses the room with a somnambular walk, touches the bells and walls, kisses me on the forehead with her long rhinoceros teeth, she goes through me, she dreams me, the fork or the moon or a glass of water, these harmless objects exploding in my hand like a button that a child plays with until he swallows it, they meet, smell each other, breathe each other, greet and kill each other with a hunting rifle, they part carrying in their bleeding hearts a bayonet or a nightingale, at the first corner the lamp's smoking chimney will caress the antelope skin of a wrinkle grown into the forehead of this 14-year-old girl, or will make love to the leaves, the lamp's chimney can become an infernal machine in my hand if instead of watering it like a garden I put it over lips next to the lightning, the automatons pass by me or through me, I rub against them with my arms or tissues, I hide behind the door in order not to be seen by the table, I hide under the table in order not to be found by the Swiss Army knife, the forest also joins in this tender game between no and no, and the elements, and the four birds of prey whose loneliness is the most ferocious, my pearl necklace also joins in, the black gloves, the pallor and the echo, the voluptuous clitoris of this echo lightens my room like a lamp and an agony, a silver tray falling from the armoire onto the floor and passing from the floor directly into nothingness as if nothing had existed, as if nothing had happened, reminds me of the gestures of that witch doctor who in my childhood charmed away my epilepsy with two straws pulled from the broom and a few grams of lead, instead of falling on the rug the ashes from the cigarette that I smoke in the dark rise, they are a vibrating tree where a bird of ashes is singing, large chunks of asphalt peel off its voice as if from an unearthed city, a magnifying glass under my eyes I follow the microbe of that voice, its movements of a melted beast, its unresolved, heartpounding struggle on the edge of the real, its returning to flame, the microbe of this flame, the landslides in this match, the no littering of these compasses, the no admittance of those dentures, the rear exit of the window or the entrance by the back stairs of stones, here are so many possibilities of doing exactly the opposite of the things imposed on us and so many corridors that confer on the way we walk the freshness of a pack of wolves chasing a sleigh, here is this piece of domesticated dynamite for my personal use while the tie becomes a noose, without any scruples I would launch the axiom with two mirrors one in front of the other that reflect a third, a fourth, a fifth, I bathe in mirrors, all the objects that surround me are mirrors, they reflect and reflect me, my bones are inside them, my nerves fly at the window instead of a flag, my ear is stuck to the floor so I can listen to the galloping of bricks, maybe I haven't left the house yet, maybe I haven't left my childhood yet, maybe I'm still running in the field on a wooden horse, my nostrils scattered by swords that cross in the wind, my lips unraveled by feverish murmurs, my narcissistic teeth thrust into my own tongue while in my bed ravaged by passions, a comb and hair couple scandalously like two snakes.

ROMANIAN POETS:
THE 60'S GENERATION

SUMMER PHOSPHORESCENT

translated by Nadia Marin

1.
THE CITY this multitude of solitudes
a drunk folded near a sewer's red mouth
the small eves of indifference
for how many years have we remained in '77?
the voices of those who left echo still
on the Dumbrava road
                        ding deng dong
                ding deng dong
an earthquake in the other world—
I hear it collapsing in me

2.
IN CIGARETTE SMOKE the woman
sips her coffee: magic filter
of love and the man
drinks her face in the way
she sips her coffee—
sterile dreams of marble arms
a mad world dancing on its optic
nerves
it has been Sunday for many days—
Sterile dreams of felicity
woman for one night

3.
IN DREAM a slice
from the still steaming body

DUMITRU CHIOARU

301

the brain/the heart
melting in the babble of unconsciousness
the stomach: poor rodent
dies a suicide—
is dreaming a chance?
this devouring of the diurnal mask

4.
AFTER ALL THIS the flower-grinder
next to a roast
"after the third glass wine drinks the man"
the woman's hand squeezes the life from the man's neck
or caresses the jugs
for many Sundays it's been day all the time—
in every newspaper: "after long suffering
we announce death"
for how many years have we been in '77?

5.
AT DAWN everything the same:
the clones of cronos god of the alarm clock
start a working day
the earth still runs on oil
medicines get the blood flowing
the head on its shoulders—
Adrian tells me:
Sometimes you're so alone you can't be counted

6.
SOLITUDE: smell of ink—
                    poetry
when words are more real
than things

ARS AMANDI

translated by Adam J. Sorkin and Angela Jianu

I'm looking for Ovid's grave
it's still there
in Constantsa
part nectar
part hemlock
an ancient Greek goblet

DENISA
COMANESCU

delivered over by the Romans
appeals to the emperor
love letters
in bottles
thrown into a dead sea.
Ovid
with his doctorate in despair
awarded by the Getae
and the Thracians
honores
honors
half a coin from beyond a sea.
"Under this tombstone lies
the singer of the tenderest loves
by his own art undone.
Stop, traveler,
if thou didst ever love,
and for him pray
that he may sleep in peace."
With a freedom fighter's zeal
we each went near
and each of us prayed
though the emperor would not hear
but mercy has a thousand hands
a station master eyeing a deserted station
Ovid's grave is here to redeem
our hope once more
that prehistoric ghost
dreamed up somewhere
in this land.

HIBERNATION

translated by Adam J. Sorkin and Angela Jianu

I need a line
you give me one.
The spark of fire in the alfalfa.
I'd invent a deity
but my mind is barren.
And the soul no longer holds back
devastated.
Doltish overseer! Who gave this life into your hands?
With stones and clods.

The earth devours trails of fire.
O give me a line.

AUTUMN SCENE

translated by Adam J. Sorkin
and Angela Jianu

Two-bit sadness is biting her tongue.
You pinch her cheek
like a girl's too young for her makeup.
On a bench the lonely lover
kept slapping the woman's face
just like a doctor trying
to bring back a suicide.
(All around leaves kept falling and falling,
leaves and newspapers.)
The man was beside himself
to get her to go away.
As if her soul had tangled
in his fingers
he continued to sit by her side
until both disappeared under a mound
of leaves and newspapers.

THE KINETIC MOMENT

translated by Adam J. Sorkin and Sergiu Celac

Plywood painted as nymph
taxpayer painted as tree
roar painted by synthesizer
lion tamer painted on a handbag
black painted grey blue white
violent white

Ballerina painted as ellipse
anyone painted as the Good Guy
roof painted by footprints
descending from the Northern Cross

Words as food
and food as words

IOANA IERONIM

I as any woman
you as any man

Embrace me white
Embrace me black black black
all-devouring black

IMPERFECTION

translated by Adam J. Sorkin and Sergiu Celac

you operate according to objective laws
            and yet...
you comply with various statistics
            yet...
you believe in the lovely myths of science
you don't steal don't kill don't covet
            and yet...
terror pain a mere fleeting word
these close in on you from every side
            and yet...
he says: I know ALL about you
            —you're in my power!
            yet...
(by a hand's breath—father taller than son)
/don't rely on the lame octopus
of Memory/

you toss the dice. you wait for a number
that isn't there
you thirst to have it
all all all /but hold on!
how fast can you fade to the color of the wall?
how fast can you hide
(without noise without being seen without shadow)
in the color of your enemy?

GROUND

translated by Lidia Vianu

I thought I was
a word
turned upside down in his huge pupil
which forgives
all my sins
in his pupil which bears with me and keeps me
under the Ray
in his pupil which is always awake.
And so it was
when I still thought I was deciphered
by his great bounty
until I felt my
a-ni-mal smell
until I saw rotting in the ground
the stone claw
of the sad tiger that's me.

OXYGEN

translated by Lidia Vianu

Within the frame of a cover,
within the frame of an open window, on its edge
like a character from Tolstoy
I
in the whirl of the red dress
my forgetful, shameless body.
I like this image.
Below, very low, a lot of people and dogs.
Shouts, firemen, open nets.
Well, no!
Let it burn
I like this image.
But I have never had
a red dress.
But I live on the ground floor
par-terre.

THE MAGDEBURG HEMISPHERES

translated by Lidia Vianu

My flesh will get bored
your fingers are tired already.
Soon we shall see the false teeth, the plastic,
the mechanism of this supernatural mood
soon we shall be able to conjugate again, self-assured,
I am, you are
separately, separately
our intact cells
will forget absolutely everything
our instincts will lean their
muzzle and disarray
against their dizzy paws.
I am not afraid of the explosion lurking in the ventricle
or of the bright red of that state
or of the adrenalin shock
or this small flame,
smaller
I am afraid of the almost incestuous love
between our almost twin, despairing
occipitals thinking
the same word at the same time.

METAPHOR

translated by Adam J. Sorkin and Sergiu Celac

You know, some younger friends just back from Athens
(it's good for the young to travel)
reminded me of the word metaphor which there
means street car or subway or even train
I thought to myself well, you take a metaphor
and you're in an entirely different part of Greece
or of the world
you board a metaphor and, well, you just go
you leave everything behind sorrow and joy alike
and other contradictory-contrary feelings
that used to torment you in whatever place
you've been stranded for so long
everybody gets to work there by metaphor
everybody escapes (outside on picnics) by metaphor

NICOLAE PRELIPCEANU

307

everybody has just one notion (an idée fixe)
in joy or in sorrow
and it is called metaphor
you buy a ticket for the metaphor
and you're on your way
but they forgot to tell me
what you're supposed to do when the metaphor is on strike
perhaps you just hoof it or hit the road on your own (by foot)
pure and simple as in the old days
when metaphor didn't mean mass transit
but rather your own transition
solo going

UNTITLED

*translated by Adam J. Sorkin
and Sergiu Celac*

because all the
words
are nothing but
seeds of fruitlessness
and poetry
a machine for forgetfulness
of what in any case nobody
ever remembers

BEHIND THE SCENES BEFORE THE JAZZ HOUR

in English by the author

jacques knows you
just as i do
though you believe him dead of cancer in belgium
though you can't make him out in the confusion of those
twilight soirées
trying to forget me beneath your eye shadow
to erase me from the memory of your skin
smoking starving yourself frantically
brainwashing yourself with liquor
from the story above throwing yourself over the berlin wall
but what trick wouldn't you devise

VIRGIL MIHAIU

ideal woman alarmed by my idealism
you may even vanish forever
leaving the radio to play on in the emptiness
with the fatalist's voice *ne me quitte pas*
ne me quitte pas after which my program begins
for solitary hearts solidarity through jazz

STATISTICS

in English by the author

height—medium
expectations—so-so but not too-too
territory—of average dimensions
climate—temperate
way of life—middling
reaction to stimuli—restrained in feeling
preferred tempo—moderato
grade for conduct—satisfactory
truth—somewhere in between

FROM *THE EMPIRE OF AFFINITY*

AND SO

translated by Sasha Vlad and Zack Rogow

We walked on tiptoe not to awaken the Beast Two simple ones two beings just summoned from the void We looked for something: I yellow she white She had put on a caparison and it suited her very well it broke the roughness of the slide from ecstatic to anxious Some salt dunes told me "from her eyes we grew up" but I didn't remember having milked her tears maybe I was a shy merlin back then and I didn't know what I was asking her for It was crawling among arts an incipient grating

    (Smashed in the forehead by the airplane transporting poppy seeds the Hulk had grown silent All together there were nine Big Numbers placed in a semicircle on the field The only ones left on the floor were the azure-red pair slashing the vault with their arms I bend down to pick up a piece of paper she bends down to pick up an

DAN STANCIU

309

Etruscan Dollar and bent like this we receive the fire flame We spun around on our heels and the Number 29,430 points to the black stripe I take my partner by the waist and we disappear

The Neverending brings us back It fed on jade and it belches dim and dull sparkles We stand in front of it like H and G from the fairy tale It says "play nicely and falls asleep)

A MIDSUMMER NAUGHT'S DREAM

translated by Sasha Vlad and Zack Rogow

Whereas you (having what you have and being only the thousandth part of a multitude of coagulated rains) can (or could if you wanted to) get off the streetcar at a place that's too humid (as humid as the mother's limit) and there (controlling the hands that have the tendency to articulate a sentence and are burning) to enter the film

Something would stop you from enjoying the magic canvas The ashes on the seats or the smell of knives only that sweetdarkness You would like to disappear when—look a plump little rabbit shows up and asks you to be his wife You ask your father in your mind what to do: to accept or flee the fortress—but he sits mutely on his chicory island Then you cry When the tear duct is finished the scene turns completely upside down

In a house in the lower part of the city a pilot's son brings you on his silver moped Now (face to face) you drink each other Outside the truck with stones is passing by

THE TRUTH WITH TWO FOREHEADS SEEMS TO START COLORING US

translated by Sasha Vlad and Zack Rogow

It was Thursday or it was evening

At the hour when the wounds of the day retreat into shells or boxes A part of his head had filled with silence

The other still rang He (a psychopath on a psychotrail in front of a half-burned table) was a golden someone between four white walls Or close to white because the light is from the missing planet He had eaten some hearts before getting to where we see him At rest

Emptying mirror or rim

Separated from him by an open door (see Musset) that woman I avoided until now connecting to a

name stares at the threshold
She has become calm She puts on her lips a red of a lower degree
She undresses and covers herself with the cat

Here kitty he whispers from the next room

THE FORM OF FEVER

translated by Sasha Vlad and Zack Rogow

Discrete disasters happen the light when it doesn't start working at erod-
ing is breaking into perfect spherical parts The edges are wavy because of
the heat but in the middle where they (the mother und the daughter) are
and each one of them gets a taste of an apple—the transparency is complete Not doing anything black the hands can touch at will They can sew
eyes They can hit a description with a piece of a jaw bone they can annul
a smile that was damaged Everybody's face is continually improved by
this The empire of affinity is expanding
    The one sent by a breath becomes the equal of the one received in
metal Dressed in a white mystery the creator of disappearance has to
gather cruel results and he does It's using a rake to control a powerful
fraying Or a bed arched over a river
    The mother and daughter's clothes have disappeared and they sit
naked on two rocks waiting for linen to move (But who could steal
clothes in this pitch dark It's thought instead that they wanted to leave
this way and this is the way they appeared and only a destroyed sense of
sight mistook the smoke that protected their bodies for clothing) They're
both the same age One has red hair the other very red hair They seem
like a body of water chained for a year
    The mother stood up and now whistles toward the mountains she
has the Voice The daughter has remained crouching and covers a mirror
with sand To both of them (both having a hot Y in the center of their
foreheads) the coal animals that have formed around them seem dead or
have no substance
    They are not

BETWEEN SILICA AND CARBIDES

translated by Sasha Vlad and Zack Rogow

Between transparency and explosion I stood and scattered my thoughts
(if I had had a Webster inside my head I still would have gotten it
out anyway, even if it had taken me a year to do so. but I

had only seven or eight not too good ideas about how to make a warm film. I chased them away)

The witness found me on the ground She lifted me up and delivered the news I didn't understand

I chewed that stuff long ago I told her I digested it and spat it out She repeated it I fell flat on my face In front of me I saw a cloud of oranges a red Ford with a rubber giraffe at the wheel and a glass drawer filled with shoelaces in all colors I chose one of them and I offered it to a star falling from the ceiling The star lifted me up and gave me a drink of water

"Water" I asked and I drank a sheet of paper covered with sour writing Then a break appeared between 2 and 3 or between M and N because I can't read anything

GOD FORBID

translated by Lidia Vianu

History seems to be carrying us in its belly
and has forgotten to give birth to us,
the holy ones are nearsighted
they sip the borscht of dogma which drips in their cap,
and daily bow to all things
since who knows what archbishop sleeps
in the ladle, in the rag basket,
in the barrels of these sad guns
where the Madman hatches his crime
and kills us just because he loves us,
when we are hungry he draws fish,
when the cold comes he jails the weather
stop History—I must get off at the next stop
stop at the God forbid stop
                    stop

MIRCEA DINESCU

KOVERSADA, CROATIA

One day I decided I wanted to see 25,000 naked people all at once. So I set off on a pilgrimage to Koversada, Croatia, the largest nudist camp in the history of clothing.

I have already blasphemed by using the word "nudist," abhorred by real "naturists." I knew about the naturist camps of California, Sweden and France. But they were nothing compared to the Adriatic nude enclaves of Catholic, and at the same time communist, Croatia. Why there? Neither communists nor Catholics are known for their celebration of the body. The puritan tradition in North America is so strong that over the years several groups have actually campaigned to put clothes on statues and even animals. Alan Abel received wide media attention and support in the 1960's for his Society For Indecency To Naked Animals (SINA), and is famous for the battle slogan, "a nude horse is a rude horse." In Koversada 25,000 people couldn't all be wrong. Or could they?

My pilgrimage was not an easy one. I had to book an expensive airflight to Zagreb, in the Republic of Croatia, where I avoided the robber baron taxi drivers by getting a ride from a long lost cousin, who drove in from Duga Resa to meet me. He hadn't heard from my branch of the family since my grandfather vanished from the farm without a trace and ran away to America in 1905. "Why you here?" he asked in broken English. "I came to see 25,000 naked people in Koversada." He did not appear surprised. Back at his modest house, surrounded by the ubiquitous Croatian chickens, geese, and free roaming cows and goats (all nude), we took out a map and located Koversada about halfway up the Istrian Peninsula on the west coast. I still had 300 kilometers to go.

I took a 4-hour bus ride from Karlovac to the ancient Roman city of Pulla, then another bus to Vrsar. The rest I had to do on foot. I was the only passenger to get off at Vrsar, little more than a boat dock and a few vegetable stands, although historically a playground for bishops (compliments of the peasantry). The few people I saw were dressed.

I walked up a long path to a series of buildings which I thought were the outskirts of Koversada. Not wanting to embarrass myself by being caught with my pants up, I prepared to disrobe. But then I saw an old peasant woman wearing the traditional black triangular scarf tied under the chin and a dark dress buttoned up to the neck. She was walking toward me with a laundry basket. I tried to ask her where the nude people were. She chatted on in Croatian as if I understood her perfectly.

I continued down a narrow road flanked by fields with blue jays stripping kernels from naked cobs. I came to a gate like a toll booth and a sign that said "Koversada." A policeman

313

manned the gate. A *uniformed* policeman. Which made sense, otherwise where would he pin the badge? After fumbling in pidgin Croatian learned from a phrase book, I got the message that I could just walk in for free. But with strict Stalinist authority he pointed to a sign with pictures of a campfire, a camera, and clothes—all with slash marks through them. I didn't want to end up in some gulag for outraging the public decency, so I slipped out of my clothes and carried them.

I walked happily down the road, experiencing the ultimate in roominess when I saw a car coming. As it passed I was disturbed to notice that the occupants were fully clothed. Self consciousness came over me like a body suit. I checked my map again. According to the position of the sun I was heading south and Koversada was supposed to be south of Vrsar about 1 kilometer. I figured I'd walked at least that far already. With the historic multiplicity of Balkan languages, was it conceivable I misunderstood the directions from the gatekeeper? I walked up a side road that looked like it led to a campsite. All I saw were clothed people. Then, like the sight of land to a lost ship, I saw my first nude human, a man who looked like a tanned Winston Churchill carrying a hibachi to his car.

So here I was at the end of my 5,000 mile journey. As I walked further into the camp ground I saw thousands of men, women, kids and pets, all going about their business as in any other resort except in various stages of undress. Tennis players, picnickers, kids on skateboards, sail boaters, campers. There were indeed thousands of naked people. Apparently, the whole idea of naturism is to neutralize the taboo of nudity. This was accomplished in part by the evident fact that I saw more pot bellies than flesh pots. I began to take an interest in the now quite obvious diversity of human physique. Outsize necks, asymmetrical shoulders and hips, beer barrel legs, hirsutism (male and female) naked humanity in all its realness. Male circumcision was not popular, but a surprising number of older people bore the scars of nasty traumas, an apparent reminder of how much closer Europeans were to the last War.

I approached a nude man changing a tire and told him in Croatian, French and Italian that I was a journalist and wanted to ask some questions. He tried to answer in French, but that failed, so he settled into a pidgin of English and German. Meanwhile, his two naked daughters, about 5 or 6, chased each other around my legs like squirrels around a tree trunk. I pretended I understood what he was saying about "christentum," but it wasn't until later, when I played back my tape for a German speaking friend that I finally understood he was trying to tell me Christianity introduced the concept of body shame. A Croatian man wearing only an unlit cigarette asked me for a light, probably because I was carrying a bundle of clothes. I could tell he was Croatian by his bad teeth.

"How did you know I was Croatian?" he asked. "Uh, just a

guess. How did you know I was American?" "Sunglasses. Only Americans wear sunglasses." I looked around and he was right. "Why doesn't anyone here wear sunglasses?" "American TV. Only bad guys wear sunglasses." I took them off and put them in my camera case. He said he was a shipworker, married to an English woman and glad to be out of Croatia because of its economic problems, like 200% yearly inflation and a shortage of dentists. He was visiting his native land on a tourist visa. Feeling I could take the chance I asked him very frankly, "Is there any problem here with, you know, sex offenders?" He laughed. I laughed too. Flashing was certainly pointless. "All *that* happens in America. Not here. America, Middle East. Sex is big problem."

As I wandered about Koversada for the rest of the day I saw that nudity had a variety of interpretations. Some people were topless, others bottomless. Some wore shoes, some hats and necklaces, some wore knapsacks or money belts. I talked to people from both western and eastern Europe and learned that nudity has its hazards. Barbecuers were always getting burned in strange places and male tennis players had to be careful of those tight inside back swings. Life was like any other bustling small European metropolis except everyone was more or less nude. They sailed, swam, shopped or just lay around spread-eagled, getting burned in the bright Adriatic sun. On a higher level, Koversada was not so much about the N word, as about the M word—money. This part of what was then Yugoslavia—the western coast and the northern republic of Slovenia—was notoriously liberal and politically incorrect, showing all sorts of capitalist tendencies. Yugoslavian rednecks didn't like it at all. They considered it unpatriotic. But that didn't stop the likes of Jerko Sladojev from founding Koversada in 1960, or Valter Velenik, camping director, from stripping $7 million dollars a year from foreign tourists. The money is divided, with traces of socialism, among a consortium of businesses that make up the naturist mecca.

By this time I'd worked up an appetite. I went to a restaurant on a little island reached by a bridge loaded with fishermen, bare as what they were catching in the emerald waters. Feeling somewhat vulnerable, I stepped carefully around them as they swung back with their baited hooks.

At the restaurant I was given a nice table on a patio outside. I was surprised to see that the waiters were dressed, possibly to avoid any social discomfort of sitting customers in close proximity to them standing. After some initial fumbling over where to tuck the napkin, I dug into a fabulous meal which cost me the equivalent of 4 U.S. dollars. At the table next to me were a group of naked Italian teenagers. One boy wore only an earring, a girl wore only a cowboy hat, and another girl, about 14, the most rebellious of all, was sitting there in broad daylight, in public view, and in a restaurant, no less, completely and entirely *clothed*. But tolerance is the order of the day along the Croatian coast. She was allowed to remain, and all she got were a few disapproving scowls from some older naturists nearby. She was probably just trying to bug her parents.

Clothed, back at the bus stop at Vrsar, I studied a sheet Xeroxed from a British travel guide. It listed dozens of naturist beaches strung along the Adriatic from Istria to the Dalmatian Coast. Each had a notation that said either, "suitable for children," "very suitable for children," or "not as suitable for children." A few said, "definitely *not* suitable for children. " I put a little mark by those and waited for the first of several buses that would take me through a labyrinth of transfers and faded Croatian timetables back to the ancient city of Pulla.

MANIFESTO

Translated from Serbian by Charles Simic

Greetings law-abiding folk! Greetings lovers of truth!

If you deign to guild these words with your gaze, you'll see the irreverent form of manifesto come to life with no signature and independent of any Movement. The form unites in itself several others... Our song composed under the morning shower to the rhythm of the shivers brings fresh air into your rooms! The spirit of rebellion of heroic movements dating back to the beginning of this century comes to life again in it!

We are showing you a city square in winter inside a bell jar where no sound reaches. A madman waves his arms as if he is about to fly away, dispersing the voices of priests and speechmakers who continue to read quietly around him. He breathes only through words. He removes the spiderweb off his face with a habitual gesture and preaches to the empty square!

Our outbursts are the points with which we pin down the reader's attention! They deny us until the moment our existence seems a usurpation, and these words wait to be heard only when our name becomes worthy of them! You will watch the rise and fall of our nervous tension, the quiver of our heart waves! Your name was entered in The Guest Book when you were born; this is The Book of Complaints!

With a calm voice suitable for truth-telling, we direct a weak protest against the injustice of death... We are afraid that what we see is the reverse of what is really there!

While your eyes flow back and forth over these pages, the clouds flow like a river over the city. The clowns spread their arms slowly like accordion players, and embrace each other.

Harlequin wears ice skates and stands with his arms hanging by his side, his head bowed and sleepy, while the wind makes his submissive body execute various classic figures over the frozen lake. The shadows in his mind are arabesques in a turned-over coffee cup. His hair has withered out of sorrow.

To dream up plots is infantile! Naive and cruel, the action in our lives is in short supply; only invective makes it eternal! Who cares for the plot! We write to create a certain autonomy apart from our life. Action is the Christmas tree on which the writer hangs ornaments. Let them remain suspended like quiet fireworks, pulsing and changing in the air.

Man works occasionally and thinks all the time. Most of our life is doomed to anonymity: the world of our pulse; the space on this side of the face; the sequence of our inner cinema ...

Events, they are just the noise distilled into thoughts and feelings. Who grasps the mood, grasps everything. Reality is the ore from which after many rinsings we get the dream!

O painful mortality of all beings! The movements of our pens are no more premeditated than the innocent movements of a deer, even when we write so well that the lady readers experience us as their lovers! Literature is nothing but endless bragging and apologizing.

The dusk has the color of ink diluted in water. A wind full of medicinal properties is blowing. The branch is swaying from which the snow just fell. Over the chime one can hear the soft steps of a deer. Man is that which he notices ...

For the one who knows how to look, the world is always showing off. We'll get hold of it and circle it with our heads spinning just like the billiard ball when it connects all the points of the pool table at once!

If the intimate was not universal, all art would be shameful like a bared wound!

The era always seems older than it is! The elements which characterize it later are now hidden and in opposition. In the present thoughts collide loudly like billiard balls. It's hard to separate the voices from the noise.

Many in the audience pay no attention to what we are singing. They just watch our efforts to draw the next breath.

Opponents cry out in a husky voice of a crow who has learned how to speak. They pronounce words as if they were punishing them, striving to drown in erudition every revolt. The purpose of theory is to scare off. The ignorant eternally believe that the New is the same as the Old—only badly made! They are always claiming that the soapsuds are more important than the soap! Soon they'll announce that the metronome is music and not the violin!

They place traps on the boundary of poetry and prose.

Spirituality in its finer forms tires them and they see in it only conspiracy. They hate beauty and continue to call shapelessness by its name. They pretend that they understand each other while in truth they are just protecting each other's asses.

Art is not a space for machinations, but a ghetto of tenderness! Enough flirting with Indifference! Bright-colored pictures are laid out before cataract-covered eyes!

This book was written in sleeplessness, in the midst of whispering choirs lamenting the fate of the sorcerer who fell out of grace with the known laws of the universe.

The witness, as it's true everywhere, either feels or doesn't feel sympathy. Everything else is two-faced bickering! People who stick to truth like burrs will give us the right. We believe in affection, contagious like yawning, initiated by our voice more pleasant than a cello.

Our soul purer than tea!

Loving us is as easy as plowing snow!

HERAKLES

Translated from the Slovene
by the author and Anselm Hollo

Now Herakles performed many more great labors
back there on the Peloponnesus
and then went to Aetolia, its capital city, Kalydon
ruled by King Oineos.
Now Oineos had a most desirable daughter, named Deianeira
whose multitudinous suitors were so persistent and forward
as to make her quite miserable,
more miserable than any other girl in Aetolia.
Now she had been reared in Pleuron, the second city
and there Acheloos, the river god, had seen her and become
quite hideously infatuated! And thus
he kept appearing before her father
asking for permission to marry her—
1) in the ensorcelled flesh of a genuine bull
2) as a continuously mutating dragon
and 3), and last, in human form, but with a steer's head
from which curly head poured rivulets of the clearest water.

TOMAZ SALAMUN

YUCATAN

Translated from the Slovene
by the author and Elliott Anderson

Maruska, Ana, Francie, Bob and me
we are going to Mexico for Christmas '71
I'll meditate on people I like, watch
the desert through a pane of glass, Ana will piss

I'll meditate on sin crushed in a white glow
for I love Bob, I will love Moon's body when she
is grown up as Maruska is, we are rested
tired of lifting the dam between soul and meat

tender, as though blessed with wine
grateful, a clean mellow fruit in the new
balance between earth and sky, hiding before
hostile waiters of gasoline, wounded by the

glitter of freedom of our bodies, persisting
in hostile jealousy, we are traveling, cradling
laughing, with a river of tigers swinging
sliding south, living birth

KING OF BIRDS

Translated from the Slovene
by the author and Michael Waltuch

Decadence is haziness. What do you babble
and pile on bricks for, as if they were
entrails of differentiated strata which
almost wrung you out, caught you in a sticky,

meager trap, sucked you up, you dumb-ass insect.
You have paid 51 cents for milk which is
good, much better than the last time when
you paid 54 cents. First cut off this tree.

With total devotion read a list and an
itemized bill of things which belong
to Cornelius Doremus, baptized in
Acquackonock in 1774. You won't be

knocked down, a color will carry you
around the world immediately. There will
be no diagrams trickling slowly like
pitch out of a cork tree, and if there

are, they'll be there at once. There is
no need to fertilize the image. The image
doesn't need rain. It's got to be created
out of nothing. It has to be stamped

like a seal of the universe. Like this
dance of the king of birds. He didn't
waddle on earth, he didn't get dust on
his feet with history. We get him directly

from Lesbos. On the way he only visited
his friend, Catullus. He is the highest
leap in this magic sphere, named Iowa City,
he is the most glittering Bob Perelman.

EUROPEAN SONG

NINA ZIVANCEVIC

The unification of Europe, scheduled for 1992 seems to me a
somewhat murky enterprise: The NY Times headlines
read almost every day: West Germans started feeling before
East Germans as an endangered species; Italy fears that its art
treasures will scatter in unified Europe; Hungary would like
to become Austria, and the Basques won't speak
Spanish again in their new
and improved country. Europe fears
that its unification might deprive it
of its own history, oh history,
when will you stop fearing the future,
and you future, when will you
start obeying the present just once,
say, it's not a Zen method—it's
humanity, or what am I
talking about?

THE MEMOIRS OF A SPLIT GROUP (A BALKAN SYMPHONY)

NANOS VALAORITIS

When I came out here to the West in the late sixties, I ran into some very fine rascals. All dressed up to go at low prices. There was not much I could do since everything seemed to be centered on me; it's they who got the best part of the bargain, which was no big deal anyway. In those days a dollar was still worth ninety-five cents. Today it's no more than fifty-five. My childhood in Bucharest was, to say the least, stormy. I went to study at the University of Beograd. I was fluent in Latin, which helped greatly my advance in *Slavic and Arabic languages*. My surprise was immense when we were invaded by the Greeks. The Emperor had always coveted Illyria—but the Illyrians themselves, poor people, have only survived biologically in the Yugoslav cultural capsule. My days in Sophia were numbered, because I had set out for Istanbul where my old friend from medical school, Ahmed Arlsan, had a very beautiful sister. They promised me the sister in exchange for my passport. Turks have some difficulty in getting passports. They cost too much. So I sold my identity (Romanian then) very cheap and presented myself to the Greek Consulate as a displaced Armenian. They took me in after some questioning. There was no question that I was Armenian of Albanian descent. That didn't matter a bit to them. All they wanted to know was if I had been born in Athens. I named famous princes I had known in Romania: The Mourouzi, the Cantacouzene, the Callimachi, the Soutso. They all vouched for my good name and character and soon I became the most coveted of all citizenships, second only to Swiss—Americans in the East. It was at that time, as a medical student in Istanbul that I met two other medical students who called themselves respectively Tristan Tzara and Eugene Ionesco. I met Ionesco fifty-two times in the same evening. He always thought I was someone else. In the end he said, It's *you* again. I thought it was *you* from the beginning. No, I said, it's me. But I'm never the same twice running. "Si jeune et déjà le même," he murmured and walked away. My South American friends in Istanbul were numerous. As a Grecian spy I had become very popular among the riff-raff who thought I would put them on the payroll for "indecent information" about senators. They knew a lot. But it was expensive. So I made a deal with them. Two scandals a week only for a set price. All this information later fell in the hands of the Germans and that is how they kept Turkey out of the war. My friend Souleiman the Magnificent, as his pals called him, gave a party where I met Nanos Valaoritis, Cyril Connolly and other members of the London intelligentsia— marked by the Russians as potential fellow-travelers. They

321

were wrong. However I will come to this later.

The best years of my life were spent in Split, near Tito's old house.

CUCKOO D'ETAT

JEFF KOEHLER

I was appalled to hear the horrible news from Russia this week, especially given its graphic and humiliating nature. After the new oligarchs stated that Mikhail Gorbachev was suffering from "unspecified health problems," I later heard an announcement which, to my shock and disgust, stated flatly that "Gorbachev has been purged by his colleagues." No wonder he suffers! These men were not trained in the art of colonic irrigation. In fact, kissing ass is probably the closest thing any of them have done to giving an enema. It fell to Solzhenitsyn to explain how the torturers in Stalin's gulags preferred enemas of a stiffer kind: red hot pokers and glass rods, mainly. Fortunately, it appears that Gorbachev has recovered. He can thank his colleagues for purging him with nothing stronger than tepid rhetoric.

ed note: then it was over

FROM THE E.C. CHAIR

ANDREI CODRESCU

The Soviet Union is no more. It's strange. For the whole of my life the Soviet Union was always there, part of my mental and emotional geography. When I was a schoolboy in Romania I swore allegiance to it. Occasionally, I heard someone curse it but in a tone of resignation. Its eternal nature was not in dispute. We knew that empires had collapsed but that was in the past, in history, in school. In America, the Soviet Union was the stodgy official enemy for most of the 20th century. We based our foreign policy on it. We based our domestic policy on it. It was the springboard for political careers and the excuse for witch-hunts. It was our mirror. The US, like the USSR, was also founded as a utopia, and the two utopias were mutually exclusive. For some, who found the promises of America disappointing, the USSR held the promise of a different way. They closed their eyes when the utopia's gritty idealism brushed them with its all too real wings. But no matter how we felt about it, one thing was indubitable: the Soviet Union was there, part of the landscape of our minds. It isn't just the physical geography, though that's hard enough to conceive of. It's the fact that among the few facts that comprise our picture of the

322

world the Soviet Union was one of the essential ones, a kind of Archimedian support that lent coherence to the others. What, for instance, is one to think of the modern State itself in the absence of an ideological enemy? Is there any reason now for the clumsy militarized mechanism of the state? The USSR, that clumsy acronym that was as familiar a part of our speech as WWI, DDT, UN, PHD, NATO or, for that matter US of A, is no longer part of living language. Nor is the geographical entity part of our world. "America love it or leave it," and "Go back to Russia," the once-popular slogans of unthinking conservatism have become meaningless. Where can one go now? What's there to leave when there is no longer a place to go to? Which is not to say that I miss the vast concentration camp that was the USSR. I miss only the certainties of yesteryear. Which were pretty horrific in their seeming coherence.

INSTRUCTIONS BEFORE DEPARTURE

translated from Russian
by Ann Vinograde and Robert Wiltsey

Yesterday l finished my shift at the forge
It was a double shift
And left to go on a business trip abroad
The soot and grime I washed off
In the shower—ate some cold fish
And listened to the travel-guide
What to do there and what not.

Living conditions are better there—for the time being
I shouldn't ask questions about that
The guy ordered me to read a booklet
So I wasn't tempted to act the fool
Like we always do here.

He talked to me like a brother
About the tricky West
About a trip to the friendly democracies
To the Czech city of Budapest:
They have a special way of doing things
We can't understand it right away
You must try and respect them, my friend.

There'll be debates with vodka—you better say:
No thanks, fellow democrats only tea for me!
Refuse their gifts absolutely

VLADIMIR VYSOTSKY

323

We have all those things and plenty more.

He continues: Living comfortably there
You can save your money
But don't act like a fool
And watch out—no nonsense
Or you'll be in trouble
In Polish Budapest times are such
That they might say:
Eat and drink with us!
Or perhaps they won't give you a drop.

Oh in Hungary you'll try the markets
And stare at Germans and Romanian women
They won't take a single kopeck
From Soviet citizens
My advisor assures me.

But the bourgeois infection is everywhere
Tagging at your heels
Avoid all extramarital connections
The women are all spies
With fine bodies well-built
They'll hang in the doorways
They'll peek in your windows
Just let 'em know we've finished
With that sort of thing long ago.

But they do act so smooth
Show up in your compartment
Pretending they are men
Slip something beneath their girdles
Be sure and check it out
Be aware of your neighbor's sex.

So then I ask my friend
Okay, so I'm suspicious
How do I check her out?
Feel under her dress?
She'd slap me in the face!
But then he skimmed over all that
And went on about the devious West
Then I explain to my stupid friend
Going to Budapest to see Bulgarians

If certain types come up—I'll cut them off right away
No need to argue with them
If they don't get it
I'll just explain again.

But I don't think I can handle it
Or make up speeches
I know how to forge a hammer
I'm no agitator just a plain blacksmith
Better give up the trip
To the Poles in Ulanbator.

Now I'm safe at home
In bed with my wife
But I can't sleep:
Luce, old Luce
Perhaps I'll manage without this trip
I'd just screw up—better forget it
I'm not cut out for that
And that's the truth
Lucy's dozing like a child
Her hair up in curlers.

She answers back still half-asleep:
Now look here Kolya don't nag
You're just too timid Kolya
I'll have to get another man
Twenty years I've dealt with you
And all you say is:
Luce, old Luce.

You promised you would go
Now don't deny it
You'll bring the tablecloth
from Bangladesh!
Spend what we've saved
Don't argue
Bring me something
Even the devil in a can!

I fall asleep embracing my Lucy
Tender little wife
Then had a dream: I forged myself
A suit of armor, shield and sword

Out there they have their ways
They they don't like you
They'll eat you alive!
I dreamed of women in Hungary
Who all wore beards and packed a gun.

I dreamed of Lucy's tablecloth
A fine beige one
Of sexy spies in Bangladesh
Perhaps I'd better stick to Romania
They came from the Volga
Same as us

IRA COHEN

FRANCE, GERMANY, THE CZECH REPUBLIC

PEPE LE MOKO LIVES

—for Yasha & Gherasim Luca

I would like to write a poem in French
as if I were a man with only one arm
returning from an alligator hunt
in the sewers of New York
It should be avant garde as a menu
& could be titled *Service Non Compris,*
something really soulful
like the howl of a wolf
looking for food in the streets
of Paris during that terrible winter
when François Villon died
The poem should contain the black
lunettes worn by God
to protect Himself from his admirateurs,
O Mon Dieu, a poem without price
written for an audience not for sale,
something unforgettable as white excrement,
something with panache
and the taste of next year's
Beaujolais
It should also be practical
as selling chemicals for poison gas

to Saddam Hussein
or arms to both sides
during a civil war in a backward country
like Rwanda
Long live Haute Couture
Like a whore I want to please you
I would like to write a poem in French
which would last forever,
not a button without a buttonhole,
something logical and purposeful,
something mesmerizing & really feminine
with no regrets
like the high kick of a can can dancer
exposing everything just for fun
Like Boris Vian
I would like to spit on your grave
Artaud, Cocteau, Crapaud
Vive la France
The Power & The Glory
Let there always be injections
of surrealist intelligence
March on March on
Long live Hemophilia!

VIEW FROM THE AUTOBAHN

Driving across Germany
passing Koblenz & Pfaffenheck
where we consider picking up
a few cartons of Wild Banana condoms
Exotische-Erotische
Somewhere there must be an electronic
                                  grapefruit
waiting to be violated
The forehead begins contracting
between the eyebrows
The Germans have become a nation
of television stripteasers covered
                          in fat patches,
the new method of effortless schlimming
They practice in front of mirrors
on the best way to unhook the national
bra

327

You can sense magical vibrations
born of ritual blood dancing,
but one feels safe on the Autobahn
passing Kisselbach and Bachrach
Though we don't take the Ausfahrt
to Bad Kreuzbach
Not much to be seen from the Autobahn,
but it's comforting to know,
as we pass Hockenheim for a dump,
that *Schmutzfinkery* will not be tolerated
Auslanders are Different
is a sign placed over the doorway
as an indication of German hospitality
& a desire to encourage a better
human rights record
Take it from me, the best jokes were told
on the way to the ovens
You never get to hear the best stuff
It was too small for me anyway
It was a bird that flew
There goes Chaplin running along
the Autobahn heading for PILSEN.

You'd think I had nothing to lose,
but, baby, what you don't know
will hurt you.

CZECHMATE

—for Curtis who, when asked how he likes Czechs,
replied, "Czechs are OK, but I prefer Cash."

I met a hooker in Brussels
who had very big muscles
I must confess
when I took off her dress
it was Curtis Jones
working one of his hustles.

In Prague at the Velryba Café
we enjoy Czech cuisine
Here you can order Tartar Sauce
as a main dish—

Philippe wants to know about the sexual mores,
the seduction games as he puts it
I note that there is a lot of public demonstration
of kissing et cetera
usually at the base of one of the innumerable statues—
I'm sure it's a good town for plumbers
& Penta laughs
Confessions of a Window Cleaner is the name of the movie
Kafka undresses in a dark room
while Milena ascends a ladder
leaning against the moon...
Penta tells me that there are
a lot of dogs in Prague, but not
so many cats
I guess the dogs just have to make it
with each other
A blonde gypsy woman sits sadly
on the Charles Bridge
& in the full moon over the city
you can see the abundant rump
of the Czech Republic gleaming whitely
& lit by a phallic candle,
all of it hand tinted by Jan Saudek.

SMEARED VELVET:
THE LAST DAYS OF
CZECHOSLOVAKIA

JOE SAFDIE

The 10-year anniversary of the End of the Cold War passed as most such commemorations do: a few expressions of nostalgia from the leaders, articulate speculation about how the revolution lost its way, editorials in the local papers. NPR did a week's tour of Central Europe, joined by CNN and a few of the other networks. For most people in the West though, it was still, in the immortal words of Neville Chamberlain, "a land far away, of which we know nothing."

The land Chamberlain was specifically referring to was Czechoslovakia, now the Czech Republic, and it got its share of the spotlight too; Václav Havel, despite having lost most of his moral authority among Czechs some time ago, wound up on the front page of the NY Times. I lived and taught in that region for three years in the

329

early nineties, and wrote the piece that follows for Exquisite Corpse *in the winter of 1993.*

The editors had originally and graciously allowed me to add an "interlinear" (a way of cutting in and out of time, not, certainly, a gratuitous "update"), but I eventually decided the piece could stand on its own terms. There are, of course, ironic echoes in the ten years of history that have followed: the Klaus-Zeman power-sharing "handshake" that has infuriated so many current Czech citizens, for instance, is a mirror-image of the infamous Klaus-Meciar agreement to partition the country, and the walling-in of Labem's Gypsies is a reminder that the likes of John Rocker are not limited to North America. But perhaps what we most need relief from are those obvious Orphic looks back, frequently destructive, rarely enlightening. What follows then, in all its short-sightedness, is a view from the trenches.

28 December 1992

Cold, dreary, smokestacked skies; slick, frozen streets; neither the church bells from the reconstructed cathedral around the corner nor the occasional streetcar rumbling down the cobblestones do much to lighten the gloom outside. Some kind of weird high-pressure zone has settled in over Central Europe for the last two weeks—the Czech meteorological term gets translated as "anti-cyclone"—and has frozen everything in an icy grayness. The sun does come out, for a few hours a day, but it never gets above 5° or 6° Celsius. It's a perfect parallel to the political mood here, another kind of frozen paralysis, as the clock slowly ticks away the last days of the doomed federation.

I've been here 18 months now, teaching English in a Moravian university town called Olomouc ("oh-low-moats"). In three days the country's going to split apart, and there'll be a new international border set up about 70 kilometers to the southeast, the one that will mark the sovereign country of Slovakia. Word is that some new border guard jobs will be created; that's about the only rational reason I can see for the split. But then, I'm not Czech, or Slovak ... I'm just a foreign hired hand.

I don't really want to write about the split itself: the politics are too devious, and too far-removed, probably, for most people to care about. But it might be worth giving a "Report to the Academy," as Kafka had it, about some of the things that have been going on here at the eastern edge of the New World Order ... because it's getting pretty obvious that the folks here have their own ideas about what that order means.

Those, that is, who aren't too shell-shocked to notice.

≈

First, why am I even here to witness this? You might remember that there were a few upheavals in Central Europe in 1989; some people even called them "revolutions." After the buzz wore off, the various new governments realized that, besides money, they needed a massive infusion of native English-speakers: it seems there was no "infrastructure" to handle the intense demand along the newly liberated students for the language of millionaires. Besides, large numbers of Czech teachers whose specialty was teaching Russian were suddenly, as the euphemism goes, "made redundant," and had to go back to school to get requalified to teach English if they wanted to keep their jobs. So the new ministries of education in Poland, Hungary and Czechoslovakia petitioned the international community for help. My wife and I saw an ad in our local paper in California, thought it would be exciting to live in a country that had recently made a playwright of its president, and some months later signed on for a two-year gig.

Looking out at these icy and almost deserted streets, it's funny to remember that the last few days we spent in the states were in the middle of downtown Atlanta at a local Radisson Hotel, the black attendants all dressed in attractive black uniforms. The air-conditioning in our room made a lot of noise but didn't seem to get the place any cooler—a matter of some importance, as it was mid-summer, pushing 100° and unbearably humid—so we spent a lot of time in the company of Alvin, a big and friendly maintenance man who couldn't figure out the problem. But that *smile!* Unfortunately, we couldn't move to another room, they're all booked at the moment, Gee I wish I could help you, I really do ... so as a result we also spent a lot of time at the rooftop bar.

"Czechoslovakia? Jeezus Christ—whaddya want to throw your lives away for?" This provocative question came from a semi-pretty bleached blonde with callow features who, at the moment of asking, was being playfully tied up by her jock boyfriend at the other end of the bar. Everything's relative, I guess. We mumbled something about wanting to see Europe for free—the boyfriend nodding his head slowly with that pseudo-concerned look that usually means "I don't care about a word you're saying"—but she just curled her lower lip further down in disgust. "That ain't Europe; that's fucking *Russia!*"

Alvin and the floozie might be a good place to start this report, because Alvin's service-economy friendliness is what Czechoslovakia is definitely *not*—sometimes it seems like every face in the shops and streets over, say, 35 years old is wizened, care-worn and decidedly unfriendly— and because what my friend in bondage meant may yet turn out to be pretty close to the truth. But nobody knows that now. Nobody knows much of anything now. "Czechoslovakia," in fact, is only going to exist for a few more days, and it seems more like a giant train-station than a country, a waiting room where people wander about dazed, searching for their connections, not realizing that the routes have all been changed, the tracks derailed...

Except for the followers of Czech Prime Minister Václav Klaus. They know exactly what's going on, and aren't shy about letting you know. Their view of the forthcoming split can be summarized pretty simply: it's just a recapitulation of the last 40 years, right here on this ancient patch of ground, for those of you who missed it the last time... the Cold War! In one corner, the sober, rational, free-marketeer Václav Klaus, courageously leading the Czech lands back into democratic Europe; in the other, ex-Commie rabble-rouser and populist Vladimír Meciar, preying on Slovak fears and resentments to drag the eastern third of the country back into state-controlled enterprise. "Let 'em go," say the members of ODS, Klaus' party, "the sooner the better." (One of the less attractive features of Czech political culture is a tendency towards anonymous unanimity: a majority of people in Bohemia and Moravia, the "Czech lands," signaled by their votes in the national elections last June a desire to preserve the common state; now they're the ones pounding the drum for separation.) And if you ask them why, exactly, these two men, Klaus and Meciar, have decided the fate of the country instead of something a little more democratic—a vote of the people, for instance—they say, well, the elections in June were the referendum, and the people who voted for Meciar knew exactly what they were getting.

Which has a certain fatalistic logic, except for the facts that 1) Meciar never actually mentioned anything about an outright split in the election campaign, and at least some of his supporters voted for him because they thought he would engineer more concessions for Slovakia while preserving the common federation; and 2) by all accounts (and a poll was conducted as late as November), if there *had* been a referendum with one question, "Should the common state between Czechs and Slovaks be preserved?," a majority of the people would have voted "yes"— including, presumably, the tens of thousands of Czechs and Slovaks who happen to be married to each other. As one of my colleagues on the law faculty here told me last month, there's definitely something rotten in the state of Denmark. He then went on to repeat the argument that the June elections were the referendum and, after all, two such radically different views of economic and social policy as Klaus' and Meciar's really couldn't survive in one state.

Except that they can. The entire political history of the United States, for example, is an object lesson in compromise: any two radically different ideas can be compromised eventually. In fact, the main function of political parties is to ensure just that. But it's probably not realistic to expect such tarnished wisdom to take root in a country that's enjoyed exactly 23 years of independence in the last 500. Instead, in harmony with Czechoslovakia's long history of passive resistance, we're getting something called "the velvet divorce"...a process, insists Mr. Klaus unctuously at every opportunity, that need not disturb the dreams of western financiers.

Well, maybe it won't. Maybe it's a good thing, this split. As my students are forever telling me, you don't know, you haven't lived here, you can't understand what it was like. But in a few days, a 75-year-old country is going to dissolve; the people who used to be its citizens will not have had the chance to vote on it; and the creepy thing about it is, they don't seem to care. Nobody's demonstrating; nobody's raising their voice; nobody's even clearing their throat. Here's a small example of what I'm talking about: two months ago, in October, the truncated federal parliament refused to pass a piece of legislation that would have made the forthcoming split legal and constitutional. Mr. Klaus—plummeting out of velvet mode for a moment—exploded, and was quoted to the effect that the country was going to divide anyway, and whether it would do so legally or illegally was besides the point! And when I asked my students—law students—what they thought about this, a very bright young girl said "You know, a lot of things happen in our country that aren't strictly legal." Fine...then what's the point in having a revolution, velvet or otherwise? What's the point of trying to create a democracy? (Seeing my displeasure, she went on to ask me if it wasn't true that George Bush could do whatever he wanted, but that's another story.) At any rate, the question became moot a few days later, as the last few opposition groups that had been clinging to the idea of preserving a common state—somewhat ironically, they're all left-wing—were outflanked by Mssrs. Klaus and Meciar: the separate republics assumed federal powers, and "divorce" became an absolute certainty.

It's a divorce, like any divorce, of incompatibility: there are real historical tensions between the two republics, and more than enough bad faith on both sides to go around. But it's also a divorce, it seems to me, of disillusionment. People here are disappointed that the "revolution" didn't bring them the instant affluence they saw over the borders in Germany and Austria and, by satellite, further west. A joke I heard is that Czechoslovaks expected to consume like the Germans, be provided for like the Swedes, and work like the Russians (I expect you have to have lived in Europe for a while to know how funny that is). When none of that happened, people started looking for someone to blame. Some blamed the Communists they said were still in power, the only ones who could afford to buy the newly privatized stores, and who were thus enjoying the same privileges they always had. Some blamed Havel for not bringing about a Golden Age. But for the Slovaks, the obvious enemies were the Czech politicians around Prague, who had always treated them like second-class citizens. When the unemployment rate in Slovakia rose rapidly to 13% while stalling in Prague at about 2%, some Slovaks felt that they'd seen this movie before, and started making noises about leaving the theater. Now that they're almost at the exit, it might be wise to roll the film back a few reels.

29 December 1992

This morning I saw, again, CNN's endlessly recurring promo for its "hard-hitting documentary reports on (among other things) Eastern Europe: its hopes... and fears." The old guy's face in the corner as the narrator solemnly intones these words looks a lot like one of my neighbors here in Olomouc, a tanned, weather-beaten gentleman who studiously inspects the dumpsters outside our old flat every day for any valuable—or edible—refuse. He's quite dignified, though; and even though the less desirable aspects of capitalism have already started to affect most Czechoslovak citizens, it strikes me that I've never, in 18 months, seen anyone asking for a handout. A small thing, maybe; certainly subject to change in the coming months. In both republics.

Empires are out of fashion these days (except, of course, for CNN's media empire), so it's probably not very politically correct to remember that the Hapsburg version managed to rule over an increasingly cosmopolitan group of 12 different "subject-races"—for hundreds of years—with a modicum of enlightenment... especially compared to the Nazi and Soviet systems that succeeded it. The main problem that Czechs and Slovaks are dealing with today stems from the fact that, in 1867, a weakened Austria determined that it had to split the dynasty and share power with the Magyars in Hungary. This new "Austro-Hungarian Empire" had disastrous results for many segments of the Hapsburg monarchy, but most of all, perhaps, for the Slovaks.

Because while Czechs and Slovaks are certainly ethnic cousins and neighbors, the similarity stops there. Slovakia was considered part of Hungary for almost a thousand years, never once achieving its own independence until 1939, when Hitler created a brief puppet fascist state led by a priest, Monsignor Tiso. And the Magyars were absolute in their dominion: no other ethnic groups of any sort were to have any rights, and anyone wishing to participate in the government had to "become" Magyar. This naturally discouraged the formation of a Slovak intellectual core, keeping those of them who didn't forsake their identities completely poor, rural and uneducated. The Slovaks didn't really even have a language, other than local dialects in isolated villages, for the greater part of the 19th century; and in 1918, the first year of the Czecho-Slovak state, it was estimated that there were from 750 to 1,000 educated Slovaks... period.[1]

The Czechs of Bohemia and Moravia, on the other hand, did have

334

1. Polisensky, J. V., *History of Czechoslovakia in Outline*, Vydala Bohemia International, Prague, 1991, p. 114.

some experience of independence, albeit an ancient one. The "Great Moravian Empire" lasted for about a hundred years until the Magyars invaded in 896 A.D. (thus taking Slovakia); and the state of Bohemia even contributed two Holy Roman Emperors to the roll-call, Charles IV making Prague the center of Europe in the Golden Age of the 14th century by means of his aggressive building program, much of which survives today. Jan Hus' form of Protestantism (the Hussites, later called Utraguists) spread throughout Bohemia long before anyone had ever heard of Martin Luther; Hus was deemed a dangerous heretic and burned at the stake in 1415, but his followers became an integral part of Czech political and religious culture. The kingdom of Bohemia survived until 1620, when the Czechs and their few Central European allies were wiped out by the united forces of Catholic Europe in the disastrous Battle of the White Mountain near Prague.

It took over 200 years for Czech patriots and intellectuals to recover, but finally, under the stimulus of the "national revival" of the 19th century, poets, historians, scientists and journalists joined together to create a kind of "Slav consciousness" in the Czech lands. For one thing, Czechs—unlike Slovaks—had the chance to participate in the Austrian Civil Service, especially when language ordinances allowing them to speak Czech while doing so were temporarily adopted. But perhaps most important was the development of industry. When aristocratic feudalism broke down in the countryside during the industrial revolution, thousands of displaced peasants swamped the cities and coal-mines of northern Bohemia: the introduction of mechanized crops forced a job re-training program on a massive scale. Strong mining and textile industries were the inevitable result.

So that when Dr. T. G. Masaryk engaged Woodrow Wilson's administration in a fierce letter-writing campaign in 1917, agitating for independence and urging the Americans to enter the war against Austria, he was able to point to the existence of a thriving economy that had been exploited by "totalitarian" rulers. Masaryk—a professor of Slavic studies at Charles University in Prague, who was soon to become the republic's first president—knew this wasn't exactly true, but felt he had to get America on his side somehow. In this he was helped by a group of Slovak immigrants who had come to the United States in the 19th century and done what immigrants dream of doing: namely, get rich. This "Slovak League of America" joined with Masaryk's supporters, the Bohemian National Alliance, in a coordinated campaign for recognition. And they were successful: one of Woodrow Wilson's "14 Points" mentioned complete autonomy for "Czecho-Slovaks" and other subject races—until that coining, the word had hardly been used. (Another new word was "Yugoslavia.")

So it was an unnatural marriage to begin with, contra

naturam, and it soon became clear that the Czechs weren't interested in sharing their new power with their backward cousins from the east. Masaryk's and Wilson's invention was to last 20 years, until the treacherous Munich Agreement of 1938, when the Prime Minister of one of the countries that had helped create it called Czechoslovakia "a far-away country of which we know nothing." Then came a Nazi "protectorate" in Czech lands and Tiso's puppet regime in Slovakia, followed, in 1948, by the Communist *putsch*—further proof, if any was needed, that the historic destiny of the Czechs and Slovaks until this moment has been to be dominated by every conceivable terrible system of government on earth.

Life under Communism in Czechoslovakia is not something that any citizen of "The West" can easily imagine, and that's especially true, I think, for those of us whose natural sympathies are with the left. Because, as Richard Rorty wrote last spring in the *Yale Review*:

> We are all accustomed to thinking of World War II as a good war, but many of us are not yet prepared to think of the Cold War as a good war. Yet this is just how the Czechs think of it. The Czechs and Slovaks would be...outraged by the suggestion that the West should have avoided the Cold War.[2]

After 18 months in this country, I know this is true. A broad majority of my students—those, that is, who cared at all about the U.S. elections—were "for" George Bush, because they believed that even such a carefully manicured creation as Bill Clinton would prove to be "soft" on Communism; they would have been infinitely responsive to the shrill attacks on Clinton's patriotism (i.e., that he visited Moscow and Prague in 1969 and stayed with Communists) which apparently fell on deaf ears in the States. And this is so not because these people have been "sheltered" from the supposedly sophisticated political dialogues of the West, but because they bore the full brunt of a system that forced them to live a lie, that was profoundly anti-human.

This is starting to sound a little like Jean Kirkpatrick, for which I extend my apologies. But there is an element of *mea culpa* here that I shouldn't ignore. Before coming to Czechoslovakia, I was actually excited about the chance to live in a place where the boundaries between rich and poor were more fluid than the ones with which I'd grown up, thinking I could garner fresh evidence about the sickness of capitalism, etc., etc. I'd thought, in fact, that the problems of Communism were mainly those of a civil libertarian nature, and that once the freedoms of speech and press and assembly kicked in, people would start to realize the real benefits of a more egalitarian economic structure.

---

2. Rorty, Richard, "The Intellectuals at the End of Socialism," *The Yale Review*, Spring, 1992 (excerpted in *Harper's*, May 1992).

I couldn't have been more wrong.

What survived here after 40 years of Soviet domination was a carcass, an empty shell of a country ... and I'm not just talking about the environmental damage. You have to imagine a real saturation job: a parasite attacking your body until there's almost no body left, only parasite. For example, I teach in the building that used to be the Communist Party District Headquarters, one of the few modern structures in town, complete with sauna on the ground floor. Our flat is more typical: it's in a building that once housed the Soviet Army in Olomouc, a great concrete slab of a structure, a peeling hulk. Along with many other examples, it's a square-jawed legacy of socialist realist architecture, which offers a strange counterpoint to the Baroque churches that also dot this small town. The most grotesque example of this culture clash may be the neo-Gothic astrological clock of the town square. Originally, a circle of saints blessed the populace on the hour, much like the more famous clock in Prague's Old Town Square. But the Nazis destroyed it in 1945 as they were pulling out of town. Ten years later, the Communists restored it, but they replaced the saints with noble workers—welders, cobblers, farmers, athletes—and added a gold-lamé rooster that clucks pathetically after the procession is over.

But the real effects of Communism were psychic, and for those you have to listen to someone who was here. Václav Havel's description of the 1970s in Czechoslovakia isn't his most profound paragraph, but may suffice as a snapshot of the kind of atmosphere that prevailed:

> A long period of moribund silence began. A new ruling elite, which was in fact much like the old one, quickly formed and carried out all those purges, prohibitions, and liquidations. An exhausted society quickly got used to the fact that everything once declared forever impossible (in 1968) was now possible again, and that an often unmasked and ridiculed absurdity could rule once more. People withdrew into themselves and stopped taking an interest in public affairs. An era of apathy and widespread demoralization began, an era of grey, everyday totalitarian consumerism. Society was atomized, small islands of resistance were destroyed, and a disappointed and exhausted public pretended not to notice. Independent thinking and creation retreated to the trenches of deep privacy.[3]

Things have gotten a lot better, my Czech friends always tell me; you should have been here ten, five, even two years ago. I nod my head; I'm happy for them. But in most places outside Prague—even in this peppy university town—much of this paragraph of Havel's still rings true today.

At any rate, as everyone was equal under socialism, Slovakia too began to emerge from its centuries of provincialism. After the crushing of

---

3. Havel, Václav, *Disturbing the Peace*, Vintage Books, New York, 1990 (translated by Paul Wilson).

the Prague Spring in 1968, in fact, the republic of Czechoslovakia became a federation of two republics, thus diverting Dubcek's reform energy into a mild Slovak nationalism. The party fathers' further contribution to this process was to increase the level of heavy industry there: steel plants, chemical works and, above all, arms factories became the new engine of the nascent Slovak economy.

But as Communism in Slovakia was just as demoralizing and anti-human as it was in the Czech lands, Slovaks joined enthusiastically in the Velvet Revolution of late 1989. Their excitement, however, dampened somewhat when Havel announced one of the first policies of his new post-revolutionary government: that Czechoslovakia was no longer interested in selling arms. No one, apparently, had thought to ask the Slovaks what they thought about this. (It's rumored that there was also some pressure applied to Havel from the U.S. government, who of course would never dream of selling arms to unstable regimes.)

Meanwhile, Havel turned the job of economic reconstruction over to his finance minister Václav Klaus, who after years of quiet economic study was convinced that free markets à la Milton Friedman were the way to go. Klaus is an admirer of Maggie Thatcher's dictum "no third way," meaning that he opposes any government intervention whatsoever in the invisible hand of the marketplace: in the other new democracies of Central Europe, they call this idea "shock therapy." And while the full effects of his ambitious large-scale privatization program won't be felt for some time, the initial stages, as I mentioned in talking about the unemployment rate, went over a lot better in Bohemia than in the factory-dependent Slovakia.

(And not for the first time. I found this quote in a Czech history book published just after the revolution in 1990:

> Equally resented was Czech economic policy, or rather the lack of it, with respect to Slovakia. The Slovak enterprises were treated as equal to the Czech ones; it was up to market forces which of them were to prosper and which were to perish. The latter was more likely to happen to Slovak than to Czech firms. In the credit shortage caused by the deflationary policy the Slovak enterprises were particularly vulnerable.[4]

The kicker, of course, is that the author is talking not about 1990, but about 1918!)

But modesty is not one of Mr. Klaus' virtues, and in fact he consistently scorned his critics—both in Slovakia and in certain other portions of Mr. Havel's government—as being "too soft," both in this matter of economic policy and in their approach toward ex-Communists.

338

4. Krejcí, Jaroslav, *Czechoslovakia at the Crossroads of European History*, I B Tauris & Co Ltd, London, 1990, p. 139.

Indeed, the most controversial and divisive piece of legislation passed by Czechoslovakia's velvet government had nothing to do with economics, but instead banned all officials of the previous regime—including party members above a certain rank and any suspected collaborators with the StB, the former secret police—from holding any governmental position for a period of five years. The problem with this seemingly just proposition, called the "lustrace" law from the Latin for "purification by sacrifice," was not just that it shifted the burden of proof onto the (presumed) innocent—as the international human rights organization Helsinki Watch gently informed its former clients in Havel's government—but that the list of "collaborators" was kept by the StB themselves. Many such lists began appearing in Czech newspapers and periodicals. And when such people as the wife of famous Czech writer Josef Skvorecky—and Havel himself!—turned up on some copies, people began to compare the atmosphere to America in the 1950s and started talking about witch hunts.[5]

But not Klaus. It had been his party that had forced the law through Parliament, and he and his deputies strongly support it today. Havel wavered, stressing the need for Czechoslovaks to forgive each other and forget the past; he eventually signed the bill, but suggested it be further modified in Parliament. And Meciar? Ten days before the June elections, a report surfaced that he was undoubtedly an StB collaborator: his code name was "The Doktor," he had shredded important documents that proved his guilt, he was still a Communist sympathizer. The many thousands of people who voted for him in Slovakia chose either to ignore or disbelieve these charges, perhaps seeing them as yet another Czech slander against Slovaks. Meciar himself apparently believed Havel was behind the story, as the former playwright, in a speech a few days before the elections, urged the people not to vote for "divisive populists." They ignored him: Meciar's party was the big winner in Slovakia, while Klaus' party won the majority of votes in the Czech lands.

In such a polarized atmosphere, it was probably inevitable that the two men, charged by Havel with the task of forming a new federal government, found nothing to talk about, and decided instead to split the common state into two separate republics. Moreover, since under Czechoslovakia's constitution the president is elected not by the people but by Parliament, Meciar withheld his support and that of his allies for Havel's candidacy. Whereupon Václav Havel—poet, playwright, philosopher king—resigned his post as President of Czechoslovakia.

That's a lot of material for one day … but then, people have been living in these parts for a long time; and like most people in Europe, they

5. Lawrence Weschler has a good piece on the slimy contradictions of the "lustrace" law in the October 19, 1992 issue of *The New Yorker*.

wear their history on their sleeves. I'll try to explore some of the implications of all this tomorrow.

30 December 1992

The weather report on TV this morning says the ground temperature's -22°! (That's -7°F for you westerners.) I guess we'll have to put on two pairs of socks before going out today. But then, maybe we'll just stay put: the only shops open this week are liquor stores, or "vecerkas," which cater to a seemingly inexhaustible appetite. Czech alcoholism is a serious problem, some people say, and it's true that it's a rare morning when the beer halls aren't already doing a thriving business ... at 7 A.M.! The beer is great—*really* great—but I've never gotten used to that.

Other stores that might have been open this week are closed for "inventory"—largely a matter, one suspects, of raising prices for the new year in accordance with the new value-added tax that will be tacked onto most goods and services in the Czech Republic. Czech inflation is actually pretty moderate compared to other Central European countries, but you can't help wonder whether the worst is yet to come.

So ... if these tensions between the two republics are real (and one could hardly have missed Klaus' absence from Alexander Dubcek's funeral in Slovakia in November), why not just split and be done with it? Apart from a certain sentimental attachment to the only democratic structure these folks have ever known, what's the problem here? Self-determination, after all, is a fundamental democratic right: at least that's what Woodrow Wilson wrote, in enunciating the principles that underlie the origins of Czechoslovakia. And it can certainly be argued that self-determination is the reason there's no Soviet Union today, the reason why some conservative intellectuals have declared "the end of history."

Well, one problem—to take one last plunge in that obsolete tidepool—is that Woodrow Wilson developed terminal brain cancer a year after the publication of his 14 Points, his idea for an effective League of Nations fatally comprised by the refusal of his own nation to join. But what's not as well known is the incredible arrogance (sometimes called "idealism") with which he, a few Brit allies, and a secret committee called The Inquiry proposed to re-write the European map along ethnic lines. This latter group of five people (among whom the most prominent was the young journalist Walter Lippman) studied various maps and charts and lists of statistics, trying to determine how to grant sovereignty to the various ethnic groups of Central, Eastern and Balkan Europe without doing too much damage to the interests of the victorious Allies. The solution they came up with, under a good deal of pressure from the émigré groups already in America, they called "Czechoslovakia" and "Yugoslavia." It took a while—the Iron Curtain had a way of

340

smothering ethnic tensions—but now those particular chickens are coming home to roost.

Because the problem with ethnic states is that they can never be 100% ethnically pure: notwithstanding the aggressive cleansing campaign being carried out a few hundred miles south of here, there's always going to be minorities to deal with. And any state that defines itself along ethnic lines must, by definition, be threatened if equal rights are accorded those minorities. Thus the current concerns in Nagorno-Karabach, in Moldova, and, closer to home, with the 600,000 or so ethnic Hungarians living in Slovakia: the new Slovak constitution doesn't mention anything about their rights. (Given the long historical enmity between Slovaks and Magyars, this is probably not accidental.) And then there's the Gypsies, or "Romanies," as they're officially called, a darker race of people whose language derives from Sanskrit and who are, indisputably, the niggers of Europe: the one ethnic group the overwhelmingly white Czechs and Slovaks can agree in dumping on. "They're not civilized," said many of my students last year; "if you give them a flat to live in, they just destroy it." Shades of Selma, Alabama. And, of course, there's Sarajevo, a formerly cosmopolitan city where Muslims, Serbs and Croats had lived together peacefully for many generations, and which may or may not still be standing by the time you read these words. We're a long way, here on the plains of Central Europe, from universal brotherhood.

So it makes little differences that, as Mr. Klaus unfailingly repeats to all his western interviewers, "Czechoslovakia isn't Yugoslavia." The point is not whether one country or another might manage to avoid armed conflict for a while ("We're not like the Czechs," sneered one Solidarity member in Warsaw a few years ago; "we fight"), but what it is they envision as the peace. This is a land of kings and princes, upon which was grafted a peculiarly brutal form of the workers' paradise. It's not a place where anything called democracy has ever flourished for long, and the way in which it's going about its division doesn't offer a lot of hope for the future. Or as noted office worker Franz Kafka had it, in *A Country Doctor* (1919, one year after independence):

> "What is going to happen?" we all ask ourselves. "How long can we endure this burden and torment? The Emperor's palace has drawn the nomads here but does not know how to drive them away again.... It is left to us artisans and tradesmen to save our country; but we are not equal to such a task; nor have we ever claimed to be capable of it. This is a misunderstanding of some kind; and it will be the ruin of us."[6]

"But we are not equal to such a task" ... Czechs and Slovaks achieved a certain comfort level under Communism because they were

6. Kafka, Franz, *The Penal Colony*, Schocken Books, New York, 1948 (translated by Willa and Edwin Muir).

told what to do all the time, and never had to make their own decisions or assume personal responsibility for anything. Habits like that aren't going to change overnight by the infection of the invisible hand of the marketplace. An example: down the street from our flat a restaurant called "Neptune" had been under construction for some months, and we waited impatiently for its opening, hoping to experience the taste of fish again, even fish flown in from New Zealand (the only fresh fish served in this land-locked country is carp, a notorious bottom-feeder that eats things no other fish would touch). One night as we were walking home down the deserted cobblestone streets (which empty out soon after night-fall), I expressed the opinion that the restaurant really should open on the coming weekend, as there was a big flower festival in town and they might be able to attract some international customers. To which my wife said "Joe, they don't *think* that way." Sometimes it's painful to realize the assumptions capitalism creates, but she was right: Czechs and Slovaks simply don't think—yet—in terms of business, of making a profit, of getting more customers through better service, etc. No one thinks about "raising their station"; upward mobility is an alien concept outside of Prague, and even there monetary success still has a taint about it. Most shops aren't even open on weekends! Weekends, after all, are family days: time to put the kids in the old Skoda and go visit the grandparents. On weekends Olomouc becomes a ghost town, as *all* the university students go home to be with... their parents! (If American politicians really cared about "family values," they'd use Czechoslovakia as a role model.) And it's in this environment that Mr. Klaus seeks to introduce the forces of market capitalism, forces that have been destructive to every known family value since their inception. All I can say is, don't hold your breath. (By the way, "Neptune" finally did open in August; it closed in October. Apparently it was too expensive, and there was some dispute over who owned the furniture. But the god who lent his name to a temporarily unsuccessful business venture still has a 17th-century, pre-capitalist fountain on the town square that gushes tribute on warm days.)

But Klaus is still popular in the Czech lands, and his party has enough power in the Czech parliament to force through most, if not all, of his economic reforms. So like it or not—and a sizable minority of left-wing parties don't—Bohemia and Moravia seem destined for a bumpy ride through the shoals of western-style capitalism. And Slovakia will finally have its cherished independence ("for the first time in a thousand years," say some of its nationalist politicians), but will go slower on economic reforms and, fairly obviously, preserve some of those jobs in the arms industry. "Arms exports," said Meciar the other day, "are an internal issue of Slovakia." Neither republic figures to become an exemplar of democratic values. Meciar recently fired the director of the Slovak TV network, apparently for being hesitant to grant the new Prime Minister a daily forum, and closed down the leading opposition newspaper; Meciar now only grants interviews to a few selected friends in the media. But Klaus has his problems with the media as well. He thought that the minority opposition parties were getting too much coverage on TV at one point, and came up with the astonishing suggestion that because ODS had won the majority of votes in the election, they should also receive the preponderance of featured time on the nightly new telecasts! "That's democratic," he said. As all TV networks in the two republics are still owned by the state, there's nobody to say otherwise.

The main problem in the political spectrum, however, is that there's no middle, no potentially unifying constituency that would help to promote tolerance and mediate between polarized extremes. Havel might have been that kind of figure, and he did want to preserve the common state; but even if, as seems certain now, he becomes the first president of the new Czech Republic, his influence will never be the same. Havel called himself a "non-political politician" who didn't want to stoop to the ignominious position of identifying himself with a political party; he doesn't in fact, believe in political parties: he wants to stay "above the fray." But while he continued to promote his moralistic and unquestionably profound reflections, Klaus and Meciar were busy organizing powerful constituencies. Meanwhile, the party led by the former Foreign Minister Jiri Dienstbier—like Havel, a former dissident who had spent some years in jail—was perceived as being too vague, and failed to receive the necessary 5% of votes that would have allowed it representation in the parliament. All this left Havel without a leg to stand on. (In this, his similarity to Woodrow Wilson is eerie and a little ominous.) But as I said, he's apparently going to lend his prestige and credibility—still intact in the west—to Klaus' government, and serve as a largely ceremonial president. It's a little hard to figure out why.

31 December 1992

Last-minute news reports mention a flood of Slovaks applying for Czech citizenship ... I certainly didn't want to suggest, in any of the preceding analysis, that Meciar was some sort of angel. For all I know, he was an StB collaborator-thug, and he *will* lead Slovakia into chaos. What I think is important, though, is that whatever pain and suffering result might have been avoided if Mr. Klaus hadn't been so ideologically determined to cut what he saw as his losses. There was nothing historically, politically, or economically inevitable about this split; it didn't need to happen.

But I want to get back, finally, to the proposition I started with: that people don't care, that they seem oblivious to it all. There certainly haven't been any outward signs of alarm among the people of

343

Olomouc as they've gone about their daily business, wheeling baby carriages, staring through shop windows, crowding onto streetcars. And while a vocal minority of my students tries all the time to engage me in political arguments, a larger group professes no interest at all in the subject. Some are discovering religion; others carry on the long-established Czech tradition of drinking beer and telling stories at pubs, without ever really *doing* anything (see *The Good Soldier Svejk* by Jaroslav Hasek, a long and mostly hilarious novel about a Czech soldier's misadventures during World War I, thought by some to epitomize the "typical" Czech character). It's this tendency towards a faceless anonymity—developed to a fine art as a survival technique under the long years of Communism—that bothers me the most: it's a passivity that goes beyond even the slothful inactivity in the states. Searching for a metaphor once last year, I came up with a late-summer baseball game at the Astrodome, when there's only a few thousand people in the stands desultorily eating their hot dogs and the score-board operator has to flash N-O-I-S-E! on the message screen to get any response at all. There are times, in fact, when Marx' description of Czechs in the late 1850s as "inferior beings who had lost the race"—whose only hope lay in submissive loyalty to the culture-bringers, the Germans—seems almost understandable. And I start to remember the litany of passive resistance: didn't fight back against the Nazis, didn't fight back against the Soviets, didn't fight in the Velvet Revolution, don't care about their country's splitting apart...

Am I overstating the case? Maybe. One quality that's taken root here, over the long years of occupation of one sort or another, is a healthy dose of skepticism, or disbelief that any government structure could ever be telling the truth. "If we couldn't laugh," said the rector of the university to me one day, "we wouldn't have survived." Granted; but once you've learned to live at an ironic remove from things, it's a little hard to bring it all back together. "We're a small country," wrote one of my better students last year, "and we've never thought the world revolves around us." It was an implied affront to the imperial dreams of superpowers; it was realistic; it was even wise. But what it wasn't was passionate: passion doesn't combine too well with skepticism. And without passion a certain portion of the human spectrum of experience remains unexpressed.

It's presumptuous, of course, to think you can judge anyone's essential instincts. But I see new examples of this overwhelming impassiveness every day. When we first came here, people told us it would take at least a generation for the revolution to become "real" in people's minds: it now seems to me that that estimate is a little generous. Not because there's any lack of intellectual curiosity, or of liveliness, or humor, but because there doesn't seem to be any goal to which people feel they can commit themselves passionately: everything's been compromised. Nothing's of any intrinsic *worth*. Nothing's worth fighting for.

Which makes any political discussion, finally, irrelevant. I mean, nobody really cares if Meciar's government goes slower or faster in adopting economic reforms; nobody *really* cares (despite bankers' propaganda to the contrary) if they go back to socialism altogether ... though some might care if they begin to officially discriminate against the Hungarians. But it's the more intangible feeling of being adrift that's the real problem: the feeling of being set free from intolerable restraints only to find that this is everyone's problem—but it seems more magnified in a country with no real democratic traditions, whose last feeling of independence dates back to the 14th century.[7]

"The feeling of being adrift" ... in this, as with other maladies that affect the spirit, I frequently have recourse to poetry. One of the earliest Central European poems I learned to love was "To Raja Rao" by the Polish Nobel Prize winner Czeslaw Milosz, which contains these lines:

> Ill at ease in the tyranny, ill at ease in the republic,
> in the one I longed for freedom, in the other for the
> end of corruption.

But he learns "at last to say: this is my home ... in a great republic, moderately corrupt."

The Czech and Slovak republics are a few years away from being "great," and the level of corruption could not honestly be described— December, 1992—as moderate. But it's necessary, as Havel insists, to view politics from a sphere that's outside their provenance, perhaps even from a sphere of Chinese philosophy over 3,000 years old. Just before we left for Czechoslovakia, I consulted—for the first time in many years— the *I Ching*, and received one of the most unequivocal hexagrams in the book: The Well. It contains these lines:

> The town may be changed,
> But the well cannot be changed.
> It neither decreases nor increases.

---

7. At least the Czechs remember their medieval successes. Contemporary Serb leaders like Radovan Karadzic constantly invoke the 1389 battle of Kosovo to rally the troops, a battle in which the Serbs were totally wiped out.

I also wish to cite Edward Crankshaw's *The Fall of the House of Hapsburg* (Viking Press, New York, 1963) for valuable historical material and an entertaining, quirky and extremely persuasive analysis.

The gloss says that "political structures change, as do nations, but the life of man with its needs remains eternally the same—this cannot be changed." There's further commentary that anyone seeking a homeland—Czech, Slovak or American—might find useful.

Time to get dressed: there's a new café on the town square that's having a New Year's Eve celebration tonight. I wonder how many people will be celebrating.

DEFENSE OF (SMEARED) VELVET

Z. F. DANES

Joe Safdie (EC, No. 42, pp. 14–18, 1993) published an excellent article, observing the attitude and reaction of the Czechs (not the Slovaks, mind you!) to the fact that their country should divide into two separate countries. Excellent, too, in analyzing the historical background and presenting that complicated matter in a highly readable and easily comprehensible manner. But he failed in probably the most important point: he failed to understand the Czech psyche. Yes, the *Good Soldier Svejk* has a lot to do with it: but he is not the creator of Czech mentality: he is only its epitome. Certainly, I cannot speak for every single Czech: but I feel comfortable to speak for a great majority of my nation. First, Safdie is amazed that we were not more concerned about our country's unity; the answer is, that we do not see anything sacred in unity. We are willing and determined to create a good state with good government. Something we may be proud of. If anybody wants to join us and comes with good intentions, he is welcome. But if you don't like the rules of our home, find another home. The Slovaks were not our subjects: they were given the privilege of becoming our citizens. And the tens of thousands of Slovak immigrants since the partition speak for themselves. Second is the matter of fighting: yes, we can fight, if we have to. Those who forced us to fight them have learned their lesson the hard way. But we don't enjoy it. (Our last wars of conquest date from the thirteenth century.) To us, violence is revolting. We fail to comprehend the American lust for it: when their children play with guns and pretend to kill each other (for no reason, except for the joy of killing), our children play hide-and-seek. While the Americans watch one television program after another, all of them very primitive to our taste and all of them soaked with blood, we listen to the music of Dvorak and Smetana. Finally, and mainly, we always ask the question: WOULD IT BE WISE? Would it be wise to try to hold the Slovaks who do not want to stay? Won't we be better off without the neighbor who costs us billions each year and still wants to go? Yes, that is the question. And our answer is NO. If we don't fight, it is because we are civilized. And it would not be wise. If we don't force the Slovaks to stay with us, it is because we respect their freedom. And because it would not be wise. And we avoid ruining our country—and the countries of others—because it is not right, and not wise. Our heroes are not warriors, but teachers. (Prestige-wise, you cannot climb above the university professor, no matter how much more money you have or make.) Our nation does not produce Hitlers, Napoleons, Stalins, Ceaucescus, Mussolinis, Francos and their likes: those we get as unwanted imports from our generous neighbors. We produced Hus, Chelcicky, Comenius, Masaryk, Havel. We are civilized. And we are wise.

ED. NOTE: *We will not climb over* Professor Emeritus *Danes but these Czech children who play hide-and-seek while listening to Smetana while ours go boom-boom struck us as deficient in precisely those moral areas the professor claims superior. To wit: it's no great honor to debarass oneself of the poorer kids because they smell and prefer folk music to the bourgeois stiffness that made Kafka so unhappy. Furthermore, this imaginary nation of Gandhis appears to be oddly nostalgic for the professoriat, which we remember as socialism with a human face. And one more furthermore: Czech non-violence is not the last repository of either hippies or the apotheosis of diplomacy. If Talleyrand and Abbie Hoffman had a baby he would not be Czech, he would be a lesbian Beavis (and) Butthead. In short, nationalism is kitsch.*

FRANZ KAFKA: THE WRITING, THE BABES

KIRBY OLSON

Franz Kafka, when not writing nightmarish stories that reveal the horrific absurdity of modern bureaucracy, spent his time fucking Czech maids, streetwalkers, Jewish actresses, plump bourgeois beauties, and their secretaries. He even said that he considered his sister the ideal mate. Kafka was a Jew in Prague, writing in German. Aside from his literary chums, his only links to life were erotic ones. Surrounded by Protestant Czechs with whom he shared few values, his only way out was to make love to them, and make love to them he did. One autumn he wrote to his friend Max Brod, "There have been at least six since summer." Often considered an introvert, Kafka could obviously come out with it when called upon! Prague is the most beautiful city in Europe, as it was never bombed in World War II. Its golden spires remain thrust into the crystalline skies as the shapely women of Prague stroll unsuspiciously past—no longer monitored by the KGB. Eighty years ago, before Russian tanks and Soviet occupation, this city was Kafka's playground. Now it is once again ours. It is said that only when Kafka was deep inside some Czech maid on the pantry floor did he really feel that he and the peasantry were one. Only when he was being given one of those quick nervous blowjobs the bourgeois upper crust are noted for did he really feel the pleasures of his class. Besides his hallucinatory fiction, in which, for example, a young man awakes as a cockroach; or a man sits on top of a pole to practice the unappreciated art of hunger; Kafka wrote thousands of pages of light love letters, had innumerable liaisons with ladies of the night, but rarely included a full-length love scene in any of his fiction. What was Franz doing? Did the prohibitions of the era prevent Kafka from writing directly about fucking, or was there some peculiar aberration that he wished to avoid exposing? There is a short, lurid scene in his novel *The Castle*, in which K., a land survey- or, has been summoned to a mysterious fortress. As he enters the town, continual phone calls are made to the higher-ups to ascertain his identi- ty—but even these higher-ups aren't sure. Certainty breaks through in the form of a bar-maid named Frieda. Soon enough, K. and she are mak- ing love on the floor, K. poking Frieda like a dog—amidst sticky beer- puddles. A brief overview of Kafka's love life is given in Nahum Glatzer's book *The Loves of Franz Kafka* (Schocken Books, 1986). Glatzer gives generalizations of each major lover in Kafka's life—but to glimpse the intercourse between Kafka and his babes, and the endless stream of let- ters that ejaculated from these liaisons, one must turn to Kafka's diaries. Kafka's mind and cock were at odds. He wrote thousands of pages of love letters to Felice Bauer, his first fiancee, for example, a Berlin business woman with bad teeth. The nature of their engagement can best be described as Kafkaesque—the closer Kafka got to this woman the more he wanted a separation; the further she kept her distance, the closer he wanted to be. Halitosis? Bauer's go-between, a woman named Grete Bloch, became Kafka's lover. She gave birth to Kafka's only son, but kept it a secret from the father, as she was embarrassed by the circumstances. During the unsuccessful Bauer siege (Kafka's parents thought the Bauers were beneath them—the Bauers returned the sentiment), Kafka had many short trysts—a young Swiss woman he spent ten days with—which he included among the horniest of his life. In his private diary he wrote, "I can't resist, my tongue is fairly torn from my mouth if I don't give in and admire anyone who is admirable and love her ..." In the same peri- od, he wrote an imaginary rape scene, "He seduced a girl in a small place in the Iser mountains where he spent a summer to restore his deli- cate lungs. After a brief effort to persuade her, incomprehensibly, the way lung cases sometimes act, he threw the girl—his landlord's daughter, who liked to walk with him in the evening after work—down in the grass on the river bank and took her as she lay there unconscious with fright...." Kafka apparently relished teenage girls with their nipples budding, but could not accept society's disapproval, and so half-heartedly courted more mature women as a cover. His first lover was a shopgirl he took to a hotel while studying for the law. When she pointed to her asshole with a silly grin, he was offended, and didn't want to see her again. His first romantic interest was an obese Jewish thespian named Mrs. Tschissik whom he followed like a dog, and bought flowers to be handed to her during her performance. Kafka comments in his diary, "I had hoped, by means of the flowers, to appease my love for her a little, but it was quite useless. It is possible only through sleeping together." He probably did get to pop his cork with this blimp, but he was too discrete to mention it in his journals. After his lengthy engagement with Felice Bauer, the woman with bad teeth, he met an attractive and fashionable young woman at a health spa. Kafka's father, for whom he worked as a minor clerk, was pissed off when he met Julie Wohryzeck, and told his son to go to a whore house if he just wanted to fondle a pretty blouse. Kafka's most literary courtship was with Milena Jesenska, a Czech journalist. She translated a few stories of his into Czech, and thus commenced a typically Byzantine correspondence. Kafka wrote, "I love the whole world and this includes your left shoulder—no, it was first the right one, so I kiss it if I feel like it (and if you are nice enough to pull the blouse away from it) and this also includes your left shoulder and your face above me in the forest and my head resting on your almost bare breast." There were ten times as many letters as trysts, and at the end of her life, Jesenska had this to say about literary love: "The real thing never happened ... I have often wished I had a lot of children and had to spend my time milking cows and looking after geese, and had a husband who beat me occasionally." Ah, there's something about clean country life! Another brief exchange of letters developed with a Jewish girl named Minze Eisner. She had a wonderful neckline. She soon became engaged and Kafka politely withdrew himself from her. During the early twenties, Kafka lived in Berlin with a simple blonde named Dora Dymant. Kafka was dying from tuberculosis, unable to afford adequate food or medical care in the years of inflation in Germany after the first World War. When he died, Dora Dymant screamed, "Dearest!" Franz Kafka was a tender lad whom women could not help but embrace, pressing their cheeks close to his lower tummy. He was often described by them as a saint, but it should be clear from his life that he was also possessed by a bit of the horny gentleman in red pj's. Too, all that remains of a writer's life is what he put on paper; so what of his casual liaisons—to which he frequently alludes in his diary—his walks in the night with Czech prostitutes and young shopgirls? Were not these short trysts the *real* staple of his emotional life, and the rest a cover story to present to the world? In Kafka's novel *The Trial*, the judge's lawbooks are in fact porno novels. The breezy nature of justice in pre-Nazi Eastern Europe is one of Kafka's strongest obsessions; and yet Kafka's central theme in his private journals is the simple opposition between having a good time and family life. Romance in its sheer physical appeal was his replacement for a wife. He could not afford commitment, as it would get in the way of his two chief pursuits: literature and pussy. He wrote in his diary of 1911, while still in his early thirties, "Should I be grateful or should I curse the fact that despite all misfortunes I can still feel love, an unearthly love but still for physical objects?" Kafka's work at his father's factory, and at his writing desk at night, only left him time for fiancées, and he tried to drag them out as long as possible—only to nip them just before the ceremony. Kafka's payload found its way into bevies of bouncing Czechs before he would waltz off without paying the tab. At this historical remove, one can only applaud. Franz Kafka never marched to wedding music. He did the hoky poky to his own private organ.

AND WE KEEP LOOKING FOR JUSTICE

translated from Hungarian by John Batki

Let our legs wear down to a stump,
who cares. We march on whistling,
we keep looking for justice, although
we find it nowhere we go.

We have no packs, only our backs,
we are Abels fingering the axe,
nobody asks if our hearts contain beasts,
our thoughts are the devil's feasts,
but our souls are driven by God
who cracks the whip so we plow hard.

If it is winter, then we shiver
without knowing that we shiver,
our eyes and ears freeze together,
we thaw them out with words of fever,
we don't sleep in the shade in summer,
our pockets are full of promises made,
we ourselves are the bread we ate,
we always win, even in defeat,
nothing beats us, not woman, or hunger,
north and south, we move on yonder,

we slap hands with every beggar,
camp out in the worst weather,
our two hands have stuck together,
so we don't pray, and don't sin, either.

We may starve but we won't hunger,
we keep arriving ever earlier,
we launch the future from our mouth,
a humaner world! we shout,
it is love, and freedom we want,
blessed our faces, our feet are wind,
we eye every thorn and stone
where nobody has gone before,
hey, ho, we sing our solace,
have no tables but words of grace—
we keep looking for justice.

ON THE DEATH OF A FELLOW POET

written for Gyula Juhasz,
translated in memoriam Darrell Gray
translated from Hungarian by John Batki

The telephone rings, the news hurts
that you have killed yourself, my friend,
now lying so stubbornly on your bed.
Not even among madmen could your heart

bear its fate. Nowhere did you find balm
to soothe the pain of imagined
torments in this earthly sphere that
now opens for you its peace, the tomb.

What should I say now? Good-by? That
long ago imagination had made you die?
Your beautiful hair and beard still grow.

We have your many fine poems to recite.
They are washing you now. Your mother cries
and a fellow poet writes an epitaph.

MARCH, 1937

translated from Hungarian by John Batki

I

Mild, misty rain drizzles on
downy young spring wheat bud.
The stork returns to the chimney,
beaten winter to the icy north.
Green explosions announce
the merry vernal violence.
In front of a carpenter's shop
fresh pine scent gives a whiff of hope.

What's in the news? In Spain
the gang ravages and rages;
in China a dumb general chases
peasants from their few small
acres. Hordes utter threat,
clean linens soak in blood.
The poor are being tormented.
War mongerers wave their claws.

I am happy. My soul is a child;
Flora loves me. But see how slyly
against our naked beautiful love
heavy metal tanks are matched
by the vilest men. I am alarmed
by the zealousness of this scum.
I find solace in the two of us
and life-strength to carry on.

II

Mercenary man and his paid slut,
their hearts I am unable to touch.
Their evil may be overamplified
yet I still fear for my life,
for it is all I have.
The careful mind has thought ahead.
If violated Earth grows cold,
Flora, my heart's love will still glow.

For we shall create a lovely, bright girl
and a brave, understanding manchild

who will save of us some shred
—as sunlight in the Milky Way reflected—
so even as the Sun wanes tired,
our offshoot will chat full of faith
in their fine craft, flying on
to cultivate the arable stars.

AN ANCIENT RAT

translated from Hungarian by John Batki

An ancient rat spreads disease among us,
the thought that is unconsidered, un-thought,
its snout sticks into what we have cooked up,
it runs from one human to another, caught.
It is what makes the drunk unaware
when he drowns his mood in champagne
he is swilling down the meager soup
of many a shuddering impoverished man.

And since the spirit of nations cannot
express the fresh juice of human rights,
all sorts of new infamies of race
stir humankind against humankind.
Oppression descends in crowing flocks
upon living hearts as on carrion
and misery trickles over the globe
like saliva from an idiot's chin.

Summers pinned down by starvation droop
their wings in misery's collection.
And over our souls machines troop
the way bedbugs roam over a sleeper.
Faith and gratitude burrow deep inside us
and our tears are dropping into flames.
We are caught in an alternating dance
of craving for revenge, and conscience.

And like a jackal that turns to the sky
to disgorge its howling at the stars,
it is at heaven where agonies shine
that the poet sends up his bootless cry ...
Oh you constellations! So many rusty
rapacious iron daggers all around

stabbing my soul over and over—
(death is the only success on this ground).

Still, I have faith. With tears in my eyes
I beseech you, future, be less harsh ...
I have faith, for unlike the forerunners
today we are no longer drawn and quartered.
Some day the peace of freedom will have arrived
and torments will become more rarefied
until we too will be forgotten at last
in arbors where peaceful shadows are cast.

BIRTHDAY POEM

translated from Hungarian by John Batki

So I lived to be thirty-two
this poem is a surprise too:
     pretty
     pretty

gift that came my way
in a corner of this cafe
     from me
     to me.

My thirty-two years have flown,
never had two hundred a month of my own.
     That's right,
     My Homeland!

I could have been an educator,
instead of a fountain pen pusher,
     free
     booter.

But at the university in Szeged
I was summarily expelled
     by a weird
     laird.

His reproof came quick and hard
for my poem "With a Pure Heart"
     he'd guard
     this land

against me with drawn sword.
And so my spirit has conjured
    his game,
    his name:

"You sir, as long as I am competent,
will not be a teacher on this continent,"
    he blusters,
    illustrious.

But if Professor Horger is full of cheer
that this poet is not a grammar teacher
    control
    your joy—

I shall teach a whole nation,
not only the high-school population,
    just wait
    and see.

REPORT FROM EGYPT

I was on the proverbial slow boat, in this case the Ra from Luxor to Luxor to Luxor. Two-thirds of the monuments in the world are said to be in Luxor. Every day I was made to admire antiquities, commentary by a lecherous and lame old Egyptian who was always trying to get my hand near his cane. "That's Horus's wife and 7-year-old son, see her tit in his mouth as she is given the sun, a necklace, lotus, incense." Then we'd slide up (south) and down (north) the Nile and back to Luxor, a country town of markets and mud. The Ra served the worst of English food but the crew was cute. I drank a lot and was bored and decided to learn Arabic.

The bartender started me on "intercourse." OK I may be a dumb American but no talking dirty, darlin'. Turns out "*ente coise*" means "how are you." Soon I was told superciliously that I was speaking Arabic with a Nubian (black) (hick, that is) accent. Nubian vocabulary too.

So I bought a phrase book, obviously written by someone who learned English from a phrase book: This is the lady whose dress you have. Which way to the Israel boycott office? And my favorite: The workers themselves have said so.

The Egyptians see in their own faces the ancient dead, carved in stone. How can anything change in a country of stone and sand

ELINOR NAUEN

and one strip of water? Egypt's literature like the Nile is a thin fertile line between violence and monochrome. A dead end. Dead or just abandoned? The carved profiles—unanimated and haughty—rarely interact, leaving them (and us) disengaged. However, they certainly had the mechanics down. How, I wonder, did the workers see inside to carve and paint? A system of foil mirrors reflected sunlight into the gloom. Did the ancients have a sense of humor? I get no hint of their lives, what they did when it wasn't for display. What I liked best at Stonehenge were the trinkets left behind by centuries of picnickers. The unguarded moments are never in tombs. The unfinished vault of Ramose, however, moves me, the women with kohl tears filing like toy soldiers down their faces. Despite spending half his life preparing for his death, Ramose died before the grief was ready.

The strength of the Egyptian is in staying put. They are not a roving people, not like the Greeks, who also live on the Mediterranean. Apartments are expensive in Cairo, so lots of people live in the cemeteries near the Citadel. It's quiet, free, and they take care of the tombs.

And now toddlers sit on stone steps, silent as mummies, flies twitching around their unblinking eyes. Is this why there are so many one-eyed Egyptians? The Nubians, men and women, are often incredibly sultry. One of the journalists on our press trip proposed marriage to a dark-eyed 18-year-old, a scarf-seller by the temple of Dendera. "You will instantly take precedence over all Eurotrash and never have to wait on line again," Mark explained. She made a face, no thrill for her, New York.

No matter how much we told our driver we didn't want to see tourist sights, that's exactly where we were taken: the tower, the Citadel. "No problem," everyone says. "Why not? Of course!" And then they show you what they assume you really must want to see. Why else are you here? Salespeople are equally importuning. My "do you have" invariably translates as "I must have." People are friendly but have no manners. You can even get circumcised—men or women—at the circumcision bazaar. "Takes one second, doesn't hurt and you walk right off. Sure I'll wash if you like. For you, my friend, no problem. Anesthesia—not necessary, my friend." The jewelry and scarabs in the Egyptian Museum look like the junk everyone sells everywhere.

Riches is a filthy restaurant in Cairo, serving bad coffee and bad pastries and full of foreign students. On the walls are framed photos of Arab luminaries, all identified, for example as "cynical writer" (A. Al Aziz Ali Beshri) "slang poet" (Fouad Haddad) and "singer" (Om Koulthoun, a woman). Most prominent—largest and colored—is Mr. Mahfouz, local hero, the first (1988) Arab winner of the Nobel Prize for Literature.

A few days later, I'm having coffee in the Café Naguib

Mahfouz in an alley in the Khan el Khalili—the Times Square/East Village of Cairo. The waiter is insistent on correct Arabic pronunciation and given to pronouncements. "Behind every successful man..." he begins. I interrupt, "...is a *mara*" (Arabic for woman). He laughs. "*Immara* is woman," he says. "Mara is language." Pointing to a portrait of Mahfouz, I say, "Behind every successful writer is *mara*" and crack up. The waiter doesn't. He doesn't get "pun" or "play on words." It probably wasn't a pun in Arabic and wouldn't have worked if I had more command of the language. Like hearing "horse" and "house" so similarly that you lay one over the other end and call it a joke. It's not. It's just a mistake. And because no Arab speaker gets it, I finally see that translating isn't just memorizing the words as they come rolling off the assembly line. It's not yourself in a mirror. It's more like having an affair and then meeting his twin brother. Two words can't occupy the same spot at the same time. Now, a year later, a war on, I can still say "thank you" and "get away from me, cur."

PENIS CAN'T FACE MECCA

According to a report in Holland's *De Gay Krant*, the late Ayatollah Khomeni condemned passive homosexual intercourse but would tolerate the active role. The newspaper also said Khomeni believed that only certain fingers should be used when holding the penis to urinate and that it was improper to point one's penis in the direction of Mecca.

On the issue of sex during religious fasting, Khomeni said the penis could enter the vagina only to the circumcision ring and must not ejaculate in order for the fast to remain valid. But if a man couldn't tell how far his penis actually went in, well, the fast was still valid. Also OK: The semen may "stir" but not "spill."

Khomeni said the fast was invalid, however, if the man had sex with a camel or other animal to the point of ejaculation.

ERICA HERRMANN

ZIMBABWE'S BEAT GENERATION

BRIAN EVENSON

The Black Insider by Dambudo Marechera. Baobab Books, 1990.

Sitting on a park bench in Africa, all his possessions (a typewriter, a packet of paper, 5 review copies of a previous novel)

357

contained in a plastic bag, Dambudo Marechera writes *Mindblast* (1984). The city park is his home, his office is any bench on which he can rest long enough to take out his typewriter and put it on his knees. If it isn't raining too hard and if the police will leave him alone for a few hours—he begins to create worlds at least as hopeless as his own.

Marechera was the African version of the Beats, had read Bukowski, Burroughs, Ginsberg, Kerouac, and the rest, and lived a similar sort of life style. But while America managed to support its Beats, Africa didn't. We bought Burroughs' *Naked Lunch*; we idolized Ginsberg as the man who simplified, appropriated, and Americanized Eastern philosophy. But nobody idolized Marechera. In Zimbabwe, Marechera *is* the only member of the beat generation—a community of one. When out of fear his fellow students refused to protest march against the Rhodesian government, he marches alone, a lonely and ignored figure carrying a placard through empty streets. In his novels, his characters are solitary as well: to validate any power outside of oneself is self-betrayal. Marechera is a complete anarchist: "I am against everything/Against war and against those against/War. Against whatever diminishes/The individuals' blind impulse."

Upon winning a prize for his short story collection *The House of Hunger* (1979), Marechera shows his gratitude by hurling plates at the chandeliers and at the heads of guests. Three years later, trying to leave Zimbabwe, he is detained at the border. He spends the next five years on a park bench in Harare, sleeping on the streets, tapping out novels on his typewriter (some of which were banned, most of which remained unpublished) until he runs out of paper. He eats nothing but cabbages—the only thing he can afford. In 1987, at the age of 35, he dies of lung collapse.

At his death, a parasitic, necrophilic Trust springs up, a so-called artist's appreciation society who, having failed to help Marechera publish anything while alive, decide now to crack his bones and suck out the marrow. Now that he is dead, they extol his virtues—he can be recuperated for a profit. Flora Veit-Wild, the head of the Trust and editor of Marechera's posthumous work *The Black Insider* (1990), fashions an academic career for herself from pieces of Marechera's corpse (which is hardly exquisite), despite the fact that her editorial decisions are questionable and her footnotes (and lack thereof) leave serious doubts about her academic prowess.

Marechera's *The Black Insider* is a sort of intellectual garbage dump, full of scraps of different philosophies and fetishized fragments of erotica, mixed up with twisted and hardly recognizable allusions. It is similar in style and mood to Acker's *Don Quixote*. The same confusions take place in both works; both manage to keep the reader slightly off balance. Marechera has no inhibitions, linguistic or otherwise.

He wanders through the ruins of his books, picking things up only to throw them away a moment later, plunging his hands deep into shit, occasionally finding a nihilistic treasure which he plays with then destroys. Through incredible literary acrobatics, he manages to jam *Playboy*, Hieronymous Bosch, Dylan Thomas, Wole Soyinka, and Coca-Cola into the same sentence; then, instead of bowing when you applaud this feat, he spits in your face. His paragraphs are word-labyrinths that make the reader claustrophobic, but in these dark passages lie concealed phrases and thoughts that drive like nails into your skull, changing the way you think. Marechera inspires hatred or awe, but never indifference.

The characters of *The Black Insider* are all the same character, different versions of Marechera, a whole community of his selves. Their conversations are meditations on the nature of being, long painful essays. Words and actions fade in and out of each other in a battleground in which Marechera pits himself against everything.

Marechera's life view? "We are like matches being systematically scratched alight and put out in a dark and confused room." His reason for writing? "[T]here will be no silence in the cemetery because always there are burials and more burials of people asphyxiated by words." Marechera through his writing wants to "bridge the gap between intelligence and mass terror."

The Black Insider is a remarkable and frightening book, despite Veit-Wild's editing (which is also frightening, but in the wrong way). But as far as I know, I have the only copy in America. Maybe if you ask nicely I will let you read it. The rights are available for almost nothing: why hasn't an American press picked it up yet? Two reasons. First, nobody knows about it since the world ignores (often with good reason) the literary affairs of Zimbabwe; second, most publishers have a definite, safe idea of what an African author is and Marechera refuses to fit in with their ideas: he doesn't beat the right political bongos. A press that had an anarchistic or Beat audience would find plenty of readers for *The Black Insider*. And then Marechera's ghost would haunt the parkbenches of this country as well.

SOUTH KOREA: BELLY UP

ROBERT PERCHAN

"You got a name to go with that face?" I ask the bargirl who has slid her slim buns onto the barstool next to mine in the downstairs Dallas Club, a GI beer joint across the street from Pusan's Camp Hialeah, the southernmost US Army installation on the Korean peninsula.

"My name Ae-joo."

"Yeah? You're kind of cute. How old are you?"

"Twenty-three. You buy me whiskey coke, okay?"

"Korean age, or American age?"

"Korean age. Only four thousand *wun*. One whiskey coke."

She means that she is in fact twenty-two years old, as we Occidentals would style it. When Koreans calculate a person's age, they invariably count the ten months spent inside Mom. (Ten months, yes. We're talking lunar calendar here.) This makes some sense to me, as we in the West have had it pounded into our heads since Freud that one's fetushood is the best time one will ever have had in one's life, and of course that cherished experience is always more and more dimly receding into the past. And Sandor Ferenczi told us, if I recall rightly, that male penetration of the female is nothing other than an attempt to climb back up into that cozy, moist heavenly space vehicle. No doubt this curious idea would provide powder and shot for the Pro-Lifers' blunderbuss. But in Korea it reeks of contradiction. A recent article carried in the English-language *Korea Herald* reported that by the time they reach the age of forty, eighty percent of Korean women will have artificially aborted at least one fetus, virtually all of them female. Ultra-sound tests to determine the gender of the little booger or boogerette caged in the womb are illegal over here—and performed on a routine daily basis in private clinics. Elementary school teachers report a disproportionately large number of little boy students in their classes. In the interests of socialization, Korean teachers like to alternate boy-girl-boy-girl in their seating arrangements, and the little boys like this a lot too, but there just aren't enough little girls to go around. One teacher intimated to me that she receives monthly bribes from many a worried, frantic mother who wants her son seated beside a girl so that he'll grow up "balanced and erect." Maybe even as "balanced and erect" as I am right now, perched on my barstool with my paw on Ae-joo's mini-skirted bare thigh. Yes, a lot of little girls get waylaid long before they even have a chance to begin to dream of kindergarten. Twenty years from now, when these millions of little boys reach marriageable age, a resounding hue and cry is going to go up: WHERE ARE ALL THE FUCKING WOMEN? THERE AREN'T ANY FUCKING BROADS IN THIS COUNTRY! And they will be right. If I had a time-machine right here next to me in the Dallas Club, I would slip it into fast-forward and plunge ahead those two decades into the future. Ae-joo here beside me at the bar would generate a steady and respectable income about then on a time share basis, single-minded and flat-chested and whiney as she is:

"*Four thousand wun. One whiskey coke. Then I go away no bother you some more.*"

And about then I'll probably need the money, having pissed away my Peak Earning Years in a country that is coming more and more to regard foreigners as greedy, evil-smelling interlopers, adipose barbarian jowls nudging their unwelcome way into the national family trough. And getting bonked smack on the nozzle for their impudence. Foreigners who teach their native tongue and its literature over here are hunkering down, bracing for the storm. This is not Old Dictatorship. This is New Democracy. And its weird double-clutch dance with Eternal Xenophobia. Last year when the President-for-Life of my university was finally dethroned, the first act of the newly-elected Faculty Senate was to strip all foreign faculty members of tenure, boot them off the pension plan, and jack up their school-sponsored medical insurance premiums by 600%. That this was against Korean law as interpreted by the Ministry of Education was no obstacle: we were simply ordered to voluntarily resign our professorships so that we could be rehired under new one-year contracts. If we didn't resign, we would be fired, and then we definitely could not be rehired, because if we were fired, it would have to have been *for a reason*. And the only possible reason for which an honorable foreigner could be fired would have to be that the honorable foreigner must be *a bad professor*. (And maybe I am, looking back and trying to parse the verbs of those last couple sentences.) And if the honorable foreigner is *a bad professor*, he certainly ought not to be rehired by an upstanding institution. And if I am straining at my feeble handle on the English language trying to convey this Catch-22 to you, imagine what an effort it would take to dump my load of woe on thirsty, mousseheaded polymath Ae-joo on the barstool to my left:

"*One whiskey coke. No ploblem. Four thousand wun. Don't be the Cheap Chollie.*"

But I don't want all this to sound like a glum, spiteful down letter home. And, really, xenophobia can be a gruesome kind of entertainment, as long as it's directed at somebody else. One fellow wrote in to the *Korea Herald* just last month:

To the Editor:

I woke up at 5:30 last Sunday morning to find my arms pinned to my chest by some thug. Three of his buddies were swaggering around my apartment with metal pipes. They thought they owned the place. I thought otherwise.

Over the course of the next ten minutes, one of my uninvited guests smashed me in the head and legs with a pipe, while the other held me down and used a razor to slash a six-inch slit in my thigh.

They were clearly not professional burglars: They did not take money I had laying right out on my desk. Aside from a Walkman and a pair speakers, they didn't get much. That is, if you don't count the $250 I had to pay the hospital to patch me up.

Although we can't prove it, we suspect that we were attacked because we had a party that same night, a loud party that may have disgruntled some of our neighbors. Koreans who came to the party told us, rather belatedly, that entertaining in your home is a big social "no-no" in Korea. One Korean friend who heard of the attack immediately reacted by assuming that our neighbors had paid off those thugs to rough us up because of the party. Of course this is all speculation, and I am not sure whether I believe it.

However, one thing is for sure: We were targeted because we were foreigners. The attackers came upon a Korean who slept over in our apartment and said: "Oh, you're Korean, get out of here." They were interested in attacking foreigners. Also, this is not an isolated incident. It happens all too often here in Seoul, no matter how reluctant Koreans are to admit it.

I am not writing this letter just to vent my spleen. I have two warnings for the foreigners living here: 1. Make sure all your doors and windows are locked when you go to sleep, especially if you are living in a house. This is not a joke. It could save you a trip to the hospital...or to the morgue. 2. Do not have a large party at your home. If you want to entertain, keep it small and quiet. All those stupid commercials on American Forces Korea Network about "blending into the local populace" may not be so far off the mark after all.

Terronce Kiernan
Seoul

As enthralling as Mr. Kiernan's narrative is, it is but a single instance. (Though I have a single instance or three I could recount, as does just about every expat I've run across over here—save my six-foot-six three-hundred-pound Kraut neighbor, colleague and friend, author of the forthcoming *Dining with Rage: Adventures in Korean Cuisine* "Where else in the world can you order lunch and be served a meal that looks like it had just crept live out of the Burgess Shale?") And a Korean associate (a personal, idiosyncratic euphemism I employ to mean—take your pick—drinking buddy, translator, informant, gofer, shill, squeeze, procuress, etc.) of mine argues forcefully that the real object of enmity in this country is not us "true" foreigners at all, but rather those Koreans who left the homeland a decade or two ago, earned an M.D. or a Ph.D. in Robotics at M.I.T. or Stanford or Ludwig-Maximilians-Universität, obtained American or German or British citizenship, spawned a family, made a pile, and have now returned to the Land of the Morning Calm (pace Mr. Kiernan) with their prestigious diplomas and First World expertise to cash in on the economic boom and high-tech explosion that are presently "sweeping the land." What's the gripe? Well, besides being viewed as crass opportunists and even traitors who split when the going was tough, many of these fellows skipped out on performing their military service, South Korea having—with rogue-shark, nuke-brandishing North Korea only fifteen minutes away by Moped from downtown Seoul—mandatory universal conscription. To keep these unpatriotic gents from having it too good on their return to the fatherland, the Korean Government and other democratic institutions like my university have formulated exclusionary regulations that prevent "foreigners" (we're all lumped in together) from getting such goodies as cost-of-living raises, tenure, anything longer than a one-year contract, access to pension plans and other desirables devoutly to be wished for—unless the renegades renounce their foreign citizenship and become True Koreans once again. Personal grumbling, I confess, since I can hardly yield up my US passport and don the trappings of Korean National Character. That, of course, is something you are born with, like a caul or a tail. It's all very much like being a houseguest caught in the middle of an escalating family squabble. ("YOU WALK OUT AND LEAVE US AND NOW YOU THINK YOU CAN JUST COME SASHAYING BACK IN THE DOOR!") This very morning the *Korea Herald* carried an article warning foreigners that henceforth residence visas will have to be renewed every six months instead of the customary one year. The Brit columnist who broke the story—no Jonathan Swift by a long shot, admittedly—waxed so livid that the area of his brain that controls grammar simply caved in and the article trailed off in a jumble of disconnected morphemes that resembled nothing so much as the final score of a cricket match between rival mental institutions.

But let's give the culture its due. Military service is more than simply a moral obligation or a sacred duty in Korea—it is a two-year-long rite of initiation into a special kind of Manhood that no outsider can ever be expected to comprehend—a ritual that is excruciatingly more painful, and certainly more protracted, than, say, teenage circumcision. Of course it has its plusses: most young conscriptees have the first sexual encounter of their lives on an overnight pass—with a prostitute naturally—and return to their barracks with a hard, secret knot of knowledge in their bowels of what a woman can do to a man if given half a chance. And it is in the military that a young lad with abstruser musings and inclinations will find expression to more forbidden stirrings in the dick-tweaking antics of the shower room. Officially gays do not exist in Korea, and consequently they have found small opportunity to develop a "subculture." That is, they have little finesse and even less style. A young man stepped out of an alley and confronted me one evening just as I was about to enter the American Legion Club, another GI beer joint across the street from Camp Hialeah, my sole intention being to lean up against the bar for a couple of hours and angle for whatever doll-size bottomfeeder gash with doll's eyes that might stray into the shadow of my keel and rudder. "Good evening," the apparition announced in passable English. "I'm a homo." We gaped silently at each other out there on the dark street for a few seconds, he in a blue salaryman's business suit and dark monochrome necktie, and me in threadbare jeans and an ancient

Firesign Theater t-shirt that proclaimed: *Everything You Know Is Wrong.* "That's fine," I said. "I fuck carp." And skirted my way past the poor wandering soul and slipped through the door under the Legion Club's neon sign. Women have a decidedly different and more domestic row to hoe toward initiation and social acceptance. They simply spread their thighs for X number of months or years until they give birth to a bouncing baby boy, at which point they become fully and unassailably human, a Son's Mother. What the Sapphic tribe is up to I have no knowledge of, probe as I have my dwindling set of female contacts. There are some doors that must remain closed to even the most persistently inquisitive. Probably they emigrate to the States and found a minority.

But I digress. Army life does indeed fullfil its social function—and maybe even the promise of the topic sentence of the previous paragraph: it does indeed make Men out of Boys in Korea. If we Americans didn't learn that in the Korean War, we certainly did in Viet Nam. A week before I was to rendezvous in Korea for my first full-time teaching job in my life on land, I sat in the lounge of Manila's Admiral Hotel waiting for a pretty and selfless Filipina named Josie to show up with my laundry. The U.S. Marine eighteen-year-man sergeant who bellied up to the bar alongside me and bought a round had a serpentine latticework of tattoos that slithered from his wrists straight up under the mat of hair on his arms and disappeared into his shirtsleeves. "Say you're goin' to Koh-REE-ah? Man, them little Koh-REE-ahn bastards is tough. In Nam the U.S. Marines wasn't afraid of no suckers. 'Ceptin' those little Koh-REE-ahn Marine bastards—and they was on our side! Man, I seed a platoon of them guys lined up at attention for inspection one afternoon. Cap'n walks down the line tappin' each one of 'em in the balls with a whip handle sort of approval-like. Not hard. But by no means gentle. I wouldn't fancy it. Then he comes to one guy—a big sucker—and the cap'n looks down at the poor feller's crotch and barks somethin' in gook. Turns out the poor fucker had his cock and balls on the wrong side of his trouser seam. Before you could say jake the guy was on the ground in a heap bleedin' from every pore on his body. I never seed a man reduced to mush so fast. 'Ceptin' in combat, of course. Them was the Koh-REE-ahn Marines. Tough." I took a long, slow, silent pull on my San Miguel. "But they's women is all right. Got to get yourself down to Texas Street in Pusan some time. Pretty. Don't got them jungle noses like these here Filipinas sometimes got. Just don't cross one. Just don't cross one. One of them whores prett' near tore me a new asshole one night just for dancin' in another club. Territorial, that's what I calls them. Territorial." About then Josie breezed in off Roxas Boulevard, in her arms the laundry bag with my name and USS DECATUR stenciled on the side. "You Navy?" Sarge inquired. "You don't *look* Navy. Navy don't allow a moustache like that." "Civilian," I explained, stammering a little, flushing at the wimpishness and absurdity of what I did for a living in the presence of a Man of War. "A teacher. PACE Program. Program for Afloat College Education." "Yeh? I heard of you guys. Teachin' on the ships." "I teach English." "Yeh? I heard of that." "Composition. Introduction to Literature." "Well, I don't know about that." "For sailors who are interested. Nothing special. Those Wespac cruises can last nine months. Nothing to do. Study." "Navy's okay," Sarge allowed. "But I wouldn't want to spend my whole military career walkin' around with a cork stuck up my butthole. Not me." Sarge turned to Josie and seemed to notice for the first time that she was a female. "Sorry, ma'am. For my language. For my English." Together Josie and I edged toward the plastic-vine-covered arbor with the EXIT sign above it. But I wasn't quite finished: "Sarge. The *Decatur* put into Pusan a couple of months ago. That's how I landed the job up there in Korea." "Yeh?" "That woman on Texas Street. Was her name In-ja?" "I don't rightly recall. Could've been. Had no bush at all. I remember that." "That was her." "Well, if it was, you better watch your ass. She's a tiger." Out in the lobby I stole a sidelong glance at Josie and her nose. It was tiny, but the nostrils were round and open and the tip upturned and I knew I could see almost all the way into her soul if I looked hard enough. Just as I can sit right here at the bar in the Dallas Club and gaze into Ae-joo's open mouth and marvel at her uvula vibrating like a fleshy diminutive sex-toy:

"*You buy me whiskey coke. I no got a momma. I no got a poppa. Only got a Mama-san. Only four thousand wun. Mama-san gonna be angly anybody no buy me whiskey coke tonight.*"

But one wants to be careful what one says in print about Korea. You never know whom you're going hurt. There are victims more innocent than might first come to mind. In the run-up to the '88 Seoul Olympics—the only Olympics, to my knowledge, in which a boxing referee had to take a standing eight-count—the foreign press made a big deal out of the fact that Korea was the world's largest "exporter" of babies for adoption, permitting as many as 9000 parentless infants and children per year to find permanent homes overseas, mostly in the U.S. and Europe. Once the world was alerted to this cold fact, the quota of babies allowed to leave the country dropped precipitously—to less than 6000 the next year. The Korean Government had saved face, or a cheek and a chin and part of a nose anyway. A woman who had been adopted as a child and raised in Sweden returned to the land of her birth and was allotted ample KBS-TV air-time to wail and bemoan the miseries she had had to endure throughout her life in the West—the most trying of which turned out to be the fact that she had divorced three times. Author Chung So-dang penned a novel in which a Korean child is adopted by an American couple so that his heart can be ripped out and transplanted into the chest of their ailing natural son. Under such a barrage of

365

propaganda, few protested that some 3000 orphans would not get the exit visas they needed to join waiting surrogate families abroad. Had Woody Allen coaxed young Soon-Yi Previn out of her drawers a few years earlier, that whole business would no doubt have been part of the action too. Even now it doesn't much help the real humanitarians over here make their case. The foreign press, characteristically, never followed up on the orphan-export sensation it had so dutifully exploited. They had had their scoop. You never know whom you're going to hurt, what misery the pen can leave in its inky wake. Yea, the field is strewn with the fallen crying out for succor:

"Anybody not buy me whiskey coke tonight! Only four thousand wun! Mama-san she gonna scold Ae-joo too much! Gonna put me in a kitchen wash a dish!"

In the kitchen. Poor female Ae-joo. But that's as Confucius would have had it. (And ever since the Red Guards pulverized all the Master's shrines during the Cultural Revolution over yonder in the Middle Kingdom, Korea is officially "the most Confucian culture in the world.") And the Master's teachings are still very much alive here, however adulterated over the slow roll of the centuries by the need to apply them to new and unique situations, as our hapless author of that letter-to-the-editor probably learned if he snapped open the pages of the *Korea Herald* a week after posting his own epistle:

To Editor,

Torrence Mr. Kiernan the man (letter May 14st) cannot understanding the Korea culture because of he not try hard. Korea peoples loves the foreigner as the brother. Some time beat up the guy, sure. Because of not understanding the culture. Let me explain you;
Story my Confucius scholer Uncle tell to me: Soo-hyun was boy love his momma & his poppa too much and very love his teacher too. Because of they say Soo-hyun about Korea people always loves and respecks a foregn people. Every day his momma & his poppa and his teacher too say about Korea peoples loves the foregner. Yes, one day Soo-hyun he walking street with his freind and see a Korea guy to be hitting the foreigner head and neck. Foregner all blood. So Soo-hyun he say his freind; "Foregner love to be hitted! Strange peoples! I cannot understanding them!" See?
Or other story my Uncle tell; When he was the young man time he always dream he going to take the dump at Haeundae some day. Always dream this dream about certain place he some day going take the dump exactly there. Time pass, and a Germany guy he build his house at there Haeundae beach. Big house of rich. Come a night my Uncle he drunk some soju liquird and he enter rich house of Germany man and take the big dump there. Dream full fill! But Germany man find Uncle he squat. "What you here? Take the dump my living room! Low fellow!" But! "No!" my Uncle

say. "Why you build house at a place I always going to take the dump there? You cannot understanding the Korea. Go back the Germany country!"

Mr. Torrence! Must understanding the Korea culture. So!

Yi Mu-hak
Seongshim Jeongshin Byeongwon
Haeundae-gu

Yes, Soo-hyun loves his momma and his poppa and his teacher too. I suspect he loves his momma the most though, and I suppose I can guess why. Mrs. Kim stops by my place once a week or so. She's been divorced half a dozen years and is thoroughly at sea in a culture which invariably awards the child of a divorce suit to the father. Her only son is thirteen and has just entered middle school, where the pressures of competition for top grades border on the unbearable. The signs of stress have been unmistakable—a vacuous stare, loss of appetite, hypochondriacal whimperings—and on the one day a month the kid is able to sneak out of his father's house and visit his mother, she does what she can. She started with back rubs that graduated to "brief, innocent massages" of his buttocks and wang. She had heard of mothers doing it in Japan, had discussed it with a friend over coffee. Kids get so depressed about their schoolwork they jump off apartment buildings, swallow packets of rat poison. *Stressuh*. One afternoon, after ministering me rather perfunctory head, she fessed up that she had been doing it *eep-aw-ro*—"by means of the mouth"—to her version of little Soo-hyun for some time. I had clearly stumbled into an Oedipal thicket. Worse, she was asking me for advice. Was she wrong to do such a thing? She was not a well-educated woman, but she had heard about "psychological damage." Her friend had dropped hints that she too was concerned about what she was doing for/with/to her child. But then she slipped and upped the ante by letting her boy have her in the bung and the kid had talked and now Soo-hyun wanted it that way too. Mrs. Kim was uneasy. She was sad. She wanted to know whether she was evil or not. Was it unnatural? She wasn't even sure if it was permissable for a husband to have it that way, let alone a son. As far as she could tell, Confucius was silent on the issue. She hoped I wouldn't be. She wanted the opinion of an outsider, a foreigner: "What will he want next? My vulva?" Yes, there still is a Korean or two who want us to stick around here awhile longer. If just to try to help make a little sense out of things.

"YOU NO BUY ME WHISKEY COKE? I NO SIT HERE SOME LONGER! YOU GO! YOU THE CHEAP CHOLLIE! YOU GO BACK THE YANKEE AMERICA COUNTRY! ONLY FOUR THOUSAND WUN!"

Okay, okay, Ae-joo. You've earned it. Okay, okay.

ROBERT PERCHAN

SOUTH KOREA: AT PLAY
IN THE YEAR OF THE DOG

"NO!" I howl. "I CAN'T!"

Mr. Choi glowers down at the small oblong plate on which lies the pathetic fountain-pen-size tube of boiled flesh. Gentle Mr. Ku sits stiffly upright, nervously fingering his stainless steel chopsticks with the ginseng root patterns on the handle-ends, fidgety fearful that he has been made an accomplice in some terrible breach of etiquette—at the expense of an honorable foreigner, no less. Impish Mr. Kim, who has been rubbing his palms together with gleeful anticipation, knocks back a glass of clear, potent soju. Once a month the four of us dine out together, trading ribald jokes, ribbing each other about our respective governments' blunders and inexhaustible capacities for mismanagement, consoling one and all on our own respective failures to "get ahead," rambling on in our cups about sex and money and power and corruption—that which concerns all men at all times in all lands. The principal at the high school in Seoul where Mr. Kim's brother-in-law teaches was recently arrested for taking hundreds of thousands of dollars in bribes from parents who wanted their kids' grade transcripts doctored. The President-for-Life at a local university was dethroned not so long ago by mobs of student demonstrators for permitting the matriculation of students who had failed the entrance exam but had succeeded in life by having rich, well-connected fathers and steel-willed mothers of vise-like tenacity who would not see their children's lives flushed down the tubes just because the pampered, indolent brats had no brains, nor ambition, nor talent. Nobody quite understood why this university president bothered to take these bribes —he was already one of the wealthiest men in the province. Perhaps it was only because, as one Korean Sage-cum-Wag puts it, "For a Korean with a desk and a nameplate of inlaid mother-of-pearl, going a month without a bribe is like going five hundred years without a woman."

But tonight was to have been a special night. The focus was to have been on the meal itself, and not on peripheral concerns like our indignation and utter amazement at what blatant sleaziness our fellow professionals have proved themselves capable of. My three Korean high school English teachers had been on me for months now to overcome my deepest personal inhibitions and narrow cultural prejudices and try *gae-gogi*—boiled dog meat. And, I decide, I have acquitted myself well this evening, munching through a respectable portion of slices of abdominal wall of pooch, a large platter of dark, tender morsels of haunch of pooch, and a helping of sweet and succulent, fork-flakey, melt-in-your-mouth neck of pooch. I even managed to handle my share of the four steaming paws we had been served up, soft budlike footpads intact. When the "auntie" set them down on the low table where the four of us sat crosslegged, I at first mistook them for a version of braised pussywillow, so difficult it is for the mind to recognize on a plate what it has a thousand times registered in living rooms and backyards: *Shake hands. Abelard. Now roll over. Now beg. Don't you have the cutest little footsies. Kiss.*

"I'm sorry, Mr. Kim. I just CAN'T!"

Mr. Choi and Mr. Ku stare at each other and then down at the little weenie that has been cut for us into four equal measures, uncertain whether it would be polite to partake. This final delectable of the meal would be getting cold. It has always been my friends' custom to offer me the first, choicest morsel of anything set before us. I am a foreigner and in middle-middle age—that laughable euphemism whose threshold is crossed with only the deepest misgivings—nearly a decade their senior to boot. And a college professor, or at least a reasonable simulacrum thereof. A man of profound learning and broad experience. A man who washed down a bull's-testicle tapa with a pitcher of tinto in the shadow of the bullring in Jerez on that other *peninsula de tristeza*. Hemingwayesque. Almost a hero in the eyes of my nephews, who applauded the snapshot I sent home to my sister of yours truly running the bulls down main street in Arcos de la Frontera. But this little finger of canine flesh, licked a thousand times under summer suns by its former owner—

"Professor Bob," Mr. Kim coaxes. "Couldn't you just close your eyes? I'll slip it right in your mouth."

"He's chicken," Mr. Choi grumbles.

"I'm sorry," I whine. "I just don't think I can. You never told me we'd be eating the dog's *juh-jee!*"

Which is true. Mr. Kim had extracted the dogmeat promise from me that afternoon over the phone. But he never mentioned juh-jee. Like a lover wheedling a kiss out of his virginal sweetheart, Mr. Kim had insisted that I didn't know what I was missing. *It not only tastes good. Gaegogi is good for you too. You've been in Korea long enough. It's time!* This was only too true too. I had been making jokes in poems and stories about Koreans and dog meat for long enough, maintaining the practice was symptomatic of a darker and graver malevolence lurking just behind the culture's sunny smile—packed between its molars, in fact. But, in all fairness, did I know whereof I spoke regarding pooch and Culture and the culinary arts? *And Mr. Ku hasn't been feeling up to par lately. He needs it for his health. His stamina.* Which, of course, had always been my point. That Korean men eat dog to give their sex lives a boost and a boast—to produce rock-hard erections that must last well into the matutinal ministrations of amor. A stiff prick is just plain good health. "Never loan money to a man who wakes up in the morning without a hard-on," runs a venerable Sino-Korean proverb, meaning, obviously, Be careful the fucker doesn't croak before he has the chance to pay you back. *And I'm sure Mr. Ku's wife would appreciate it too. They're still hoping for that male offspring. And they're not getting any younger.* That the birth of a bouncing baby boy might hinge on a dog hanging by its neck from a hook on the ceiling of a butcher shop and slowly choking to death because the adrenaline invoked by the suffering is thought to tenderize the meat is, of course, my point even more poignantly.[1] *And this is The Year of the Dog! Professor Bob, please!*

Clearly it is now or never. The success or failure of the evening rests in my carnivorous claws. Gruff, rock-jawed Mr. Choi sits in gloom as the boiled dog's boiled *juh-jee* cools to a *tiempo*. Mild, self-effacing Mr. Ku looks on with pained resignation. Convivial Mr. Kim leans forward and beams boyishly in my face. He has already taken pains to make his point that the "auntie"—who is in fact the owner of the establishment—graces only the most "esteemed" clients with this special "cut." I make an effort to recall that eminently versatile syllogism a Real Man is trained to employ in difficult circumstances: *In this situation everybody is having a good time. I am in this situation. Therefore I am having a good time.* With trembling chopsticks I lift my quarter of dog *juh-jee* and deposit it on my tongue. Chew and chew and finally gulp and swallow, stifling the gag reflex with that same power of sheer will a man might beseech a novice fellatrix to summon in the throes of an analogous consummation. Wash down whatever debris remains with a toss of sweet, viscous *soju*. The welkin does not open up. Nor does a bolt of lightning come bursting through the window of the restaurant to split me in half like a forlorn, solitary oak in a thunderstorm. No Marlow out of Conrad comes chugging slowly upriver to carry my final whispers back to genteel drawingroom civilization. Dog pizzle, it is clear, when properly prepared, is—well, edible. And yes, since you're dying to ask, there indeed is a bone in it. The lucky stiffs.

$$\approx$$

At a beer house far enough off the beaten track to be reasonably priced—a *dan-gol jip* or "regular haunt" of Mr. Kim's and our *ee-cha* or "second stop" for the evening—a waitress in a miniskirt and about a quart of cheap domestic perfume sets down a bilingual menu before us. Mr. Choi, eager to show off his English in front of the young and aromatic sexpot,

---

1. I might note here that once the pooch has been released by death from its final agonies, its fur is expeditiously blowtorched off before it's skinned and dragged over to the chopping block. Curiously, an old Korean folk remedy for dog-bite is to grab the cur that got you, yank out a sizeable handful of its hair, singe it, and apply this as a kind of poultice to the wound. "A little hair of the dog that bit you," as one Occidental lush might offer to another.

orders four bottles of OB beer and something called "Dried Slices of Dish," which turns out to be regular old *marun anju*, a mixed plate of dried anchovies, tissue-thin squares of dried seaweed, peanuts and tiny strips of dried cuttlefish. As a professor of literature I feel obliged to suggest the "Dried Poe"— I wonder how long the poor bastard had been walled up before adjudged desiccated enough to serve as provender—but Mr. Ku waves me off and indicates that what we really need to balance (this is yin-yang country, after all) the *marun anju* is the "Fruited Prate" which, in due turn, manifests itself as a simple platter of sliced apples and bananas and segments of mandarin orange, and not, thank God, a round of idle, epicene prattle. In Korea it is considered barbaric and "unreasonable to your health" to drink without a snack at your fingertips—even if you have just polished off a sizeable portion of Man's Best Friend, pecker, neck, haunch and paw.

"I've got good news for you, Professor Bob," Mr. Kim announces as he pours me a glass of beer from one of the oversize bottles of OB. In Korea it is regarded as the epitome of anti-social audaciousness to pour your own. Koreans may be among the world's most prodigious boozers, but every form of excess here is governed by principles of etiquette ignored only at the risk of jeopardizing the eternal serenity of one's dead Ancestors. A man reckless enough to be found drinking alone in a bar might as well be declaring to all the world that he doesn't have any family or friends—and doesn't give a shit, either.

"Shoot."

"You mentioned on the phone that you wanted to start putting away some money."

"I suspect it's about time."

"Well, there's a terrific savings plan at the Korea Finance Bank. For teachers only. Twenty-four percent a year."

"Twenty-four percent? You think I'm eligible?"

"Why not? You're a teacher—just like us."

"Yeh, but I'm a foreigner too. My own university won't even let me in on its pension plan. And I pay six times more for health insurance than my Korean colleagues do."

"Here," he says, removing a slip of memo paper from his pocket.

"I wrote down the name of the savings plan for you in Korean. Just show it to the people at the downtown branch. No problem."

I pocket the note, sit back, and hoist my glass of beer. Mr. Choi, an exuberant master-of-ceremonies now that he has half a bottle of soju and a goodly portion of pooch under his belt, proposes a toast and we all drink to something I don't quite catch. Something about "your ancestor's dog's corpse." Mr. Kim senses my confusion and offers to translate: "May wild dogs rummage your grandmother's bones."

"That's not a toast," I cry. "That's a curse."

371

"Yes," Mr. Choi laughs. "But it's a Family Curse! Ha! My father used to shout it when he drank with his friends in the old days. Then the others would join in and recite their own favorite curses. I learned a lot from them."

I allow that it's a heck of a good curse and Mr. Choi scribbles it down for me in Korean on another piece of memo paper. I pocket this note too, with the notion of committing it to memory when I have a clearer head, certain that I will have the opportunity to use it sooner or later—no doubt the next time a taxi driver refuses to stop for my Caucasoid Mug in front of my school or some bargirl tries to hit me up for a 4000 *wun* whiskey coke. Mr. Ku asks me the most effective curse in English and I tell him my old stand-by. He begs me to write it down for him (it's the one about *You and the horse you rode in on*) and soon curses and slips of white memo paper are flying so fast and thick we probably look like four drunken louts simultaneously stricken with a wacky strain of Gilles de la Tourrette's Syndrome in the middle of an arctic blizzard.[2] My three friends have spent much of their waking professional lives studying and teaching textbook English, but they often fess up to an uneasiness about certain gaps in their knowledge. They are innocent of the "juicier" recesses of my native tongue and sometimes feel like bewildered outsiders (a condition of the spirit I know only too well) when they view Hollywood films laced with racy slang and raunchy obscenities. In the Korean subtitles to American movies, "asshole," "cocksucker," and "motherfucker" all come out as the blandly comprehensive *napun-nom*, "good-for-nothing low-fellow." There is, really, no appropriate lexicon for my friends save for a native speaker with a few too many beers in him. They need me—and if world politics are any guide—this may be the only real foundation for international friendship.

"What's a 'cunt head'?" growls Mr. Choi. "I cannot imagine this. Or a 'dick head'? I cannot imagine this either."

"They're just other words for 'asshole,' I suppose. Like 'shit for brains' or 'dog breath' or 'butt face'."

"Well, why do you Americans need so many words for 'asshole'?"

Which is a hell of a good question. Signifiers and Things Signified. Signs and Wonders. But it is late in the evening—not the hour to mutate from a beer-swilling dogeater into a Theory-spewing frogeater. "I guess it just goes," I say, "with the territory."

---

2. My favorite Korean curse, for what it's worth, is *Nee ddong-jjip saeng-in-dae-ro nol-ah-ra* and means "Have it your way, dammit." Literally translated, however, it's a bit more fun: "Okay then, play it according to the shape of your own asshole!"

Mr. Choi and Mr. Ku live near each other on the other side of town and, after conferring secretively with Mr. Kim on some arcane matter that involves the exchange of fistfuls of banknotes, choose to share a taxi home. The cab gets only a dozen yards down the street when Mr. Ku springs out and dashes back into the beer house. He emerges minutes later with the foil packet of leftover *gae-gogi* that his wife had entreated him to bring home. She wants that little puer heir as much as he does. Mr. Ku waves as the taxi lurches off again. Mr. Kim and I wave back. The gentle English teacher hadn't forgotten about his "doggy-bag"—which, I have the opportunity to observe, is no mere figure of speech over here. I stand on the street corner ready to flag down the next cab while Mr. Kim circles around me in an eccentric orbit, eyeing me up and down appraisingly. Above us a streetlamp buzzes and flickers. It is a weeknight and Greater Pusan has long since turned in.

"How do you feel?" Mr. Kim asks.

"Fine. A little bushed, I guess."

"You didn't eat much of the *gae-gogi*."

"I had my share, I think. Thank you."

"You look like you could do with a haircut."

"Don't be silly," I snap. "I had one just last week."

"A trim then," he says flatly. "I know a place nearby."

"Mr. Kim, it's almost midnight. There aren't any barbershops open now. Even if I wanted a haircut."

"This one is special."

Mr. Kim hooks my arm and ushers me across the street. A taxi without a fare slows to a crawl and I motion for it to pull over but Mr. Kim tugs on my coatsleeve insistently and the cab draws off. We walk down a narrow sidestreet of darkened, closed shops that opens on a broad thoroughfare. Beside the entrance of a new office building a carpeted flight of steps leads down to a subterranean glass door curtained on the inside.

"That barber pole is not lit up, Mr. Kim. It isn't revolving. This place is closed."

"The police," he says conspiratorially. "You've read about the crackdown."

As indeed everyone has. Korea has been polishing up its public image ever since its capital won the venue for the '88 Olympics. This involves, naturally enough, the eradication of all appearances of public vice—particularly lewd services for hire. But Mr. Kim has never seemed the type to frequent such places. He is happily married, or so he says. I met his wife once and liked her. No beauty, she has that grace that comes when a woman is sincerely content with her husband. Teachers are underpaid in Korea, but thanks to Confucius and Mencius and all that crowd their social status is high. Traffic cops will let you off with a warning if you flash your school ID card. You are a *son-saeng-nim.* *Son-soeng* means "teacher." *Nim* is a special tag used with certain forms of address and means 'honorable.' (*Nom*, as you may recall, is its precise opposite, as in *napun-nom.* You watch your vowels over here.)

Mr. Kim pushes open the glass door and I follow him into a small, low-ceilinged waiting room lined on three sides with sturdy, well-worn sofas. There is a hint of mildew and a clammy closeness in the air; we are indeed underground. A young woman in heavy makeup and a sort of beautician's uniform sits on one of the sofas engrossed in a dubbed Hollywood movie on a tiny portable TV. Gregory Peck is taking lip from a woman at a lavish party. Then the woman is crying and people around them are beginning to notice. He appears about to visit the face of the teary-eyed beauty with the back of his hand when the young woman notices us standing inside the door and jumps off her sofa and bends down to remove my shoes. She sets down a pair of plastic shower sandals and guides my feet into them.

"I'll wait here," Mr. Kim says solemnly. "I'm a married man. I get twinges of consciousness. You're a bachelor. You don't get enough relief. Besides, I haven't seen this movie before. I like William Holden."

Enough relief. I had long learned to keep my male Korean friends in the dark about my nocturnal forays, lest they beg to accompany me. Korean men hunt in packs. Serious Westerners more often than not go it alone. And the surest way to strike out with a Korean woman is to show up with one or more of her countrymen in tow. Intimate relations with outsiders are frowned upon. More than once I've strolled past the fashionable shops of Nampo-dong with a decent-looking squeeze on my arm only to be greeted by a shrill, resonant *Ship-pal seki!* (probably the most insulting term in the Korean language's arsenal of abuse, which curiously enough translates literally as the ineffectual "You goddamn Son of The Number Eighteen") from the proprietor of a cigarette kiosk or pushcart vendor. Like a wild dog of the savannah, a foreign man often enough has to wait for his prey to detach herself from the herd, hobbled as she is by some hidden psychic wound. My Kraut neighbor, colleague and friend (author of the unjustly ignored *From Earthiness to Dirtiness: The Transformative Power of El Bucko in the Developing World*) is convinced that the only Korean women who are attracted to foreign men are "flawed" in some indefinable way. When I press him on this point, he waves me off and mutters into his blackmarket schnapps about "table leavings." Apparently it hurts. And fully a quarter of the strays I have worried into the sack in this tragic-comic cul-de-sac of a country have confessed to having been ruined for life by a father or a step-father or an uncle. That's a pretty high percentage by my reckoning—and the repressed memory syndrome is not even in vogue yet over here—and has skewed my perception of my hosts. I see them darkly through a glass smudged with the soot of my own infernal imaginings.

"That's Gregory Peck," I say. "That's not William Holden."

"Of course." Mr. Kim stares hard at the television screen and squints.

In a cubicle barely spacious enough for jumpingjacks the young woman in the beautician's uniform settles me in a barber chair, tucks my collar inside my shirt, and checks the length of my fingernails, all the while discretely averting her eyes. From underneath all that makeup nothing specific, nothing individual shines through, save that she has a widow's peak and a dimpled chin. Such Asian women, a likeable but thoroughly unreliable ex-friend once titillated me, sport no foliage on their fleshy little venereal escarpments. But clothed she might be any porcelain doll in a row of identical porcelain dolls in a toy shop window, passive, wide-eyed, inert yet hypnotically alert.

A barber in a starched white tunic enters and wordlessly goes about the business of giving me a trim. The straight razor is dull and rasps at my nape, and I think about weasels ripping my flesh and the late Frank Zappa and middle age and inoperable cancer of the prostate. The barber doesn't so much finish the job as seem to lose interest and give up. He packs up his tools in a drawer beneath the large mirror in front of the barber chair and sort of melts away. I don't know how else to describe it—he is there in the mirror one moment and then he is smaller and then he is gone. Dimpled Chin returns—perhaps she ducked out to catch part of the Gregory Peck flick with Mr. Kim—and pulls a lever of some sort underneath the chair and suddenly the back of the chair collapses and I am staring up at the ceiling, my legs stuck straight out and supported by a part of the chair that has risen magically up out of nowhere. A neatly gadget, I decide. Dimpled Chin places a small towel over my eyes—some small concession to female modesty, no doubt—but I can see fairly well out the lower edge, as in cheating at pin-the-tail-on-the-donkey. Then the overhead light goes out and a red lamp above the mirror comes on. Apparently there are hidden levers and toggles all over the place, like a state-of-the-art torture chamber. She sits down beside me on a low stool and massages my arm, popping my fingers on one end and squeezing my pectorals on the other. Occasionally her hand drifts over my belly and brushes lightly across my lap, each time tarrying there a little longer, applying just the slightest bit more pressure. It is all very coy but my chest tightens just the same and my breathing begins to labor. With cool precision she unzips my fly and unbuckles my belt, guiding me to arch my back just enough for her to slide my slacks and undershorts down to mid-thigh. There are stirrings. The sluggish juices have begun to roil.

By methodically squinching and unsquinching my face I am able to dislodge the towel enough to clap eye fully on my manly part.

That poor, abused appendage is engorging admirably. Perhaps it is the angle of perspective or a trick of the red glow in the background, but the thing looks huge, alien, and eerily majestic, like an inscrutable dolmen thrust up on the horizon at the scarlet dawn of time. (Rosey pose, empurpled prose.) No better hung than the next White Dude, I have to allow that maybe there is something to this dog-meat aphrodisiac business after all. And then my cock vanishes and the silhouette of her head appears in its place, bobbing up and down, up and down, her lips doing all the heavy work, her teeth carefully tucked away in the soft, pliant flesh inside her mouth. I close my eyes and try hard not to think of epileptic seizures or the set of barber's tools packed in the drawer just an arm's length away in the dark. That morning's editorial in the paper complained that not only had Lorena Bobbit been found innocent by reason of temporary insanity, she has been released from the looney bin with a clean bill of mental health as well. In Thailand, the editorial went on, wronged, indignant wives refer jocularly to the act of castrating one's husband as "throwing him to the ducks." More poetically, in the Philippines, where surgeons are adept at reattaching severed organs, one feminist critic has suggested tying the bloody thing to a helium-filled balloon and releasing it to the sodden, moon-drenched Manila night sky.

≈

Yea, never lend money to a man who wakes up in the morning without a hard-on. A stiff pecker equals good health and good health is the firmest foundation on which a bright future can be erected over here. A fair translation of the Sino-Korean *boo-shin tang* is "good health soup" and its main ingredient is sliced dog. A young newlywed husband whose bride is a bit more amorous than he had anticipated will be prescribed a thick, syrupy decoction of boiled dogmeat to be swigged down every morning after breakfast during the first half dozen or so months of matrimonial ardor. An older gentleman who suffered a claustrophobic, arranged marriage in his early manhood will resort to it as he finds his circumstances grown solid enough to permit him to take on a mistress. Westerners turn their noses up at such quaint folk beliefs and mutter about the inhumaneness of it all, recoiling at the spin their Asian cousins have put on the old adage that *A dog is a man's best friend.* And then they concede, whispering among themselves and nodding knowingly, "Well, of course there could be something to it. Look at ginseng!"[3]

---

3. And there indeed may be something to this. The amino acid sequences in dog flesh are reputedly quite similar to those in human beings, making dog easily digestible for us bipedals, especially on those hot summer nights—*gae-gogi*'s high season is August, the Dog Days, believe it or not—when we don't really feel like eating much of anything at all.

Though Korea is considerably less bawdy and phallocentric than Folk Japan and its Shinto lingams, the male member begins with a starring role in a little tyke's life. Traditionally male toddlers are free—encouraged actually—to swagger about the neighborhood unclad below the waist, their maleness proudly on display. It is a gesture of approbation and goodwill for an older man to bend over and fondle the little one's prepuce and shaft and pronounce the equipment adequate.[4] Unjustly, no such ritual is reserved for the inculcation of gender pride and sexual identity in the female, and little girls are expected to keep their nether parts out of sight and mind, though in my own neighborhood little preschooler Sook-hee or Mee-ran is free to drop her drawers and empty her bladder at any time right there on the street, usually within spattering range of my spanking-new Reeboks. Penis Envy is pretty much a fact of life over here—after all, what sex wouldn't begrudge the other the license to strut about and dangle for all the world to see the Instrument for the Ensurement of the Continuation of the Family Line. Young boys who grow up in the same neighborhood together and attend the same elementary schools refer to each other proudly ever after as *juh-jee chingu*, "penis friends." When, during a moment of intercrural intimacy, I asked a female Korean acquaintance if there was a corresponding term for girls who had passed the earliest years of their youth in a like manner—"I mean, do you say *buh-jee chingu*, 'pussy friends,' or what?"—she gave me such a look of bewilderment and incredulity that I backed off and tacked into a wholly different line of crosscultural inquiry and sharing.

As they grow older, boys are expected to identify their thickening and lengthening doopers with the distinctive main staple of Korean cuisine, the *gochu*, or hot pepper. The condom machines in the men's rooms of bars and other like establishments are decorated with a picture of a bright red *gochu* superimposed on a packed throng of faceless people and carry the advisory that Zero Population Growth is foremost in the minds of all loyal citizens. Anyone who has mashed a tiny Mexican pequin pepper between his molars can appreciate the hoary Korean saying *Chagun gochu mepda*, which is what a young lanceman who fears he is less well-endowed than his peers will whisper into the ear of the coy damsel he is wooing: *The smallest pepper is the hottest.* When in the old days a traditional village household produced a newborn baby boy, a string of bright red peppers was hung across the entrance gate to 'notify'

---

4. The source of considerable embarrassment and shame to old Korean codgers who emigrate to the States with their ambitious, upwardly mobile grown children and on a sunny afternoon suburban walk decide to apprise little tow-headed Johnny Peterson from down the street of his future cocksmanhood. Intercultural misconstruances can be a melting-pot bailbondsman's boon.

the other villagers of the good fortune. For a newborn baby girl, lumps of charcoal were sometimes set out.[5]

But I digress. The only absolutely convincing attestation I have run across of the aphrodisiacal properties of anything in the Korean larder has been the testimony of a former Peace Corps volunteer who slurped down a bowl of *dok-baem tang*—"venomous snake soup"—for lunch one afternoon and later that day hopped the ferry in Pusan for Shimonoseki, Japan. It's a twelve-hour trip on a clear evening, and the crossing that night was particularly rough, especially for a guy prone to motion sickness, his cock swollen to such obscene proportions that he began to think about "bleeding" it, as indeed old-time leeches might well have prescribed. It is difficult—even piquantly painful—to try to recollect in the tranquillity of middle-middle age a cock grown so thick and rigid that it actually hurts—but I've got to take the guy's word for it, his ashen face as he recounted leaning over the side of the ship every fifteen minutes to upchuck and grinding the aching head of his pecker against steel railing and brass belt buckle. Every fifteen minutes. For twelve solid hours. When I asked him why he didn't just go into the head and masturbate and get it all over with, he took a long slow drag on his Marlborough Light and held the toke in his lungs till the color came back into his cheeks. "Christ, I jerked off half a dozen times the first hour. Until even my cock had the dry heaves!"

≈

Mr. Kim is watching the credits of the Gregory Peck movie when I step back into the waiting room, struggling to control the fool smirk of the blissfully undone torturing my lips. Dimpled Chin bows deeply to the two of us as I lift my feet out of the plastic sandals and settle them into the familiarity of my loafers. Mr. Kim slips her a small pad of banknotes and she bows again. She says something in dialect that I do not catch and Mr. Kim laughs and agrees with her. He tells her I am an important professor from a foreign country and her hand covers her mouth in a manner that suggests reverential awe—or panicked confusion, sometimes it is hard to tell which. She bows hurriedly a third time and backs away and disappears through the narrow archway that leads to the cluster of hidden cubicles, shielding her face as from, I muse, the Brightness and Glory of My Countenance. After all, I am still grinning like a loon.

"Mr. Choi and Mr. Ku and I were worried about you," Mr. Kim

---

5. Possibly a couple of cultural universals here—as I do recall collecting a specially wrapped stogie or two from proud new papas during my graduate school days as well as that fist-size chunk of coal stuffed into the toe of my Christmas morning stocking one year, an event that led me to wonder if my parents had found out I had discovered the joys of self-gratification.

remarks as he levers me into a taxi out on the street again. "You're a bachelor. You never talk about a girlfriend."

"You guys all chipped in, didn't you?"

Mr. Kim smiles paternally. The taxi driver drums his fingers on the dashboard.

"We are all thankful for what you have done for us."

Toward dawn I awake in my bed, bolt upright and shivering, my torso and arms rigid in a straitjacket of cold sweat. I have been tossing a stick in a green meadow and a prancing, eager mixed-breed—it is my Natasha whom I had had to let a vet put down so many years back—is retrieving it for me. Each time she brings it back I pat her on the head and let her lick my face and nuzzle me down below. On the last throw she returns with a limp human penis clutched gingerly in her jaws. I look down between my legs but there is nothing there, only a bloody round hole the size of a half dollar. Natasha ducks and feints playfully and dashes away with her prize in her mouth as I stand fast, frozen, unable to pursue, a shock of her tawny hair in my clenched fist.

≈

I slip the piece of memo paper out of my wallet and present it to the pretty young teller with bangs and a button nose at the downtown branch of the Korea Finance Bank. She unfolds it, scans the message and pauses, mumming her lips as in silent prayer. Then she gapes up at me, her bright, innocent eyes wide with incomprehension and her lips slightly parted, as if one of us has suddenly been revealed a couple of beads short in the old abacus.

"*Son-saeng imnida*," I mince with an ingratiating, rehearsed smile. "I'm a teacher. Special account. Twenty-four percent. For teachers only."

Bangs and Button Nose eases herself nervously off of her tiny stool behind the counter and hurries the note to a desk along the back wall of the bank where a serious man in a salaryman's blue suit is flipping mechanically through a stack of canceled checks. They confer, whispering behind cupped hands and glancing over at me from time to time. Bangs and Button Nose's expression has changed from bewildered confusion to pallid, abject terror. Salaryman turns the note around and around, as if reading it upside-down or backwards might yield up the information he seeks. A security guard eyes me with suspicion—it is, of course, not all that wise to hand a handwritten note to a bank teller, regardless of the culture you find yourself in. I stare impatiently at the pair, summoning an air of indignation at the delay. No doubt I will be asked to produce a ream of documents to prove I am a teacher and eligible for the savings plan. When at long last Salaryman rises from behind his desk and approaches the counter, he clears his throat and

379

bows slightly. Tiny pearls of sweat glisten on his forehead just below the hairline.

"Sir," he says in crisp, polite English. "Miss Gong is new to her position at our bank. This is her second week only. Clearly it would be better if I spoke with you."

"I understand completely," I say, pitying poor Bangs and Button Nose, who is now a terror-stricken silhouette against the blank wall. Her pose reminds me of a postcard someone once sent me from Pompeii. She has probably never met a foreigner face to face before. Whatever English she might have been able to muster in a high school classroom a year before has failed her in the breach. The challenge of a simple conversation in a foreign tongue is an impossible burden for such kids, like being asked to play ping-pong with a bowling ball.

"On the other hand," Salaryman continues, creasing and smoothing out the note in his hands, "clearly there has been some mistake. This—"

Some mistake. I know that song and dance. I hear it from Immigration Officials every year when I try to renew my residence card. I heard it from the Ministry of Education when they demanded copies of my dusty university diplomas if they were to approve me to teach here in The Land of the 10,000 Bureaucratic Rudenesses. I heard it from the City Courthouse when I went to apply for the form I would need to apply tor the documents necessary to apply for a marriage license, documents finally procured the day before I got dumped. Now it is the banks' turn.

"I'm not eligible for the account? Because I'm a foreigner? Fine," I snap sarcastically, not bothering for an answer. "Thanks." I grab the note out of his hands, thrust it into my jacket pocket, spin around on my heels and storm out of the building.

Outside I look up and down the street for a taxi stand. Behind the glass doors of the bank Salaryman is speaking at length with a nodding security guard. Traffic whizzes by a few feet from my nose, swirling the air and sending scraps of paper in dizzying spirals high above the cracked, uneven sidewalk. A sewer opening reeks at my feet. And suddenly a queer sensation sweeps over me. That twinge of paralysis you feel when you realize you can't remember for sure whether or not you unplugged the coffee pot before you left home in the morning. I fish the note out of my pocket and uncrumple it and translate the scribbled Korean with gut-wrenching humiliation and a blinding rush of profound sympathy for poor Miss Bangs and Button Nose: *May wild dogs rummage your grand—*

"You awake?" I said.

"Okay."

"Nice butt."

"Humm."

"Look at the crack on you."

"What?"

"It barely comes up to your coccyx,"

"Cock-licks? Don't know cock-licks."

"Your tailbone. The crack of your butt just barely comes up to your tailbone."

"Same-same crack everybody else."

"No way. It's lower on a Korean woman. Look."

"You crazy. Anybody can't see own butt. No got turn around head like Exercise lady."

"Exorcist lady."

"Oh."

"You want me to get a mirror?"

"No! Why anybody want a see own *ung-dungee*?"

"Well, look at mine then."

"Ugh! Don't show me white man hair butt in a morning!"

"I just want you to see the difference."

"Ugh! You got one *byo-roo-jee*."

"A what?"

"*Byo-roo-jee*. I don't know English. Jit?"

"A zit."

"Okay."

"Hey. Be careful."

"Fat one."

"Hey, I'm human. What the hell. Ouch!"

"Bloody."

"OW!"

"Sorry. No white stuff. Only blood. You go herb doctor. Give you some medicines."

"That hurt, Ae-jin."

"Not my name."

"Sure it is."

"My name Ae-*joo*."

"Sorry."

"You no remember Ae-joo name? You too much drinky last night Dallas Club."

"Sure I remember. You're *My name Ae-joo. You buy me whisky and coke. Only four thousand wun.*"

381

"Not funny."

"Maybe not. But I see a big smile right here in front of me. Just look at the crack of your butt. It's like a big round yellow Happy Face."

"Hey! Why you kiss a butt?"

"I'm a sick man, Ae-joo."

"So you kiss a Ae-joo ung-dung-ee?"

"It's the only cure. The only balm. Kiss a Happy Face and you'll live one more day."

"You go herb doctor. Give you some medicines you brain. No want a kiss Korean woman butt any more got a live one day."

"You don't understand."

"I understand all thing American man say Korean woman butt."

"No you don't, Ae-joo."

"You think you pretty smart guy."

"Smart enough to know some things."

"What?"

"Your butt, for example."

"Shit."

"Your butt, darling, begins right here. At the coccyx. At the tail-bone. And proceeds downward and inward to here."

"Hey! Don't touch a poop place!"

"And passes the perineum. Which is a sort of fleshy little door-mat. You can wipe your foot here and go in the back door—'

"HEY! I SAID DON'T TOUCH A POOP PLACE!"

"Or, if the fair maiden will not permit such a liberty, you can step back out and wipe your foot on the little doormat again and enter the front door like a gentleman. Like this."

"Oh!"

"And once you're inside, it's pretty dark in there. So you just feel along the wall for the light switch. Like this."

"You nice guy. Nice hand. Nice finger."

"Thank you."

"So why you no got a girlfriend?"

"I do."

"Why come she no here?"

"Because you're here. And I've got my finger inside you. Don't let's talk about her."

"She don't love you?"

"So you just feel along the wall for the light switch."

"Maybe she gone a come here kill Ae-joo."

"There once was this guy who had a girlfriend whose hole was huge. Mammoth."

"Ae-joo hole too much big?"

"One night while they were making love, he thrust too hard and fell tumbling inside her."

382

"Your girlfriend hole too much big?"

"By the time he came to his senses, he realized he had fallen so far in that he couldn't find his way back out again."

"Bullshit. Anybody woman no got a hole too much big like that."

"For hours he wandered around in the darkness trying to find his way out again."

"This true story? Four hours?"

"As God is my witness, Ae-joo. Finally, after he had completely lost track of even what day it was, he sat down and buried his face in his hands and wept softly."

"This guy you?"

"At the very nadir of his despair, he heard a sound off in the distance."

"This girlfriend you girlfriend?"

"There was somebody else inside there with him!"

"Bullshit. Now Ae-joo know bullshit."

"Hey! he cried. Is there somebody else in here too?"

"Hey. Why you put a other finger in a pussy? Ae-joo too much small. Two fingers."

"It's part of the story, doll. Two fingers. Sure, said a Voice from the blackness. I've been in here for weeks."

"Hurt. Don't waggle a fingers."

"You know how to get out of here? said the man. I'm lost."

"This long time story."

"Sure. No problem, said the Voice. I'll tell you what."

"What?"

"I'll tell you what, said the Voice. You help me find my damn car keys and we'll drive out together!"

"HA!"

"Too long time story. You hurry finish."

"It is finished. That's the story, Ae-joo."

"Yeh? What a girlfriend say she see two guys drive out a she's pussy in a car?"

"I have no idea."

"Dumb story."

"It's a joke. Just a joke."

"Oh."

"You don't get it at all, do you?"

"Ae-joo think story girlfriend you girlfriend."

"Bull crap."

"Ae-joo think you got *goo-mung dong-suh.*"

"What the hell's that? Some kind of disease?"

"You girlfriend got a other boyfriend. You got *goo-mun dong-suh.* Same-hole brother-in-law."

"Shut up."

"Like right now. You got a two fingers in Ae-joo pussy."

"And it's warm and wet in there, my sweet."

"Too much tight. No space."

"Well, spread your legs little."

"Okay?"

"That's better."

"What you do now? You gone a climb on Ae-joo back? Make a morning time doggy jiggy-jiggy?"

"Umm."

"No put a cock in poop place. Okay?"

"Never fear."

"OH!"

"You okay, baby?"

"Uh."

"Better?"

"Why come American peoples all of time make morning time jiggy-jiggy?"

"Don't talk."

"Korean peoples think morning time jiggy-jiggy too much bad."

"Cultural differences, my love. You're Confucian. I'm a Dionysiac. We all have to make adjustments. Hitch your butt up an inch or two, could you?"

"Uh."

"That's better."

"Morning time work time. Not a jiggy-jiggy time. Sweep a floor time. Boil a rice time."

"Shhh."

"Care a babies time."

"This *is* work, baby."

"OW!"

"Hold it right there. Now move up and down ever so slightly."

"Okay?"

"That's it. You got it."

"Oh!"

"Woooo."

"You gone a come?"

"Just hang on. Now suffer me to—"

"HEY! DON'T PUT IN A POOP PLACE! YOU PROMISE!"

"Just for a second."

"OW! "

"Oooh."

"Put back in a pussy, okay?"

"Wooo-ooh. Hooh!"

"You finish? You a liar. You promise. No put in a poop

place. Now take out."

"Okay. Sorry."

"Hurt."

"Couldn't resist."

"You girlfriend okay put a cock in a poop place?"

"The word is 'asshole', Ae-joo. Not 'poop place'."

"Okay, you girlfriend okay put a cock in a asshole?"

"Don't let's talk about her?"

"Who she is?"

"She's nobody."

"Can't be nobody."

"I don't have any girlfriend. Just you."

"Bullshit."

"No bullshit."

"Last night Dallas Club you all of time watching door. Somebody maybe come. Maybe you girlfriend come. You no buy Ae-joo whiskey coke long time."

"You're wiser than your years, baby."

"She no come, huh?"

"She no come. That's right."

"Who she is?"

"Why do you want to know?"

"Girlfriend find out Bob and Ae-joo jiggy-jiggy Ae-joo big trouble time."

"She doesn't care."

"She come Dallas Club?"

"Sometimes."

"Who she is? Got a know. Work Dallas Club. Maybe she come make Ae-joo big trouble time."

"Her name's Mi-ra, for Christ sake."

"Big titty Korean girl?"

"Nice talk."

"You like big titty?"

"Big tits are okay. A nice tight ass is okay too. Like yours."

"Hey! Don't put afinger in there! Ae-joo got a take some dump soon."

"Well, don't do it here in my bed."

"Big titty girl name Mi-ra. I know she. She got a boyfriend."

"You know him?"

"Sure. I see all of time Dallas Club. Big titty Mi-ra girl too. Together. Everybody know they."

"You sure?"

"Everybody know."

"Never mind. It's not important."

"You angry? You got a angry face."

"Let's change the subject."

"You love a big titty Mi-ra girl, huh?"

"Are you going to can it?"

"Sorry. Don't understand."

"Forget it."

"But you love a big titty Mi-ra girl. For sure."

I lifted myself off the thick quilt—quaintly called a *yo*—that serves as bedding over here in Korea and went into the bathroom and took a long, hard, blind piss into the toilet bowl and watched a cockroach climb the wall and disappear behind a broken tile. Mi-ra once remarked that her mother told her there were no cockroaches on the peninsula until the Yankees—Koreans pronounce it yanqui, the way Latin Americans do—steamed over for the Korean War and off-loaded the hardy little newcomers along with hundreds of tons of processed American cheese in brown cardboard cannisters that sat around unopened in the alleys of the cities because the half-starved war-bitten locals couldn't stomach the bouquet of the stuff. Perhaps it is true. You never really know in Asia, where the past is forever being reinvented to bring it more in line with the tenor of the present. And vice-versa. When I finished pissing I swung my mug around in front of the mirror above the sink and started to floss out the chunky brown debris of last night's Dallas Club beef jerky. Ae-joo came in and sat down on the commode and commenced her business, both holes, sucking in air and letting it out slowly as she purged.

"Hey, Bob," she said.

"Yes, my little hebephrenic breech-loader?"

"Look at you cock."

"Oh man."

"Full of shits."

P.C. PATROL

D. W. WRIGHT

R. Perchman's rude comments on Koreans made me angry. Reading *EC* gives you lots of chances to think about the meaning (the usual meanings) of offensiveness—and I'm offended by very little you print. But! ugly slurs on racial groups ... does this guy hang out on the back stoop with Duke or what? I wish you had said (as you have before): Get a conscience!

Ed. Note: *We repudiate Mr. Perchan's rude statement that ancient Koreans "fucked" horses. We think they fucked sheep, like everyone else.*

THE GOLDEN ORIENT

After sixty days in Taiwan not even Polo Bros. had the connections to keep me in the country. They had to send me out to renew my visa. Dandy called it a business trip. "We need you to be a messenger, it's a small thing, you do a little work then you can take two days off and get your new visa." He bought me a ticket to Hong Kong and returned my passport to me. "You can make a lot of money with this extra work. Mr. Yeh thinks you are O.K., you didn't run away like your friends and the theaters like your show. You won't run away will you? You still have a contract with us and we have many friends in Hong Kong to look after you. You have more work when you come back. You'll be going to Bangkok from Hong Kong. You get your ticket from Peter at this address. It's on Hong Kong Island, just take a taxi from the airport. You know it's so easy for you to travel anywhere you want. We Chinese cannot go whenever we want or wherever we want. We must have an invitation, a visa and exit permit. Very difficult to get even a passport."

So I got ready for a trip to Hong Kong. I thought about running away but why? And run back to what? I didn't even have the Chevy van anymore. I had a little money but not much really. I wanted to go back to California with enough to live in a house for a while. Maybe even enough to go back to college. Besides I was getting used to the vaudevillian adventure of it all so I decided not to run away. I flew to Hong Kong and met Peter. A very businesslike man in a suit and jacket even in the sweltering heat of Hong Kong. He was friendly and polite, offered me tea in a clean cup in his office. It was a much nicer place than what Polo Bros. had. Mahogany panels, carpeting, heavy wooden doors. He asked me to please wait while he did something in his private office.

Three men entered through the main door. They wore jackets zipped up to the neck. They were sweating but moving very slow. Their steps seemed heavy and deliberate. Sliding a wall panel aside they entered what looked like a conference room. The panel slid shut. I heard the muted sing-song of Cantonese from inside and a light rush of activity. Then a heavy clunking sound as something was unloaded on the table.

"Can you come in please," Peter spoke softly. I walked into his private office. "You will be our messenger. We have something which must be delivered to Bangkok. It's gold. Can you carry ten kilos?"

There on the table sat a pile of gold. Ten million dollars worth of gold. "You carry only ten kilos, the rest we have other people carry. This is Shiao Chen, she will show you what to do." Shiao Chen fitted me with a canvas belt. It had pockets to hold the gold bars. Each bar was marked, pure South African gold, one kilo.

387

Adrenaline pumped into my veins. "You want me to carry this to Bangkok?"

Shiao Chen spoke only Mandarin but had no trouble making herself understood. "Kuai Yi Tien," she said sliding one bar after another into my belt. The concentration of its weight crushed my insides. She fitted in the last two bars and I groaned. Next she arranged a long scarf around my neck and handed me a summer jacket.

"Tsou Tsou," walk around.

I walked as normally as possible with this tremendous weight resting on my hips. My hair stood up on my arms. I said again, "Is this what you want me to carry ?"

"It's no problem." Peter said. "We have messengers every week. If you have any problem with customs in Bangkok you can quietly give the officer one of your bars. It's enough for two generations of his family to live in luxury. But try to deal with only one officer and don't give away more than half of what you carry."

I sank into the deep plush couch and the gold embedded itself in my abdomen painfully. Sitting up straight to pull my lungs out of the crush, I tried to breathe. "About how long will I have this on? Don't people normally use Brinks trucks, security guards, for this kind of thing?"

Peter answered. "Get up and take it off and I will explain what to do. First you must not talk about this with anyone, not one word. We want to take this to Bangkok quietly do you understand? Second, you must be willing, if not, forget it. Since now you have seen it we must be very careful. Are you willing?"

I stood up with one million five hundred thousand dollars strapped around my waist. I found I could walk normally as long as I kept the weight centered. I understood very well that they wanted me to smuggle this gold into Thailand. I asked a lot of questions. "Why me? Does this stuff even belong to you? Wouldn't professional security guards be better? This is a lot of money! What makes you think I won't run away with it, get on a different plane or disappear in Bangkok?"

"Don't worry there are people watching you along the way, but if you try to run away with it, I should warn you that it happened once before, but we caught up with him and took care of him with our special methods."

"Are there other people who know about this, people who would not mind blowing my head off to get the gold?"

"Haha, they have only these," with his thumb and forefinger he made a pistol. "But we have these." With his two arms he made a machine gun.

"Who does this amount of money belong to any way?"

"A group of investors," was all he would say about that. And the the next thing, "don't ask so many questions."

A pile of gold sat on the table, yellow shining metal worth more than I could imagine. I unloaded my belt and as I held a bar in my hand I knew why gold drove people crazy to have it. I felt a whisper of something very ancient crawl up the back of my neck. I wanted to touch it and feel its immensely concentrated weight. It was hard to take my eyes off it. "I'm willing."

"Good," Peter said. "Take this shoulder bag with you to the airport. I will meet you in the the coffee shop after you go through immigration. You come and sit beside me and I will put the gold in your bag. Then you take the bag on the plane with you and keep it under your feet all the time. Don't eat anything for lunch, maybe one small thing but you will have problems because the gold is so heavy it will press the food out, so be careful. After lunch take the bag with you to the toilet. There take it out and load it very carefully into your belt. Put it in exactly the same as you did in here, same positions. Now here is the Bangkok Airport."

He spread a sheet of paper with a line drawing of Bangkok Airport's arrival and immigration area. "If the plane lands at the farthest terminal then you have to walk a long way. So use the electric walkways here and here. The passport check is on a balcony over the customs tables. From there you can see the number ten table, nothing to declare. Just walk through and go to the taxi stand. You must still be very careful because there are plainclothes policemen in the arrival area and outside. I will meet you at the taxi stand and we will share a taxi into the city. I will pay you one thousand dollars when we get there."

By the time I arrived at the taxi stand my legs were turning to jelly. Sitting down with great relief in the taxi I looked at Peter. He spoke softly. "You must still be careful." So we didn't talk in the taxi but by now the gold around my waist really felt like it was going to cut me in half. I'd felt it against my spine as the plane made its descent. Then I had to stand in line at passport control, then descend a flight of steps to the crowded baggage claim area. I managed to smile at the officer standing at the 'nothing to declare' counter and walked right out of the airport into the unbelievable heat of Thailand. That did it. As soon as I stepped outside sweat rolled down my back and my knees began to get weak.

By the time we arrived at our destination in Bangkok—some place on the second floor—my legs were shaking out of control. Maybe it was my bottled up fear but it took my last bit of strength to climb those stairs.

Peter gave me a card with the name and address of a good hotel. "Stay in this place. It's not too expensive and it's very good." He seemed in a hurry to get me out of there. He paid me, one thousand cash.

I thanked him and staggered down the stairs, relieved to be out of there myself. My body was so pumped up with adrenaline I barely made it to the hotel. After a blissful shower I collapsed on the bed and went to sleep. When I awoke my room was freezing because I'd left the air conditioner on. When I got up to pee and flushed the toilet the whole toilet went off like a fountain. Water shot straight up from the bowl and flooded the bathroom. I called the front desk right away and they sent a boy to fix it. He was no plumber. He could not stop the water from shooting out of the bowl. After a frantic telephone call for help he smiled at me as only Thai people can smile and suggested I get another room. There was not another available room until midnight. The clerk suggested I go eat dinner maybe do some shopping and then come back. He suggested I go to Patpong.

I ate a really fine meal of Thai food at a banquet restaurant. I was eating alone but it did not bother me. The food was so delicious and I had a huge appetite. I wandered around Patpong noticing there were a lot of Westerners around, mostly in groups and mostly drunk. I went into the Pink Panther Bar thinking to have a drink myself. The minute I sat down at the bar a really beautiful Thai girl came and sat next to me.

"Hello Lady, you wanna drink?"

"Yes, a shot of Chivas or Suntory with ice please."

"For me too? I like you, you are so pretty, you buy me a drink too?"

There were girls dancing on a platform in bathing suits, there was an average of three girls at every table and they were rotating constantly.

"Where you come from? What's your name? You like the dancing girl? You tell me which one I send her to you, what you want. You like lady boy?"

"Just a whisky please, with ice." Two whiskies appeared on the bar, though hers was probably tea. It cost the same as whisky. She was a hard hustler, my heart really went out to her. The place was packed with girls. She sat closer to me and put my hand on her leg. "You like me? My name Sim. You ask mama san, we go to hotel, O.K.?" Now I really felt sorry for her. Hustling like mad to sell her sex to anyone. What did she do for her soul? Did she love anyone? I bought two more drinks and made chitchat conversation with her. Her vocabulary was very limited. I thought, You're wasting your time trying to hustle me, we are practically in the same business. As soon as she realized I was not interested in buying her for the evening she disappeared from the bar and another girl took her place. Before this new one could open her mouth I paid for my watered-down whisky and left. The next place I went into there were no dancing hostess girls in sight ... for a while. I ordered another whisky, sat sipping it, lost in myself thinking about the hostess at the Pink Panther. We practically were in the same business. Hers was a lot heavier, though. I did not have to sit at tables with customers or hustle drinks or sex. Even though there seemed to be an unspoken assumption that if I was a dancer I was also a prostitute. In China especially. All the way back to the T'ang dynasty, the wine-shop sing-song girls wandered from place to place offering a wide spectrum of entertainment. Sim had it rough, I thought, having to fuck a lot of fat sweating tourists night after night, though she had the enthusiasm of a Girl Scout at a bake sale. Her eyes were clear, innocent and completely free of any remorse.

The next girl I saw did not strike me so. She wandered completely naked on to the stage-set right in the middle of the bar. Junkie eyes seeing a completely different world. She wandered back and forth like a sleep-walker in her high heels. After a few minutes she knelt down and began pulling razor blades out of her vagina. She got about twenty of them out all linked together as a chain. The mama san tending bar gave her a sheet of colored paper which she cut into a beautiful paper orchid with the razor blades. The mama san then gave her a thick marking pen. Still on her knees she inserted the marking pen into her vagina and wrote, 'I love you john,' with her hips. When I was finally able go get my glass the rest of the way to my mouth, which I realized was hanging open for some time, I downed the rest and ordered another one. It came with a balloon. The mama san told me, "Hold just like this, O.K.? Now look." She pointed to a corner stage across the room from me. A naked girl lay on her back with her knees up and open. She was sliding a large plastic drinking straw in her vagina. Loading the straw with a wooden golf tee, she took aim. My balloon took a direct hit.

WHY DO ALIENS LOOK THE WAY THEY DO?

Frequently mentioned by UFOlogists is the fact that Aliens, as described by those who claim to have seen them or been abducted by the buggers, look alike. 85% of reports indicate that the visitors share a common origin.

Skeptics note that the Aliens described not only look like each other but also look like those depicted in the media: giant head, big almond-shaped eyes, slit mouth, hairless body, skinny limbs.

There is no doubt that a particular physical version of the extraterrestrial has entered contemporary folklore—and I believe it does not require tabloid gullibility to discern the creature's true origins.

Who is this Alien? An Oriental whiz kid. I use the word "Oriental" rather than "Asian" deliberately, for the perception is based on American racist perceptions. The extraterrestrial is an amalgam of Oriental and "egghead" characteristics.

The big brainy head hardly needs explaining. The tiny

DENISE NOE

391

atrophied limbs show that Space-Nerd does not stoop to manual labor. It also reflects the anatomical fact that on a species-to-species level there is a trade-off in the amount of energy given over to muscle and to brain.

The shape of the eyes reflects the dominant white culture's repulsion-fascination with our "model minority." Their large size tells us that these wonderfully evolved humanoids are the All-Seeing Ones.

The tiny mouth does not correspond to an anatomical feature but to Oriental "Silence is Golden" inscrutability—as perceived by white racism. Relative hairlessness is an Oriental characteristic, and also an advancement over our ape relatives.

TOBY KOOSMAN

IN OSAKA, SAKE

In Osaka, sake
is God.

Today we wrote dirty haiku
and abused the denizens
of many nations,
a special place being reserved
for Swedes.
(A Swede sent me to the ward
for shots, traveling in China:
his directions to the facilities
led me not to the commode
but to the sewer itself;
In the dark, I stepped out,
Splash. The big Swede
meant to say left, not right
Excuse him, his English).

In Osaka, sake
with tonic,
Full House red wine,
vodka, beer and Soju
(Korean rocket fuel)
were my pacific spirit.
In my three years in this
        country
I have refined
the consumption of alcohol
to a zenlike degree.
Five times drunk since
        Thursday

I twice slept two days
and I would be staring blankly
into Nothing
even now, except it seems
such a pathetic waste of time.

In search of the superior life
I made a Master copy
of the forged transcript
that landed me my first job here
(at Berlitz).
That earned me a position
at Osaka U. teaching
technical English
to Ph.D. students, who marveled
that any woman knew a widget
from a wrench. (Lars and I
drank twelve of them under the
        tatami
putting down ten
liters of beer and three bottles
of vodka between us two
but unfortunately
although we outdrank them we
outbarfed them also
which didn't daunt them at all
they just held us at arm's length
whenever they needed to use the
        loo).

In Thailand you can buy speed
and valium
over the counter, one of the many

great things about that country
along with the paucity of
    Americans.
I met these two Danish
pubcrawlers
on the proverbial slow boat
(How can you have adventures
if you travel first class?)
up the Yangtse to Nanjing; we
    drank
three bottles of maotai
in two days. The Chinese waiters
were surly and lethargic.
When I was waiting tables
back in Tennessee, at the Bahou,
Fouad used to tell us
to bring the food quickly
and set it down slowly,
but there they swagger
at their leisure to the table
maybe detouring through the
    local park
slam down the plate suddenly
with no apology.

Back at the office
I'm getting ready for my latest

intercontinental move
dropping socks and vital papers
interviewing the poor sods
who wish to succeed me
(or exceed me, perhaps)
all losers so far
and we already have
one of those, Nick,
who spilled a bowl of noodles into
the computer printer today and of
    course
totally fucked it up.
In an office where everyone
has a specialty, this
is his only field of expertise.
(For tax purposes
the company is buying my ticket
instead of paying me
and writing it—and me—off.
A one-way business trip).

I'll miss the yakiimo man
who comes round
with his little pushcart
tinkling a recording
of the only Japanese folk dance
known in America.

OISO, JAPAN

DAVID HIPLE

I was trying to find one more sea urchin on the mammoth gourmet platter of sushi in the middle of the table when out of the buzz of Japanese around me I heard Omura-san's voice say in English that I ought to go to the toilet. I wasn't sure I heard it at first because I was seated near the floor-model CD player connected to the white baby grand player piano which was entertaining us very loudly with what sounded like Liberace's greatest hits. Then he said it again.

By now conversation had stopped; everyone was smiling at me knowingly. Omura-san said they were talking about Fukuyama-san's special order toilet and that I should go see it. I didn't really feel like an inspection tour of the toilet in the middle of dinner, but it was clear they all wanted me to go, so I smiled and did my duty.

The toilet was a red, state-of-the-art rocket seat. The

only thing it lacked was a seatbelt. I sat down and my fingers fell on the control panel at the end of the right armrest. I entered combinations randomly. I pushed and the digital clock flashed. I pushed and elevator music enveloped me. I pushed and the toilet flushed.

I pushed once more anticipating lift-off, but the countdown was halted when a squirt of warm liquid washed the seat of my pants. I sat for a moment contemplating the malfunction. What would John Glenn do?

We had left Tokyo for the beach house in Fukuyama-san's silver Mercedes. My mind's eye projected us cruising along a scenic coastal highway past Yokohoma and Kamakura to Oiso. Instead we joined a jumble of bumper-to-bumper traffic snaking from grey Tokyo to grey Oiso through urban, suburban, and exurban sprawl.

Door to door, our feet never touched the ground, our noses never exposed to Essence of Tokyo. It was the Bossman, Fukuyama-san; two salarymen, Omura-san and Yamada-san; and I, the guest of honor, Gaijin-san. We passed from the climate-controlled office, to the climate-controlled Mercedes in the subterranean garage, to the climate-controlled beach house.

We approached the compound, and the electronic gate admitted the Mercedes to the grounds. We approached the house, and the electronic garage door admitted the Mercedes to its carpeted space in the mothership. The house cast a shadow over its neighbors, resembling nothing more than the home version of one of those Marriott hotels, a self-contained space station with too much lobby and too much glitz.

After a futile damage control effort in the rocket room, I sidestepped back to the table, quickly took my seat, and continued with the sushi, hoping I wasn't making a wet spot on the chair. I complimented Fukuyama-san and his wife on their toilet, their good taste, and their beautiful home, which featured, among other things, a vaulted ceiling reminiscent of the Mormon Tabernacle, a miniature Roman fountain spouting orange Kool-Aid, and a stand of plastic Miami Beach palm trees. Lost in space in the Oiso Marriott.

When we could eat no more, Fukuyama-san led us to the squash court, which now doubled as the home karaoke bar; Noriko-san and I had played squash there before dinner. Noriko-san was a supporting actress in this production. She was an office lady in the company who had been invited to take the train from Tokyo to join us: she was intended to be good company, a pretty face, a pourer of drinks. Noriko-san was a game squash player, too.

Now, we all sat in the upper deck, the spectator lounge above the squash court, and watched as the arena became an electronic home entertainment center. The opposite wall became the screen, and the side bar next to us revealed the laser disk library. Fukuyama-san produced a leather-bound menu of karaoke selections and circulated it among our group.

As the book of selections made the rounds, Fukuyama-san inserted a laser disk into the player, and a life-sized pinball game lit up the opposite wall. A string of beach balls waited in the lower right-hand corner of the animated scene to be launched into play. Fukuyama-san handed me the remote, and I sent the first beach ball into the action on the beach. A lifeguard flexed his muscle and batted the ball down the wall; a reclining bathing beauty with one leg crossed over the other lifted her foot and kicked the ball back up the wall to the lifeguard. Lifeguard, in turn, muscled the ball back down the wall and off of the head of a toddler playing in the sand at the surf's edge.

Noriko-san applauded and handed me a Bud. This space bar was stocked with the best, Kirin, Asahi, etc., but Fukuyama-san sent me a Bud because it was an expensive import and because it was the beer of cowboys. One hand on the Bud, one hand on the remote. The beach ball sailed into the middle of a volleyball game, and one of the jocks spiked it back to the bathing beauty. Miskick. Bathing Beauty sent the ball sliding down the wall into the ocean and the waiting mouth of Jaws. Game over. Then it was time to sing.

Fukuyama-san told Yamada-san to go first. Yamada-san made his choice from the leather-bound menu and Fukuyama-san put on the disk. It was a sad, moody song of lost love. We saw a beautiful young woman in reverie standing on a cliff and watching the surf below her. Before long the picture faded into a soft-porn make-out scene as the nymphette relived her love affair. All the while, the Japanese lyrics paraded across the bottom of the screen. Yamada-san sang into the microphone loudly and passionately and got high approval ratings from the crowd. Then it was Noriko-san's turn.

Noriko-san lit into a rock song, the visual accompaniment a bootlegged MTV rock video with seemingly no connection to the Japanese lyrics. Everyone applauded enthusiastically. Noriko-san said I should sing with her, and I calculated the risk of offending my hosts by declining or exposing my rocket-seat-stained pants by accepting. I decided I should risk it.

The squash court wall gave a panoramic view of New York as the full-orchestra anthem echoed from corner to corner in the pit below. Despite all of those trips to Yankee Stadium, I realized I still didn't know the words, and the Japanese characters flashing on the skyline did not help me. "…*hmmm hmm hmm…be there in the city that never sleeps, NEW YORK, NEW YORK…*" Then it hit me that, since no one else knew the lyrics either, I could sing anything at all. At that moment, I became a star; Noriko-san settled into the role of back-up singer. Las Vegas lounge lizards had nothing on me. Wild applause. Encore.

Fukuyama-san handed me the book and pointed to a page with a special section of English selections. I surveyed my options and narrowed it down to *Blue Hawaii, Rudolph the Rednosed Reindeer* and *Tallahatchie Bridge*. Finally I went for *Rudolph*, a good choice for any occasion, and the story played out on the squash court wall with an animated Santa, sleigh, and team of reindeer. As Santa and the crew flew through the night sky, Rudolph's red nose became the bouncing ball that we followed through the lyrics. More wild applause. I took advantage of my success to announce my retirement and passed the mike on to Omura-san.

We had many more lost-love, soft-porn, make-out sing-alongs until everyone had sung again and the supply of Bud was exhausted. Then Fukuyama-san called it quits, and Yamada-san, Omura-san, and I sweated in the sauna in the basement before retiring to our assigned rooms in the upper floors of the Oiso Marriott.

I was pulled out of sleep by an overwhelming need to escape the space station and re-enter earth's orbit. I got into my running gear and let myself out of the back gate and into a walled alley that deadended at the freeway. I ran along the narrow path beside traffic, down a ramp, and into a damp tunnel under the roadway.

When I came out into the light, I was on the beach. I ran up the strip of empty brown sand with the black ocean on my right and the grey highway on my left. The morning was not quite sunny. I approached the beach house standing tall above the freeway, its glass facade shining transparently. As I passed, I tipped my Yankee's cap at the four figures standing in rank order, noses pressed against the window, hands waving in unison at the man who fell to earth.

THE ACCIDENTAL RE-APPEARANCE

The whole art of poetry reduces itself to this, that anyone who wishes to excel as a poet must unlearn all his native language and return to the pristine beggary of words; by this necessity he will express the feelings of his mind by means of the most obvious and easily perceived aspects of things; he will, by the aid of the senses and the imagination, paint the most striking and lovely images of things, manners and feelings...
—Giovanni Battista Vico, 1668–1744

The following is an essay written by Yasuko Miyamoto, a 20-year old Japanese college student. Yasuko is a lower-level English student. The assignment for which this essay was written was quite simple—"Write a short essay about your weekend."

CLARK LUNBERRY

Recently I am saying, "You are losing heart, don't you?" or "You are losing the brilliancy eyes, don't you?" Talking with my friends, eating the lunch, attending the lectures on, too!!

The present day I am the cast-off skin of human being: there is the soul and not energy. I know the reason why I change into like this thought.

In spite of my became college student, I am taken "ill of dullness of study." The ill is not related to the result, but is related to my posture against study of English literature.

I think I am not attending lectures that have only to get credits for it and I am studying English very hard. But the truth is not studying. I have a difference of speaking and doing. Then I thought. Surely this words is like the word that explain me that made for me. I startled this phrase. When I heard the result of an entrance examination, I noticed the fact that clearly say at that time.

If that regular business of that company don't give me this words, I will have graduated from college without noticing such a thing.

I think I try to reconsider my thought!

I want it to be clear that I am not suggesting that Yasuko's essay in any way approaches the levels of brilliance found in Mallarmé or that it shares any specific stylistic devices. The connections and affinities between the two exist in another realm.

Mallarmé was a supremely self-conscious artist, intensely aware of history and tradition, in command of his language and capable of achieving extraordinary results by employing the language in conventional and unconventional ways. By the time he wrote "A Throw of the Dice" in 1897, he was clearly striving to break through the boundaries of his inherited, tradition-laden language. What he desired to say could no longer be articulated through 19th-century methods of syntax, poetic structure, typography and grammar. Mallarmé's poetry was created through a knowing disregard of poetic conventions, a self-conscious fragmentation of syntax, a willed ignorance of inherited expectations.

Yasuko's essay is built upon parallel but reversed principles—an un-knowing disregard of poetic conventions, an *un*-self-conscious fragmentation, and an *un*-willed ignorance. In the process, Yasuko achieves, *by accident*, fascinating, strange and highly suggestive combinations of word, fragment and image.

Yasuko did not write a poem, but instead, and largely by chance, unconsciously created what I will call a kind of para-poetics. Not a sustained, unified and coherent poem, built upon a solid understanding of and reaction to poetic traditions and modern innovations, but rather an accident of language; poetic fragments that transcend Yasuko herself. Yasuko's English could scarcely have allowed her to be clearly aware of what she was writing. She must have felt herself that she was, in a sense, throwing the dice.

Her low-level grasp of the English language undoubtedly gave her *some* idea of what she was writing but she lacked the conventional grammar and syntactical skills to clearly articulate what she hoped to say. Her mind continues to operate in her native language—Japanese—dominated by the culture and language of which she is a part. Thinking in Japanese and writing in English, she transfers ideas formed in her native language into an alien one—a direct transference that does not take into account the cultural and historical grounding of language, naively assuming that words *mean* what the dictionary says. This alien imposition implies a kind of linguistic warfare as the student struggles to make room for alternative forms of expression found in the new language ... a foreign agent scratching up against the mother tongue.

A metaphor in Japanese transferred quite literally into English will often seem meaningless—or rather, imbued with a meaning at variance with the original Japanese thought. Some possible examples of this are Yasuko's use of "brilliancy eyes" of which she may have been thinking of the Japanese "me no kaga yaki"; or "the cast-off skin of human being" from the Japanese "dape nuke gara"; or "I have a difference of speaking and doing" from "gendo no fuichi"; or "I am taken ill of dullness of study" from "gogatsu byo...."

Yasuko's intentions and the way her mind conceived of what was written are certainly beyond our comprehension or elaboration. However, all of the expressions mentioned above are quite familiar in Japanese and it seems likely that she was trying to squeeze them into English.

Regardless of Yasuko's awkwardness, it is fascinating how the transferred, "translated" metaphor maintains meaning ... *a* meaning ... however ambiguous and imprecise. The individual words are still clearly recognizable, possessing associations in the native speaker's mind that the non-native writer could not have anticipated. Combinations of words are brought together forming fragments, shards of language which create bizarre, jarring images—images that the mind is not prepared to receive and comprehend. An example of this is Yasuko's line: "Then I thought. Surely this words is like the word that explain me that made for me" or "I noticed the fact that clearly say at that time." The native speaker follows the line of words. The correct spelling and careful punctuation provide the illusion of familiarity, but a comprehensible "meaning" is not allowed to settle on to these jagged fragments. Each word in isolation is understood, the combinations at times are clear, but as sentences and paragraphs the English tentatively suggests far more than it gives.

Another point of disturbance and uncertainty for the native reader of Yasuko's essay involves the strange, indeterminate rhythms which emerge while reading the written lines. How does the reader pace the lines, where is the stress, where is the focus and emphasis? In the absence of a clear and readable rhythm, the mind cannot flow smoothly over the words but must hesitate before each one, momentarily wondering how to proceed. Like a composition of atonal music, each word is heard in isolation...a familiar rhythm, a memorable melody, though suggested, is denied. Our linguistic habits, habits which dissolve words into concepts, are stymied leaving each letter clearly on the page...the blinded eye temporarily restored to vision.

The persistence of meaning within error, ambiguity and readerly confusion suggests that the power and freshness in this student's paper has less to do with Yasuko and her creative, expressive intentions than they do with the structure and power of language necessarily existing prior to any speaker. Jean-Jacques Lecercle, in a fascinating essay entitled "Postmodernism and Language," elaborates on this idea of language preceding the speaker, alluding to the Heidegerrian concept that "*Language* speaks." "One does not speak language as one uses a tool," Lecercle writes, "rather, one is spoken by it: language is a social practice and not an individual faculty...There is no master of language. Its speakers are only travelers along the pathways that have emerged in the course of what is a collective and organically developing phenomenon...Language is not a timeless synchronic structure. It is historical through and through, a treasury of words, phrases and temporary rules...all sedimented within language...On the one hand, language is so powerful that it determines all meaning, making the speaker or writer a mere linguistic puppet...On the other hand, language may be seen as talking to us and offering us the freedom to explore innumerable paths..."*

Yasuko's essay possesses rich associations even in the absence of a self-conscious, well-trained, confident user. It 'talks to us' through its fragments, errors and disjunction. To speak, it does not necessarily require complete sentences, correct grammar or conventional. As Lecercle points out later on in his essay, "Language is more plastic than the rules of grammar allow." Like an airplane set on automatic pilot, language itself flies along. Whether or not a competent, knowledgeable person is seated behind the steering wheel, the flight proceeds. Granted, the airplane cannot go far and it may very well crash and break up into a thousand pieces, but in the process, movement is made, utterance recorded.

*Lecercle, Jean-Jacques. *Postmodernism and Society.* Eds. Roy Boyne and Ali Rattainsi. London: MacMillan, 1990.

PAT NOLAN

Enclosed a selection of haikai no renga (renku). Keith Abbott and I have been linking verse for quite a few years now and we roped Mike Sowl, an old friend from our Monterey days, into joining us about six years ago. It was about that time that we got serious and looked up the rules of prosody for this peculiar form. Our reference is Early Miner's *Japanese Linked Poetry* as well as his *The Monkey's Straw Raincoat*. Doubling the stanzas inhibits the tendency to read through the renku as if it were a single unit. In our case it is thirty-six separate units brought together as a plotless lyric narrative. Linked verse can have as many as a hundred linked stanzas (some have gone to a thousand) but we tend to go for the 36 stanzas—it's less complicated and was the length of Basho's renga. The rules for composing linked verse are incredibly complex, foreign, maybe even simplistic to anyone schooled in the rules of Western prosody. Two stanzas in a row can "link" but not three so that there is always a change of vector or inclination as the links progress. The poets link with the previous stanza either by allusion, pun, tenor, or suggested relation, and the link can either be "close" or "distant." The judicious use of these factors among many others determines the warp and woof of the final tapestry. There are also three designated moon stanzas and two flower stanzas that appear at predesignated spots. There are so many rules and nuances to these rules that we don't bother with too many. The three-line stanzas are supposed to be 17 syllables and the two-line ones are supposed to be 14 syllables, but since the masters of the form didn't always follow this count we certainly didn't feel held to it either. There are also two broad classifications as far as subject matter is concerned: seasonal and miscellaneous. The idea is to start with a seasonal bent (spring and autumn being the preferred seasons) and then lard in the miscellaneous verses throughout the body of the poem, and then ending once again on a seasonal footing. As you will no doubt see in the enclosed renku, we followed the rules when it was convenient and/or when we remembered. Some people are very finicky (anal) about following the rules, but what we've tried to do is synthesize the form to fit our own particular "modern" esthetic to allow for the max in spontaneity and creativity while still working within the basic structure of renku and not forgetting that we are in the 20th century after all. At any rate, Maureen Owen and I did one together and then she joined us (the Totem Pole School) on "No Hat". The idea of a guest hokku (the lead stanza) as in "No Hat" is Keith's innovation; it is a place of honor and usually reserved for the renku master, and of course that's Kerouac's haiku. The traditional setting for renku composition is on straw mats gathered around the hibachi and knocking back warm rice wine and it usually takes place over the course of a couple of hours with the renku master correcting links or even deeming them inappropriate. Our chain mail approach is not so demanding and if there's any correction, it's usually self correction. And of course they're composed over months rather than hours. I think the bottom line on renga is the relation between stanzas, not so much the focus on any particular stanza, and which gives it that unique disparate unity—a lot like the modern novel in some ways. The "Japanese" idea of relations and harmony opens up a whole new realm of classification upon which to base our rationalism. Well, I'm obviously overstating the obvious. If any of this piques your interest in haikai no renga, the Miner book is quite thorough if not a tad academic: *Japanese Linked Poetry*, Princeton U. Press, 1979. Keith and I (I think) are the only ones out of the Totem Pole School who have read both tomes on renga and tried to make any sense out of the prosody, and that may have hindered (constipated) us to some degree—Mike and Maureen seem to do perfectly fine winging it.

NO HAT RENKU

guest hokku: Jack Kerouac
renku master: Keith Abbott
renku poets: Pat Nolan, Maureen Owen, Michael Sowl
late winter/early fall, 1991

All day long
wearing a hat
   that wasn't on my head

   all day long
wearing a hat
   that wasn't on my head
her foot on the running board
"you sure look good in a truck"

her foot on the running board
"you sure look good in a truck"
   below zero out
neighbor's pickup protesting
   battery gone dead

   below zero out
neighbor's pickup protesting
   battery gone dead
cacti shoulders pop apart
icy cut-outs catch the light

cacti shoulders pop apart
icy cut-outs catch the light
   woke up only once
Sierra Nevada snow
   in my shining cup

   woke up only once
Sierra Nevada snow
   in my shining cup
steam rising a thousand feet
Superior burns to ice

steam rising a thousand feet
Superior burns to ice
   windows wet inside
I let the water boil away
   no tea for me

   windows wet inside
I let the water boil away
   no tea for me

socks hot out of the dryer
a long war   now a ground war

socks hot out of the dryer
a long war now a ground war
   what she thought was
a mourning woman a Soto monk
   weeding the lawn

   what she thought was
a mourning woman a Soto monk
   weeding the lawn
parka'd against the west wind
kneeling on ice three feet thick

parka'd against the west wind
kneeling on ice three feet thick
   kerosene kindling!
in front of a ball of fire
   they left the ice house

   kerosene kindling!
in front of a ball of fire
   they left the ice house
insistent sea bird's whistle
a break in the bad weather

insistent sea bird's whistle
a break in the bad weather
   a few leftover cabbage leaves
add color to
   the cleared garden plot

   a few leftover cabbage leaves
add color to
   the cleared garden plot
bright moon and the aurora—
first bouquet for our new Spring

bright moon and the aurora—
first bouquet for our new Spring
   sweep off the stone path
beams yellow as daffodils
   coming to visit

   sweep off the stone path
beams yellow as daffodils
   coming to visit
irritating dream woke me late
cobwebs won't brush away

irritating dream woke me late
cobwebs won't brush away
   neighbor hanging out
early morning wash don't step
   on the violets!

   neighbor hanging out
early morning wash don't step
   on the violets!
what old Albert saw that he
decided not to tell us

what old Albert saw that he
decided not to tell us
   bugs enjoy days like this
heat and the odor
   rising off tall dry grass

   bugs enjoy days like this
heat and the odor
   rising off tall dry grass
the right tool is broken and
it's time for lunch anyway

the right tool is broken and
it's time for lunch anyway
   staining Charlie's deck
"Hmm ... 'bout five gallons of
   stain,
   five cases of beer"

   staining Charlie's deck
"Hmm ... 'bout five gallons of
   stain,
   five cases of beer"
hurry to the corner store
pick the lottery numbers

hurry to the corner store
pick the lottery numbers
   green checkered lawn
birds play a game of chess
   tossing mulberries

   green checkered lawn
birds play a game of chess
   tossing mulberries
no lights in the nursing home
TV flickers across empty chairs

no lights in the nursing home
TV flickers across empty chairs
   unopened 12-pak
sits in the fridge three weeks now
   where's my thirsty friends

   unopened 12-pak
sits in the fridge three weeks now
   Where's my thirsty friends
only the sound of the screens
ricocheting off bug feet

only the sound of the screens
ricocheting off bug feet
   long into the wee hours
"I already answered that question!"
   —heat lightning

   long into the wee hours
"I already answered that question!"
   —heat lightning
—unfaithful—bored—she tries
lying even to her housemaid

unfaithful—bored—she tries
lying even to her housemaid
   almond sliver moon
what a grating tone it has
   the old cat's meow

almond sliver moon
what a grating tone it has
   the old cat's meow
in dark nights he remembers
a day of blue dragonflies

in dark nights he remembers
a day of blue dragonflies
   sweater full of holes
a chill creeps up the sleeve
   where laughter used to go

   sweater full of holes
a chill creeps up the sleeve
   where laughter used to go
ah, nothing like breathing your last
to put new life in you

ah, nothing like breathing your last
to put new life in you
   her dog leash a toaster cord
crazy lifts her skirt
   a big red flea bite

   her dog leash a toaster cord
crazy lifts her skirt
   a big red flea bit
I tripped on a crown of thorns
as I was crossing the yard

I tripped on a crown of thorns
as I was crossing the yard
   flag up bounding leap
a doe now there/not there gone
   vibrant empty space

   flag up bounding leap
a doe now there/not there gone
   vibrant empty space
now all that's missing's
a flowering plum stick in a vase

JAPANESE FOR TRAVELERS

Collage poem from the Berlitz Book of
Japanese for Travelers

THE ARRIVAL
Greetings!
Good afternoon!
Good morning!
See you later.

I'm very pleased to meet you
Do you speak Italian?
Can you lend me a chambermaid?

CUSTOMS
I have nothing to declare
I have 4000 cigarettes
a bottle of wine
and an exploding samurai sword.

These are not my hostages.
They are only for my
personal use.

SETTLING IN
Please turn on the ranpu
That's the raijo
Does your terebi have kara?
No, I was never in Iowa or Ohio

Please knock up the ceiling
if you can bring a chambermaid
on a stand.

TABLE TALK
Good evening
I'd like a table for three.
A table in the corner
    by the window
    outside on the terrace
    in the washroom
    behind the stage,
404   preferably

Wild boar ketchup
will be exquisite.
How big is the fishnet soup?
Is it safe for swimming?
Yes, we each have our own
        roboo.

I would also please
like a ticket to
Chicago, St. Louis, and
        Moncton.

Where is the water table?
It must have at least
three legs.
Haven't you anything cheaper?

We will need some ski equipment
with a hot air mattress
and a handful of mercenaries.

TRAVELING
Where is the radio station?

Please get me a helicopter, fast
or a bicycle, as well!

Is this the main point of Interest?
Can you recommend a toilet
with reinforced support beams?
Do you have anything larger?
Are tidal waves frequent here?
Who is the Samurai in the
        roboo?
I don't speak much Japanese.

I don't want any cream.
The chambermaid has just
        surfaced.

PRESIDENT PROFFERS POST-PRANDIAL PUKING TO PRIME MINISTER

D. R. BLUMEN

TOKYO—At a state dinner honoring the President and the first lady, there was a brief moment for concern when the President appeared to lose consciousness and slump into the lap of Prime Minister Kiichi Miyazawa of Japan, instantly creating a poetry so rich as to astound the poetic community world-wide.

"GOTTA HURL!"—The President murmured almost incoherently as he coughed cuisine, chunky-style, in the lap of the Prime Minister. Mrs. Bush, who rushed to her husband's side, ostensibly to lend aid, was heard to say afterwards, "I thought they were just having sex."

RIVALRY—Also with the President were the Secret Service, who denied reports of it being a situation. "It was an incident. We are taking every precaution to see that it does not become an occurrence," an unidentified agent said. "The President is always trying to outdo his former boss. Mr. Reagan merely fell asleep in front of the Pope."

REACTION—"Life is a metaphor," Prime Minister Miyazawa reflected. Other reactions have been diverse. "What are the odds of something like that happening?" asked a surprised Jimmy the Greek. "Who knew?" says Letitia Baldridge, etiquette consultant to the White House. "It's square one," she said of her edacious employer.

IRONY—In an earlier conversation with Prime Minister Miyazawa, Mrs. Bush asked, "I simply LOVE your dinner tux. Is it new?"

LUCID MOMENT—Vice President Dan Quayle stated that he and the President often discussed Japan in relation to bodily functions. He said, "Mr. Bush often said Japan's economic trade policies made him want to vomit. I guess he felt the time was right."

SENSE OF HUMOR—As the President recovered and was being assisted to his feet, he waved to the state gathering, exclaiming, "It's a little late, folks, so, goodnight!" He was taken directly to his hotel where he remarked to a member of the entourage, "From now on, I'm sticking to good old American values I understand. Steak and potato, yes. Sushi, no."

EVALUATION—Caribbean poet Derek Walcott observed, "Nothing is beyond poetry. Men do this to each other. That is what's important."

405

When Stuart makes biltong, he takes raw steaks and rubs them with salt and saltpeter and hangs them in a dryer improvised from a plastic table and a screen. There is a fan blowing on the meat at all times. The steaks get smaller and smaller as the weeks go by. The breeze and the saltpeter preserve them. When the steaks shrink to the size of hamburgers they are sliced and eaten. The slices look like blood red marble. I have walked into Stuart's kitchen and seen all counter space occupied by large steaks waiting to be biltonged. You are familiar with the drooping watches in *The Persistence of Memory*? The unexpectedly large and unrefrigerated steaks evoke this painting by Dali. The biltong is the idea of Stuart's South African girlfriend, Peta. Peta says that there is antelope and even elephant biltong. I make jokes about sneaker biltong, holding up Stuart's shoe by its lace. Much to Peta's lack of amusement, I hang a ring of keys and a plastic skull between the steaks. When Peta describes antelope and elephant biltong, she opens my Pandora's box. I think that everything is biltong. What the Grecian urn was for Keats the biltong is for me. I imagine the planet Mars big and wet. Bang! It is knocked from its orbit. The salt and the saltpeter rain down. The watery planet is slowly desiccated. It's up there in the sky, but what for? Biltonged. On earth there are dinosaurs, undulating dinosaurs, so liquid sensuous in their very bigness. They soak in lakes, unaware of what they are marinating themselves for. Bang! comes the meteor, throwing dinosaurs up into the trees. The small ones hang by their necks—and dry like biltong. The Egyptians biltong themselves, confusing God with beef jerky. Cats, birds and vegetables are biltonged with them. Pontius Pilate tried to have Jesus biltonged. It didn't work. Closer to home, the Great Salt Lake slowly desiccates a state capital. Across the face of the earth, salt and saltpeter rain down. We swim in the hotel pool. Marinating ourselves for what? I don't want to be the capital of Utah. I have a freshwater lake inside me, and I like it that way. Stuart and Peta tell me I must try the biltong or I cannot make another biltong joke. But I do not want to eat a metaphor. The biltong makes me sad. As they dry, the steaks cry salty moisture beads. Even the parts of an animal can have a sense of loss. Since I have sought to understand biltong, I cannot bear the sight of hay, as hay is biltonged meadow. How am I to eat the biltonged cow? The biltong is put into my hand. I take a bite and it tastes like beef which has imploded. It is like eating a black hole. I drink a whole pitcher of water to flush the taste from my mouth. I will not taste any more of this substance till the grim reaper runs after me with his biltong hook. I will hold on to what moisture I have.

LU LI & WENG LI TRANSLATED

LEN U. DARIEN

We are delighted to introduce an extraordinary discovery to our readers: the recently found and translated Chinese poets Weng Li and Lu Li. The story of how these poems were found has already created a great deal of excitement in China. Nothing was known of these poets from the Mongol Century (1279–1368) until a recently discovered archive was made available to scholars. Not much is known now beyond what they tell us in their poems. But they tell us so much! Weng Li was a warrior, Lu Li was a courtesan. They were either brother and sister or lovers or, perhaps, both. They wrote poems for each other without any certainty that the other would ever read them. In fact, these poems are so intimate, so shatteringly honest, one imagines that their authors wrote them entirely without hope of an audience. After the manuscript—carefully bound together as if someone was preparing it for publication—was found in 1989, two more years passed before a Chinese edition by Wang Shih appeared. The first translation in the West was into Portuguese by Dr. Alberto S. Figueroa, a scholar from the University of Lisbon. This superb translation into English by Len U. Darien is from both the Chinese and the Portuguese. This is the first publication in English of Weng Li and Lu Li, two poets who speak across the ages clearer than most of us speak across the room.
    —Exquisite Corpse

LU LI

Lying on my back
the emperor's astrologer on top of
    me
I thought of the stars
years ago they foretold this
they could not tell that their
    astrologer's labors were in
    vain
even the stars have no say
in who works for them

≈

The emperor's waiting rooms
reek of perfumes
I can tell who has visited here
for many years
their scents are stacked like paper
in the imperial library

they were all greedy and fearful
I like the market better
the sweat of humans and horses
fears no one there

≈

All their days and nights
my friends count things
how many robes they have
how many rings the courtiers wear
how many fields the fat merchants
    have
how many cows and horses they
    can see
from their windows
their minds must be an abacus
an unseen hand moves the
    beads

407

until one day they die
we all die one day
there is only one on that one day

≈

Li Chen's silk worms work day
        and night
he has thousands of trees in many
        valleys
travelers sometimes stumble there
are woven into his cocoons
my new robe has two lovers on it
hand in hand one night they
        wandered
foolishly into Li Chen's fields

≈

one of the emperor's dwarfs
parted my robe
kissed the crease under the fold
when warriors dismount
they are all this short
I can't wait until Weng returns

≈

today we had games
in the purple chamber
two rows of ten little feet
made a bed
for the emperor
mine were the collar
around his neck

≈

I saw some writing
in a stream
I couldn't read
what it said
it said Lu Li
Lu Li Lu Li
there is a gray hair
among your black ones
    it said that
        I couldn't read it

408

≈

no one came for me today
all the windows were shuttered
the emperor's son lay ill
the bad wind from the north
brought news from the war
Weng Li is there
on his horse riding
against the wind

≈

I did not feel like being dressed
        today
I sent away my maid
I made a hill of my clothes
in the middle of the floor
the wind rattled the shutters
all day
I am no one without my clothes
I could have stayed like that
        forever
In the evening a messenger came
I stepped into my clothes
and was Lu Li again

≈

ten red beans
ten white beans
a black stone
ten times in a day
I move them
no one else
can play my game
the cook surprised me
one of them I said
will make a meal
for the whole palace
she smiled knowingly
her hair is white

≈

the cobra in the jade pot
was our dinner

our appetites differ

In autumn
the vulgar tongue
tastes my egg
secretly

≈

he had so much flesh
it took three days to unravel
his wide belt
he was the emperor's treasurer
the empire was in his belly
even the moon did not rise
that night

≈

it is always dark
in the winter
it is always winter
in the palace chamber
once the sky
was my window

≈

The sweet smelling one
left at dawn
a rainy day
he is going to translate
indian poetry
for our emperor
whose mind is far away from war
my beloved Weng Li
makes war far away

≈

The moon is no joke
to a bald woman
In winter
her feet burn

≈

A half a man
goes by my window

his manly parts
are twice-hidden

≈

My friend's jade comb
looks better in my hair
the man who gave it to her
sleeps better on my pillow

≈

I lie down for a moment
clouds pass
summer is beginning
I think I will visit
my parents
in the country

≈

An egg yolk in the pan
the sun in the sky
a goldfish in the pond
the gods made many round things
to make Lu Li laugh

≈

Magical ducks lay gold eggs
in places no one can find them
I find them
but I paint them black
like swans' eggs
I do not want my neighbors
to know that I'm rich

≈

In the tree by my window
birds often lay each others' eggs
in each others' nests
I sometimes leave pretty
         underthings
in strange houses

≈

They called her
The Queen of Heaven

409

she was the charwoman's
daughter
I for one never doubted it

≈

The man a woman bathes
becomes her egg

≈

In the pockets
of her pantaloons
she carried eggs home
from the market

≈

Foreigners
find her in her tub

≈

The eyes of men
are hen's eggs
when they look at my breasts
they hatch fantasies

≈

the rice wine was sweet last night
today I do not dare to open my
mouth
for fear a foul wind
made of all the words I
thoughtlessly spoke
will blow out of it
they are still laughing at the palace

WENG LI

The village henchman
poisoned the well
threw himself in it
for good measure
everyone else fled
we set fire to the empty sheds
we were thirsty for water
not for blood
that night I heard
laughter from the well
next day we rode far

≈

The snow fell all night
when I stepped out of my tent
the beards of old men
had wrapped everything
wisdom has come to us I thought
I heard a white mound groan
and another grunt
and one farted loudly
the snow is kind
but wisdom is far away

≈

The crows read my writing
in the snow
soldiers write in the snow
for crows
the crows take our messages
to the cities
to make the merchants tremble
they gather in fear behind their
walls
soldiers are pissing just outside our
walls
they say and tremble and wait

≈

The barbarian sang before we
killed him
he was too weak to work
but he had a melodious voice
his stories were about spirits
he was already home among them

≈

it might as well be said
hun and sen live together
like man and wife
and they quarrel the same
today hun cut the gold tassel
on sen's saddle
he bawled so much the enemy
came to spy on us from the hill
they thought our prince died

≈

on a lone tree in a clearing
autumn left an apple
it is wrinkled and stubborn
an old whore's behind
everyone wants to eat it
no one wants the others to see him
the emperor's best men
are afraid of an apple
the shame will make us kill
more people will die tomorrow

≈

there was no one to greet us on the
    street
the houses were on fire
we torched them all
a stubborn old man
sat on an ancient stump
in front of his blazing pig sty
singing a song to himself
I tipped my lance to him
he did not see me

≈

Sometimes there are three of me
one walks in monk's garb
alongside my horse
the other follows
with bent head
behind
he will be the one
to see me depart this world

each one of me lives in his own
    season
the dark-hooded one who follows
lives in the heart of winter

≈

peace was concluded
yesterday between my lord
and our enemies
but today we rode into battle
to fight for ourselves
I held high the head
of a soldier I killed
no one knows why

≈

Lu Li my beloved
sits on a cloud of incense
pleasing the emperor's
translator
this news has clouded my mind
I hit my horse hard
he looked at me without
    understanding

≈

The headman presented our lord
with two jade lovers
we passed them from hand to
    hand
each man thought of his loved one
when the figures were returned
the jade was dark
the lovers were many

≈

tonight our cook
found only a little dog
the broth was thin
the star in the sky
some call "the dog"
filled our empty bowls

≈

411

Treason was twice punished today
the foot soldier was torn to pieces
tied to four horses
the noble was halved by sword
from the hills the enemy watched
tomorrow we meet in the field
I whiled the night drinking silently
with my lord

≈

Some of my fellows believe
that a man and his horse
go to heaven together
but why ride there
when you are lighter
than sunlight
we will ride alongside
each other there
horse and men mere friends

≈

In the purse
I cut from around his neck
were three gold coins
bearing the script
of another empire
a lock of black hair
and a small plain stone
the hair was the same shade
as Lu Li's
the stone was like the many stones
I skipped on the Yantze River
when I was a boy
for a moment
I thought the strange soldier
was myself
he was not
he was dead

≈

They tell a story
about a country
  where no one could read
        a monk could live there

unafraid that one day
they will see
what he wrote of them

≈

My master thought poetry
was for the idle
I have been wearing armor
these many years
I think he was wrong

≈

The smell of burning
villages
is not poetry
the smoke on the empty
autumn sky
writes something there
it is not poetry either

≈

My head hurts
the armies haven't done this
the emperor's service
does not require this pain
I will march against myself
when I am better

≈

The philosophers argue
about how the world was made
some say the planets made us
others say gods did
I take no part in their discussions
I watch a young boy watch a
        young girl
the grass whispers after they pass

≈

Seven times in one year
I have written Lu Li
not once did she answer
seven times she read
every letter
she knows them by heart

≈

By the side of the road
to Nanking
a monk so fat
three boys had to hold him upright
the dust of my horse's hooves
made a cloud of them
what stories were they telling?

≈

When I was a boy
in our village
was a fountain
a demon lived in it
one time I saw him
he was eating a leaf
war is coming
my father said
I am that demon

≈

My fellow soldiers
have their way
with frightened girls
in burning villages
I do not play their games
I think of Lu Li

≈

I have served under seven lords
some were generous with their gold

I like my horse best of all
We have ridden so far from home
he sometimes looks at me
I know that he remembers

≈

I have no use
for the village I conquered
for my lord
the big house in the middle
of the town
looks at me
through the eyes of a young girl

≈

When I am killed
my fellow soldiers
will find my poetry
under my saddle
they will laugh
they will say
all this time
we thought he was like us

≈

I have killed another boy
flying the pennant of my enemy
I think about Lu Li
in the faroff city
she would have liked him

PETER'S CHINESE SYNTAX

Tornado.
We're fucked.

HOWARD MCCORD

In the spring of 1955 took a course in Mexican Folklore with Soledad Perez at Texas Western College. I was interested in the Tarahumara, and decided to do a paper on their uses of peyote. The Tarahumara called the cactus "Tio Hikuri" and ascribed great magical powers to it. They did not have as elaborate a peyote cult as did the Huicholes to the south, but it was the most important drug in their pharmacopeia and was used to treat everything from tuberculosis, prostate disease, to rheumatism and palpitations. In researching the names for peyote in Thord-Grey's dictionary of the language, I found that several different cacti were judged by them to be brothers of Tio Hikuri. I was interested in finding more out about these brothers. Peyote was easily available in the *hierbarías* of Ciudad Juárez, and I had talked with the local Mexican herbalists of the lore associated with it. But they did not seem to know much of the brothers. So I decided to travel into Tarahumara county on the eastern slope of the Sierra Madre about a hundred miles west of Chihuahua.

In those days there wasn't much trouble in getting a permit for a pistol and a rifle in Mexico, though the .45 ACP was prohibited because it was the military caliber. That's why the .38 Super had such a following south of the border. Same old familiar 1911 Colt, but a civilian caliber. That it shot flat and hard was also appreciated. I stuck some water bottles, food, and wandering gear in my VW, and the 1911 in a Sam Myers holster and headed south to Chihuahua, then west toward the Sierra Madre. In those days the pavement petered out rather quickly, and the dirt roads weren't any worse than terrible. Late in the afternoon, the foothills of the Sierras looming large in the west, I figured I had bounced enough for one day. I pulled off the road and guided the Bug slowly through the mesquite until the car was well hidden from the road, maybe a quarter of a mile. I don't need much space to camp—just a spot for a sleeping bag beside the car. I heat water on a Primus stove, and forego a campfire. Don't like the mess, or the trace.

Peyote is a ground-hugging cactus, maybe three inches across the crown, and rising up no more than an inch or two. The brothers were similar. All of them grew in the rocky soil of the low foothills and the immediately adjacent desert. I was just about where I could expect to start seeing them. My legs needed a stretch after a day in the car, so I scouted the area for an hour or so, chewing on some beef jerky I'd brought, and keeping my eyes open. I followed an arroyo a ways, then climbed out of it up a low rise. I could see a few miles back to the east from there. Not a rancho, not a windmill anywhere. Just a lot of Chihuahua. There were, as in most deserts, far more plants than your average New Yorker would expect, and I wished I were a better botanist. I had done a little flower gathering in Laos and Burma the year before, and could name a few rhododendron and slipper orchids, but small, undramatic cacti tended to blur together in my mind, and it was going to take some work to get whatever I found identified, though Dr. Berkman had said he'd help when I got stuck. I also wanted to get the Tarahumara names for the ones I found, and hoped the Padre at the Mission could get me a "native informant." I'd watched Ben work with plenty of those in Burma, and sometimes thought he'd get as much information just by guessing. It was weird work.

The sun was starting to hit the edge of the Sierra, and I turned back, chewing the last of the jerky. By the time I got to the car, the sunset was rich as a volcano, and I had three specimens to mull over and check against the pictures in the cactus book, Britton and Rose, 1920, which still remains an authority. In the twilight, the country softened, and a little draft of cool wind breathed down the slopes of the Sierras. They were there, growing black. Seven hundred and fifty miles north to south, and 150 miles across, and cutting deep into them, six barrancas, nearly as deep as the Grand Canyon, each with hundreds of miles of rim rock, tiered cliffs, and hidden globes. I had dreamed of wandering them someday, and still do. But they are wild and rough beyond imagining, and no one has ever known them all. As I tell this tale of nearly forty years ago, I cannot think I will ever visit them again.

I lit the Primus, made tea, heated a can of creamed corn for supper, and finished with a can of pears. Goatsuckers had darted in the dusk, followed by some bats just before dark. They were probably still up there, acrobatic predators, as silent to my ears as fish. In the desert around me, the night life began. A coyote howled, and a friend replied. Things would be out now, attending to the business of living. Far more things than in the day. The mouse sought the seed, the snake sought the mouse, the owl would eat either one. The last grizzlies in Mexico were somewhere in the Sierra, and would be happy to eat me, though a mule deer would be much preferred.

I lay on my army blanket much of the mild night, until 3 A.M., when a chill awoke me and I slid under half the blanket. The moon had risen, and cast its white-gray radiance so that a kind of lunar dust seemed to cover everything. The pistol was cold and hard under my leg, and I slipped it up on the blanket beside my waist. The coyote clan yipped happily and I wished them all a full belly by morning.

Breakfast was a strip of jerky, three flour tortillas from the dozen I had bought in Ciudad Chihuahua and a can of refritos with a few slivers of cheese. The jerky was from a mulie I had shot in the Sierra Diablo in November. I still had a roast and a bag of the jerky in the freezer back home, and tried to save it for my walks. I finished, cleaned up, took a canteen and an apple, locked the car, checked my pistol and started toward the Sierra. I planned to walk one of the slow rising out-reaches of the foothills for a few miles, cross to the next north, and make my way back, making a circuit of fifteen miles or so slowly enough to scan the ground for cactus possibilities. I had a day pack for specimens, and a hand trowel. Before I leave a campsite I always make a circle, and check for signs of anyone's approach. When I come back, I do the same, a little further out, and more carefully. I don't like surprises.

I saw no tracks, but saw a way I would approach on my return, by which I could approach my car without being easily seen by anyone waiting. This may seem paranoid to some readers, but there are places where my paltry possessions are a treasure, and back country Chihuahua was one of them. Out here a person didn't need to be much of a criminal for the idea of latching on to my stuff to strike as a real possibility. People like me were always getting lost and dying in the cruel desert. It was only natural. The long ridge rose slowly, and I ambled over it like one of those ants you've watched who are going somewhere particular, but have to examine everything of interest along the way, even if it means detours, circles, and backtracking. By noon I was up high enough to be moving out of mesquite and into juniper, and when I raised my head I could see piñon mixing in farther up, and then a few straggling pines, where the foothill started to be mountain. Down on the ground, where I kept my eyes, I watched for *Tio Hikuri*, and *Astrophyrum-capriconne* and *Ariocarpus furfuraceus*, my guess as the brothers, as the three are found in association, though all are very scarce. Lophophora williamsii was the first described by Lemaire in 1845, but it was not until the 1880's and the researches of Dr. L. Lewin, who isolated an alkaloid he called anhalonin, and the later work of Dr. Erwin E. Ewell that anything of its pharmacology was known. Lumholz wrote of it in his magnificent *Unknown Mexico*—still the best book on the Sierra Madre, published in 1902, over ninety years ago. That was a man I would have loved to travel with.

But this is not a story about peyote and the Tarahumara. It is a story which explains a poem, a sort of narrative footnote which will never be mentioned in the critical apparatus of my next anthology, should there be one. So I will leave cacti and ethnopharmacognosy behind except to say that somewhere in the archives of the Texas Folk-lore Society is a copy of my paper, "Species of Peyote Used by the Tarahumara," which won an honorable mention in the 1956 competition. It was my first academic honor. From the heights I had risen to, I could see dozens of miles into the east, out across the vast Chihuahua desert. I saw the thread of my road winding out of the east, then turning north along the flank of the Sierra a ways beyond my parking spot. No windmills, no ranchos. But this does not mean little *jacals*, shacks, each with a family and some stock, were not out there someplace. And at this moment I could be the object of a patient Tarahumara's musings higher up. I did not worry about the Tarahumara. Their favorite relaxation is to gather in groups, and drink *tesguine*, a corn beer, till they are wildly, stupidly, cosmically drunk. But they are not a predatory people, nor even a little aggressive when drunk. But the lowland mestizo had a different culture, one which included machismo, banditry, and an exposure to the good things in life money could buy. Most were kind and delightful souls—ordinary people, but there were a few who lived out the old Roman adage, *homo hominii lupus*. They were wolves to men, and respected others only as prey. I had met a few in my day. In Texas, in California, in Laos. And I'd meet others on the faculties of universities, doubtless destined for high administration.

The downhill slope was easy after I'd crossed the small canyon to the next ridge. I like ridge walking, but had learned enough to stay below the crest. You'd be surprised how far away you can spot a skylined dot. Just hang below, and occasionally cross over to the other side using some concealment, and see what's over there. You can't hunt mule deer or elk in mountains and not learn that. If you lack the woodcraft of a deer, you've got a better brain, so use it. Remember the different range of senses in creatures, too, and how the eye of a man who's looked for cattle in brush, or tracked deer notices things someone who is asphalt and sidewalk bound will never see. I paid attention to what I was doing, watched the ground for cacti, found a few, ate my apple, and eased down the ridge, enjoying the afternoon. The wind, a jay or two, some insect buzz, the crunch of my footsteps, and the rest was a lovely silence.

I was back at the car by five o'clock, and busied myself with supper. I had walked a lot on one apple. I opened a can of Dinty Moore stew—an old staple—and broke up a piece of jerky and added it. Helps the flavor. Made some tea and had a can of fruit cocktail for dessert. I cleaned up and got the gear all packed away before the first trace of sunset. The sky was just beginning to slip into alpenglow in the slanting rays, and I sat on my folded blanket, leaning against the bumper, as content as an old iguana on a warm rock before night falls. It was lizard time in the mindlessness of pure perception, and I think it was because I wasn't thinking, I was just sensing everything around me that I first smelled something new. I think I smelled them before I heard the soft, nearly inaudible footsteps. I smelled what I first thought was horseshit, though it turned out to be burroshit still moist on the backside of a burro with the runs. Then there was a tiny scent of human sweat. As my mind processed these odors my hand had slipped across my belly and loosened the Colt in its holster, and my thumb edged the safety down. I always carried in condition one—a round in the chamber, hammer cocked, and safety on. John Browning meant it to be carried that way. While I did this I rocked over on my left knee, pivoted, and kneeled, looking over the left fender. My pistol was out and some heavy adrenaline sprucing up my attention. There was a fellow about fifty feet away, shielding himself behind his burro, looking down the sights of a rifle pointed right at me. I pulled back behind the cover of the fender slightly, extended my pistol, got him in the sights, and fired. He fired at nearly the same time, a millisecond before or after, I am not sure. I later found the spot behind me where his bullet struck the ground. When I shot, the burro kicked and bawled, the man dropped his rifle, grabbed his gut, and fell to the ground as the burro danced away, kicking. The man yelled as the burro brayed, and he grabbed at his fallen rifle. My second shot took him in the head and he collapsed. I waited behind the fender, watching him closely, trying to calm my heartbeats. He did not move again, and in a moment or two, or three, I got up, just as I realized I had not looked for anyone else, and cursed my stupidity. I turned quickly, and made sure there was not a second bandit. I saw no one, and heard nothing. His burro had trotted away.

I was a little reluctant to approach him, but settled down and walked over to his body. His hat had fallen off, and the head wound was considerable; there was no doubt he was dead. He was a Mexican, about forty, scrawny, denim pants, a khaki shirt, city shoes. He had 23 pesos in his pocket and nothing else. The rifle was a beat-up Winchester 94. He hadn't ejected the one he fired, and there were three more shells in the magazine. No other ammo. I went over to the car and got my canteen and took a long drink. It was time to figure out what to do. I thought about the burro, and checked the ground where its tracks were. There was fairly heavy blood sign, so it was hit hard, too. You don't let a wounded animal wander off and die slowly, so I started following the sign. He had gone about half a mile, then lay down to consider things. He started to get up when he saw me, but couldn't quite do it. I got close and shot him in the head. I was sorry I had shot low and through him, but there wasn't anything I could do about it. I did bless the penetrating power of the .38 Super though, because if I hadn't hit the bandit on the first shot, I might well be the one lying back there with a hole in my head. A .45 ACP might have stayed in the burro. I'd still carry a .45 elsewhere, since it's not usual to have to shoot through a burro to take out a bandit. But I was very pleased with the .38 Super that day.

I left the bandit where he had fallen, put his rifle in the car, and drove back to El Paso to write my paper on cacti. I read the daily paper from Juarez, *El Fronterizo*, for a month just out of curiosity, but there was nothing there. The desert has a big appetite, and so do buzzards. It took a good many years, but the experience finally settled in to that part of my mind where poems work themselves out, and long after his bones were whitened by the sun, he came back, as distant, alien, and objective as he had been on that day. The story doesn't explain the poem, nor the poem the story. It was all too simple to need an explanation.

They stand as corollary formulations of a moment's act, and the only memory left of that moment.

> *Shot a goddamn bandit*
> *right through his burro*
> *when he threw down on me*
> *Wanted my fucking gringo*
> *money, got a bad hole*
> *in his kidney and would have*
> *howled till he died*
> *if I hadn't ended it right*
> *there, the burro too.*
> *Not one to leave a gut-shot*
> *animal or man*
> *out in the sun.*

MEXICO: THEY WANT THE KANGAROO, NOT YOU

There were a lot of final blows that knocked me out of the United States. Those North Dakota boxing kangaroos for one. But I don't want to get ahead of myself. First things first. I'm in show biz. I'm a stage hypnotist. Yeah, yeah, I know, if you've seen one you've seen them all. Anyway, for years I made a pretty good living in night clubs out in the sticks getting people to do things in front of an audience they'd never live down. Bark like dogs, hop like chickens, mate like sheep, etc. All under hypnosis. Not real sophisticated, but it put food in my dish. That was then. Now it's back to traditional values. People act like Quayles. They're afraid to do anything. People are scared of their own minds. They even think I do "the devil's work." So they go for the "safe" stuff like amateur Jell-O-wrestling or those damn boxing kangaroos, stealing all my business.

The very final blow came in some cowboy dump in the Badlands. I was walking down the stairs to the dressing room in the basement when I suddenly slid on something. My feet flew out from under me and I skidded the rest of the way down the steps on my tailbone. I looked over my shoulder. The stairs were covered with something too revolting to describe. A few feet away, staring at me sideways, was a monster in a sequined robe. A kangaroo. On the other end of the leash was a shaggy human.

JOHN-IVAN PALMER

419

"Sorry man, he got into some bad salad."

It was a hell of a way to find out I wasn't the headliner, but a mere warm-up act for an overgrown rodent. What a blow to my ego. I stuck around afterwards to see how the kangaroo did and sure enough, all the local loudmouths lined up to go a couple of rounds.

They wanted the kangaroo, not me, so I said, fuck it. I'm going to Mexico. Maybe they'll like me there.

I jerked all my contacts and came up with an ex-hand-balancer turned agent named Jose Gutierez. I signed a contract with him to tour Mexico for five grand a week. Sounded good. I used to speak Spanish as a kid in Texas, but since I knew I'd be a little rusty I had Gutierez put in the contract that I'd be furnished with a translator, Humberto Ramos, whoever that was.

On Jan. 15, 1989, I was supposed to meet Ramos in the lobby of an old hotel in the small border town of Douglas, Arizona. At the appointed time I was met by a big Mexican woman with a magnificent mane of black hair. "*Humberto?*" she said. "*Si,*" I answered. This was only the beginning of many language problems.

She drove me across the border into Mexico in an old Ford with Sonoran license plates, the back seat a veritable garage sale of wigs and dresses, and chatted in Spanish while I pretended to understand. She drove around deep potholes, rusted oil drums, abandoned refrigerators, old car chassis and dead dogs and came to a club called *El Cache del Cid*. On the door was a small poster that said, *Humberto Ramos Autentico Travesti Show.* "*Travesti*" wasn't in my Spanish/English dictionary, but I got the message soon enough. It was a female impersonator show, Mexican transvestites for Christ sake, and the "woman" who drove me into Mexico was not a woman but Humberto Ramos himself, a.k.a. "Marie." At that point my fingers were at least 1,500 miles from Gutierez's windpipe.

The show consisted of an MC, "Marie," and three young *Mexicanos* who carried their incredibly tattered dresses and wigs in boxes and plastic sacks like bag ladies and traveled together in the old Fairlane. They were all in their early 20's and looked like three alluring babes when in female drag, but out of disguise they were three very different guys. Marie (Humberto) always looked like, and dressed as, a female. Every so often she'd catch me looking at her a little too closely and say in front of the others, "*Tu quieres ver mi cocho* (You want to see my cunt)?" and I'd say politely, "No thank you, not right now."

But who knows. Mexico is full of illusion. In fact, Mexico *is* illusion. The whole country is put together with mirrors. Anything fake becomes real and anything real becomes fake. Nothing stays the same. Bogus vanilla is sold as authentic, designer labels are put on cheap jeans, the hideous carcasses hung up in the *carnicerias* and fobbed off as goats are sometimes large dogs, and someone who gets a knife across the cheekbone one night might get drunk with his attacker the next. Things are simply not in as fixed a state of drab authenticity as in the States.

About 11 P.M., with 30 people in the place, Marie, in a low cut black evening dress that revealed a lot of jiggly, genuine (hormone induced?) tit, went out and did 10 minutes of jokes in Spanish. Beforehand, I tried to talk to her about translating, but I realized she couldn't speak English any better than I could speak Spanish. So I drank tequila straight out of the bottle and tried to work up some boozy machismo before she introduced me.

Through the tinny microphone I said, reading off some notes palmed in my hand, "*Voy a demonstrar a ustedes los poderes fantasticos del hipnotismo* (I'm going to demonstrate to you the strange powers of hypnotism)." They laughed. I continued, and they laughed louder. Marie took the microphone and said something to the audience in Spanish, which made them laugh even harder, then gave it back to me.

From where I was standing I could see the door. I told myself, just run, it will take only four or five strides. Just keep running and in another few minutes you'll be back across the border working cowboy bars again. But no. I didn't have the guts.

I rambled for a sentence or two in Spanish, but then my tongue groped in my mouth for words that weren't there. I cupped my hands around the clay of nothingness in front of me, trying desperately to form those mispronounced words into some kind of meaning, but it failed. They only laughed harder and louder than ever before, and the drunks, in mock sympathy, stumbled right up to me in the floodlights to offer their open pints of José Cuervo.

Somehow Marie and I managed to get two hypnotic subjects to close their eyes and slump in their chairs. For all I knew they could have really been hypnotized. At this point I didn't care. I told Marie (mostly in pantomime) to tell the guy to stick his arm out so he couldn't bend it. She said something I didn't understand and sure enough, his arm became stiff as a rod. The audience loved it. I reached for the mike to go on to the next stunt, but Marie wouldn't give it up. Power went to her head. She said something in Spanish and the two people flapped their arms like birds. "Tell them their legs are getting heavy," I said. She translated, and for some reason they kicked off their shoes. At what point did I lose control? I know, when I passed through Mexican customs earlier that night.

So we hit the Mexican night club circuit, from Agua Prieta to Hermosillo. These weren't resorts like Cancun or Cabo San Lucas. There were no *turistas* in these depressing, windblown towns that made Appalachia look like Palm Springs. Some clubs were just four walls and a stack of Tecate cases in the corner. As far as a bathroom, you simply hosed it out the back. Sometimes we'd have to string an extension cord 200 feet to an outlet in the next block just to run the lights and sound.

Surface Catholicism notwithstanding, there's a lot of voodoo in Santeria Mexico. Lots of belief in the evil eye and blood sacrifice, death, morbidity and pain, which maybe accounted for my backhanded "success" with hypnosis. As long as I was a laughingstock, I was OK. However, in Caborca I was taken too seriously and Marie hustled me out the back because she said someone wanted to drain my blood.

My biggest cut of the cover charge so far was 50,000 pesos (around $20), but as we climbed up into the mountains toward Durango, my cut fell to 5,000 pesos.

On the outskirts of Durango the car died. We opened the hood and all I saw was a mass of coat hangers, electrical tape, sheet metal—and smoke. "*Somos chingados* (We're fucked)," said Marie, pushing a huge preponderance of black hair out of her broad Mayan face.

So we walked through the nuclear winter of Durango's outer slums and came to a building with a faded sign barely visible in the dark that said: "Waldorf Astoria." I'd seen a lot of this kind of borrowing in Mexico, just like we take their "Loma Linda's" and "Sierra Vista's." I paid an ancient woman 1,000 pesos for a private room (about 50 cents), and was glad to have a roof over my head at last, but that turned out to be an illusion too. On the floor was a bare mattress and a torn blanket. That was fine. I expected that. What I didn't expect was to find only three walls, the fourth having been burned away in a fire. I looked over the edge of the charred boards into the alley below and saw several laughing hobos roasting what looked like animal guts over a fire made from parts of the hotel. They seemed a lot happier than I was.

One of the funniest things you can do is try to call the U.S. from a Mexican pay phone. The only thing I reached was something big, black and fuzzy that crawled out of the coin return, then, seeing me, crawled back in again. But that was nothing compared to the tarantulas I had to shake out the legs of my tuxedo pants while working those oil rig shows in Guatemala, but that's another story.

At the Caballo Blanco Disco, Marie, after a great deal of hesitation, asked me for money to help repair the car. I told her, more or less truthfully, I didn't have it. She reached out with her dark fingers with ruby nails, tweaked me on the cheek and informed me my salary was now zero pesos a show.

I hung in there for about a week, settling into the Waldorf where my reputation had spread to the alley. The hobos invited me down one night for food and drink. I have to admit, the chicken tripe tasted pretty good. Such friendly people. But here's where the story reaches its end, or where another story begins. I could tell there'd been a lot of discussion about me in Spanish the past week and I knew something bad was going to happen. That final night as I trudged over to the Caballo Blanco, blasted on rum and paregoric, my worst fears became real. When I entered the so-called dressing room, I thought I was hallucinating. I'd seen a lot of strange things in Mexico so far. Guys at the faucet washing out rubbers for the second or third time, eleven year old mothers begging for food, cockfights and scorpion races, unkempt adolescent cops with their zippers open standing in front of banks carrying machine guns and reading comics—yes, I thought I'd seen it all. But what I saw that night was too strange and twisted, even for Mexico. I want to emphasize I have nothing against kangaroos per se. They have a right to exist and pursue free enterprise like any other species, but circumstances can make them unwitting jinxes. Can make any of us jinxes. And a jinx is a jinx. You can't pretend it's something else. At the Caballo Blanco Disco, Durango, Mexico, winter, 1989, right there in my very presence, in the dressing room, haunting me like a voodoo demon, was a goddamn boxing kangaroo. No, it was not the same sick act from the Badlands, that would have been too outrageous. For that I'd commit 'rooicide. This was just another borrowing, like the Waldorf Astoria. The beast was full of dandruff and had a scaly bald patch behind its neck and something liquid draining out the corners of each eye. It seemed to look and not look at me both at the once. Typical kangaroo attitude.

The *travestis* all looked guilty. *"Quieren el canguro, no tu* (They want the kangaroo, not you)," said Marie, almost crying. Even though we were from different planets we had shared hardships together and become friends.

But it went beyond that. Their car was dead, they needed money, transportation, wig repair, everything. In all fairness they gave me first shot at the quarter million pesos (about $100) to fix the car, but I lied and told them I didn't have it. Durango's a big city. They apparently searched around and made a deal with someone else to share the expenses.

I downed the rest of my rum and paregoric. Since Marie, Chichi and Jesús truly wanted me to like them nonetheless, they invited me to join them for chicken feet soup at someone's house near a tape cassette factory. Inside was an altar full of plaster virgins and rosary beads. The opium in the paregoric had been giving me visions, so I'm not sure about what I saw. I thought I noticed on the altar, next to a plastic Halloween skeleton, a scrap of cheap offset printing. It appeared to be soaked in blood.

I looked at Marie, Jesús and Chichi who seemed to look at me with that helpless expression that says *you're on your own*.

My Spanish had improved considerably over the weeks and so I was sure, or almost sure, I heard her (him) say, *"No se preocupe, todos tienen que morir algun dia.* (Don't worry, everyone has to die sometime.)" Was that really my picture torn off a poster and soaked in blood? Did I really see Marie cross herself three times, or was I in a state of Mexican hypnosis?

I don't know if I was in any actual danger of having my blood drained that night. I probably wasn't. Mexicans on the whole seem more caring and emotionally secure than *Americanos*, but one never knows. As far as I was concerned Gutierez's contract was now full of leaks. So I let it sink to the bottom of my memory.

I left awkwardly and abruptly, then caught a late night bus lit inside with red bulbs and smelling of the pungent, accumulated perfume of Mexican females packed all around me.

Fuck it, I said, I'm going to Guatemala.

PANAJACHEL, GUATEMALA

JOEL LIPMAN

The previous trip out of Guatemala ended on a Bluebird bus with a peasant woman dying in the aisle, machete-clutching passengers clambering on from milpa paths that led to thatch-roofed clusters of houses a few hundred meters off the road in the slash-and-burn scrub jungle of the Peten.

This time, Panajachel was the bustle between hospadajes and hotels, kids of six or seven selling bracelets for a dime, colorful chemises for a dollar, working a strip thick with skinny, coked-out Germans and their ruddier, just-off-the-bus-from-San Diego girl-friends, a kilometer-long vendor-lined cobblestone street that ends hygienically at the stones of Atitlan's depths and across the conic lake to a triad of volcanoes overladen with moody mauves and duskier purples, midnight darkest-against-lightest echoes of moon and sky and rock. A longer horizonline, less immediate in its fatalism than the rusty one trapped along the blood seeping down wrinkles in the plastic dropcloth she'd been wrapped in that jungle-hot day along the road to Benque. Atitlan is inherently healthier and more life-enhancing than a hacked and hemorrhaging woman on a jarring, provincial bus, that much can breathlessly be claimed for the splendid lake and its sere rim of cones. I was looking for some time out of time with beauty. Looking for—those expectations, they really knock you down, not that they have much to do with the clotheslines and straps that hold chickenbaskets, huge cloth bundles and rucksacks to Esmeralda's green bustop rails. But of course expectations have everything to do with ropes and knots and bags and bundles. What's a chicken in a basket atop a bus about if not expecta-tions? What firewood or two melons? Along the stone wall at the

424

end of the road boats pull up to the docks, depart with a tossing of lines and splash of motor wake, all the waving and mugging of a carnival afternoon in the tropical wintertime of the high mountains on the day after Christmas. Everywhere the pop and smokehaze of firecrackers.

The drug deal set-up the night before had gone sour, was lame from the go. I was just hopeful, one key to disillusion's door. Not that it was more than delay and no-show tension in a bar only generically familiar. I was there, a source for my expectations, that's about all—a place called ExPort, at night a proletarian connection point and beery bistro thick with EcoHeads and mint Greens, tattooed druggies and tooters, bus-hardened wanderers and escapees on holiday. Locals. I was not of the last group but the previous, committed to nothing except nothing. I figured to score a few day's smoke and ease along in a chair with the local tienda's stock of cheap Chilean Cabernets and Argentine Burgundys. It was an occasion to twist the clock off dead center and I was at ExPort mid-afternoon to meet this guy who reminded me of Jim Croce's mustache and who, last night, rapped fast enough to juggle deceit and charm—there was his girlfriend who, powerless against her husband's rage over their affair, offered him 5,000 Quetzals out of affection. "Hunff, I threw the money to the floor, said she could buy me a Cabro." The pulpy melodrama of taking a beer and sniffing at $1,000 and his curiously commingled syntax made for memorable bar art. "Belgium," he said when I asked where he was from and, of course I thought, or Switzerland or Amsterdam. This great stache, weighty and almost archetypal, like a long session in front of a hotel mirror looking back past yourself at the bathroom window and out into the yard behind your reflection, while past and instant swivel and fuse and the long zippers on canvas bags are yawns of volcanoes awakening from sleep, as was the narcotic homesong beneath the drugdealer's walrusmouth of whiskers. He was to be here at 1 and it was after 2. The afternoon fresh ground coffee was hot and cheap at ExPort, the patio florid with bougainvillea.

I saw him later that afternoon. Sitting on the curb across from the bar, his head hung between his knees, I slid alongside while he raised up just enough to reveal the junkie's clawing want and denial. Wrecked, gone, slouchy and vague, Jim Croce's mustache helped locate his mouth and nose, adding a bracing, hairy horizontal to his face, for without its support he'd have emulsified or softly exploded into the bits of gray paper from last night's firecrackers blowing about in downy tatters across the street's uneven stones.

"50 quetzals. I'll be gone 10 minutes," his palm more open than his eyes.

"No, man, Won't do. It's not important." I didn't care

about the terms of our short, forgettable history—it was an afternoon bright and dry, fresh with light highland air, no longer the addictive cabaret halflight of the previous evening where everybody chain smoked 40¢ a pack Guatemalan cigarettes and murmured into one another's knots of bone in hoarse, inarticulate bits of speech. Now, mid-afternoon shifting ripples of shade were radiant enough to cause me to shield my eyes. A child came by, a basket with 3 hands of bananas balanced on her head. "De nada," I waved. Her alert and hopeful eyes gestured toward my companion. "OK, a tardes," and processionally she moved along the street trailed by 2 other kids, one with a cloth bundle of small tangerines, the last armladen with strands of shoelaces and sashes.

"50 quetzals. Be right back. Red hairs fine as the sweetest pussy."

Who knows—sex and drugs, the red line of some immediate moment's integrities? I'd been there a few times. "How you feeling?"

"That's my problem. I won't stiff you. Here, hold my coat till I'm back."

"I don't want your jacket (though it's a sharp white heavy cotton tanker, my size and worth a few dimes) and won't even think about whether I'll get stiffed—it's uncool. I'm not giving you my money, then sit here wearing your threads. Maybe tomorrow."

"Tomorrow I may be dead."

It was left at that.

JORGE GUITART

MEXICO

i live in mexico
which others call buffalo

i julio agosto drink vamos
the polish twins drink somav

that was my life
starring sintagma

well pragma dude
is it all necro now

or is there room
for a nudo

A GUSTO

SAUL YURKIEVICH

translated from Spanish by Cola Franzen

This glutton I know loves long Augustinians in snap sauce, but he says they are the very devil to catch. First he screams at the top of his voice to chase them down, then rips off their clothes. The spine prepared, he puts in this and that, reduced to pap, mashed with pinches of jiffy, and leaves it all incarnated, soaking until dawn. He drowses three carats with fissures. When it is clarified, put in the specific, grasp the keel, and throw the spine into the gulp. It's not easy to attract long Augustinians. You have to throw them virgules and pieces of essential, you have to swindle forcefully until the pack cracks, warbles, goes into the layer house and the long Augustenant can close the whathisname with one blow. Later they are skewered with a pinnule. And now you add pepper, syrup, guimpe and pimpernel, and capillary them and roast them on a fire of bags, carefully and lovingly, and in a gluttonous spree, they are placed in the cheek then in the throat. And the confiscation laughs and feasts without chiton and without kid while dancing the fang dance:

> compose cousins with me
> I invite you to this feast
> strongpoint my long Augustinians
> assail in the throat
> grasp the dredge and pickle
> there is no impudent more spruced up
> than a platterful of long Augustinians
> to the fang Si
> to the fang No
> for this pack of long Augustinians
> fills me up
> fills me up
> Yaaahoooooooooo

SOMETHING GIVES HIM AWAY

translated from Spanish by Cola Franzen

Something gives him away: the simulacrum never manages to be entirely complete. To keep it from deceiving us, God prohibited Satan from appearing totally identical to man. His feet, for example, couldn't be shaped the same as ours. (Feet, in the mystical sense, are allegories for sensual passions. Bare feet enhance the desire for camel contact. Worshippers kiss the feet of their idols with great pleasure.) The devil's feet usually point backward. We find them disgusting. The deformity means that, although subject to the Supreme Command, they go contrary to it at the same time, are disrespectful of the harmonious designs of God.

They say the devil adopts goose steps. Perhaps the goose possesses evil qualities that we are not aware of and that suit the infernal order. Its irritating croak or its urge to splash around in the mud rooting in search of slimy morsels link it with the perverse and the filthy, with the world of darkness.

Someone, certainly, among the people we see must be a devil, but it turns out to be difficult to discover him. We should become intimate enough with the suspect until some unmistakable sign reveals him to us, always late, as devil. Subtle signs can give him away: horny armpits covered by hair, a toothed foreskin or a spiny clitoris, a distinct umbilical floriation, some lacerating thorn behind the ear, a certain conformation and certain consistency of the elbow.

NEW ORLEANS: QUARTER NOTES

RENE NEVILS

My balcony in the Vieux Carré faces the Jesus Place, from which the personally saved storm the streets nagging repentance from tourists too stoned to be of any use to Christ. In the apartment above this haven of holiness lives a nest of transvestite hookers. Since they have more wigs than Eva Gabor, it was hard at first to tell how many people actually live there. After a while I realized there is only one couple, Delores and Juanda, who rent the place. They do have a lot of sleepover company especially on the weekends with parties that last all night, the guests coming and going as business calls them away. Some of the visitors stow beepers in beaded evening bags to keep in touch with regular clients like college students and married men who don't have the time or the guts to cruise New Orleans looking for what they need. The purses squawk all night sending their owners racing for the phone. The routine never varies. Ten minutes past the *BEEP* a Mercedes or an Alfa Romeo with a Tulane parking sticker will sidle up to wait at the corner or a black and white cab with Mardi Gras beads swinging from the rearview mirror will call someone down with an annoying blast on the horn. Juanda and Delores' friends totter up from the bar next door wearing working clothes of spike heels and clinging knits, but their bodies are too heavy and muscular to look natural. They move like a cloud of butterflies who have been dosed with steroids and the whole place must smell like a combination of Shalimar and fart. The older ones like Juanda are expert with make-up. Some of the younger guys attempt a chemical maquillage by taking massive doses of female hormones to melt their masculinity until their endocrine systems must be a confused goo of "who's on first?" What cannot be altered is foot size, and women's shoes are not designed to fit them. The shoes are cut too shallow and the large veins atop their feet scream WRONG. The wrought iron balcony that fronts this apartment is always decorated according to the season. At Christmas the railing is swagged in garlands of cedar studded with twinkle lights and in the spring there are baskets of plastic red geraniums. Juanda sprinkled gold and purple glitter on the leaves to make them sparkle with Mardi Gras colors. Sometimes a new wig will trip out onto the balcony to tend the garden with a feather duster. The apartment has one feeble air conditioner which must be quite useless against the horrible heat in this humid city. The French doors stay open most of the time making it easy and enticing to look in on my neighbors' lives. There are lots of posters tacked on the wall. I recognize one of Marilyn Monroe in her chanteuse costume hanging over the battered sofa. James Dean is there too in that Jett Rink cowboy hat. The furniture is old and covered with the kind of third world couch throws sold at Pier One. The place would look quite sad and shabby if it weren't for Delores. Somewhere in another life before he took to the streets, Delores worked construction. He has built an entertainment center for Juanda and has redone the kitchen cabinets dressed in a black satin teddy and his carpenter's apron. He does odd jobs for the neighbors and once without telling my husband (who would have sworn to do it himself and badly) I asked Delores to fix a broken shutter. He came wearing a jumpsuit and purple wedgies. He worked quickly, anxious to get away because street folk are not welcome in our building. The "Are you ready for HIM?" stickers on some of the apartments made him uncomfortable. Daytime is a sad in-between world for people like Delores. To supplement their income some of the transvestites have regular jobs. It is a particularly strange sauté of sexes who trudge past my door in waiter's jackets or khaki uniforms with names like Jason or Michael stitched on the front. Always there is the telltale smudge of eyeliner and sometimes they forget to remove those scarlet press-on claws. Night is their quality time when they come out to frolic in the moonlight. Summer and winter they sashay back and forth between the two transvestite bars along the street, their voices raised an octave higher with the setting of the sun. It is hard to talk or write about people without using gender reference. My husband and I argue about this. I call the transvestites "guys" even when they are trussed up in faux lamé and breakaway pantyhose. The prominence of the adam's apple, flat hips and that hard knot of muscles at the

429

back of the calf precludes speaking of them in the feminine. To me it is a practical matter. You can buy silicone tits, but if you have gonads you are a man. You can call yourself a lamppost but if you can pee up a wall, I'll call you mister. My husband is kinder about it than I am. He says they are girls because that's how he sees them and girls are what they call themselves. My husband gives them their wish and when he speaks of them he uses only the feminine forms of speech. We chat with Delores and Juanda across the balconies as civilly as neighbors can who distrust each other's lifestyle. They like my husband more than me because he teases them and makes them laugh. There are no feminazis among the transvestites. They are the prototypes for Blanche DuBois and flirt outrageously with any man. When they work the streets shaking that money maker they are impossible to ignore. I have seen Juanda make dates with everything in pants from a movie actor to a Soviet sailor. I have often wondered if the clients knew what they were getting ahead of time or if they just liked to be surprised. The women Juanda and Company encounter give them disgusted looks which have little to do with morality. Speaking for myself I am a bit jealous of all the attention that the transvestites' exaggerated femininity gets them. My only contributions to conversation with them are banal comments on the weather or the traffic. I find it intimidating to be around people who threaten to usurp something as basic as my sexual identity. I feel no real animosity towards them. I leave that to the street Christians who really despise their gaudy neighbors. The two groups often clash in serious shouting matches that feature some mean name calling by both sides. If rosary bracelets and pastel Medjagordje medals are clues then most of the transvestites are Catholic. I see many of them going to mass at the cathedral. Since Catholics are not reckoned to be true Christians by this full gospel church, this is just another reason to dislike them. Granted Delores and Juanda and their friends are dope addicts, prostitutes and sexually reckless beyond reason but, all this aside, what really seems to piss off the Christians is that the transvestites appear to be having such a good time on the way to damnation. The Christians work hard at making Jesus seem like a fun guy. They clown for Christ and play Christian hard rock which sounds like an unlikely collaboration between Keith Richards and Karen Carpenter, appealing mostly to the deaf unshriven. I find it hard to believe that Jesus will come back with all this noisy crap going on. The religious sect acts just as reckless as the transvestites in the way the members collar and harass pedestrians. The faithful tend to forget they are proselytizing in a combat zone. Often in an effort to snag an errant soul some novice will wander past the police barricades into the dark zone of the Quarter. The cross is no protection there. The transvestites have better sense than to go into those dangerous places even to buy the drugs that fuel their midnight rambles. They place an order with a dealer to have the goods delivered C.O.D. by a teenager on a bicycle. From my balcony I watch this endless neighborhood carnival and feud. Peace between the two groups is impossible. The transvestites, who are easy to judge and hard to pity, may die from their excesses. But there is no returning to the lives that first claimed them. They are in this for the long haul no matter how short that may be. The Christians with their shiny new souls will never cease trying to convince the uninterested that their way is the only way. Silent and dispassionate I hover above them sipping my communion of Johnny Walker Red. The role of observer is both my sin and my penance. My cup runneth over.

BATON ROUGE: THE SUMMER OF PURPOSE

MATT CLARK AND JOSH RUSSELL

In March, Louisiana is Mardi Gras country. This July, we got us a new festival. Operation Rescue's "The Summer of Purpose." Tennessee Williams once wrote a play called *Summer and Smoke*. This has got more sturm and drang, cher.

The best parking is at the 24-hour market. They're one of the last merchants not to charge three bucks.

Next door: The Sizzler Steakhouse manager is in tears. His shrubbery is infested with sweating, middle-aged men dressed for the golf course, but bearing larger than Pro-Life sized photos of mangled fetuses, which they brandish at lunchtime patrons like four irons or pitchforks.

"What's wrong, honey?" one diner asks his wife. "You don't like them baby-back ribs?"

Big Frank's got it all outside his nightspot for teens: lemonade, hot dogs, iced-tea, cold drinks, hot coffee, sausage-on-a-stick and inside, air-conditioning and pool tables. Today's special—2 cars, five bucks, free Bomb Pops for the kids.

"There's some choice babes down there," Big Frank says. "Get it? Choice? Babes?"

The Cyclone fence they could have used in Kansas—300 yards long, six feet high, festooned with rosary beads and signs reading: POLICE LINE DO NOT CROSS. It runs down the center line of Bennington Road, gleaming in the sun, a zipper, a metal serpent, a strong suggestion which is sure to lose out in the end.

What's missing at this carnival:
1) Rides. The EMBRYONIC DERVISH! The ASCENSION/ DAMNATION PARACHUTE DROP! The FETALWHIRL!

431

2) Food. Big Frank's got a lot, true. But he doesn't stock what we need. Blue coconut snowballs! "Where's the cotton candy man?" "I think I saw him over by the Jesus Is Lord Command Post."

3) Etc. Ring toss, skee-ball, Guess Your Weight for a Prize?, target shooting (however, with a garrison of very hot, very annoyed Baton Rouge cops, don't rule that one out).

What's not missing at this carnival:

1) Crowd control.

2) Freaks galore.

3) Anti-fashion run amuck. Our favorite t-shirt? The New Jerusalem Polo Club featuring the four Horsemen of the Apocalypse doing a *pretty* accurate Prince Charles. Best in Class—THIS IS YOUR BRAIN. THIS IS YOUR BRAIN IN HELL. (Do they have frying pans in hell? Should I capitalize hell?)

4) Colorful tents. Some brimming with policemen and policewomen snatching some shade, some with turkey salad sandwiches and Gatorade for the God Squad.

5) Kewpie dolls. Dismembered and glued to signs reading "It Hurts, Mommy, It Hurts." (In keeping with the family theme, Barbie's torso is clothed in a stylish Stay Soft Fabric sheet.)

6) The sour smell, the crush of humanity.

The Man, Himself:

Keith Tucci. Like Gucci, but with a T. "That's our leader," a woman whispers. She looks down at our feet. "You're standing on Holy Ground."

Remember Eb from Green Acres? What's he done with himself lately? Dressed up in blue Dickies work pants and a flesh colored golf shirt with a Kachina doll embroidered over his left breast? In Baton Rouge? With a bull-horn and a wet Bounty towel pressed to his forehead? ("He doesn't stand back and point fingers," a fellow observer notes, "he gets down and crawls with his people.") Rumor has it they're *not* going to take New York, they're going to pitch camp here through August. "Keep Manhattan and give me that countryside!"

Overheard "Praise Jesus, brother. Is that ice-cold watermelon?"

Covert Operations: Code Name "Pearly Gates: The Back Door":

Boris and Natasha lurk in tunnels under the street trying to find a way into the Delta Women's Clinic. Natasha: pregnant with "the child of Moose." Boris: looking up through manhole peep slots. "Hairy legs, dahlink. Hundreds of them. We must be directly beneath the camp of feminists. We're homefree."

Now that the front door is blocked à la God's Red Rover team, (they want NO ONE to come over, those snobby bastards!) alternate entrances must be found. The entire block, cordoned off Colonel Klink-style, affords a variety of entrances. "Friendly" businesses offer sneaky access to the no man's land between the fences and the clinic. It worked, too, until the press, in their infinite wisdom and greed for ratings shares, leaked the info. Did it occur to channels nine, two, thirty-two, forty-four (HUT!) that these folks have tv's in the rv's? Once the righteous got the cable-call, all hell broke loose. (Well, sort, of.) Back-door Bathshebas, hot to trot any gauntlet for the J-meister, had a holy-rolling hay day, complete with bone-jarring open-field tackles by body-armor clad B.R. peace officers. (If only Marv Albert was here: YES! You know that had to hurt!) "Get Smart" get lost; this is slapstick espionage at its finest.

Parade at High Noon:

Mothers with bibles under their arms push baby strollers up and down the fence line. "We love *all* babies!" "Mommy, I'm hot." It's 97 with a heat index of 106. The asphalt is steaming, tar patches bubble. "It's a lot hotter where these sinners will be going, dumpling. Don't pick at your scabs."

There's money to be made, I think. A new line of trading cards. The stats: arrests, time in jail, number of prayers said in a twenty-four hour period, number of Big Reds consumed during daylight hours, number of body cavity searches endured stoically, passive resistance record holders: "Look, there's Cigar Store Pete. It took seven officers to lift him off that lesbo hell-bitch in Seattle. What a guy!"

Back at Big Frank's:

The watermelon man and a kid in a "Choose Choice or Fuck Off" t-shirt are shooting eight-ball for Tucci's soul. The watermelon man, on his knees, one eye closed in prayer, one eye sighting a shot. The kid, mugging for CNN and three balls up. SCRATCH! Neither player's any good. What're in the pockets got there by luck, not by skill or divine guidance. Big Frank interrupts, "Time's up, my good men. I've got a business to run and need table space for the lunch rush."

THE DIARY OF NANETTE JENKINS

I was telling Stanley the other night that I was going to make Seattle my own personal Paris of the soul. He lowered the paper at my pronouncement. His brow furrowed. He was trying to understand me, the poor dear, but he never would. Still, I loved him. I loved the simple things he brought me, like a lot of money, but I longed for understanding, too. Finally, Stanley spoke.

"I just don't get this Larson guy. Everyone thinks he's funny, but I don't get it. Look at this. Is this supposed to be funny? You know, what I think—I think only a bunch of goddam posers

DAVID FEWSTER

433

can laugh at this stuff. That's what I think."

I am going to make Seattle my own personal Paris of the soul. Fuck Stanley.

≈

I think I love him. He says he understands me, too, but I wonder, as he can't even feed himself without help. Oh, he can eat all right, it's just going into the supermarket he can't handle. He will walk in, get a cart, and fill it to overflowing with one item, say, kidney beans. Then he'll go to the express line and exclaim "I am a poet. I need beans." The trouble is, then he'll try to buy all the beans for the price of one can, indignantly yelling at the cashier, "After all, it is only one item." I am taking care of Roberto right now, because he is a genius.

≈

Went to Walter's today to discuss the publication of my book of erotica, *The Tongue-Lashing and Other Wet Punishments*. Walter said it was very fine. The writing, he said, reminded him of a female Bukowski. Either that, or he said I looked like a female Bukowski. I couldn't tell— Walter's office is located over the Greyhound Terminal, and it gets pretty noisy sometimes. I feel he understands me, though, and that's the important thing.

≈

Life with Stanley is suffocating me. Tonight, I decided to tell him that we mustn't limit ourselves to each other so much—we should go out, grasp new people, sensations, experiences. Of course, such an arrangement would be a bit unfair—I have the advantage of being intriguing, mysterious, beautiful, and talented, while Stanley is as interesting as a bowl of soggy cornflakes, and about half as good-looking. Still, perhaps I could make the suggestion in such a way as to make him see the benefits of such a plan, artfully phrasing my thoughts in a way to spare his feelings. Haltingly, I began.

"Stanley, you bore the shit out of me. We need to start having sex separately, preferably with other people."

Stanley put down the paper. "What are you talking about? Is this a joke? You're not making up captions for that Larson strip and testing them out on me before sending them in, are you?"

"I'm not doing this for me—it's for both of us. I want to see you expand before my eyes and drain the cup of life to its sludgy dregs. Have your own affairs—there's Miss Stone next door. I've seen her give you the eye many times."

"Miss Stone is 87 years old and lives with her collection of grasshoppers collected from all 50 states."

"But darling, I want you to have these experiences. And later on, if you promise not to tell me about yours, I'll promise not to tell you about mine."

Well, after a few hours of discussion Stanley reluctantly agreed to try the idea. Later, I let him make love to me, out of pity. He was so grateful he spent the remainder of the night polishing all the doorknobs in the house.

≈

Roberto is proving difficult. For one thing, since I've been supporting him, he's given up on beans entirely and lives on Mumm's and Chateaubriand, which I have to cut up for him because he doesn't trust himself with a knife.

"You are the only one to understand my pain, Nanette, the pain that would make me plunge the steely blade into my artist's heart if it weren't for your love." This is all very fine, but explaining the $567.23 grocery tab to Stanley is not going to be easy.

Also, the other afternoon Roberto asked me to pose for him in the nude. "But I thought you were a poet," I said.

"Silly goose, haven't you ever heard of a wordpicture?"

This sounded reasonable to me, but when I came out of the bathroom to stretch out on the divan, I found that he had run out in the street and sold tickets to a roomful of passersby for a "$1.00 Peep-Show." Face it, I am by nature a giver, but this "take, take, take" is leaving me deeply dissatisfied.

≈

I knew I'd never be able to keep my relationship with Walter on a purely intellectual plane. It's for my mind that I want to be esteemed, the selfsame mind that can claim authorship of such works as "Steaming Ropes of Jism" and "Gardenhose." Walter, unfortunately, has reached the groveling stage.

"You are a goddess, Nanette, have pity on a mortal man. All I ask is for one time. Just touch it once. You can even wear gloves. I beg you—you are Life to me, Nanette," etc., etc.

I'm not really attracted to Walter, who resembles a young Peter Lorre covered with a form of Dutch Elm blight that he calls a "beard," but the curse of my woman's soul is its terrible excess of compassion. Also, my book isn't off the presses until next Tuesday, and I would sorely hate any complications. I finally gave in, on the condition that Walter laminate himself from head to foot with quick-drying plasticene and supply me with surgical garb, after which I grudgingly masturbated him with a pair of salad tongs.

Making Seattle the personal Paris of my soul is becoming

435

more of a chore than I had expected. True, both are gray most of the time, but the similarities end there. O, where are the beloved madmen I dream of, the sort that take their pet lobsters for walks on a leash, beat pigeons in the square with magical canes given them by Celtic priests, and discharge firearms in crowded restaurants? True, Roberto will ofttimes spit in public, but, while this is certainly anti-bourgeois of him, it somehow lacks the epic grandeur that I'm yearning to find.

Still, I try to do my part. Sitting in B & O Espresso, I drink lattés and write surrealist poetry while singing Broadway showtunes at the top of my lungs. On alternate days, I write Broadway poetry and sing surrealist showtunes, but the clientele here is too unsophisticated to appreciate the difference. In any case, I've been asked to take my business elsewhere. God, how I hate Provincialism. Perhaps I should start my own salon.

≈

Both Walter and Roberto were wildly enthusiastic when I broached the subject of a salon to them. Roberto promised to bring all the artists he knew who felt the way we do (and, at times like these, I feel that despite his shortcomings Roberto does understand me), and Walter has arranged for the entire proceedings to be videotaped by George Lubetkin, the avant-garde filmmaker, who will use his influence to get a possible airing on the public access channel. It's exciting to be part of the vanguard.

The plan is for me to start the evening by reading from my novel-in-progress, *Shimmering Lard*, after which the floor will be open to any and all displays of self-expression. Walter was, as usual, somewhat overly effusive.

"Nanette, you are a star, bless you for your light. It is only through you that the nebulous gases of our existence are crystallized and given form and life, life that is only a reflection of the goddess from which it springs, whose shape is Beauty and whose ways are inscrutable, save that we know she is called 'Nanette.'"

Fortunately, I've heard this song before, and when Walter suggested I don a leather bikini and pour scalding sauerkraut on him while he lay at my feet in a weenie suit, I pled another appointment and left.

≈

RANDOM THOUGHTS WHILE SITTING IN A SIDEWALK BISTRO DRINKING A BOTTLE OF WHITE ZINFANDEL AND LISTENING TO OLD JONI MITCHELL ALBUMS THROUGH THE P.A. ....

I feel very French today. Maybe it is the wine, or the sun. Yes, the sun is out today, its reflection glaring off the concrete sidewalks, bathing the scene in a blinding whiteness that would remind me of Morocco if I had ever been there. The people around me sense the alienness, too. I see them walking into lampposts, tripping over curbs and unconscious transients, driving their cars into parked vehicles and straight over pedestrians who made the mistake of crossing with the light. An inexplicable strangeness pervades the air, as if we were all possessed by spirits. On the other hand, maybe it's just that the sun is out in Seattle, and everyone's too retarded to know what it is. Of course, they act like this in the rain, too. Life is a mystery.

How appropriate that "Blue" is playing in the background as I write these impressions. Dearest Joni—her soul is so French. If only she'd move there. Face it, nobody understands her here. We have much in common, she and I. Perhaps I should take some guitar lessons.

≈

It was at the open mike last night that I met Raoul. His exotic swarthiness and workingman's physique made the other acts, mostly anemic suburban cowpokes whining about life in A-minor, seem pale in comparison. He sang songs of rage and revolution out of a cruel, sensual mouth furnished with white teeth made pointy through years of being ground in frustration at the injustice of the ruling classes. True, all his songs were in A-minor, too, but they sounded different coming from him, somehow. I decided then and there that here was a man who would understand how to teach me to play guitar.

After the show, I introduced myself. Raoul's life is as romantic as his songs are inflammatory—he lives in a houseboat on Lake Union. We went to the Marina, only to find that Raoul had misplaced his keys, necessitating his having to break the window of his boat. The next morning, I found myself alone in bed until the two policemen arrived. Luckily, Walter was able to cover my bail as an advance against future royalties.

≈

Last weekend I held my first and last salon. I can barely bring myself to write of it so soon after the event, but I remind myself that the entire point of this diary is its searing honesty in which I face even the most painful experiences, thus showing the world my clear-headed bravery, compassion, hatred of hypocrisy, blinding intelligence, and spiritual beauty. Anyhow, that's how I want the reviews to read, so I guess I'd better get it over with.

I had timed the salon to coincide with one of Stanley's trips to Denver, where he periodically goes for executive meetings to do whatever business he does in order to make a lot of money. Frankly, I'm not even sure what company Stanley works for. The whole thing bores me terribly. I would encourage him to quit his job to become an artist, but luckily I'm not criminally insane yet. Also, Stanley is already drawing a comic strip that he says is a lot funnier than the one that Larson draws, so at least he's occupied during his off-time.

I spent the day before the reading decorating the living room in an Egyptian-French-Greek-Arabic-Inca-Mongolian-Navajo-Italian Renaissance-Eskimo-Cubist-Druid-Surrealist motif, something to reflect the various aspects of my soul, which had the misfortune of having been born in Beaverton. Finding all this stuff in K-Mart took an entire day's shopping. I set up a table laden with caviar and champagne, and through Roberto's romantic underworld connections I had acquired a block of hashish, which I planned to unveil after the prepared performances so that we could all sit in a circle and tell about our visions. A transcript of our talk, I felt, would be an important artistic document in its own right.

At nine, Walter arrived with Greg Lubetkin to set up the camera, which he assured me was the very same type of equipment used for segments of "America's Funniest Home Videos." Walter suggested that the film should open with an image—shocking, yet laden with symbolic overtones, not unlike the slit eyeball Buñuel used at the beginning of *Un Chien Andalou.*

"What did you have in mind?" I asked.

"I was thinking of something along the line of a huge close up of a penis entering a vagina." Walter looked around the room. "Gee, you wouldn't know where I'd be able to find something like that around here, would you?"

Luckily, or tragically, for me, the doorbell rang and guests started pouring in. Roberto had generated a huge wave of interest in the salon by telling everyone he met in bars across the city that I was the person responsible for approving grant applications for the Arts Commission. I was immediately very popular. In fact, I had never before seen such a group of fawning sycophants who hung on my every word, complimented me outrageously for work which they hadn't even read, promised all sorts of sexual favors, and in general acted like a bunch of puppies who would be happy to spend their days licking me from head to foot, using their tongues so I would never have to spend another dime on toilet paper as long as I lived. I liked it. I liked it a lot. This, I felt, would be the kind of audience that would truly understand me. No doubt the reading from Chapter 11 of my novel *Shimmering Lard*, where François wakes up to find that he has been transformed into a trombone mouthpiece, would be well received by such a discerning group.

My fatal mistake, unfortunately, had been telling Roberto that he could be Master of Ceremonies. He took his responsibilities for this very seriously, preparing himself beforehand by getting totally blasted. Entering the room, he shouted something about the kingdom of heaven being visible only to those who have achieved total derangement of the senses (I think he got the phrase from McKuen, but I'm not sure), after which he drained Stanley's liquor cabinet, then proceeded to drink bottles of cologne, furniture polish, rubbing alcohol, and Listerine, finishing the performance by guzzling a gallon jug of Pinesol. On the bright side, his breath smelled fresher than it had for months, but this was only the beginning.

"All you bastards care about are manifestations of your own egos," he screamed. "My mission here is to purge you of these pretensions." So saying, he took out a pair of handcuffs and locked himself onto the tripod of Greg's camera, so that the only thing that could be seen through the viewfinder was Roberto's head yelling "Death sucks" over and over again.

Well, this was going too far, even for Art. Besides, he was ruining my film. Visibly upset, I cried, "Can't somebody do something?" This was a bad request to make in a roomful of people desperately tlying to second-guess my every wish. Sounds of breaking furniture immediately followed, and dozens of hands bearing sofa legs, bookshelves, ashtrays, coffee tables, and the like started beating Roberto about the face and neck. This certainly helped in quieting him, but it didn't do much to get him out from in front of the camera lens, which was getting caked in blood, anyhow. Finally, Raoul came out of Stanley's shop with an acetelyene torch, but, in trying to burn off the cuffs, set fire to a Byzantine tapestry I had bought at Walgreen's.

In any event, to make a long story short, the whole damn house burned to the ground. When Stanley got back I told him it started when the cat knocked the lava lamp off the mantelpiece. We're staying now in our condo, where Stanley's mother had been living. We put her in the rest home yesterday. True, she put up quite a fuss, but nobody can tell me anything about sacrifices.

≈

Got a call from Greg Lubetkin today. He says he'll show the video to Stanley and the home insurance people unless I come up with $5,000. I'm not sure whether to pay him or submit it to the Seattle Int'l Film Festival. The more I think about it, the more our little documentary seems to be a blistering statement of our times. Decisions, decisions.

LONG POND, NY/NJ

Have you ever studied a map & noticed: at the borders of the county or state you see abstract lines cross & vanish into a void—& a map of the *next* county or state shows lanes & turnpikes evaporating just over *its* borders, disappearing out toward the edges of the paper. If you juxtaposed these two maps you would indeed find that a sort

HAKIM BEY

of *Border March* exists, an area of vagueness or in-betweenness, where back-country roads become one-lane blacktop then unimproved dirt then nothing at all in a sudden silence of obscure forest. And that's where I live.

After the revolution (which was always yesterday) we'll estivate like alchemical hermits in this run-down lake resort on the border. The feng-shui's excellent, dragon/phoenix valley with a spring-fed serpent-shaped long pond stocked with bass & pickerel. Used to cut ICE here for the Cuban trade (1890s?), slabs of diamond down by rail to NYC. Summer cottage dates from art deco '44 or '45, yellow paint peeling under the pines, broken flagstone steps, Cold Mountain bar-b-q, Li Po with a 6-pack. All I need is a cauldron of bhang & one or two acolytes to lean on while smashed & laughing at the moon in Taoist america. Jade cinnabar jasper motor-boat in the distance—"OHHMMmmm..."—wu wei, Slack, rural sloth, spaghetti & Chianti for supper like old-time anarchists. Down in the village half the shops are boarded up, an old roadhouse offers "female revue & Jell-O wrestling"; the season's over, the hillsides are dripping with ferns.

The lake's gray with inkbrush tendrils of Sung mist, fishermen in tiny rowboats, scarlet sumac by the road. A good time to go looking for Ramapo Mountain People or "Jackson Whites," legendary local Lovecraftian degenerates lurking in the hills. Like the Kallikaks (of the Jersey Pine Barrens) or the Jukes (Upstate NY), "triracial isolate communities," accused by 1920s Eugenics Movement of incest, fur poaching, six fingers, selling votes for liquor, "feeblemindedness"—the Jacksons a mixture of Dutch-Indian/Black, all named Van Dunk. Jump in the jeep, bounce back in the woods where the Govt. Topo map shows only green, & little crossed-pick symbols for abandoned iron mines, there's a "Van Dunk Rd," gravel, then dirt... Near the cyclopean vine-encrusted ruins of 19th cent. furnace-foundry & huge rust-cracked waterwheels deep in German-fairy-tale green & amber, back in the in-between, streams & marsh exuding a silvery haze into the orange obscurity of October, into the topaz of late afternoon, abandoned factories, ice-houses, burnt-out church choked by the forest... Sure enough, right away we find them, just as we imagined: Tobacco Road rural slum of sagging trailers, log cabins, trash cars, gypsy junk, too many children with ghost-ashgray skin & beautiful Indian eyes.

The Jackson Whites! Our motto: "Live Like Them"—but secretly and unknown to sociologists. Mutant hippies of the future. Out on the patio under moon & rain & Chinese evening mist, bathrobe undone, dick hanging out, dancing with earthworms & snakes, false intellect dissolving in old Jersey genes.

THE PROBLEMS OF TRANSLATION

You are sitting in the apartment of a famous man discussing the subtleties and nuances of translation. You have been talking for nearly two hours and your head is starting to feel like an attic laced with dirt. You say something he obviously disagrees with and he frowns slightly, then asks if you would care for a cup of coffee. You say yes so he goes into the kitchen which leaves you time to spy through the inscriptions in his many books. You return to where you are sitting, which is the bed, because although he is a very famous translator, there is no money in translation and there is no other place to sit except the other chair which looks uncomfortable. Also, you want to convey how much at ease you are talking with a famous translator about his subject. You find yourself listening to make sure he is still rummaging in the kitchen, then slump down because your brain is feeling like swirling dust. He returns with a tray bearing two cups, cream and sugar. You look at him, your head resting on the pillow, hear yourself say, "I think it is a good idea for us to have sex now." He jumps backwards, spilling coffee and gazes at your pubic hair which is in full view since your knees point to the ceiling, you've shoved your tights around your ankles and thrown your skirt around your hips. He stands gazing and thinking. Your brain feels like a nicer place to be already. Steam rises up to his face, you have to remind him he's holding hot coffee, then sit up, pull your skirt down and say "No, seriously, I think it is a good idea," adopting the grave tone of voice you use to talk about translation. But he says he has an appointment, has to go out and leaves you there dreaming in two languages, feeling the fleshiness of your fingers moving over and over.

TALES OF HARLEM

MILTON BEYER

While walking back to work from lunch last Friday, two police cars sped past me down First Avenue. By the time I had walked the three blocks to 102nd Street, where the police had stopped, a small crowd had gathered in front of Bull's saloon on the corner. I looked through the window. I saw Frankie looking strange and lying very still on the floor. He was dead. I did not recognize him immediately because his fair complexion had turned dark and his blond hair was covered with blood and with sawdust from the floor.

I entered the saloon and heard Bull telling the police, "Frankie was standing at the bar with Izzy when the killer came in, fired three shots from behind and ran out."

441

Frankie was a well-known and much loved figure in the Harlem Market. The market extended from 101st Street to 106th Street and from First Avenue to the East River.

Frankie had worked in Izzy's garage until last year when he developed arthritis in his knees and couldn't do the work anymore. He then got into the numbers racket as a runner and retained his popularity in the neighborhood. He continued his generous activities and would lend a helping hand when needed. Often he would drive a truck for our produce company when we were short-handed.

Within a very few minutes, an ambulance, detectives and more police converged on what is normally a quiet corner. Last to arrive was Frankie's mother. On hearing of the tragedy she was refused permission to see her son and then attempted suicide by throwing herself in front of a moving truck. The attempt was frustrated by the quick thinking of the driver and his good brakes.

Frankie, dead at 28, was survived by his widow and small daughter. Izzy took up a collection to provide funds for the funeral and life resumed its normal course on First Avenue.

The Harlem Market has been going to seed. The Long Island and New Jersey truck farmers have deserted it for the new Bronx Terminal Market. The merchants and peddlers have followed the farmers and taken with them the activity and prosperity of the old market.

As a result of the exodus north, Sam, the stable man, was going out of business. His final liquidation took place at noon. The setting was a melancholy one. The wagons, some 50 in number, were lined up in the open farmers square at the edge of the East River. The buyers and onlookers were a motley group. They shivered and stamped their feet on the uneven cobblestones, for the wind from the river was biting and the snow blew in their faces and settled on their clothes. The wagons were quickly auctioned off; many bringing less than the worth of the wheels.

The auctioneer then led the way into the stable proper and took his place in front of a round-topped table placed in an open wagon. At his side sat an assistant recording the purchases.

The stable was poorly lit. The ceiling beams were split and sagging. Straw, mud and manure had been made insoluble by the trampling of the crowd. The smell of horses and of men was pungent and the cries of the auctioneer, the horse dealers, the peddlers and the stable owners who had come to buy made a clamourous and noisy confusion.

Hay, oats, bran, wheels, wiffletrees and harnesses were sold. Everything, even a family of goats and the spotted dogs that lived in the stable, was put on the block and knocked down to the highest bidder. Finally the horses were led out. Eager hands reached up and pried apart the jaws of the animals to determine their age and condition. Hands slapped great rumps and powerful legs. A whip flicked over the back of the first animal and he ran up and down the stable, demonstrating his step. Sam was noted for the good horses he kept and expressions of approval were made as each horse was examined.

The bidding began. It was spirited and fast. The auctioneer gesticulated with a cane as he rapidly shouted the progressive offers and exhorted the crowd for the next bid. Buyers stepped up to pay for their purchases and took from worn pants' pockets rolls of bills—small money—hard come by.

The sale was over. Men, animals and merchandise left the stable. The snow drifled in the open door and the wind blew through the cracks in the walls. Sam remained, left with the familar smells and with his memories.

≈

Orson Welles and John Houseman created the Black Theatre in Harlem, an offshoot of their W.P.A. federally funded Mercury Theatre. They produced *Macbeth* there in 1936 and I took a school chum, Ruth, to see it on a date. I was 19; she was 18.

The witches scene: a Carribbean island and a voodoo ceremony. Celebrants are painted, feathered and bedecked around a blazing fire; pounding drums and raising dust with dancing feet. Goats and chickens wait for the sacrifice.

It was off putting; either the production or the date or both. Ruth was a hip young radical and I was striving to get ahead in a business career. I had the hots for her. She didn't have the hots for me. We drifted apart.

Harlem is my fate. I was born on West 130th Street in 1917. I met my date at City College on 133rd Street and now I'm into a Black *Macbeth* on 135th Street.

Four years later the story resumed.

The shadow on the wall speaks, "My father is the sun, my mother the casement window. My straight black lines on the wall of the living room frame a tableau of a young woman taking a picture of a newly married couple. They are smiling and happy and beautiful. It is their first weekend in their first apartment."

The building is a cooperative at 433 West 21st Street in Chelsea. New York. The Theological Seminary, occupying a square block, is visible through the open window. The sun is streaming into the room. Bessie, the bride's friend, is snapping the picture.

Bessie has just arrived at the apartment after a session posing for the sculptor, Chaim Gross, in his Greenwich Village studio. The nude figure of a chunky, nubile young girl will find its way

443

one day to the Hirschorn Museum.

They met in the common room of City College at the standup lunch counter. She asked him for a cigarette. It was the beginning of the fall semester, 1936.

Their first date, a few days later, was riding the Fifth Avenue bus downtown after school. They went on top and sat on one of the front seats. The beginning of love was ever after associated with views into second story windows on Fifth Avenue. They were seeing moving pictures of oriental rugs, antique furniture, portraits, sculptures and Beaux Arts architecture.

They stopped at the Brass Rail for coffee and cherry cheese cake before parting; she to Queens and he to the Bronx by subway.

Four years later he was living at the Regent Hotel on upper Broadway. They had recently resumed a relationship that had been broken off for three years. After their long delayed lovemaking that evening at the Regent, they drove to Gallagher's Steak House on West 52nd Street. They arrived after midnight, dined on steaks and left after 3:00 A.M. Both basic drives were appeased and the feeling was bliss. They pledged their love and decided to marry as soon as possible.

Christmas holidays delayed blood tests and it was January 6th when Henry Schimmel, City Court Judge, performed the wedding ceremony in his chambers in the Municipal Court House at City Hall Plaza.

Judge Schimmel, a good and sweet guy, was a Tammany Hall stalwart. He was secretly married to Kitty, an Irish American school teacher, who lived with her parents in Jersey City. The judge lived with his widowed, Jewish mother in Manhattan. The union was secret because all the parents were violently opposed to a "mixed marriage." The loving couple did share a Manhattan apartment on weekends until time, curing all things, removed all the objectors.

After the wedding supper at Cavanaugh's on 23rd Street, they drove to Herald Square, home of Gimbel's and Macy's. At midnight, flower wholesalers load the sidewalks with fresh cut flowers from far and near to supply the city's florists with their flower needs for the new day. They bought armfuls of California-grown jonquils, purple heather and mimosa and drove to their new apartment in Chelsea. The flowers were placed in a laundry bucket, a wood fire was lit in the fireplace and a fifty-year tradition of anniversary flowers began.

Later he mused, "What did the shadow see?"

Three things are too wonderful for me;
 Four I do not understand:

The way of an eagle in the sky,
The way of a serpent on a rock.
The way of a ship on the high seas,
And the way of a man with a maiden.
—Proverbs XXX 18

CALIFORNIA DREAMING

Nineteen twenty-five was a good year for film pioneers. Charlie Chaplin made *The Gold Rush*. Sergei Eisenstein made *Battleship Potemkin*. MGM made *Ben Hur*, directed by Fred Niblo. It was a costly spectacle and the budget soared to a reported four million dollars. It is a tale of a Jew and a Roman who were friends as children and became bitter enemies during the time of Christ. Ramon Navarro was in the title role, Francis X. Bushman played Messala and I contributed as an extra in Ben Hur's army.

At age eight, I was living in Hollywood with mother, father and older brother. Our home was a small bungalow at the bottom of a hill in the San Gabriel Canyon. Antonio Moreno, silent film star, lived in a large house at the top of the hill.

My Aunt Esther had a Russian friend who came from her home town near Kiev. He was an assistant director at MGM in Culver City. When he had calls for children as extras, he would call her and her children would get work in films with Douglas Fairbanks, Mary Pickford and Harold Lloyd. This time the call was for a large number of boys and men. Her two sons, my brother and I, caught the trolley-car before 7:00 A.M. and rode to Culver City and the MGM studio.

I joined over 150 men and boys, tall, medium-sized and small, in a large tent holding Bedouin costumes and make-up artists. I dressed in a flowing robe and turban, put on greasepaint and make-up and left with a lance with pennant attached.

The crowd was assembled in a valley between papier-mâché-mountains supported by two-by-fours on the back side. They were Ben Hur's army recruited to rescue Jesus. Ben Hur said, "No bloodshed, please," and the rescue was a non-starter.

Full-grown men were in the front rank, facing the cameras and the wind machines, and everyone else in order of diminishing size brought up the rear. Four-and five-year-old kids, plus smaller-sized dolls stuck in the sand and on the side of the papier-mâché mountains, completed the illusion of a vast host gathered together to liberate Jesus from Pontius Pilate. After rehearsing the lance raising, the shouting, and the backing and filling for about two hours, the wind machines were turned on, the cameras started rolling and the shooting began.

August 1988, *The New Yorker* magazine assigned a writer to invite Irene Mayer Selznick (L.B. Mayer's daughter) to attend and report on a showing of *Ben Hur*. It was the same newly-restored version presented by the British film historians, Kevin Brownlow and David Gill. The performance was in Purchase, New York, a Pepsico Summerfare offering. It was the first time in 60 years that Irene Selznick had seen the film.

The reporter remarked at what seemed to be thousands of extras up on the screen. "Little dolls," she said. "Little dolls." That, to me, was the real *Valley of the Dolls*.

Nineteen twenty-six was the year I lived in the small town of Alhambra, California. Today it is swallowed up in Metro LA and is twenty minutes east of downtown LA.

Our skyscraper was four stories high and posters posted in the town announced that "The Human Fly" was to scale the immense height on the outside of the building to its roof at eight P.M., Saturday night.

Mr. Smith, my dad's partner in a fruit and vegetable market on Main Street, bet me 10¢ that it wouldn't happen. I wagered and lost. He won on a technicality. The "Fly" was late and accomplished the death defying feat at nine P.M.

Mr. Smith soon after made up for his tricky deed by presenting me with my first puppy. My dog, "Spot," a fox terrier with a black spot over one eye was frisky, friendly and yappy. We both ate and enjoyed my mom's noodle and rice puddings. As a young puppy, he cried in the night for his mom. My mother, thinking him cold, covered him with an old sweater. He threw it off. She then fastened it with safety pins. Her mother's heart.

≈

A bright memory like a fate morgana or mirage still dazzles me—walking home from school in June at the end of my third year and looking up at the blue sky and seeing in the distance the snowcapped San Gabriel Mountains. I returned in 1976 and looked out at the same mountains, saw Mount Atlas at 10,000 feet elevation and it was still snowcapped in June. I drove my grandson up the mountain until we reached the snow line. We parked and I made him a square snowball as promised.

Very deep is the well of the past. Should we not call it bottomless? I can still inhale the strange fragrance of eucalyptus and pepper trees and see the Spanish missions along El Camino Real. The neighboring town of San Gabriel is the home of the mission San Gabriel Arcangel. It was the 4th mission built of the twenty-one created by the Spanish Franciscans between 1769 and 1823 from San Diego to Sonoma.

With a pal, I climbed the brick adobe wall enclosing the cloistered courtyard of the mission, reached out to a pomegranate tree and picked the fruit. The stolen fruit was more exciting than the retail variety that I knew from the family fruit market.

In the spring, when California poppies bloom, astonished Spanish conquerors, gazing from their ships at flaming hillsides cried, "This is the land of fire!"

And that was long before Watts and Rodney King.

BROOKLYN

A Scream is a System of Breathing Derived from the Kabala

Worlds within worlds kill worlds
Cities inside neighborhoods
Racism in ethnocentricity
The bourgeoisie in the proletariat
The flower in the seed, the fascism in liberality
The capitalist in the communist
The socialite in the socialist
The consciousness of the subconscious
The prescription within the freewill
The will-to-power behind humility
The buying of giving, the selling of salvation
The materialism within spirituality
The methodology of recklessness, the sameness in difference
The conformity of eccentricity, the contrived anxiety
The iconic in the arbitrary
The cunning behind impulse
The intent within precognition, the hindsight in prophecy
The design that guides coincidence
The fabrication in recognition
The perpetrator in the victim, the crime within nonviolence
The aggression within passivity, the flattery in damnation
The repressor in the repressed
The exhibitionism in inhibition
The indulgence in absention, the greed in ambiguity
The sexuality of celibacy
The masochism behind lip-service
The patronage within seduction
The poison of compulsion within judgement

CARL WATSON

447

The echo in the consequence
The guilt within gratuity, the knife inside respect
The thermodynamics within psychodynamics
Instinctual 'Reich' within abstract 'Rights'
The heresy of sincerity
The alibi of conviction
The opiate in poverty, the cowardice in ownership
The sterile seed in abundance
The producer in the purchaser
The advertiser in the wage-earner
The rapist within the inert consumer
The receiver in the donor
The chauvinism within feminism
The segregation within integration
The motivation of the majority within the minority
The money behind the mass
In the narcosis of narcissism, the narcissism of gregarity
The coercion in virtue, love, altruity
The auto-eroticism in religious ecstasy
The police mentality of the prisoner
The prison mentality of the police
The biter in the bitten, the container in the contained
The fashionable habit of the covertly mundane
The vagina inverted into a phallus
The accidentally on purpose
The hubris of the murder in beneficent creation
The stone age in the aquarian
The judaism of the protestant, the pagan-catholicism
The feudalism within gestalt
The madman in the saint, the impotence of aggression
The indoctrination in education, isolation in matrimony
The incitement in oppression, oppression in eventuality
The wrath within wit
The cajolery in sympathy
The woman in the man
What we can never know in what we seem to
Is it the we in you again, or the you in me this time
Or simply the rage of me in you.

THE DEAD, UNGRATEFUL

BEN MARKS

"Mammoth epiphanies." It's a phrase used to describe a Grateful Dead concert, as in "A series of." But the other day, I had one of my own, more unexpected than anything I had previously experienced as a long time fan of the band that lives in my former home town. It all started out innocently enough. I had gone to the newsstand to buy a copy of the Sunday *New York Times*. There, in a full color and full page ad for the over-priced men's store called Barney's, stood none other than Bob Weir, a musician who I had always felt got more from the rhythm guitar than anyone else, with the possible exception of Keith Richards. In the ad, wearing almost a thousand dollars worth of jet black clothes, Weir is standing alone with a Cheshire cat grin on his face and a lit Bic lighter in his hand. The caption reads, *THERE'S MORE TO LIFE THAN APPLAUSE. (We're grateful to shed some light.)* The next week, the company was employing Tom Jones to convey an equally obtuse message having to do with *pussycats* and things *not unusual*. To say that the ad, which I now seem to see everywhere, was a shock was putting it mildly. It's not that I want my former heroes to stay in the past, unchanged forever and ever; it's just that the contrast is so great, so overwhelming that it flouts all I know to be true about the world, and especially about the Grateful Dead. I first saw the Dead in 1970. I was too young to see them in the sixties, and as far as my parents were concerned, even too young to see them when I did. But at least the show was local, taking place in San Rafael at a venue which was called, for a while anyway, Pepperland. It cost three bucks to get in and was a benefit for the Hell's Angels. I found out about it on 4th Street near the old courthouse (before the city fathers had it torched to make way for an ugly office building) by a couple of members of this illustrious organization who assured me that it would be "fuckin' great, man." Being in no position, physically, to challenge the accuracy of their assessment of the impending "party" (Dead concerts were always called parties; maybe they still are), I bought a ticket on the spot. The show was a blur. There were lots of big hairy bikers in leather jackets drinking ferociously. None of the women, I noted with pre-teen delight, appeared to be wearing bras. Several fights broke out but somehow I never felt in any great danger. I vaguely remember lots of drum solos and have an equally hazy recollection of Janis Joplin singing "Turn On Your Lovelight" with Pigpen and trying to give Jerry Garcia a kiss onstage which he seemed to resist. By the time I started seeing the Dead on a regular basis, I was a sophomore at San Rafael High School. Going to Winterland with my best friend Mark to see the Dead, the New Riders of the Purple Sage and the Sons of Champlin became something of a bi-monthly pilgrimage. It was an occasion to take acid and get absolutely and blissfully lost in the best music ever made. Period. Of course, it had its weird moments, like during the third set on a New Year's Eve when someone had crawled way up into the ceiling's rafters and was accidentally kicking stuff onto the drummer. Bill Kreutzmann was more pissed off than concerned for this moron's safety, and duly flipped him off before leaving the stage in midwhatever. After being gently coaxed down by none other than Bill Graham himself, this poor guy was shoved in front of a microphone to tell the stunned and stoned crowd what it was he was doing up there, a public speaking task barely manageable since words were clearly optional at this point. He went off the stage into the grasp of several hulks who looked like they were going to relish tearing him limb from psychedelic limb. The Hell's Angels show would not be the last benefit I'd see. There were benefits for an organization called Seva, which brings eyesight to the blind. There was another for the American Indians, and there was even one to buy the Dead's roadies their own home. I knew about all this because I knew this woman (who wore a ring in her nose and whose name absolutely escapes me) who was going with a guy named Mr. Sparks, or simply Sparky, as in, "Sparky and the Ass-Bites from Hell," the Dead's sound test band. Another roadie named John Hagen used to shop where we both worked, buying the most expensive coffee (Jamaican Blue Mountain) we sold. This was always impressive. He even gave me a stage pass once to a show at Stanford but I was so high that I totaled my father's Alfa on the way there. I heard the show was great. Later, while attending school in upstate New York (where there is a sub-species of the genus Deadhead that is much more intense and financially committed than I ever was) I managed to use these tenuous connections to get backstage at a show in Buffalo, one of the band's infamous and ill-fated experiments with a horn section. At one point the horns were so off key and generally awful that bassist Phil Lesh (who has perfect pitch) made a hand motion usually reserved for masturbation to express his displeasure. But the show did provide my one and only audience with Garcia. Since I wasn't quite sure how I was going to get home, and was even facing the prospect of hitchhiking after the show, I only consumed half my usual dose of acid that night. It was a good thing too because what would follow took all the coherency I could muster. In an increasingly desperate search for the can, I found myself in a locker room with Garcia, Lesh and two women who I concluded were not their wives. They were eating plates filled with steak, baked potatoes and string beans, I think. Somehow, I managed to get into a conversation with Garcia who seemed quite willing to fulfill my every fantasy. An idle comment on his guitar turned into "here, you wanna hold it." A discussion of their new sound system designed with time delays for major stadium shows became a session in which I was grilled over the sound quality of a concert I had attended the previous summer at Kezar

Stadium in San Francisco. It was Deadhead heaven! During the show, standing off to the side in the backstage crowd, I was certain that Garcia was winking at me. That year, returning to Marin for spring break, I again made the pilgrimage to Winterland, only this time as someone who had actually spoken to the band. My old friendships were never quite the same after that, but Winterland was. Even though I had decided not to drop acid that night the place looked exactly the same inside, and I felt exactly the same after the show. It was as if my brain was encoded to react a certain way to the place, a bona-fide contact high. After one of the many encores, Bob Weir, observing what must have looked like a sea of lit Bic lighters (which were gaining popularity as a substitute for actual applause) mumbled to the crowd in his best northern California drawl, "You all ought to know better than that in a fire trap like this." Which brings us full circle to Barney's and the irony of Weir holding the lighter. I mean, I was there when he publicly renounced the practice. In fact, there were about 5000 other witnesses. I don't care about the clothes, I don't even care about the generational irony implicit in a member of the Grateful Dead doing a fashion ad, but the lighter; how could he! It's like Smoky the Bear all of a sudden saying it's OK to play with matches in a cigarette commercial. What a sell out! Years later my wife and I would cater for the band in Seattle, even doing the first one for free in repayment for all those benefits, an offer at first not wholly believed by the band's management. But after a few years we stopped, the thrill was gone. People like John Hagen had been replaced by these arrogant assholes who ran sections of the stage like mini-fiefdoms. It was depressing and demeaning and worst of all, I couldn't concentrate on the music. These days drug use is no longer cool but the Dead are more popular than ever. I haven't seen them in years and would probably purchase a ticket with the same sheepish anxiety an adolescent might feel buying his first copy of *Penthouse*. But I gotta admit, I'm glad their library is out on CD.

IN A FORGOTTEN TIME AND PLACE

I.
Haight Street, 1967.
It was all there for the asking.
Doyle and Naatsi panhandled
for twenty minutes and scrounged
up forty-five clams from tourists
who thronged to the human zoo
and threw their spare change at
　　the freaks.

They bought a matchbox of
　　gold,
some strawberry rolling papers,
a gallon of burgundy,
a large order of fish and chips,
one pack of Kools, one pack of
　　Marlboros,
two barbecued fried bologna
　　sandwiches,

ADRIAN C. LOUIS

451

ten pirogies from the Ukranian
    bakery
and some spearmint gum.
And then they trucked down
to Golden Gate Park
to trade all their supplies
for some sleek pelts of beaver.

II.
Winter rain after
THE SUMMER OF LOVE.
No tourists, no gain.
Saint Anthony's beans for lunch.
For dessert, a roach stuck
between two matches is ignited
for a few seconds of happy pain.

The next day up in North Beach
down on Broadway past the barkers
into the darkness with enough
    money
for two drinks, Doyle and Naatsi
chortled at Carol Doda and her mind
blowing tits and then went
looking for a pawn shop
to hock their high school rings
so they could score
the milk-blood of bliss.

III.
1968. Brautigan was looking
so safely bohemian
with a floppy gray fedora
and flaxen hair dangling
onto his new pea coat.
The cat was sipping steam beer
at the MDR on Grant.
Naatsi smiled and said, "Cool"
when his pal Doyle
who was zippered into goofiness
on reds and short dogs of tokay
told Brautigan: "Say us a poem."
  Naatsi giggled, thinking that
        probably

Brautigan was plastic and
    perhaps
really straight, but then
    (epiphany!)
he felt embarrassed and walked
    away
because his hands couldn't clutch
    a pen
and he had no poems to show
    but the holes
in his soles which were covered
with cardboard to hold
in the stink.

IV.
In an alley off Grant
China Girl and Naatsi
tripped on poor Bob Kaufman
that old beat poet who wrote
about golden sardines and such
and was dog-howling at the
    neon,
perhaps, or shrieking at invisible
    light
bulbs dancing upon his tongue.
They stopped and passed him a
    lit doobie
and he mumbled something at
    them
and smiled when he passed it
    back.
Naatsi toked from a distance
never touching his lips
to where madness had kissed
deeper madness.
He gave the eerie poet the roach
and floated off with China Girl
to Chinatown to buy her
fried shrimp and the white rice
of her race.

V.
Naatsi was unwashed
and stinky, red-eyed

and unholy when
he once crashed
with some speed freaks
in their crab-infested
Stanyan Street pad.
In the tense darkness,
he watched their half
moon eyeballs flit
from wall to wall
and bounce off
blacklight posters.
They tied off,
shot up and peeked
out grimy windows
all night waiting
for the American KGB
to burst in
and cover their groins
with molasses and fire ants.
When the morning sun
spoked rays through
their India print curtains,
they jitterjived
like trapped vampires.
An ambulance screamed
up the sunny street
and pure fear sweated
out all their meth.
When he saw them
fixing up for breakfast,
he threw his toothbrush
into his backpack
and escaped to the park
where he sat under
a eucalyptus tree
and prayed for them,
for all those lost souls,
yes, he did Lord,
yes he did.

THE WAR IN SAN FRANCISCO

RONNIE BURK

Well now that all hell has broken loose I can report that I was arrested as an act of civil disobedience on Thursday morning at the federal building along with about a thousand other people. The night before about 30,000 demonstrators crowded downtown S.F. A cop car was burned and dramatically exploded. Set afire by a bunch of wandering punks in road warrior drag. I suppose it is redundant to say "dramatically exploded," is an explosion ever not dramatic? But a cop car set on fire and exploding, I suppose that's the ultimate punk art event. There were in truth few acts of violence. I saw also a window at Macy's get trashed, considering 30,000 people that was all rather amazing that there was nothing more than these few acts of vandalism but the media (of course) played up the violence and played down the numbers (papers and television reported three to seven thousand people on the night the war broke out, it was more like 30,000). The next few days I fell ill with flu and sat at home. So I was able to work on a few things. I visited Diane DiPrima the night Israel was bombed (the first time). I had just gotten out of jail that day and was, needless to say, quite frazzled. She is collaborating with a bunch of "kids" on a tabloid street sheet kind of anti-war peace anthology that will be sold by

453

homeless people who will keep the spare change and help circulate the message. So I am plugging into that. It seems the entire world is sinking towards some kind of Buddhist hell realm. Yesterday morning warming tortillas on the stove I forgot about the tortilla so glued was I to the television. The tortilla caught on fire and filled the kitchen up with smoke. I ran back into the kitchen to put out the burning tortilla when the smoke alarm went off. Hearing the alarm I ran immediately back to the television set thinking Tel Aviv had been bombed again, it was my roommate who came in to explain that it wasn't Tel Aviv but the house smoke alarm that had gone off. Such is the scene at the home front. I am taking valarian root capsules at night to sleep.

MONTEREY

On Thursday afternoon, when we came past the sand dunes on the freeway and saw Monterey Bay, tears came to my eyes. I always get choked up when I return, and I try to return as often as possible. I consider Monterey my spiritual home. It's where I landed when I was lost, on the run from a Gothic Pacific Northwest. It's where, when I hesitantly admitted that I was a writer, a businessman asked, "A poet? Great! Need a part-time job?" It's where I set two of my novels, where my daughter was born. It's where I embraced the Mediterranean California life. Where Lani and I lived on free mussels, bummed French bread and borrowed wine. From our Cannery Row boarding house balcony above Lee Chong's grocery we used to yell down to the military types from Fort Ord or the Defense Language School or the Naval Institute—"Hey, you can come up and see how artists live, if you bring us some fooood."

It wasn't always idyllic, but it was real.

My buddy Price had promised us a place to stay, but when we got to his girlfriend Robin's apartment early Thursday night, no one was home. So Lani checked the local paper for interesting events and we selected the horse show at the Monterey Fair Grounds. It was the first time I'd been inside there since the Monterey Pop Festival in 1967. It looked ridiculously small, like a house from childhood.

There was another *déjà vu* available, too. Before we left Berkeley I'd had a powerful dream, a jet landing on a freeway, but I understood in dream logic that it could be any public place. This dream worried me during our drive. As we had turned off for the interstate freeway exit in San Jose, I'd carefully scanned the skies for any incoming aircraft—that section being in the flight path of San Jose International. But in Monterey, as we stood in the cool evening, watching the horses, a

KEITH ABBOTT

454

corporate Lear jet came skimming over the Fairgrounds low, on its way to the Monterey Airport. I almost cried out in relief. Because of the advance warning systems of our media, one gets so used to bad dreams arriving on schedule. It was somewhat comforting that my *déjà vu* turned out to be only mundane reality.

Despite my incoming impending dooms, the rich folk hadn't changed. Mink stoles, designer hair, preppy gear, English tweeds and tat. The horses were housed in monogrammed tents, tastefully color-coordinated, hung with little homey touches such as family crests and photographic pedigrees, many festooned with the wide, blue, red, and yellow ribbons of past triumphs. Some of the buggies were fashioned out of rare rain forest woods, sporting immaculate chrome axles, and enough black leather to drape an S&M convention. The horses were as beautifully groomed as their owners. And some showed a scootch more intelligence.

While viewing pricey horseflesh up close, I overheard a Republican joke. This emitted from a fellow in English country gentleman drag—green jacket with green riding pants and knee-high boots. Chubby, and with the superb social ease of the terminally dim, he related his *chose drôle.*

A woman goes to the pet store. Sees some puppies. Owner says, "These are rare Democrat puppies. If you don't want them just bring them back and full money refund." So the woman buys but brings them back. Owner says, "Sorry, we can't buy these back. These are Republican puppies." "Hey, when I bought these you said they were Democrat puppies." "Yeah, but now they have their eyes open."

Back in the fairgrounds arena we sat in the stands watched the show and tried to guess why Scarabande or Pooky got the blue ribbon. These were beautiful, high-stepping horses, some five-gaited, able to shift effortlessly in and out of various choreographed steps, as high-strung and manic and obsessed with pleasing the crowd as any game show host.

Accompanying the events was the music of the former organist for the California Angels ballpark. I assumed this escapee from Southern California culture had been invalided out of the service for dementia. Because of the announcer calling out the changes in horses' routines, none of the tunes were ever finished, or even, in most cases, allowed to get their choruses. Hearing this was like listening to a juke box run on crack cocaine.

Foxtrots and sambas and waltzes and gavottes from the 1930's and 40's and 50's musicals reeled out. "Put On Your Easter Bonnet with All the Frills upon It"—"Don't Sit under the Apple Tree with Any One Else but Me"—"Chattanooga Choo-Choo Why Dontcha"—"49 Ford, Tankful of Gas, Handful of Titty and a Carload of Ass"—did I hear that? No, not really. That was a Greaser Flashback to my Puyallup Rodeo Days.

455

Speaking of flashbacks, these musical hallucinations sparked off some of my own nostalgia. I recalled the afternoon I looked north across this dirt arena and the nearly extinct Rolling Stone, Brian Jones, was there: a blond gnome looking *très* diseased, dressed in white feathers and blue suede, sunken in a seat, a smirk on his face.

After all but the last bouts of the horse show routines, we motored back by Robin's place late, but no one was still there, so we took a turn around the peninsula to check at Asilomar Convention Center and see if any rooms were vacant from no shows. No such luck. We drove along the golf course in Pacific Grove and checked motels. Almost everyplace had rooms.

We couldn't believe it. Easter Weekend? Vacancies? Finally, around 11 P.M. we got a cottage at (Scout's Honor) the Bid-a-Wee Motel, $49. A "cottage," slightly smaller than our house, facing the ocean, one empty lot away. (Turned out Price and Robin had a dinner date out in the valley, argued over our ETA, *no, they're coming on Good Friday,* dawdled and got home too late to respond to our note.) We ate well, drank well, woke up to a fantastic blue-green ocean and a ice-plant purple vacant lot, took a roll in the hay and a stroll in the spray, and then read all about Hemingway's Paris in a picture book—reliving his youth as we simultaneously relived ours. Thrill-crazed and physically double-jointed as always. Paradise! Why'd we ever leave?

That afternoon we drove around Carmel Valley and Carmel, where we noticed a large number of houses for sale. In twenty-six years of living in or visiting Monterey fairly regularly, I'd never seen so many homes available on the peninsula.

On the main drag in Carmel, I asked the clerk at the Sierra Club Bookstore for directions to another bookstore.

"There was one down the block oh a month ago, but that doesn't mean anything. It could be gone."

He said businesses were winking out of existence every month. Said $40 a square foot commercial rents were one reason.

"Of course, these properties were paid off eons ago, so it's just pure greed. But still these investors come like lemmings, leasing places and then going bankrupt in a couple months. I can't imagine what these people are thinking. Surely they can't keep coming."

The major hurdle has been a big falloff in tourists. This was Easter weekend and there were a *few* folks around, fewer yet buying goods. It was as if the situation had been reversed: the shop owners were looking longingly *out* at the parade outside.

Lani was fascinated by the changes in Carmel shopping patterns. The town has lost entirely its upscale antique stores, a former staple of commerce. Now there are mostly specialty shops for the trivial—salt water taffy, Origami, sticker tape vending outlets—or T-shirt/

stuffed toy sea-otter emporiums for tourists doing cheap. The two visibly successful antique shops—i.e. ones with customers in them—were a shop for antique golf equipment and another for rare medical instrumentals, presumably solvent because doctors and golf addicts always have disposable income and time to kill when they're not hacking.

Checking the real estate windows showed mostly long lists of low end commercial ops readily available: laundromats and sub sandwich franchises. More telling was that any type of house you would like is up for grabs. Any. Seaside duplexes, Goat Hill Renovated Fisherman Shacks, Carmel Cottages, Pacific Grove Victorians, Carmel Valley Ranch Houses, Pebble Beach Grossere spreads—you name it, you can buy one. (Later we were informed that "400–900k houses were black holes on the Market.") The famous Rock House out at Point Lobos, 5+ prime acres overlooking the mouth of the Carmel River and the ocean, was going for a measly 1.9 million.

Around five o'clock that day, Cannery Row was sparsely populated. I was able to park on the street! An unheard of event in recent years, due to the intensely popular Monterey Bay Aquarium. But the foot traffic was light, too. Used to be that derelict canneries provided *tempus fugiti* color. Now abandoned 1980's development has created new ruins. Dotted among the T-shirt traps, Authentic Ethnic Restaurants and yogurt venders are for sale lots with only large cement foundations in pools of stagnant water, their rusting tie rods poking into the air.

One abandoned investment op is surrounded by a plywood fence hung with fading, chipped murals painted by various local artists portraying Olde California Life As It Used To Be. The dates on the panels stopped at 1989. This was remarkable evidence that recession-proof California is deep into an economic *malebolge*. And this is what Monterey looks like now, even before Fort Ord and the other assorted Armed Service bases close for good. But what were those wide-open puppy eyes seeing now?

On the downscale upbeat side, Price has recently scored a Priest's Hole out in sunny Carmel Valley at "Cripple Creek" as he calls the Senior Citizens Housing center. His rent remains at an affordable one-third of his income. His apartment is stuffed with books for entertainment and he exists on disability from his hearing loss and arthritic condition. However, Price was exultant and triumphant because, as often happens in Monterey when you live next to the Quality Folks and pray to the Trash Gods, they both do deliver.

On Saint Patrick's Day he went to the Goodwill to check in with Manual, his inside man on the new incoming goodies, and Manual told him that a 1979 Datsun station wagon had just been donated. Price looked at it, *one owner car, 125K. Good tires. All the heater defroster radio blinkers speedometer lights working! Original owner's*

manual in the jockey box and!!!and!! all the repair papers from the day it
was bought! No rust!

Only one *screw on the chrome top luggage rack was rusted!*
And only $750.

Well, Price had fortunately brought Robin along and even though they were tapped out for the month, Robin still had her dad's rental property account clear and they kited a check for the car until the first when they could do the old roll-around.

When he called me and told me that he had new wheels (his old one died a week before), I said, *That's funny I just yesterday mailed you a check for $750* (proceeds from some rare book sales). Price was so happy, he said that he was going to go to the Village and hang some paper for lunch. He later contacted the former owner of his car and it turned out it had 25K on it, not 125K. It had sat in a garage for years waiting for someone to get well.

For the rest of that Easter weekend we buzzed around the Peninsula, never getting in the endemic traffic jams that have plagued the tourist-choked streets in the past. It was like time-travel to 1966—with major exceptions, of course.

As we drove out of Monterey, heading for Santa Cruz, we saw apartment complexes near Fort Ord advertising *A Move-in Bonus!* That never happened in the Good Old Days. Of course, neither did 17% "official" unemployment—and this with all the local bases still open. So that is what the fabled "peace dividend" has trickled down to: after living high on the sword, time has come to die on our own swords. Those soldiers in the street aren't going to be coming up with the food and drink much longer.

DETROIT: WHY I SMOKE CRACK

J. MICHAELS

Detroit—It's 6:45 P.M. on Thursday night and I'm standing in a doorway of a boarded up party store on the comer of Cass and Alexandrine. I'm pretty much in the bowels of the Cass Corridor part of town that's a combination of Cannery Row and the Black Hole of Calcutta. I'm not really sure if I'd tell you who I am or what I'm doing here, or if it really matters. I am just staring at my shoes and thinking about smoking crack.

Everyone down here thinks about smoking crack. You don't need to be on crack to dig the weird tense psychotic vibe here, but it might help. The weirdness floats in the sewer steam. It throbs in the eyes of the transvestite whores and the legless Vietnam vet-homeless. It's just a sense that everything could get way out of control really fast but you pretend you don't give a shit.

There's a police station 3 blocks from this corner but it could be in Iceland for what it's worth. It's not that the cops are scared or bought out or anything like that. It's just that things happen here the way they happen and a few cops really aren't going to change that. Maybe the Army Rangers could. But no one down here is really worth the effort and everyone knows it.

It's drizzling September cold. The streets are usually empty in Detroit and it's not any different here. All motion is photon motion. Intense bursts of energy, then nothing. A few blocks away I hear someone popping off a few rounds. If I could stand here until midnight I'd hear that sound a dozen more times.

No one ever really gets used to that sound—the sound of gunshots. People say they do. People even sometimes believe they do. I figure some people go to such lengths to believe they don't cringe at the sound of gunfire that they go a little crazy. They rape old ladies and babies and stuff. They do crazy shit with their city face on.

It's the face pulled taut by pretending things which are totally false, are true. That violence is normal and that pain is pleasure. That's the face of the zombie dead boys and girls on their way to school in Sarejevo, in Detroit. It's the glassy-eyed crazy motherfucker look of any crack-head.

Every drug cycle is defined by the times. Maybe even more than the times are deemed by the drug. Nineteen ninety-four and crack cocaine is the sweetest poison you could ever suck. Crack is every great blow job you ever had but even less satisfying. It's not like any hallucinogen which chills you out or makes you think you know something, or smack which numbs the pain, crack just makes you crazy.

It makes you psychotic, just psychotic enough to make you understand Oprah or OJ, or Tel Aviv, or Newt Gingrich. For once in your pathetic life you have as much power as all the other assholes on TV, on the box, and down the street. For once you're the man.

You don't feel really good but you really don't care because you're crazy as shit and no one is going to mess with you. If they did you'd just gash their throat and maybe set their momma on fire. No one fucks with you no more, man. Smoking crack is the ultimate American experience. It's every back breakin' power trippin' white boy wet dream roped into one. It's the hearty and rugged individualism of the early pioneers-yippie! It's the snap of the slave whip—cower nigger! It's the Trail of Tears. It's Donald Trump and it's Iran-Contra.

Crack is the city man's information superhighway. Ten dollars a pop and you're cruising into virtual hyperspace. Your cyberhead is so in touch it just hurts. Every synapse crackles and even your hair is like some tragic tribal king. Too strong to be colonized, yet not

459

malleable to survive as European spineless. Time stands still as an angel spits down from heaven. Not even she knows where this highway heads, but everyone is on-line, baby.

Still, there is no community. There is no equality. There is only me.

Judging by what folks say and what the media reports, people are just pretty much fed up with everything. There's no toleration of nobody or nothing that ain't going to change my life now. If it don't affect me I don't care, if it does I want it fixed now. For only $10 a bang I can rip away every ugly thing I've ever known.

Sometimes you appreciate crack for what it means to you. Sometimes when you're not rocked off. Sometimes like at two in the afternoon when you're watching TV. You realize that it's become more than just a fun thing to do. You realize it makes you feel like shit. It makes you barf and beg and fuck and steal. You realize your brother is dead. Your cousin is dead. It makes you pissed as hell, but you don't say a word. You know no one would listen. Crack is your revenge.

I think it's easier nowadays to smoke crack hardcore than it was for any other junkies. No one expects nothing. No one feels guilty about anything. Our society has moved beyond any notion of a conscience. Nietzsche would be proud.

So the rain stops now and the wind shifts. The stench from the city trash incinerator burns my nose. I think of my mom's cooking. I think of being 11 years old and my drunkass daddy putting a gun to my head. I don't remember a word he said. I just remember my mom hitting him in the head with a whiskey bottle. It was like a stupid movie. My memories turn in slow motion.

It's 1994 and crack is the drug of hate. It's the drug of the racist cop, three strikes and you're out, and Rush Limbaugh. It's the drug of lost daddies and whore mommies. It's the drug of every lie society told you about opportunity and hope.

I think nowadays people have pretty much given up on this whole idea of hope anyway. It's not to say that folks are hopeless. They're just non-hope. Hope is a notion that is so far removed from everyday existence that it's indistinguishable from Mars or Neptune or God.

I can't remember a time without crack. It's just there. Like the guns. Like the screaming in my head. Like everything else that never really changes. Life has a funny way of crawling under your skin and dying. You spend half your time wondering what the smell is and the other half trying to get rid of it. You never really can, though. The odor lingers.

I asked one lady down the street why she smokes crack. She's young, smart, funny. She has three kids that were taken by the State into foster care because she was leaving them alone while she was out using. She said because it can't matter if she do or if she don't, so why not?

I figured this was not much of a reason. But then I guess most people don't have a reason for half the things they do. I know I don't. Not just one easy to think of, easy to say reason. Most of the time I can't think of a reason for shit I do until a year after I do it. But I still do it.

I'm pretty much chilled to the bone now. I pull my collar tight around my neck to cut out the wind. My toes are numb. I need some new boots before the winter gets here. I came down here tonight to not think about anything. To just see what was going on and check things out. The thing that's happening here is happening across Woodward Avenue, it's happening in Chicago, in New York. It's happening in Davenport, Iowa, and Kalamazoo. People are standing in the cold, thinking about smoking crack.

MICHIGAN MILITIA VISION

Once the UN takes over our country, teeming masses of Chinese Communists armed with meat cleavers will fall upon every last American broiler chicken in one last gigantic mindless Gengis Khan-style massacre, lopping off their ugly heads in the billions, the horde preceded on foot by an advance guard of old crones with gold teeth and dressed in quilt jackets and with massive gnarled old hands twisting the necks of hapless hens as they go along, tossing them into big steaming pots drawn on carts by blond and blue-eyed insurance executives abducted from Witchita, Kansas and set to work still wearing their Abercrombie and Fitch wash and wear suits.

ALAN KAUFMAN

WEST POINT (TWO THOUSAND YOUTHFUL MOUTHS)

ANNE WALDMAN

They come for me in a big limousine. The driver, a military man, tips his cap. I am suddenly a Mam. Yes Mam, No Mam. I dress in a skirt of many flowers, white blouse, ladylike. Hair brushed to the maximum. Underneath I wear the poet's uniform: *skin of the jaguar*. The world prays here in unison at lunch. Then two thousand spoons move synchronistically into two thousand

461

youthful mouths. A young woman tells me it has been her childhood dream to land here. Another traces his family lineage to be strictly "held in line." A black daughter of the army is gracious and direct; she likes the precision of awakening at dawn. The light is friendly as it slices off trees. Flags move slightly in the spring breeze. Down a road I spy a maneuver in battle fatigues. Three soldiers in battle fatigues silently blow up two men and a cannon. Now they are hiding something. Another group is seeking what they have hidden. Across the road men are marching in tight formation. There is some remorse in the conversation about the long ago war in Southeast Asia after I read the poem with the lines "Then gathers strength into something monstrous/right here along the coast of your feelings." But many of these officer gentlemen never had to go there. I shout "Mega Mega Death Bomb—Enlighten!" to some polite applause. Now I want to make them laugh. Who is to say who's more awake? The heads and shoulders of the cadets move harmoniously in the bright light. Their shadows march against clean buildings. Spit and shine. Spit and shine. Tamed to be fierce, unbending under the seasoned officer's eye.

CHICAGO

JOEL LIPMAN

Met Rosalie in the Greasy Lake. At Burrito Jungle met David, at Cup & Saucer Diner one A.M. Jennifer and Lou, 3 times over 4 nights met Bette at Saddleshoe Lounge, at Reggie's Pancake Palace was Sid, then Jerry and Jerry's sister—a forgotten name, but poems sharp as leopards' eyes. At Hamburger Heaven met Roberto spooning yat ca mein, washing down hangover humming scat song ricocheting through his head. At #1 Golden Nugget met Amengo, all gospel at the table, at #2 Golden Nugget Annie and luscious Maribelle spooning strawberry jam and butter onto hotcakes, she once a lover of James Dickey, now Chicago librarian sitting at yellow table in sunlight spooning sweets at 8 in morning, book of poetry propped on sugar canister, nine blocks further another Nugget, me, Gene and Rama chanting on corner next to paper box. In Sweet Pickle met George and wife Linda, through them or rather because of George's introduction met Mary and another Mary and wispy beard poet from north Halsted called Swifty—he opened his bag and pulled me to their table, talking strange streams of words I couldn't make out but read his gestures and lightning rhythmical changes. Met Mean Mac at whole food cafe. "Whoa," I thought, "this guy is doing a bean growl, nasty lettuce incantation, drumming for earth spirit by porcelain vegetable cooler. If I introduce myself it'll be weird legume arpeggio poems, all leafy." But beyond store door six saris in breeze dancing and chinging fingers. 6 little bows, I, my hands before chin like fishy envelope sandwich. Met Rudy at Sally's Ice Cream Bazaar, waiting between the roller skating waiters. Emily at the Shrimp Machine, Emily again at Noodle and Struedle, she reading the other morning paper, drinking coffee, thinking about indian infant mortality rates and patterns of population migration during her lifetime. Chiaparra Singh & 2 male friends over savory lamb curry & yogurt at late night middle east coffee shop, they spooning sugar into volcanic black coffeecups and passing pages of poetry. Esther at ice cream window, Chino Jones on curb sucking italian ice thru straw, working on his ear, extemporizing about brownstone row houses. Met Roger in Hiawatha Grill— "try the cherry cobbler with cream," he called out waving a spoonful, "I got some stuff to show you." We closed the joint and went to Sad Ella's Backalley Tavern, met Joyce met Ted and Alice, met revested publisher of little magazine *Milk*. Turner and the Cozmic Cadence rhythm section in late afternoon submarine port eating torpedoes & drinking Coca Cola, they trying to stretch out refrain from Turner's bad streetlight howl and he raspy-throated going over and over an imponderable measure, Phil the drummer rapping four fingers on the tabletop, saying "come on man, quit fuckin' around, quit the artsy fartsy bullshit and belt." Janet at Buttercup Tap in a room full of gay women, I felt safe and out-of-place when my neighbor's sister asked me to dance. "Any poets hang out here?" I asked Lennie and she a smile and sweep of the arm around the half-lit yellow room. Met Rudy Estigenian at Herb's Vienna Red Mots, his cousin Mac over falafel in nameless corner souvlaki counter, wiping grease off line 3 in 4th stanza. Met Diane at Crown and Crumpet, Terri at Halfshell, Phil Lang, Michael Rosenstein, Daisy Fallish, Karl Rukowski and Joe something all in windmill of paper passing at Bagel Sunday brunch. Met Shari at Blinky's Disco, a Mrs. Courtney who writes carport lyrics, her young daughter, Cloister, at Winnetka steak house salad bar. Left Sugar Shack with drunken poets & stumbled over park fountain into dogbath water, met Peter at Wise Fools, Mickey from Connemora at Shaugnessy's, his poems in travelsack of blue canvas on incredibly thin onionskin. Met Estelle at Berghoff's drinking dark beer at marble bar. Met apocryphal poet Ned Chones eating fish in fingers Sunday morning Maxwell Street, bobbing huge head to Sweet Clara's bottleneck blues, he slapping my palms twice over, hugging my head to his chest. Met Marge at Contemporary Spoon, Sharon at Stalagtite Tap, Kenneth and lover Darryl in revolving 67th floor overlook lounge, they writing on low coffee table alongside panoramic window, offering me third chair, watching over gulls and the wrinkling lake.

NEW MEXICO

JOHN KNOLL

Feeling sluggish and slow I take myself outside into the snow to walk across Hwy 4; south into Indian Land: half crazy from the emotional freeze of another Christmas passed. Looking back to last New Year's Eve I see me with middle-aged angst, crying in the night, hitting my head against a Ford steering wheel; crying. "I'm a man. I'm a man. I'm not a baby. I'm not a baby." Old funny winter psychosis. I was unemployed then and I'm unemployed now, walking on Indian Land. I walked for about an hour and I was tired when I found a dry spot beneath a cedar tree, surrounded by snow-laced hills; huge Grandma doilies covering tierra de muerte, patches of green chamisa peeking through snow, cholla cactus, a pinyon here and there. The cedar I sat under was in a low spot beside an arroyo, overcast sky, muted light rooted in stone, pink underbelly of clouds over Sangre de Cristo. Truchas Peak, Trout Mountain, holding the bloody eastern horizon. I lay beneath the cedar tree. My hand examined tiny cedar needles; twigs that dropped on this spot for how many years? A blanket of twigs. I wonder if I could sleep here all night without freezing to death? My hands dug into the blanket of needles to the damp earth. I opened her skin, dug a hole. The Mother was with me. I reclined on her, started to cry again. For joy or pain, who can say? Laughing at myself; crying, I sculpted cedar needles into pubic hair around the Mother hole. I got on my knees, unbuttoned my green army fatigues, and began to masturbate. Howling and crying I came and dripped my juice into the earth's vagina. I tasted my cum; thought of Maria, Dionysus. My sperm dripped into the hole, I covered it with wet earth, cedar needles, small stones, and tears; and walked away, wondering if I was going crazy, wondering if anything would grow in me now that I've impregnated the Mother? Now I see a tiny white lily with turquoise Apache eyes growing where I planted my sperm. The moon overhead, my daughter. I walk home a changed man, desperate for the community of moons and madmen. Rising and falling my breath flows out into Jemez Valley River Canyons. A bone rattle shakes the stars. Walking home. I am walking home leaving this desert in peace.

LYING DOGGO TAI CHI IN COLORADO

KEITH ABBOTT

Since moving to Longmont, Colorado from the San Francisco-Berkeley area, my wife and I have felt a certain cultural dropoff in public events. It was not gradual and it was not insubstantial. This lack was not completely satisfied by the biggest theatrical extravaganza, the "What The Dickens" Christmas Faire at a local Christian church. This Faire consisted of several store fronts in the Ye Olde England Style propped against the facade of the church. Folks dressed in approximations of Dickensian garb circled throughout and imitated Pierce Brosnan as they failed to talk Brit. But this was a ruse, one to get the rubes in the tent for The Message.

Inside the church, a thespian dogrun through the Christmas Story wended its way around the church's adjoining school classrooms out into the playground which had been turned into Biblical landscapes through the magic of hay bales and theatrical playettes of typical Jerusalem urban scenes. Along the route to the Nativity street jockeys in bed sheets imitated Jews trying to palm off costume jewelry while diminutive Roman soldiers in plastic armor sported plastic swords. Because the Baby Jesus was a petroleum product, the burro definitely stole the Nativity scene, although the chickens were working hard.

Such experiences have induced us to manufacture our own cultural amusements.

Although we had previously been Only Cat Owners, we got a dog. That and a pair of snow tires were our main attempts to Blend in with the Coloradans. So, here is the Longmont Dog News.

Our Keeshond Kody has been going through some rigorous training: Frisbee Aerobics. Because of an inbred trait, intelligence, he soon learned to refuse to drop the Frisbee and chase another Frisbee. Instead, because of the need to establish alpha dog credentials and inflict humiliation on others in the pack, he A) droops the Frisbee and scrapes it along the cement, showing you he can make noise and you can't; B) turns the Frisbee over inset side up, so he can scoop up gravel and toss it about with gay abandon having noisy rattle fun when you can't; and C) jabs the level Frisbee into the back of your knees, should you tire of this "I got the toy and you don't" display and walk away, to remind you of what high hilarity you're missing watching him frolic with your Frisbee. This last trick has led to an extension of Frisbee Aerobics, Tai Chi Frisbee.

So far, Kody has mastered counter moves for almost all the basic kicks which remove the Frisbee from between his jaws and send it cartwheeling across the driveway (occasioning the exhilarating Mad Scramble with Noisy Plastic on Cement which he enjoys with all his doggy heart). He still gets distracted by the hand movements of Snake Creeps Down (prelim to Golden Pheasant Stands on One Leg and therefore rarely spots the hidden kick coming), and pooch has difficulty not going slackjawed in admiration for Wave Hands In Clouds (a bewitching prelude to a non-Tai Chi Kung Fu side kick). But this just shows a budding aesthetic sensibility, admirable in a mutt.

The basic tenant of the Tai Chi martial arts combat Push Hands has been also mastered by Woofie, although this was very hard since he had to retool his basic Wolf instincts, refined by many ancestral

465

hours around the familial carcass, i.e. to keep neck muscles taut, sink his teeth in and keep them sunk. But he's smart so it took only three times for his cranial bulb to light up on this. The principle is "Love to Lose Ground." Le Grand Lou-Lou (as the French charmingly call Keeshonds, trans. The Big Little Wolf) had to understand that in a tug of war *avec Fresbi*, I was perfectly willing to let him pull me all over without resistance, but once he relaxed the tiniest bit at the end of a yank, ZANGO! The Frisbee was MINE, just as in Push Hands you may legitimately dump your partner on ass end as a Mystical Experience, should he/she be foolish enough to force any push or pull through your Perfect Circle Taoist Space Void.

So now doggo and *moi* go around and around in circles with me barely hanging on to the Frisbee and Kody barely toothing onto it, each waiting for the other to try a yank and then go with it enough to pull the other off balance and expertly remove the Frisbee. It's very funny and satisfying in a masculine way, because we both growl at each other to make up for the lack of aggression. Sort of like the mouthoff preliminaries for a bar fight—but one that's being run in reverse.

And lastly, the Kodymeister and I do "Whoa Husky Sled Dog" stamina training in lieu of long distance jogging. This involves a retractable leash, a sturdy shoulder harness and 235 pounds with bad knees on a bike. Basically I let Kody yank me and my bike around Longmont for ten to sixteen blocks at top speed, spreading massive envy and jealousy among the neighborhood penned curs and inspiring loud barking. As a social service, we perform this around 6:30 to 7:30 some mornings to make sure folks get to the job on time and also so we don't get hit by late to work cars.

My wife Lani, who persists in her effete University of Berkeley notions of learning, read in her Keeshond book that "the dog needs to be warmed up before any exercise. She warned me accordingly and worried about pulled muscles in canine hams while she sleeps in—the paradigm of the Classic Dysfunctional Liberal in a Conservative Age. Our warm-up consists of Kody twisting in circles and frantically badgering me to get my helmet on, the gate open, and the show on the road.

DALLAS WIEBE

CANADA

You can't laugh at Canadians. They just aren't funny, You can't satirize them. You can't parody them. You can't belittle them. You can't burlesque them. You can't call them bad names. You can't joke about them. You can't make caricatures of them. You can't make ethnic, racial, religious or gender slurs against them because they have no national character. It's an interesting phenomenon and needs to be addressed. Consider the evidence.

First of all, for instance, Canadians are never from Canada. If you ask a person from north of the U.S. border where he's from, he'll say he's from Ireland, Germany, Lebanon, Russia, Pakistan, Japan or East Timor, but never from Canada. If he speaks English he will say that he is from Quebec, Winnipeg, the Yukon Territory, Guelf, Waterloo, Chilliwack or Manyberries, but never from Canada. That's because no one knows where Canada is. It's an anonymous suburb of the U.S.A. It's like a pond in an unused park. The Quebecers couldn't secede from Canada because there's nothing to secede from. When immigrants to Canada take the oath of allegiance to the country, the entry for "country of citizenship" is left blank. Some immigrants write in "none." No one knows who issues a Canadian passport.

Secondly, try to tell a Canadian a joke about Canada or Canadians. He won't understand what you're trying to do. He won't even know that you're telling a joke. Telling a Canadian a joke is like trying to tell an impervious man that he is impervious. I tried to tell Johnny Canookie a joke once. He's from New Brunswick, one of the maritime provinces. Think of it, Canada has maritime provinces. One of them is called "Nova Scotia" and one is called "Prince Edward Island." How can an island be a province? Get real, Canookies. It's an island, for heaven's sake. Like "Nova Scotia" and "Newfoundland." Who thinks up such cockamamie names? "New Brunswick"? So I made up a joke about Canadians. The joke I told Johnny Canookie was this: "Johnny, which hand does a Canadian wipe with?" Johnny said, "With his right hand." I said, "In the U.S. people use toilet paper." Johnny said, "What brand?" I said, "Quilted Northern." "Oh," he said, "we can't afford that."

Number three for-instance. Have you ever seen a Canadian in a cartoon? In cartoons we see white Americans, black Americans, Russians, Mexicans, Brits, Frenchmen, Germans, Laplanders, Chinese, Japanese, Arabs and Indians. But no Canadians. In cartoons we see rabbits, coyotes, road runners, chicks, dogs, cats, mice, blackbirds, elephants, hippos, horses, mammoths, snakes, fleas and worms. But no Canadians. In cartoons we see presidents, secretaries of state, congressmen, governors, mayors, councilmen, policemen, garbage men, dog catchers, bookies, crooks and the mentally handicapped. But no Canadians.

Number four for-instance. Even here in the U.S., a place referred to by Canookies as "The States," have you ever heard a joke by or about Canadians? Of course not. Because there is no Canadian culture—that's a contradiction in terms if I ever heard one—there are no Canadian comedians. More than that, try to write a joke about the Canookies like I once did. Here are some examples:

1. Question: Why is the Canadian flag red and white? Answer: Because they ran out of colors.

2. Question: Why is the maple leaf on the Canadian flag? Answer: Because it falls to the ground and rots.

3. Question: What is the national bird of Canada? Answer: The mosquito.

4. Question: Why do the Canadian Royal Mounted Police wear red coats? Answer: So they'll make better targets.

5. Question: Why does Canada have two national languages? Answer: So they'll have an excuse for not being able to read.

6. Question: Why do Canadians ice-skate? Answer: Because their legs are too short to walk.

7. Question: What is a Canadian paraplegic? Answer: A person with no ice skates.

8. Question: Why do Canadians play games with sticks? Answer: Because their fingers are too numb to grip a ball.

9. Question: Why is ice hockey the national sport of Canada? Answer: Because playing it requires no brains.

10. Question: Why is the southern border of Canada the longest border between two nations? Answer: So the Canadians can find it.

11. Question: How does a Canadian make a U-turn? Answer: He kicks her in the head.

See, I told you it couldn't be done.

Number five for-instance. Try to write a satire of Canadians. Here's an example: "Alfonse Quebec falls in love with Minnie Winnipeg. He courts her by taking her out to see the Northern Lights. Her feet freeze to the ground. He's forgotten his ice pick. He unbuckles her ice skates and, taking her in his arms, skates back to Yellow Knife where he is given two minutes in the penalty box for high sticking. When his penalty is over, Alfonse and Minnie skate across the blue line and the red line and are offside. They face off in the right corner. Minnie knocks out his front teeth with her hockey stick. He slaps the puck into her stomach. The game ends and they go home together to play Stanley Cup, which is a game played in the woman's igloo. There, under a moosehide blanket, they tie the laces of their hockey skates together so neither can escape. They get out some sandpaper and polish each other's blades. When the blades sparkle he cross-checks her and she pulls the starter rope on his snowmobile. They get colder and colder as their passion increases. He rubs her icicle and she licks his." See, I told you it can't be done.

Number six for-instance. Try to laugh about the history of Canada. Here's what they teach the little Canookies in the first grade which is also the last grade because it is the only grade they have in their schools: "Canada was formed by leaking water. The water came from the mouth of Pisstofferos, who was at the North Pole and sucking his snowball. One day, while he was polishing his ice skates, he heard a word and the word was 'Saskatchewan.' He said, 'This too must come to pass.' So Pisstofferos created the Ice Age so he would have a path to Saskatchewan where he could practice his slap shot. As he skated toward Saskatoon, his blades cut through the ice and left trenches in the earth. Where he fell, he created Lake Superior. Where he planted his toe he made the Great Slave Lake. Where he cut to the left he made Lake Winnipeg. When he got to Saskatoon he spit and created the Columbia River. At Saskatoon he slapped his puck southward and scored a goal when it became the United States of America. Pisstofferos looked back on his journey and said, 'I think I'll call this pile of ice Canada.' And so it was that the Canadian national boundary was formed and that's why it's hard to find because every once in a while it melts. And so it was that Pisstoferos made the Arctic Circle to run through Canada so that it would remind all the little Canookies who they are and where they came from."

See, I told you it can't be done.

Number seven for-instance. Try to burlesque the Canadian national character. They have no religion because they can't pray and they can't pray because they can't remember when to say "Amen." Canadians can't read because the Northern Lights aren't bright enough to see by. Canadians can't write because grammar is illegal in Canada. In Canada the three R's are red line, red light and the road to Yellow Knife. Canadians can't sing because their tongues are frozen to their teeth. Canadians have no theaters because the stage lights melt the ice proscenium. What did I tell you?

Number eight for-instance. Nothing so well defines the non-character of the Canookies as their military forces. They've never won a war. When they got into WW II, they landed at Dieppe and got wiped out because they thought they were landing at St. Johns, Newfoundland. "The Royal Canadians" were, for heaven's sake, a dance orchestra. We know how bad their armed forces are and what a joke they are because whenever the U.N. wants to maintain peace between some insane African tribes the U.N. sends Canadian soldiers. Don't tell me the Secretary General of the U.N. doesn't have a sense of humor. OK, so the Canadians slapped the snot out of Louis Riel and some hapless half-breeds at the Assiniboine River. Giving that as a great victory is like saying that the Battle of the Little Bighorn was the high point of U.S. military history.

Number nine for-instance. Name two Canadian poets. Name two Canadian novelists. Name two Canadian painters. You can't. Try none and you might have better luck. There just isn't any art in Canada. When they try to paint landscapes, the paintings are all white. When they try to paint portraits the canvases are all black. When they try to write novels they can't find the edges of the white sheets of paper and they

469

don't know which edge of the white paper is up. The poem they sing as their national anthem, written by "The Sweet Songstress of Saskatchewan, Sarah Binks," goes as follows:

> Oh Canada, discovered by lost sailors
> And settled by the children of the Marquis de Sade,
> We salute you in the voice of the Wapiti
> And in the slapstick pucks of your destiny.
> Oh Canada, ice sheet of the slipshod north,
> We cry out to you in our bad sledding
> And in the voices of our lost snowflakes.
> May you be our loving father, mother, sister, brother,
> Grandfather, grandmother, cousin, second cousin
> And all the little children lost on icebergs.
> May our ice skates always fill your crevasses
> And our hockey sticks grow into maple trees.
> We salute you, oh Canada, and pledge to shiver forever
> In service to you, God and the Montreal Canadiens.

What did I tell you? Just try to sing that Canookie ditty written in Yellow Knife in 1914, where Sarah Binks had gone to eat muktuk in the Bush, and adopted it as the national anthem in 1993. Try to sing that anthem before a game between the Calgary Flames and the Edmonton Oilers. Had enough? Have I made my point?

Canadians will not like this essay. That's because they have never seen themselves in a cartoon. That's because they've never heard a good joke about themselves. That's because they don't know what the word "satire" means and because they have no history. The Canookies will not like what is said here because they have no national character and no art to prove it. But no one need worry. There will be no retribution from the Canadians. They won't like this essay mainly because they won't understand a single thing that's been said here and they'll never get the joke because they have no sense of humor.

BARRY GIFFORD

LISTENING TO THE NEWS

My favorite radio stations when I was a kid were WOPA and WAAF in Chicago and WLAC in Nashville. This was during the 1950s, when I'd lie awake in the small hours of the morning and dig Big Bill Hill's Shopping Bag Show on the weak Oak Park, Illinois, frequency. (WOPA was broadcast from the Oak Park Arms Hotel—thus the call letters OPA.) Big Bill called it the

Shopping Bag Show because he kept a shopping bag full of liquor bottles by his feet while he broadcast blues records. A listener could hear the bottles clanking against one another as he pulled one up and played a disc by Eddie Clearwater ("A-Minor Cha-cha") or the latest Magic Sam release on Crash or Cobra. More than once I heard him play a tune by, say, Eddie Boyd, then announce, "Man, I like that one so much I gone play it *again*. Don't care whether *nobody* else care for it. My opinion the onliest one that count!" And, of course, he'd spin Eddie Boyd until he got tired of it. Occasionally, Big Bill would do a remote from The Phoenix Club in Harvey, Illinois, where there was live music, like J.B. Hutto and the Hawks. Hutto was a marvelous slide guitarist, and Big Bill loved the slide. "Play 'Hip-Shakin'' again!" Bill would shout at him; invariably, J.B. would oblige.

WAAF was highlighted for years by Daddio's Jazz Patio, an afternoon show hosted by Daddio Daylie. Daddio played all kinds of records: blues, R&B, pop, jazz, soul—everything from James Brown to Jerry Lee Lewis. WAAF was a "black" station—on Sundays they broadcast church services—but Daddio didn't care about that; when he heard something he liked, he played it. This was in contrast to Purvis Spann over at WVON, a straight soul station, which I also loved. It was on WVON that I first heard The Valentinos do "Lookin' for a Love" by Bobby Womack. But Daddio Daylie had a personality that didn't quit. He became famous in Chicagoland to the extent that politicians fiercely contested for his endorsement.

WLAC played a combination of hillbilly, rock 'n' roll, and pop. Since it was a 50,0000-watt AM channel, I could get it at night either in Chicago or in Tampa, Florida, the two cities I lived in most often in those days. Randy's Record Shop in Murfreesboro, Tennessee, was the sponsor I remember best on WLAC. Randy's offered great deals on collections of 45s. I listened to and dug Pee Wee King, Bill Monroe, The Everly Brothers (they did a show out of Shenandoah, Iowa, I believe, with their father, Ike, that made it to Chicago—in fact, they may have broadcast *from* Chicago for a time), Jerry Lee (even after he married his thirteen-year-old cousin, Myra), and, of course, Elvis.

Living in the Midwest and the Deep South gave me access to stations from Macon, Georgia; Memphis, Tennessee; Little Rock, Arkansas; even, on a clear night, New Orleans, Louisiana. The music that was broadcast during the fifties and early sixties changed and formed my existence. I'll never forget hearing the rhythm section intro to Little Richard's "Lucille"—that sound made me realize right then, at ten years old or however old I was, that the world truly had to be a wild and mysterious place. I wanted to find out where that sound came from, what made it happen. It cut into the deepest part of my being, as did, a few years later, Wilson Pickett's scream or Maria Callas's stunning and dangerous arias. Great art is always dangerous, daring the listener, viewer or reader to go over the edge with the artists. The music I picked up on back in those days was like that, and I'm still listening for it. It's the real news.

MEMORIES OF STATES 1938 (LAUNCH, EPIPHANY, SPHINCTER)

JACQUES SERVIN

A rabbit for Lucinda Sanders

My earliest recollection is of a washboard in Missouri and a large Asian man doing his shoes on it. I don't believe a thing my mother told me about my past, like that the washboard couldn't have happened. I also remember the man screwing in a template; maybe he's tired. My mother said it was ridiculous. (Missouri is a state for wonder, it grows on you as you get to know it. It's somewhere in the Midwest, I know that, the Midwest of this country, and lots of people move there from the outer states. If you look at books about it you'll have no idea.)

I'm going out with Pucky, a gentle soul from Kansas. She admires my shoes, which pleases me no end because they're from Illinois, the state of my father's birth. Pucky tells me I wear them akimbo. I show her akimbo and she laughs mouth open; she knows what she means.

We're going to the Arkansas. I say "the" because that's how my uncle says it, that's where he's from. Pucky picks the motels and loads the car; I feed the dogs. I'm slothful to the point where Pucky says she's in masochism with me.

I admire her turn of mind.

When I was twenty I sought a guru for my spiritual pain but there wasn't any, no pain and no guru. It was kind of weird to realize all that, I still remember and I remember only important things, which Pucky says is stupid. "That's stupid," she said when I told her. Anyhow, in no pain I sought a guru and now I realize I just need someone to know, like Pucky.

We're starting for the Arkansas!

Pucky likes South Carolina a lot. She says it makes her tingle. She tells me about the Gaster book in which the Carolinas unite over cold roast and parsnips, even though I've read it twice with a headache.

We stop for lunch in a little town in Georgia, it's kind of ugly in all the sun but the food is reasonable and reminds me of a dinner at three with largish feting relatives at ease. We admire the waitresses in velveteen and the schoolchildren in full romp. Pucky nudges my elbow and stares into my eyes, not really vacantly but she's

472

definitely somewhere else. I grin.

The car doesn't start. I zone out on the local paper, admiring the bingo-club feel, the luncheons and parties and quotes that evoke for me a certain childhood, not mine but very intense. The mechanic takes forever but doesn't really overcharge; he insists I keep my change. We drive!

Alabama treats us to a real show. In one city are the Dancing Elite, a group of "headstrong but lithe" young women who breeze about to classical music, occasionally contorting in ways that recall to one one's sadism. In one town we encounter "races of speed," which are biathlons featuring splendid young men in green and red. Finally, right on the splendid border, by a deep and fragrant lake, hundreds of youths dive from rocks, splitting our heads with their manifold hubbub.

In-between the car nearly explodes and we find a nice mechanic for not too much money.

The upshot of our Mississippi experience is unfortunately small, almost insignificant. Mississippi in our eyes comprises a poverty-absorbed territory and a good fistful of muddy waters, unprofitable except to Pucky's generous sponge of an imagination: she thinks of crocodiles and worms. Exactly that, in fact, is the upshot: and it takes us two days.

Later suddenly I develop a rare case of ankle swelling and Pucky pretends not to notice. I limp and swear and we argue like demons for hours but then suddenly she's in my position, driving the car, adoring the sights I won't notice, experiencing the driving need of dual solitude. We enter the Arkansas, examine what we've come for, experience the values, and leave.

Mississippi is again a cruel disappointment. Alabama grants us joy in the form of troupes and then in Georgia we visit the birthplace of (a) a President, and (b) a famous composer of music. South Carolina turns my stomach and overjoys Pucky; and home I am full of memories, despite mother.

Hallelujah. The land of our fathers is still a major voyage.

IN HEAVEN

In Heaven, all the women are from the west coast
six feet tall, half Cherokee
and know how to drink.
In Heaven, men wash dishes without breaking a
    single one,
know how to dance,
& think about fucking all the time.
Because, in Heaven, while there is no birth control,

JIM NISBET

473

there is trilateral social responsibility
nurtured by all three sexes
—we'll get to them in a moment—
and plenty to eat.

And in Heaven, there is Absolutely No MSG
you can plug your guitar into any wall
and Newt Gingrich is in jail for parking tickets.
Because, in Heaven, Justice is more than a
        personal pronoun,
mercantilism is strictly limited
to wholesale pubic hair wigs, untaxed—
that's it for Mercantilism!

Moreover, in Heaven, all people got the beat,
—just like here, except in Heaven they know it—
but if you get too rich
in Heaven, you turn into a permanent
tongue involved in a geometrically festering
        rimjob
—the Last Job at last. Take a tip, folks,
before you get to Heaven
Give It All Away
to someone
anyone
who needs it
because the best thing about Heaven
is not only can you not take It with you
you can't take You with you.
Ciao, motherfuckers!

CONTRIBUTOR NOTES

ANDREI CODRESCU (www.codrescu.com) has edited *Exquisite Corpse* since 1983. He is a poet, novelist, and essayist. His commentaries can be heard regularly on NPR. His film, *Road Scholar*, won the Peabody Award. He teaches at Louisiana State University in Baton Rouge.

LAURA ROSENTHAL is a Louisiana-born poet, editor, and critic. She has written the "Body Bag" column in *Exquisite Corpse* since 1990, and has been a Co-Editor since 1994. Her poetry has appeared in *New American Writing, Hanging Loose*, and other magazines. She writes on poetry for the *Minneapolis Star Tribune*.

KEITH ABBOTT teaches fiction workshops and "The Contemplative Brush" at The Naropa Institute. Selections from his unpublished novel, *Arfy Darfy Love*, are currently undergoing movie-option negotiations along with his novel *Mordecai of Monterey*. Forthcoming publications include an introduction to a Houghton-Mifflin edition of Richard Brautigan's early works.

MICHAEL ANDRE is the Editor of *Unmuzzled Ox*. He lives in New York.

ERIC BASSO (decius@mail.bcpl.lib.md.us) was born in Baltimore, 1947, with work appearing in *Fiction International, Exquisite Corpse, Central Park*, and the British magazine *Margin*. The author of 21 plays, his *The Golem Triptych* was published by Asylum Arts.

JOHN BATKI is a poet and translator from the Hungarian. He has brought into English the poetry of Attila Joszef.

HAKIM BEY is a zealot for new ideas and concepts necessary for the birth of our intellectual new age. He spends his life shaking the foundational structures that impede agreement, and publishes his ideas on the web at www.gyw.com/hakimbey/.

BOB BLACK is an anarchist writer who has pissed off more people than *Exquisite Corpse*.

DONALD R. BLUMEN lives and works in Nashville, Tennessee.

DANUTA BORCHARDT was born in 1930, in Wilno, Poland, graduated from medical school in Dublin, Ireland. She has lived in the Boston area since 1959 and worked as a psychiatrist until 1993. Her translation of Witold Gombrowicz's *Ferdydurke* is the first unabridged edition directly from the Polish translation.

ROBERT BOVÉ worked as a cattle farm caretaker in W. Virginia, a stage carpenter's apprentice with the New York Stagehands Union, & writer & editor in DC, but now adjuncts English in NYC universities. The pay falls short. Profits from his last poetry chapbook *Nine from Metronome* (Pisces Press) don't, alas, take up the slack.

DAVE BREITHAUPT lives in Grambier, Ohio, with his family and works the night shift at Kenyon College's Olin and Chalmers Libraries. Dave was formerly employed by the late, great Allen Ginsberg in NYC to help organize his literary archives. His work has appeared in various other *Corpse* wanna-be magazines. He often wears black like the Amish when it fits his mood.

RONNIE BURK is a member of the controversial AIDS dissident organization ACTUP/SF and wants everyone to know HIV does not cause AIDS!

MAX CAFARD, pre-ancientist philosopher and prophet of surregionalism, lives on a floating island in a dream state. He edits *Psychic Swamp: The Surregionalist Review* and teaches Yat Studies in New Orleans.

RICHARD CARR's poems and essays have appeared in a variety of magazines, and Frank Cat Press published his poetry collection *Letters from North Prospect*. Abandoning a lucrative teaching career at Bowling Green State University, Richard bought Fitzpatrick's Tavern in Toledo and now exercises his talents tending bar.

CYDNEY CHADWICK is the author of seven books and chapbooks of stories and prose poems. Her writing has been translated into French, Russian, and Portuguese. Additional information about Cydney can be found at: www.litpress.com/avec/ and www.jps.net/penoak/Chadwick.html.

MAXINE CHERNOFF is Professor of creative writing at SFSU and Co-Editor of *New American Writing*. She's the author of six books of poems, two collections of stories, and three novels, most recently *A Box in Winter* (Crown, 1999).

MATT CLARK's novel is *Hookman Speaks* (Avon Books, 2000). He was Assistant to the Editor of *Exquisite Corpse* from 1993 to 1994, and for several years after he taught writing and literature at Louisiana State University. Matt died on May 7th, 1998.

TOM CLARK's books of poetry from Black Sparrow Press include *Junkets on a Sad Planet: Scenes from the Life of John Keats* (1994); *Like Real People* (1995); *Empire of Skin* (1997); and the novel *The Spell: A Romance* (2000).

IRA COHEN is well known for his photography and film making as well as his poetry. His work is being translated into Japanese, French, German, Hungarian, and Serbo-Croatian. He is a contributing editor to several magazines among which are *Nexus* and *X-press*. His video of the Kumba Mela in India, *Kings with Straw Mats*, is available from Mystic Fire.

RICHARD COLLINS, author of *John Fante, A Literary Portrait* (Guernica Editions), lives in New Orleans.

LEN U. DARIEN is a scholar and translator from the Chinese. He is currently a Visiting Professor at the University of Venice.

MAGGIE DUBRIS is the author of *Willie World*, a sixty-page prose-poem based on her experiences as a 911 paramedic in New York City (Cuz Editions, 1998). She recently completed a novel, *Skels*, and a screenplay, *The First Strange Adventure of the Bird*. She is also a guitarist and principal songwriter for the band Homer Erotic.

BRIAN EVENSON is the author of five books of fiction, including *Contagion, Father of Lies* (1998), and *Altmann's Tongue* (Knopf, 1994). He teaches at the University of Denver and is a senior editor for *Conjunctions Magazine*.

DAVID FEWSTER lives in the mythical city of Pugetopolis in the Pacific Northwest. His work has appeared in the *Seattle Times, Cups, Urban Spelunker*, and the anthology *Revival: Spoken Word* from Lollapalooza 94. It will be 15 years before his daughter, Hannah Rose, is old enough to read the scabrous pages in this volume.

EDWARD FIELD's newest book, written with his partner Neil Derrick, is *The Villagers* (Painted Leaf Press, 2000). Field has published two books with Black Sparrow Press, *Counting Myself Lucky: Selected Poems 1963–1992* (1992) (which won a Lambda Award); and *A Frieze for a Temple of Love* (1998). He has also edited two volumes of the work of Alfred Chester.

TEODOR FLESERU is the mysterious chronicler of *Hermanstadt*, Sibiu, Romania.

DENNIS FORMENTO is Editor of *Mesechabe: The Journal of Surre(gion)alism* and publisher of Surregional Press. Currently, he's working on an oral history of the underground publishing scenes and Bohemia of New Orleans, where "nothing happens but everything goes."

COLA FRANZEN is a distinguished translator from Arabic and French.

JAMES GALLANT has been published in *Story Quarterly, Mississippi Review, North American Review, Press, Georgia Review, Massachusetts Review, Transatlantic Review* and *Exquisite Corpse*.

BARRY GIFFORD's books include the novels *Wild at Heart, Night People* and the forthcoming *Wyoming*, as well as a memoir, *The Phantom Father*. He also co-wrote the feature films *Lost Highway* and *Perdita Durango*, which is based on his novel.

MIKE GOLDEN is the Editor and Publisher of *Smoke Signals* (www.carmine-street.com/smokesignals.html). A poet, novelist, journalist, playwright, and screenwriter, his most recent books are *The Buddhist Third Class Junkmail Oracle* (the art and poetry of d.a. levy) and that "big 60's novel we've all been dreading," *Been to the Mountaintop, Went over the Edge*.

MARIA GOODWIN is the pseudonym of a respected scholar in French studies.

JORGE GUITART teaches Spanish linguistics at the State University of New York at Buffalo. He is the author of *Foreigner's Notebook* (Shuffaloff Press, 1993) and *Film Blanc* (Meow Press, 1996).

477

JIM GUSTAFSON, Detroit's poet extraordinaire, wrote poetry (*Tales of Virtue and Transformation*, among other books), novels (*Discount City*) and essays for Detroit newspapers and magazines. He died in 1997, leaving behind a large unpublished œuvre and a store of legends.

PHILIP HERTER has lived in Mexico City, New Orleans, Los Angeles and New York. He is the author of a play, *Pursued by Happiness* and the novels, *Baby Farm Circus, Felix Easter,* and *The Uptake.*

DAVID HIPLE is a transplanted New Yorker who lives in Honolulu when he's not traveling.

GREGORY HISCHAK is the Editor of the zine *Farm Pulp*. He lives in Seattle.

ANSELM HOLLO, poet and literary translator, was born in Helsinki, Finland. After sojourns in Germany, Austria, and the United Kingdom, he came to the United States and has lived here for thirty-odd years; for the last ten, he has been teaching at The Naropa Institute's Kerouac School of Poetics in Boulder, Colorado. His most recent books of poems are *Corvus* (Coffee House, 1995) and *Ahoe* (Smokeproof Press, 1997).

BOB HOLMAN's most recent poetry is in *The Collect Call of the Wild*; CD: *In with the Out Crowd*. He is a founder of the NYC Poetry Calendar, former Coordinator of the Saint Mark's Poetry Project, and for seven years was Slam Impresario at the Nuyorican Poets Café. He produced the PBS series, *The United States of Poetry*, and is currently working on a digital anthology, *The World of Poetry*. He is Visiting Professor of English at Bard College.

CLIFF HUDDER is an Adjunct Professor of English at Houston Community College, and a lecturer in creative writing at the University of Houston. His fiction has appeared in *The Missouri Review, The Kenyon Review, Alaska Quarterly Review, Cream City Review* and other journals.

STEFAN HYNER is an artist, poet, and translator. He lives in Germany.

DANIEL KANE has poems published in *Exquisite Corpse, The Denver Quarterly, Hanging Loose,* and other journals. His book on the Lower East Side poetic community of the 1960's should be out relatively soon.

ALAN KAUFMAN lives in San Francisco. He is a poet and the author of several books. The most recent, *Who Are We?* (Wordland Books/Davka Limited Editions), is his first full-length collection.

JAN KEROUAC, the daughter of Jack Kerouac and Joan Haverty, was born in Albany, New York, February 16, 1952. She is the author of several novels, and of a memoir, *Baby Driver*. She died in 1996 of kidney disease, her battle over the disposition and control of the Kerouac estate left unfinished.

JOHN KNOLL is the author of *Opera of Virus.*

ERIC KRAFT is the author of the novels *Herb'n'Lorna, Reservations Recommended, Leaving Small's Hotel,* and an ongoing serial novel entitled *The Personal History, Adventures, Experiences & Observations of Peter Leroy.*

WILLIAM LEVY won an Erotic Oscar for "Writer of the Year 1998" awarded at the Sex Maniac's Ball in London. Recent books include poetry (*Billy's Holiday*), as well as essays on art (*Politische Pornos: Eine illustrierte Einfuhrung* and *Unser Freund Otto Muhl: Eine Studie zum Kulturschock*).

JOEL LIPMAN is the author of *The Real Ideal.*

ADRIAN C. LOUIS spent the '99–2000 year teaching at Southwestern State University in Minnesota. A new book of poems, *Ancient Acid Flashes Back,* is due out in 2000 from University of Nevada Press.

CLARK LUNBERRY is a doctoral candidate in the Modern Studies Program at the University of Wisconsin-Milwaukee. He is currently writing a dissertation on articulations/disarticulations of silence in literature, music and the visual arts. His work has appeared in *Discourse, Journal of Dramatic Theory and Criticism, Kyoto Journal,* and *LVNG.* A book of his poetry and photography, *StonePoems,* was published in 1999 from Kalligram Press, Bratislava.

HOWARD McCORD was born in 1932 in El Paso, Texas. He's been a university teacher for 42 years. His most recent book is *The Man Who Walked to the Moon* (McPherson, 1997). Three more books will soon be published. He's married to Jennifer Revis and has six children.

NANCY MacKENZIE lives in Minnesota where she makes masterpieces of fiber art and hunts for morels and chickens-of-the-woods.

KEN McLAUGHLIN is a fiction writer and artist from Baton Rouge, who was part of the Deborah Salazar Aktup Group which disbanded in 1996.

MINNESOTA MAGGOT, aka Chris Bennet, was last seen heading to Northern California to save the trees and live in a geodesic dome.

ELINOR NAUEN is the author of *American Guys* (Hanging Loose) and Editor of *Diamonds Are a Girl's Best Friend: Women Writers on Baseball* (Faber & Faber) and *Ladies, Start Your Engines: Women Writers on Cars and the Road* (Faber & Faber).

RENE NEVILS is writing a biography of John Kennedy Toole, the author of *A Confederacy of Dunces.* She lives in Baton Rouge.

479

GERALD NICOSIA is a biographer, historian, poet, and critic, best known for his biography of Jack Kerouac, *Memory Babe* (University of California Press). His most recent work is *Home to War: A History of the Vietnam Veterans' Movement*. He lives with his wife Ellen, son Peter, and daughter Wu Ji in Corte Madera, California.

RICARDO L. NIRENBERG was born in Buenos Aires, Argentina, in 1939. He taught math at several institutions of doctoral ignorance. He's the author of a novel, *Cry Uncle* (Latino Press, 1998) and various shorter works. Nirenberg edits *Of(f)course*, an internet literary journal: http://www.albany.edu/offcourse.

JIM NISBET, Co-founder (with Darrel Gray) of the Actualist Movement, poet and essayist, also writes crime novels. His most recent *roman noir* is *Prelude to a Scream* (Carroll & Graff).

DENISE NOE has been published in *The Humanist, Georgia Journal Catalyst, The Lizzie Borden Quarterly, Exquisite Corpse, Gauntlet*, and other places. She is featured in *Here and Now: Current Readings for Writers*. She is interested in the ape language experiments and social welfare issues.

PAT NOLAN has put down roots among the redwoods in Monte Rio, California, where he lives to write. His translation of Philippe Soupault's "Comrade" appeared in *Poems for the Millennium* (Vol. 1). Most recently he has privately published a limited edition of a four-volume poetry document entitled *Made in the Shade*.

JULIA OLDER is a story writer, poet, and translator whose work has appeared in *New Directions, The New Yorker*, and many other journals.

KIRBY OLSON is a frequent contributor to *Exquisite Corpse*. He is a sometime academic who would prefer to win the lottery and exist in a sleepy suburb of Geneva, but he is currently living with his family and working on a novel in Finland.

JOHN-IVAN PALMER has appeared in print under a variety of pseudonyms. In 1974 he was "John Pilcrow" in Pushcart Prizes. He has written a novel about male strippers and is currently finishing a book about scandals specific to stage hypnotists (see john ivanpalmer.com). He is the grandson of a Cherokee snake oil salesman and operates out of Minneapolis and Tokyo.

ROBERT PERCHAN is the author of a book of fiction, *Perchan's Chorea: Eros and Exile* (Watermark). His poems and stories have appeared in recent issues of *The Prose Poem, Libido* and, of course, the *Corpse*. He lives in South Korea.

ROBERT PETERS, prolific poet, dramatist, critic, editor, writer of memoirs, and fiction writer, is also a fine satirist and humorist, as his parodies here show. These pieces are from an epic poem called "The Heniad, or Seventy-Five Ways of Considering the Rooster Mounting His Hen," in the voices of numerous American and British poets. Peters resides in California with his life-partner of nearly thirty years, Paul Trachtenberg, a poet and dictionary maker.

PAMELA QUINLAN lives in Portland, Oregon. She provides lyrics and vocals for the band Fez Fatale, which recently released its first CD on Wild Hair Records, available at www.localsonline.com.

EDOUARD RODITI was born in Paris in 1910. He began publishing poetry in 1928 in *transition*, the expatriate Paris periodical to which James Joyce, Gertrude Stein and Hart Crane, among others, were contributing. In 1934, T. S. Eliot published some of his poems in *The Criterion*. His books include *Poems 1928–1948* and *The Delights of Turkey* (New Directions), *Emperor of Midnight* and *Thrice Chosen* (Black Sparrow Press), *Magellan of the Pacific* (Faber & Faber) and *Dialogs of Art*.

ZACK ROGOW's most recent book of poems is *The Selfsame Planet* from Mayapple Press (www.concentric.net/~Jkerman/). He also translates French literature, and was a co-winner of the PEN/Book-of-the-Month Club Translation Award for "Earthlight" by André Breton, and winner of a Bay Area Book Reviewers Award (BABRA) for his translation of George Sand's novel *Horace*. His personal web page is www.dark. void.org/~sayings/zrogow/zack.html.

JOSH RUSSELL was Assistant to the Editor of the *Exquisite Corpse* numbers 38 to 42, and is the author of the novel *Yellow Jack*.

JOE SAFDIE was born in Oklahoma City, April 4, 1953. He's lived in Seattle since 1994. Before that, he spent many years on the California coast (Venice Beach, North Beach, Bolinas) and three years in the early 90s teaching in the Czech Republic (Olomouc and Prague). Books he's published include: *Saturn Return* (Smithereens Press, 1983); *Spring Training* (Zephyr Press, 1985); *September Song* (Oasia Press, 2000). He edited the literary magazines *Zephyr* and *Peninsula* in the 80s and early 90s.

CATHERINE SCHERER is the author of *Objects Left Too Long in One Place* and *Billy Smith in New Guinea*. She lives in Chicago.

PAT SCHNEIDER is the founder/director of Amherst Writers & Artists and Editor of Amherst Writers & Artists Press. She's been published widely in literary journals and magazines, including *Sewanee Review, Minnesota Review, Ms. Magazine,* and *Negative Capability*. She has published three books of poetry, *Olive Street Transfer, White River Junction* and *Long Way Home*.

PETE SEEGER, born 1919, is one of America's best-loved folksingers and an untiring environmentalist. He has been at the forefront of the labor movement, the struggle for Civil Rights, the peace and anti-war movements, and the fight for a clean world. Once blacklisted from national television for being unafraid to voice his opinions, he was given the nation's highest artistic honors at the Kennedy Center in December, 1994. In January 1996 he was inducted into the Rock and Roll Hall of Fame.

JULIAN SEMILIAN's poems, translations, and essays have appeared in *Exquisite Corpse, Arshile, Syllogism, Ribot, Transcendental Friend, Trepan, Suitcase, Mr. Knife & Miss Fork,* and *Callaloo*. Green Integer/Manifest Press will publish his translations of Paul Celan's Romanian poems in 2000. His episodic novel/essay *The Skeuromorph Detective* appears as a regular feature in *Exquisite Corpse*. He teaches film editing at the North Carolina School for the Arts.

JACQUES SERVIN is a hero of the hacker underground. He is also the author of two collections of stories, including *Mermaids for Attila*. His whereabouts are never known in advance or after the fact.

CHARLES SIMIC was born in Belgrade, Yugoslavia in 1938, and came to the United States with his family at the age of 15. He has published more than 60 books of poetry, among them *The World Doesn't End*, for which he received the Pulitzer Prize for Poetry in 1990. He is Professor of English at the University of New Hampshire.

WILLIE SMITH. Born on a hilltop in Maryland. Killed him a roach when he was only three. Reasonably sober, relatively clean, happily married, no kids, no career. Black Heron Press published his novel *Oedipus Cadet* in 1990. 26 Books has just published *Execution Style*, a chapbook of short stories. He was always deeply honored to be counted among the *Corpse*'s contributors.

PETE SNIEGOWSKI, alias "Extreme," teaches in an all-girl Catholic high school. Somehow, he passed the urinalysis.

SPARROW is currently reading G. K. Chesterton's *The Club of Queer Trades* and losing weight.

MARK SPITZER, Assistant Editor of *The Corpse*, darkles Toledo nonstop chucklehead. Do not patronize his authorship: *Bottom Feeder, The Collected Poems of Georges Bataille, The Church, Chum,* and sundry other novels and translations.

MARIANNE STEELE was born in San Francisco in 1959, and grew up in Northern California. She lived and worked as a dancer in China from 1983 until 1990. Since 1991 she has lived in Germany with her husband and daughter where she practices Tao Shiatsu and works as a gardener.

HARIETTE SUROVELL (RP@Panix.com) is a true-crime reporter and a film critic as well as a short-story/creative writer. Her first publication, at age 16, on the *New York Times* Op Ed Page, was a plea for sex education in high schools. After many years of adventures and dates from hell, she finally met and married a man who exhibits no Men's Planetary sensibilities whatsoever.

NANOS VALAORITIS was born in Switzerland in 1921. He spent nine years in London and ten years in Paris where he was connected with André Breton's surrealist group. He taught at San Francisco State University from 1968–1993. He edited *Magazine Pali* in Greece from 1963–1967 and *Synteleia* from 1989–1997. His most recent book is *My Afterlife Guaranteed, Narratives and Poetry* (City Lights, 1990). Nanos lives part of the time in Oakland, California and the other part in Athens, Greece. He's married to American painter Marie Wilson.

SASHA VLAD translates Romanian surrealist poets. His co-translation of the surrealist novel *Zenobia* by Gellu Naum was published by Northwestern University Press. His co-translation of the series of poems *The Advantage of Vertebrae* by Gellu Naum is soon to be included in *The Knife and Mrs. Fork, An Anthology of International Poetry* published by Sun and Moon Press.

ANNE WALDMAN co-founded, with Allen Ginsberg, the Jack Kerouc School of Disembodied Poetics at The Naropa Institute in Boulder, Colorado. She is the author of many books of poetry, most recently, *Iovis II* (Coffee House, 1997), *Au Lit / Holy: Of Transgressions of the Maghreb*, with Eleni Sikileanos and Laird Hunt, and *Young Manhattan*, with Bill Berkson (Smokeproof Press, 1998, 1999).

CARL WATSON is the author of several books of fiction and essays, including the novel *The Hotel of Irrevocable Acts* (Gallimard, Paris) and *Beneath the Empire of the Birds* (Apathy Press, Baltimore). His upcoming book of horror stories is called *Psychosomatic Life*. He lives in New York City.

PETER WEVERKA, a freelance writer, lives in San Francisco.

DALLAS WIEBE's latest book is *Our Asian Journey: A Novel*.

NINA ZIVANCEVIC, poet, fiction writer, essayist and translator was born and raised in the bomb-ridden Belgrade. She went to school in England and the U.S. Presently she lives and works in France at the University of Nancy II. She has published nine books of poetry and four books of fiction.

MISSING IN ACTION:

Elliott Anderson	Don Bapst	Milton Beyer
Joel Brouwer	Casey Bush	Sergiu Celac
Jane Dalrymple-Hollo	Z. F. Danes	Brahm Eiley
Paul Grajnert	Ted Grossman	Erica Herrmann
Jason Horwitch	Angela Jianu	John Kehoe
Toby Koosman	Gàbor Kovàcsi	Ben Marks
J. Michaels	Don Monaco	Wendy Mai Rawlings
Janet Rodney	Adam J. Sorkin	Nathaniel Tarn
Lidia Vianu	Ann Vinograde	Vladimir Vysotsky
Michael Waltuch	Dana Wilde	Robert Wiltsey
D.W. Wright		Saul Yurkievich

Printed November 2000 in Santa Barbara &
Ann Arbor for the Black Sparrow Press by
Mackintosh Typography & Edwards Brothers Inc.
Text set in Sabon and Albertus by Words Worth.
Design by Barbara Martin.
This first edition is published in paper wrappers;
there are 300 hardcover trade copies;
125 hardcover copies have been numbered &
signed by the editors; & 22 copies lettered A–V have
been handbound in boards by Earle Gray
and are signed by the editors.